# Atlas of Dragonflies in Britain and Ireland

Edited by Steve Cham, Brian Nelson,
Adrian Parr, Steve Prentice, Dave Smallshire
and Pam Taylor

Brilliant Emerald *Somatochlora metallica*
Courtesy of Richard Lewington

Text and maps © Natural Environment Research Council and
British Dragonfly Society (2014)

Cover image: Red-eyed Damselfly © Richard Revels

Title page image: Brilliant Emerald © Richard Lewington


Published for: Biological Records Centre
NERC Centre for Ecology and Hydrology
Maclean Building
Benson Lane
Crowmarsh Gifford
Wallingford
Oxfordshire
OX10 8BB

With: British Dragonfly Society
www.british-dragonflies.org.uk

By: Field Studies Council
Unit C1
Stafford Park 15
Telford
TF3 3BB

ISBN: 978 1 906698 49 2

# Contents

# Foreword

Sir David Attenborough visiting the BDS stand at the British Birdwatching Fair, Rutland Water. *Pam Taylor*

A dragonfly settled on a rush within a few inches of where I was sitting. I was, I suppose, about thirteen or fourteen years old and I was sitting by a small pond in rural Leicestershire. The dragonfly, I am fairly sure, was a female Southern Hawker – but that is a later realisation. At the time, I simply sat enchanted as it perched motionless beside me with its wings outstretched. I looked at its cocked head and gigantic mosaic eyes. I examined in detail the brown and green markings on its abdomen and the glinting reticulation of its transparent wings. It was as wonderful a creature as I had ever seen. And then it was off on a high-speed circuit of the pond. I could hear the tiny clatter of its wings as it banked steeply to catch a mosquito in its legs crooked beneath its head like a net. Within a few seconds it was back and sitting on exactly the same perch to allow me, once again, to examine it in all its tiny details. It was one of the most vivid and unforgettable images of my childhood.

In later years, as I learned more about these astonishing insects, they became even more firmly entrenched in my imagination. Palaeontologists have shown that some of the first dragonflies were giants with wingspans of some 30 centimetres that appeared 290 million years ago, long before flying reptiles like the pterosaurs or those comparative latecomers, birds. Dedicated entomologists have explained the extraordinary details of dragonfly reproduction that require them to make such spectacular aerial couplings. And film-makers using high speed recordings have revealed that, almost unbelievably, they are able to beat each one of their four wings independently. Marvel upon marvel.

Of course I am not alone in cherishing my childhood vision of one. This book is the incontrovertible evidence that a host of people have had just such a bewitching experience. For how else could there be the experts with a passion and dedication to compile this authoritative book.

The rest of us can only be deeply grateful to them for having done so.

*David Attenborough*

Sir David Attenborough,
Patron, British Dragonfly Society

# Preface

The pages contained within this atlas are the outcome of many painstaking hours of field observation undertaken by a network of dragonfly enthusiasts. They are mainly volunteers and without their hard work and dedication this atlas would either not have been possible, or very deplete in its coverage. With an increasing demand on the greatest resource we all have, that of time, the Dragonfly Recording Network and DragonflyIreland are indebted to all those who have submitted their records and observations. It is to them that this publication is dedicated.

Atlases of fauna and flora are mere snapshots in time, summarising our understanding of distribution at that point. The previous atlas was published in 1996, utilising records up to and including 1990. It was the first comprehensive statement about the national status of the British and Irish dragonfly fauna and formed the baseline on which to build for this atlas. Prior to that there had been two provisional atlases in the late 1970s and a small number of workers recording dragonflies and publishing their findings in specialist journals and local atlases. It was agreed at a Dragonfly Recording Network meeting at Wytham in 2002 that the time was right to compare current dragonfly distribution with the previous atlas. It also seemed appropriate because a number of species were showing signs of range change and there would be a 'good story' to tell by the publication of a new atlas. So the wheels were set in motion to plan a way forward.

A meeting of vice-county recorders for the Dragonfly Recording Network and representatives from other interested organisations was held in Oxfordshire and a project proposal subsequently drafted for the setting-up of a more sustainable and targeted recording scheme. One tangible outcome of the proposed project would be a new dragonfly atlas. Funds were sought for the project and when these were secured, a project officer was appointed and the process begun.

Alongside these developments, the National Biodiversity Network was formed in 2000 and was looking for Recording Schemes to work with and pilot the functionality of the NBN Gateway. The Odonata Recording Scheme had been running for some time with a growing network of active recorders and so the British Dragonfly Society was delighted to provide wider access to dragonfly data and work with the NBN. Up to this point the BDS had valued the support provided by the Biological Records Centre at the Centre for Ecology & Hydrology, which had formerly managed the Odonata Recording Scheme. Paul Harding and Trevor James were especially supportive in the early stages of setting up the DRN, helping us to find the sources of potential funding to sustain regular recording and data collection. This support continued with the NBN, helping the DRN to improve verification of dragonfly data and to pilot some of the early Gateway developments.

Climate change and its potential impact on the human population have been high on the political agenda for some time, with responsible governments attempting to mediate its effects. The last decade has seen enormous interest in how rising temperatures influence the distribution of a wide range of organisms and their ecosystems. Dragonflies have a key role as indicators of a changing climate. One of the outcomes planned for this atlas was to demonstrate trends in the distribution of our resident breeding species as well as document the spread of new colonists arriving on our shores. Using a combination of the maps, associated texts and statistical analysis the reader should be able to gain an appreciation of how our species are faring and reacting to climate change.

Dragonflies are one of the most visible and readily identified taxa dependent on freshwater habitats to complete their life cycle. As such they represent one of the best indicator groups with which to assess the quality and well-being of our waterways and waterbodies. Changes and trends can be subtle and go undetected for many years. They can start with the loss of a particular species from some sites, or the first appearance of a new species in a new area. Whilst isolated sightings have limited value they can, when collated and combined into a single large database, be used to show trends.

We have encouraged recorders to send in records of sightings for all species. Many naturalists have anecdotal knowledge of their favourite sites which often remains

Common Darter resting on a BDS cap. *Dave Smallshire*

# Acknowledgements

hidden in notebooks for years, never to be appreciated by a wider audience. One such sighting, that of a Southern Damselfly in Oxfordshire, went unrecognised for a number of years until it was followed up and a previously unknown breeding population was discovered in the area. Such findings are the 'stuff' that motivates and drives many naturalists to explore new areas in search of their 'quarry'.

There are new species arriving on our shores and the questions inevitably arise of when does a migrant or vagrant become an established species? When does the process of colonisation start? For the first time in dragonfly recording history we have been able to track the colonisation and establishment of several species from their first tentative wanderings across the Channel, or Irish Sea, or northwards into Scotland, to becoming regular breeding species spreading across new areas. Collaboration with our friends in The Netherlands during the 1990s had informed us of a significant spread of Small Red-eyed Damselfly across their country and that we should expect its arrival at any time. As a result of this early warning dragonfly recorders have been able to document the arrival and subsequent dramatic spread of this damselfly across southern Britain since 1999.

Recording schemes are only as good as the information they provide to conservation action plans and site management. There are now over one million records in the DRN and DragonflyIreland databases. The DRN has always been resolute that data should be used to further the cause of conservation and to protect our dragonflies and their habitats. So the DRN has provided, and will continue to provide, dragonfly data to maintain its online presence through the NBN Gateway, making the data available to conservationists and scientists.

An atlas of this nature is the result of co-operation between many individuals and other organisations and societies exchanging records. Citizen Science has seen significant interest in participation in many recording schemes and plays an important role in increasing public involvement and awareness of our native wildlife. Sightings backed up by a good quality photograph have added many new records to the DRN database. New technology continues to bring more sophisticated digital cameras and mobile phones fitted with GPS, enabling sightings to be located on the map with great accuracy. Future generations of naturalists and dragonfly enthusiasts will have an increasing armoury of sophisticated tools to aid and enhance recording accuracy. It is hoped that this atlas will serve as their benchmark and enable them to continue the 'good story'.

Steve Cham.

This atlas would not have been possible without the hard work and input from a large number of people at every stage of the process, from recording to publication.

**Field recorders:** The number of records in the DRN database exceeded 1 million in January 2013. The effort and dedication of everyone who sent in records has contributed to this atlas. So first and foremost we would like to extend our heartfelt thanks to all recorders. These are listed individually in Appendix A5.

The editors would also like to thank the following:

**For substantial editorial support:** Helen Roy (Biological Records Centre, Centre for Ecology & Hydrology) and Peter Mill especially for their expertise and diligence at picking up our typographical, grammatical and technical errors and promptly returning the proofs to meet the deadlines.

**For guiding us through the publication process:** Rebecca Farley-Brown (FSC Publications).

**For trends analysis:** Nick Isaac (Biological Records Centre, Centre for Ecology & Hydrology).

**Vice-county Recorders:** For stimulating observers to gather and submit records and for collating, checking and inputting those records throughout the atlas recording period: Peter Allen, David Anderson, Paul Ashton, Mike Averill, Pat Batty, Ted Benton, Allan Brandon, John & Gill Brook, Andrew Brown, Anthony Brownett, Richard Chadd, David Clarke, Anne Coker, Stephen Coker, Steve Covey, Bob Dennison, Helen Dinsdale, Harry Eales, Gareth Ellis, Lin Gander, Peter Garner, Keith Gittens, Dave Goddard, Penny Green, Tom Hubball, Chris Iles, Dave Jackson, Steve Jones, Alistair Kirk, David Kitching, John Luck, Sue McLamb, Alistair McLean, Ian Merrill, Alan Nelson, Keith Noble, Adrian Parr, Val Perrin, Mike Powell, Peter Reeve, Eugenie Regan, Elaine Rice, Christine Shepperson, Perry Smale, Dave Smallshire, Pam Taylor, Nick Tribe, Mike Turton, Ingrid Twissell, Mark Tyrrell, Ted Waring, Steve White and Roy Woodward.

**For drafting species' sections:** Mike Averill, Pat Batty, Allan Brandon, Steve Brooks, Andrew Brown, Steve Cham, Dave Chelmick, David Clarke, Craig Emms, Dave Goddard, Claire Install, Stuart Irons, David Kitching, Peter Mill, Brian Nelson, Adrian Parr, Val Perrin, John Phillips, Pam Taylor, Mark Tyrrell, Graeme Walker, John Ward-Smith and Jonathan Willet.

**Photographers:** We would like to acknowledge all the photographers who supplied images and without which the atlas would be much less visually appealing. Unfortunately, it has not been possible to include all images, but those that are included have been individually credited. We would especially like to thank Richard Revels for the use of his photograph of Red-eyed Damselfly used on the atlas cover and pre-publication flyer.

**For funding and supporting the Dragonflies in Focus Project, for which the production of this atlas was a major outcome:** Environment Agency for their partnership funding of the BDS throughout the project; Esmee Fairbairn Foundation for a grant enabling the first half of this project to proceed; Natural England for grant funding the BDS Conservation Officer in the initial stages of the project and for hosting both the BDS Conservation Officer and the BDS Dragonflies in Focus Officer since 2002; Natural Resources Wales and Scottish Natural Heritage for grant aiding all stages of the project; NBN Trust for its funding support during the planning stages of this project and for its practical support throughout; Scottish Environmental Protection Agency for its funding support during the initial stage of this project.

**For sponsoring and supporting DragonflyIreland:** National Parks and Wildlife Service; Northern Ireland Environment Agency; National Museums Northern Ireland; the Heritage Council and National Biodiversity Data Centre; Eugenie Regan (Irish Regional Recorder 2011-2013) coordinated the final transfer of the DragonflyIreland data.

**For providing additional national/regional datasets:** Philippa Tomlinson (Manx Biological Recording, Isle of Man); National Biodiversity Data Centre, Ireland; CEDaR, Belfast, N. Ireland.

**For producing UK climate change maps:** Adam Scaife and Dan Hollis (Met Office).

**For allowing the use of British wetland data:** Chas Holt (British Trust for Ornithology) and the Wetland Bird Survey partnership.

**For producing the wetland maps for Ireland:** Jochen Roller.

**For funding the publication of this atlas:** The Biological Records Centre, Centre for Ecology & Hydrology. BRC is jointly funded by the Joint Nature Conservation Committee and the Centre for Ecology & Hydrology within the Natural Environment Research Council (NERC).

Finally, we apologise humbly for any omissions and accept responsibility for any inaccuracies that remain in the text.

The Dragonflies in Focus Project began in April 2007 with initial funding from:

# About the editors

## Steve Cham

Steve has had a life long interest in all aspects of natural history and a passion for dragonflies from an early age. He has served as Vice-county Recorder for Bedfordshire and was National Co-ordinator for the Dragonfly Recording Network after it transitioned from the Biological Records Centre at Monks Wood. He is the author of a number of books on dragonflies, including the popular field guides to larvae and exuviae. Steve was elected to honorary membership of the NBN Trust in 2008 in recognition of his services to biological recording in the UK and awarded the Royal Entomological Society Marsh Award for Insect Conservation in 2011.

## Brian Nelson

The discovery of a new site for Irish Damselfly in his native county of Fermanagh sparked Brian's interest in dragonflies. He has served as Irish Dragonfly recorder from the latter stages of the previous atlas through the DragonflyIreland project to this point. He works as Invertebrate Ecologist in the Irish National Parks and Wildlife Service and his interests extend to the whole Irish insect fauna but especially those found in freshwater.

## Adrian Parr

Adrian has been involved with dragonflies for over 30 years, joining the BDS shortly after its inauguration. He has long-term interests in both bird and insect migration, and functions as the Society's migrant specialist and as secretary of the national Odonata Rarities Committee. In recent years he has also acted as Vice-county Recorder for Suffolk. Other interests include dragonfly phenology, and he is an active field recorder both for dragonflies and several other insect groups.

## Steve Prentice

Steve is one of the three paid staff of the BDS. As the Dragonflies in Focus Officer since 2007 his major role has been managing the records of the Dragonfly Recording Network. After a career in computing working for international banks and financial institutions he saw the light and took a degree in Conservation Management. The post of Dragonflies in Focus Officer combines his many years computing experience with his interest in the countryside and nature conservation.

## Dave Smallshire

Dave's interest in dragonflies came through a 50-year passion for birds and other wildlife and their conservation in Britain and abroad. Since retiring as an agroecology policy adviser to Defra and Natural England, he has led a series of dragonfly-watching tours to countries in Europe, Africa, Asia and central America. Together with his colleague Andy Swash, he authored the highly praised Britain's Dragonflies, now in its third edition. He is the dragonfly recorder for Devon and since 2008 has been Convenor of the BDS Dragonfly Conservation Group, which oversees the Dragonfly Recording Network.

## Pam Taylor

In common with many dragonfly enthusiasts, Pam began her wildlife interests as a childhood birdwatcher, moving on to mammals, plants and butterflies as her experience increased. She only discovered the fascinating world of dragonflies after moving to Norfolk and becoming involved with the local wildlife trust. Following her contributions to a county dragonfly atlas in the late 1980s, she became Vice-county Recorder for dragonflies in Norfolk during the mid-1990s; publishing a revised county atlas in 2003. Her involvement in dragonfly recording and conservation led Pam to becoming a BDS trustee in 2000 and Convenor of the BDS Dragonfly Conservation Group a year later. She continued in this latter role until 2008 when she was elected BDS President. Having seen the BDS through a number of major developments and its 30th anniversary year, Pam stepped down as President at the end of 2013. She now continues her dragonfly interests at a more local level once again.

# The dragonfly fauna of Britain and Ireland

The dragonfly fauna of Britain and Ireland (Table 1) amounts to 57 species, with 56 of these recorded from Britain and 32 from Ireland. A total of 46 resident and regular migrant dragonflies have been recorded in Britain and Ireland since 2000. Of these, 25 breed or are regular migrants to Ireland, including Irish Damselfly which is not found in Britain. In addition to these species Norfolk Damselfly and Orange-spotted Emerald have not been recorded since 1958 and 1963, respectively, and are considered extinct in Britain. There have been no recorded extinctions from Ireland. A further nine species from the current fauna of 55 have been recorded as vagrants, all but one since 1989. This includes one North American species and one pantropical species, the rest being European resident species.

Biogeographically, the Channel Islands and its fauna are closer to that of France, and hence continental Europe, and for this reason are not included in this atlas. Two species, Southern Skimmer (*Orthetrum brunneum*) and Southern Darter (*Sympetrum meridionale*) have been recorded in the Channel Islands, but not in Britain or Ireland, while Scarlet Darter (*Crocothemis erythraea*) – a vagrant to England – has bred there.

Being islands with a temperate climate, Britain and Ireland have a naturally limited dragonfly fauna. As a general rule, continents support more species than islands and island biodiversity decreases with increasing remoteness and decreasing size. Hence Britain has more species than Ireland. Dragonfly diversity also declines generally from south to north again following the broad global trend of all biodiversity in the northern hemisphere. However, the region with greatest species diversity in Europe is the central region from France east to Russia (Kalkman *et al.*, 2010). To put the total number of species for Britain and Ireland into perspective, it is considered that there are currently nearly 6,000 species recognised worldwide, with perhaps a further 1,000-1,500 awaiting formal description (Dijkstra *et al.*, 2013). Only 125 of these (43 Zygoptera and 82 Anisoptera) breed in Europe and this represents the pool of species from which the British and Irish fauna is drawn.

All the species present in Britain and Ireland would have had to recolonise the islands since the end of the last glaciation. The potential for this will have been limited by the loss of land bridges from Britain to the continent and from Ireland to Britain, respectively 6,500 and 16,000 years ago.

Although dragonflies and damselflies are capable of flight, the impoverishment of the British and Irish fauna compared to the neighbouring continent suggests that some species, especially damselflies, have difficulty in making the relatively short sea crossing. There are 13 species that breed in coastal areas of France, Belgium and The Netherlands just across the English Channel from southern and eastern England. To reach southern Britain would require a sea crossing of some 32-200km. This has happened with a number of species since 1990, with a net increase in the number of breeding species in Britain of 7%. However, for the remainder the sea currently appears to present an obstacle.

Ireland has also experienced an increase in breeding species, with colonisation by Migrant Hawker and Emperor Dragonfly since 2000. Further changes in the Irish fauna are unpredictable, requiring new species to fly against prevailing winds across the Irish Sea. This would seem most possible for species which are well-established and increasing in western and northern Britain. The most likely candidates to become residents in Ireland are Southern Hawker (this has already reached Ireland as a vagrant with good evidence the specimen originated from southern Europe rather than Britain) and Red-eyed Damselfly.

If and when individuals successfully make such sea crossings, permanent colonisation will only be possible if the right habitat and climatic conditions (i.e. appropriate temperatures) exist. A lack of sufficient suitable habitat and a cooler climate result in a lower diversity of dragonflies in the fauna of Ireland, the Isle of Man and the many small Scottish islands compared with Britain. The potential exists for the British and Irish dragonfly lists to increase further as a result of increasing temperatures. This already appears to be happening at a rate unprecedented during the history of dragonfly recording in Britain and Ireland and is well illustrated in the maps of several species. No less than seven species have been recorded in Britain and five in Ireland for the first time since the previous atlas. In particular, two damselflies, Willow Emerald and Small Red-eyed, have established strong breeding populations in Britain during this period, and a third species, Dainty Damselfly, has recolonised. Southern Emerald Damselfly, Southern Migrant Hawker, Lesser Emperor and Yellow-winged Darter have also bred on occasions.

In addition to the species known to occur naturally, at least 11 exotic species have been introduced accidentally into Britain (see page 245). These records have come principally from aquatic nurseries (Brooks, 1988), but some have been reported outdoors (Parr, 2010). There are no indications that any of these have bred. To date there are no known occurrences of exotics in Ireland.

Table 1. The status of species recorded in Britain and Ireland.

| | | Britain | Ireland |
|---|---|---|---|
| Willow Emerald Damselfly | *Chalcolestes viridis* | B (1979) | |
| Southern Emerald Damselfly | *Lestes barbarus* | M+ (2002) | |
| Scarce Emerald Damselfly | *Lestes dryas* | B | B |
| Emerald Damselfly | *Lestes sponsa* | B | B |
| Winter Damselfly | *Sympecma fusca* | M (2009) | |
| Banded Demoiselle | *Calopteryx splendens* | B | B |
| Beautiful Demoiselle | *Calopteryx virgo* | B | B |
| White-legged Damselfly | *Platycnemis pennipes* | B | |
| Small Red Damselfly | *Ceriagrion tenellum* | B | |
| Norfolk Damselfly | *Coenagrion armatum* | X (1958) | |
| Northern Damselfly | *Coenagrion hastulatum* | B | |
| Irish Damselfly | *Coenagrion lunulatum* | | B |
| Southern Damselfly | *Coenagrion mercuriale* | B | |
| Azure Damselfly | *Coenagrion puella* | B | B |
| Variable Damselfly | *Coenagrion pulchellum* | B | B |
| Dainty Damselfly | *Coenagrion scitulum* | B | |
| Common Blue Damselfly | *Enallagma cyathigerum* | B | B |
| Red-eyed Damselfly | *Erythromma najas* | B | |
| Small Red-eyed Damselfly | *Erythromma viridulum* | B (1999) | |
| Blue-tailed Damselfly | *Ischnura elegans* | B | B |
| Scarce Blue-tailed Damselfly | *Ischnura pumilio* | B | B |
| Large Red Damselfly | *Pyrrhosoma nymphula* | B | B |
| Southern Migrant Hawker | *Aeshna affinis* | B (1952) | |
| Azure Hawker | *Aeshna caerulea* | B | |
| Southern Hawker | *Aeshna cyanea* | B | M |
| Brown Hawker | *Aeshna grandis* | B | B |
| Common Hawker | *Aeshna juncea* | B | B |
| Migrant Hawker | *Aeshna mixta* | B | B (2000) |
| Norfolk Hawker | *Anaciaeschna isoceles* | B | |
| Vagrant Emperor | *Anax ephippiger* | M (1903) | M |
| Emperor Dragonfly | *Anax imperator* | B | B (2000) |
| Green Darner | *Anax junius* | M (1998) | |
| Lesser Emperor | *Anax parthenope* | M+ (1996) | M (2000) |

Table 1 continued.

| | | | |
|---|---|---|---|
| Hairy Dragonfly | *Brachytron pratense* | B | B |
| Common Clubtail | *Gomphus vulgatissimus* | B | |
| Yellow-legged Clubtail | *Stylurus flavipes* | M (1818) | |
| Golden-ringed Dragonfly | *Cordulegaster boltonii* | B | M (2005) |
| Orange-spotted Emerald | *Oxygastra curtisii* | X (1963) | |
| Downy Emerald | *Cordulia aenea* | B | B |
| Northern Emerald | *Somatochlora arctica* | B | B |
| Brilliant Emerald | *Somatochlora metallica* | B | |
| Scarlet Darter | *Crocothemis erythraea* | M (1995) | |
| White-faced Darter | *Leucorrhinia dubia* | B | |
| Large White-faced Darter | *Leucorrhinia pectoralis* | M (1859) [2] | |
| Broad-bodied Chaser | *Libellula depressa* | B | M [4] |
| Scarce Chaser | *Libellula fulva* | B | M [4] |
| Four-spotted Chaser | *Libellula quadrimaculata* | B | B |
| Black-tailed Skimmer | *Orthetrum cancellatum* | B | B |
| Keeled Skimmer | *Orthetrum coerulescens* | B | B |
| Wandering Glider | *Pantala flavescens* | M (1823) | |
| Black Darter | *Sympetrum danae* | B | B |
| Yellow-winged Darter | *Sympetrum flaveolum* | M+ (1862) | M (1995) |
| Red-veined Darter | *Sympetrum fonscolombii* | B [3] | M |
| Banded Darter | *Sympetrum pedemontanum* | M (1995) | |
| Ruddy Darter | *Sympetrum sanguineum* | B | B |
| Common Darter [1] | *Sympetrum striolatum* | B | B |
| Vagrant Darter | *Sympetrum vulgatum* | M (1836) | |

B   Breeding species; (year): year of first recorded individual.

M   Migrant, vagrant or not-established species; M+: has bred; (year): year of first recorded individual.

X   extinct in Britain; (year): year of last record.

[1]   includes dark specimens in the north-west formerly treated as a separate species, Highland Darter *Sympetrum nigrescens*.

[2]   Large White-faced Darter was reported in the mid-nineteenth century from an ill-defined site possibly off the coast, the first clear mainland records were in 2012.

[3]   Red-veined Darter is a migrant that now breeds quite regularly in Britain, but its exact status is difficult to define.

[4]   Broad-bodied and Scarce Chaser are on the Irish List based on single nineteenth century records. There is no evidence either were established species.

# Environmental factors influencing dragonfly distribution

## Climate and weather

The distribution of dragonflies and their habitats is influenced strongly by climate. Climate, particularly rainfall patterns, interacts with geology, landform and altitude to determine the general distribution of wetland habitats. Wetlands, suitable for dragonflies to breed in, cover only a small proportion of Britain and Ireland and their distribution is uneven (Figures 14 and 15, pages 13 and 22). For example, it has been estimated that Devon's key dragonfly sites cover no more than 0.145% of the county (Smallshire, 1995). Even the extensive Broads area of Norfolk and Suffolk covers little more than 3% of those counties. Northern Ireland is better endowed with potential dragonfly habitat with over 4% of the land area being open water. However the diversity of dragonflies is lower in Northern Ireland than the two English areas so quantity of habitat is not necessarily equated with species richness.

Temperature strongly influences dragonfly distribution at the continental scale and dragonfly species-richness is correlated with latitude. In general, temperatures become lower with increased latitude with a reduced species diversity (Figure 28, page 39). However, temperatures in the British Isles are ameliorated somewhat by the buffering influence of the sea and the Gulf Stream in particular. This means that winters here are milder and summers cooler than in many other regions on the same latitude. These lower summer temperatures appear to influence species diversity more than winter temperature as the regions of lowest species diversity in Europe are on the Atlantic fringe from Ireland through Scotland to western Norway.

High rainfall has led to the formation of peat bogs, especially in parts of upland and western Britain and Ireland, as seen here at the bog pools of Buachaille Ètive Mòr, Glen Etive, Argyll. *David Clarke*

Such is the quantity of rainfall in Britain and Ireland that, except where they flow over porous rocks such as chalk and limestone, watercourses in Britain and Ireland maintain their flows all year round. High rainfall has led to the formation of peat bogs, especially in parts of upland and western Britain and Ireland. Elsewhere, impeded drainage of surface and sub-surface flows have created mires and fens in valleys and other depressions. The streams, flushes and areas of open water associated with bogs, mires and fens hold a rich variety of dragonfly species, many of which are of great conservation significance and have protected status. In some cases, this interest has actually been enhanced by human action, where ditches have been dug to channel water or where water has flooded after peat extraction.

Climate and short-term weather factors can affect larval development time and adult survival. The temperature of water plays an important role through influencing prey availability and the rate of larval growth. Higher numbers of adults are active and therefore likely to be recorded in warm summers compared to cooler summers. Extended periods of warm and sunny weather are potentially conducive to the spread of species within Britain and Ireland, especially when numbers of adult dragonflies are high.

It is well-established that warm airflow from the continent encourages the movement of insects (and birds) across the English Channel and Irish Sea. These insects include several dragonfly species that have already colonised Britain and Ireland and others that look set to do so soon. The species most likely to spread and successfully establish new populations are those with more general habitat requirements rather than 'habitat specialists'. The latter are typically restricted in their distribution by the scarcity of their preferred habitat.

## Climate change

Data from the Met Office show an increasing trend in UK temperatures and rainfall, albeit with a pattern of considerable year-to-year variation. A comparison of mean temperature and rainfall for periods before and after 1990 (Figures 1-8) shows how the UK climate has changed since the previous atlas. Both summer and winter temperatures and rainfall have been higher since 1990. UK mean summer temperature has exceeded 15°C in seven years since 1975, compared with only three in the previous 65 years. Temperatures in most parts of the UK have increased by about 2°C in summer and 1°C in winter. Despite predictions of increased summer drought, July average rainfall amounts have risen, no doubt influenced by the notably wet Julys from 2007 to 2010 (which incidentally affected recording for this atlas).

Similar trends are apparent in Ireland, with annual temperatures showing an increase of 0.5°C between the

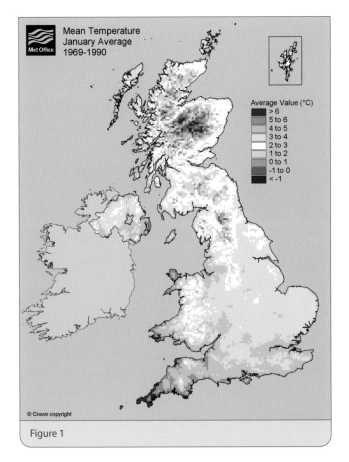

Figure 1

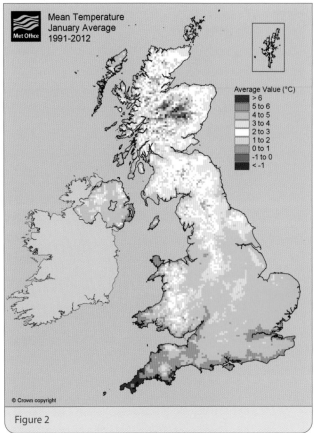

Figure 2

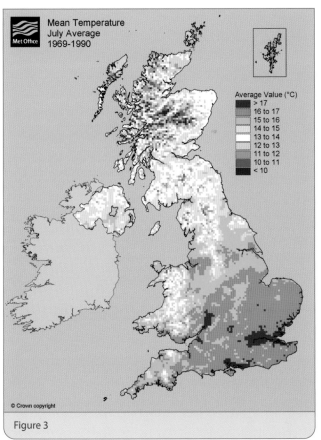

Figure 3

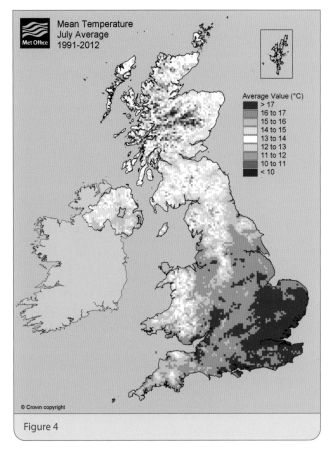

Figure 4

Figures 1-4. Mean UK January and July temperatures (°C) for 1969-1990 and 1991-2012 inclusive, from UK weather station data. Courtesy of Adam Scaife and Dan Hollis at the Met Office, Crown Copyright.

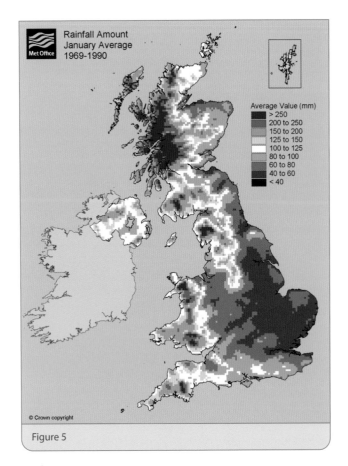

Figure 5

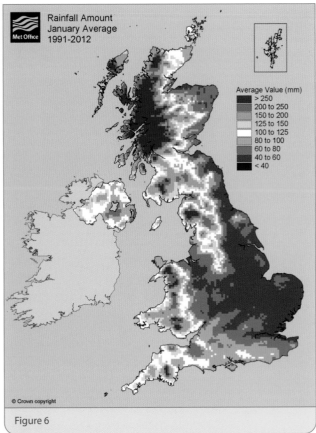

Figure 6

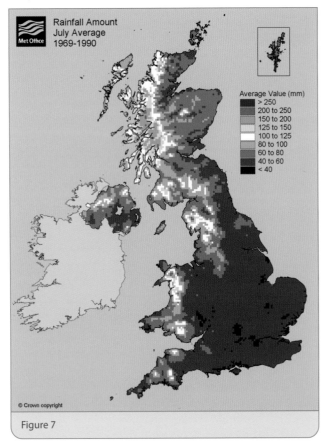

Figure 7

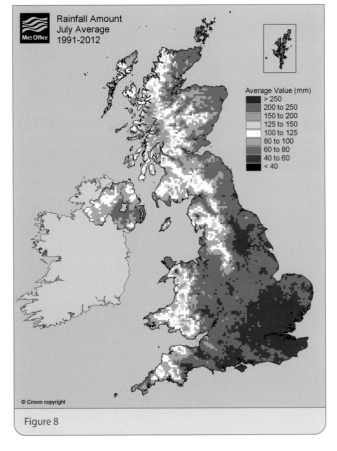

Figure 8

Figures 5-8. Monthly average rainfall (mm) for 1969-1990 and 1990-2012 inclusive, from UK weather station data. Courtesy of Adam Scaife and Dan Hollis at the Met Office, Crown Copyright.

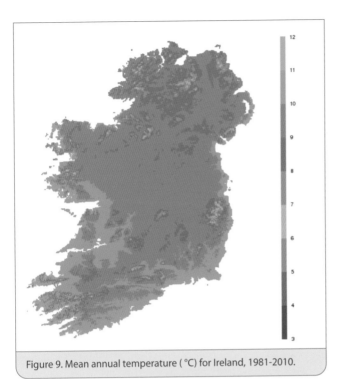

Figure 9. Mean annual temperature ( °C) for Ireland, 1981-2010.

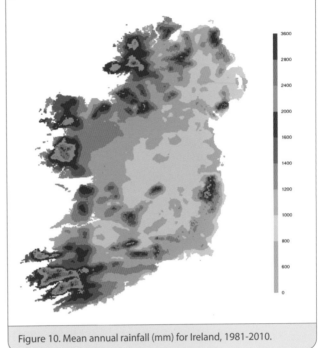

Figure 10. Mean annual rainfall (mm) for Ireland, 1981-2010.

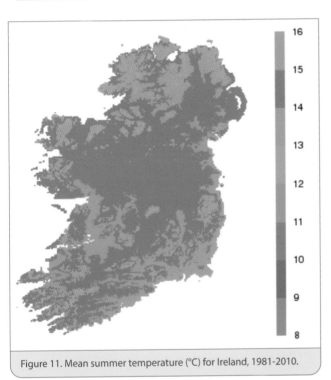

Figure 11. Mean summer temperature (°C) for Ireland, 1981-2010.

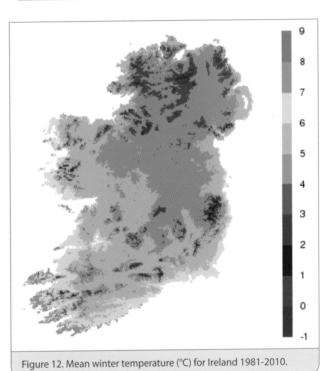

Figure 12. Mean winter temperature (°C) for Ireland 1981-2010.

means for 1961-1990 and 1981-2010, with the greatest increases in the south-east (Figures 9-13). Maximum and minimum temperatures have also increased by approximately 0.5°C. Rainfall also increased across all seasons in Ireland.

The climate maps for Britain and Ireland should be compared with the distribution maps in the species section. Whilst no analysis of climate data and dragonfly distribution has been made it is interesting to note that the distribution of some species appears to be influenced by climatic factors. The distribution of Keeled Skimmer particularly has a strong association with areas of Ireland and western Britain with high rainfall.

The ability of dragonflies to withstand drought in Britain and Ireland is poorly understood, although many species cope in drier parts of Europe and elsewhere. Even less is known about the effects of the serious summer or winter flooding that has been a feature in recent years. In particular, the effects of these events on species associated with running waters are unknown but it is likely that floods may transport larvae downstream. Open water species may also be able to spread through floods which create temporary linkages between ponds and lakes.

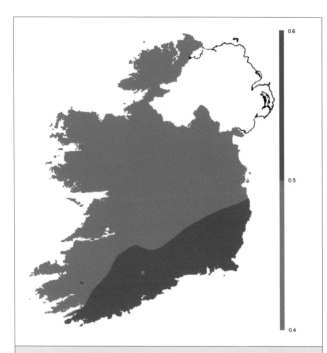

Figure 13. Ireland: Difference between 1981-2010 averages and 1961-1990 averages (°C).

Source for Figures 9-13: Walsh, S. (2012). A Summary of Climate Averages for Ireland 1981-2010. Met éireann Climatological Note No. 14. (Accessed via www.met.ie/climate-ireland/SummaryClimAvgs.pdf on 3 October 2013).

The effects of climate change on dragonfly flight periods are discussed further in Phenology, page 64.

## Altitude

Dragonfly diversity and abundance decline with altitude due to a combination of lower temperatures and the lack of certain habitat types in comparison to low altitude localities. In Ireland, many species reach an upper limit around 250m and only Common Hawker and Common Blue Damselfly are generally observed above 300m. On slopes, where standing waters are generally scarce and running waters rapid and often nutrient-poor, dragonfly species diversity is low, whereas lowland waters are typically rich in nutrients, biomass and dragonfly species.

In the same way that rising temperatures have enabled some dragonfly species to spread northwards, species typical of lowland areas should theoretically be able to colonise suitable wetlands at higher altitude. This may pose additional threats to upland/northern specialists in the form of competition for food, predation and aggression from territorial adults.

## Geology

Bedrock geology influences soil type and acidity, which in turn influence the trophic status (nutrient content) of waterbodies and watercourses. Low nutrient levels and acidic conditions are typical of many upland areas dominated by hard rocks such as granite. Such oligotrophic conditions are characterised by few aquatic plants and little organic matter. Conversely, minerals are more easily dissolved from softer sedimentary rocks, such as calcareous limestone and chalk that also give rise to alkaline water. These result in mesotrophic or eutrophic waters, which typically have luxuriant plant growth. Nutrient levels, however, are also influenced heavily by anthropogenic sources: sewage effluent (especially phosphates) and diffuse pollution from agricultural fertilisers (nitrates and phosphates), especially in the lowlands where human settlement and agricultural intensity are greatest.

The scarcity of surface waterbodies over porous rocks such as chalk and limestone in Britain is apparent from the absence or low numbers of dragonfly records from these areas. A glance at the maps for several species reveals areas of blank hectads around Salisbury Plain and in an arc from Wiltshire to west Norfolk where standing waters are scarce. Conversely most Irish lakes are on the limestone plain and the regions of habitat scarcity are some of the upland areas. Very locally, aquifer fluctuations cause standing waters to come and go erratically, producing turloughs (Ireland and Wales) and pingos (English Breckland).

## Water quality

Rivers and streams, and the wetlands that they flow into and through, have been altered significantly by human activity since prehistoric times, as first woodland was cleared and then the land tilled, exposing the soil to the elements. Centuries of erosion and leaching of soluble chemicals have deposited mineral and organic matter into watercourses and waterbodies. These processes were often accelerated during wartime (e.g. after tree-felling to build ships and after grassland ploughing in the Second World War). Nitrate fertiliser, leached during heavy rainfall, finds its way, via surface and sub-surface routes, into watercourses, resulting in eutrophication (enrichment) and often the consequent loss of submerged aquatic plants as they are suppressed by algae and duckweeds.

Eutrophication also occurs, in a more persistent fashion, as a result of phosphates bound to sediment being carried and deposited into watercourses and waterbodies by the considerable power of floods. Such flood events have increased in recent years possibly as a consequence of the current climate change scenario. Phosphate comes in organic matter originating both from agricultural land and sewage. In recent decades, the expanding human population has added pressures to wetland systems, through the increased disposal of treated (and sometimes untreated) sewage. Spillages from agriculture and industrial sources, mainly accidental, have exacerbated problems locally.

Flood events not only increase eutrophication, but in coastal regions they can also contaminate freshwater areas with saline water. The increased frequency of powerful tidal surges in recent years has led to areas of low lying ground and freshwater ditches being inundated with salt water. For example, the tidal surge in the North Sea of December 2013 led to salt water flooding of coastal grazing marshes from the Tees estuary south to Essex.

## Habitat specialists and generalists

Habitat types are determined by distinct combinations of environmental factors leading to specific vegetation structure and associated communities including dragonflies. Dragonflies that can be regarded as habitat generalists tend to be widespread because they occupy a range of habitat types. Specialists have a more restricted distribution due to their specific requirements.

Dragonfly distribution will also be affected by the ability of each species to disperse to new areas of suitable habitat, so the proximity of suitable sites and the intervening landscape are also important. Unfortunately little is known of the ability of most species to disperse and find suitable new habitat in which they can breed. Anecdotal evidence suggests that generalists are good dispersers, while limited scientific studies have shown that some specialists such as Southern Damselfly are not, although others might be. An outstanding example of the latter is Black Darter, where the distribution map clearly shows a number of records well outside the expected breeding range, particularly in the south and east of Britain. Only a few of these wandering individuals will find suitable habitat in which to establish a colony.

Another habitat specialist that is apparently a good disperser is Scarce Blue-tailed Damselfly. This species is regularly found at new sites some distance from known populations and evidence suggests it is capable of arriving

The second British record of an andromorph female Scarce Blue-tailed Damselfly came from Winterton, Norfolk, on 8 September 2012. *Adrian Riley*

in Britain from continental Europe on a regular basis. The finding of an andromorph female in the Forest of Dean in 2011 and another in Norfolk the following year suggests a continental origin for these individuals, since this form is almost unknown from the British and Irish populations. Therefore, it should be borne in mind when interpreting the maps within this atlas that records from areas lacking suitable breeding habitat are not distinguished from those that have it. This is one of the reasons why records of breeding stages are important.

Range expansion and the sustainability of new populations is dependent on new habitat becoming available, or already being available, and climatic factors being appropriate. New habitat may result from pools forming in mineral extraction sites, newly dug ponds or modification to a habitat through succession or site management. Changes to existing environmental conditions caused by human intervention and the interaction of these changes with other environmental factors are therefore of significance to dragonfly distributions. The recent range expansion of Scarce Chaser, a species that requires lush emergent vegetation at the breeding site, can be attributed to a combination of more sympathetic management of riverside vegetation, maintenance of adjacent meadows and scrub, improved water quality and climate change. Broad-bodied Chaser is another species heavily influenced by human intervention. It is an early coloniser and a species of early successional stages. It breeds in shallow water, even laying eggs into wheel ruts, although sites like this may dry up subsequently. The creation of new ponds and the management of other waterbodies to return them to previous successional stages influence the distribution of this species.

## Conclusions

Environmental factors encompass a wide range of physical, chemical and biological attributes that influence dragonfly distributions. For example, geology and rainfall combined will influence the chemical composition of water and the type of waterbody created in any particular area. Climate and the availability of suitable wetlands greatly influence the range of a species but weather events caused by climate change can also bring disaster to dragonfly populations in the form of more frequent floods, saline conditions and drought. This atlas marks a point in time during a rapidly changing phase of altering environmental conditions, some of which are entirely natural, whilst many more are influenced by human behaviour. In the main, the current changes seem to be of overall benefit to most dragonfly species but only time will tell if this is to continue. Trends in dragonfly populations are discussed on pages 58-63.

# Dragonfly habitats

A habitat is defined as the place where a given species or community lives (Corbet, 1999). The distribution of a dragonfly species is ultimately determined by the availability of suitable conditions that enable it to complete its life cycle and sustain a population. Such habitat normally comprises a complexity of varying elements, each of which is required for either egg, larval or adult survival. Any given habitat type rarely occurs in isolation and many wetland sites comprise a mosaic of different types with varying shape, size, water flow and associated terrestrial habitats. Habitat for dragonflies must include water for breeding and development, as well as surrounding land for adults to find food and shelter. For example, following emergence, Common Clubtail dragonflies leave their breeding sites and fly some distance from water, with mature males returning to the river about a week later to hold territory and find a mate.

Habitat features include the physical, chemical and biological characteristics of the environment (page 4). Aquatic habitats where dragonfly larvae are known to complete the majority of their life cycle are described in general terms here, whilst species-specific elements are covered in more detail in the species accounts.

Generally accepted habitat groupings are based mostly on vegetation communities, yet the aquatic stages of dragonflies are less closely associated with particular plant species and more with specific niches and microhabitats. The aquatic habitat in which egg and larval development takes place is the most critical factor for a dragonfly species. The successful development of eggs (either in or on plant material and debris or in mud) and larvae, together with secure locations for adult emergence, will determine whether a viable population can be sustained. The terrestrial habitat surrounding the breeding site should also be able to support sufficient prey for the more mobile adult dragonflies.

## Plants

Vegetation structure and the growth habit of plants play a major part in creating suitable conditions for many dragonfly species. They also serve as cues for habitat recognition and selection by dragonflies. The species, shape, structure, extent and position of submerged, floating and emergent plants all influence site selection. Damselflies and hawker dragonflies insert their eggs into plants or other organic material (endophytic), while other species normally scatter their eggs into water (exophytic). The morphology of the ovipositor reflects the interspecific variation in mode of oviposition and determines the type of habitat sought by breeding females. Most of the emerald damselflies select habitat with an abundance of emergent plants of the right type and stage of succession. Willow

Emerald Damselfly is the only British species that oviposits into trees, such as willows, Hawthorn, Elder and Ash. Tandem pairs of this species select branches overhanging water and, after the eggs hatch, the larvae drop into the water. In contrast, soft plant tissues are important for oviposition by Southern Damselfly, one of our smallest species. The feel and firmness of the oviposition site may also be important for larger species. For example, females of the larger hawkers probe the substrate with their ovipositor before depositing eggs.

Sometimes, dragonflies do seem to be particularly associated with specific plants. For example, Rigid Hornwort often dominates still or slow-flowing eutrophic waters in ditches, ponds, sluggish streams and disused canals. It has a predominantly southerly and easterly distribution in England, with more scattered populations in Wales, Ireland and the southern half of Scotland. It is particularly attractive to coenagrionid species such as Small Red-eyed Damselfly. In addition, Norfolk Hawker has historically been noted to be strongly associated with Water-soldier in Britain. While this is less the case at some of its new sites in Suffolk and Kent, the plant clearly provides key features for this and other hawker dragonflies. High numbers of exuviae of Brown, Migrant and Southern Hawkers have been found on both native and naturalised varieties of Water-soldier. A new Norfolk Hawker colony in Cambridgeshire is associated with the commercially grown variety of the plant. In The Netherlands, where Norfolk Hawker is recorded somewhat more generally, it is Green Hawker (*Aeshna viridis*, a species not recorded in Britain and Ireland) that has a strong association with habitats containing Water-soldier.

Concern has been expressed about the spread of non-native species such as New Zealand Pigmyweed (Australian Swamp Stonecrop), Parrot's-feather, Floating Pennywort and Water Fern. In the New Forest and elsewhere, ponds have become dominated by New Zealand Pigmyweed to the detriment of native plants. Despite this undesirable situation for plant communities, there is no evidence to suggest that this particular non-native species has had a deleterious effect on dragonflies. Indeed, at many sites the plant is used by several species for oviposition.

The shallow pools at Greenham Common, Berkshire, have been colonised by large expanses of New Zealand Pigmyweed. These pools attract large numbers of Common Darter. *Steve Cham*

## Microhabitats

Microhabitat elements influence the availability of prey and the occurrence of predators throughout all stages of a dragonfly's life. The survival of any individual adult or larva, or indeed the species as a whole, will obviously be maximised where prey items are most abundant and predators are either scarce or most easily avoided.

It appears that visual cues are used by female dragonflies to select the preferred habitat, through the choice of the oviposition site. Tactile cues are used by female hawkers and damselflies when selecting plants or other material in which to insert their eggs. Mate-seeking and pairing in most species typically occurs at or near potential breeding sites. The patrolling behaviour of males at water is often determined by the behaviour of females and their preferred locations. This is well illustrated by species such as Emperor and Hairy Dragonflies. The size of a waterbody may also influence habitat selection, with Common Blue Damselfly in particular being attracted to large expanses of open water.

Although habitat selection by dragonflies is determined in the first instance by a mated female selecting a suitable place to lay her eggs, oviposition may not always yield progeny. Eggs may not survive or larvae may fail to develop. For species that overwinter as eggs it is essential that oviposition sites are selected that maximise protection of the eggs from predation and/or infection, enabling them to develop successfully. However, there are many instances of female dragonflies ovipositing onto cars or gravestones (e.g. Horváth *et al.*, 2007), presumably where highly polished surfaces have confused the dragonfly's use of polarised light as a visual clue for water surfaces. Clearly these events will not lead to viable progeny.

Vegetation structure and other microhabitat details, including physical features, water depth, shading and nutrients, will all determine the success of a given site for the development of dragonfly larvae. Some waterbodies, particularly shallower ones, are prone to drying out during periods of drought or warmer weather. This is potentially disastrous for larvae, but a number of species have demonstrated the ability of larvae to withstand drought. During 1982, a series of settling tanks associated with a former tin mine in Cornwall dried out for a period of about six weeks. The mud was kept moist by occasional light rain and larvae could be found under stones awaiting the return of normal water levels. The following season, at least ten species emerged from these tanks and Scarce Blue-tailed Damselfly was recorded present in greater numbers than in the previous year (Jones, 1985).

As larvae grow, they ultimately seek out areas in which to emerge, either individually or en masse. Once again, microhabitat features, including vegetation structure, water temperature and the physical characteristics of the waterbody, will play a role in site selection. The aspect of the site is also important, with many species seeking to emerge in unshaded places which are warmed by early morning sunshine.

After emergence, the adult's maiden flight is away from water, to find suitable habitat in which to feed and attain sexual maturity before returning to water to breed. The surrounding areas are especially important for feeding, roosting and sometimes mating. Whilst the proximity of water usually means a guaranteed supply of small flies with aquatic larval stages, notably chironomid midges, a diverse terrestrial habitat will harbour many other potential prey items from aphids to butterflies. Although the quality of the terrain surrounding breeding sites is of special importance for foraging, protection from predators and the weather is another major factor. For many dragonfly species, trees, shrubs, heathland or grassland provide safe areas for roosting and shelter during inclement weather.

Shelter for roosting is an important criterion in site selection as can be seen by Red-eyed and Variable Damselflies taking shelter in nettles. *Steve Cham*

## Human influence

Most of the surface of Britain and Ireland has been highly modified by centuries of human intervention. Many wetland habitats are man-made or at least modified. Without continued management, these habitats go through a succession of changes in floral composition combined with the deposition of organic and mineral sediments, which influence the range of dragonfly species present. Intervention is required for most habitat types to maintain the continued breeding success of certain species. Site management aimed at maintaining a range of successional stages will support a wider range of species.

# Rivers and streams

**Rivers** can be defined as watercourses with a unidirectional flow of water that exceeds 3m in width, whereas **streams** are narrower than this, but more than 30cm wide. Both are dynamic in nature, showing marked fluctuations in water level and flow rate, particularly when in spate. Watercourses may overflow and cause flooding and their course may be changed by a variety of factors.

Rivers and streams can be divided into upland watercourses that are mainly eroding and those in the lowlands that are mainly depositing. To some extent these are related to the gradient and hardness of underlying rock. Relatively coarse mineral sediment is produced from the erosion of hard rocks, while smaller silt and clay particles come from softer rocks and topsoil and are deposited in alluvial plains. Geology has a clear influence on the trophic status and acidity of rivers, with low nutrient levels and acidic conditions typical of many upland areas dominated by hard rocks such as granite. In lowlands, watercourses collect more dissolved nutrients from soft sedimentary rocks like chalk and limestone that give rise to alkaline water. However, nutrient levels are influenced by anthropogenic sources, e.g. sewage effluent (especially phosphates) and diffuse pollution from agricultural fertilisers (nitrates and phosphates), especially in the lowlands where human settlement and agricultural intensity are greatest.

Upper reaches of the River Nene in Northamptonshire provide suitable conditions for Beautiful Demoiselle. *Mark Tyrrell*

These physical and chemical characteristics will determine to a large extent the plant and animal communities in the rivers and streams. Channel dimensions, the river bank vegetation and human impacts all influence stream and river communities. Channels may contain deep pools, islands of gravel, sand or mud and, of particular interest to dragonflies, sluggish backwaters and fringing beds of emergent plants. Shading by trees can influence the distribution of adult dragonflies and larvae. Near their tidal limits, rivers become brackish. While no European dragonfly species can breed successfully in seawater, some can complete larval development in brackish water (e.g. White-legged Damselfly emerging just below the limit of tidal influence on the River Exe at Countess Wear, Devon).

Floating and submerged plants are often scarce in rivers, although the margins and banksides are frequently clothed in emergent and other plants. Beds of River Water-crowfoot may be present in larger rivers, while Chalk-stream Water-crowfoot prefers faster-flowing streams, especially those with alkaline waters; both provide good oviposition sites for demoiselles. Slow-flowing waters may also have water-lilies, pondweeds and water-starworts. Sediments that accumulate under beds of tall emergents such as Common Club-rush, Common Reed, Yellow Iris, Reed Canary-grass and Unbranched Bur-reed provide microhabitat for the larvae of White-legged Damselfly and Scarce Chaser.

Water Crowfoot growing in streams and rivers provides perches favoured by both Banded (male below) and Beautiful Demoiselles. *Bob Carpenter*

The terrestrial habitats through which watercourses flow are important for shelter and feeding by adult dragonflies. The presence of semi-natural and/or rank vegetation close to watercourses is beneficial. Countryside Survey 2007 (Carey *et al.*, 2008) showed that the richness of plant species by streams decreased by 7.5% in Britain between 1998 and 2007 while, since 1990, vegetation has become taller and with a higher proportion of more competitive species. Bankside trees may cast shade onto the water, reducing opportunities for aquatic plants to grow and for adult dragonflies to perch in sunlight. Both Beautiful and Banded Demoiselles often occur on watercourses with partial shading and Golden-ringed Dragonfly frequently breeds in woodland streams. Excessive shading caused by dense tree growth, however, reduces or eliminates dragonfly usage, at least by adults. Shade from Purple Moor-grass, Black Bog-rush or Bog Myrtle along heathland streams used by Southern Damselfly can severely limit their use by that species.

River Teign, Dartmoor, Devon. A fast flowing upland river that supports Beautiful Demoiselle and Golden-ringed Dragonfly. *Steve Cham*

The Warwickshire Avon at Marcliff is a proven breeding site for Common Clubtail and White-legged Damselfly. Scarce Chaser has also been recorded. *Kay Reeve*

The fast flow rate, combined with lower temperatures, typical of upland rivers and streams reduces the opportunities for dragonflies to breed. In contrast, the slow flows in floodplain streams and mature rivers allow silt and organic matter to accumulate and emergent vegetation to develop. Riffles, rapids and waterfalls occur in some lowland water courses, providing habitat where Beautiful Demoiselle and Golden-ringed Dragonfly can breed. Overall, microhabitats for larvae are more abundant in lowland watercourses and a total of 31 species have been recorded breeding in the lowlands compared with at the most nine in upland water courses, principally in streams.

The data for Britain is based on the Wetland Inventory of the UK's Wetland Bird Survey (WeBS*), developed by WeBS following extensive cross-validation of Ordnance Survey Mastermap® 1:10,000 coverage (sourced in 2005) with OS® 1:25,000 and Google Maps®, undertaken using ArcMapTM 9.2 GIS (ESRI Inc. 2006). The Irish data is derived from Ordnance Survey Ireland and Ordnance Survey Northern Ireland 1:50,000 Discovery Series geometry.

Metres (000s)

<20

20-40

40-60

60-80

80-100

100-200

200-500

500-800

800>

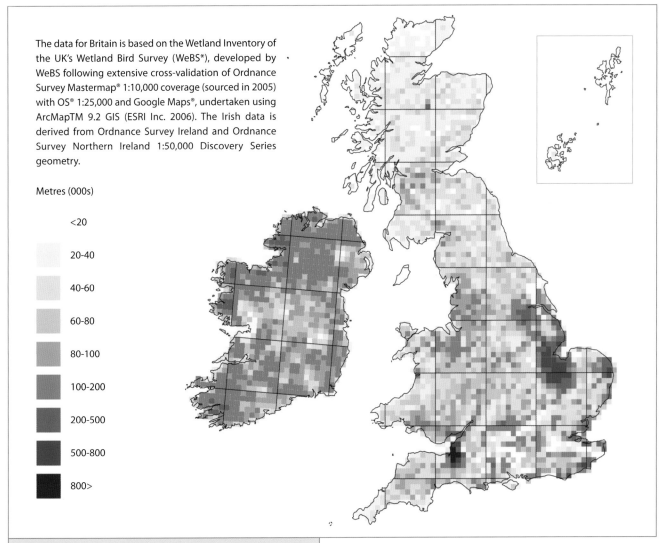

Figure 14. The combined length of rivers, drains, ditches and canals in each hectad.

* WeBS is a partnership between the British Trust for Ornithology, Royal Society for Protection of Birds and Joint Nature Conservation Committee (the last on behalf of the statutory nature conservation bodies: Natural England, Natural Resources Wales and Scottish Natural Heritage and the Department of the Environment Northern Ireland), in association with the Wildfowl & Wetlands Trust.

## Threats and influences

The threats to species living in rivers and streams vary in different regions. In the past, watercourses flowing through urban areas were frequently polluted by industrial effluents. Such events are now mainly accidental and modern clean-up and containment operations for them are likely to be more successful than they were in the past. Point source pollution events have eliminated some species in pastoral areas where silage, slurry or sheep-dip have been allowed to escape into watercourses. The effects on dragonflies of such incidents may be temporary, provided that a source of recolonisation remains (upstream, for example) once the pollution has dissipated. In England and Wales, the number of serious pollution incidents (involving both water and air pollution) halved from 2000 to 2012. However, the waste, agriculture (especially dairy), water and sewerage sectors continue to be of concern, accounting for 60% of the more serious incidents in 2012 (Environment Agency, 2013).

Watercourses that pass through agricultural land also receive fertiliser and sometimes pesticide run-off, the former increasing nutrient levels, encouraging plant growth and reducing oxygen levels. The seriousness of pesticide run-off depends on the concentration and type of product involved. The EU Water Framework Directive (2000/60/EC) requires member states to improve the ecological condition of watercourses and standing waters, especially through controlling diffuse pollution. The difficulty in achieving the required standards has been acknowledged. However, the aim is to achieve good ecological status by 2015.

When grassland is converted to arable land and soil erosion occurs, nearby watercourses may receive sediments that alter their character, for example by the concretion of gravel beds. Afforestation of catchments can also have severe impacts on streams and rivers through nutrient release and acidification of watercourses, as shown by numerous studies in Britain and Ireland (e.g. Ormerod et al., 1993). Wooded streams may become too shady near their sources, when trees are left unmanaged and the canopy cover increases. Climate change, through an increase in extreme drought or rainfall events, threatens flow rates generally. A reduction in river flow rates because of excessive abstraction from rivers represents a potential threat.

Very few rivers and streams remain in a completely natural state in Britain and Ireland, although some still meander freely across their floodplains and flood during and after heavy rain. Embankments have been constructed in many upland and, especially, lowland rivers to reduce the risk of flooding, especially in times of high rainfall. Such efforts to control water flow in rivers have modified the majority of river systems to the detriment of most aquatic life. The flooding in the winter of 2013/14, especially in the Somerset Levels, resulted in the call to increase the amount of dredging of rivers draining low lying land. This in turn

will have a negative impact on aquatic life. In conjunction with losses in the natural regulation provided by upland blanket bogs as well as woodland cover in catchments, river flows are no longer ameliorated and there is consequently greater and more rapid variation in flow rates. This variation has been exacerbated in recent years by extreme weather events. The current climate change predictions include increased summer droughts and winter flooding.

Some lowland watercourses have been canalised, straightened and/or dredged and have trapezoid cross-sections to improve flow, limit flooding and reduce erosion. Dredging and trapezoid cross-sectioning of streams (and ditches) reduce microhabitat and are generally unfavourable for dragonflies. Even apparently natural watercourses may have been dredged or deepened. The engineering of watercourses to improve flow has not been without modification to the margins. Rock barriers have been used to prevent bank erosion. Sometimes trees, but more often woody debris, have often been removed. Access for livestock typically results in at least localised poached ground, if not more extensive degradation to banks. Although some specialised invertebrates benefit from this, it is unlikely to have helped dragonflies, with the possible exception of providing bare substrate for territorial or basking Black-tailed Skimmers and Common Darters. There is now recognition that canalisation decreases biodiversity and action is being taken in some areas to reverse the process. Thus, in Norfolk, the River Wensum is undergoing reinstatement of meanders and similar work has been carried out, or is proposed, for many streams, e.g. the New Forest, Hampshire. Where it has been carried out, combined with tree clearance, it has resulted in a greater range of microhabitats that in turn has benefited dragonflies.

Re-instatement of meanders in the New Forest, Hampshire.
*Steve Cham*

Modifications such as weirs, common in parts of France, are rare on lowland rivers in Britain. Many watercourses have been dammed to produce reservoirs or ornamental lakes and ponds and rivers associated with mills have mill ponds that produce areas of calmer water. The discharge from

Confluence of the River Hertford and River Derwent, Yorkshire. This site has both Banded and Beautiful Demoiselle. *Paul Ashton*

deep upland reservoirs comprises cold water from near the bed; this may reduce populations of aquatic invertebrates, including dragonflies, in rivers downstream. Most watercourses flow permanently, though some, notably those flowing over porous rocks, may disappear temporarily, especially in periods of summer drought. The effects of this on dragonflies are not fully known, although emerging dragonflies have been observed within cave systems.

Abstraction for industry or agriculture has been of concern in recent years, as the flows of some rivers have been markedly reduced in summer during periods of drought. Some watercourses have dried up completely, with likely (but perhaps only temporary) consequences for dragonflies. In a few places, water is piped long distances from rivers in areas with spare water capacity to reservoirs for storage in places where demand outstrips local supply. In times of drought water may also be piped from storage reservoirs to alleviate low river flows. In East Anglia, water is currently transferred from Norfolk to the Abberton and Hanningfield Reservoirs in Essex through a network of large pipelines and rivers. The bulk movement of water at this scale must be responsible for some spread of aquatic species, including dragonflies, across potentially large distances.

## Water quality

Many watercourses receive treated water in the output from sewage treatment works. The quantity and quality of these are controlled by consents from the relevant bodies in Britain and Ireland. Effluent standards have improved significantly in recent decades, as methods such as phosphate stripping have become available. Biological and chemical sampling of rivers has revealed general improvements in both of these elements of water quality. The UK Sustainable Development Indicator 30a (chemical quality of rivers) showed that, between 1990 and 2007/8, the percentage of river lengths of 'good' chemical quality rose to 95% in Wales, stayed at about 85% in Scotland, rose from 55% to 79% in England and rose from about 50% to over 70% in Northern Ireland (source: http://webarchive.nationalarchives.gov.uk/2011022309355

0/defra.gov.uk/sustainable/government/progress/national/ 30.htm, accessed 5 February 2014). Similarly, the biological quality of rivers improved in England and Wales during the same period but in Ireland fell, with 77% with good quality in 1990 falling to 69% in 2008 (McGarrigle *et al.*, 2010). Since then, the assessment methods have changed in order to measure ecological status for reporting for Water Framework Directive targets.

Water pollution may take a variety of forms. Point sources of pollution include the unlicensed discharge of sewage, accidental discharge of silage liquor, slurry and milk and accidental or deliberate release of industrial waste, including the release of heavy metals (e.g. arsenic) from mines. Levels of phosphate and nitrate have fallen in England and Wales in recent years. However, in England, 50% of river length was still rated 'high' for phosphate content and 29% for nitrate in 2009, with the highest percentages in central and eastern England and the lowest in the north-west. A much smaller proportion of rivers in Wales have high levels of these pollutants; the comparative figures for phosphate and nitrate falling to about 6% and 1%, respectively, by 2009.

The acidification of watercourses has been associated with the ability of conifer plantations to trap and concentrate acidifying air pollutants. Extensive areas of conifers have been planted, especially in upland areas where many watercourses are already naturally acidic, but the effects of further acidification on dragonflies have not been quantified. Similarly, the effects on dragonflies of levels of contaminants such as PCBs and organochlorine and organophosphate pesticides are imperfectly known. In any case, the long term effects of pollution are influenced by the ability of species to recolonise after any mortality (Corbet, 1999).

Increased sedimentation in many eroding rivers is considered a problem for spawning salmonid fish; conversely, it is not implausible that this increases microhabitats for dragonfly larvae. A few watercourses may have sediment in suspension, including clay particles in quarry outflows, but typically this is removed at mining sites by sedimentation tanks before the outflow reaches larger watercourses off-site. As mentioned above, access to watercourses by livestock, especially cattle, for drinking purposes creates muddy areas. This can add to the sediment load and is believed to contribute to the concretion of gravels used by salmonid fish for spawning. Many such areas have been fenced in recent years to restrict the access of livestock to short sections and thereby protect the quality of the watercourse (e.g. in the Tamar Valley, Cornwall/Devon). Broad-bodied Chaser, Black-tailed Skimmer and a few other species may be attracted to such trampled areas and it is possible that some dragonfly larvae benefit from the same sedimentation that causes problems for salmonids. Where livestock movements are concentrated to cross heathland and moorland streams, these muddy 'pinch points' are attractive locally to Scarce Blue-tailed Damselfly.

The temperature of flowing waters is influenced to some extent by the fact that they mainly flow from higher altitudes where temperatures will generally be lower. An important exception to this, at least as far as Southern Damselfly is concerned, is the temperature buffering in winter provided by springs feeding the streams in which they breed. Water temperatures can also be affected by industrial processes. Coal-fired power stations and steelworks abstract water for cooling purposes, returning the water downstream with unnaturally high temperatures. It is likely that such warmed water has enabled the rapid development and early emergence of some dragonflies (see Phenology, page 64), although the numbers of these industrial discharges has declined in recent years.

Historically, boats have used calm, lower stretches of many rivers for commercial trade but, in recent years, generally smaller leisure craft have been the norm. Such boating probably has very limited effects on dragonflies, although propellers on motorised craft can stir up sediments causing turbidity. Additionally, the waves these boats create may erode banks and bankside vegetation and, at certain times of the year, this may disturb adult dragonflies as they emerge from the water. Emerging Common Clubtails have been known to suffer from boat wash on the River Thames (e.g. at Goring, Oxfordshire).

Flowing waters tend to have more sustainable densities of fish than standing waters and stocking poses less of a threat to dragonflies. Stocking in rivers may occur where fish have been lost during a pollution incident or where angling, such as that for trout, has a commercial value.

## Species of rivers and streams

The species common to both upland and lowland watercourses are Beautiful Demoiselle, Large Red Damselfly, Golden-ringed Dragonfly and, more locally, Blue-tailed and Small Red Damselflies, Broad-bodied Chaser, Keeled Skimmer and Common Darter. Up to about 300m above sea level in the south of Britain (lower further north), typical species may also include Banded Demoiselle and White-legged Damselfly, joined in sluggish sections by species more usually associated with standing water, such as Azure, both red-eyed, Common Blue and Blue-tailed Damselflies, Brown and Migrant Hawkers, Emperor Dragonfly, Black-tailed Skimmer and Common Darter.

Less frequent species breeding in slow-flowing lowland rivers and streams include Emerald Damselfly, Hairy Dragonfly, all three chasers and Ruddy Darter. Acidic flushes, seepages and/or streams in heathland may hold Scarce Blue-tailed and Small Red Damselflies, Common Hawker, Keeled Skimmer, Black Darter and Northern Emerald. Scarce Blue-tailed Damselfly is closely associated with shallow water that warms up quickly, including artificial watercourses associated with quarrying. Southern Damselfly occurs very locally in base-rich streams and flushes flowing through heathland, fen and chalk river valleys.

Crockford Stream, New Forest, Hampshire, a lowland heath stream. *Ian McColl*

Irish streams and rivers support fewer species than British examples, although the length of rivers and streams is relatively higher in Ireland than in most of Britain. Lowland rivers in Ireland are occupied only by the two demoiselle species. Upland streams are similarly devoid of dragonflies, apart from the Large Red Damselfly and Common Hawker. Golden-ringed Dragonfly is a notable absentee from Irish stream and flush habitats. Although it is present along the entire west coast of Britain, the Irish Sea has, until recently, proved a barrier (there have been three recent sightings in Ireland but no confirmed populations have been found). This species is also absent from the Isle of Man, although it is found in many of the Inner Hebrides, showing that short sea crossings are possible. It is absent from the Outer Hebrides.

While, as outlined above, many species are able to utilise rivers and streams for breeding in Britain and Ireland, it is worth mentioning that we have a relatively restricted number of species that largely specialise in such flowing habitats when compared to many parts of Europe. Such species in Britain include our two demoiselles, White-legged Damselfly, Common Clubtail, Golden-ringed Dragonfly and Scarce Chaser. On the Continent, a wider variety of white-legged damselflies (also known as Featherlegs) and Gomphids (Clubtail species) are found and there are frequently two species of Goldenring present. This reduced biodiversity in Britain and Ireland is to some extent associated with several species being on the edge of their range in northwest Europe.

# Bogs, fens, mires and swamps

Wetlands are areas of permanently saturated ground, occurring throughout Britain and Ireland, with most types attracting and providing breeding opportunities for dragonflies. As they exist in many forms and often in a mosaic with other habitats, classifying wetlands can be problematic. Additional confusion can be caused by the variety of colloquial names that exist for the types of wetland. So the same name may be used to mean different things in different areas. For some a bog just means any area of saturated, wet ground but to a wetland ecologist it has a precise meaning. The situation is further complicated through intervention and human influence. In Britain and Ireland the most significant types of wetlands for dragonflies are fens and bogs. These are peat-forming wetlands and collectively are termed mires in ecology. **Swamp** refers to a wetland that is normally inundated by nutrient-rich neutral or alkaline water and comprises tall, dense beds of grass-like vegetation, often Common Reed.

Mires are areas of peatland, characterised by saturated ground with low growing vegetation dominated by sedges and mosses. The nature of the water feeding the mire creates the fundamental ecological distinctions between a bog and a fen. The chemical composition of the water is the major influence on the species of flora and fauna (including dragonflies) that will inhabit the wetland. **Bogs** are entirely rain-water fed (ombrotrophic), whereas **fens** receive some or all water from ground water sources (minerotrophic).

Fens can, therefore, be acidic or alkaline depending on ground water chemistry. This can be fresh, acid or alkaline, nutrient rich or nutrient poor, unpolluted or polluted by enrichment. Bogs can develop on top of fens and equally fens can be found within blanket bogs. Fens may also be found in association with raised bogs and heaths.

As rain-water is naturally acidic and nutrient poor, bogs are home to species which can tolerate these harsh conditions, such as the peat-forming species of bog moss, cotton grasses and sedges. Heather is usually present on bogs but it is not as dominant or as strongly growing as it is on better-drained heaths. There are two main types of bogs: raised and blanket bogs. Raised bogs are dome-shaped peatlands that form over a lake basin or natural depression. They are also lowland features and only found in areas experiencing moderate rainfall (800-900mm annually), whereas blanket bogs are the large expanses of bog that literally blanket the upland landscapes of the north and west of both Britain and Ireland. Blanket bogs can also be found at sea level in the high rainfall areas of the north and west. Raised bogs naturally have few areas of open water unlike blanket bogs, which can have many areas of open water in the form of pools covering extensive regions, such as the Flow Country of northern Scotland.

Aerial view of the pools created at Brackagh Moss NNR, Co. Armagh, N. Ireland. This site is a fen that formerly held a colony of Irish Damselfly. The site has become much more enriched in recent decades and populations of some species including Variable Damselfly have declined. *Robert Thompson*

Bog pools at Silver Flowe NNR, Dumfries & Galloway, provide ideal breeding habitat for Azure Hawker. *David Clarke*

Fens are also peat-forming systems and will develop along seepages and flushes, as these are ground water fed. As noted above, fens can be acidic and lacking in minerals but in many areas of England and Ireland there is a calcareous base rock and hence the water is alkaline and base-rich. Consequently, fens in general are richer places than bogs and are dominated by small sedges and brown mosses. Fens can often be small in extent around springs and flushes but extensive fens still exist in some areas. Fens can also develop secondarily when bogs have been modified by removal of peat. This can create pools or areas of peat where ground water influence replaces the solely rain-water-influenced bog surface. Some of the richest Irish dragonfly sites are these cutover bogs. The Somerset Levels and Moors and the Norfolk Broads have a similar origin and constitute two of the most significant areas of fen in Britain and Ireland.

Bog lakes above Maentwrog, Merionethshire: an area of acidic lakes with mats of Marsh St John's-Wort and bog-moss providing breeding conditions for Large and Small Red Damselflies and Four-spotted Chaser. *Allan Brandon*

There are few intact raised bogs left in either Britain or Ireland but extensive areas of blanket bog exist, especially in Scotland and western Ireland. Raised bogs have been exploited for peat for fuel and horticulture and blanket bogs have been altered, especially by large scale afforestation. Blanket bogs are harsh places for dragonflies, which have to cope with cool summer temperatures and low productivity. Typical species across Britain and Ireland are Common Hawker, Large Red Damselfly and Four-spotted Chaser, which are also found in pools on heathland in the south of Britain. Azure Hawker is found in Scottish bog pools, while White-faced Darter occurs in just a few areas of England and Scotland, where it breeds in small pools filled with bog-moss. Raised bogs offer slightly more benign conditions for species and Black Darter in particular seems to favour raised bogs over blanket bog. Many of the interesting species found on mires are associated with fens within bogs and heaths. Northern Emerald breeds in wet bog-moss with hardly any open water and appears to be found mostly where there is some ground water influence, although conditions are still acidic. Small Red Damselfly is also found where there is some ground water movement and sometimes where the water is calcareous. Keeled Skimmer is the most widespread species of this flush and spring community, which is present widely in the south and west as far north as western Scotland.

Wildmoor Heath NR, Berkshire, comprises valley mire and wet and dry lowland heath. The building of dams and sluices has aided the creation of bog pools that support locally rare species such as Small Red Damselfly, Common Hawker and Keeled Skimmer. *Des Sussex*

Although Ireland has an abundance of bogs, some of the bog-living species are absent. This is probably a result of the timing of colonisation. Bogs did not exist at the end of the last Ice Age and most that exist now developed much later, when the climate changed to a cooler and wetter phase. Bog development in Ireland happened after the island became separated from Britain, which prevented species like White-faced Darter and Azure Hawker colonising.

Cothill Fen, Oxfordshire, is a calcareous fen supporting a population of Small Red Damselfly and Keeled Skimmer. *Steve Cham*

Much of the peat layer in bogs was formed in past millennia, when rainfall amounts were significantly greater. This makes the human-induced damage of recent decades difficult to repair. Some attempts have been made to restore blanket bog after plantation forestry, for example in the Scottish Flow Country, and after degradation by overgrazing and/or burning, for example in Exmoor (Devon/Somerset). These restoration projects have achieved some successes with regard to dragonflies. Where the peat layers in bogs and fens have been cut for fuel or horticulture, and allowed to flood, the open water is very attractive to dragonflies. At Thorne Moors, part of the Humberhead Peatlands NNR, Humberside/South Yorkshire, a high water level is being maintained after the cessation of peat extraction to encourage the restoration of the former raised bog; dragonflies are among those groups expected to benefit from this.

Where water flows over and through calcareous bedrock it becomes alkaline, producing **rich fens** where it meets flat landscapes. These are very different in the plant communities which they support compared to their acidic counterparts described above. Rather than peat accumulating from decaying bog-mosses, here it is formed from the remains of plants such as Common Reed and Great Fen-sedge. The vegetation is typically lusher and more species-rich than more acidic poor fens, which means that dragonflies are essentially restricted for breeding purposes to areas of open water, including artificial ditches.

Thursley Common NNR, Surrey, is considered to be one of the best dragonfly sites in Britain. Boardwalks provide easy access to the bog areas and reduce the impact on this fragile habitat. *Steve Cham*

Rich fen specialities include Variable Damselfly and Norfolk Hawker (e.g. at Upton Fen, Norfolk), while poor fens, especially in the south, may support quite a wide range of species, including Scarce Blue-tailed and Southern Damselflies, Golden-ringed Dragonfly and Keeled Skimmer.

# Lakes and ponds

Lakes and ponds cover all types of standing water from tiny water-filled holes to areas of water covering thousands of hectares, such as Lough Neagh or Loch Ness. Whilst most people have no difficulty recognising a lake or pond, providing a succinct definition that encompasses this huge diversity is problematic. In Britain and Ireland, size is used to distinguish lakes from ponds, the latter being those that are less than 2ha in area (Freshwater Habitats Trust: www.freshwaterhabitats.org.uk/habitats/pond/).

Lakes and ponds take a wide variety of forms, reflecting their origin, purpose, permanence, chemical and botanical characteristics, depth, successional stage and landscape setting. All of these strongly influence the presence, relative abundance and fecundity of dragonfly species. Standing waters can be classified according to their nutrient status, which represents the concentration of dissolved chemicals, especially nitrogen and phosphorus. These nutrients feed the entire food chain from algae and higher plants to animals, including predators such as dragonfly larvae. As a general rule, greater nutrient concentration gives rise to higher biomass production that, in turn, tends to benefit generalist dragonflies. At lower nutrient levels, specialist species typically occupy scarce niches, where presumably they can harvest more localised prey species.

**Dystrophic waters** are highly acidic (pH below 5.5, low in nutrients and typically stained brown from humic and other acids in the peat substrate). Most dystrophic waters are peat pools and lochans within blanket bogs. Among the aquatic plants supported are bladderworts, some pondweeds (Broad-leaved and Bog) and Bogbean, while some bog-moss species (e.g. *Sphagnum auriculatum* and *S. cuspidatum*) may be present.

**Oligotrophic waters** lack plant nutrients and organic matter, resulting in a scarcity of floating or submerged plants and a high concentration of dissolved oxygen. They may be acidic or, as in limestone/marl lakes in Ireland, base-rich.

**Mesotrophic waters** have moderate trophic or nutrient conditions, being neither oligotrophic nor eutrophic. Such lakes in the middle of the trophic range are relatively infrequent and largely confined to the margins of upland areas in the north and west of Britain and throughout Ireland. Moderately rich in nutrients, mesotrophic waters are sometimes discoloured by algae and have beds of submerged aquatic plants. The plant growth is typically lusher than in oligotrophic lakes. Characteristic aquatic plants include White Water-lily, Yellow Water-lily, pondweeds and often stoneworts.

**Eutrophic waters** are base-rich and usually discoloured or turbid from algae and large amounts of suspended mineral and organic matter, which results in abundant growth of plants, especially algae, and low levels of dissolved oxygen. Some waterbodies are naturally eutrophic but most waters become eutrophic as a result of anthropogenic (human influenced) enrichment. Typical aquatic plants include duckweeds, pondweeds, waterweeds, water-crowfoots, Rigid Hornwort and Spiked Water-milfoil. Submerged plants are usually restricted to marginal shallows. Dense stands of emergent swamp vegetation, such as Common Reed, Reed Sweet-grass and bulrushes are common around sheltered margins, although few dragonflies breed in such dense cover.

## Origins of lakes and ponds

Relatively few standing open waters in lowland England and Wales are natural in origin. In contrast, in the lake-rich areas of northern England, north Wales and the north and west of both Ireland and Scotland, natural waterbodies predominate. In lowland England, dragonflies have had to adapt to the lack of natural standing waters and occupy some of the many types of man-made ponds and lakes instead. The dragonfly fauna of the north and west of Britain and Ireland is still largely found on naturally occurring sites. However, few lakes can be considered genuinely natural and untainted by human influence. Invariably, those that sit within extensive areas of semi-natural habitat, such as heathland or moorland, comprise some of the most valued sites for dragonflies.

Llyn Tecwyn Isaf, Merionethshire. This acidic rock basin lake supports locally rare or uncommon species including Small Red Damselfly and Hairy Dragonfly and the only known population of Downy Emerald in North Wales. *Allan Brandon*

Since Roman times, fish ponds have been created to supply fish for human consumption. During the Industrial Revolution, many mill ponds were created by damming, or channelling water from, watercourses in order to provide power for mills and other factories. On farmland, many pits were dug for marl, subsequently flooding to become a valuable source of freshwater. Whilst some lakes and many ponds have been drained or infilled in the more recent past (half of Britain's ponds were lost in the 20th century), many new sites have been created through the flooding of mineral extraction sites, peat workings and areas of mining subsidence. Other new sites have resulted from the digging of livestock drinking ponds, balancing ponds, and the construction of water storage reservoirs, mainly for human consumption and, more recently, crop irrigation, as well as the direct creation of many different types of pond. Artificial or ornamental standing waters may be found in parks, gardens, golf courses or in the grounds of stately homes. The nutrient status of these artificial waterbodies is variable and may be very high, for example in hypertrophic waters found in urban parks, where the water has been excessively enriched with nutrients as a result of large numbers of wildfowl.

Balancing pond adjacent to a housing estate, Isle of Wight. *Dave Dana*

Carlin's Cairn, Galloway Hills, Dumfries and Galloway. These upland pools 630m above sea level are good for Large Red Damselfly and Common Hawker. *Richard and Barbara Mearns*

## Lake and pond statistics

Standing open waterbodies covered only about 1% of Britain and Ireland in 2006/7: 204,000 ha (0.9%) in Britain and 188,935 ha in Ireland (2.2%) (Carey *et al.*, 2008; the figure for Ireland is derived from Ordnance Survey Ireland and Ordnance Survey Northern Ireland 1:50,000 Discovery Series geometry). There was a significant increase in the area of standing waters in England between 1998 and 2007, with an overall increase in Britain and Ireland of about 7,500 ha (Carey *et al.*, 2008; Cooper *et al.*, 2009; ERA-Maptec, undated).

Countryside Survey 2007 (Carey *et al.*, 2008) estimated that there were 478,000 ponds in Britain. Overall, the number of ponds in Britain increased by 12.5% between 1998 and 2007, following a 6% increase in lowland ponds between 1990 and 1998. For individual countries the figures are: 234,000 in England (up 18.3% since 1998), 199,000 in Scotland (up 5.5%) and 47,000 in Wales (up 16.9%). Comparable figures for Ireland are not available. The same survey also found that only 8% of British ponds were in good ecological condition and that pond quality had declined since the previous survey in 1997.

## Typical species of lakes and ponds

All but five of the regular breeding species in Britain and Ireland are known to have bred in ponds. Fewer species breed in lakes, particularly upland lakes, which are generally

cooler and have lower nutrient status than ponds. Six species are common to both upland and lowland lakes and ponds: Emerald, Large Red, Common Blue and Blue-tailed Damselflies, Four-spotted Chaser and Common Darter. Given the widespread nature of these habitats, it is no surprise they are the most widely distributed species in Britain and Ireland.

Lakes are typically more exposed to wind and hence wave action than ponds and have a smaller proportion of the shallow water favoured by most plants and invertebrates. For these reasons, lakes tend to have lower species diversity per unit area than ponds, with exposed margins being less attractive to dragonflies than sheltered areas. Among the more conspicuous species able to benefit from large expanses of open water are Common Blue Damselfly – often present in huge numbers over eutrophic lakes and, especially, reservoirs – and Red-eyed Damselfly, where water lilies are present.

## Distribution of lakes and ponds

Lakes and ponds are widespread and their distribution obviously has a major influence on the distribution of many dragonfly species. However, like other wetland habitat types, lakes and ponds are not found uniformly across Britain and Ireland. Figure 15 shows that lakes and ponds are common features of the north and west of both Britain and Ireland, but note that the map only shows features that are visible at the scale of the map and therefore many smaller waters are excluded.

There is a relatively small total area of standing water across most of the southern parts of Scotland, England and Wales. There is a striking pattern across northern Scotland, with lakes common in the western Highlands but relatively few in the north eastern Highlands. Many of the Scottish Islands have large areas of standing water but lakes and ponds are rare features of the Isle of Man.

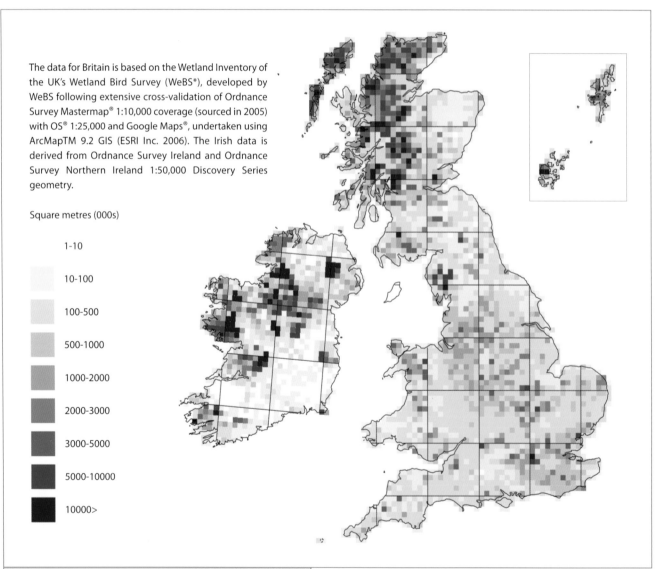

The data for Britain is based on the Wetland Inventory of the UK's Wetland Bird Survey (WeBS*), developed by WeBS following extensive cross-validation of Ordnance Survey Mastermap® 1:10,000 coverage (sourced in 2005) with OS® 1:25,000 and Google Maps®, undertaken using ArcMapTM 9.2 GIS (ESRI Inc. 2006). The Irish data is derived from Ordnance Survey Ireland and Ordnance Survey Northern Ireland 1:50,000 Discovery Series geometry.

Square metres (000s)

1-10

10-100

100-500

500-1000

1000-2000

2000-3000

3000-5000

5000-10000

10000>

Figure 15. The density of standing waters. (The map shows the area, per hectad, of lakes, lochs, lochans, pools, ponds and reservoirs in Britain, lakes and ponds in Ireland; hectads with darker colour contain more standing water.)

* WeBS is a partnership between the British Trust for Ornithology, Royal Society for Protection of Birds and Joint Nature Conservation Committee (the last on behalf of the statutory nature conservation bodies: Natural England, Natural Resources Wales and Scottish Natural Heritage and the Department of the Environment Northern Ireland), in association with the Wildfowl & Wetlands Trust.

In Ireland there is a huge contrast in the density of lakes between the lake-rich counties west of the River Shannon and across the north in Co. Donegal and Co. Fermanagh and those in the south and east. Most of the lake area in the north and west is in the lowlands and under 100m above sea level. The south and eastern counties from Meath in the north-east to Kerry in the south-west have very little standing water, with the exception of the Wexford coast and the uplands of Wicklow, west Cork and Kerry. Similarly, Co. Tyrone, Londonderry and Antrim are a region with relatively few standing waters.

## Oxbows

Oxbow lakes and ponds are formed naturally by cut-off river meanders. The water levels in these may fluctuate widely. Some have been fenced off and become wooded to some extent, while others may remain within grazing units. Where water is retained permanently, a diverse and well-structured aquatic flora may develop, such as at

Langham Pond at Runnymede, Surrey, is an oxbow lake where Variable Damselfly has been recorded for many years. *Dave Smallshire*

Langham Pond, Runnymede (Surrey) where Variable Damselfly breeds. Species may include both red-eyed damselflies as well as Banded Demoiselle, White-legged Damselfly and Common Clubtail, species usually associated with slow-flowing watercourses.

## Urban ponds

Many ponds have been created in gardens and other built-up areas in recent years, often with wildlife conservation in mind. Some 17 species can be considered as widespread breeding species in such ponds, while eight others breed in them only rarely. Even in such built-up areas, often devoid of any semi-natural surroundings, dragonflies may colonise or be introduced on plant material. Garden and school ponds take many forms, from natural hollows to highly ornamental features. They vary hugely in shape, size and the amount of sunlight received. The type and diversity of both native and non-native plant species and the nature of the margins (the naturalness and extent of shallow water) determine their attractiveness to dragonflies. From a dragonfly viewpoint, there is little evidence to suggest that non-native plants are necessarily worse than those occurring naturally in the area. Better quality garden ponds, with submerged plants providing a good range of structure and niches, may support Azure, Large Red and Blue-tailed Damselflies, Southern Hawker, Emperor Dragonfly, Broad-bodied Chaser and Common Darter, with other species more rarely. Ponds in rural surroundings are likely to attract a wider range of species than those within large conurbations.

Rodley NR, Leeds, Yorkshire, is situated just four miles from the centre of Leeds next to the River Aire. The reserve was created in 1999 on the site of the old Rodley water treatment works on land owned by Yorkshire Water plc. It is managed by Rodley Nature Reserve Trust Ltd. *Peter Mill*

Garden pond. *Isaac Scaife (aged 12)*

Small ponds typically go through a series of stages. During the first stage, soon after construction, the bare open habitat quickly attracts coloniser species, such as Broad-bodied Chaser and Common Darter, the former disappearing as plants become established. More mature ponds, well-stocked with aquatic plants, may support species such as Emerald Damselfly, whose larvae prefer denser submerged vegetation. However, many garden ponds are maintained to favour open water. In those ponds stocked with fish, both the survival rate of larvae and the extent of microhabitats in debris and among pondweed will be reduced. The presence of decaying logs and stumps often attracts female hawkers to oviposit.

## Rural ponds

Ponds in rural surroundings potentially have a more diverse dragonfly community than their urban counterparts, influenced in part by their typically larger size and potential proximity to semi-natural habitat, but also by their origin. In Ireland, most ponds in rural localities are natural. In contrast, most ponds in Britain are artificial: the rest of this section concentrates on these.

Many ponds date back more than a century and are hence well-established, while others are more recent, such as the community ponds created to celebrate the new millennium in 2000. Dragonfly populations at artificial ponds are determined by the initial design, the degree and the nature of any subsequent vegetation planting or clearance work and by the presence of fish and wildfowl, as well as by the proximity of farmland, roads and drainage that can lead to enrichment.

Many farm ponds are used for multiple purposes, such as providing water for livestock or irrigation, stocking or attracting wildfowl for amenity or shooting, or recreational angling. The overall balance of these various uses will strongly influence the diversity of dragonfly species they can support. Unfortunately, very large numbers of ponds have been infilled in recent decades, for example in the Cheshire Plain, where flooded marl pits traditionally provided drinking water for livestock. Some ancient dewponds on downland still survive and some provide suitable breeding conditions for dragonflies in landscapes with little other standing water. From the distribution maps it is apparent that several species are virtually absent in landscape areas such as this because of the lack of any standing water. Regardless of their origin, ponds accessible to livestock are susceptible to poaching (trampling), especially by cattle. This creates bare ground adjacent to the water and helps to maintain an early successional stage favoured by Broad-bodied Chaser. The bare mud may also be attractive to basking and/or territorial Black-tailed Skimmers.

Many irrigation reservoirs have been constructed in recent years to alleviate drought problems. Reservoirs, impounded for water storage or irrigation, often have water levels that fluctuate widely in the course of a year as a result of abstraction. Artificial margins, such as concrete dams or retaining walls, provide poor habitat for most dragonflies but, where semi-natural margins are allowed to develop, generalist species may occur. Additionally, where pondweeds are allowed to thrive, they often provide habitat for large populations of Common Blue Damselfly. The intensive nature of most farmland over the last 50 years has increased the risks of artificial fertiliser reaching farm ponds, especially where they have stream inlets (which provide the additional problems of sedimentation and associated phosphate enrichment and rapid infilling). Many larger farm ponds, including reservoirs, have multi-purpose use and may be stocked with fish, such as trout or coarse fish for angling, at unnaturally high densities. It is becoming increasingly common for fisheries to practise stocking. Currently, some 6,000 separate fish introductions take place each year in England and Wales alone, involving some two million fish. Eutrophic lowland sites may also attract high densities of water birds and this too will increase nutrient levels and inhibit colonisation by dragonflies.

## Flooded mineral and peat workings

Lakes and ponds resulting from the flooding of areas excavated for minerals or peat have long provided dragonflies with suitable habitats. The Broads of Norfolk and Suffolk derive from medieval peat diggings. Together with adjacent rich fens and grazing marsh ditch systems, they provide a rich combination of dragonfly habitats, although the habitat specialists such as Norfolk Hawker breed in the ditches (known locally as dykes), rather than in the open water areas. Water quality in some places has been diminished through phosphate enrichment in the past from sewage but the installation of improved treatment works in recent years has done much to alleviate this problem.

Aerial view of Cleveland Lakes, Cotswold Water Park, showing the mosaic of habitat. *Robert Bewley*

More recently and controversially, industrial-scale digging has taken place in many areas of peat, such as that at Whixall Moss (Shropshire) and Thorne Moors (Humberside/South Yorkshire). This has resulted in the creation of relatively small areas of open water that often have important dragonfly populations. Similar cutting of 'sedge peat' (derived from circum-neutral reed swamp rather than acidic *Sphagnum* peat) in the Somerset Levels and Moors has produced open waters and reed-swamp within more extensive areas of grazing marsh ditches (known as rhynes locally) and drains. Such wetland, in the Avalon Marshes of the Brue Valley around Shapwick Heath National Nature Reserve, is one of several sites in England now famous for spring gatherings of up to 100 Hobbies that feast upon emerging damselflies and dragonflies, thus demonstrating the importance of such sites to these insects.

Bog pools created by hand cutting of peat provide some of the most valuable dragonfly habitat in Ireland. The ponds created, if left undisturbed, become overgrown and less suitable with time but new ones are relatively easy to create. The Montiaghs Moss in Co. Antrim is perhaps the best example surviving and it supports a diverse assemblage of the original bog species, together with those of fens, including Hairy Dragonfly, Black Darter, Variable Damselfly and Irish Damselfly.

Quarrying for minerals has provided convenient holes for the disposal of domestic and other refuse in the past and many of these have subsequently been returned to agriculture. However, more recently, pits have been allowed to flood and been given over to multiple uses, including nature conservation. Sand and gravel extraction for the construction industry has provided the most widespread example of such pits, typically along river valleys. In the early stages after flooding, mobile generalist dragonflies such as Common Blue Damselfly, Common Darter, Emperor Dragonfly and Black-tailed Skimmer colonise. Depending on the water source, a series of shallow pools and associated flushes and runnels can be attractive to Scarce Blue-tailed Damselfly and Broad-bodied Chaser. These species tend to disappear within a few years as vegetation grows up. Natural succession in deep waters can take many years. However, with time and plant colonisation, the typical dragonfly community diversifies and 30 species have been recorded breeding overall. Hairy Dragonfly has colonised many flooded pits when suitable beds of emergent plants have become established. Unfortunately water quality can be variable and pits are often deep, with limited areas of shallow water, unless some judicious profiling has been done before flooding. The close proximity to rivers results in periodic flooding that may result in the re-distribution of larvae. Scarce Chaser, a species typical of flowing water, has bred in gravel pits and other standing waters near to rivers. A good example of mature gravel pits can be found at Meadow Lane, St. Ives (Cambridgeshire), which has significant populations of Variable Damselfly, Hairy Dragonfly and Scarce Chaser.

Rookery Clay Pit, Bedfordshire, is a vast disused quarry where a series of pools of varying sizes has formed, creating a diversity of habitat for species including Black-tailed Skimmer and Emerald Damselfly. *Steve Cham*

The open habitat at this gravel pit at Willington, Bedfordshire has large numbers of Common Blue Damselfly and Black-tailed Skimmer. *Steve Cham*

The mature gravel pits at Paxton Pits NR, Cambridgeshire, support large populations of Azure and Variable Damselflies, the latter being more abundant. *Steve Cham*

Sand extraction results in waterbodies with different chemical and botanical composition. Being porous, sand quarries often have pools of a temporary nature. Downy Emerald occurs at sand pits near Leighton Buzzard (Bedfordshire), while at Woolmer Forest (Hampshire) a range of shallow pools host a diverse dragonfly fauna. The temporary nature of some ponds favours Emerald Damselfly (and Natterjack Toad).

Pools form in chalk and limestone quarries if underlying clay is present, or if the water table is high enough. The porous nature of these minerals results in the formation of spring line flushes, often at the base of cliffs. Such sites have supported transient colonies of Scarce Blue-tailed Damselfly (e.g. at Sundon, Bedfordshire). Long-lived colonies have persisted in abandoned quarries in Ireland, such as at Tonnagh in Co. Fermanagh. Shallowly flooded quarries in Ireland are attractive to Black-tailed Skimmer, due to the combination of bare ground and shallow warm water. Deep marl lakes are less attractive to many species and have an impoverished fauna.

Both china and ball clay deposits have been quarried in south-west England since the 19th century, with early workings being small-scale and leaving ponds good for dragonflies, such as those in Devon in the Bovey Basin (e.g. Little Bradley Pond, which has Downy Emerald) and on the south-west fringe of Dartmoor (e.g. Smallhanger, which has Scarce Blue-tailed Damselfly). Modern clay quarries are much larger and deeper and any open waters tend to be milky with suspended clay particles, so these are of more limited value to dragonflies. In the absence of pumping, particularly large deep lakes may form. These are often the last places to freeze in cold winters and they suffer bank erosion from wave action. Nevertheless, large populations of Black-tailed Skimmer and Common Blue Damselfly can occur, the latter where submerged plants grow just below the water's surface. More interesting though are the seepages, flushes, streams and drains that are common in working pits. These, and any shallow pools that form, are quickly colonised by emergent plants and may dry out in summer. Such vegetated pools can support large populations of Emerald Damselfly. Clay extraction sites are increasingly targeted as landfill sites and sites of conservation importance for dragonflies can be lost as a result.

As with agricultural ponds, a large proportion of ponds and lakes created by mineral extraction are also stocked artificially with fish and many are stocked for angling, often for commercial purposes. A range of coarse fish and Rainbow Trout are added to natural populations, leading to stocking densities that are well above natural levels. This inevitably brings an elevated risk of predation to dragonfly larvae and/or the loss or reduction of larval habitat quality by disturbance of the substrate (by bottom feeders) and/or the consumption of submerged aquatic vegetation. The ecological balance of waters can easily be disturbed by the introduction of Common Carp. Due to the feeding behaviour of this species, large numbers can rapidly lead to increased turbidity in the water and a reduction in submerged aquatic vegetation. With fewer plants, reduced light penetration and an increase in available nutrients, algae often increase. This process is extremely hard to reverse (Environment Agency, undated). By contrast, the activities of anglers themselves, including the clearance of patches of emergent, floating and submerged vegetation from banks and water to create better angling conditions, may result in some increase in the structural diversity of the habitat. The limited clearance of dense, bankside vegetation may aid some species, such as Four-spotted Chaser, Scarce Chaser and Black-tailed Skimmer, the males of which use the open ground created for basking and territorial perching. At least 23 species are believed to breed in fishing ponds, suggesting that a wide range of dragonflies can co-exist with fish, although anecdotal evidence suggests that populations may be lower at such sites than those with few or no fish.

## Heathland and bog pools

Lowland heathland, with its associated ponds, bogs and streams, provides some of the richest dragonfly habitat in Britain and Ireland. Once widespread across southern England, such habitat is now more restricted, with some of the best examples in Berkshire, Devon, Dorset, Hampshire and Surrey. The diversity of microhabitat types formed under these conditions supports very high species diversity.

Where bog-mosses and Marsh St John's-wort grow in pools (and flushes) associated with valley bogs, Small Red Damselfly and Keeled Skimmer are often found. While it is tempting to conclude that these species require this type of habitat, they also occur at calcareous fen sites and it is more likely that the plant structure is the key factor. Dersingham Bog NNR and Roydon Common (both Norfolk) are examples of valley bogs that support outlying populations of Black Darter, particularly in the associated pools. In the New Forest (Hampshire) the poached margins of shallow heathland ponds support significant populations of species such as Broad-bodied Chaser and Emerald Damselfly.

## Woodland ponds and lakes

The proximity of trees and woodland to lakes and ponds can have a significant influence on their attractiveness to dragonflies. A high density of trees close to the margins will reduce the penetration of sunlight to the water, thus reducing water temperature and therefore having a negative effect on larval development and reducing areas suitable for adults to be active. Densely shading tree growth will limit the species visiting such pools. However, woodland can provide valuable shelter from prevailing winds and sunny areas within it produce good foraging for adults. Where shading is limited and good levels of sunlight reach the water's surface, aquatic vegetation can flourish and a good range of breeding species may be present.

Long established lakes, often associated with large country estates, support strong populations of Downy and Brilliant Emeralds. Downy Emerald favours woodland pools or pools with close proximity to extensive woodland. Although it is generally regarded as a poor coloniser, in the last decade new colonies have been recorded in Bedfordshire and Northamptonshire where pools occur in or adjacent to woodland. At an area of private woodland in Northamptonshire, the species is locally abundant at a complex of small pools formed by the creation of ammunition dumps by the Ministry of Defence.

The damming of woodland streams has also resulted in pools attractive to dragonflies, supporting high numbers of Downy Emerald, such as Oval Pond (Berkshire). The creation of pools by damming streams for the Wealden iron industry created ponds and lakes that support a range of rare species,

Swinley Brick Pits, Berkshire, is an area of former clay pits used for brick production. The former diggings, which cover a large area, have left an array of troughs in wet heath where water collects. A few areas of open water have always existed, but the site was largely covered by plantation and regenerated pine until 1995. *Steve Cham*

Eyeworth Pond, New Forest, Hampshire, was formed by damming of a stream during the second half of the 19th century to provide water to a gunpowder factory. This site now supports Red-eyed Damselfly and Downy Emerald. *Steve Cham*

including Brilliant and Downy Emeralds. Furnace and hammer ponds were often created in woodland where charcoal was made for use in blast furnaces and forges. The head of water was also used to drive tilt hammers. Some of these pools in Sussex are very old.

Brilliant Emerald is a species with a curious distribution in Britain. It occurs in Central Scotland and in southern England from east Kent through Sussex, Surrey and into Hampshire, where it is most commonly found in forest lakes and ponds. These English sites are usually in excess of 1 ha and have relatively little emergent vegetation, but trees and shrubs overhang the margins and provide good breeding habitat. While the received wisdom is that lakes good for fish are bad for dragonflies, in England Brilliant Emerald is found most abundantly in lakes where large carp and their associated anglers predominate. These wooded lakes were, more often than not, originally formed by the damming of rivers and streams for industrial purposes or as fish ponds. It is therefore not surprising that White-legged Damselfly is often found along with Brilliant and Downy Emeralds.

Despite the often manicured edges of lakes within landscaped gardens, if some wooded edges remain the lake may support Brilliant and Downy Emeralds, especially those waterbodies with minimal disturbance to the bottom substrate. Perhaps the greatest threat to forest lakes is tidiness. Manicured waters with minimal emergent vegetation and tidy, surrounding shrubs, linking tightly mown fishing stations, leave little room for wildlife, including dragonflies. The very best lakes are sympathetically managed with dead trees left overhanging and clearance only around fishing platforms; large patches of Yellow Water-lily, favoured by Red-eyed Damselfly, are left, even though anglers dislike them.

Small, heavily-shaded, woodland ponds are less attractive to dragonflies than those exposed to plenty of sunlight. However, where sunlight allows vegetation to develop, they can provide good conditions for Southern Hawker, a species that utilises this type of pond more so than other dragonflies. When woodland ponds become choked with leaves and overgrown, this limits the species that will utilise them. The release of tannins as leaves break down and the build up of gases when such ponds freeze over in cold winters may be toxic to larvae.

## Temporary ponds

Ponds that dry out naturally each year represent a potentially hostile environment for a dragonfly because larval development is dependent on aquatic habitat. Most temporary ponds experience drying as the water table lowers in summer, filling again over winter and remaining wet through the spring and early summer period. Such sites often develop stands of emergent plants presenting a vegetational architecture that attracts certain species. A one-year life cycle with rapid larval development is a key mechanism for survival at these sites.

Emerald damselflies are well adapted to survive the drying period at such temporary ponds. The large ovipositor typical of these damselflies is well suited to cut into emergent plant stems, leaving the eggs protected during the latter part of the summer. The eggs hatch in late winter when water levels have risen and the larvae feed and develop rapidly in the shallow water, which is warm and fish-free. The adults emerge in early summer after as little as ten weeks as larvae.

Ruddy Darter may also be found in such habitat conditions, often in association with Emerald and Scarce Emerald Damselflies. Tandem pairs of the darters often oviposit around the dry margins of temporary ponds, scattering their eggs onto mud and grass. The eggs hatch as water levels are restored during the winter months and larval development takes place rapidly in the spring. Emergence of adults occurs through the summer period before water levels drop again.

Temporary ponds can form almost anywhere where water can accumulate in a depression in the ground. Those that are filled infrequently from surface water rarely last for long and are less likely to provide suitable dragonfly habitat. Ponds that fill from naturally-fluctuating aquifers can persist for long periods of time and develop unique habitat. In Breckland (Norfolk/Suffolk), the nationally important pingo systems form extensive areas of pits and pools with shallow water. Unusually, pingo pools can be wet in summer but dry in winter. Shallow pingo pools at Thompson Common, Hills and Holes and Frost's Common (Norfolk) represent the inland strongholds for Scarce Emerald Damselfly. In the west of Ireland, there are many temporary wetlands, which go by the local name of turloughs. They are very variable in their nature, depending on the topography, duration of flooding and water quality. The best examples support a rich and varied community of plants and invertebrates including the strongest Irish populations of Scarce Emerald Damselfly. The Irish name of Turlough Spreadwing signifies the importance of this type of habitat for this species. Ruddy Darter is the only other regular inhabitant of turloughs.

Temporary ponds can also result from heavy rainfall, or develop where the water table is exposed, such as in mineral extraction sites. At the latter sites, water seeping from pit walls may also add to ponds that subsequently dry out. The bare and shallow nature of these ponds makes them attractive to Scarce Blue-tailed Damselfly, although the extent to which they and other species can survive desiccation is not known.

Although highly localised, dune ponds (often artificial) can support a rich dragonfly assemblage. Their often-ephemeral nature makes them suitable for Emerald Damselfly and it is perhaps no coincidence that colonisation attempts by Southern Emerald Damselfly have occurred at such ponds

at Winterton Dunes (Norfolk) and Sandwich Bay (Kent). The strategic position of dune ponds makes them good sites to look for migrant dragonflies in general. Seasonal ponds away from the coast, such as the Breckland pingos and Irish turloughs, hold only about half of those species associated with dune ponds. Flooded dune slacks in western Ireland can support large populations of Common Darter, Common Hawker and, occasionally, Black-tailed Skimmer.

Winterton Dunes, Norfolk. These shallow dune ponds are temporary in nature yet support a range of species including Southern Emerald Damselfly and Common Hawker. *Adrian Riley*

## Brackish waters

Only a few species can tolerate the brackish water, either in ponds or ditches, most often found adjacent to sea defences. Blue-tailed Damselfly and Migrant Hawker are the most likely species to be found near brackish water, with Southern Hawker, Emperor Dragonfly, Black-tailed Skimmer and Common Darter occurring less often. Scarce Emerald Damselfly has been recorded breeding in brackish ditches in grazing marshes in eastern England (Drake, 1990). Brackish coastal lagoons in south-east Ireland in Co. Wexford are the most regular locations for migrant sightings in Ireland including Red-veined Darter and Lesser Emperor. It remains to be seen whether Red-veined Darter will use brackish waters more widely, as it does use saline lagoons on the Continent.

Ballinduff Turlough, Co. Galway. A large turlough in the karst of western Ireland and important habitat for Scarce Emerald Damselfly and Ruddy Darter. *Robert Thompson*

# Canals, ditches and dykes

## Canals

Canals are a major part of the network of inland waterways in England and eastern Wales, but to a much lesser extent in Scotland and Ireland. The English and Welsh canals are a single interlinked system, connecting the main river systems and forming dispersal routes for a number of dragonfly species. White-legged Damselfly in particular, has dispersed between river systems using the canal network. The main Irish canals radiate out from Dublin across the central plain to the Shannon and the Barrow Rivers. Canals are important to dragonflies as they can provide still-water conditions in areas that have few natural waterbodies.

Canals have a long and colourful history, having been used for irrigation and transport, through becoming the focus of the Industrial Revolution, to their current use for recreational boating. Despite periods of abandonment, the use of the canal system is again increasing, with neglected and derelict canals being reopened, and the construction of some new routes. Most canals in the Britain are maintained by the Canal & River Trust, previously British Waterways, but a minority of canals are privately owned.

The Basingstoke Canal, Surrey (seen here in 2009) was one of the best sites in Britain for aquatic plants, which in turn attracted a large assemblage of dragonflies, including Brilliant and Downy Emeralds. *Des Sussex*

Irish canals come under the remit of Waterways Ireland, the all-island intergovernmental agency tasked with maintaining navigation on inland waterways.

Canals can provide excellent habitat for dragonflies depending on the amount of boat traffic and bankside vegetation. Although they appear similar to rivers, the water in canals is generally static, so they attract a dragonfly fauna that favours still water habitat, as well as species of slow flowing rivers. Boat traffic can affect the habitat in a

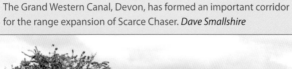

The Grand Western Canal, Devon, has formed an important corridor for the range expansion of Scarce Chaser. *Dave Smallshire*

number of ways through direct pollution, turbulence creating turbid water and reduced sunlight penetrating the water. Canals may also be actively managed to control bankside and aquatic vegetation to allow for easier navigation. The nature of canals varies tremendously across Britain and Ireland. This variation will be due to the source water that feeds the canals and the amount of traffic. Canals also bring wetland habitat into areas where none existed before. For example the Royal and Grand Canals in Ireland both flow through Dublin creating linear wetlands fed by water from base rich aquifers many miles distant from the city. Some dragonflies have clearly benefitted from this although the situation may have been reversed somewhat with the reinstatement of the canals for leisure traffic.

The demise of the Basingstoke Canal that passes through Hampshire and Surrey serves to illustrate how the fortunes of these linear habitats influence the species of dragonfly that can breed at such sites (Rand & Mundell, 2011). Since the late 1800s the canal had been a magnet for botanists attracted by the lush diversity of aquatic plants growing in the clear water. By the mid-1960s parts of the canal were derelict and lacked boat traffic and it was regarded as one of the best botanical sites in Britain. The varying acidity along its length further enhanced the diversity of plants which in turn attracted a large assemblage of dragonfly species, including a number of notable rarities. Following dredging of important stretches and the resulting re-instatement of boat traffic the water became turbid and many of the plant species disappeared. The introduction of large bottom feeding fish by anglers further exacerbated the problem. The canal still has a rich assemblage of dragonfly species supplemented by individuals from nearby sites, but the population numbers are unlikely ever to recover to the levels when there was less disturbance.

## Ditches and dykes

Ditches and dykes can be very similar to canals. In parts of the East Anglian fenland the drains or lodes were extensively used for the transportation of reed, sedge and fen litter, as well as drainage. Their use for transportation is much reduced now, but some reed and sedge is still removed from site in this way and there has been an increase in the recreational use of some larger channels. Water courses important for boat traffic and drainage require regular management to keep them open, although actual water movement within them is often limited. This work creates habitats similar to linear ponds held at a mid-point in vegetational succession. Such habitats can be important for a diversity of dragonfly species including Red-eyed and Common Blue Damselflies, Four-spotted and Scarce Chasers, Brown Hawker and Emperor Dragonfly.

A fenland drain at Horseway Lock, near Chatteris, (Cambridgeshire), supported significant populations of Variable Damselfly and Hairy Dragonfly, until the cessation of boat traffic resulted in vegetation encroachment and the loss of open water.

Ditches and dykes used for drainage and as 'wet fences' within grazing marsh systems tend to be narrower than those historically used for transportation. Water levels and water movement within them can alter according to local conditions such as rainfall, but levels and flows are often managed to maintain the overall integrity of the system. Ditches of this kind in eastern England often support species such as Large Red, Azure and Emerald Damselflies, Four-spotted Chaser, Black-tailed Skimmer, Hairy Dragonfly and Norfolk Hawker.

# Recording and data collection

The *Atlas of the Dragonflies of Britain and Ireland* by Merritt *et al.* (1996), referred to throughout as the 'previous atlas', was published by the Biological Records Centre (HMSO) in 1996 and included all dragonfly records collated by the Odonata Recording Scheme up to 1990, plus some selected later records of particular interest. It also contained a chapter on the history of recording that outlined developments from the early collectors of the 1800s to the establishment of an Odonata Mapping Scheme in the late 1960s. The mapping scheme was initially administered by Dave Chelmick but later became the Odonata Recording Scheme and, in 1980, Bob Merritt was appointed as national recorder. During this period, the study of dragonflies became popularised by the publication of several useful field guides, beginning with that by Cyril Hammond in 1977. By the mid-1980s, the overall patterns of species distribution were reasonably well known thus enabling the publication of the previous atlas.

In addition to collecting records for large scale distribution mapping, dragonfly recording has since focused more on identifying and monitoring key sites and gaining detailed knowledge of the occurrence and habitat requirements of species at a local level. At the time of the previous atlas, the standard method of reporting sightings was to complete and post the RA70 recording card (subsequently superseded by the RA74 and RA83 – Figure 16) to the vice-county or national recorder. During the period of collecting records for this atlas, the use of recording cards has declined significantly and the RA83 has become almost obsolete. The majority of records are now submitted electronically on spreadsheets or, increasingly, via online recording forms shown in Figures 17 and 18. The number of records submitted up to the end of 1990 was 108,793. This new atlas has seen a more than tenfold increase compared to the previous publication and is based on 1,095,972 records up to the end of 2012. The dataset is made up from British records from the Dragonfly Recording Network and Irish records contributed by DragonflyIreland.

The Channel Islands have not been included in this atlas, as they do not form part of the cohesive, biogeographical unit covered by Great Britain, Ireland and the Isle of Man. However, for species that are otherwise rare in Britain and Ireland, selected records from the Channel Islands are described within the texts, where relevant.

Figure 16. Odonata RA83 recording card.

| Odonata RA83 | Locality | | | | | | | Grid Reference | | | | | | | | | | |
|---|---|---|---|---|---|---|---|---|---|---|---|---|---|---|---|---|---|---|
| VC No | VC Name | | DRN Site Recording Form | Day | Month | Year | Alt (m) | Conservation Status / Threats | | | | | | | | | | |
| Code | Zygoptera (Damselflies) | | | Ad | Co | Ov | La | Ex | Em | Code | Anisoptera (Dragonflies) | | Ad | Co | Ov | La | Ex | Em |
| 0103 | Calopteryx splendens | Banded Demoiselle | | | | | | | | 2201 | Aeshna caerulea | Azure Hawker | | | | | | |
| 0102 | Calopteryx virgo | Beautiful Demoiselle | | | | | | | | 2209 | Aeshna cyanea | Southern Hawker | | | | | | |
| 0405 | Lestes dryas | Scarce Emerald Damselfly | | | | | | | | 2207 | Aeshna grandis | Brown Hawker | | | | | | |
| 0404 | Lestes sponsa | Emerald Damselfly | | | | | | | | 2212 | Aeshna isosceles | Norfolk Hawker | | | | | | |
| 0407 | Lestes viridis | Willow Emerald Damselfly | | | | | | | | 2204 | Aeshna juncea | Common Hawker | | | | | | |
| 1010 | Coenagrion hastulatum | Northern Damselfly | | | | | | | | 2210 | Aeshna mixta | Migrant Hawker | | | | | | |
| 1009 | Coenagrion lunulatum | Irish Damselfly | | | | | | | | 2401 | Anax imperator | Emperor Dragonfly | | | | | | |
| 1002 | Coenagrion mercuriale | Southern Damselfly | | | | | | | | 2403 | Anax parthenope | Lesser Emperor | | | | | | |
| 1007 | Coenagrion puella | Azure Damselfly | | | | | | | | 2101 | Brachytron pratense | Hairy Dragonfly | | | | | | |
| 1006 | Coenagrion pulchellum | Variable Damselfly | | | | | | | | 1502 | Gomphus vulgatissimus | Common Club-tail | | | | | | |
| 1101 | Erythromma najas | Red-eyed Damselfly | | | | | | | | 2601 | Cordulegaster boltonii | Golden-ringed Dragonfly | | | | | | |
| 1102 | Erythromma viridulum | Small Red-eyed Damselfly | | | | | | | | 2701 | Cordulia aenea | Downy Emerald | | | | | | |
| 0601 | Pyrrhosoma nymphula | Large Red Damselfly | | | | | | | | 2804 | Somatochlora arctica | Northern Emerald | | | | | | |
| 0901 | Enallagma cyathigerum | Common Blue Damselfly | | | | | | | | 2802 | Somatochlora metallica | Brilliant Emerald | | | | | | |
| 0801 | Ischnura elegans | Blue-tailed Damselfly | | | | | | | | 3903 | Leucorrhinia dubia | White-faced Darter | | | | | | |
| 0805 | Ischnura pumilio | Scarce Blue-tailed Damselfly | | | | | | | | 3201 | Libellula depressa | Broad-bodied Chaser | | | | | | |
| 1301 | Ceriagrion tenellum | Small Red Damselfly | | | | | | | | 3202 | Libellula fulva | Scarce Chaser | | | | | | |
| 0504 | Platycnemis pennipes | White-legged Damselfly | | | | | | | | 3204 | Libellula quadrimaculata | Four-spotted Chaser | | | | | | |
| | | | | | | | | | | 3309 | Orthetrum cancellatum | Black-tailed Skimmer | | | | | | |
| | Recorder(s) | | No. | | | | | | | 3302 | Orthetrum coerulescens | Keeled Skimmer | | | | | | |
| | Card Complier | | No. | | | | | | | 3812 | Sympetrum danae | Black Darter | | | | | | |
| | Source of Record | | | | | | | | | 3809 | Sympetrum flaveolum | Yellow-winged Darter | | | | | | |

Estimated Nos.

| | |
|---|---|
| A | 1 |
| B | 2-5 |
| C | 6-20 |
| D | 21-100 |
| E | 101-500 |
| F | 500+ |
| + | Present |

Key to Columns

| | |
|---|---|
| Ad | Adult (Total number) |
| Co | Copulating pair |
| Ov | Ovipositing |
| La | Larva |
| Ex | Exuvia |
| Em | Emergent |

Habitat / Comments

Tick if this record comes from a full site-visit list at a wetland that is likely to be a breeding site for dragonflies ☐

Transect ☐    Map on back of form ☐

| 3807 | Sympetrum fonscolombii | Red-veined Darter |
| 3810 | Sympetrum sanguineum | Ruddy Darter |
| 3803 | Sympetrum striolatum | Common Darter |

**IMPORTANT:** By submitting information on this form you agree that it may be collated and disseminated manually or electronically, including the Internet, for environmental decision-making, education, research and other public benefit uses in accordance with the Dragonfly Recording Network's data access policy. Names and contact details of data suppliers will be used in accordance with the Dragonfly Recording Network's privacy policy. Both these policies can be found at http://www.british-dragonflies.org.uk/.

April 2013

## Record collection

Dragonfly recording in Britain is currently carried out under the auspices of the Dragonfly Recording Network (DRN). Formerly administered by the Biological Records Centre (BRC), it is now overseen by the British Dragonfly Society (BDS). The DRN comprises Vice-county Recorders (VCRs), most of whom are members of the BDS, and a growing network of recorders and observers. In some cases, the respective Local Records Centre (LRC) fulfils the role of a VCR. VCRs encourage, collect, collate and verify records contributed by recorders in their area. In recent years, the network has increased its coverage and most vice-counties have a nominated VCR. Fifty VCRs cover the 70 vice-counties of England and Wales, while a single coordinator is responsible for all 41 Scottish vice-counties.

Dragonfly recording in Ireland since 1990 has taken an independent path. Recording is organised on an all Ireland basis with a single record coordinator, a structure that was put in place during the period of the previous atlas. The main phase of dragonfly recording in Ireland was between 2000-2003 for the DragonflyIreland project. The records are kept and maintained in Ireland jointly by the two record centres, CEDaR in Northern Ireland and the National Biodiversity Data Centre in the Republic. The records are displayed on the websites of both data centres. The data from Northern Ireland is also shared through the NBN Gateway.

At regular intervals (at least annually), the DRN dataset is exported to the NBN Gateway (data.nbn.org.uk) ensuring that data on British dragonflies is publicly available. The precision at which records have been made accessible has increased, such that currently data can be downloaded at 1km resolution but better access can be requested through the NBN Gateway. The latest data contained in this atlas will be transferred to the NBN Gateway shortly after publication in 2014.

A valid biological record should, as a minimum, contain at least four pieces of information: What, Where, When and Who. The RA83 and its predecessors collected this data whilst also allowing additional optional information to be added, which – unlike many other recording schemes – includes details of abundance and evidence of breeding. One advantage of a paper record card is the reverse can be used for a site map, showing the location of unusual species and/or habitat features etc.; this information is generally lacking with electronic record submissions. Wherever possible a record should also be linked to a vice-county (appendix A4) for Britain or Ireland. Unfortunately, vice-county boundaries are rarely if ever shown on maps used for biological recording and this can sometimes lead to errors allocating a record to the correct vice-county. Record Cleaner (www.nbn.org.uk/record-cleaner.aspx) software, a tool to help individual recorders and organisations, such as LRCs and national recording schemes, to verify and improve the quality of records submitted electronically, can be used to check the accuracy or allocate the vice-county to a record. Whilst vice-counties provide a useful, yet parochial, means to collate records at a local level, their relevance to national recording is increasingly diminished. Modern location and positioning tools, such as GPS, have enabled recorders to accurately locate the position of their observations on the national grids.

## Record verification

The normal flow of records in Britain is from the recorder to the VCR, who verifies the species, location and time. A similar process is in place in Ireland with record verification by the Irish recorder before display online. Records with insufficient detail or of a suspect nature are queried with the original observer and may be rejected at that point. Verified records from Britain are then sent, usually annually, to the DRN for inclusion in the national database. Since 1998, British records of rare species have been assessed by the BDS Odonata Rarities Committee, a small group of experienced enthusiasts.

In recent years, the DRN has made use of Record Cleaner, which was launched by the NBN Gateway in 2011 to intercept suspect records passing through to the NBN Gateway based on a set of rules. These spatial and temporal rule sets were provided by the BDS for all resident dragonfly species, so records could be validated for potentially incorrect species, locations and dates. Rejected records were checked manually and subsequently accepted, rejected or referred back to original recorders. Record Cleaner has worked well as a first line filter for potentially erroneous records but cannot fully replace the judgement brought by an experienced VCR.

## DRN database management

The central database of DRN is held currently in the Recorder biological record management system. Recorder 3 was developed in the late 1980s by the Nature Conservancy Council and was made generally available from 1992. The package has been updated periodically, the latest version, Recorder 6, being launched in 2004. A prerequisite of any computerised recording and data management system has always been the ability to export records for import into Recorder. Software suitable for recording Dragonflies has included Darter, BioBase, AditSite and MapMate. Mike Thurner developed Darter, a bespoke version of BioBase for Odonata, which was adopted by the DRN in 1998 as the recording package of choice. When support for Darter was withdrawn in 2006 after Mike's retirement the rights of the system were transferred to Adit Limited. Subsequently, Adit Limited was commissioned to produce a Darter-like input screen as a front end to the AditSite recording system. The resulting system was recommended for use by VCRs but was adopted by only a relatively small number. MapMate is used by some VCRs where it is the preferred recording software of their local county natural history society.

In addition to these bespoke systems, DRN Species Recorder has also been used since 2007 by some recorders and VCRs. This was a modified version of Sussex Biological Records Centre's Microsoft Excel based Species Recorder. It comprises a user-friendly input screen that compiles records in a spreadsheet form compatible for import into Recorder.

## Online recording

In general, records have been submitted in many different forms, from letters, record cards, telephone messages and emails through to spreadsheets and data files exported from a range of recording software packages. With an increasingly computer-literate population, a greater proportion of records have been submitted electronically in recent years with online data inputting becoming increasingly popular.

During the period of the Dragonflies in Focus project (see page 35), online recording has become an important means of acquiring records. As is often the case with new technologies, several systems have become available, but unfortunately with no agreed national standard. However, a multiplicity of systems need not be a problem so long as there is reliable dataflow between the systems, such that all records, irrespective of the source, can all ultimately be made available through the NBN Gateway.

The BDS launched basic online recording for the 2010 season, at the end of which a new website was developed with the Drupal Content Management System. This enabled the development of a new online recording system the following season with increased functionality (Figures 17 and 18). It uses Indicia, an open source wildlife recording toolkit, funded by Open Air Laboratories (OPAL) network and managed by Centre for Ecology & Hydrology (CEH). Indicia simplified the development of a suitable recording system by providing the components needed to build an online recording system that met the unique requirements of dragonfly recording.

Subsequently, iRecord (www.brc.ac.uk/irecord) was developed by BRC (part of CEH) as a generic online recording system for all species. Also built using Indicia, iRecord was designed to make it easy for wildlife sightings to be collated, checked by experts and made available to support research and decision-making at local and national levels. Although relatively new, it enables dragonfly records to be input and thence imported into the DRN database. Another online environmental recording system, Living

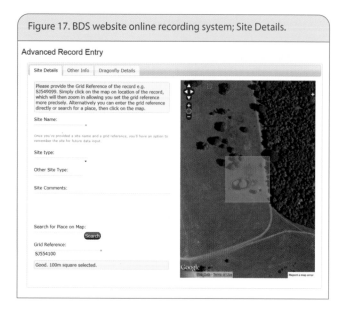

Figure 17. BDS website online recording system; Site Details.

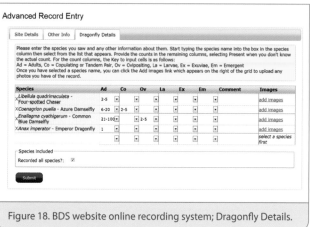

Figure 18. BDS website online recording system; Dragonfly Details.

Record (www.livingrecord.net), was launched in 2010 by mc² Data Innovation Limited, primarily for use by groups such as local dragonfly groups. It enables rapid verification by the VCR and ensures that high quality records filter through to the DRN.

The BDS has also been fortunate in cooperating with larger nature conservation organisations that have been willing to share their experience and knowledge (Table 2). Since 2008, recorders for Butterfly Conservation's Wider Countryside Butterfly Survey (WCBS) have been able to submit optional counts of dragonflies. Since 2011, recorders for the British Trust for Ornithology's (BTO) Garden BirdWatch (GBW) have provided a valuable source of records. Following the success of this, observers contributing to BirdTrack, a partnership between the BTO, RSPB, Birdwatch Ireland, the Scottish Ornithologists' Club and the Welsh Ornithological Society, can also now submit dragonfly records. These three sources have contributed a substantial total of records (21,802) during 2009-2012, inevitably – given the lack of focus on wetland sites – comprising mainly common and widespread species. Nevertheless, from an atlas perspective, these helped to put some dots on maps, although their value for population monitoring has not yet been evaluated.

Table 2. Total records received from incidental recording of dragonflies during Wider Countryside Butterfly Survey, Garden BirdWatch and BirdTrack surveys.

| Survey | 2008 | 2009 | 2010 | 2011 | 2012 | Total |
|---|---|---|---|---|---|---|
| WCBS | 300 | 569 | 546 | 442 | 716 | 2,573 |
| GBW | | | 66 | 6,732 | 6,407 | 13,205 |
| BirdTrack | | | | | 6,024 | 6,024 |
| Total records | 300 | 569 | 612 | 7,174 | 13,147 | 21,802 |

## Key Sites Project

The Key Sites Project, initiated in 1988, aimed to identify important sites for dragonflies. For conservation purposes, Key Sites are classified as being important for maintaining breeding populations of nationally- or locally-important species, or a high diversity (assemblage) of species and hence can be ranked of national (i.e. of SSSI quality) or local importance. Intrinsic in this aim was the need to identify where scarcer species were breeding and hence it promotes the recording of life stages other than the adult. The RA70 recording card was developed to allow observers to record not just the presence of copulating pairs, ovipositing females, larvae, exuviae and pre-flight emergents, but also counts or estimates of their numbers. Following a review of the British Red List and the publication of definitions for proof for breeding, national criteria were developed to define Key Sites (www.british-dragonflies.org.uk/content/key-sites). This initiative has encouraged increased recording of abundance and breeding evidence and the identification of important sites. Records containing breeding evidence (probable and confirmed) increased from approximately 4% of the DRN database in 2007 to 15% in 2012. In order to encourage recorders to submit larval and exuviae records as proof of breeding, an easy-to-use photographic field guide was published by the BDS, to improve the identification skills of recorders. The volume for Anisoptera was published in 2007 and that for Zygoptera in 2009. A combined volume including some new resident species was produced in 2012 (Cham, 2007, 2009, 2012).

## Dragonflies in Focus project

During 2005-06 a short-term project to collate recent dragonfly records, and in particular to make available detailed data from the BDS Key Sites Project, was supported by funding from Defra. Data compiled during this project were made available through the NBN Gateway. The continuation of this work and the development of the future infrastructure of the BDS were the objectives of a project plan that led on to the Dragonflies in Focus (DiF) project in April 2007. DiF was initiated with funding from the then Countryside Council for Wales, Environment Agency, Esmée Fairbairn Foundation, Natural England, Scottish Environment Protection Agency and Scottish Natural Heritage. The six-year DiF project aimed to produce robust and repeatable methods of recording and monitoring the status of dragonflies in Britain by:

• Developing a sustainable system for gathering, managing and using information about the status of dragonflies in Britain.

• Providing access to authoritative and reliable information on dragonflies, in particular through the National Biodiversity Network (NBN).

• Putting dragonflies more securely 'on the map', through increased involvement of the BDS membership and the broader public.

• Producing a new revised national dragonfly atlas.

These were to be achieved by:

• Developing the recording and monitoring programme.

• Improving the scope and quality of records.

• Developing, in partnership with local organisations, a national system for collating and managing dragonfly records.

• Increasing participation by volunteers in a range of surveillance activities.

• Sharing information with other organisations via the NBN.

## Pilot dragonfly monitoring scheme

While distribution mapping using non-systematic recording can show graphically how species have spread in recent years, it has significant limitations for monitoring dragonfly populations (see pages 58-63). As one of the objectives of the DiF Project, a pilot British Dragonfly Monitoring Scheme ran from 2009 to 2012. Following experience in The Netherlands, this involved counts along fixed transects or at fixed points, using a standard method. However, it differed in that sites were not randomly selected. The pilot was intended to determine the practicality of gathering counts from a large number of sites in order to provide national population indices. There were 53 recorder-selected transects at 28 sites in 2009, but the number reduced in subsequent years. The results from these were insufficient to produce national indices, but some lessons were learned concerning likely take-up of a count-based method. As a national initiative it was discontinued but the methods can still be used as a local site monitoring tool (available at www.british-dragonflies.org.uk/content/british-dragonfly-monitoring-scheme). The recent development of site occupancy modelling and similar analytical tools saw a shift in emphasis to the promotion of complete day lists as a viable alternative means of obtaining trends (see pages 58-63).

During the five year recording period in Britain from 2008 to 2012, progress maps were published annually in Darter (DRN's recording newsletter), which also contained detailed local information and feedback to recorders. The maps showed the 2858 English, Welsh and Scottish hectads for which records had been submitted and imported into the DRN database. An interactive map was available on the BDS website that allowed VCRs to click on their area and check progress for each hectad. Progress maps were only produced for Britain as the DragonflyIreland records came as a complete dataset so no annual progress reports were available for Ireland.

The progress maps used three colours to represent recording progress against a vice-county Diversity Threshold (VCDT). The VCDT (Figure 19) was calculated as a proportional measure of each vice-county's dragonfly species diversity, based on 60% of the number of breeding species occurring

within each vice-county. The actual percentages were modified in the light of local expert knowledge and the species diversity in adjacent vice-counties. Vice-counties were then allocated to one of three diversity groupings: high (at least 14 species: predominately in southern England), intermediate (11-13 species: predominately in central and eastern England and Wales) and low (8-10 species, occurring in northern England and Scotland).

Area maps were produced annually for each VCR to show the progress of recording in specific vice-counties (Figure 20) and were linked to the interactive map on the Atlas page of the BDS website. They were used as a tool to help identify gaps and target recording activities during the following season.

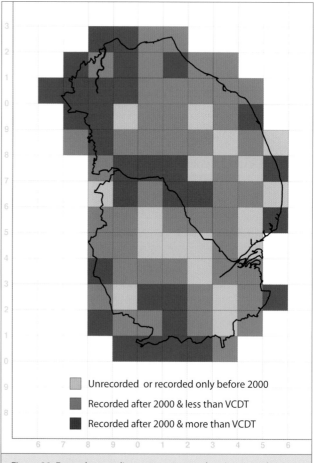

Figure 20. Example recording progress map, showing recording progress for hectads in Lincolnshire (vice-counties 53 and 54) up to the end of the 2010 season.

Figures 21-26 show how recording progressed from 2008 to 2012. Due to a disproportionate number of recorders living in south-east of England hectads were rapidly recorded in that area before recording intensity increased in the other regions. The maps encouraged all recorders to survey and submit records for poorly recorded hectads. Scotland covers a large area with few resident dragonfly recorders, so recorders from south of the border were encouraged to take holidays in Scotland and cover a few unrecorded hectads.

Figure 19. Vice-county Diversity Threshold (VCDT) depicted on map of Britain.

- 8-10 species
- 11-13 species
- At least 14 species

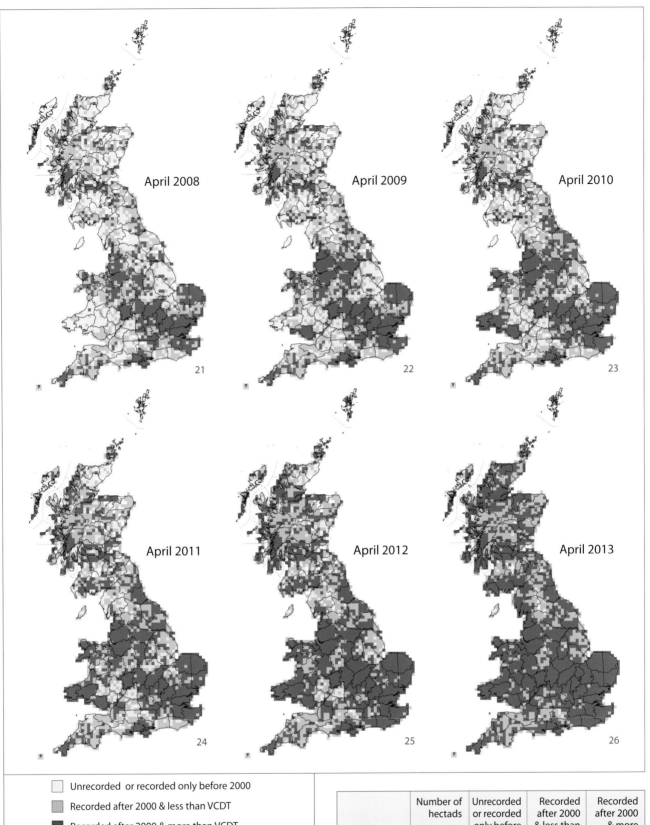

| | | April 2008 | | April 2009 | | April 2010 |
|---|---|---|---|---|---|---|
| | | | | | | 21 22 23 |
| | | April 2011 | | April 2012 | | April 2013 |
| | | | | | | 24 25 26 |

☐ Unrecorded or recorded only before 2000

▨ Recorded after 2000 & less than VCDT

■ Recorded after 2000 & more than VCDT

Figures 21-26. Recording progress maps for Great Britain, 2008-13. (Note that the maps are dated April, by which time records from the previous year, together with any data received for earlier years, had been collated, verified and incorporated into the national database.)

Table 3. Final recording status in Britain (see page 36 for an explanation of VCDT) after 2012 fieldwork. It is testament to the efforts of the DRN Scottish Coordinator that 87% of the hectads in Scotland were surveyed for this atlas.

| | Number of hectads | Unrecorded or recorded only before 2000 | Recorded after 2000 & less than VCDT | Recorded after 2000 & more than VCDT |
|---|---|---|---|---|
| England | 1,511 | 52 | 386 | 1,073 |
| Scotland | 1,119 | 153 | 378 | 588 |
| Wales | 287 | 8 | 47 | 233 |
| Britain total | 2,917 | 213 | 811 | 1,894 |
| Percentage of total | | 7% | 28% | 65% |

# Mapping the data, species richness and recording intensity

By definition, an atlas is a collection of maps. Throughout this atlas, maps are used to show the past and present distribution of British and Irish dragonflies in a readily accessible manner. In the previous atlas, the maps were printed in monochrome. Now with the availability of high quality digital printing, it is possible to show the core range for each species combined with gains and losses at a hectad resolution. Whilst many vice-counties have a wealth of data at a tetrad or monad resolution, the coverage is insufficient to be able to map at a higher resolution across Britain and Ireland in this atlas. The colour palettes used were designed to be distinguishable by those with colour impaired vision. All the maps were produced using *DMAP* mapping software written by Dr Alan Morton (www.dmap.co.uk)

One of the major trends in the current atlas period is the significant northwards spread of species compared with the previous atlas. Whilst there is no doubt that this can partially be explained by increasing temperatures, resulting from climate change, there has also been an increase in the number of recorders actively involved in recording dragonflies. This increase in recording intensity, therefore, needs to be considered when using the maps to interpret change. Figures 27 and 28 compare species richness ('diversity') for all species recorded in the previous atlas period with those from the new atlas period up to 2012.

Figures 29 and 30 compare the recording intensity for the current atlas period with that of the previous atlas. This comparison shows the considerable effort across much of southern Britain with fewer recording visits further north and in Ireland. These maps generally show a representation of where the majority of active recorders live. However, the greater number of visits in the south-east of England compared to other regions also coincides with where the highest diversity of species is to be found. As one progresses further north and west, considerable effort has been made to visit the often-remote hectads, particularly in the north of England and Scotland. The areas of high recording intensity in Scotland tend to show the areas for the key 'must see' species. In Ireland, coverage in the current atlas period is much more complete than in the previous atlas.

Table 4 shows the number of records for each species and the number of hectads in which each species has been found. These data are also expressed as a percentage of the total number of hectads with records. The data up to 1990 is compared with that from 1991-2012. Hectad presences are shown in Table 5, expressed as a percentage of the total number with records in each country. Table 6 shows the occurrence of each species in the vice-counties of Britain. Table 7 shows the occurrence of each species in the vice-counties of Ireland.

During the current atlas recording period, recorders were also encouraged to submit any records from previous time periods. This resulted in a large number of new records coming to light that improved our understanding of distribution patterns for earlier periods. For example, only 61,014 records (Figure 31) of some 160,434 (Figure 32) imported into the DRN database during 2012 were from that year. It was therefore important that these newly acquired records should be reflected in any analysis of change.

## Grid reference precision

Since the production of the previous atlas, there has been a marked improvement in the precision of records submitted to the DRN. Prior to 1991, 31% of all records submitted were at a 10km or 1km precision, this proportion falling to 15% post-1991 (Figure 33). In contrast, 80% of records submitted between 1991 and 2012 were at a 100m precision (6 figure grid reference) or better (Figure 33), including 626,198 records submitted at 100m precision (Figure 34). With the advent and increased use of GPS devices more records are being received at 10m precision (8 figure) and 1m (10 figure) precision.

In common with other atlases produced at the scale of entire countries, the hectad is the basic recording unit plotted on the maps. The term 'hectad' is used throughout in preference to the potentially misleading '10-km square' (strictly-speaking, this is a 10 km × 10 km square, often badly abbreviated to 10km$^2$, which is mathematically incorrect, as the area of a hectad is actually 100km$^2$).

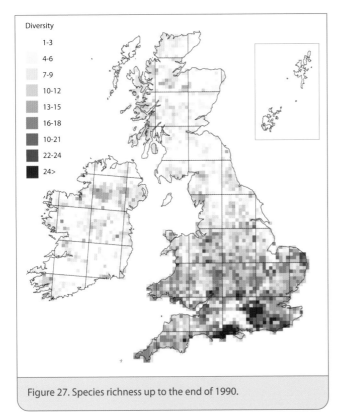

Figure 27. Species richness up to the end of 1990.

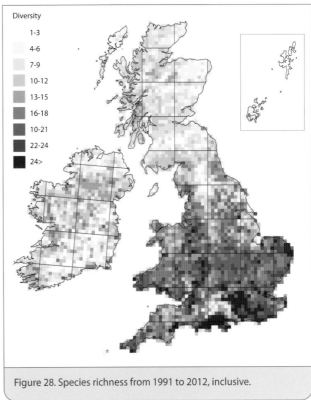

Figure 28. Species richness from 1991 to 2012, inclusive.

The colour density of each square in Figures 27 and 28 indicates the number of species recorded in each hectad whereby the dark squares relate to higher number of species than the light squares.

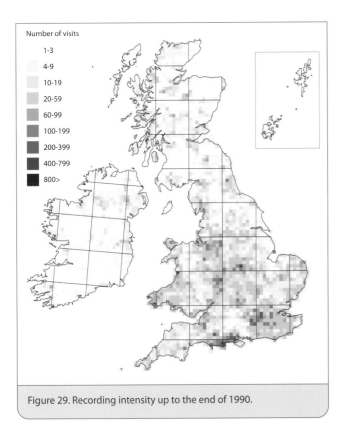

Figure 29. Recording intensity up to the end of 1990.

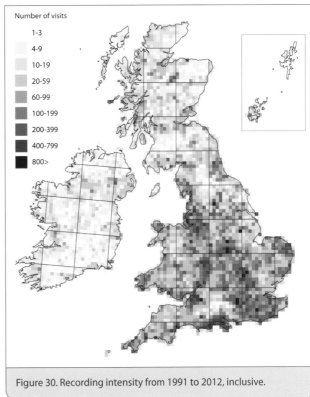

Figure 30. Recording intensity from 1991 to 2012, inclusive.

The colour density of the squares in Figures 29 and 30 indicates the number of visits to each hectad whereby the dark squares relate to higher number of visits than the light squares.

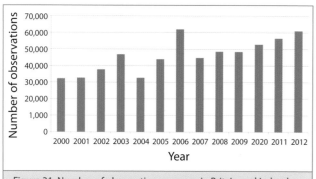

Figure 31. Number of observations per year in Britain and Ireland since 2000.

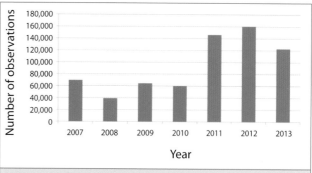

Figure 32 Number of observations submitted annually to the DRN during the Dragonflies in Focus project.

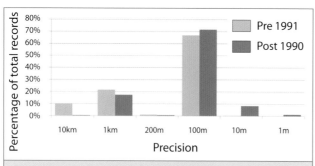

Figure 33. Percentage of records at different precisions comparing the two atlas periods (pre 1991 and post 1990).

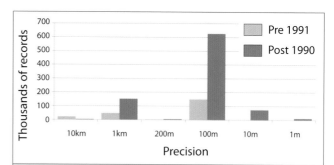

Figure 34. Numbers of records at different precisions comparing the two atlas periods (pre 1991 and post 1990).

Table 4. Numbers of records received and hectad occupancy in the two atlas periods. In the earlier period 3,195 hectads had records; this number increased to 3,595 hectads between 1991 and 2012.

| Species | Up to and including 1990 | | | 1991-2012 | | |
|---|---|---|---|---|---|---|
| | Records | Hectads | | Records | Hectads | |
| | | Number | Percentage | | Number | Percentage |
| Willow Emerald Damselfly | 1 | 1 | 0.03 | 463 | 4 | 1 1.14 |
| Southern Emerald Damselfly | 0 | 0 | 0 | 91 | 10 | 0.28 |
| Scarce Emerald Damselfly | 290 | 64 | 2.00 | 538 | 81 | 2.26 |
| Emerald Damselfly | 9,196 | 1,405 | 43.97 | 27,403 | 2,150 | 59.97 |
| Banded Demoiselle | 8,293 | 937 | 29.33 | 36,158 | 1,436 | 40.06 |
| Beautiful Demoiselle | 4,819 | 709 | 22.19 | 12,028 | 901 | 25.13 |
| White-legged Damselfly | 2,256 | 234 | 7.32 | 9,687 | 401 | 11.19 |
| Small Red Damselfly | 1,989 | 111 | 3.47 | 4,191 | 112 | 3.12 |
| Northern Damselfly | 177 | 8 | 0.25 | 354 | 16 | 0.45 |
| Irish Damselfly | 101 | 33 | 1.03 | 240 | 53 | 1.48 |
| Southern Damselfly | 795 | 34 | 1.06 | 7,129 | 33 | 0.92 |
| Azure Damselfly | 17,284 | 1,632 | 51.08 | 66,504 | 1,981 | 55.26 |
| Variable Damselfly | 2,147 | 484 | 15.15 | 4,567 | 478 | 13.33 |
| Dainty Damselfly | 13 | 2 | 0.06 | 12 | 3 | 0.08 |

Table 4 continued.

| | | | | | |
|---|---|---|---|---|---|
| Common Blue Damselfly | 21,988 | 2,343 | 73.33 | 78,871 | 2,810 | 78.38 |
| Red-eyed Damselfly | 3,238 | 346 | 10.83 | 21,519 | 673 | 18.77 |
| Small Red-eyed Damselfly | 0 | 0 | 0.00 | 3,711 | 393 | 10.96 |
| Blue-tailed Damselfly | 26,681 | 2,321 | 72.64 | 88,694 | 2,761 | 77.02 |
| Scarce Blue-tailed Damselfly | 1,111 | 184 | 5.76 | 3,680 | 215 | 6.00 |
| Large Red Damselfly | 18,698 | 2,248 | 70.36 | 65,499 | 2,864 | 79.89 |
| Southern Migrant Hawker | 1 | 1 | 0.03 | 51 | 12 | 0.33 |
| Azure Hawker | 244 | 58 | 1.82 | 354 | 77 | 2.15 |
| Southern Hawker | 9,326 | 1,066 | 33.36 | 40,977 | 1,526 | 42.57 |
| Brown Hawker | 11,486 | 950 | 29.73 | 43,010 | 1,347 | 37.57 |
| Common Hawker | 6,565 | 1,350 | 42.25 | 17,554 | 2,075 | 57.88 |
| Migrant Hawker | 4,879 | 622 | 19.47 | 35,998 | 1,286 | 35.87 |
| Norfolk Hawker | 176 | 14 | 0.44 | 1,336 | 41 | 1.14 |
| Vagrant Emperor | 14 | 9 | 0.28 | 62 | 42 | 1.17 |
| Emperor Dragonfly | 6,025 | 684 | 21.41 | 42,668 | 1,450 | 40.45 |
| Green Darner | 0 | 0 | 0.00 | 36 | 4 | 0.11 |
| Lesser Emperor | 0 | 0 | 0.00 | 1,045 | 157 | 4.38 |
| Hairy Dragonfly | 2,179 | 368 | 11.52 | 10,192 | 712 | 19.86 |
| Common Clubtail | 889 | 89 | 2.79 | 1,816 | 98 | 2.73 |
| Golden-ringed Dragonfly | 5,791 | 908 | 28.42 | 14,344 | 1,157 | 32.27 |
| Downy Emerald | 1,757 | 149 | 4.66 | 6,161 | 194 | 5.41 |
| Northern Emerald | 220 | 48 | 1.50 | 401 | 87 | 2.43 |
| Brilliant Emerald | 561 | 44 | 1.38 | 2,515 | 59 | 1.65 |
| Scarlet Darter | 0 | 0 | 0.00 | 16 | 6 | 0.17 |
| White-faced Darter | 529 | 53 | 1.66 | 1,325 | 56 | 1.56 |
| Broad-bodied Chaser | 6,702 | 836 | 26.17 | 26,486 | 1,307 | 36.46 |
| Scarce Chaser | 595 | 47 | 1.47 | 3,221 | 163 | 4.55 |
| Four-spotted Chaser | 7,996 | 1,322 | 41.38 | 34,517 | 2,199 | 61.34 |
| Black-tailed Skimmer | 3,485 | 451 | 14.12 | 27,083 | 1,141 | 31.83 |
| Keeled Skimmer | 3,106 | 302 | 9.45 | 9,244 | 477 | 13.31 |
| Black Darter | 5,577 | 943 | 29.51 | 12,626 | 1,408 | 39.27 |
| Yellow-winged Darter | 229 | 99 | 3.10 | 1,264 | 254 | 7.09 |
| Red-veined Darter | 144 | 64 | 2.00 | 3,425 | 327 | 9.12 |
| Ruddy Darter | 3,219 | 565 | 17.68 | 22,776 | 1,220 | 34.03 |
| Common Darter | 17,147 | 1,864 | 58.34 | 86,104 | 2,748 | 76.65 |
| Vagrant Darter | 16 | 14 | 0.44 | 35 | 14 | 0.39 |

Table 5. Percentage of hectads occupied by each species in England, Scotland, Wales, Britain and Ireland. Hectad occupancy is expressed as a percentage of the total number of hectads that have dragonfly records in each country and includes records for all periods up to 2012.

| Species | | England | Scotland | Wales | Britain | Ireland |
|---|---|---|---|---|---|---|
| *Number of recorded hectads* | | *1481* | *998* | *280* | *2759* | *948* |
| Willow Emerald Damselfly | *Chalcolestes viridis* | 2.84 | 0.00 | 0.00 | 1.52 | 0.00 |
| Southern Emerald Damselfly | *Lestes barbarus* | 0.68 | 0.00 | 0.00 | 0.36 | 0.00 |
| Scarce Emerald Damselfly | *Lestes dryas* | 6.08 | 0.00 | 0.00 | 3.26 | 2.95 |
| Emerald Damselfly | *Lestes sponsa* | 73.80 | 60.52 | 82.86 | 69.23 | 51.69 |
| Winter Damselfly | *Sympecma fusca* | 0.00 | 0.00 | 0.36 | 0.04 | 0.00 |
| Banded Demoiselle | *Calopteryx splendens* | 72.05 | 1.20 | 52.50 | 43.82 | 38.29 |
| Beautiful Demoiselle | *Calopteryx virgo* | 39.16 | 5.21 | 77.50 | 30.16 | 21.52 |
| White-legged Damselfly | *Platycnemis pennipes* | 28.43 | 0.00 | 8.57 | 15.80 | 0.00 |
| Small Red Damselfly | *Ceriagrion tenellum* | 7.29 | 0.00 | 13.57 | 5.29 | 0.00 |
| Norfolk Damselfly | *Coenagrion armatum* | 0.14 | 0.00 | 0.00 | 0.07 | 0.00 |
| Northern Damselfly | *Coenagrion hastulatum* | 0.00 | 1.60 | 0.00 | 0.58 | 0.00 |
| Irish Damselfly | *Coenagrion lunulatum* | 0.00 | 0.00 | 0.00 | 0.00 | 6.86 |
| Southern Damselfly | *Coenagrion mercuriale* | 2.03 | 0.00 | 5.00 | 1.59 | 0.00 |
| Azure Damselfly | *Coenagrion puella* | 87.58 | 21.14 | 92.86 | 63.18 | 47.36 |
| Variable Damselfly | *Coenagrion pulchellum* | 14.99 | 2.61 | 13.57 | 10.33 | 43.78 |
| Dainty Damselfly | *Coenagrion scitulum* | 0.34 | 0.00 | 0.00 | 0.18 | 0.00 |
| Common Blue Damselfly | *Enallagma cyathigerum* | 92.17 | 81.36 | 93.21 | 87.31 | 66.56 |
| Red-eyed Damselfly | *Erythromma najas* | 46.25 | 0.00 | 6.07 | 25.34 | 0.00 |
| Small Red-eyed Damselfly | *Erythromma viridulum* | 26.47 | 0.00 | 0.36 | 14.24 | 0.00 |
| Blue-tailed Damselfly | *Ischnura elegans* | 92.78 | 67.43 | 93.57 | 82.42 | 80.80 |
| Scarce Blue-tailed Damselfly | *Ischnura pumilio* | 7.22 | 0.00 | 40.71 | 7.97 | 9.07 |
| Large Red Damselfly | *Pyrrhosoma nymphula* | 88.25 | 86.47 | 92.50 | 87.13 | 76.27 |
| Southern Migrant Hawker | *Aeshna affinis* | 0.88 | 0.00 | 0.00 | 0.47 | 0.00 |
| Azure Hawker | *Aeshna caerulea* | 0.00 | 10.92 | 0.00 | 3.95 | 0.00 |
| Southern Hawker | *Aeshna cyanea* | 85.48 | 10.52 | 82.50 | 57.27 | 0.11 |
| Brown Hawker | *Aeshna grandis* | 67.72 | 0.20 | 24.29 | 38.24 | 41.14 |
| Common Hawker | *Aeshna juncea* | 49.29 | 81.76 | 77.86 | 63.36 | 62.66 |
| Migrant Hawker | *Aeshna mixta* | 74.68 | 1.10 | 47.86 | 44.87 | 6.96 |
| Norfolk Hawker | *Anaciaeschna isoceles* | 2.90 | 0.00 | 0.00 | 1.56 | 0.00 |
| Vagrant Emperor | *Anax ephippiger* | 2.23 | 0.80 | 2.50 | 1.74 | 0.32 |
| Emperor Dragonfly | *Anax imperator* | 79.34 | 2.10 | 79.29 | 50.82 | 7.49 |

Table 5 continued.

| Green Darner | *Anax junius* | 0.27 | 0.00 | 0.00 | 0.14 | 0.00 |
|---|---|---|---|---|---|---|
| Lesser Emperor | *Anax parthenope* | 9.25 | 0.10 | 2.86 | 5.29 | 1.16 |
| Hairy Dragonfly | *Brachytron pratense* | 29.51 | 1.40 | 27.86 | 19.10 | 29.64 |
| Common Clubtail | *Gomphus vulgatissimus* | 6.95 | 0.00 | 8.21 | 4.28 | 0.00 |
| Yellow-legged Clubtail | *Stylurus flavipes* | 0.07 | 0.00 | 0.00 | 0.04 | 0.00 |
| Golden-ringed Dragonfly | *Cordulegaster boltonii* | 33.22 | 58.92 | 78.93 | 46.83 | 0.21 |
| Orange-spotted Emerald | *Oxygastra curtisii* | 0.27 | 0.00 | 0.00 | 0.14 | 0.00 |
| Downy Emerald | *Cordulia aenea* | 13.91 | 0.90 | 2.14 | 7.97 | 1.05 |
| Northern Emerald | *Somatochlora arctica* | 0.00 | 10.32 | 0.00 | 3.73 | 0.42 |
| Brilliant Emerald | *Somatochlora metallica* | 3.17 | 1.50 | 0.00 | 2.25 | 0.00 |
| Scarlet Darter | *Crocothemis erythraea* | 0.41 | 0.00 | 0.00 | 0.22 | 0.00 |
| White-faced Darter | *Leucorrhinia dubia* | 1.62 | 5.61 | 0.71 | 2.90 | 0.00 |
| Large White-faced Darter | *Leucorrhinia pectoralis* | 0.14 | 0.00 | 0.00 | 0.07 | 0.00 |
| Broad-bodied Chaser | *Libellula depressa* | 76.64 | 0.60 | 83.57 | 49.40 | 0.11 |
| Scarce Chaser | *Libellula fulva* | 11.82 | 0.00 | 0.36 | 6.38 | 0.11 |
| Four-spotted Chaser | *Libellula quadrimaculata* | 72.72 | 59.92 | 77.86 | 68.03 | 59.18 |
| Black-tailed Skimmer | *Orthetrum cancellatum* | 65.50 | 0.30 | 42.14 | 39.29 | 8.86 |
| Keeled Skimmer | *Orthetrum coerulescens* | 15.06 | 6.51 | 45.36 | 15.04 | 16.14 |
| Wandering Glider | *Pantala flavescens* | 0.14 | 0.00 | 0.00 | 0.07 | 0.00 |
| Black Darter | *Sympetrum danae* | 34.71 | 67.03 | 54.29 | 48.17 | 39.24 |
| Yellow-winged Darter | *Sympetrum flaveolum* | 18.50 | 0.30 | 11.43 | 11.20 | 0.11 |
| Red-veined Darter | *Sympetrum fonscolombii* | 20.39 | 1.00 | 11.07 | 12.40 | 1.90 |
| Banded Darter | *Sympetrum pedemontanum* | 0.00 | 0.00 | 0.36 | 0.04 | 0.00 |
| Ruddy Darter | *Sympetrum sanguineum* | 64.96 | 0.20 | 23.93 | 37.15 | 28.27 |
| Common Darter | *Sympetrum striolatum* | 92.71 | 55.31 | 95.00 | 78.40 | 78.38 |
| Vagrant Darter | *Sympetrum vulgatum* | 1.82 | 0.00 | 0.36 | 1.01 | 0.00 |

Table 6. Vice-County distribution of species (England, Wales and Scotland only). Recorded before 1899 only (⊠), up to the end of 1999 only (O) and 2000 onwards (Δ).

| Species | West Cornwall | East Cornwall | South Devon | North Devon | South Somerset | North Somerset | North Wiltshire | South Wiltshire | Dorset | Isle of Wight | South Hampshire | North Hampshire | West Sussex | East Sussex | East Kent | West Kent | Surrey | South Essex | North Essex | Hertfordshire |
|---|---|---|---|---|---|---|---|---|---|---|---|---|---|---|---|---|---|---|---|---|
| Willow Emerald Damselfly | | | | | | | | | | | | | | O | Δ | O | | Δ | Δ | |
| Southern Emerald Damselfly | | | | | | Δ | | | | | | | | Δ | Δ | Δ | | Δ | | |
| Scarce Emerald Damselfly | | | | | | | | | | | | | | Δ | Δ | Δ | O | Δ | Δ | O |
| Emerald Damselfly | Δ | Δ | Δ | Δ | Δ | Δ | Δ | Δ | Δ | Δ | Δ | Δ | Δ | Δ | Δ | Δ | Δ | Δ | Δ | Δ |
| Winter Damselfly | | | | | | | | | | | | | | | | | | | | |
| Banded Demoiselle | Δ | Δ | Δ | Δ | Δ | Δ | Δ | Δ | Δ | Δ | Δ | Δ | Δ | Δ | Δ | Δ | Δ | Δ | Δ | Δ |
| Beautiful Demoiselle | Δ | Δ | Δ | Δ | Δ | Δ | Δ | Δ | Δ | Δ | Δ | Δ | Δ | Δ | Δ | Δ | Δ | O | Δ | O |
| White-legged Damselfly | | | Δ | Δ | Δ | Δ | Δ | Δ | Δ | Δ | Δ | Δ | Δ | Δ | Δ | Δ | Δ | Δ | Δ | Δ |
| Small Red Damselfly | Δ | Δ | Δ | Δ | | Δ | | Δ | Δ | | Δ | Δ | Δ | Δ | | O | Δ | | | |
| Norfolk Damselfly | | | | | | | | | | | | | | | | | | | | |
| Northern Damselfly | | | | | | | | | | | | | | | | | | | | |
| Southern Damselfly | O | | Δ | Δ | O | | | | Δ | | Δ | | | | | | | | | |
| Azure Damselfly | Δ | Δ | Δ | Δ | Δ | Δ | Δ | Δ | Δ | Δ | Δ | Δ | Δ | Δ | Δ | Δ | Δ | Δ | Δ | Δ |
| Variable Damselfly | | | | Δ | Δ | | | | O | | Δ | Δ | Δ | Δ | | | Δ | Δ | | O |
| Dainty Damselfly | | | | | | | | | | | | | | Δ | Δ | | O | | | |
| Common Blue Damselfly | Δ | Δ | Δ | Δ | Δ | Δ | Δ | Δ | Δ | Δ | Δ | Δ | Δ | Δ | Δ | Δ | Δ | Δ | Δ | Δ |
| Red-eyed Damselfly | | | Δ | Δ | Δ | Δ | Δ | Δ | Δ | Δ | Δ | Δ | Δ | Δ | Δ | Δ | Δ | Δ | Δ | Δ |
| Small Red-eyed Damselfly | | | Δ | | Δ | Δ | Δ | Δ | Δ | Δ | Δ | Δ | Δ | Δ | Δ | Δ | Δ | Δ | Δ | Δ |
| Blue-tailed Damselfly | Δ | Δ | Δ | Δ | Δ | Δ | Δ | Δ | Δ | Δ | Δ | Δ | Δ | Δ | Δ | Δ | Δ | Δ | Δ | Δ |
| Scarce Blue-tailed Damselfly | Δ | Δ | Δ | Δ | | Δ | Δ | Δ | Δ | Δ | Δ | Δ | | O | | | Δ | | | O |
| Large Red Damselfly | Δ | Δ | Δ | Δ | Δ | Δ | Δ | Δ | Δ | Δ | Δ | Δ | Δ | Δ | Δ | Δ | Δ | Δ | Δ | Δ |
| Southern Migrant Hawker | | | | | | | | | | | Δ | | Δ | | | | O | Δ | Δ | Δ |
| Azure Hawker | | | | | | | | | | | | | | | | | | | | |
| Southern Hawker | Δ | Δ | Δ | Δ | Δ | Δ | Δ | Δ | Δ | Δ | Δ | Δ | Δ | Δ | Δ | Δ | Δ | Δ | Δ | Δ |
| Brown Hawker | | O | | Δ | Δ | Δ | Δ | Δ | Δ | Δ | Δ | Δ | Δ | Δ | Δ | Δ | Δ | Δ | Δ | Δ |
| Common Hawker | Δ | Δ | Δ | Δ | Δ | Δ | Δ | Δ | Δ | Δ | Δ | Δ | Δ | O | | | | Δ | O | O |
| Migrant Hawker | Δ | Δ | Δ | Δ | Δ | Δ | Δ | Δ | Δ | Δ | Δ | Δ | Δ | Δ | Δ | Δ | Δ | Δ | Δ | Δ |
| Norfolk Hawker | | | | | | | | | | | Δ | | | | | Δ | | | | |
| Vagrant Emperor | Δ | Δ | Δ | | | | | | Δ | Δ | Δ | | | Δ | Δ | O | Δ | | | |

Table 6 continued.

| Species | West Cornwall | East Cornwall | South Devon | North Devon | South Somerset | North Somerset | North Wiltshire | South Wiltshire | Dorset | Isle of Wight | South Hampshire | North Hampshire | West Sussex | East Sussex | East Kent | West Kent | Surrey | South Essex | North Essex | Hertfordshire |
|---|---|---|---|---|---|---|---|---|---|---|---|---|---|---|---|---|---|---|---|---|
| Emperor Dragonfly | Δ | Δ | Δ | Δ | Δ | Δ | Δ | Δ | Δ | Δ | Δ | Δ | Δ | Δ | Δ | Δ | Δ | Δ | Δ | Δ |
| Green Darner | O | O | | | | | | | | | | | | | | | | | | |
| Lesser Emperor | Δ | Δ | Δ | | | Δ | Δ | Δ | Δ | Δ | Δ | Δ | | Δ | Δ | Δ | Δ | Δ | | Δ |
| Hairy Dragonfly | Δ | | Δ | Δ | Δ | Δ | Δ | | Δ | Δ | Δ | Δ | Δ | Δ | Δ | Δ | Δ | Δ | Δ | Δ |
| Common Clubtail | | | | | | | O | | | O | Δ | Δ | O | | | O | O | | | |
| Yellow-legged Clubtail | | | | | | | | | | | | | | ⊠ | | | | | | |
| Golden-ringed Dragonfly | Δ | Δ | Δ | Δ | Δ | Δ | Δ | Δ | Δ | Δ | Δ | Δ | Δ | Δ | Δ | Δ | Δ | Δ | | |
| Orange-spotted Emerald | | | O | O | | | | | | O | O | | | | | | | | | |
| Downy Emerald | | | Δ | | Δ | Δ | Δ | Δ | Δ | Δ | Δ | Δ | Δ | Δ | Δ | Δ | Δ | Δ | Δ | Δ |
| Northern Emerald | | | | | | | | | | | | | | | | | | | | |
| Brilliant Emerald | | | | | | | | | | | | | Δ | Δ | Δ | Δ | Δ | Δ | | |
| Scarlet Darter | O | | Δ | | | | | | | Δ | Δ | | | | | | | | | |
| White-faced Darter | | | | | | | | | | | | | | O | O | | O | | | |
| Large White-faced Darter | | | | | | | | | | | | | | | | | | | | |
| Broad-bodied Chaser | Δ | Δ | Δ | Δ | Δ | Δ | Δ | Δ | Δ | Δ | Δ | Δ | Δ | Δ | Δ | Δ | Δ | Δ | Δ | Δ |
| Scarce Chaser | | | Δ | Δ | Δ | Δ | Δ | Δ | Δ | Δ | Δ | Δ | Δ | Δ | Δ | Δ | Δ | Δ | Δ | Δ |
| Four-spotted Chaser | Δ | Δ | Δ | Δ | Δ | Δ | Δ | Δ | Δ | Δ | Δ | Δ | Δ | Δ | Δ | Δ | Δ | Δ | Δ | Δ |
| Black-tailed Skimmer | Δ | Δ | Δ | Δ | Δ | Δ | Δ | Δ | Δ | Δ | Δ | Δ | Δ | Δ | Δ | Δ | Δ | Δ | Δ | Δ |
| Keeled Skimmer | Δ | Δ | Δ | Δ | Δ | Δ | | Δ | Δ | Δ | Δ | Δ | Δ | Δ | Δ | Δ | O | Δ | O | Δ |
| Wandering Glider | | | | | | | | | | | | | | | | | | | | |
| Black Darter | Δ | Δ | Δ | Δ | Δ | Δ | Δ | Δ | Δ | Δ | Δ | Δ | Δ | Δ | Δ | Δ | O | O | O | O |
| Yellow-winged Darter | O | O | O | O | | Δ | | | O | Δ | Δ | Δ | Δ | Δ | Δ | Δ | O | O | Δ | Δ |
| Red-veined Darter | Δ | Δ | Δ | Δ | O | Δ | Δ | Δ | Δ | Δ | Δ | Δ | Δ | Δ | Δ | Δ | Δ | Δ | | Δ |
| Banded Darter | | | | | | | | | | | | | | | | | | | | |
| Ruddy Darter | Δ | Δ | Δ | Δ | Δ | Δ | Δ | Δ | Δ | Δ | Δ | Δ | Δ | Δ | Δ | Δ | Δ | Δ | Δ | Δ |
| Common Darter | Δ | Δ | Δ | Δ | Δ | Δ | Δ | Δ | Δ | Δ | Δ | Δ | Δ | Δ | Δ | Δ | Δ | Δ | Δ | Δ |
| Vagrant Darter | Δ | | Δ | | | | | | Δ | O | O | Δ | | O | Δ | O | ⊠ | O | | O |
| **No of species** | 29 | 26 | 35 | 27 | 28 | 32 | 28 | 28 | 35 | 32 | 39 | 34 | 33 | 40 | 37 | 37 | 37 | 34 | 27 | 31 |
| **Britain ranking** | 28 | 46 | 7 | 40 | 32 | 15 | 32 | 32 | 7 | 15 | 2 | 9 | 12 | 1 | 4 | 4 | 4 | 9 | 40 | 19 |

| Species | Middlesex | Berkshire | Oxfordshire | Buckinghamshire | East Suffolk | West Suffolk | East Norfolk | West Norfolk | Cambridgeshire | Bedfordshire | Huntingdonshire | Northamptonshire | East Gloucestershire | West Gloucestershire | Monmouthshire | Herefordshire | Worcestershire | Warwickshire | Staffordshire |
|---|---|---|---|---|---|---|---|---|---|---|---|---|---|---|---|---|---|---|---|
| Willow Emerald Damselfly | | | | | Δ | Δ | Δ | | | | | | | | | | | | |
| Southern Emerald Damselfly | | | | | Δ | | Δ | | | | | | | Δ | | | | | |
| Scarce Emerald Damselfly | O | | | O | Δ | Δ | Δ | Δ | O | O | O | | | | | | | | |
| Emerald Damselfly | Δ | Δ | Δ | Δ | Δ | Δ | Δ | Δ | Δ | Δ | Δ | Δ | Δ | Δ | Δ | Δ | Δ | Δ | Δ |
| Winter Damselfly | | | | | | | | | | | | | | | | | | | |
| Banded Demoiselle | Δ | Δ | Δ | Δ | Δ | Δ | Δ | Δ | Δ | Δ | Δ | Δ | Δ | Δ | Δ | Δ | Δ | Δ | Δ |
| Beautiful Demoiselle | Δ | Δ | Δ | Δ | | | O | Δ | | Δ | | Δ | Δ | Δ | Δ | Δ | Δ | Δ | Δ |
| White-legged Damselfly | O | Δ | Δ | Δ | Δ | Δ | | | Δ | Δ | Δ | Δ | Δ | Δ | Δ | Δ | Δ | Δ | Δ |
| Small Red Damselfly | | Δ | Δ | Δ | O | | O | Δ | O | | | | | | | | | | |
| Norfolk Damselfly | | | | | | | O | | | | | | | | | | | | |
| Northern Damselfly | | | | | | | | | | | | | | | | | | | |
| Southern Damselfly | | Δ | Δ | | | | | | | | | | | | | | | | |
| Azure Damselfly | Δ | Δ | Δ | Δ | Δ | Δ | Δ | Δ | Δ | Δ | Δ | Δ | Δ | Δ | Δ | Δ | Δ | Δ | Δ |
| Variable Damselfly | O | Δ | Δ | Δ | Δ | Δ | Δ | Δ | Δ | | Δ | Δ | | O | Δ | O | | O | Δ |
| Dainty Damselfly | | | | | | | | | | | | | | | | | | | |
| Common Blue Damselfly | Δ | Δ | Δ | Δ | Δ | Δ | Δ | Δ | Δ | Δ | Δ | Δ | Δ | Δ | Δ | Δ | Δ | Δ | Δ |
| Red-eyed Damselfly | Δ | Δ | Δ | Δ | Δ | Δ | Δ | Δ | Δ | Δ | Δ | Δ | Δ | Δ | Δ | Δ | Δ | Δ | Δ |
| Small Red-eyed Damselfly | Δ | Δ | Δ | Δ | Δ | Δ | Δ | Δ | Δ | Δ | Δ | Δ | Δ | Δ | | Δ | Δ | Δ | |
| Blue-tailed Damselfly | Δ | Δ | Δ | Δ | Δ | Δ | Δ | Δ | Δ | Δ | Δ | Δ | Δ | Δ | Δ | Δ | Δ | Δ | Δ |
| Scarce Blue-tailed Damselfly | | Δ | Δ | O | | | Δ | | O | Δ | | | Δ | Δ | Δ | Δ | | Δ | |
| Large Red Damselfly | Δ | Δ | Δ | Δ | Δ | | Δ | Δ | Δ | Δ | Δ | Δ | Δ | Δ | Δ | Δ | | Δ | Δ |
| Southern Migrant Hawker | | | | | | | Δ | Δ | | | | | | | | | | | |
| Azure Hawker | | | | | | | | | | | | | | | | | | | |
| Southern Hawker | Δ | Δ | Δ | Δ | Δ | Δ | Δ | Δ | Δ | Δ | Δ | Δ | Δ | Δ | Δ | Δ | Δ | Δ | Δ |
| Brown Hawker | Δ | Δ | Δ | Δ | Δ | Δ | Δ | Δ | Δ | Δ | Δ | Δ | Δ | Δ | Δ | Δ | Δ | Δ | Δ |
| Common Hawker | Δ | Δ | Δ | Δ | Δ | | Δ | Δ | O | O | O | Δ | Δ | Δ | Δ | Δ | Δ | Δ | Δ |
| Migrant Hawker | Δ | Δ | Δ | Δ | Δ | Δ | Δ | Δ | Δ | Δ | Δ | Δ | Δ | Δ | Δ | Δ | Δ | Δ | Δ |
| Norfolk Hawker | | | | | Δ | Δ | Δ | Δ | Δ | | Δ | | | | | | | | |
| Vagrant Emperor | O | | | | | | Δ | Δ | | | | | | | | | | Δ | |

Table 6 continued.

| Species | Middlesex | Berkshire | Oxfordshire | Buckinghamshire | East Suffolk | West Suffolk | East Norfolk | West Norfolk | Cambridgeshire | Bedfordshire | Huntingdonshire | Northamptonshire | East Gloucestershire | West Gloucestershire | Monmouthshire | Herefordshire | Worcestershire | Warwickshire | Staffordshire |
|---|---|---|---|---|---|---|---|---|---|---|---|---|---|---|---|---|---|---|---|
| Emperor Dragonfly | Δ | Δ | Δ | Δ | Δ | Δ | Δ | Δ | Δ | Δ | Δ | Δ | Δ | Δ | Δ | Δ | Δ | Δ | Δ |
| Green Darner | | | | | | | | | | | | | | | | | | | |
| Lesser Emperor | Δ | Δ | Δ | Δ | Δ | | Δ | Δ | Δ | Δ | Δ | Δ | Δ | Δ | Δ | | Δ | Δ | Δ |
| Hairy Dragonfly | Δ | Δ | Δ | Δ | Δ | Δ | Δ | Δ | Δ | Δ | Δ | Δ | Δ | Δ | Δ | O | Δ | Δ | |
| Common Clubtail | O | Δ | Δ | Δ | | | | | | | | | O | Δ | Δ | Δ | Δ | Δ | Δ |
| Yellow-legged Clubtail | | | | | | | | | | | | | | | | | | | |
| Golden-ringed Dragonfly | O | Δ | | | | | | | | | | | Δ | Δ | Δ | Δ | Δ | O | Δ |
| Orange-spotted Emerald | | | | | | | | | | | | | | | | | | | |
| Downy Emerald | Δ | Δ | Δ | Δ | O | | Δ | O | Δ | Δ | | Δ | Δ | Δ | | Δ | | | Δ |
| Northern Emerald | | | | | | | | | | | | | | | | | | | |
| Brilliant Emerald | O | Δ | | O | | | | | | | | | | | | | | | |
| Scarlet Darter | | | | | | | | | | | | | | | | | | | |
| White-faced Darter | | | | | | | | | | | | | | | | | | | Δ |
| Large White-faced Darter | | | | | Δ | | | | | | | | | | | | | | |
| Broad-bodied Chaser | Δ | Δ | Δ | Δ | Δ | Δ | Δ | Δ | Δ | Δ | Δ | Δ | Δ | Δ | Δ | Δ | Δ | Δ | Δ |
| Scarce Chaser | | Δ | | Δ | Δ | Δ | Δ | Δ | Δ | Δ | Δ | Δ | Δ | Δ | O | | Δ | Δ | |
| Four-spotted Chaser | Δ | Δ | Δ | Δ | Δ | Δ | Δ | Δ | Δ | Δ | Δ | Δ | Δ | Δ | Δ | Δ | Δ | Δ | Δ |
| Black-tailed Skimmer | Δ | Δ | Δ | Δ | Δ | Δ | Δ | Δ | | Δ | Δ | Δ | | Δ | Δ | Δ | | Δ | Δ |
| Keeled Skimmer | | Δ | Δ | Δ | | | Δ | Δ | O | | | | | | Δ | Δ | Δ | Δ | Δ |
| Wandering Glider | | | | | | | ⊠ | | | | | | | | | | | | |
| Black Darter | | Δ | O | Δ | Δ | | Δ | Δ | O | O | O | Δ | O | Δ | Δ | Δ | Δ | Δ | Δ |
| Yellow-winged Darter | O | Δ | Δ | O | Δ | Δ | Δ | Δ | Δ | O | O | O | | O | O | O | O | O | Δ |
| Red-veined Darter | Δ | Δ | Δ | Δ | Δ | Δ | Δ | Δ | Δ | Δ | Δ | Δ | O | Δ | Δ | Δ | Δ | Δ | Δ |
| Banded Darter | | | | | | | | | | | | | | | | O | | | |
| Ruddy Darter | Δ | Δ | Δ | Δ | Δ | Δ | Δ | Δ | Δ | Δ | Δ | Δ | Δ | Δ | Δ | Δ | Δ | Δ | Δ |
| Common Darter | Δ | Δ | Δ | Δ | Δ | Δ | Δ | Δ | Δ | Δ | Δ | Δ | Δ | Δ | Δ | Δ | Δ | Δ | Δ |
| Vagrant Darter | O | | | | | | O | | | | | | | | O | | | | O |
| **No of species** | 31 | 34 | 31 | 33 | 32 | 25 | 38 | 32 | 31 | 28 | 27 | 28 | 29 | 33 | 31 | 28 | 27 | 31 | 29 |
| **Britain ranking** | 19 | 9 | 19 | 12 | 15 | 55 | 3 | 15 | 19 | 32 | 40 | 32 | 28 | 12 | 19 | 32 | 40 | 19 | 28 |

| Species | Shropshire | Glamorganshire | Breconshire | Radnorshire | Carmarthenshire | Pembrokeshire | Cardiganshire | Montgomeryshire | Merionithshire | Caernarvonshire | Denbighshire | Flintshire | Anglesey | South Lincolnshire | North Lincolnshire | Leicestershire & Rutland | Nottinghamshire | Derbyshire | Cheshire | South Lancashire | West Lancashire |
|---|---|---|---|---|---|---|---|---|---|---|---|---|---|---|---|---|---|---|---|---|---|
| Willow Emerald Damselfly | | | | | | | | | | | | | | | | | | | | | |
| Southern Emerald Damselfly | | | | | | | | | | | | | | | | | | | | | |
| Scarce Emerald Damselfly | | | | | | | | | | | | | | O | O | | | | | | |
| Emerald Damselfly | Δ | Δ | Δ | Δ | Δ | Δ | Δ | Δ | Δ | Δ | Δ | Δ | Δ | Δ | Δ | Δ | Δ | Δ | Δ | Δ | Δ |
| Winter Damselfly | | Δ | | | | | | | | | | | | | | | | | | | |
| Banded Demoiselle | Δ | Δ | Δ | Δ | Δ | Δ | Δ | Δ | Δ | Δ | Δ | Δ | Δ | Δ | Δ | Δ | Δ | Δ | Δ | Δ | Δ |
| Beautiful Demoiselle | Δ | Δ | Δ | Δ | Δ | Δ | Δ | Δ | Δ | Δ | Δ | Δ | Δ | | | O | Δ | O | Δ | Δ | Δ |
| White-legged Damselfly | Δ | O | Δ | Δ | | | | Δ | | | Δ | | | Δ | | | Δ | O | O | Δ | |
| Small Red Damselfly | | O | O | Δ | Δ | Δ | Δ | Δ | Δ | | | | Δ | | | | | | | | |
| Norfolk Damselfly | | | | | | | | | | | | | | | | | | | | | |
| Northern Damselfly | | | | | | | | | | | | | | | | | | | | | |
| Southern Damselfly | | Δ | O | | | Δ | O | | | | | | Δ | | | | | | | | |
| Azure Damselfly | Δ | Δ | Δ | Δ | Δ | Δ | Δ | Δ | Δ | Δ | Δ | Δ | Δ | Δ | Δ | Δ | Δ | Δ | Δ | Δ | Δ |
| Variable Damselfly | Δ | Δ | Δ | | Δ | | O | | O | Δ | O | O | Δ | Δ | Δ | Δ | Δ | | Δ | | |
| Dainty Damselfly | | | | | | | | | | | | | | | | | | | | | |
| Common Blue Damselfly | Δ | Δ | Δ | Δ | Δ | Δ | Δ | Δ | Δ | Δ | Δ | Δ | Δ | Δ | Δ | Δ | Δ | Δ | Δ | Δ | Δ |
| Red-eyed Damselfly | Δ | Δ | | | Δ | | Δ | | | Δ | Δ | | Δ | Δ | Δ | Δ | Δ | Δ | Δ | | |
| Small Red-eyed Damselfly | | | | | Δ | | | | | | | | | Δ | Δ | Δ | Δ | Δ | | | |
| Blue-tailed Damselfly | Δ | Δ | Δ | Δ | Δ | Δ | Δ | Δ | Δ | Δ | Δ | Δ | Δ | Δ | Δ | Δ | Δ | Δ | Δ | Δ | Δ |
| Scarce Blue-tailed Damselfly | Δ | Δ | Δ | Δ | Δ | Δ | Δ | Δ | Δ | Δ | | | Δ | | | | | | O | | |
| Large Red Damselfly | Δ | Δ | Δ | Δ | Δ | Δ | Δ | Δ | Δ | Δ | Δ | Δ | Δ | Δ | Δ | Δ | Δ | Δ | Δ | Δ | Δ |
| Southern Migrant Hawker | | | | | | | | | | | | | | | | | | | | | |
| Azure Hawker | | | | | | | | | | | | | | | | | | | | | |
| Southern Hawker | Δ | Δ | Δ | Δ | Δ | Δ | Δ | Δ | Δ | Δ | Δ | Δ | Δ | Δ | Δ | Δ | Δ | Δ | Δ | Δ | Δ |
| Brown Hawker | Δ | Δ | Δ | Δ | O | | | Δ | Δ | O | Δ | Δ | O | Δ | Δ | Δ | Δ | Δ | Δ | Δ | Δ |
| Common Hawker | Δ | Δ | Δ | Δ | Δ | Δ | Δ | Δ | Δ | Δ | Δ | Δ | Δ | Δ | Δ | Δ | Δ | Δ | Δ | Δ | Δ |
| Migrant Hawker | Δ | Δ | Δ | Δ | Δ | Δ | Δ | Δ | Δ | Δ | Δ | Δ | Δ | Δ | Δ | Δ | Δ | Δ | Δ | Δ | Δ |
| Norfolk Hawker | | | | | | | | | | | | | | | O | | | | | | |
| Vagrant Emperor | | Δ | | | | Δ | | | | Δ | | | | | | | Δ | | | | |

Table 6 continued.

| Species | Shropshire | Glamorganshire | Breconshire | Radnorshire | Carmarthenshire | Pembrokeshire | Cardiganshire | Montgomeryshire | Merionithshire | Caernarvonshire | Denbighshire | Flintshire | Anglesey | South Lincolnshire | North Lincolnshire | Leicestershire & Rutland | Nottinghamshire | Derbyshire | Cheshire | South Lancashire | West Lancashire |
|---|---|---|---|---|---|---|---|---|---|---|---|---|---|---|---|---|---|---|---|---|---|
| Emperor Dragonfly | Δ | Δ | Δ | Δ | Δ | Δ | Δ | Δ | Δ | Δ | Δ | Δ | Δ | Δ | Δ | Δ | Δ | Δ | Δ | Δ | Δ |
| Green Darner | | | | | | | | | | | | | | | | | | | | | |
| Lesser Emperor | | Δ | | | Δ | Δ | | | | | | Δ | | Δ | Δ | Δ | Δ | Δ | Δ | Δ | Δ |
| Hairy Dragonfly | Δ | Δ | O | Δ | Δ | Δ | Δ | Δ | Δ | Δ | Δ | Δ | Δ | Δ | Δ | Δ | Δ | | | Δ | Δ |
| Common Clubtail | Δ | | | Δ | Δ | O | Δ | Δ | | | Δ | Δ | | | | | | | Δ | | |
| Yellow-legged Clubtail | | | | | | | | | | | | | | | | | | | | | |
| Golden-ringed Dragonfly | Δ | Δ | Δ | Δ | Δ | Δ | Δ | Δ | Δ | Δ | Δ | Δ | Δ | | Δ | | O | Δ | Δ | Δ | Δ |
| Orange-spotted Emerald | | | | | | | | | | | | | | | | | | | | | |
| Downy Emerald | Δ | Δ | | | | | | Δ | Δ | O | | | | | | | | | Δ | | |
| Northern Emerald | | | | | | | | | | | | | | | | | | | | | |
| Brilliant Emerald | | | | | | | | | | | | | | | | | | | | | |
| Scarlet Darter | | | | | | | | | | | | | | | | | | | | | |
| White-faced Darter | Δ | | | | | | | | | | Δ | | | | | | | | Δ | | |
| Large White-faced Darter | | | | | | | | | | | | | | | | | | | | | |
| Broad-bodied Chaser | Δ | Δ | Δ | Δ | Δ | Δ | Δ | Δ | Δ | Δ | Δ | Δ | Δ | Δ | Δ | Δ | Δ | Δ | Δ | Δ | Δ |
| Scarce Chaser | Δ | | | | | | | | | | | | | | | | | | O | | |
| Four-spotted Chaser | Δ | Δ | Δ | Δ | Δ | Δ | Δ | Δ | Δ | Δ | Δ | Δ | Δ | Δ | Δ | Δ | Δ | Δ | Δ | Δ | Δ |
| Black-tailed Skimmer | Δ | Δ | Δ | Δ | Δ | Δ | Δ | Δ | | Δ | Δ | | Δ | Δ | Δ | Δ | Δ | Δ | Δ | Δ | Δ |
| Keeled Skimmer | Δ | Δ | Δ | Δ | Δ | Δ | Δ | Δ | Δ | Δ | | | Δ | | | | | Δ | O | | |
| Wandering Glider | | | | | | | | | | | | | | | | | | | | | |
| Black Darter | Δ | Δ | Δ | Δ | Δ | Δ | Δ | Δ | Δ | Δ | Δ | O | Δ | O | Δ | Δ | Δ | Δ | Δ | Δ | Δ |
| Yellow-winged Darter | O | Δ | | Δ | Δ | Δ | | | O | O | | | | | Δ | Δ | Δ | O | O | O | Δ |
| Red-veined Darter | Δ | Δ | Δ | Δ | Δ | Δ | | | O | Δ | | Δ | | | Δ | Δ | Δ | Δ | Δ | Δ | Δ |
| Banded Darter | | | | | | | | | | | | | | | | | | | | | |
| Ruddy Darter | Δ | Δ | Δ | Δ | Δ | Δ | O | Δ | O | O | O | Δ | Δ | O | Δ | Δ | Δ | Δ | Δ | Δ | Δ |
| Common Darter | Δ | Δ | Δ | Δ | Δ | Δ | Δ | Δ | Δ | Δ | Δ | Δ | Δ | Δ | Δ | Δ | Δ | Δ | Δ | Δ | Δ |
| Vagrant Darter | | | | | | | ☒ | | | | | | | | | | | | | | |
| **No of species** | 30 | 31 | 26 | 25 | 29 | 27 | 25 | 26 | 24 | 26 | 27 | 24 | 24 | 25 | 26 | 26 | 26 | 25 | 31 | 23 | 21 |
| **Britain ranking** | 27 | 19 | 46 | 55 | 28 | 40 | 55 | 46 | 61 | 46 | 40 | 61 | 61 | 55 | 46 | 46 | 46 | 55 | 19 | 65 | 69 |

Table 6 continued. Recorded before 1899 only (⊠), up to the end of 1999 only (O) and 2000 onwards (Δ).

| Species | South-east Yorkshire | North-east Yorkshire | South-west Yorkshire | Mid-west Yorkshire | North-west Yorkshire | Durham | South Northumberland | North Northumberland | Westmorland & N. Lancs | Cumberland | Isle of Man | Dumfriesshire | Kirkudbrightshire | Wigtownshire | Ayrshire | Renfrewshire | Lanarkshire | Peeblesshire | Selkirkshire | Roxburghshire |
|---|---|---|---|---|---|---|---|---|---|---|---|---|---|---|---|---|---|---|---|---|
| Willow Emerald Damselfly | | | | | | | | | | | | | | | | | | | | |
| Southern Emerald Damselfly | | | | | | | | | | | | | | | | | | | | |
| Scarce Emerald Damselfly | O | | | | | | | | | | | | | | | | | | | |
| Emerald Damselfly | Δ | Δ | Δ | Δ | Δ | Δ | Δ | Δ | Δ | Δ | Δ | Δ | Δ | Δ | Δ | Δ | Δ | Δ | Δ | Δ |
| Winter Damselfly | | | | | | | | | | | | | | | | | | | | |
| Banded Demoiselle | Δ | Δ | Δ | Δ | Δ | Δ | Δ | Δ | Δ | Δ | | Δ | Δ | | | | | | | Δ |
| Beautiful Demoiselle | Δ | Δ | O | | | Δ | | | Δ | Δ | | | Δ | | | | | | | |
| White-legged Damselfly | | | | | | | | | | | | | | | | | | | | |
| Small Red Damselfly | | | | | | | | | | | | | | | | | | | | |
| Norfolk Damselfly | | | | | | | | | | | | | | | | | | | | |
| Northern Damselfly | | | | | | | | | | | | | | | | | | | | |
| Southern Damselfly | | | | | | | | | | | | | | | | | | | | |
| Azure Damselfly | Δ | Δ | Δ | Δ | Δ | Δ | Δ | Δ | Δ | Δ | | Δ | Δ | Δ | Δ | Δ | Δ | Δ | Δ | Δ |
| Variable Damselfly | Δ | O | O | Δ | | | | | O | Δ | | Δ | Δ | Δ | | | | | | |
| Dainty Damselfly | | | | | | | | | | | | | | | | | | | | |
| Common Blue Damselfly | Δ | Δ | Δ | Δ | Δ | Δ | Δ | Δ | Δ | Δ | Δ | Δ | Δ | Δ | Δ | Δ | Δ | Δ | Δ | Δ |
| Red-eyed Damselfly | Δ | | Δ | Δ | | | | | | | | | O | | | | | | | |
| Small Red-eyed Damselfly | Δ | Δ | | | | | | | | | | | | | | | | | | |
| Blue-tailed Damselfly | Δ | Δ | Δ | Δ | Δ | Δ | Δ | Δ | Δ | Δ | | Δ | Δ | Δ | Δ | Δ | Δ | Δ | Δ | Δ |
| Scarce Blue-tailed Damselfly | | | | | | | | | | | | | | | | | | | | |
| Large Red Damselfly | Δ | Δ | Δ | Δ | Δ | Δ | Δ | Δ | Δ | Δ | Δ | Δ | Δ | Δ | Δ | Δ | Δ | Δ | Δ | Δ |
| Southern Migrant Hawker | | | | | | | | | | | | | | | | | | | | |
| Azure Hawker | | | | | | | | | | | | | Δ | | Δ | | | | | |
| Southern Hawker | Δ | Δ | Δ | Δ | Δ | Δ | Δ | Δ | Δ | Δ | Δ | Δ | Δ | | | | | | | Δ |
| Brown Hawker | Δ | Δ | Δ | Δ | Δ | Δ | Δ | Δ | Δ | Δ | Δ | | ⊠ | | | | | | | |
| Common Hawker | Δ | Δ | Δ | Δ | Δ | Δ | Δ | Δ | Δ | Δ | Δ | Δ | Δ | Δ | Δ | Δ | Δ | Δ | Δ | Δ |
| Migrant Hawker | Δ | Δ | Δ | Δ | Δ | Δ | Δ | | Δ | Δ | Δ | Δ | Δ | | Δ | | | | | |
| Norfolk Hawker | Δ | | | | | | | | | | | | | | | | | | | |
| Vagrant Emperor | | O | O | | | | | | Δ | | Δ | Δ | Δ | | | | | | | |

Table 6 continued.

| Species | South-east Yorkshire | North-east Yorkshire | South-west Yorkshire | Mid-west Yorkshire | North-west Yorkshire | Durham | South Northumberland | North Northumberland | Westmorland & N. Lancs | Cumberland | Isle of Man | Dumfriesshire | Kirkudbrightshire | Wigtownshire | Ayrshire | Renfrewshire | Lanarkshire | Peebleshire | Selkirkshire | Roxburghshire |
|---|---|---|---|---|---|---|---|---|---|---|---|---|---|---|---|---|---|---|---|---|
| Emperor Dragonfly | Δ | Δ | Δ | Δ | Δ | Δ | Δ | Δ | Δ | Δ | Δ | Δ | Δ | Δ |  |  |  |  | Δ |  |
| Green Darner |  |  |  |  |  |  |  |  |  |  |  |  |  |  |  |  |  |  |  |  |
| Lesser Emperor | Δ | Δ | Δ | Δ | Δ | Δ | Δ |  |  | Δ | Δ |  |  |  |  |  |  |  |  |  |
| Hairy Dragonfly | Δ |  | Δ | O |  | O | O | O | Δ |  |  |  | Δ | Δ |  |  |  |  |  |  |
| Common Clubtail |  |  |  |  |  |  |  |  |  |  |  |  |  |  |  |  |  |  |  |  |
| Yellow-legged Clubtail |  |  |  |  |  |  |  |  |  |  |  |  |  |  |  |  |  |  |  |  |
| Golden-ringed Dragonfly |  | Δ | Δ | Δ | Δ | Δ | Δ | Δ | Δ | Δ |  | Δ | Δ | Δ | Δ | Δ | Δ | Δ | O | Δ |
| Orange-spotted Emerald |  |  |  |  |  |  |  |  |  |  |  |  |  |  |  |  |  |  |  |  |
| Downy Emerald |  |  | ⊠ |  |  |  |  |  | Δ | Δ |  |  |  |  |  |  |  |  |  |  |
| Northern Emerald |  |  |  |  |  |  |  |  |  |  |  |  |  |  |  |  |  |  |  |  |
| Brilliant Emerald |  |  |  |  |  |  |  |  |  |  |  |  |  |  |  |  |  |  |  |  |
| Scarlet Darter |  |  |  |  |  |  |  |  |  | Δ |  |  |  |  |  |  |  |  |  |  |
| White-faced Darter |  |  | O |  |  |  |  |  | Δ | Δ |  |  |  |  |  |  |  |  |  |  |
| Large White-faced Darter |  |  |  |  |  |  |  |  |  |  |  |  |  |  |  |  |  |  |  |  |
| Broad-bodied Chaser | Δ | Δ | Δ | Δ | Δ | Δ | Δ | Δ | Δ | Δ |  | Δ | Δ |  |  |  |  |  |  |  |
| Scarce Chaser |  |  | O |  |  |  |  |  |  |  |  |  |  |  |  |  |  |  |  |  |
| Four-spotted Chaser | Δ | Δ | Δ | Δ | Δ | Δ | Δ | Δ | Δ | Δ | Δ | Δ | Δ | Δ | Δ | Δ | Δ | Δ | Δ | Δ |
| Black-tailed Skimmer | Δ | Δ | Δ | Δ | Δ | Δ | Δ |  |  | Δ | Δ |  |  |  |  |  |  |  |  |  |
| Keeled Skimmer | Δ | Δ |  |  |  |  | O |  |  | Δ | Δ |  |  | Δ | Δ | O |  |  |  |  |
| Wandering Glider |  |  |  |  |  |  |  |  |  |  |  |  |  |  |  |  |  |  |  |  |
| Black Darter | Δ | Δ | Δ | Δ | Δ | Δ | Δ | Δ | Δ | Δ | Δ | Δ | Δ | Δ | Δ | Δ | Δ | O | O | Δ |
| Yellow-winged Darter | Δ | Δ | Δ | O |  | Δ | Δ | O | O | O |  |  |  |  |  |  |  |  |  |  |
| Red-veined Darter | Δ | Δ | Δ | Δ | Δ | Δ | Δ | O | Δ | Δ | Δ |  | Δ | Δ |  |  |  |  |  |  |
| Banded Darter |  |  |  |  |  |  |  |  |  |  |  |  |  |  |  |  |  |  |  |  |
| Ruddy Darter | Δ | Δ | Δ | Δ | Δ | Δ | Δ | Δ | Δ | Δ |  |  |  |  |  | O |  |  |  |  |
| Common Darter | Δ | Δ | Δ | Δ | Δ | Δ | Δ | Δ |  | Δ | Δ | Δ | Δ | Δ | Δ | Δ | Δ | Δ | Δ | Δ |
| Vagrant Darter | O |  | O |  | Δ |  |  |  |  |  |  |  |  |  |  |  |  |  |  |  |
| **No of species** | 28 | 25 | 28 | 24 | 19 | 23 | 22 | 18 | 26 | 26 | 14 | 16 | 23 | 14 | 12 | 10 | 9 | 9 | 10 | 11 |
| **Britain ranking** | 32 | 55 | 32 | 61 | 71 | 65 | 68 | 72 | 46 | 46 | 80 | 75 | 65 | 80 | 87 | 97 | 106 | 106 | 97 | 92 |

| Species | Berwickshire | East Lothian | Midlothian | West Lothian | Fifeshire | Stirlingshire | West Perthshire | Mid Perthshire | East Perthshire | Angus (Forfarshire) | Kincardineshire | South Aberdeenshire | North Aberdeenshire | Banffshire | Moray | East Inverness & Nairn | West Inverness | Main Argyll | Dunbartonshire | Clyde Islands |
|---|---|---|---|---|---|---|---|---|---|---|---|---|---|---|---|---|---|---|---|---|
| Willow Emerald Damselfly | | | | | | | | | | | | | | | | | | | | |
| Southern Emerald Damselfly | | | | | | | | | | | | | | | | | | | | |
| Scarce Emerald Damselfly | | | | | | | | | | | | | | | | | | | | |
| Emerald Damselfly | Δ | Δ | Δ | Δ | Δ | Δ | Δ | Δ | Δ | Δ | Δ | Δ | Δ | Δ | Δ | Δ | Δ | Δ | Δ | Δ |
| Winter Damselfly | | | | | | | | | | | | | | | | | | | | |
| Banded Demoiselle | Δ | | Δ | | | | | | | | | | | | | | Δ | | | |
| Beautiful Demoiselle | | | | | | O | O | | | | | | | | | | Δ | Δ | | |
| White-legged Damselfly | | | | | | | | | | | | | | | | | | | | |
| Small Red Damselfly | | | | | | | | | | | | | | | | | | | | |
| Norfolk Damselfly | | | | | | | | | | | | | | | | | | | | |
| Northern Damselfly | | | | | | | | Δ | Δ | | | Δ | | | Δ | Δ | Δ | | | |
| Southern Damselfly | | | | | | | | | | | | | | | | | | | | |
| Azure Damselfly | Δ | Δ | Δ | Δ | Δ | Δ | Δ | Δ | Δ | Δ | | Δ | | | | | Δ | Δ | Δ | Δ |
| Variable Damselfly | | | | | | | | | | | | | | | O | | Δ | | | |
| Dainty Damselfly | | | | | | | | | | | | | | | | | | | | |
| Common Blue Damselfly | Δ | Δ | Δ | Δ | Δ | Δ | Δ | Δ | Δ | Δ | Δ | Δ | Δ | Δ | Δ | Δ | Δ | Δ | Δ | Δ |
| Red-eyed Damselfly | | | | | | | | | | | | | | | | | | | | |
| Small Red-eyed Damselfly | | | | | | | | | | | | | | | | | | | | |
| Blue-tailed Damselfly | Δ | Δ | Δ | Δ | Δ | Δ | Δ | Δ | Δ | Δ | Δ | Δ | Δ | Δ | Δ | Δ | Δ | Δ | Δ | Δ |
| Scarce Blue-tailed Damselfly | | | | | | | | | | | | | | | | | | | | |
| Large Red Damselfly | Δ | Δ | Δ | Δ | Δ | Δ | Δ | Δ | Δ | Δ | Δ | Δ | Δ | Δ | Δ | Δ | Δ | Δ | Δ | Δ |
| Southern Migrant Hawker | | | | | | | | | | | | | | | | | | | | |
| Azure Hawker | | | | | | | | Δ | | Δ | | | | | O | Δ | Δ | Δ | | |
| Southern Hawker | Δ | Δ | | Δ | Δ | Δ | | | | | | | | Δ | Δ | Δ | Δ | Δ | | Δ |
| Brown Hawker | | | | | | | | | | | | | | | | | | | | |
| Common Hawker | Δ | Δ | Δ | Δ | Δ | Δ | Δ | Δ | Δ | Δ | Δ | Δ | Δ | Δ | Δ | Δ | Δ | Δ | Δ | Δ |
| Migrant Hawker | Δ | | | | | | | | | | | | | | | | | | | |
| Norfolk Hawker | | | | | | | | | | | | | | | | | | | | |
| Vagrant Emperor | | Δ | | Δ | | | | | | | | | | | | | | | | |

Table 6 continued.

| Species | Berwickshire | East Lothian | Midlothian | West Lothian | Fifeshire | Stirlingshire | West Perthshire | Mid Perthshire | East Perthshire | Angus (Forfarshire) | Kincardineshire | South Aberdeenshire | North Aberdeenshire | Banffshire | Moray | East Inverness & Nairn | West Inverness | Main Argyll | Dunbartonshire | Clyde Islands |
|---|---|---|---|---|---|---|---|---|---|---|---|---|---|---|---|---|---|---|---|---|
| Emperor Dragonfly | Δ | Δ | Δ | Δ | Δ | | | Δ | | | | | | | | | | Δ | | |
| Green Darner | | | | | | | | | | | | | | | | | | | | |
| Lesser Emperor | | | | | | | | | | | | | | | | | | | | |
| Hairy Dragonfly | | | | | | | | | | | | | | | | | Δ | Δ | | |
| Common Clubtail | | | | | | | | | | | | | | | | | | | | |
| Yellow-legged Clubtail | | | | | | | | | | | | | | | | | | | | |
| Golden-ringed Dragonfly | Δ | | O | | Δ | Δ | Δ | Δ | Δ | Δ | Δ | Δ | O | Δ | Δ | Δ | Δ | Δ | Δ | Δ |
| Orange-spotted Emerald | | | | | | | | | | | | | | | | | | | | |
| Downy Emerald | | | | | | Δ | | | | | | | | | Δ | | | Δ | O | |
| Northern Emerald | | | | | | Δ | Δ | Δ | | | | | | | Δ | Δ | Δ | Δ | | |
| Brilliant Emerald | | | | | | | | | | | | | | | Δ | | | Δ | | |
| Scarlet Darter | | | | | | | | | | | | | | | | | | | | |
| White-faced Darter | | | | | | | | O | | | O | Δ | | | Δ | Δ | Δ | Δ | | |
| Large White-faced Darter | | | | | | | | | | | | | | | | | | | | |
| Broad-bodied Chaser | Δ | | Δ | | | | | | | | | | | | | | | | | |
| Scarce Chaser | | | | | | | | | | | | | | | | | | | | |
| Four-spotted Chaser | Δ | Δ | Δ | Δ | Δ | Δ | Δ | Δ | Δ | Δ | Δ | Δ | Δ | Δ | Δ | Δ | Δ | Δ | Δ | Δ |
| Black-tailed Skimmer | Δ | | | | Δ | | | | | | | | | | | | | | | |
| Keeled Skimmer | | | | | | | | O | | | | | | | | | Δ | Δ | | Δ |
| Wandering Glider | | | | | | | | | | | | | | | | | | | | |
| Black Darter | Δ | Δ | Δ | Δ | Δ | Δ | Δ | Δ | Δ | Δ | Δ | Δ | Δ | Δ | Δ | Δ | Δ | Δ | Δ | Δ |
| Yellow-winged Darter | | | | | | | | | | ⊠ | | | | | O | | | | | |
| Red-veined Darter | Δ | Δ | O | | Δ | | | | | | | | | | | | | | | |
| Banded Darter | | | | | | | | | | | | | | | | | | | | |
| Ruddy Darter | Δ | | | | | | | | | | | | | | | | | | | |
| Common Darter | Δ | Δ | Δ | Δ | Δ | Δ | Δ | Δ | Δ | Δ | Δ | Δ | Δ | Δ | Δ | Δ | Δ | Δ | Δ | Δ |
| Vagrant Darter | | | | | | | | | | | | | | | | | | | | |
| **No of species** | 17 | 12 | 13 | 10 | 14 | 13 | 11 | 15 | 10 | 11 | 9 | 11 | 9 | 9 | 15 | 16 | 17 | 20 | 10 | 12 |
| **Britain ranking** | 73 | 87 | 83 | 97 | 80 | 83 | 92 | 77 | 97 | 92 | 106 | 92 | 106 | 106 | 77 | 75 | 73 | 70 | 97 | 87 |

| Species | Kintyre | South Ebudes | Mid Ebudes | North Ebudes | West Ross. | East Ross. | East Sutherland | West Sutherland | Caithness | Outer Hebrides | Orkney | Shetland |
|---|---|---|---|---|---|---|---|---|---|---|---|---|
| Willow Emerald Damselfly | | | | | | | | | | | | |
| Southern Emerald Damselfly | | | | | | | | | | | | |
| Scarce Emerald Damselfly | | | | | | | | | | | | |
| Emerald Damselfly | Δ | Δ | Δ | Δ | Δ | Δ | Δ | Δ | Δ | Δ | Δ | |
| Winter Damselfly | | | | | | | | | | | | |
| Banded Demoiselle | | | | | | | | | | | | |
| Beautiful Demoiselle | Δ | Δ | Δ | Δ | | | | | | | | |
| White-legged Damselfly | | | | | | | | | | | | |
| Small Red Damselfly | | | | | | | | | | | | |
| Norfolk Damselfly | | | | | | | | | | | | |
| Northern Damselfly | | | | | | | | | | | | |
| Southern Damselfly | | | | | | | | | | | | |
| Azure Damselfly | Δ | | | | | Δ | | | | | | Δ |
| Variable Damselfly | | | | | | | | | | | | |
| Dainty Damselfly | | | | | | | | | | | | |
| Common Blue Damselfly | Δ | Δ | Δ | Δ | Δ | Δ | Δ | Δ | Δ | Δ | Δ | Δ |
| Red-eyed Damselfly | | | | | | | | | | | | |
| Small Red-eyed Damselfly | | | | | | | | | | | | |
| Blue-tailed Damselfly | Δ | Δ | Δ | Δ | Δ | Δ | Δ | Δ | Δ | Δ | Δ | |
| Scarce Blue-tailed Damselfly | | | | | | | | | | | | |
| Large Red Damselfly | Δ | Δ | Δ | Δ | Δ | Δ | Δ | Δ | Δ | Δ | Δ | Δ |
| Southern Migrant Hawker | | | | | | | | | | | | |
| Azure Hawker | | | | Δ | Δ | Δ | Δ | Δ | | Δ | | |
| Southern Hawker | Δ | | Δ | | Δ | Δ | Δ | | | | | |
| Brown Hawker | | | | | | | | | | | | |
| Common Hawker | Δ | Δ | Δ | Δ | Δ | Δ | Δ | Δ | Δ | Δ | Δ | Δ |
| Migrant Hawker | Δ | | | | | | | | | | | |
| Norfolk Hawker | | | | | | | | | | | | |
| Vagrant Emperor | | | | | | | | | | Δ | Δ | O |

Table 6 continued.

| Species | Kintyre | South Ebudes | Mid Ebudes | North Ebudes | West Ross. | East Ross. | East Sutherland | West Sutherland | Caithness | Outer Hebrides | Orkney | Shetland |
|---|---|---|---|---|---|---|---|---|---|---|---|---|
| Emperor Dragonfly | | | | | | | | | | | | |
| Green Darner | | | | | | | | | | | | |
| Lesser Emperor | | | | | | | | | | | Δ | |
| Hairy Dragonfly | Δ | | | | | | | | | | | |
| Common Clubtail | | | | | | | | | | | | |
| Yellow-legged Clubtail | | | | | | | | | | | | |
| Golden-ringed Dragonfly | Δ | Δ | Δ | Δ | Δ | Δ | Δ | Δ | Δ | Δ | Δ | |
| Orange-spotted Emerald | | | | | | | | | | | | |
| Downy Emerald | | | | | | Δ | | | | | | |
| Northern Emerald | Δ | | Δ | Δ | Δ | | Δ | Δ | Δ | | | |
| Brilliant Emerald | | | | | | | | | | | | |
| Scarlet Darter | | | | | | | | | | | | |
| White-faced Darter | | | | Δ | Δ | | | | | | | |
| Large White-faced Darter | | | | | | | | | | | | |
| Broad-bodied Chaser | | | | | | | | | | | | |
| Scarce Chaser | | | | | | | | | | | | |
| Four-spotted Chaser | Δ | Δ | Δ | Δ | Δ | Δ | Δ | Δ | Δ | Δ | Δ | Δ |
| Black-tailed Skimmer | | | | | | | | | | | | |
| Keeled Skimmer | Δ | Δ | Δ | Δ | Δ | | | | | | | |
| Wandering Glider | | | | | | | | | | | | |
| Black Darter | Δ | Δ | Δ | Δ | Δ | Δ | Δ | Δ | Δ | Δ | Δ | |
| Yellow-winged Darter | | | | | | | | | O | | | |
| Red-veined Darter | | | | | | | | | | | | |
| Banded Darter | | | | | | | | | | | | |
| Ruddy Darter | | | | | | | | | | | | |
| Common Darter | Δ | Δ | Δ | Δ | Δ | Δ | Δ | Δ | Δ | Δ | | |
| Vagrant Darter | | | | | | | | | | | | |
| **No of species** | 15 | 10 | 12 | 12 | 13 | 13 | 11 | 10 | 10 | 10 | 9 | 5 |
| **Britain ranking** | 77 | 97 | 87 | 87 | 83 | 83 | 92 | 97 | 97 | 97 | 106 | 112 |

Table 7. Vice-County distribution of species (Ireland). Recorded before 1899 only (⊠), up to the end of 1999 only (O) and 2000 onwards (Δ).

| Species | H1 South Kerry | H2 North Kerry | H3 West Cork | H4 Mid-Cork | H5 East Cork | H6 Waterford | H7 South Tipperary | H8 Limerick | H9 Clare | H10 North Tipperary | H11 Kilkenny | H12 Wexford | H13 Carlow | H14 Laois | H15 South-east Galway | H16 West Galway | H17 North-east Galway | H18 Offaly | H19 Kildare | H20 Wicklow |
|---|---|---|---|---|---|---|---|---|---|---|---|---|---|---|---|---|---|---|---|---|
| Scarce Emerald Damselfly | ⊠ | | | | | | | | Δ | Δ | Δ | | | | Δ | O | | | O | O |
| Emerald Damselfly | Δ | Δ | Δ | Δ | Δ | Δ | Δ | Δ | Δ | Δ | Δ | Δ | Δ | Δ | Δ | Δ | Δ | Δ | Δ | Δ |
| Banded Demoiselle | Δ | Δ | Δ | Δ | Δ | Δ | Δ | Δ | Δ | Δ | Δ | Δ | Δ | Δ | Δ | Δ | Δ | Δ | Δ | Δ |
| Beautiful Demoiselle | Δ | Δ | Δ | Δ | Δ | Δ | Δ | Δ | Δ | Δ | Δ | Δ | Δ | Δ | Δ | | | Δ | Δ | Δ |
| Irish Damselfly | | | | | | | | | Δ | | | | | | | | | Δ | Δ | |
| Azure Damselfly | Δ | Δ | Δ | Δ | Δ | Δ | Δ | Δ | Δ | Δ | Δ | Δ | Δ | Δ | Δ | Δ | Δ | Δ | Δ | Δ |
| Variable Damselfly | Δ | Δ | Δ | Δ | Δ | Δ | Δ | Δ | Δ | Δ | Δ | O | Δ | Δ | Δ | Δ | Δ | Δ | Δ | Δ |
| Common Blue Damselfly | Δ | Δ | Δ | Δ | Δ | Δ | Δ | Δ | Δ | Δ | Δ | Δ | Δ | Δ | Δ | Δ | Δ | Δ | Δ | Δ |
| Blue-tailed Damselfly | Δ | Δ | Δ | Δ | Δ | Δ | Δ | Δ | Δ | Δ | Δ | Δ | Δ | Δ | Δ | Δ | Δ | Δ | Δ | Δ |
| Scarce Blue-tailed Damselfly | Δ | Δ | | Δ | | | Δ | Δ | | Δ | Δ | O | | Δ | Δ | Δ | | | O | Δ |
| Large Red Damselfly | Δ | Δ | Δ | Δ | Δ | Δ | Δ | Δ | Δ | Δ | Δ | Δ | Δ | Δ | Δ | Δ | Δ | Δ | Δ | Δ |
| Southern Hawker | | | | O | | | | | | | | | | | | | | | | |
| Brown Hawker | O | Δ | Δ | Δ | Δ | Δ | Δ | Δ | Δ | Δ | Δ | Δ | Δ | Δ | Δ | Δ | Δ | Δ | Δ | Δ |
| Common Hawker | Δ | Δ | Δ | Δ | Δ | Δ | Δ | Δ | Δ | Δ | Δ | Δ | Δ | Δ | Δ | Δ | Δ | Δ | Δ | Δ |
| Migrant Hawker | | Δ | Δ | Δ | Δ | | Δ | Δ | Δ | | Δ | Δ | Δ | Δ | | | | | Δ | Δ |
| Emperor Dragonfly | Δ | Δ | Δ | Δ | | Δ | Δ | Δ | Δ | | Δ | Δ | Δ | Δ | | | | | Δ | Δ |
| Vagrant Emperor | | | Δ | Δ | Δ | Δ | | | | | | Δ | | | | | | | | |
| Lesser Emperor | | | | Δ | Δ | Δ | | | | | | Δ | | | | | | | Δ | Δ |
| Hairy Dragonfly | Δ | Δ | Δ | | Δ | Δ | Δ | Δ | Δ | Δ | Δ | Δ | Δ | Δ | Δ | Δ | Δ | Δ | Δ | Δ |
| Golden-ringed Dragonfly | | | | | | Δ | | | | | Δ | | | | | | | | | |
| Downy Emerald | Δ | Δ | Δ | | | | | | | | | | | | | | Δ | | | |
| Northern Emerald | Δ | Δ | Δ | | | | | | | | | | | | | | | | | |
| Broad-bodied Chaser | | | | | | ⊠ | | | | | | | | | | | | | | |
| Scarce Chaser | ⊠ | | | | | | | | | | | | | | | | | | | |
| Four-spotted Chaser | Δ | Δ | Δ | Δ | Δ | Δ | Δ | Δ | Δ | Δ | Δ | Δ | Δ | Δ | Δ | Δ | Δ | Δ | Δ | Δ |
| Black-tailed Skimmer | O | Δ | | Δ | Δ | Δ | Δ | Δ | Δ | Δ | | Δ | | Δ | Δ | Δ | Δ | Δ | Δ | Δ |
| Keeled Skimmer | Δ | Δ | Δ | | Δ | Δ | Δ | Δ | Δ | Δ | Δ | Δ | Δ | O | Δ | Δ | | Δ | Δ | Δ |
| Black Darter | Δ | Δ | Δ | Δ | Δ | Δ | Δ | Δ | Δ | Δ | | | | Δ | Δ | Δ | Δ | Δ | Δ | Δ |
| Yellow-winged Darter | | | | | | | | | | | | O | | | | | | | | |
| Red-veined Darter | Δ | | | Δ | Δ | | | | | | | Δ | | | | | | | | Δ |
| Ruddy Darter | Δ | Δ | Δ | Δ | Δ | Δ | Δ | Δ | Δ | Δ | Δ | Δ | Δ | Δ | Δ | Δ | Δ | Δ | Δ | Δ |
| Common Darter | Δ | Δ | Δ | Δ | Δ | Δ | Δ | Δ | Δ | Δ | Δ | Δ | Δ | Δ | Δ | Δ | Δ | Δ | Δ | Δ |
| **No of species** | 24 | 21 | 21 | 22 | 22 | 23 | 18 | 20 | 22 | 19 | 20 | 23 | 18 | 19 | 19 | 20 | 17 | 18 | 22 | 23 |
| **Ireland ranking** | 1 | 11 | 11 | 6 | 6 | 2 | 27 | 13 | 6 | 18 | 13 | 2 | 27 | 18 | 18 | 13 | 34 | 27 | 6 | 2 |

Table 7 continued.

| Species | H21 Dublin | H22 Meath | H23 Westmeath | H24 Longford | H25 Roscommon | H26 East Mayo | H27 West Mayo | H28 Sligo | H29 Leitrim | H30 Cavan | H31 Louth | H32 Monaghan | H33 Fermanagh | H34 East Donegal | H35 West Donegal | H36 Tyrone | H37 Armagh | H38 Down | H39 Antrim | H40 Londonderry |
|---|---|---|---|---|---|---|---|---|---|---|---|---|---|---|---|---|---|---|---|---|
| Scarce Emerald Damselfly | | △ | ⊠ | △ | △ | △ | O | △ | △ | | | | | | | | | | | |
| Emerald Damselfly | O | △ | △ | △ | △ | △ | △ | △ | △ | △ | △ | △ | △ | △ | △ | △ | △ | △ | △ | △ |
| Banded Demoiselle | △ | △ | △ | △ | △ | △ | △ | △ | △ | △ | △ | △ | △ | △ | △ | △ | △ | △ | △ | △ |
| Beautiful Demoiselle | △ | | | | | | △ | | | | △ | | | | | | | | | |
| Irish Damselfly | | △ | O | O | △ | △ | | △ | △ | △ | △ | △ | △ | | △ | △ | △ | △ | △ | △ |
| Azure Damselfly | △ | △ | △ | △ | △ | △ | △ | △ | △ | △ | △ | △ | △ | △ | △ | △ | △ | △ | △ | △ |
| Variable Damselfly | △ | △ | △ | △ | △ | △ | △ | △ | △ | △ | △ | △ | △ | O | △ | △ | △ | △ | △ | △ |
| Common Blue Damselfly | △ | △ | △ | △ | △ | △ | △ | △ | △ | △ | △ | △ | △ | △ | △ | △ | △ | △ | △ | △ |
| Blue-tailed Damselfly | △ | △ | △ | △ | △ | △ | △ | △ | △ | △ | △ | △ | △ | △ | △ | △ | △ | △ | △ | △ |
| Scarce Blue-tailed Damselfly | O | O | O | | △ | △ | △ | O | | | O | O | △ | O | △ | △ | O | △ | O | △ |
| Large Red Damselfly | △ | △ | △ | △ | △ | △ | △ | △ | △ | △ | △ | △ | △ | △ | △ | △ | △ | △ | △ | △ |
| Southern Hawker | | | | | | | | | | | | | | | | | | | | |
| Brown Hawker | △ | △ | △ | △ | | △ | △ | | △ | △ | △ | △ | △ | △ | △ | △ | △ | △ | △ | △ |
| Common Hawker | △ | △ | △ | △ | △ | △ | △ | △ | △ | △ | △ | △ | △ | △ | △ | △ | △ | △ | △ | △ |
| Migrant Hawker | △ | | △ | | | | | | | | △ | | | | | | | | △ | |
| Emperor Dragonfly | △ | | | | | | | | | | △ | △ | | | | | △ | | △ | |
| Vagrant Emperor | O | | | | | | | | | | | | | | | | | | | |
| Lesser Emperor | △ | | △ | | | | | | | | △ | | | | | | △ | | | |
| Hairy Dragonfly | △ | △ | △ | △ | △ | △ | △ | △ | △ | △ | △ | △ | △ | △ | △ | △ | △ | △ | △ | △ |
| Golden-ringed Dragonfly | | | | | | | | | | | | | | | | | | | | |
| Downy Emerald | | | | | | | | | | | | | | | | | | | | |
| Northern Emerald | | | | | | | | | | | | | | | | | | | | |
| Broad-bodied Chaser | | | | | | | | | | | | | | | | | | | | |
| Scarce Chaser | | | | | | | | | | | | | | | | | | | | |
| Four-spotted Chaser | △ | △ | △ | △ | △ | △ | △ | △ | △ | △ | △ | △ | △ | △ | △ | △ | △ | △ | △ | △ |
| Black-tailed Skimmer | △ | △ | △ | △ | △ | △ | △ | △ | △ | | △ | | △ | △ | △ | | △ | | △ | |
| Keeled Skimmer | O | | | △ | △ | △ | △ | △ | | | △ | | | △ | △ | △ | | △ | △ | |
| Black Darter | O | △ | △ | △ | △ | △ | △ | △ | △ | △ | △ | △ | △ | △ | △ | △ | △ | △ | △ | △ |
| Yellow-winged Darter | | | | | | | | | | | | | | | | | | | | |
| Red-veined Darter | △ | | △ | | | | | | | O | | | | | | | | △ | | |
| Ruddy Darter | △ | △ | △ | △ | △ | △ | △ | △ | △ | △ | △ | △ | | △ | △ | △ | △ | △ | | △ |
| Common Darter | △ | △ | △ | △ | △ | △ | △ | △ | △ | △ | △ | △ | △ | △ | △ | △ | △ | △ | △ | △ |
| **No of species** | 23 | 18 | 20 | 19 | 19 | 19 | 19 | 19 | 17 | 16 | 22 | 17 | 18 | 16 | 18 | 16 | 20 | 19 | 18 | 16 |
| **Ireland ranking** | 2 | 27 | 13 | 18 | 18 | 18 | 18 | 18 | 34 | 37 | 6 | 34 | 27 | 37 | 27 | 37 | 13 | 18 | 27 | 37 |

# Trends in the status of dragonflies in Britain and Ireland since 1980

## Introduction

The BDS Dragonfly Recording Network (DRN) dataset exceeded one million records in January 2013 after which the DragonflyIreland dataset of over 33,000 records was combined into the dataset to produce this atlas. Over 20,000 records have been submitted each year since 1990 (over 400 records per species per year), making the Odonata one of the best-recorded groups in Britain and Ireland (most other insect groups average around 20 records per species per year: Isaac, 2012). This vast repository makes it possible to estimate quantitative trends in the distribution of each species, which can be compared directly with the collective opinion of BDS British and Irish recorders.

Estimating trends from biological records is not straightforward, for several reasons. Most importantly, records are very rarely gathered systematically using standardised survey methods. Rather, recorders have been free to visit wherever and whenever they wish and recording intensity has therefore varied markedly over space and time. The intensity of dragonfly recording has increased noticeably since the 1970s (Figure 35), with over half the total records being collected since 2000. This means that simply counting occupied monads, or even hectads, is not a reliable means for measuring change.

The data do not tell us which species might have been present but were not recorded (i.e. false absences: Tingley & Beissinger, 2009). Hence, there are many lists of species reported from a site on a given date, in which only a subset of the total species present was reported (short lists). Indeed, over 40% of species lists in the DRN database contain just a single species (Isaac, 2012). Single-species visits may reflect the fact that only one species was active and observable on the day in question but a large proportion are probably incidental records, in which other species were present but not recorded (e.g. because the recorded species was an interesting rarity or a large and obvious dragonfly, rather than a damselfly). Unfortunately, information about the exact nature of the recording patterns is not available for most visits, so when seeking trends, analytical methods need to take into account this problem.

Counting dragonflies is fraught with practical and interpretational problems (these are discussed further on pages 32-37), so it is more appropriate to measure changes in species' distributions than in total abundance. At the hectad scale, used to plot the species distribution maps, basic comparisons can be made between the proportions of hectads occupied in different time periods. Figures 36 and 37 show the relationships pre- and post 2000.

It should be noted that the proportions of hectads in which species have been recorded are influenced by changes in recording patterns, so for this reason only those hectads that were visited in both time periods were used to produce Figures 36 and 37. However, even with this constraint on the data, differences in recording intensity within the selected hectads remain. Nevertheless, Figures 36 and 37 do allow us to say that some species have increased faster

Figure 35. The number of dragonfly records gathered in Britain and Ireland per year, 1950-2012.

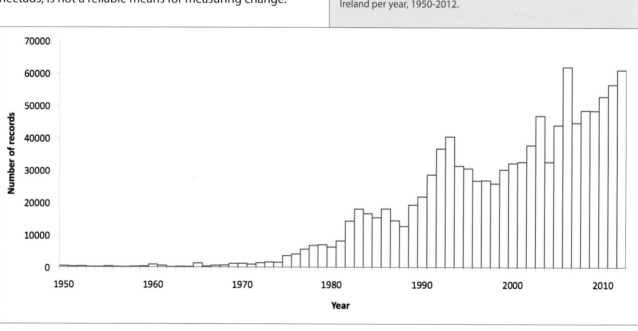

than others. Most of the dragonfly species appear to have increased in range. At occupancy levels of 1-10%, the frequencies of four out of five damselflies (Scarce Blue-tailed, Small Red, Southern and Irish) have contracted, as have those of four Anisoptera (Common Clubtail, Azure Hawker, White-faced Darter and the migrant Yellow-winged Darter). Also within this occupancy range, Scarce Chaser and the still mainly migrant Red-veined Darter appear to have increased, as have all species occurring at below 1% occupancy. While improvements in water quality may at least partially explain the range expansion shown by Scarce Chaser, colonisation and spread promoted by climate change and associated exceptional weather events is likely to have been responsible for much of the increases of these scarcest species.

Although comparisons of hectad occupancy in different time periods provide an interesting perspective on the various changes that have occurred in dragonfly distribution, they only go part way to fully analysing the data available. In particular, the growth in recording intensity over time means that we might expect hectad counts for many species to increase.

## Estimating linear trends in species' distributions

In order to derive quantitative estimates of trends in species distributions, a range of sophisticated statistical tools has recently been developed (Hill, 2011; Roy *et al.*, 2012; Szabo *et al.*, 2010). To find a robust method that takes account of the non-systematic methods of data collection, Nick Isaac

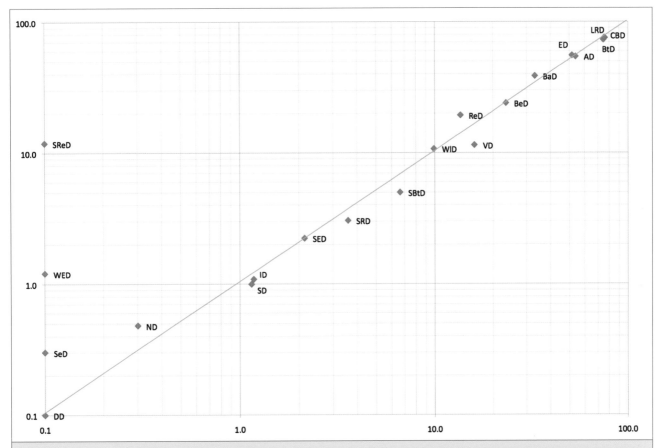

Figure 36. Percentage occupancy of damselflies (Zygoptera) in hectads, 1900-1999 (x-axis) plotted against 2000-2012 (y-axis). Only hectads recorded in both periods are used. Points indicate species with greater (above the line of no change) or lesser (below the line) occupancy since 1999. Note the logarithmic scale.

Key to species codes

**Damselflies (Zygoptera)**

| | |
|---|---|
| AD | Azure Damselfly |
| BaD | Banded Demoiselle |
| BeD | Beautiful Demoiselle |
| BtD | Blue-tailed Damselfly |
| CBD | Common Blue Damselfly |
| DD | Dainty Damselfly |
| ED | Emerald Damselfly |
| ID | Irish Damselfly |
| LRD | Large Red Damselfly |

| | |
|---|---|
| ND | Northern Damselfly |
| ReD | Red-eyed Damselfly |
| SBtD | Scarce Blue-tailed Damselfly |
| SD | Southern Damselfly |
| SED | Scarce Emerald Damselfly |
| SRD | Small Red Damselfly |
| SReD | Small Red-eyed Damselfly |
| VD | Variable Damselfly |
| WED | Willow Emerald Damselfly |
| WlD | White-legged Damselfly |

(from the Biological Records Centre which is part of the Centre for Ecology & Hydrology) compared nine different models using computer simulations and has applied one of the more robust methods to the DRN data to examine changes at a fine scale. The method, known as the well-sampled sites model (WSSM) works by selecting portions of the data for which a sufficient number of species have been recorded over a number of years. It then estimates a linear trend in site occupancy with a binomial mixed-effects model (Kuussaari et al., 2007; Roy et al., 2012). As sites are not defined accurately in the British and Irish datasets,

monads are used instead. Records were first aggregated to the monad visit level, which is defined as distinct combinations of date and monad, following van Strien et al. (2010). Records with spatial precision coarser than a monad grid reference were excluded, as were those for which the precise recording date is unknown.

Trends for 39 resident species have been estimated, based on records from Britain and Ireland since 1980. Small Red-eyed Damselfly, which has bred in Britain each year since 1999, has been included in the analysis but Southern

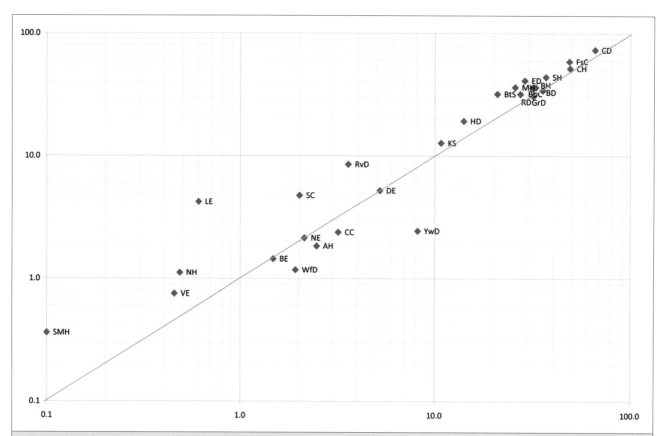

Figure 37. Percentage occupancy of dragonflies (Anisoptera) in hectads, 1900-1999 (x-axis) plotted against 2000-2012 (y-axis). Only hectads recorded in both periods are used. Points indicate species with greater (above the line of no change) or lesser (below the line) occupancy since 1999.

Key to species codes

**Dragonflies (Anisoptera)**

| | | | |
|---|---|---|---|
| AH | Azure Hawker | HD | Hairy Dragonfly |
| BbC | Broad-bodied Chaser | KS | Keeled Skimmer |
| BD | Black Darter | LE | Lesser Emperor |
| BE | Brilliant Emerald | MH | Migrant Hawker |
| BH | Brown Hawker | NE | Northern Emerald |
| BtS | Black-tailed Skimmer | NH | Norfolk Hawker |
| CC | Common Clubtail | RD | Ruddy Darter |
| CD | Common Darter | RvD | Red-veined Darter |
| CH | Common Hawker | SC | Scarce Chaser |
| DE | Downy Emerald | SMH | Southern Migrant Hawker |
| ED | Emperor Dragonfly | SH | Southern Hawker |
| FsC | Four-spotted Chaser | VE | Vagrant Emperor |
| GrD | Golden-ringed Dragonfly | WfD | White-faced Darter |
| | | YwD | Yellow-winged Darter |

Migrant Hawker and Willow Emerald Damselfly, both of which have only recently established breeding populations, have not. All 39 species have been recorded at least 300 times since 1980.

The number of species recorded per visit ranged from one to 24, but visits were excluded if less than three species were recorded. Excluding these visits with few species is a way to control the problem of incidental records (Roy *et al.*, 2012) but also leads to reliable records being discarded. The proportion of the remaining visits (i.e. those when three or more species were recorded) has been relatively constant since 1980, which is important for the trend estimates to be reliable. The dataset was then further restricted to only those monads that were visited in at least three separate years, as these are considered sufficiently well-sampled to contribute to the overall trend (Roy *et al.*, 2012). The net effect of these restrictions is seen in the distribution of the sampled squares contributing to the trend estimates in Figure 38. The relatively low number of contributing squares in much of northern England, Scotland and Ireland reflects the lower number of resident species, lower levels of recording intensity and the limitations imposed by the model. In particular, the recording emphasis in these areas has been on baseline coverage and less on repeat visits. Results were virtually identical for most species using different thresholds (two species per visit, two years per monad) for data inclusion, but the more rigorous thresholds of three species per visit and records in three years per monad were adopted for this analysis.

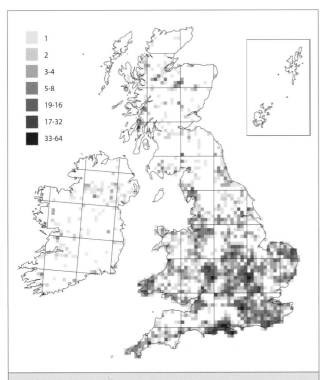

The WSSM has been shown to give unbiased trend estimates on datasets that superficially resemble the DRN data. However, it is sensitive to changes in detectability, so is not appropriate for species where recorder behaviour has changed dramatically. A further caveat is that the trend estimates will reflect the distribution of the monads that meet the analysis selection thresholds. Although the trends are estimated for Britain and Ireland, nearly 40% of the selected monads are in south-east England and just 4% are in Ireland (Figure 38). This geographical bias must be taken into account when interpreting the results. In particular, the limited coverage in Scotland and Ireland means that trend estimates for species restricted to these regions (Azure Hawker, Northern Emerald, Irish Damselfly, Northern Damselfly) are likely to be under-estimated.

The final dataset analysed contains 30,481 monad-year combinations in 5,352 monads, corresponding to 67,378 visits and 357,654 unique species records (i.e. 5 species per visit on average). Whilst the estimated trends use data from 1980-2012, the results for each species are presented as a percentage trend during the last decade (2002-2012), assuming a linear change since 1980. Technically, this trend measures change in the probability of a species being recorded during an average visit, reflecting the number of occupied sites and the abundance at those sites.

## Quantitative trends

More than two-thirds of the species (28 out of 39) show evidence of a net change in occupancy since 1980 (Table 8). Thus, there has been considerable flux in the dragonfly fauna of Britain and Ireland during this period. Of the 28 species showing significant trends, 15 are increasing and 13 decreasing, of which 12 and nine species, respectively, have changed by more than 10% since 2002. There is no significant difference between the trend estimates for common and rare species, as defined by the number of monads they occupied, or (if Small Red-eyed Damselfly is excluded from the analysis) between the mean trends for dragonflies and damselflies.

Not surprisingly, the species with the greatest rate of change are those that have recently colonised and subsequently expanded their ranges. Small Red-eyed Damselfly, which was first recorded in Britain in 1999 and has since colonised a substantial portion of central, southern and eastern England, has shown the greatest rate of change. The next most rapidly increasing species is the Scarce Chaser, the monad occupancy of which is estimated to have more than doubled since 2002. Another notable increase is shown by Red-eyed Damselfly, which, along with Small Red-eyed Damselfly, often perches in open water some distance from the margin; the trends for these species may have been exaggerated as a result of an increase in the use of binoculars among dragonfly recorders. This means that detectability of these species that are mostly found

Table 8. Trends in British and Irish Odonata since 1980.
'Number of visits' is the number of visits within the well-sampled set on which the species was recorded; 'Decadal trend' is the percentage change in distribution and abundance since 2002, assuming linear change over the period 1980-2012. 'Stable': trend is not statistically significant; 'Slight' (increase or decrease): statistically significant trend but less than 10% per decade. 'Sig': significance levels (* P<0.05, ** P<0.01, *** P<0.001).

| Species | Number of visits | Decadal trend | Status | Sig |
|---|---|---|---|---|
| Scarce Emerald Damselfly | 215 | 33.8 | Stable | |
| Emerald Damselfly | 14037 | -21.0 | Decrease | *** |
| Banded Demoiselle | 12454 | 19.7 | Increase | *** |
| Beautiful Demoiselle | 4185 | 32.4 | Increase | *** |
| White-legged Damselfly | 4044 | 25.8 | Increase | *** |
| Small Red Damselfly | 2806 | -9.4 | Slight decrease | ** |
| Northern Damselfly | 207 | -13.2 | Stable | |
| Irish Damselfly | 168 | -48.6 | Decrease | *** |
| Southern Damselfly | 1125 | 5.6 | Stable | |
| Azure Damselfly | 29646 | 1.9 | Slight increase | * |
| Variable Damselfly | 2571 | 4.9 | Stable | |
| Common Blue Damselfly | 35101 | -7.6 | Slight decrease | *** |
| Red-eyed Damselfly | 11699 | 59.7 | Increase | *** |
| Small Red-eyed Damselfly | 1697 | 369.5 | Increase | *** |
| Blue-tailed Damselfly | 39721 | -11.6 | Decrease | *** |
| Scarce Blue-tailed Damselfly | 1067 | -50.0 | Decrease | *** |
| Large Red Damselfly | 22797 | -4.0 | Slight decrease | *** |
| Azure Hawker | 131 | -10.6 | Stable | |
| Southern Hawker | 13069 | 0.1 | Stable | |
| Brown Hawker | 17765 | -10.3 | Decrease | *** |
| Common Hawker | 5509 | -22.9 | Decrease | *** |
| Migrant Hawker | 10731 | 21.4 | Increase | *** |
| Norfolk Hawker | 763 | 13.7 | Stable | |
| Emperor Dragonfly | 19511 | 18.1 | Increase | *** |
| Hairy Dragonfly | 4700 | 48.5 | Increase | *** |
| Common Clubtail | 519 | -10.2 | Stable | |
| Golden-ringed Dragonfly | 4684 | -10.8 | Decrease | *** |
| Downy Emerald | 3276 | 26.3 | Increase | *** |
| Northern Emerald | 199 | 7.6 | Stable | |
| Brilliant Emerald | 1135 | 3.9 | Stable | |
| White-faced Darter | 684 | -38.1 | Decrease | *** |
| Broad-bodied Chaser | 10561 | 5.8 | Slight increase | *** |
| Scarce Chaser | 1391 | 159.8 | Increase | *** |
| Four-spotted Chaser | 17631 | 17.9 | Increase | *** |
| Black-tailed Skimmer | 13488 | 21.9 | Increase | *** |
| Keeled Skimmer | 4612 | 4.2 | Stable | |
| Black Darter | 5187 | -28.1 | Decrease | *** |
| Ruddy Darter | 10719 | 8.1 | Slight increase | *** |
| Common Darter | 27807 | -3.2 | Slight decrease | *** |

some distance from the water's edge has increased, and changes in detectability leads to biased trend estimates in the WSSM. The results also identify nine other species that have increased significantly at more than 10% per decade: Beautiful and Banded Demoiselles, White-legged Damselfly, Migrant Hawker, Emperor Dragonfly, Hairy Dragonfly, Downy Emerald, Four-spotted Chaser and Black-tailed Skimmer. With the exception of Downy Emerald, these increases are broadly consistent with intuitive assessments made by experienced dragonfly recorders, including the atlas editors.

There are nine species for which the results suggest a significant decline of more than 10% since 2002: Blue-tailed, Scarce Blue-tailed, Irish and Emerald Damselflies, Brown and Common Hawkers, Golden-ringed Dragonfly and White-faced and Black Darters. However, for these species there is less agreement between the models and expert opinion. A decline has been suspected for Scarce Blue-tailed Damselfly, and White-faced Darter has certainly been lost from sites in southern England. However, the range of Brown Hawker is believed to be expanding, in terms of occupied hectads, and its numbers are believed to have increased in parts of its core English range and in Ireland.

## Discussion of species' trends

The use of sophisticated statistics and day lists as bases for modelling species trends have gained favour in recent years. The use of relatively low thresholds of data acceptance for the WSSM provided a reasonable geographical spread of records for analysis, but with inevitable bias in the well-populated and dragonfly-rich areas of England. Employing a stratified sub-sample of sites, randomly selecting monads in a way that reduces geographical bias, might overcome this, but the resulting dataset would be much smaller than that used in the current analysis.

Clearly, the dragonfly fauna of Britain and Ireland has been in considerable flux in recent decades. Declines are difficult to detect when data are collected non-systematically and the use of this type of model provides a counterpoint to expert opinion and provides valuable directions for future recording. Whilst analytical techniques will continue to be improved, observers are now encouraged to record all species during field visits and to denote that this is the case at the time of record submission. Such records should provide a more robust basis for future analyses. However, the problem of uneven geographical coverage, and hence bias in the results, is likely to remain given the limited numbers of skilled recorders and their uneven distribution across Britain and Ireland.

The use of monads rather than sites for the generation of day lists is pragmatic, as data are located by grid reference;

this is the only practical solution without the use of geographic information systems (GIS) to define site boundaries. Many dragonfly breeding sites are small-scale, typically smaller than the 100 ha encompassed by a monad. This means the monad is the smallest practical unit (and hence the most sensitive for recording change) into which most records can be placed automatically for analysis. Conversely, the species' distribution maps are produced at the hectad scale, which is appropriate for illustrating distributional extent in Britain and Ireland. However, hectads cover 100 times the area of a monad and losses are therefore less likely to be detected than in smaller units. This highlights the need to record absence of a species (failure to detect) or complete lists during site visits.

Twelve species are shown to have increased by more than 10% in the last decade, generally confirming the impression gained from both hectad occupancy and expert opinion. A further nine species decreased by more than 10% in the same period. At least three of these (Common Hawker and White-faced and Black Darters) have a predominantly upland and/or northern distribution and their declines may be a result of warmer temperatures. It is more difficult for recorders in general to become aware of local losses than it is to detect range expansions (i.e. new sites for a species), so some of the decreases suggested by the model were unexpected. It is possible that some of the results do not give the true picture, although the reasons for this are unclear at present. In particular, the mismatch between the model for Brown Hawker, which gives a decadal decrease of 10.3%, and the increase suggested by other information is difficult to explain. Possible explanations include: (i) the species has colonised new sites whilst simultaneously declining in abundance at existing sites; (ii) differences between the timescale of the model (four decades) and that of subjective opinion, which is more likely to reflect recent changes (the observed patterns would be consistent with recent recovery from a long-term decline); (iii) records have been affected by changes in detectability or some other bias that this model fails to capture; (iv) that, as a common species, it may have been under-recorded at the site level within its core range; and v) monads contain sites that are not visited very frequently because they are believed to hold only common species.

# Phenology

The many records within the BDS and DragonflyIreland databases can be used to increase understanding of distribution and population trends but also phenology, the study of the timing of periodic life cycle events. At present, phenological analysis is restricted to adult dragonflies, where flight periods can be easily deduced, but with improvements to recording approaches other life cycle stages may become increasingly possible.

Phenograms in the species accounts show the number of adult records for a particular species from each 7 day period throughout the year. They have not been filtered for latitude, altitude or for time period, other than a split into pre-1991 and 1991-2012 records (i.e. before and after the previous atlas). However, it is important to note that flight periods will vary dramatically across Britain and Ireland; emergences and the start of the flight period generally are later at increasing latitude and altitude, due to cooler conditions than in the south. Water depth influences the rate of warming of a site through the spring and other local microclimate effects are also important, with some sites being advanced or delayed compared to others in close proximity. Weather (particularly temperature) is one of the most important factors influencing the onset of the flight period for a species. The weather immediately prior to the period of emergence and, to some extent, during far earlier months is critical in determining the flight period of these ectothermic species. In some years, the flight period, especially of the species characterised by early emergence, can be almost a month earlier than in other years. In recent times, the springs of both 2007 and 2011 were particularly advanced, due to temperatures being well above normal. In central England, the period March to May was the warmest on record in 2011 and the third-warmest in 2007 (Met Office, 2014). During 2011, no fewer than 20 species of resident Odonata had been reported on the wing by the

end of April, mainly in southern England, whereas the usual number is close to eight. The springs of 2007 and 2011 were warmer than average in Ireland, by about 1-2°C, and early emergences were similarly recorded in both years. In addition to effects on emergence times and the start of the flight period, the weather will also have considerable influence on the time at which the flight periods peak, on the abundance of a species throughout its flight period and on the total duration of that flight period.

In England, the adult dragonfly season commences in April and ends in late November in most years. This is progressively contracted moving north and in Scotland, the season lasts from May to the end of October. In Ireland, the season usually starts around the same time as in southern England but ends earlier; mid November is the latest date recorded for any Irish dragonfly. Large Red Damselfly is usually the first species to emerge, usually occurring in southern or eastern England, and the Common Darter typically the last to be on the wing. While this refers to what may be considered a normal flight season, it must be noted that exceptions do exist. There have been sightings of Large Red Damselfly in March and, once, in late February (P. Allen, pers. comm.). December sightings of Common Darter are not too unusual in southern England, and both Migrant and Southern Hawker have also been reported at the start of December. The latest date within the BDS database relates to a Common Darter seen in Somerset on 17 December 2004. In addition to these extremes, other more exceptional sightings exist. The migrant Vagrant Emperor is of largely Afro-tropical origin and thus may occur at times that are not determined solely by local conditions. It has been reported during most months of the year, including mid-winter. Very occasional, atypical records of resident species have also been reported. For example, there is a record of an adult Broad-bodied Chaser on 17 February 1982; this individual emerged from an artificially warmed water-channel that received a continuous input of industrial waste water at roughly 27-30°C (Brinn & Nelson, 1986).

Although there are significantly more records from 1991-2012 there is sufficient pre-1991 data to allow meaningful comparisons of flight periods between the two periods. Despite there being a degree of noise in the data, whereby flight periods vary with location and from year-to-year, some general trends are apparent. Hassall *et al.* (2007) have shown that the leading edge of the flight periods of many British Odonata have advanced, on average, by about 2 days per decade over the period 1960-2004, i.e. species now start flying earlier in the year (the exception apparently being species that overwinter as diapause eggs). The authors interpreted this as being a reflection of large-scale climatic changes. However, shifts in the end of the flight period were less clear-cut, perhaps because different species respond in different ways, or because there are other factors at work (e.g. warmer temperatures may make individuals emerge earlier, but prolong adult survival).

Large Red Damselfly, usually first on the wing, has been sighted in late February and March. *Anthony Taylor*

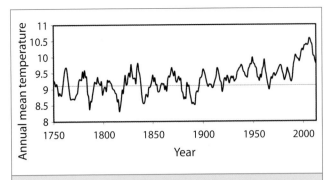

Figure 39. Plot of mean annual CET (as a five-year rolling average) against date. The thin dotted, horizontal line represents the long-term average for 1750-1920. Data from the Met Office Hadley Centre for Climate Change (www.metoffice.gov.uk/hadobs).

elsewhere, for example IPCC (2013), and see also discussions on pages 4-9). In Britain, estimates of the mean annual temperature in central England, the 'Central England Temperature' or CET, exist as far back as the mid 17th century (Parker *et al.*, 1992). A long-term trend in annual temperatures was not apparent until 1920 after which a warming trend has been observed, slight at first, apart from a good number of warm years during the mid 1930s to late 1940s, but becoming more dramatic over the last 20-30 years (Figure 39). These recent decades have seen considerable changes to dragonfly distributions and phenology, on both a local and a global scale.

Changes in the phenology of Britain and Ireland's dragonflies have continued since the analysis of Hassall *et al.* (2007) and for some species have now become quite noticeable. Inspection of the phenograms within the species accounts reveals a number of species where earlier appearances are now quite obvious. Such species include

While the long-term consequences of climate change remain unresolved, there can be little doubt that the world's climate has been shifting over recent years and that human activities have had a significant role (reviewed extensively

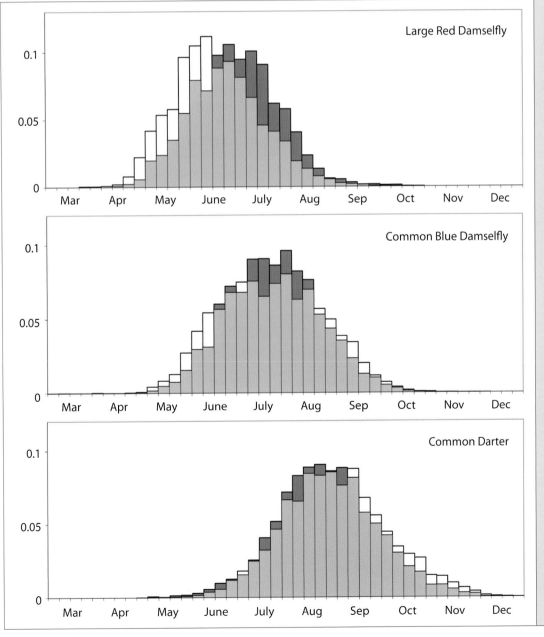

Figure 40. Flight period histograms for selected species, each showing a different pattern of shift in phenology over time. White bars relate to data from 1991-2012, whilst dark blue bars relate to the time period pre-1991; light blue is where the white and dark blue bars overlap. Individual columns represent the proportion of total records for the given species that are accounted for in any particular 7-day span (these histograms thus differ slightly from the phenograms presented in the main species accounts).

Northern, Variable and Large Red Damselflies, Norfolk Hawker, White-faced Darter, Four-spotted Chaser, Red-veined Darter and, to a lesser extent, Azure Damselfly, Hairy Dragonfly and possibly also Northern Emerald. The great majority of these are early-emerging species, where climatic effects due to warmer winters and the earlier onset of spring are likely to be most pronounced. It is interesting to note that Red-veined Darter occurs mostly as an immigrant rather than a local breeder but overall effects are clearly very similar. Perhaps changes to emergence times in source areas are involved in the early appearance of this species, in addition to possible shifts in weather patterns. Later-emerging species often show little major change to flight periods, though with a slightly increased frequency of later records, perhaps suggesting that adult life-span may have increased in recent years.

As well as increasingly early emergences, signs of a potential shift in the life cycle and voltinism of certain species have also been observed in recent years. A detailed study by Corbet (1957a) in the middle of the last century showed that Emperor Dragonfly typically emerged in early summer after a larval development period of either one or, more frequently, two years. A diapause held back and synchronised larvae that did not emerge by an appropriate date at the end of their first year. However, in recent times, several examples of emergence during the autumn have been reported and occasional adults may be encountered as late as October. Major changes in the end of the flight period of the Emperor Dragonfly are not visible in the flight period phenograms within the species accounts, because as yet any shifts affect only a small proportion of the overall population at certain localities. They do, however, clearly warrant further study, especially as the bimodal distribution shown in the 1991-2012 flight phenogram (in the species section) could imply that the previously-known one-year life cycle has also become increasingly important over the years.

Other similar cases also exist. The Red-eyed Damselfly is normally considered to have a predominantly two-year life cycle in Britain (i.e. it is semi-voltine) but an apparent strengthening in the bimodality of the flight period may imply that the one year (univoltine) strategy is now becoming increasingly common. Indeed a bivoltine strategy, with a second generation in one year, was demonstrated in Germany during 2006 (Schiel, 2006). A scattering of recent British records for October, along with the sighting of an immature adult in Northamptonshire on 3 November 2007, could imply that such a strategy may now also be possible in Britain. Given that a number of other British and Irish species, such as Blue-tailed, Scarce Blue-tailed and Common Blue Damselflies, are known to be at least partly bivoltine in more southerly areas of Europe (Corbet *et al.*, 2006), close scrutiny of their present phenology may turn up interesting surprises.

Flight periods for some species appear to be extending, Emperor Dragonflies have been sighted on the wing in late autumn.
*Steve Cham*

In conclusion, fieldwork towards the present atlas has revealed shifts in the phenology of Britain and Ireland's dragonflies, particularly in terms of flight periods. Species' life cycle duration and voltinism may also be changing but this is difficult to quantify both because of our limited base-line knowledge of these important life-history traits and the effects of increased recording intensity resulting in improved detection of rare events. As with many of the recent distributional changes seen in Britain and Ireland, recent shifts in phenology are broadly in line with those to be expected from local and regional climate change, with warmer overall temperatures and an (on average) earlier onset of spring now being encountered. Different species do not all respond in exactly the same manner but earlier appearance dates seem to be an increasing phenomenon. However, on a global scale, exceptions to this behaviour can be found. In Japan, Doi (2008) noted that the White-tailed Skimmer (*Orthetrum albistylum speciosum*) has seemingly started to emerge later in the year, a phenomenon that may be linked to some of the more advanced larvae of the spring-emerging generation of this locally bivoltine species now starting to emerge the preceding autumn. For a European perspective on recent changes to dragonfly phenology, Ott (2010a) and works therein provide the latest overviews.

# Species accounts

The species accounts in this atlas represent the input from multiple authors. It was deemed important from the outset to gain a countrywide view, with anecdotal evidence from all areas across Britain and Ireland. This approach aimed to reduce the bias that could creep in from single author accounts.

Technical terms are defined in the Glossary (Appendix A1).

## Species names

The scientific and vernacular names are included for each species. The scientific names and their sequences are those from the most recent World Odonata List (Schorr & Paulson, 2014). The vernacular names used are those advocated by the British Dragonfly Society (Mill et al., 2004). For each species the vernacular name devised for the European field guide by Dijkstra & Lewington (2006) is also included below the BDS name.

The individual species sections vary in length. It was considered important that, where there was something particularly noteworthy to say about a particular species, this information should receive additional space allocation. For example, where major range changes have occurred since the previous atlas, more details are given to provide some narrative and explanation of the maps.

Each species account consists of five sections of varying length and the purpose of each section is described below.

## Introduction

This section, accompanying a photograph of the species, briefly describes the key features and attributes of the species. It is not intended to be a comprehensive description nor a substitute for a good field guide, such as Brooks & Lewington (2004), Smallshire & Swash (2014) and Thompson & Nelson (2014).

## Distribution

This section describes the species' distribution in a global, European and local context. To avoid repetition of key references on distribution, the following publications have been used as references but are not mentioned specifically in accounts: Askew (2004); Nelson & Thompson (2004); Dijkstra & Lewington (2006); Boudot et al. (2009) and Smallshire & Swash (2014).

For some species, specific location details of the distribution in Britain and Ireland are given. Such details are particularly relevant where the species' range has changed substantially since the previous atlas.

When referring to biogeographical ecozones, the definitions and boundaries provided by Wikipedia (http://en.wikipedia.org; accessed December 2013) have been adopted. Britain and Ireland is in the Palaearctic ecozone, which includes Europe, Asia north of the Himalaya foothills, northern Africa and the northern and central parts of the Arabian Peninsula. The term boreal is applied to ecosystems with a subarctic climate in the Northern Hemisphere, approximately between latitude 45° and 65° North. In western Europe, the Boreal zone covers most of Scandinavia, the Baltic States and Finland (see footnote). The Holarctic is used in the sense of the combined area covered by the Palaearctic and the Nearctic, the latter consisting of North America north of southern Mexico.

For ease of use and clarity, mapping and recording grid units are referred to throughout as hectads (10km x 10km squares), tetrads (2km x 2km squares) and monads (1km x 1km squares). Altitude is referred to as the height in metres above sea level. Temperatures are given in °Celsius.

A flight period histogram is provided for all extant species, showing the numbers of records of adults received for each of two periods, before and after the previous atlas.

## Habitat

This section describes the main habitat type(s) for the species and may contain information about the type of waterbody preferred, water quality, associated vegetation and breeding requirements. Wherever plant or animal names are used, the vernacular name for them is given priority. Appendix A3 gives a list of scientific names for the plants and animals used in the texts. Plant names are taken from Stace (2010).

## Conservation and threats

This section summarises the actual or perceived threats to a species and/or its habitat. Reference is made to its status and category in the Red Data Lists for Great Britain (Daguet et al., 2008), Ireland (Nelson et al., 2011) and Europe (Kalkman et al., 2010), where relevant. Particular attention is given in the text to species falling in the critical categories Endangered, Vulnerable and Near Threatened. The categories are based on criteria laid down by the International Union for the Conservation of Nature (IUCN, 2005).

## National trends

This section describes significant trends and changes in distribution. Throughout this publication, the Atlas of the Dragonflies of Britain and Ireland (Merritt et al., 1996) is referred to as the 'previous atlas'. It should be used in conjunction with pages 58-63.

Footnote: http://ec.europa.eu/environment/nature/natura2000/sites_hab/biogeog_regions/maps/biogeo_map_eur27.pdf

# Willow Emerald Damselfly

## *Chalcolestes viridis*

### Western Willow Spreadwing

Willow Emerald Damselfly is a large damselfly and a recent colonist to Britain. Adults are similar in appearance to other emerald damselflies but there is no pruinescence on the thorax or abdomen and the pterostigmata remain pale, even at maturity. Although the species can be found resting on other vegetation, damselflies typically spend much of their time in trees. Females oviposit into branches overhanging water, leaving characteristic scars on the bark; the larvae hatch the following spring and drop into the water below, with adults then emerging that summer.

Willow Emerald Damselfly, male.
*Steve Cham*

## Distribution

Willow Emerald Damselfly occurs in parts of North Africa (especially northern Morocco/Algeria/Tunisia), the western Mediterranean islands and much of Europe north to about 53° 30'N. The species appears to be expanding its range northwards, with the first Danish records as recent as 2005. In the Channel Islands, it has been known from Jersey since the early 1940s. After a period in the 1980s when it was unrecorded (rare or absent or under-recorded), it has now become widespread and common once more. The species was recorded from Alderney for the first time in 2010.

In Britain, Willow Emerald Damselfly is a recent colonist. Its main stronghold is south-east Suffolk (and to some extent north-east Essex), within an area of approximately 30km radius from where the species was first recorded at Trimley, near Felixstowe, during 2007. It is now locally common and occupies a range of habitat types, including larger lakes and reservoirs such as Alton Water, smaller waters such as Staverton Lake and also slow-flowing portions of rivers such as the Rivers Deben and Gipping. Away from this core area, it occurs in south-east Essex (Hadleigh Country Park), north-east Kent (several sites in the Reculver area) and also in Norfolk (in the Strumpshaw Fen area). In 2013, a new population was located on the River Yare at Cringleford

near Norwich. Given the abundance of habitat in the Norfolk Broads that is suitable for the species, but at the same time difficult to survey, it is conceivable that Willow Emerald Damselfly is more widespread in the area.

The history of Willow Emerald in Britain is informative. In the late nineteenth century McLachlan (1884) considered the species to be of doubtful status in Britain. A specimen, apparently from Hertfordshire in 1899, is believed by some to have been mislabelled. The first confirmed record was not until 1979, when one adult specimen was found dead at Hankham Clay Pit near Pevensey, East Sussex. An exuvia was then discovered at Cliffe Marshes, Kent, during 1992, though no adults were noted either at the time or subsequently. On 17 August 2007 an adult female was observed near Trimley, Suffolk, following a weather pattern coming from the near Continent that could have brought insects over (the insect-borne Bluetongue virus, previously unknown from the UK, also arrived in East Anglia at this time). Although there were no confirmed sightings during 2008, well over four hundred individuals were reported from East Anglia in the following year. These sightings were in an area within 25km of the 2007 Suffolk sighting, with an additional record from Strumpshaw in Norfolk. In 2009,

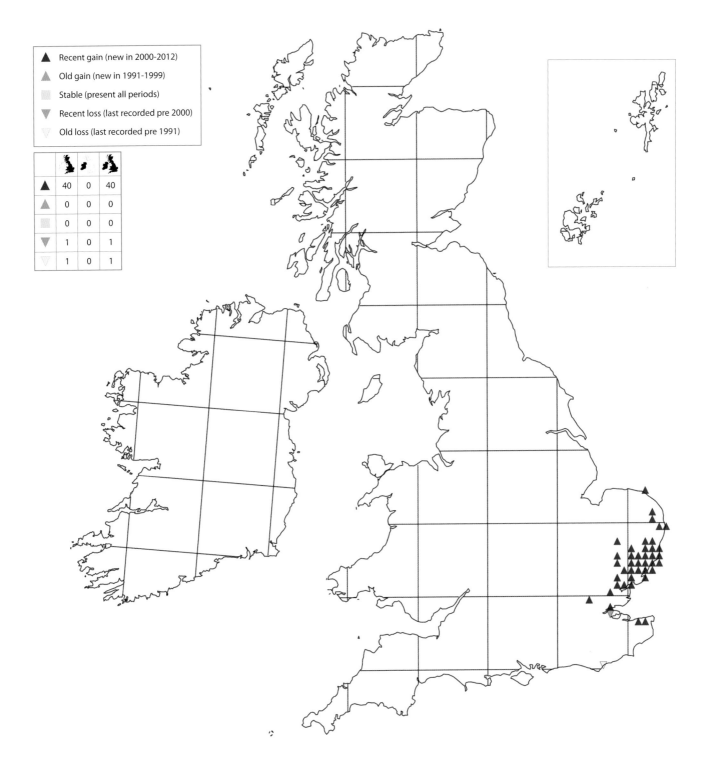

| |  |  |  |
|---|---|---|---|
| ▲ | 40 | 0 | 40 |
| △ | 0 | 0 | 0 |
| ▨ | 0 | 0 | 0 |
| ▼ | 1 | 0 | 1 |
| ▽ | 1 | 0 | 1 |

Legend:
- ▲ Recent gain (new in 2000-2012)
- △ Old gain (new in 1991-1999)
- ▨ Stable (present all periods)
- ▼ Recent loss (last recorded pre 2000)
- ▽ Old loss (last recorded pre 1991)

there were numerous records of ovipositing pairs and at least one teneral individual in Suffolk. This suggests that, by 2009, a self-sustaining breeding population had already become established in the region.

Large numbers were again reported from south-east Suffolk in 2010, with numerous tenerals being noted. Some of the out-lying sites discovered in 2009 produced no records during 2010 but new sites were discovered elsewhere in the region. Sites were also identified in new areas of eastern England, specifically near Hadleigh in south-east Essex and near Reculver in north-east Kent. Although these sites could have been occupied earlier and

initially missed, there is a suggestion that new immigration from the Continent was involved with the 2010 sightings. The Thames Estuary area also experienced a major influx of Southern Migrant Hawker Aeshna affinis at the same time. In 2011, numbers remained high in all previously-colonised areas, with some evidence for a degree of local range expansion (e.g. in Suffolk the first record for Minsmere was made on 16 September). In addition, a male was recorded near Cromer, Norfolk, during mid-October about 40km away from other known Norfolk sites. It is likely that this was an immigrant. In 2012, a probable was recorded on a willow at a balancing pond near to Biggleswade, Bedfordshire, suggesting a further westwards spread.

*Above :* Alton Water, Suffolk, where a large population of Willow Emerald Damselfly has been present. These willows had thousands of egg scars all over the branches in early 2012. *Steve Cham*

*Below:* Pond at Hadleigh Country Park, Essex, where Willow Emerald Damselfly has been seen ovipositing into Hawthorn bushes. *Andy McGeeney*

*Above:* Willow Emerald Damselflies ovipositing into a branch of willow at Strumpshaw Fen, Norfolk. *Adrian Riley*

*Below:* Willow Emerald Damselflies, mating. *Damian Pinguey*

## Habitat

Willow Emerald Damselfly favours a range of shrub or tree-lined habitats such as ponds, lakes, canals and slow-flowing sections of rivers. Unlike the other British lestids, this species does not frequent well-vegetated, shallow, standing waters prone to temporarily drying out. Adults can be found both in trees, frequently at considerable height, as well as in rough vegetation. They favour sheltered, open-structured habitat for resting but can move into deep foliage when ovipositing. These habitat preferences mean that observing or recording this species may require lengthy searching. Individuals can be found sunning themselves a long distance from water and there is a suggestion that later on in the season this might lead to significant local dispersal.

The female characteristically oviposits (in tandem) into the young branches of trees and bushes overhanging water.

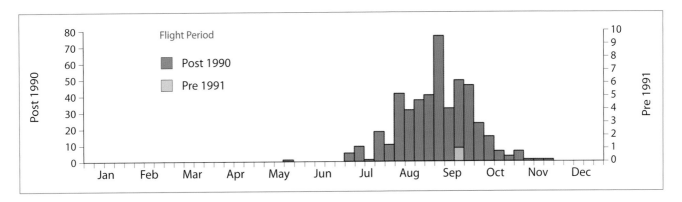

The River Gipping, Suffolk, where adults have been seen. Egg scars have been found here on willows and elder. *Steve Cham*

Oviposition scars of Willow Emerald Damselfly on willow branch showing consecutive years' growth. *Steve Cham*

Tree species currently recorded for oviposition include willows, birches, Alder, Ash, Hawthorn and Elder, with further species likely to be added in coming years. Branches chosen for oviposition typically have a diameter of 0.5–2cm. A characteristic scar pattern forms along the branches where oviposition has occurred. These can persist for several years, providing a useful means to record the species outside the main flight period.

## Conservation status and threats

Willow Emerald Damselfly was not assessed in the most recent Red Data List for Britain, by virtue of it then occurring only as a vagrant. At present, no particular conservation measures beyond continued monitoring seem necessary. However, the intensive clearing or pollarding of waterside trees does have the potential to impact on populations at individual sites.

## National trends

Prior to 2000, Willow Emerald Damselfly had been an erratic visitor to Britain, being confirmed from only two hectads. The species has been increasing in numbers and expanding its range on the near Continent for a number of years leading to a substantial influx into East Anglia since 2007. This has resulted in successful colonisation across eastern Britain and, with the increasing number of records away from the coast, further range expansion is likely.

Gaining an accurate estimate of numbers can sometimes be difficult, due to the arboreal habit of adults. However, surveying for oviposition scars on suitable trees can provide an alternative method to estimate the population size at a site and may even reveal new sites where adults have not been recorded. Numbers of adults present at sites in south-east England can vary considerably from a few individuals to the best sites with well over 100. This may reflect the availability of suitable trees for oviposition and how recently populations have become established. It seems likely that both the breeding range of the species and the number of sites holding high density populations will continue to increase over the next few years wherever suitable habitat is present.

# Southern Emerald Damselfly

*Lestes barbarus*　　　　　　　　　　　Migrant Spreadwing

Southern Emerald Damselfly is emerald green in colour and similar to most other emerald damselflies, both in terms of appearance and biology. It is distinguished by having bi-coloured pterostigmata and broad yellow antehumeral stripes. Although usually highly site faithful, under the right conditions the species has migratory tendencies. Over the last decade small numbers have started to appear in southern England, with a few localised breeding attempts made. The life cycle is one year in length, the species overwintering in the egg stage.

Southern Emerald Damselfly, male. *John Curd*

## Distribution

Southern Emerald Damselfly is a Palaearctic species that occurs in isolated parts of northern Africa (in the region that used to be referred to as the Barbary Coast, hence its scientific name), most of Europe north to The Netherlands, Germany and Poland, and also in parts of western and central Asia including Kazakhstan, Kashmir and Mongolia. It has become much more abundant in the lower latitudes of northern Europe in recent years, expanding its range to the north.

Southern Emerald Damselfly first appeared in mainland Britain in 2002, when several males were discovered at Winterton Dunes, Norfolk. Since then it has been recorded in Britain in most years, with breeding attempted on several occasions. At Cliffe, Kent, recent breeding activity is presumed successful because it has persisted there since 2010. However, unlike several other recent colonists, the species has been slow in establishing a sustained breeding population in the region. Most recent sightings have come from south-eastern coastal counties close to the near Continent, i.e. from East Sussex to Norfolk. Many records come from very close to the coast, which to some extent is typical of immigrants, but may also reflect the availability of suitable habitat in these areas. The one exception to the general trend was a female found inland near Keynsham, North Somerset, on 26 August 2006.

Well-vegetated ditch at Cliffe Marshes, Kent, where Southern Emerald Damselfly has been recorded. *Gill Brook*

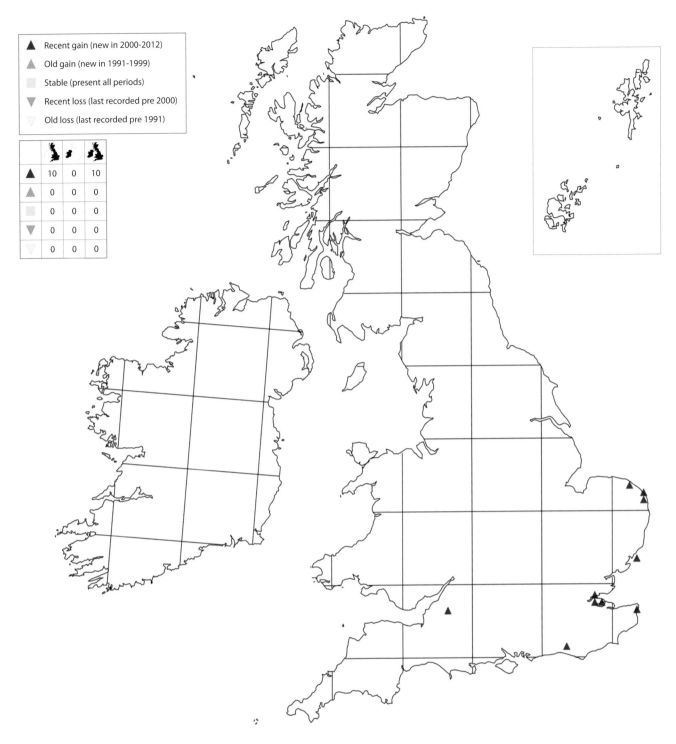

| | ![GB] | ![IE] | ![GB+IE] |
| --- | --- | --- | --- |
| ▲ | 10 | 0 | 10 |
| ▲ | 0 | 0 | 0 |
| ▣ | 0 | 0 | 0 |
| ▼ | 0 | 0 | 0 |
| ▽ | 0 | 0 | 0 |

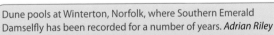

Dune pools at Winterton, Norfolk, where Southern Emerald Damselfly has been recorded for a number of years. *Adrian Riley*

## Habitat

Southern Emerald Damselfly typically favours warm shallow waters, particularly those that dry out in summer; the use of such ephemeral habitat is even more pronounced than in other lestids. Typical habitats include dune slacks, small ponds/flooded depressions and seasonally wet ditches. The species can tolerate mildly brackish conditions.

## Conservation status and threats

Southern Emerald Damselfly was not assessed on the British Red List as it was a recent colonist. The current breeding colonies are of too recent origin for their long-

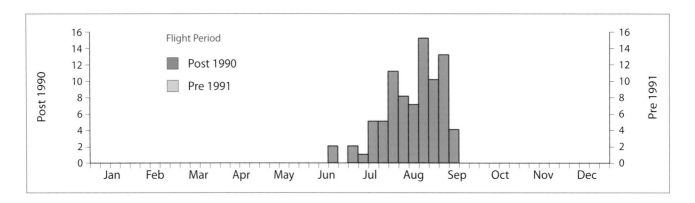

term stability to be determined. The species' use of shallow or even ephemeral waters renders it susceptible to changes in land management and drainage, while coastal sites are also at risk of flooding by seawater, which is believed to explain its failure to persist at Sandwich Bay, Kent.

## National trends

Southern Emerald Damselfly was first observed in Britain at Winterton Dunes, Norfolk, in 2002, with further records from there and from Sandwich Bay, Kent, in 2003 and 2004. The species was not found at either of these sites in the years immediately thereafter. Records at Winterton might have referred to primary immigrants rather than an established colony, and while oviposition was noted at Sandwich, the colony apparently succumbed to flooding of the site by seawater during the 2004/2005 winter. Between 2005 and 2008 only a single individual was noted (Keynsham – see above). During August 2009 singletons were recorded at Winterton Dunes and Trimingham, both in Norfolk, and from Old Felixstowe, Suffolk. In 2010, small numbers were

recorded at Cliffe Marshes and two other sites in Kent, one at Wat Tyler Country Park, Essex, and a male and a female (present on different dates) at Winterton Dunes. Oviposition was noted at Cliffe in late July and this breeding attempt appears to have been successful, with records following annually during 2011-13. Another singleton was also noted at Wat Tyler CP in 2011 and one was found in East Sussex. In 2012, several were noted at Winterton in early September, and with oviposition being observed it is possible that an established breeding colony may soon develop at this site, which is clearly attractive to the species.

Records indicate an increasing tendency for Southern Emerald Damselfly to reach British shores as a migrant. While the species' status as an established breeder is still somewhat uncertain, it is hoped that further stable colonies will soon develop. The species has been very successful in colonising much of The Netherlands in recent decades (Termaat et al., 2010), though some colony instability at the very edge of its range is perhaps to be expected.

Southern Emerald Damselfly, pair ovipositing. *Tihomir Stefanov*

# Scarce Emerald Damselfly

*Lestes dryas*

Scarce Emerald Damselfly is very similar to the much more widespread Emerald Damselfly and can easily be overlooked. Males differ in having only the basal half of abdominal segment 2 blue, while females appear relatively robust and have square dark marks on segment 1. The male's incurved inferior anal appendages and the female's long ovipositor, which just extends beyond the tip of the abdomen, are also diagnostic. The species has a one year life cycle, overwintering as eggs, which are inserted into the stems of emergent plants.

Scarce Emerald Damselfly, female. *Steve Cham*

## Distribution

Scarce Emerald Damselfly has a very extensive range in the Northern Hemisphere, being one of the few odonates found across the entire Holarctic region. It occurs in much of the USA and Canada, while in Eurasia it occurs from Portugal and Ireland in the west to Korea and Japan in the east, including Turkey, West Siberia, Kazakhstan and Mongolia. However, it is somewhat local in many regions. In Europe it is found from central Finland to the Mediterranean, although here it is largely restricted to mountainous areas. It is found also on Sicily and in Morocco.

In Britain and Ireland, the range of Scarce Emerald Damselfly is clearly localised. In Britain it has always been restricted to south-eastern England and is currently found principally in East Anglia and north Kent, with the main strongholds being around the Thames Estuary, and inland in the Breckland area of Norfolk. In Ireland, the species is found at lowland sites in the Burren and at widely scattered locations within a broad belt across the centre of the country, though several sites in the east have apparently been lost since the previous atlas. In 2013, it was rediscovered in Co. Kilkenny after a gap of more than 25 years.

## Habitat

Scarce Emerald Damselfly favours shallow still waters, with a dense growth of emergent and marginal vegetation, that frequently dry out in summer. Desiccation of its habitat reduces the impacts of fish and other species that would predate the larvae (Stoks & McPeek, 2003). Rapid larval development, following the hatching of eggs in spring, also allows Scarce Emerald Damselfly to flourish at seasonal waters. The species can withstand a degree of salinity,

Redgrave and Lopham Fen, Suffolk, where a new population of Scarce Emerald Damselfly has been recorded. *Steve Cham*

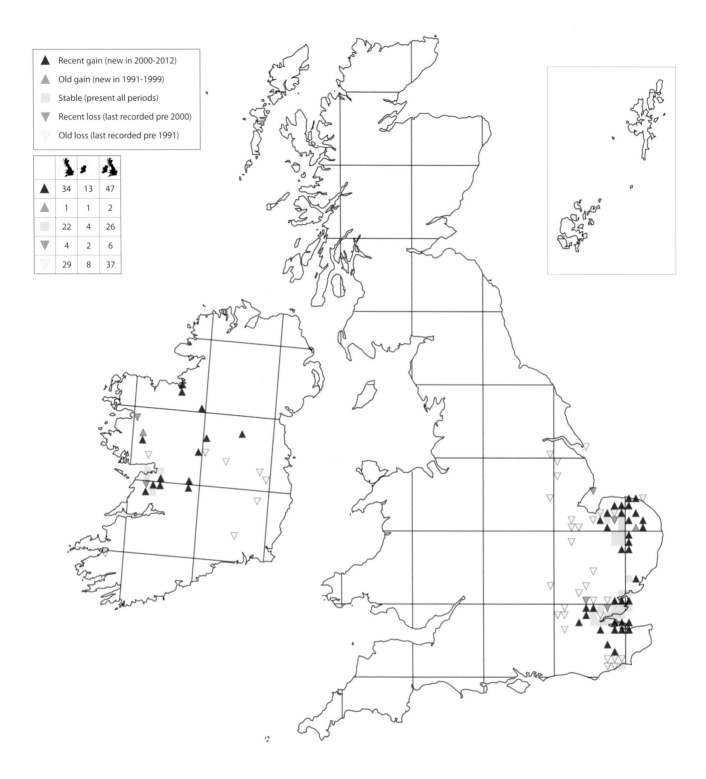

| | 🗺 | 🗺 | 🗺 |
|---|---|---|---|
| ▲ | 34 | 13 | 47 |
| △ | 1 | 1 | 2 |
| ▦ | 22 | 4 | 26 |
| ▼ | 4 | 2 | 6 |
| ▽ | 29 | 8 | 37 |

Legend:
- ▲ Recent gain (new in 2000-2012)
- △ Old gain (new in 1991-1999)
- ▦ Stable (present all periods)
- ▼ Recent loss (last recorded pre 2000)
- ▽ Old loss (last recorded pre 1991)

although the exact level of tolerance remains to be quantified. In Britain, it is found in two main types of habitat: coastal or estuarine grazing marshes, where well-vegetated (often nearly choked) ditches and drainage dykes are favoured; and seasonal ponds such as the pingos of the West Norfolk Breckland. In addition, other shallow ponds, ditches and disused sections of canal that support extensive dense, emergent vegetation may be frequented.

In Ireland the species is widespread due to the relative abundance of ephemeral habitats. The occupied habitats are much as those described for Britain, except that it has never been found at brackish sites. The largest, most stable

populations are in natural fluctuating wetlands of the limestone central plain, including the turloughs (lakes that often dry out in summer and autumn) of the karstic regions. Eastern sites are mainly wetlands in the late stages of hydroseral succession, many of which are disused and choked stretches of canals and cut-off sections of lakes.

Typical emergent plant species found at Scarce Emerald Damselfly sites include Water Horsetail, sedges, rushes and Bulrush. In coastal localities, Sea Club-rush is usually the dominant species.

Hills and Holes, near Great Hockham, Norfolk, comprises a series of shallow pingo ponds with a large population of Scarce Emerald Damselfly. *Steve Cham*

## Conservation status and threats

Scarce Emerald Damselfly is classified as Near Threatened in the British Red List. It has a restricted distribution and is currently limited to parts of south-east England. At some of its best sites the species may be quite abundant. In Ireland, it is also somewhat local, likewise being classified as Near Threatened because of the restricted number of known sites and the apparent decline in eastern parts of its range.

With breeding sites typically being shallow, or even ephemeral, waters the species is especially sensitive to changes in land use and drainage practices. There is also the likelihood of the loss of the species as a wetland becomes more permanent (no longer dries out); there is at least one good example of this occurring at a site in Co. Mayo. Reduction in the water table is a particular problem, but unsympathetic wetland management, over-grazing and eutrophication as a result of agricultural run-off are also significant issues. A small inland population, recorded during 1991-93 at Epping Long Green, Essex, was lost from a shallow pond, possibly after run-off entered it from adjacent agricultural land. Other potential threats include habitat destruction, particularly conversion of coastal grazing marsh to arable farmland and, in Ireland, the drainage of turloughs. Coastal sites are also subject to medium-term threat from rising sea level in south-east England. Habitat changes and seral progression resulting from more frequent drought might also become an issue at inland sites.

## National trends

As its name implies, Scarce Emerald Damselfly is a species of restricted abundance in Britain and Ireland. In the early part of the twentieth century, its known sites were widely scattered throughout eastern England, from Sussex north to Lincolnshire and south Yorkshire. After the mid-twentieth century there followed a marked decline in Britain (Moore,

Thompson Common, Norfolk. An area of pingos with shallow densely vegetated pools that has a large population of both Scarce Emerald and Emerald Damselflies. *Steve Cham*

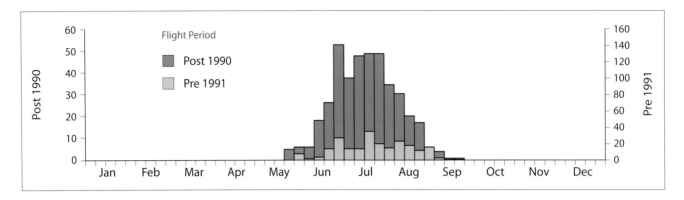

Hadleigh Country Park, Essex. The grazing marsh ditches at this site hold high numbers of Scarce Emerald Damselfly. *Steve Cham*

1980), seemingly due to a variety of factors. These factors included pollution, loss of marshy habitat through agricultural activity, urban development and natural seral progression. This species is also susceptible to periods of drought, the effects of which would have been exacerbated by changes in agriculture. In contrast, the Irish population was apparently stable. For a time in the 1970s and early 1980s, Scarce Emerald Damselfly was thought to be extinct in Britain, but more likely it was just overlooked in its few remaining strongholds. In 1983, the species was then discovered at several sites in coastal Essex and one in Kent (Benton & Payne, 1983), some of which were quite close to previously known localities. Shortly afterwards, the species was also found in the Breckland area of Norfolk.

In recent years the number of known sites for Scarce Emerald Damselfly in Britain has increased substantially. This may simply reflect better identification ability and increased recording of the species. However, it has recently appeared at well-watched sites in Norfolk well away from its Breckland strongholds. Despite substantial local fieldwork in Suffolk (Mendel, 1992), the species was considered long absent, if indeed it ever occurred. Breeding colonies were then unexpectedly discovered in the north of the county at Market Weston Fen in 2007 and at nearby

Redgrave and Lopham Fen in 2009, possibly colonised from a southerly spread of the Breckland sites. Sites in south-east Suffolk, near Brantham, were found in 2012 possibly resulting from a northwards spread of the population in coastal Essex. The range expansion of a Near Threatened species must be considered encouraging, though it remains to be seen just how many of the new sites turn out to be long-lived.

The history of Scarce Emerald Damselfly along the Kent/Sussex border demonstrates the transitory nature of this species. It was originally recorded from a number of sites in the 1940s, but was thought to be extinct from the early 1950s. Some recent sightings might refer simply to isolated migrants or wanderers, e.g. singletons at Rye Harbour, Sussex, in 2006 and near Horsmonden, Kent, in 2008. However, the discovery of a small breeding population at Sissinghurst Castle, Kent, following the creation of shallow wetlands, demonstrates that undiscovered populations may exist elsewhere in the area. In addition to the colonisation of new sites, the continuing stability of more well-established sites will also play an important part in helping to determine the species' long-term trends and fate.

Baltrasna, Co. Meath. This shallow pond in wet heath has a colony of Scarce Emerald which is one of the most easterly known sites in Ireland. *Brian Nelson*

# Emerald Damselfly

*Lestes sponsa*

Common Spreadwing

Emerald Damselfly is a relatively large damselfly with a metallic green or bronze body. Males develop blue pruinescence at the base and tip of the abdomen. The wings are typically held half-open when at rest, a feature shared with other lestids. Eggs are inserted into the stems of emergent plants, including Common Reed and rushes, where they overwinter and hatch in the following spring. It normally has a one year life cycle whereby larvae develop rapidly and emerge a few weeks later.

Emerald Damselfly, mating pair. *Steve Cham*

## Distribution

Emerald Damselfly has an extensive world range across the Palaearctic. It covers much of northern and central Europe, though largely avoiding the Mediterranean region, extending east through Kazakhstan, southern Siberia, Mongolia, northern China and as far as Japan. The species is generally common over much of this range, even as far north as Finland, where it just reaches the Arctic Circle. Its conservation status in Switzerland has recently been upgraded to Near Threatened on the basis of a decline during the 1990s. Belgium and some parts of Germany have also seen signs of localised population declines in recent years.

In Britain and Ireland, the species is widespread, having long been recorded from virtually all regions and large island groups except for Orkney and Shetland. The first record for Orkney (Rackwick, Hoy) came in 2010. In some areas it can be extremely abundant, with a few sites, such as some of the wetlands on the Lizard Peninsula, Cornwall, regularly holding over 500 adults. However, in other areas it is uncommon or even absent, reflecting a scarcity or lack of suitable habitat. Such areas include the chalk downland of southern England and the uplands of the Pennines and Scotland. There are also substantial areas apparently unoccupied in Ireland, particularly in the south-east.

Upland bog pools, Cairnsmore of Fleet NNR, Dumfries and Galloway. *R&B Mearns*

The species appears to exist at low population density in some areas, perhaps in metapopulations, disappearing at some sites from time-to-time, only to be recolonised later from nearby sites. Thus, as new sites have been discovered in recent years, others have been lost. Some of this apparent turnover may reflect variation of recording intensity. Emerald Damselfly is a relatively inconspicuous species and some small populations might not have been discovered during site visits. Analysis of distributional changes therefore is not only complicated by site turnover,

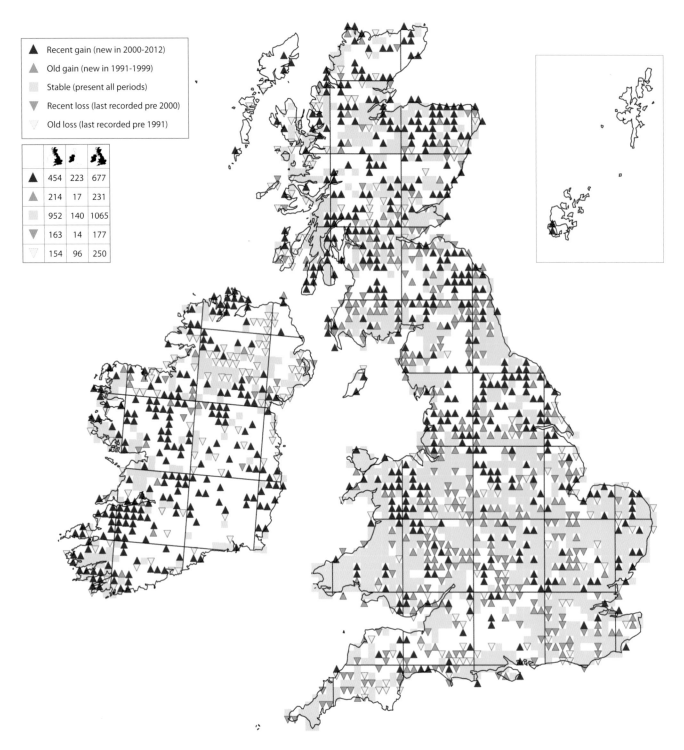

| | | | |
|---|---|---|---|
| ▲ | 454 | 223 | 677 |
| ▲ | 214 | 17 | 231 |
| ▢ | 952 | 140 | 1065 |
| ▼ | 163 | 14 | 177 |
| ▽ | 154 | 96 | 250 |

Legend:
- ▲ Recent gain (new in 2000-2012)
- ▲ Old gain (new in 1991-1999)
- ▢ Stable (present all periods)
- ▼ Recent loss (last recorded pre 2000)
- ▽ Old loss (last recorded pre 1991)

Strensall Common, Yorkshire. *Keith Gittens*

but also by changes in recording intensity and coverage. Nevertheless, there has been much apparent consolidation of its range throughout Britain and Ireland since the previous atlas.

## Habitat

Throughout its range, the species typically favours shallow wetlands, with either standing or very slow-flowing water and extensive dense emergent vegetation. The range of such wetland sites is quite broad and includes ditches, canals, ponds, lakes and vegetation-choked streams as well as acidic bog pools. The aquatic vegetation typically comprises plants with a vertical structure, such as rushes,

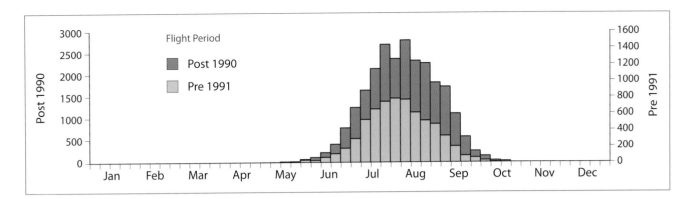

Gwern Engen, Conwy. *Allan Brandon*

sedges, horsetails and Common Reed. Emerald Damselfly fares best in waterbodies that are not stocked with fish, since its highly active larvae are susceptible to predation. Larvae have been found in slightly brackish situations. Roosting usually occurs close to the water's edge, often in tandem or *in copula*.

To a greater extent than with other lestids, apart from Willow Emerald Damselfly, many of the wetland sites occupied by Emerald Damselfly are permanent in nature. However, some occupied sites may be subject to sporadic drying out in late summer and autumn. The species is well able to cope with sites drying out, having eggs that overwinter in living plant material, and may even benefit in the long term through the associated suppression of predators such as fish. Factors important in the species' survival include the rapid larval growth rate that allows the life cycle to be completed whilst the breeding sites remain wet.

In the bog pools of northern Scotland and Ireland, Emerald Damselfly occurs at highest density at lower altitude sites. In north-east Scotland, it has been recorded at an upper altitude limit of roughly 300m, presumably being constrained by temperature.

## Conservation Status and Threats

Emerald Damselfly is widespread and locally common, sometimes even abundant, in Britain and Ireland and is thus categorised as of Least Concern in the respective Red Lists.

Warren Heath, Hampshire, holds a large population of Emerald Damselfly. *Steve Cham*

Some local populations may be under pressure from loss of habitat or from the loss of emergent vegetation through large-scale dredging of ponds and ditches. Longer-term changes in land use and in drainage practices may also have potentially serious impacts upon the species. Emerald Damselfly could, in addition, be affected by climate change. Since it largely avoids the Mediterranean region and tends to only occur at high altitude in the very south of its range, it is possible that it may ultimately respond negatively to rising temperature at low altitudes in Britain and Ireland.

## National Trends

Despite an overall increase in the number of occupied hectads compared with the previous atlas, the CEH trends analysis suggests a significant decline (pages 58-63). However, the species is still very widespread and locally common and much of the apparent infilling of records is most likely due to improved recording intensity.

In some counties, such as Suffolk, there is a suggestion that the number of smaller sites may have declined in recent decades. During recent fieldwork it was recorded from fewer tetrads compared with that in the county atlas during 1987-1992. It is suspected that changes in land management and drainage in this agricultural county may have reduced the number of wet areas that would otherwise have held the species.

# Banded Demoiselle
## *Calopteryx splendens*

Banded Demoiselle is one of the two largest damselflies in Britain and Ireland. Males have a metallic blue-green body. The wings have a metallic blue band, covering most of the wing beyond the nodus, though varying in extent from about 55% of the total wing area in southern England to only 43% in the north. Females have a metallic green body and green wings with white false pterostigmata. The larval stage normally lasts two years.

Banded Demoiselle, female.
*Neil Malton*

## Distribution

Banded Demoiselle has an extensive range and is found in much of Europe and Asia. Its European distribution extends northwards as far as southern Finland and to the south into France (except in the extreme south-west), Italy, Corsica, Sardinia and Greece. To the east it extends into Asia, through Russia as far as north-west China.

It is widespread over much of lowland England and eastern Wales and throughout Ireland. It is sparsely distributed in much of Cornwall, Devon, west Wales, the Pennines and the Lake District, particularly in upland areas where relatively few watercourses are of the type favoured by this species. Similar gaps in the distribution occur over the chalk in Dorset, Wiltshire, Hampshire, Kent, East Lincolnshire and the East Riding of Yorkshire.

In north-west England the species was restricted to north Cumbria and one area of Lancashire (River Ribble and tributaries near Preston) at the time of the previous atlas. Since then it has colonised more or less all suitable habitat in North Merseyside and Lancashire, spreading east to the Pennine fringes and north into south Cumbria. The species has also spread in north-east England, and was first recorded in Scotland in 2002 in Dumfriesshire. It has since

Female Banded Demoiselle ovipositing while the male guards her.
*Brian Smith*

been found on rivers around the Solway Firth in the west and on tributaries of the Tweed in the east since 2009.

## Habitat

Banded Demoiselle occurs typically in slow-flowing rivers and streams and is also found in canals. Favoured running waters have a muddy or silty bottom but the species can also occur where sand and gravel are present. The maximum flow rate in occupied watercourses is generally below 5-6m.s$^{-1}$, though this may be exceeded temporarily

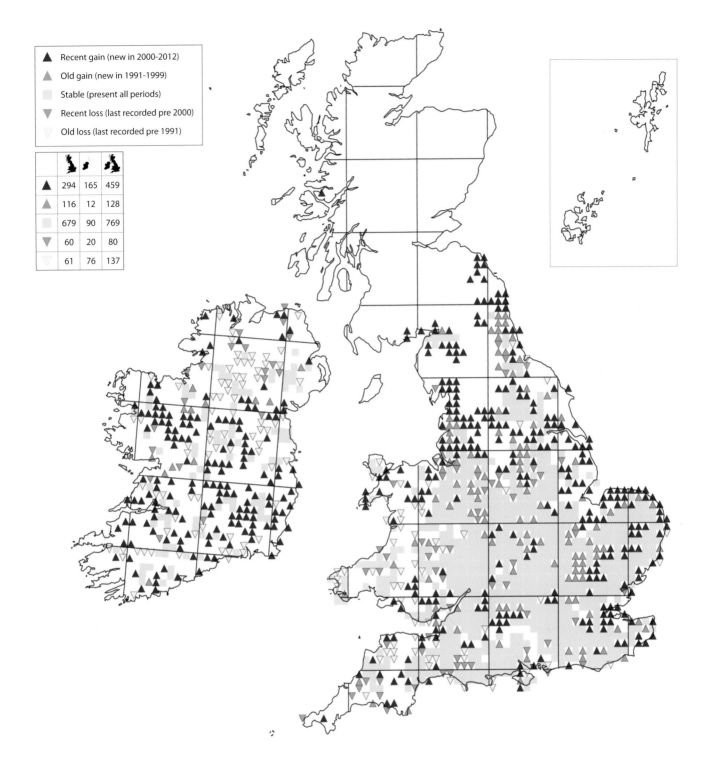

Legend:
▲ Recent gain (new in 2000-2012)
▲ Old gain (new in 1991-1999)
▢ Stable (present all periods)
▽ Recent loss (last recorded pre 2000)
▽ Old loss (last recorded pre 1991)

during periods of heavy or prolonged rainfall (Goodyear, 2000; Grand & Boudot, 2006). The species has been reported from lakes adjacent to flowing water but breeding at such sites has not been established.

Banded Demoiselle has a very strong preference for sites with lush emergent and herbaceous vegetation at the water's edge, low banks and no overhanging trees. These sites are often adjacent to open meadows on at least one bank. It avoids shaded watercourses. In Britain and Ireland it is not found at high altitude, though in France it has been recorded up to about 1200m (Grand & Boudot, 2006).

Banded Demoiselle needs aquatic plants in which to lay its eggs. It has no particular species preference, though water-crowfoots, water-milfoils, Arrowhead and bur-reeds are often used (Siva-Jothy, 2004; Cham, 2004; Benton & Dobson, 2007). For most of the year the larvae are found amongst submerged roots and vegetation such as River Water-crowfoot, Common Water-starwort and Spiked Water-milfoil, all of which require a muddy substrate in order to produce dense growth. During the winter, when flow rates may be particularly high, the larvae burrow into the mud or silt (Siva-Jothy, 2004).

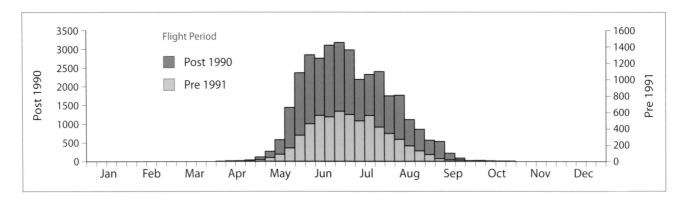

## Conservation status and threats

In Britain and Ireland, Banded Demoiselle is not endangered and is categorised as Least Concern. However, the species is sensitive to pollution and hence it is important to ensure that rivers and canals are unpolluted and that there is continued improvement in those otherwise suitable catchments that do not yet support breeding populations. Water management should aim to maintain healthy amounts of floating and emergent vegetation. Emergence takes place on bankside vegetation, including shrubs and trees, which can produce excessive shading if unmanaged.

## National trends

Banded Demoiselle has increased significantly according the CEH trend analysis (pages 58-63) and has been found in more hectads since the previous atlas. This increase is particularly noticeable in Ireland, where the uniform distribution of new hectad records suggests that the increase may be due to improved recording coverage. The increase has also been noticeable in northern England and Scotland, where the spread northwards has been real. Infilling within the previous atlas range in southern and central England tends to support the idea that improvement in water quality has been an important factor influencing the spread of the species, for example in parts of Sussex (Belden et al., 2004) and Essex (Benton & Dobson, 2007). In Lancashire, there is little doubt that improved water quality has been the overriding factor in the range expansion, which coincided with increases in the distribution of Kingfisher and other riverine birds. Equally, an improvement in the water quality of rivers in the industrial north-east has increased the amount of habitat suitable for the species.

In northern England the species has become common in recent years, in Yorkshire and Northumberland in the east, while in the west it has recently spread northwards into south-west Scotland. It is possible that increasing temperatures have played a part in this northwards range expansion, as for other largely southern species of dragonfly. It may be pertinent that the range in Finland extends some 8° of latitude further north than it does in Britain.

River Foss near York. *Keith Gittens*

River Wensum, Pensthorpe, Norfolk, is a lowland river with high numbers of Banded Demoiselle. *Adrian Riley*

# Beautiful Demoiselle
## *Calopteryx virgo*

Beautiful Demoiselle males have iridescent blue-green bodies and dark blue colouration that nearly covers the entire wings. Like Banded Demoiselle, they are conspicuous, large damselflies of running waters that use their pigmented wings in display. Females have metallic green bodies and coppery-brown wings with a white false pterostigma. Females oviposit into floating vegetation, often submerging in the process. The eggs hatch after two weeks and larvae normally develop over two years.

Beautiful Demoiselle, female. *Steve Cham*

## Distribution

Beautiful Demoiselle is widely distributed in Europe, although populations become more sparsely dispersed towards the Mediterranean and in the north of Ireland, northern Britain and Scandinavia. It is absent from most of western Scandinavia, southern Spain and Portugal and many of the Mediterranean islands. Within its range, three basic forms occur, distinguished by the extent of pigmentation in the wings: form *virgo* in the north, *meridionalis* in the south-west and *festiva* in the south-east, although there are intermediates. The species also occurs in Asia and in north-west Africa in Morocco.

Although it occurs further north in Scandinavia and Finland than in Britain, the species has a predominantly southern and western distribution in Britain and Ireland, reflecting both mild areas influenced by the relatively warm waters of the North Atlantic Drift and an abundance of fast-flowing waters favoured by the species.

In England, Beautiful Demoiselle has a predominantly western and southern distribution. There are large populations in the south-west, south-east (Berkshire, Hampshire, Sussex and Surrey) and the south and west Midlands. The species is widespread in Wales, with populations in Carmarthenshire and Pembrokeshire to the south. In north Wales it is recorded in high numbers along Snowdonian streams, especially on the west side of the area, and along the rivers of the Lleyn Peninsula and the larger rivers of Denbighshire, such as the Elwy, Clwyd and Dee.

Male holding territory at a shallow stream in the New Forest, Hampshire. *Steve Cham*

Its range in the East Midlands has expanded eastwards since 2000, through Warwickshire and into Northamptonshire. Throughout East Anglia and north-east England its distribution is sparse and highly fragmented. In Essex, for example, the species has been known from a single site along the Roman River for many years, although in 2006 another small population was discovered along a

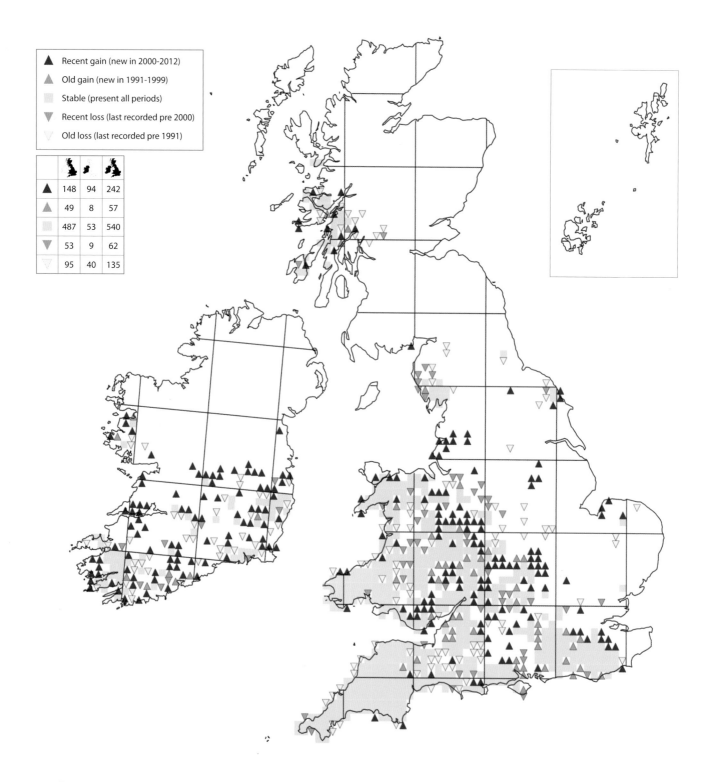

| | | | |
|---|---|---|---|
| ▲ | 148 | 94 | 242 |
| △ | 49 | 8 | 57 |
| ▨ | 487 | 53 | 540 |
| ▼ | 53 | 9 | 62 |
| ▽ | 95 | 40 | 135 |

Legend:
- ▲ Recent gain (new in 2000-2012)
- △ Old gain (new in 1991-1999)
- ▨ Stable (present all periods)
- ▼ Recent loss (last recorded pre 2000)
- ▽ Old loss (last recorded pre 1991)

small wooded stream flowing into the River Colne. There are outposts in the North Yorkshire Moors and the Lake District and, since 2000, the species has spread into Lancashire. Further north, the Scottish distribution is centred in the relatively mild mid-west: on Mull, Islay and adjacent parts of the mainland. The most northerly records are from the south of the Isle of Skye.

In Ireland the species has a distinctly southerly distribution, south of a line from Clew Bay, Co. Mayo in the west, to Dublin in the east. It is widespread in the uplands of counties Wicklow, Kerry and Cork but more local in the lowlands of Munster and Leinster. It is absent from the karst landscapes of Clare and Galway, which isolates the populations in Connemara and south-westernmost Co. Mayo from the main distribution to the south.

## Habitat

Beautiful Demoiselle favours fast-flowing streams and shallow rivers, often lined by trees. These favoured watercourses usually have sandy or gravelly bases, while muddy rivers and those with slow flow rates are avoided. Abundance is highest in shallow sections and lowest in deeper sections; this is thought to be due to the larval requirement for high dissolved oxygen levels (Prendergast, 1988).

Female ovipositing, Ober Water, New Forest, Hampshire. *Adrian Riley*

Upper reaches of River Nene, Northamptonshire, where recent colonisation and range expansion of Beautiful Demoiselle have occurred. *Mark Tyrrell*

Beautiful Demoiselle is tolerant of shade and can frequently be found in woodland streams, provided there are sections with open sunlight. Maturing adults are often found in woodlands perched in trees close to their breeding sites. Females spend much of their time close to breeding sites, returning to the water to mate and lay eggs. While completely shaded sections of rivers are avoided, those that allow sunlight to reach the water are highly attractive and adults will move between sections as light levels change through the day and season. Eggs are laid into floating or submerged vegetation, such as water-crowfoot, which can either be in mid-stream or at the margins.

In the west of Britain, in Devon, Cornwall and Wales, Beautiful Demoiselle is commonly found in shallow, spring-fed streams. In eastern England it occurs close to the sources of rivers where they are narrow, shallow, unpolluted and fast-flowing, as well as in small tributary streams (Tyrrell *et al.*, 2009). Generally, where rivers broaden and flow rates reduce, this species is replaced by the Banded Demoiselle. There are some sites, such as the River Kennet in Berkshire (where the species is especially abundant), the River Tove in Northamptonshire and the River Teme in Worcestershire, that show a diversity of habitat types supporting colonies of both species in equal abundance.

River Kennet, Woolhampton, Berkshire, is a fast-flowing river that supports large numbers of both Beautiful and Banded Demoiselles. *Steve Cham*

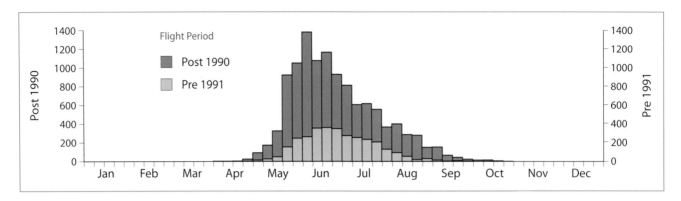

## Conservation status and threats

Beautiful Demoiselle is categorised as of Least Concern in the Red Lists for Britain and Ireland. It faces localised threats from point source pollution events that can eliminate the species, especially in pastoral areas where silage, slurry or sheep-dip has been allowed to escape into watercourses. However, the effects on dragonflies of such incidents are often temporary in nature, provided that a source of colonisation remains upstream. Watercourses that pass through agricultural land also receive fertiliser and sometimes pesticide run-off, the former increasing nutrient levels and encouraging plant growth and hence reducing oxygen levels. When grassland is converted to arable land and soil erosion occurs, nearby watercourses may receive sediments that alter their character, for example by the concretion of gravel beds. Wooded streams may become too shady near their sources when trees are left unmanaged and the canopy cover increases. Climate change, through an increase in extreme drought or lower rainfall, threatens flow rates generally. A reduction in river flow-rates resulting from unsympathetic river management represents a potential threat to this species.

## National trends

There has been a net increase in the number of occupied hectads since the previous atlas, reflecting mainly infilling of records within the earlier range. The CEH trends analysis (pages 58-63) shows that there has been a significant increase in this species. This has been less than those noted for more generalist species and not strongly in a northward direction (except perhaps in central and eastern Ireland). The range has extended eastwards on the River Nene in Northamptonshire, where it was absent prior to 2003, and in Kent there has been a recent north-eastwards expansion. In East Anglia and north-east England there have been a number of new hectad records since 2000. Records from Norfolk at Dersingham, Titchwell and the area near Hoe Rough in 2006, together with a single male seen at Salthouse the following year, have not been repeated and are all thought to refer to migrants.

Silver Stream, New Forest, Hampshire, is a heathland stream with high numbers of Beautiful Demoiselle. *Steve Cham*

# White-legged Damselfly
*Platycnemis pennipes*

Blue Featherleg

White-legged Damselfly is characterised by feather-like, laterally-flattened, white legs with a black stripe, especially prominent in males. The colours of each sex develop from a pale milky '*lactea*' colouration, with increasingly bolder black lines developing along the abdominal segments. Mature males are pale blue and appear slightly longer and paler in colour than males of other blue damselflies. Mature females develop to pale green. Mating takes place at or close to water, with tandem pairs ovipositing in floating plants, roots and other woody debris, often in groups.

White-legged Damselfly, male.
*Steve Cham*

## Distribution

White-legged Damselfly is widely distributed in Europe, with the exception of Iberia and most of Scandinavia. It has not been recorded in Ireland. In Britain, it is confined to the southern half of England and the Welsh borders, where it has a strong association with the major river systems and canal network. The links between lowland rivers and the extensive canal system have enabled this species to colonise most of the linear wetland habitats south of the Wash and the Dee Estuary. However, increasing numbers are also found breeding at still water sites.

Old arm of the Oxford Canal at Wolfhamcote, Warwickshire. This is an important conduit for range expansion of White-legged Damselfly between the River Thames and the rivers in the Midlands. *Kay Reeve*

The principal populations in England and Wales are on the rivers Thames, Great Ouse, Nene, Stour, Severn, Warwickshire Avon, Wye and Dee, together with many of their tributaries. The species is also found on the canals that link these major rivers, including the Oxford, Grand Union and Birmingham Canals. Populations also exist on many of the rivers that drain into the English Channel in Kent and Sussex and on some of the main rivers in the south-west, including the Tamar and Exe.

White-legged Damselfly breeds along much of the length of the Thames from Gloucestershire to Berkshire. Most of the tributaries in this area also hold populations, although counts appear to fluctuate significantly. In addition, the species has colonised well-vegetated still water sites within the catchment. A large population is found on the Oxford Canal, which links the Thames population to those on the canals and rivers of the Midlands. It is also found on some of the Thames tributaries in Hampshire and Surrey, including the Wey and Mole, and the Basingstoke Canal, plus many standing water sites.

The species is recorded from many stretches of the River Great Ouse and its tributaries from Buckinghamshire to the Ouse Washes in Cambridgeshire. There are also populations on the River Nene and Tove in Northamptonshire and the

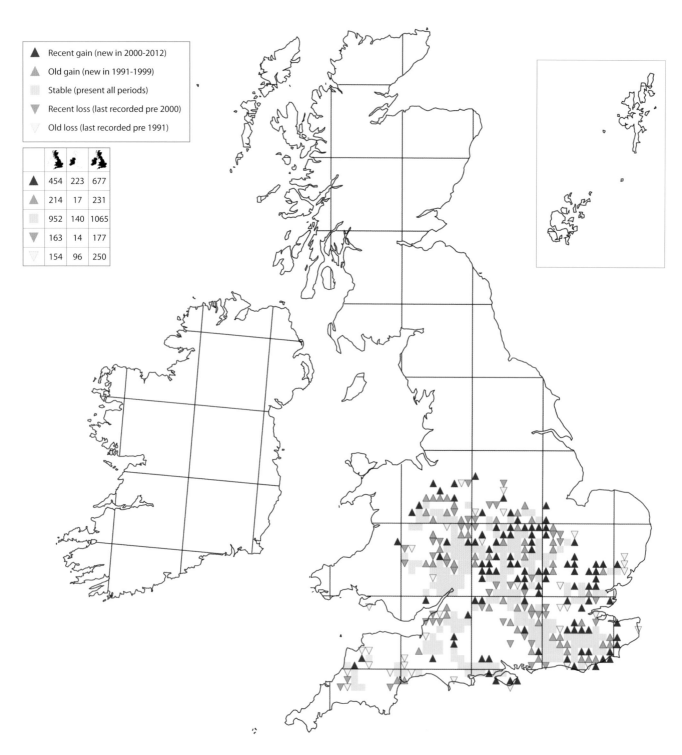

| | | | |
|---|---|---|---|
| ▲ | 454 | 223 | 677 |
| △ | 214 | 17 | 231 |
| ▦ | 952 | 140 | 1065 |
| ▼ | 163 | 14 | 177 |
| ▽ | 154 | 96 | 250 |

Legend:

▲ Recent gain (new in 2000-2012)

△ Old gain (new in 1991-1999)

▦ Stable (present all periods)

▼ Recent loss (last recorded pre 2000)

▽ Old loss (last recorded pre 1991)

Welland and Avon in Leicestershire and Lincolnshire, which mark the northern limits in eastern England. The species is also found on the extensive canal system that links these rivers.

It is found extensively on the Severn and the Warwickshire Avon and on the canals that link the Severn/Avon to the Thames. The westernmost populations in Wales are on the River Wye, its tributaries and the Montgomery Canal. The north-western limits of the distribution are along the River Dee in Cheshire and Denbighshire.

In southern England from Kent to Cornwall the species is found along many of the rivers including: the Beault,

Medway, Eden and Rother in Kent; the Cuckmere, Ouse, Rother and Uck in Sussex; Ober Water, Stour and Moors in Hampshire; Stour, Frome and tributaries in Dorset; the Axe, Otter, Exe and Torridge in Devon; and the Tamar on the Cornwall/Devon border. In Somerset, it is found at West Sedgemoor and on the rivers Avon, Chew and Tone. The species is also present on the Isle of Wight along the River Yar.

In the Weald area of Sussex and Surrey, White-legged Damselfly has long been known as a breeding species on lakes, where it often occurs with Brilliant and Downy Emeralds. Many standing water sites are occupied eastwards into Kent and to the west in the Forest of Dean in Gloucestershire.

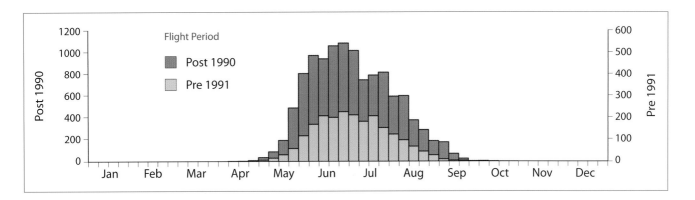

## Habitat

White-legged Damselfly favours unshaded sections of muddy rivers, streams and canals with a moderate to slow flow and luxuriant marginal vegetation. The close proximity of well-vegetated meadows or grassland is important for feeding and roosting. The species can be confined to quite short stretches of river with lush bankside vegetation, while other adjacent habitat remains unused. Although it mainly occurs on flowing water, it has increased at standing waters in recent times.

Females oviposit, whilst still in tandem, into a range of floating plants, roots and woody debris. The strap like floating leaves of Unbranched Bur-reed and Reed Sweet-grass are especially favoured and attract groups of ovipositing tandem pairs. In running waters, the flower heads of Yellow Water-lily are frequently utilised and, at still water sites, a variety of water-lily species are used for oviposition.

## Conservation status and threats

White-legged Damselfly is categorised as Least Concern in the British Red list. It requires moderately clean and good quality water with bank margins composed of lush stands of emergent vegetation. It appears to be susceptible to river management and, whilst it can occur in high numbers, populations exhibit significant fluctuation, often associated with disturbance of the habitat. Over-zealous bankside clearance of rivers and streams has been shown to result in a significant drop in numbers or loss of the species. Conversely, wherever suitable watercourses are managed sympathetically it has shown a marked expansion. It appears tolerant of high levels of boat traffic and water turbidity and on occasion is prolific on stretches of well-used canals, such as the Grand Union Canal. The species has also been shown to recover within a few years on rivers after minor pollution incidents. The restoration of some canals and the decrease in boat traffic on others, leading to better bankside vegetation, could also have aided its spread from one river system to another. White-legged

White-legged Damselflies ovipositing in a group. *Dave Smallshire*

River Severn, Bewdley, Worcestershire, where White-legged Damselfly is found alongside Common Clubtail. *Mike Averill*

Damselfly often coincides with Common Clubtail on mature rivers and is a good indicator species of water/ bankside vegetation quality.

## National trends

The CEH trends analysis (pages 58-63) suggests that White-legged Damselfly has increased significantly. Since the previous atlas there has been some limited range expansion northwards that suggests the current distribution is limited by temperature, combined with availability of suitable habitats. Although the spread has involved established populations moving along rivers and canals, the most significant increase has been in the number of proven breeding records from still water sites.

Rivers in eastern England have seen increases, including the Stour (Suffolk/Essex), Lea, Chelmer, Roding and Cam. Increases have also been recorded along the Warwickshire Avon and the Dee (Cheshire/Denbighshire). A dramatic range extension north along the Ashby Canal in Leicestershire was reported in 2006.

Whilst the species has been recorded from standing waters in south-east England for many years, there has been a recent dramatic increase in proven breeding at such sites elsewhere. Individuals are often encountered several kilometres from known breeding areas and further range

expansion is likely. In Berkshire, the population on the Thames and some of its tributaries has shown a decline since the 1990s, with the strongest breeding populations in this county now on still water sites near Aldermaston and Crowthorne, as well as on a few smaller sites.

In Devon, there have been few recent records from the River Torridge and long stretches of other rivers in Cornwall/Devon apparently lack the species. Access difficulties may account for some apparent declines, but severe point-source farm pollution incidents are likely to have had some impact on populations.

A good population of White-legged Damselfly has become established at Butter Bottom Ponds, Berkshire, and breeding activity is recorded there each year. *John Ward-Smith*

# Small Red Damselfly
## *Ceriagrion tenellum*

Small Red Damselfly has a diagnostic combination of reddish legs, eyes and pterostigmata in both sexes. The thorax is predominantly bronzy-black with fine, pale antehumeral stripes and two black lines on the yellowish sides. In males, the top of the abdomen and face are entirely red. There are four female colour forms with differing amounts of red and black on the abdomen. Larvae usually take two years to develop and their emergence in early summer is unsynchronised.

Small Red Damselfly, male.
*Steve Cham*

## Distribution

Small Red Damselfly is essentially a species of Mediterranean western Europe, being widespread through Italy, France, Spain and Portugal. It is also found more rarely along coastal North Africa, in Sicily, along the Adriatic and in Crete. Its range extends northwards as isolated pockets into Britain, Belgium, The Netherlands, western Germany and Switzerland, where it may be locally common but probably at the limits of its ecological tolerance; its distribution northwards is limited by winter cold

Calcareous fen, Cothill, Oxfordshire, where Small Red Damselfly co-exists with Keeled Skimmer. *Steve Cham*

(Clausnitzer *et al.*, 2007). It has not been recorded in Ireland or Scotland. In Greece and the Middle East the species is replaced by the similar Turkish Red Damsel *C. georgifreyi*.

In Britain the species has a patchy distribution in southern England and Wales and is often locally abundant. Its absence from apparently suitable habitats farther north in Britain indicates that climate limits its ability to complete its life cycle.

In England, its main centres of population are the boggy heathland areas of Berkshire, Surrey, north Hampshire, the New Forest and Dorset; also old tin and clay workings and heathland valley mires in Cornwall and Devon. Elsewhere it has been recorded in more isolated populations, many of which are under threat or already extinct. There is a small population in an alkaline fen at Cothill Fen on the Berkshire /Oxfordshire border. It also persists at Scarning Fen in Norfolk, an alkaline fen well away from any other known extant site. The last records from Suffolk were from Redgrave Fen in the 1940s and Fritton Warren in the 1950s. It became extinct in Cambridgeshire at Wicken Fen, Chippenham Fen and Gamlingay Bog in the latter part of the 19th century. Small populations at two Buckinghamshire heath SSSIs, Burnham Beeches and Stoke Common, were last reported in 1990 and 2000, respectively.

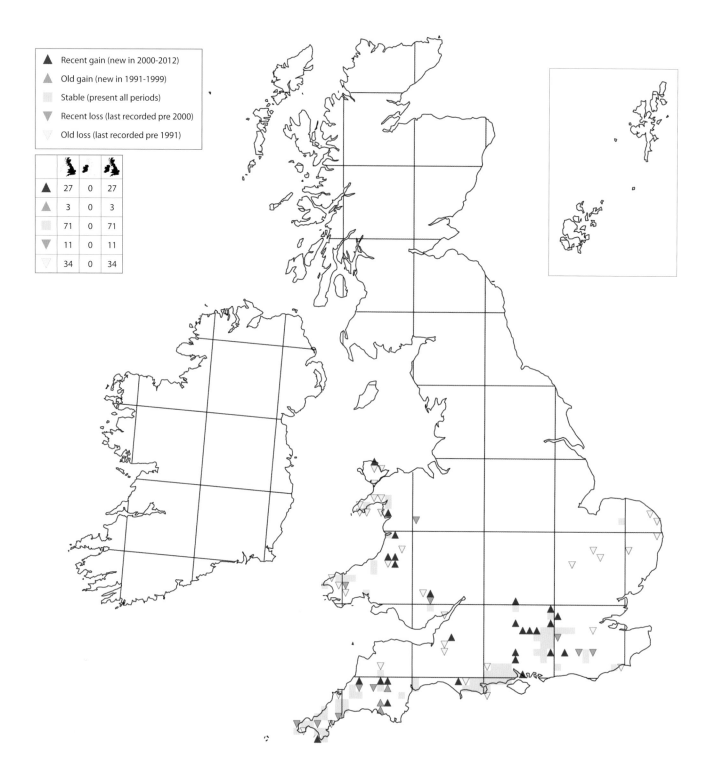

| | | | |
|---|---|---|---|
| ▲ | 27 | 0 | 27 |
| ▲ | 3 | 0 | 3 |
| ▦ | 71 | 0 | 71 |
| ▼ | 11 | 0 | 11 |
| ▽ | 34 | 0 | 34 |

Legend:

- ▲ Recent gain (new in 2000-2012)
- ▲ Old gain (new in 1991-1999)
- ▦ Stable (present all periods)
- ▼ Recent loss (last recorded pre 2000)
- ▽ Old loss (last recorded pre 1991)

The substantial Surrey/Hampshire/Berkshire population was previously thought to be in long term contraction. However, as a result of a significant amount of habitat management, to restore lowland heath, the species has recovered and is undergoing considerable range expansion in the area. There are numerous sites on the Surrey and Hampshire heaths, with large populations especially at Thursley Common, Surrey, and Warren Heath, Hampshire. In west Berkshire there are isolated colonies in the Aldermaston area and in Sussex it is now confined to small, acid heathland bogs, mainly in Ashdown Forest.

The thriving New Forest populations extend from west Hampshire, e.g. Upper Crockford Stream and Ober Water, across southern Dorset, e.g. Moors Valley Country Park, as far as the Bournemouth area.

The species was thought to be extinct in Somerset, where it was lost from several Somerset Levels sites in the early 1970s as a result of peat extraction and drainage. However, in 2006 a new site on the Mendip Hills was discovered at Waldegrave Pool, Priddy.

There are three small colonies in the East Devon Pebblebed Heaths and strong populations are scattered around

Amlwch Port heathland pond, Anglesey. This isolated pool, only 300m from the sea, holds a strong population. It is the most northerly site for Small Red Damselfly in Britain. Until this discovery in 2012, the species was thought to be extinct in Anglesey. *Allan Brandon*

Dartmoor, Devon, where several new sites were found as a result of systematic searching in 1997-8. Only one of two old clay-pit sites in north Devon remains, at Meeth. Modern ball clay extraction has caused the loss of one site in the Bovey Basin and threatens a Dartmoor fringe site (Smallhanger). Cornwall is a particular stronghold, where the main populations in the county are on Bodmin Moor, the mid-Cornwall moors and the tin-streaming areas of Kerrier.

In west Wales, it is locally widespread on the heathland bogs of north Pembrokeshire. The main site on Brynberian is a complex of small pingos. Its distribution extends through isolated small basin mires or heathland bog pools in south Ceridigion to the Cors Fochno NNR raised bog at the mouth of the Dovey Estuary. The remote Carmarthenshire site is also a raised bog. In Gwynedd the species is found in the Harlech area at a series of mainly small, rock basin, *Sphagnum* bogs within a few miles of the coast. Thriving colonies are found on Llyn Hafod-y-llyn, Hafod Garregog NNR and Llyn Tecwyn Isaf in the Penrhyndeudraeth area. The species is also common on the base-rich valley mire of Cors Geirch NNR, which transverses the Lleyn Peninsula.

As a result of afforestation, it has disappeared from the heathland pools of the Newborough Forest area, south-east Anglesey, being last recorded there in 1969. It is also extinct at the calcareous valley mires of north-east Anglesey, the last records being in 1955 at Cors Goch NNR and 1983 at Cors Erddreiniog NNR. However, a thriving population was discovered in 2012 at a small, coastal heathland pool at Amlwch, north Anglesey, this being the most northerly known occurrence in Britain. In east Wales, the present

Crowthorne Wood bog pool, Berkshire, where Small Red Damselfly is abundant. *John Ward-Smith*

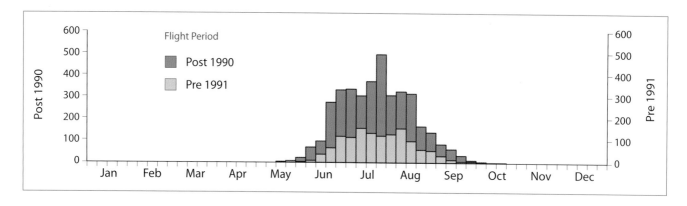

status is uncertain, but there are solitary records from Montgomeryshire (1991), Radnorshire (1989) and Breconshire (1986). The current status in Monmouthshire is also unknown, though there are records from various sites between 1978 and 2004.

## Habitat

Small Red Damselfly typically favours shallow, unshaded bog pools, abandoned small-scale peat and clay workings, peaty ditches and seepages. It is also found at small, slow-flowing streams on warm, nutrient-poor lowland heaths such as in the New Forest. These sites typically support a lush growth of bog-mosses and Marsh St John's-Wort, into which the eggs are laid. Other common plant associates are Lesser Bladderwort, Purple Moor-grass, sedges and Bog-myrtle. It also occurs at base-rich sites, such as calcareous valley mires and rich fens and the shallow, well-vegetated margins of old clay or marl pits. It will breed in the margins of large well-vegetated ponds with neutral or slightly acidic water, especially where these are close to heathlands. These sites seldom support large populations, possibly because of competition from other dragonfly species or because the larvae are susceptible to fish predation. The species does particularly well where it can exploit tiny bog pools, with very shallow water overlying mats of bog-mosses.

## Conservation status and threats

Small Red Damselfly is categorised as Least Concern in the British Red list, but its hectad frequency qualifies it as 'Nationally Scarce B' (i.e. found in 31-100 hectads). It is included in local Biodiversity Action Plans for several areas. Its shallow pools are at risk of neglect and associated scrub invasion. Lowering water tables resulting from abstraction or drainage as well as pollution events will have a negative impact. In East Anglia, the species may once have been widespread but populations have become isolated by increasingly intensive agricultural management. Its only Norfolk site, at Scarning Fen, is currently threatened by excessive abstraction from underground aquifers and by plans to widen an adjacent road.

Populations have been shown to stabilise and expand with appropriate habitat management. These include the removal

of over-shading trees and shrubs to maintain sunny conditions; the introduction of grazing livestock to control vegetation growth and create bog pools; and the construction of bunds to raise water levels. In the Bracknell Forest area, Berkshire, a considerable range expansion has occurred in recent years following extensive management work, with thriving populations now found at Swinley Brick Pits, Owlsmoor Bog, Crowthorne Wood and Caesar's Camp Pond.

Scarning Fen, Norfolk, an area of calcareous fen, holds the only colony of Small Red Damselfly remaining in eastern England. *Adrian Riley*

## National trends

It is clear that Small Red Damselfly has suffered some long-term range contraction, since the mid-1970s and probably for much longer. This is supported by the CEH trends analysis (pages 58-63). There has been an appreciable loss of sites, especially in eastern England, Anglesey and the Lleyn Peninsula, as well as locally elsewhere, as a result of habitat degradation or seral changes. Conversely, since 2000 it has been found at new sites throughout its range, largely as a result of active management for the species and greater recorder effort.

The northern edge of its distribution in Europe appears to be limited by winter temperatures and, as such, the current trend of climate change should favour some northerly range expansion in Britain. Currently, there is little indication of a range expansion to the north or west as a result of climate change. However, its apparent poor dispersal ability may restrict colonisation of the sparsely distributed semi-natural habitats that it favours.

# Norfolk Damselfly
## *Coenagrion armatum*

Dark Bluet

Norfolk Damselfly is a dark insect that resembles an *Ischnura* species. Both sexes of Norfolk Damselfly have a mainly black abdomen. Males have large inferior anal appendages, from which their scientific name derives. They also have blue markings on abdominal segments 1-3 and 8-9, with black on the basal half of segment 2. The antehumeral stripes are either reduced to dots or totally absent. Females have green antehumeral stripes and the abdominal markings are also green covering segment 1 and the basal halves of segments 2 and 8.

Norfolk Damselfly, male.
*Damian Pinguey*

## Distribution

Norfolk Damselfly is a boreal species whose range extends from Europe, across Russia to Siberia and south to Mongolia and Armenia. It is widespread in Mongolia and Siberia but highly localised or absent elsewhere. In the past there were scattered populations north of a line from Eastern England to Romania but it has now disappeared from sites across much of its former range. Within Europe, its strongholds are now in countries bordering the Baltic, as far north as the Arctic Circle. In Lithuania, a population of 100-200 adults was recorded from the Purvinas wetland in 2005 but at most other sites in this country the species is now considered extinct (Ivinskis & Rimsaite, 2009). In the Ukraine, the species could not be found at 10 of the 14 known sites searched in 2007; the last confirmed record from northern Ukraine was in 2003 (Khrokalo & Krylovskaya, 2008). The species was thought to be extinct in The Netherlands after 1956 but a small colony was discovered in the Weerribben wetlands in May 1999 (van der Heijden, 2000). Similarly, two new populations were discovered in Denmark in 2005 and at least 10 previously known populations relocated in northern Germany three years later (Bouwman & Ketelaar, 2008).

In Britain, Norfolk Damselfly was first discovered at Barton Broad, Norfolk, in May 1903, when specimens were collected by Frank Balfour-Browne. Further records from Barton Broad followed in subsequent years and others came from Stalham Broad and Sutton Broad in 1910 and 1912. Although Sutton Broad, Stalham Broad and Big Bog at Sutton are all mentioned in the literature (Brownett, 2005), they are contiguous sites with Barton Broad and it is now difficult to distinguish exactly where the species was observed within the fen habitat surrounding these waterbodies.

In May 1919 a few specimens were taken at Hickling Broad but records then ceased until 1947 when Cynthia Longfield counted about 57 in the Big Bog area of the Broads near Sutton Broad. During this period, in the first half of the 20th century, the species appears to have thrived in this localised area of Norfolk but habitat loss became an increasing threat. Records continued from the same general area until 1953 and, in that year, a further breeding colony was found about 8-9km away at Ranworth Inner Broad. The final mention of this species in Norfolk is found in a letter from Sam Beaufoy, where he states that he continued to see the species until 1958 (Brownett, 2005).

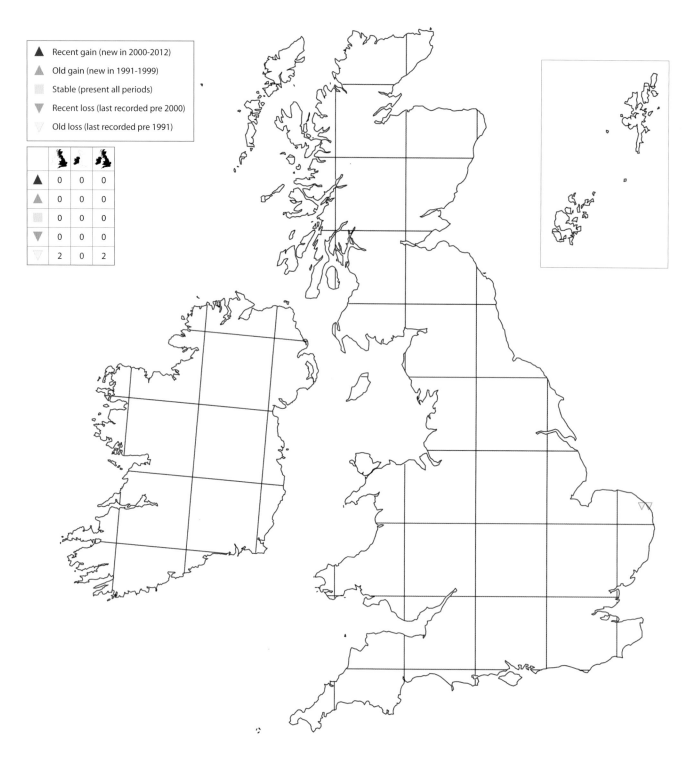

| | ▲ | Recent gain (new in 2000-2012) |
| | ▲ | Old gain (new in 1991-1999) |
| | ▪ | Stable (present all periods) |
| | ▼ | Recent loss (last recorded pre 2000) |
| | ▽ | Old loss (last recorded pre 1991) |

|  |  |  |  |
|---|---|---|---|
| ▲ | 0 | 0 | 0 |
| ▲ | 0 | 0 | 0 |
| ▪ | 0 | 0 | 0 |
| ▼ | 0 | 0 | 0 |
| ▽ | 2 | 0 | 2 |

## Habitat

Within Europe, Norfolk Damselfly breeds in shallow water with abundant emergent vegetation. Vegetation structure is a critical feature and breeding sites often contain sedges, Common Reed, Bulrush or Water Horsetail. Some sites in northern Germany are characterised by Soft Rush with a high coverage of the bog-moss *Sphagnum cuspidatum* but the vegetation structure is similar to that of other locations (Bouwman & Ketelaar, 2008). In Lithuania, Norfolk Damselfly has been observed in thick marsh vegetation beside a river (Ivinskis & Rimsaite, 2009).

## Conservation status and threats

The widespread decline of Norfolk Damselfly in Europe has several possible causes. In the Ukraine it was noted that many of its former sites had suffered from eutrophication and physical damage due to agricultural pressures (Khrokalo & Krylovskaya, 2008). In northern Germany, the species' apparent absence in the late 1970s has been attributed to summer droughts in preceding years (Bouwman & Ketelaar, 2008). Sahlén *et al.* (2004) consider habitat disturbance and alteration due to acidification, eutrophication and desiccation as possible causes.

# Northern Damselfly
## *Coenagrion hastulatum*

Spearhead Bluet

Northern Damselfly males are blue with black markings, whilst females are pea green with the top of the abdomen mostly black. The underside of the eyes and face are green and this can extend to the thorax in both sexes. Abdominal markings on males are variable, though segment 2 typically has a black spear-shape with a line at each side and segments 8-9 are blue with 2 small black spots. Larvae take at least two years to develop.

Northern Damselfly, male.
*Dave Smallshire*

## Distribution

Northern Damselfly is a boreo-alpine species, found in central and north-eastern Europe. Further south, it is present only in relict mountain populations as far as the Pyrenees and the Bulgarian Rhodope Mountains. It is also widely distributed in northern Asia.

In Britain, it has a very restricted distribution in Scotland, being confined mainly to three areas surrounding the Cairngorms: Strathspey, Deeside and Perthshire. These have a continental climate, with cold winters (January mean temperature around 2.5°C) and relatively warm summers (July mean around 14°C). Lying between 85m and 370m above sea level, these areas are lower in elevation and milder, by about 3°C, than the adjacent Cairngorm Mountains.

Northern Damselfly was first recorded from the Aviemore area, Strathspey in 1900, though an 1842 record from Sutherland, outside its present range, is mentioned by Marren & Merrit (1983). The species was recorded at 14 sites during 1978-83 (Marren & Merrit, 1983). Further fieldwork increased this to 26 sites by 1997 (Smith & Smith, 1999). Since then, yet more concerted effort, particularly looking for larvae, has increased the number of sites to a possible 52, some outside the previously known range. The 34

Strathspey sites are centred around Abernethy Forest and Aviemore, extending from north of Grantown towards Kingussie, with two recently-found sites south of Nairn. In Deeside, there are now 12 sites, nine of them concentrated around Dinnet, Glen Tanar and Ballater, and three new outlying breeding sites, one at Castle Fraser to the east and two at Braemar to the west. In Perthshire, there are six sites, four above Logierait and two new sites near Ballinluig. There has also been a casual sighting at Loch of the Lowes.

## Habitat

Northern Damselfly has been recorded from a range of standing waters, including both acidic and neutral waters, ranging from large lochs and small, well-vegetated ponds to tiny pools and an acidic basin mire. Despite this, many apparently suitable ponds within the species' range are not occupied; some of these ponds are less than 100 metres from occupied sites. Smith & Smith (1999) considered that larvae have a limited niche, occupying sites in which emergent vegetation grows sparsely, although some sites occupied recently have denser growth. Larvae cling to pondweed and Water Horsetail and are active in low temperatures.

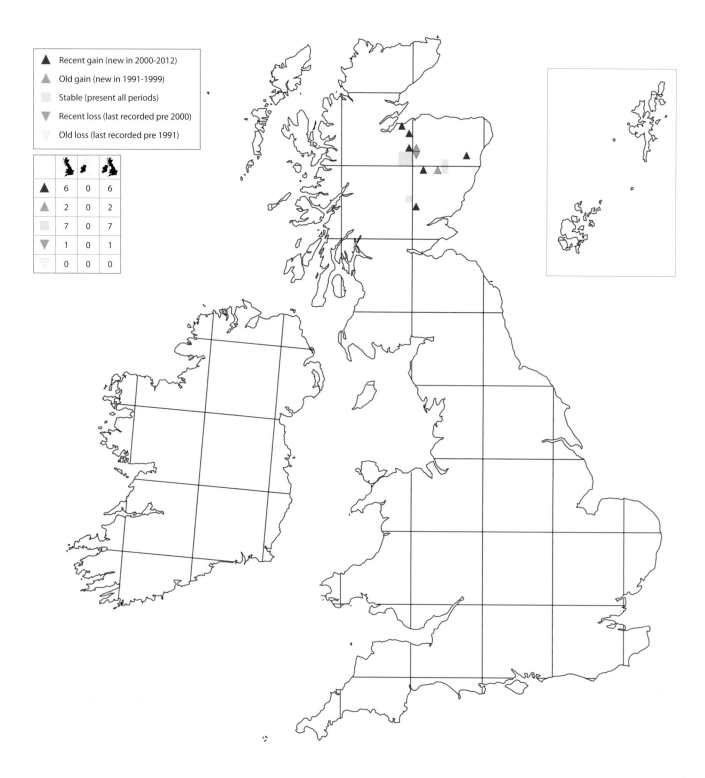

| |  |  |  |
|---|---|---|---|
| ▲ | 6 | 0 | 6 |
| ▲ | 2 | 0 | 2 |
| ▦ | 7 | 0 | 7 |
| ▼ | 1 | 0 | 1 |
| ▽ | 0 | 0 | 0 |

Legend:
- ▲ Recent gain (new in 2000-2012)
- ▲ Old gain (new in 1991-1999)
- ▦ Stable (present all periods)
- ▼ Recent loss (last recorded pre 2000)
- ▽ Old loss (last recorded pre 1991)

Sites are sheltered with stands of emergent vegetation and have a strong association with long established pine or birch woodlands. The species is less conspicuous than other blue damselflies, flying weakly amongst emergent vegetation rather than over large areas of open water. However, many recently-discovered sites are small, shallow and overgrown and, like many older sites, are threatened by infilling through natural succession.

The largest populations of Northern Damselfly are found at waters where Common Blue Damselfly is absent. This species was once the only other blue damselfly with which it co-existed in Scotland. Adults of both these species make

extensive use of the floating leaves of Broad-leaved Pondweed for oviposition. Azure Damselfly has spread northwards into Scotland and is now present at some Northern Damselfly sites. However, it is not known to what extent Northern Damselfly experiences competition with these two species and how this impacts on breeding success.

## Conservation status and threats

In view of its highly restricted range, Northern Damselfly is classified as Endangered in the British Red List. It also appears on the Scottish Biodiversity List under the Nature

Close-up view of the habitat of Northern Damselfly. *Pat Batty*

adults. More recently, even fewer sites have produced counts of this magnitude: one site in Perthshire, where a hundred larvae were estimated, and two in Deeside. Three further sites have held between 20 and 100 adults and 25 sites have produced five or fewer adults; the latter may be insufficient for long term viability. Nevertheless, larvae have been recorded at more than 50% of sites surveyed.

On a more positive note, sites in the Cairngorms National Park, National Nature Reserves and RSPB reserves all have some level of protection. The RSPB has carried out active management for the Northern Damselfly, which has spread to sites created at the Abernethy Reserve as a result of impeding drainage in burns to raise the water table. It has also been found in shooting ponds created since 2000. However, little is known about dispersal rates and extent for this species.

The main threat to the Northern Damselfly is the infilling by vegetation through natural succession of sites. Richards (1998) found that, in the Mid Garten Lochan, sedges were spreading rapidly and open water areas had almost disappeared. Three of the sites surveyed by Smith & Smith (1999) are no longer viable. Five of the current Deeside sites are rapidly infilling and have restricted open water. Some Strathspey sites are similarly threatened but a full assessment has not been made. Active management is needed to maintain sites in a condition suitable for the species. At some sites, open water has been restored and water levels raised, to the benefit of Northern Damselfly.

Conservation (Scotland) Act 2004 and is a key species in the Cairngorms Nature Action Plan. It is one of the scarcest British dragonflies, although its known range has increased since the previous atlas.

Of the 26 sites identified by Smith & Smith (1999), no more than ten were estimated likely to produce in excess of 100

Abernethy Forest, Inverness-shire. *Adrian Riley*

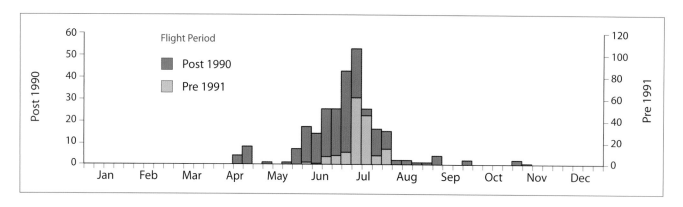

Being a northern species at the edge of its range, Northern Damselfly is potentially vulnerable to climate change, including indirectly through competition with, or predation by, newly-colonising species. Smith & Smith (1999) speculate that Common Blue Damselfly competes with Northern Damselfly: some of the best sites for the latter have none of the former breeding but where they both occur at one site, the Common Blue generally greatly outnumbers this species. Azure Damselfly was not recorded from Northern Damselfly sites at the time of their study but it has since spread northwards and is now found at the Perthshire sites, Insh Marshes, just south of the Strathspey stronghold, and at Castle Fraser. At the last site, during 2009-2013, Northern Damselfly numbers peaked at over 100 in 2010 and 2013, after prolonged cold winters, temporarily outnumbering Common Blue Damselfly. Either side of this period, peak numbers were only half that total and fewer than those of Common Blue Damselfly. In addition, numbers of Azure Damselfly, which can potentially compete with Northern Damselfly, increased annually from the first record in 2009 to almost 100 in 2013. At a new pond, created in 2011, about 80m from the established Castle Fraser site, Northern Damselfly exuviae were first recorded in 2013, indicating rapid colonisation of the new site. Work is urgently needed to determine the limits of the species' dispersal ability, the effects of increased competition with other blue damselflies and its specific habitat requirements.

The Aviemore area of Strathspey has recently undergone rapid building development. One occupied site is threatened by a building project and translocation to a suitable site is planned for 2014.

## National trends

Increases in the range and numbers of sites known to be occupied by the Northern Damselfly are due mainly to increased recording intensity, including sampling for larvae. Strathspey sites are still within the historic range, the early sites around Aviemore having been refound. However, the range has extended south-west towards Kingussie and there are two new sites in the north: south of Nairn in NH85 and NH94. Recent Strathspey records have come from 15 new sites but eight of the 17 sites recorded by Smith & Smith (1999) have not been revisited since 2000; one of these had been destroyed some time prior to 1998.

In Perthshire, there are six known sites for the Northern Damselfly, including two new locations near Ballinluig, found in 2010 and 2013 to the south-east of the known Perthshire sites around Logierait. In 2006, there was a casual sighting from Loch of the Lowes, 12km to the south-east of Logierait.

The discovery of Northern Damselfly within two new Deeside hectads in 2008 is particularly intriguing, as each is remote from the previously-known sites for this species around Dinnet. No more than five adults and larvae have been seen at one of these, 19km to the west at Braemar; a further Braemar site 5km away in the same hectad was discovered in 2013. The site in the second hectad, 32km to the north-east of Dinnet at Castle Fraser, is an established breeding site. Despite searching, no other occupied sites have been found to date in the intervening areas.

Logierait area, Perthshire. *Pat Batty*

# Irish Damselfly
## *Coenagrion lunulatum*

### Crescent Bluet

Irish Damselfly adults appear darker and stockier when compared with other blue damselflies. Adult males are extensively black above, with a contrasting blue 'tail light', and green below and on the 'face'. Females are more sombre and most are black with patches of dusky green between segments. A blue form also exists but its prevalence in Ireland and its relationship to the typical form is not understood.

Irish Damselfly, male.
*Robert Thompson*

## Distribution

Irish Damselfly is a northern Palaearctic species found from Ireland to the Russian Far East and north-east China (Kosterin, 2009; Wu & Bu, 2011) but excluding Britain. The southern limits in the west of the range are in the mountains of central France, Austria, Romania and Turkey. The distribution in Europe is patchy and, whilst it is categorised as Endangered or Near Threatened in Belgium, Czech Republic, Norway and Switzerland, it is more widespread in Finland and The Netherlands.

Since its discovery in Ireland in Co. Sligo in 1981 (Cotton, 1982), Irish Damselfly has been recorded from more than 60 hectads. The total number of known sites is 94, spread over 16 counties. The range encompasses most of the northern half of Ireland. The northernmost site is in Co. Donegal at Lough Napaste (north of Milford) and the southern limit is on the eastern edge of the Burren in Co. Clare at Skeardeen Lough (near Boston). The core of the range is in four counties – Fermanagh, Leitrim, Monaghan and Tyrone. These hold 71 (76%) of the recorded sites. Other counties have five or fewer known sites.

The increase in the range is a result of increased recording intensity away from the known core areas in the previous

atlas. Most of the new sites were found by ad hoc recording. However, there have been two important systematic surveys since 2003, one covering Co. Monaghan in 2008/09 (Woodrow 2008; Woodrow & Nelson 2009) and the other in Northern Ireland in 2012. The Co. Monaghan survey located many new sites in what was an under-recorded county. The 2011 discovery at Skeardeen Lough in the Burren of Co. Clare came as a surprise, as this area is considered one of the better-recorded areas of Ireland. However, there were no records of any dragonfly species in the DragonflyIreland database during the early summer flight period of this species, and so it would appear that it had simply been overlooked.

Skeardeen Lough, Co. Clare. The southernmost Irish site located on the eastern edge of the Burren. *Brian Nelson*

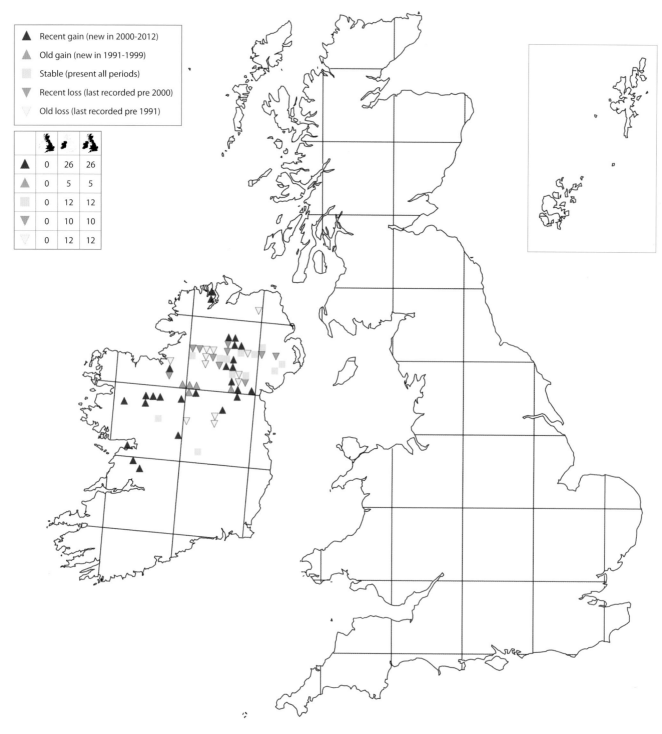

| |  | | |
|---|---|---|---|
| ▲ | 0 | 26 | 26 |
| ▲ | 0 | 5 | 5 |
| ▪ | 0 | 12 | 12 |
| ▼ | 0 | 10 | 10 |
| ▽ | 0 | 12 | 12 |

Legend:
- ▲ Recent gain (new in 2000-2012)
- ▲ Old gain (new in 1991-1999)
- ▪ Stable (present all periods)
- ▼ Recent loss (last recorded pre 2000)
- ▽ Old loss (last recorded pre 1991)

While new sites continue to be found, the status of the species at previously documented sites has not been thoroughly assessed. Many have not been revisited since the initial record. It has not been seen since 1990 in 14 hectads and the trend analysis indicates a decline in this species. It is known from Northern Ireland that individuals can stray several kilometres from breeding sites and appear regularly at unsuitable locations. The most visited colonies are in Northern Ireland, where two surveys have been undertaken. The first was in 1995, covering all sites known at that time, and the second was in 2012, when a sample of sites was resurveyed. The first survey indicated there were some losses from sites and it also revealed that most colonies were small. The 2012 survey catalogued some

additional losses but this was balanced by the rediscovery of small populations at sites where Nelson (1996) had found none. These findings highlight the need for a thorough population study of the species to determine the significance of these fluctuations in numbers.

## Habitat

Most breeding populations of Irish Damselfly are in small lakes. A small proportion of records are from pools in fens and on cutover bogs. The precise requirements of the species are still unknown but the features that seem to be necessary are mesotrophic conditions, semi-natural margins and beds of floating aquatic plants. The occupied lakes are relatively

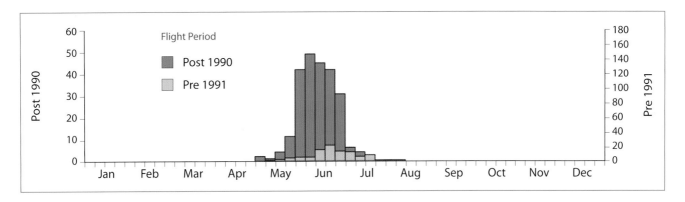

sheltered with small catchments. Some are fed by ground water. The pH of the water appears not to be as significant a factor as its nutrient status. The marginal vegetation of sites is characterised as natural and typical of mesotrophic lakes, with a low, open structure dominated by sedges, horsetails and bur-reeds. Tall species, such as Common Reed and Bulrush, are typically scarce or even absent. Submerged and floating-leaved plants do seem to be necessary as they provide males with perches and ovipositing pairs with egg-laying sites. These features are absent from some lakes and whether they are essential needs further study. The occupied lakes are usually surrounded by low-intensity farmland or semi-natural habitat. The sites in Ireland conform to descriptions of occupied habitats in Europe, which supports the view that the species is native to Ireland.

Cullentra Lough, Co. Tyrone. A typical mesotrophic lake site for Irish Damselfly with abundant floating-leaved aquatic plants. *Brian Nelson*

## Conservation status and threats

Irish Damselfly is legally protected at all times in Northern Ireland under Schedule 5 of the Wildlife Order as amended by the Wildlife and Natural Environment Act (Northern Ireland) 2011. It was listed as a priority species on the Northern Ireland BAP and was assessed as Vulnerable on the Irish Red List. Whilst it has an endangered status in some European countries, it is categorised as Least Concern on the European Red List.

Irish Damselfly is most abundant in mesotrophic water and so the main threat to the species is considered to be eutrophication and the habitat changes that result from it. Where water conditions are more eutrophic, the species appears to lose out to Variable and Azure Damselflies. Eutrophication will have many causes and is usually site specific but intensification of the land use around sites is considered to be a major factor generally. Losses at specific sites have been caused by loss of open water habitat through natural infilling or drainage. Loss of open water is the most immediate threat to the few colonies that exist in flooded peat cuttings. As this is a northern species, there may also be an impact of climate change, either through habitat changes or competition from species of a more southerly distribution.

## National trends

The current trends in the Irish population are considered to be negative. Surveys in Northern Ireland shows the species has apparently declined in abundance at individual sites or even disappeared. Determining declines in a species is difficult, as recording has been non-systematic and based on non-standardised assessments of adult numbers. The status at many occupied sites, especially in the Republic of Ireland, has not been determined. The evidence suggests there are just a few large populations and that these need to be identified and protected. This has been done in Northern Ireland, where Irish Damselfly is listed as a feature of a number of ASSIs (Areas of Special Scientific Interest). Most of the sites in the Republic of Ireland are not covered by any designation.

The absence of Irish Damselfly from Britain is an enigma, given its presence in Ireland and from the Low Countries eastwards. Apparently suitable habitat is considered to be present in Britain in former peatland areas of Norfolk, Somerset, Anglesey and western/southern Scotland. It is possible, given an increasing population in The Netherlands, that natural colonisation may occur across the North Sea at some time.

# Southern Damselfly
## *Coenagrion mercuriale*

### Mercury Bluet

Southern Damselfly is one the smallest British damselflies, found in highly localised populations along slow-flowing streams. Males are bright blue with black markings and are identified by the black 'mercury' mark on segment 2 of the abdomen. Females have a mainly black abdomen and occur in two colour forms: olive-green and a rarer blue form. Oviposition into various aquatic plants occurs in tandem. In Britain, the species has a two year life cycle.

Southern Damselfly, female. *Steve Cham*

## Distribution

Southern Damselfly is a west European near-endemic, occurring from France, Germany and Italy to Iberia and westwards to north-west Africa. It has disappeared from many sites in the east and south of this range, while at its northern limits it is close to extinction in The Netherlands, Belgium and Luxembourg. Additionally it has declined and is now local in Britain, Germany and Italy.

The highly-localised British populations are mostly below 100m above sea level. The species has a predominantly south-western distribution in Britain, in areas influenced by the North Atlantic Drift. Its strongholds include the heathlands of the New Forest, Hampshire, the Preseli Mountains, Pembrokeshire and water meadow ditch systems around chalk streams in the Itchen and Test Valleys, Hampshire. Scattered heathland populations also occur on Dartmoor and the East Devon Pebblebed Heaths, Devon, Purbeck in Dorset, and Gower in south Wales, while there are very isolated calcareous fen sites in Anglesey and Oxfordshire. Increased recording intensity for this species since its inclusion as a UK BAP Priority Species (DoE, 1995) has resulted in the discovery of populations in six new hectads in the New Forest, Dartmoor and Gower.

Several populations of Southern Damselfly in Britain have been lost since the 1950s. These include single sites in west Cornwall and south Somerset; several sites in Devon and Dorset; the most easterly New Forest and southerly Brecon Beacons populations; and two out of three populations in Pembrokeshire. One East Devon site that was lost in 1991 has been repopulated with adults translocated under Natural England licence from the New Forest.

Parsonage Moor, Cothill, Oxfordshire, is one of the more isolated sites where a small population is found. *Steve Cham*

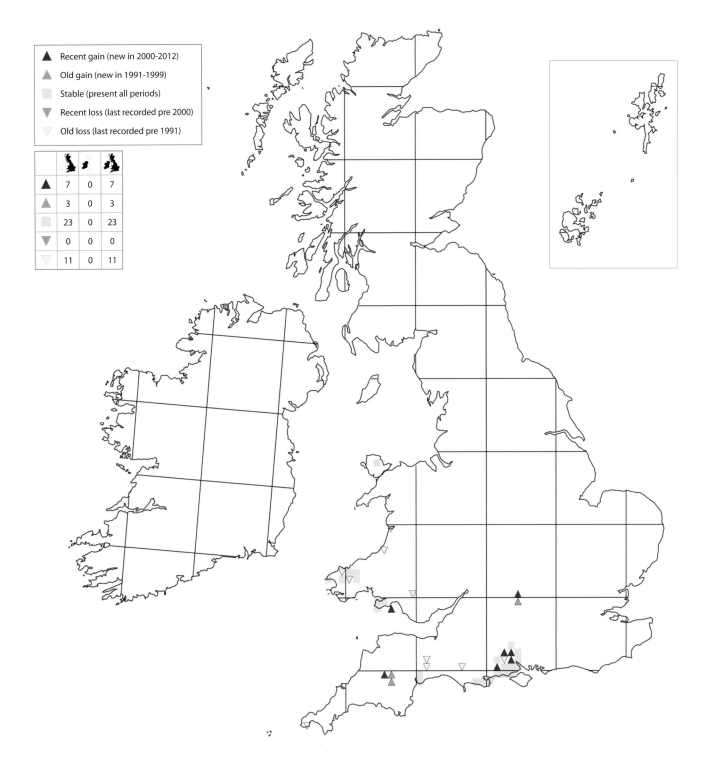

| | | | |
|---|---|---|---|
| ▲ | 7 | 0 | 7 |
| ▲ | 3 | 0 | 3 |
| ▪ | 23 | 0 | 23 |
| ▼ | 0 | 0 | 0 |
| ▽ | 11 | 0 | 11 |

Legend:
- ▲ Recent gain (new in 2000-2012)
- ▲ Old gain (new in 1991-1999)
- ▪ Stable (present all periods)
- ▼ Recent loss (last recorded pre 2000)
- ▽ Old loss (last recorded pre 1991)

## Habitat

Southern Damselfly is found in three different habitat types in Britain: heathland streams and runnels, chalk streams and calcareous fens. Within these habitats it occupies a narrow range of similar environmental conditions. The watercourses occupied have no more than a moderate flow and include: shallow flushes, runnels and streams at heathland and fen sites; and ditches, preferably with berms (raised ledges) at chalk stream sites. These berms are generally well-vegetated and result in warmer, shallower, slow-flowing areas with shelter. The watercourses are either spring-fed or groundwater-fed and most originate from soft, base-rich deposits. This provides a relatively constant temperature, reducing the risks of freezing and extreme low water levels. The occupied watercourses are well-oxygenated, more or less base-rich and with low nutrient levels (Evans 1989; Purse, 2002; Roquette, 2005). They have an inorganic calcareous substrate overlain by a shallow, dark peat or silt layer, which absorbs sunlight and helps to warm the water. Low banks reduce shading of the watercourse and allow access for livestock, which help to control the growth of plants such as Purple Moor-grass and Black Bog-rush, as well as scrub encroachment. The adults fly low and weakly along open watercourses and through low vegetation.

Tandem pairs oviposit into lush herbaceous growth in streams and flushes. *Steve Cham*

Suitable habitats support a range of plant species, with their microhabitat distribution related to small-scale variations in physical parameters. Plants often found in heathland sites include Marsh St. John's-wort and Bog Pondweed (Rodwell, 1991). At chalk stream and fen sites, typical plants include Reed Sweet-grass, which grows in unshaded conditions, Fool's-water-cress and Water-cress. Fen sites are dominated by Black Bog-rush and Blunt-

Prewley Moor, Devon. *Dave Smallshire*

flowered Rush. It is likely that the Southern Damselfly uses plant species and communities as structural cues to the suitability of a site (Purse, 2002). There must be some areas of open water, but a good proportion of the watercourse should be vegetated. First-year larvae have been found in detritus among plant roots and in the foliage of aquatic plants, whereas second-year larvae have only been found in the latter (Roquette, 2005). Eggs are laid into submerged or semi-emergent plants with soft stems and thin cuticles. Emergent plants with rigid, upright stems such as the Common Spike-rush and Jointed Rush are used as supports during emergence.

The species favours relatively open areas where bankside vegetation is sparse and includes low tussocks of grass, rush, sedge and shrubs such as Bog Myrtle, heathers and gorse species. Bankside trees are detrimental, because their shade reduces water temperature and their presence hinders flight manoeuvrability (Roquette, 2005). The habitat adjacent to Southern Damselfly sites is most frequently valley mire with grazed areas of heathland or grazed meadows at chalk stream sites (Purse, 2002 and Roquette, 2005).

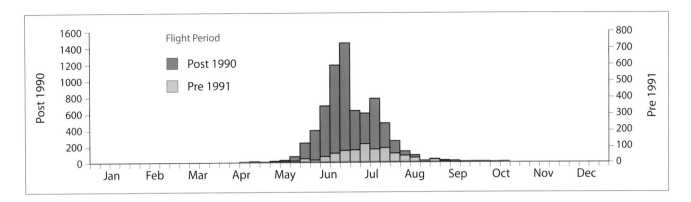

The best Southern Damselfly sites have been maintained for many years through moderate to heavy grazing, preferably by cattle and horses or ponies, with periodic human intervention, usually to control scrub. This type of grazing results in a mosaic of tussocks and shorter vegetation, reduces encroachment by scrub and emergent plants, tramples the bankside and creates areas of bare ground that floods, giving areas of diverse depth and flow that may be colonised by aquatic plants (Purse, 2002). Ideally, overshading scrub is absent, although limited amounts provide shelter for adults. Some heathland sites have been burned to control excessive vegetation prior to the introduction of livestock. Where watercourses have become deeply incised or 'piped', mechanical intervention has helped to restore open watercourses.

Upper Peaked Hill, New Forest, Hampshire where one of the largest populations in Britain can be found. *Steve Cham*

## Conservation status and threats

Southern Damselfly is listed as Near Threatened in the European Red List, Endangered in the British Red List and is listed as a UK BAP Priority Species. The species and its habitats are protected under the following European and UK legislation:

Bern Convention on the Conservation of European Wildlife and Natural Habitats (1979), Appendix II.

EU Habitats Directive (1992), Annex II.

Wildlife and Countryside Act 1981 (as amended), Schedule 5.

Natural Environment and Rural Communities Act (2006), Sections 41 and 42.

Conservation of Habitats and Species Regulations 2010 (England and Wales).

Eight British sites containing nationally or internationally important populations of Southern Damselfly have been designated as Special Areas of Conservation (SAC) under the EU Habitats Directive. It is also found in two other SACs but it was not a primary selection feature for these.

Many occupied and former sites are very small, exposing them to the risk of local extinction during periods of inadequate grazing, for example. Southern Damselflies are poor dispersers; therefore habitat fragmentation, with associated reduction in genetic diversity, is a threat (Purse, 2002, Roquette, 2005). Ideally, occupied sites should be linked, although the scarcity of suitable, base-enriched watercourses is an important limiting factor for this species.

## National trends

The British distribution contracted by an estimated 38% of occupied monads between 1985 and 2001. This followed earlier losses during 1957-65, due to reductions in cattle grazing on heathland, at a site in West Penwith, West Cornwall, and two springline mire sites in the Blackdown Hills, Devon/Somerset.

The latest report to the EU on the condition of SACs concluded that the overall British population is still declining (JNCC, 2013). It is difficult to quantify the most recent decline due to the nature of the surveys undertaken, but some sites throughout the British range have suffered as a result of inappropriate management, mainly a lack of grazing. In most places, action has been taken to try and rectify these problems, but at some sites, especially those on common land, this has been hampered by concerns over the spread of Bovine Tuberculosis and multiple grazing rights.

# Azure Damselfly
## *Coenagrion puella*

Azure Bluet

Azure Damselfly is one of the small blue damselflies. Males have a distinctive black U shape on the top surface of the second abdominal segment. Females can be either green or blue forms. Emergence often takes place over a period of about three weeks. Eggs are laid whilst in tandem, being inserted into floating and submerged plant material. The eggs hatch after 2–5 weeks and larvae take one year to develop but can take two in northern Britain.

Azure Damselfly, female.
*Steve Cham*

## Distribution

Globally this species is widespread from north-west Africa across southern and central Europe to southern Scandinavia and into central Asia. This is the most abundant species of the genus.

Within Britain and Ireland, Azure Damselfly is a common and widely distributed species, occurring in England, Wales, the lowlands of south and central Scotland and across most of Ireland. The gaps in the English distribution correspond to the upland areas of northern England and to the dry area of Salisbury Plain. There are gaps in Ireland, many of which

Canonteign, Devon. A series of well vegetated ponds and lakes provide ideal habitat for Azure Damselfly. *Steve Cham*

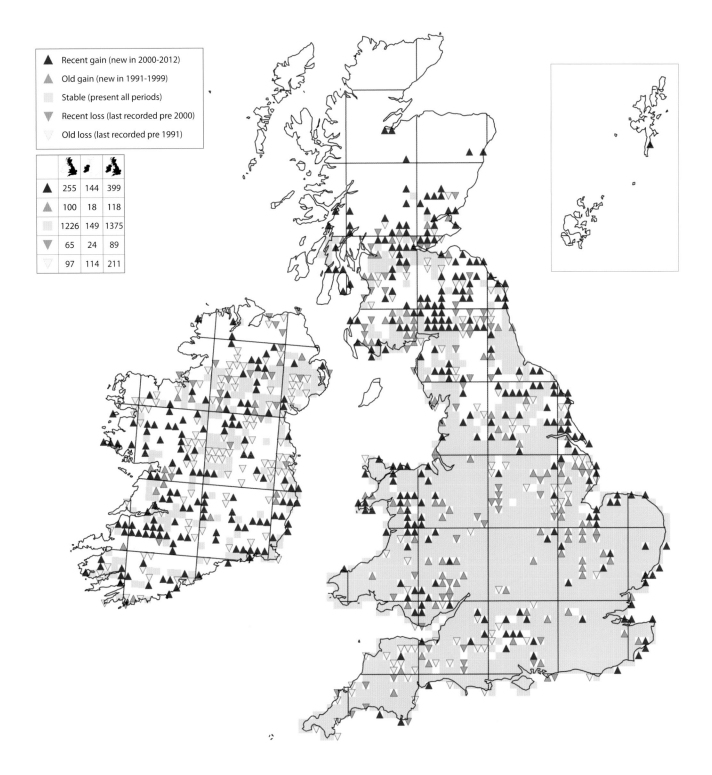

| |  |  |  |
|---|---|---|---|
| ▲ | 255 | 144 | 399 |
| ▲ | 100 | 18 | 118 |
| ▦ | 1226 | 149 | 1375 |
| ▼ | 65 | 24 | 89 |
| ▽ | 97 | 114 | 211 |

**Legend**

- ▲ Recent gain (new in 2000-2012)
- ▲ Old gain (new in 1991-1999)
- ▦ Stable (present all periods)
- ▼ Recent loss (last recorded pre 2000)
- ▽ Old loss (last recorded pre 1991)

are related to limited recording intensity. Some regions, for example north-west Co. Mayo, Co. Donegal and Co. Antrim, lack suitable habitat or, like much of northern Scotland, have an unsuitable climate.

## Habitat

Azure Damselfly breeds in a wide range of waterbodies but prefers sheltered ponds, small lakes, canals and ditches with an abundance of submerged, floating and emergent vegetation at and near the edges. It has also been recorded along slow-flowing stretches of rivers and streams and is a typical breeding species in garden ponds.

Azure Damselfly avoids acidic and exposed sites but will tolerate eutrophic waterbodies to a greater degree than Variable Damselfly. However, it is sensitive to pollution. For example, excessive nutrient levels in ditches in grazing marshes such as the Somerset Levels, typically resulting from agricultural fertiliser spreading or leaching, favour duckweed and algae, which in turn limit the amount of submerged vegetation, to the detriment of Azure Damselflies and other species.

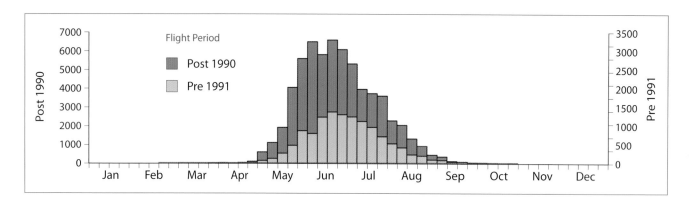

## Conservation status and threats

This species is common and widespread. It is not threatened and thus receives no legal protection. Extensive clearance of emergent, floating and submerged vegetation, which happens frequently in garden ponds and drainage ditches, may significantly reduce populations. Other threats include direct losses due to development and wetland degradation, through eutrophication from agricultural or sewage sources.

## National trends

The CEH trends analysis (pages 58-63) found a slight increase in this species. However, there is little to suggest that populations within the main part of its range have changed significantly. Previous gaps in its range now have records, most likely resulting from increased recording intensity. In Ireland there are some indications that the species has increased at sites as they have become more eutrophic, at the expense of the Variable Damselfly.

There has been a slight northward range expansion in Scotland over the last two decades, where it is now widespread and well established in the south. It has spread northwards to near Inverness and into Aberdeenshire, where it was previously unknown. Azure Damselfly now breeds in some sites alongside Northern Damselfly and this could have future implications for the population of the rarer species. The mapped record from Shetland was an introduction into a garden pond with aquatic plants and similar introductions may also have helped the spread of the species in other areas. Changes in the distribution within Ireland may also be a result of climatic change, or due to increased recording effort during the 2000-2003 DragonflyIreland project. This species is now widespread in wetlands along the Shannon valley and in the drumlin belt across the north of Ireland from Sligo Bay to Strangford Lough.

Butyl-lined garden pond in Chudleigh, Devon. The submerged vegetation is ideal for Azure Damselfly, which is the common 'blue damselfly' in garden ponds. *Dave Smallshire*

# Variable Damselfly
## *Coenagrion pulchellum*

Variable Bluet

Variable Damselfly appears similar to other blue damselflies but typical males have broken antehumeral stripes that often resemble an exclamation mark and a black marking resembling a wine glass on the second abdominal segment. However, both of these features are variable. Females have two colour forms, both of which resemble Azure Damselfly, but the blue form of Variable Damselfly has more extensive blue on abdominal segments 3-7 than its close relative. In both sexes, the distinctive three-lobed pronotum is a key identification feature.

Variable Damselfly, female. *David Kitching*

## Distribution

Globally, Variable Damselfly is recorded across Europe and western Asia, with populations present from Sweden, Norway, Finland and Russia in the north, to the Mediterranean coast in the south. Populations in the south and east often have darker males than those elsewhere and these are sometimes regarded as separate forms or sub-species.

Meadow Lane gravel pits, St. Ives, Cambridgeshire, is a complex of mature gravel pit lakes with a rich flora where Variable Damselfly breeds in high numbers. *Val Perrin*

Variable Damselfly is more common and widespread in Ireland than it is in Britain and is present in an almost continuous broad band from Co. Kerry in the south-west to Co. Down in the south-east of Northern Ireland. The species is absent from much of counties Antrim, Londonderry and Donegal to the north of Lough Neagh except for occurrences in wetlands along the Lower Bann, at several small lakes around Milford in north Co. Donegal and at Sheskinmore in west Co. Donegal. There are few locations for the species on the west coast of Ireland in counties Galway and Mayo, where its distribution appears to be restricted by the presence of oligotrophic waters and areas of upland. Similarly, in the south of Ireland in much of east Munster and south Leinster, the species is localised in distribution and limited by a lack of suitable habitats.

Within Britain, Variable Damselfly has a scattered and patchy distribution with clear concentrations of records in the East Anglian and Cambridgeshire fens, Sussex and east Kent, Somerset Levels, Anglesey, Shropshire and Cheshire meres and Dumfriesshire. It distribution therefore closely relates to the distribution of natural fens. Declines have been noted in northern England.

In Scotland the species is scarce and confined to two main areas. In Dumfries and Galloway (VC72-74) it can be found

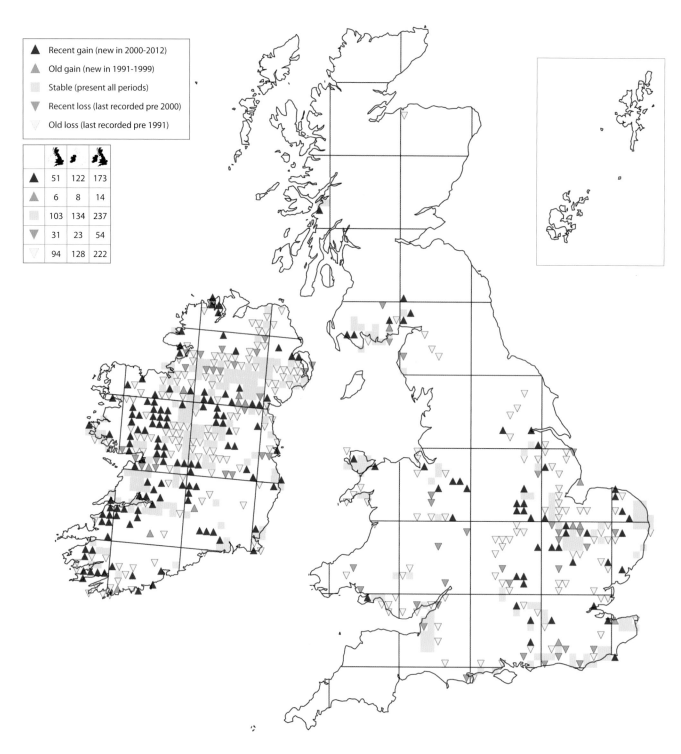

| | ![UK] | ![Ireland] | ![combined] |
|---|---|---|---|
| ▲ | 51 | 122 | 173 |
| ▲ | 6 | 8 | 14 |
| ▪ | 103 | 134 | 237 |
| ▼ | 31 | 23 | 54 |
| ▽ | 94 | 128 | 222 |

Legend:
- ▲ Recent gain (new in 2000-2012)
- ▲ Old gain (new in 1991-1999)
- ▪ Stable (present all periods)
- ▼ Recent loss (last recorded pre 2000)
- ▽ Old loss (last recorded pre 1991)

at sites along the southern coastal fringe, where it is well established and numerous in mesotrophic lochs of various sizes. There are also newly discovered inland sites in the Earshaig Lochan area near Moffat. In Argyll it occurs in good numbers in the Black Lochs area near Oban, where again increased recorder intensity has located new sites for the species in recent years.

In Wales the species is widespread, but very locally and mainly coastally distributed, with fen-rich Anglesey being a major stronghold. There are also three thriving populations near the coast in the south-east of the Lleyn Peninsula at Pen Llyn, Llyn Ystumllyn and Tomen Fawr. Further south in Wales, at Llangorse Lake in Breconshire, the

species is present in high numbers, sometimes numbering thousands on a single day. It has also been recorded from Mynydd Illtyd SSSI and the Usk valley. In Glamorgan the species is more restricted, being found only around the Tennant Canal near Neath and in the adjacent sites of Pant-y-Sais Fen and Crymlyn Bog.

In northern England Variable Damselfly is now restricted to just one hectad in Cumbria, where it inhabits an isolated kettle-hole lake, and two in Yorkshire at Broomfleet and Fairburn Ings.

There is a scattering of sites in the English midlands from Lincolnshire and Nottinghamshire in the east to Cheshire

Langham Pond, Runnymede, Surrey, is an oxbow lake with Variable Damselfly. *Dave Smallshire*

the species was formerly found on Studland Heath but is now thought to be extinct in that county. The third remaining area is on the Somerset Levels, where large populations occur in some of the less intensively managed areas. The species is most often found on dykes and along ditches but it also occurs in ponds and old flooded peat workings, where it can be fairly numerous. At all sites in Somerset where Variable Damselfly is found, it appears to outnumber the related Azure Damselfly.

## Habitat

Variable Damselfly in Britain and Ireland is mainly a species of lowland areas with fens and similar mesotrophic freshwater habitat. Breeding sites are typically small but where it is found on larger sites these are often sheltered, but not shaded, by surrounding carr or other woodland. All habitats are usually characterised by good quality water, abundant aquatic vegetation and still or slow-flowing conditions. Marginal vegetation in these waterbodies often includes Reed Sweet-grass, Yellow Iris, bur-reeds, sedges and rushes. The presence of submerged and perhaps floating vegetation can also be an important attraction for ovipositing pairs. The wetlands are usually surrounded by relatively unmodified and sheltered vegetation which will attract the adult damselflies in large numbers.

In Ireland, Variable Damselfly is often the dominant damselfly at small lakes and fens throughout the central plain and in the drumlin belt that stretches from Clew Bay to Strangford Lough. Populations are also found in low-lying coastal regions, for example Connemara, where maritime influence creates suitable fen conditions.

In Scotland the species breeds in well-vegetated ditches, ponds and lowland lakes, where it co-exists with Azure Damselfly and is often the more numerous of the two species. In north Wales it is again associated with unpolluted, well-vegetated lakes in lowland fens, often

and Shropshire in the west. In Cheshire the main population is at Hatchmere, a large lake of glacial origin in the Delamere Forest and in Shropshire most sightings are from Berrington Pool.

There are a number of newly discovered locations for the species in a band from Cheshire in the west through Staffordshire and Leicestershire to Norfolk and Suffolk in the east. In Norfolk the long established stronghold is in the Broads, with new sites scattered to the south-west of this. In Suffolk the species is found mainly in the Waveney Valley area bordering Norfolk, as well as in the Fens around Lakenheath. There are a few scattered sites in the south and east of the county.

In Cambridgeshire there is a large, well-established population of Variable Damselfly over an extensive area of mature gravel pits around St. Ives. Its range has extended down the River Great Ouse to gravel pits at Little Paxton Nature Reserve where it is recorded in high numbers. At these sites it usually outnumbers other species, including Azure Damselfly, although at other sites in the same county populations remain quite small.

Sites in Berkshire include Cookham, where the species can be found on the White Brook across Widbrook Common, and in the Burghfield area where the Kennet and Avon Canal, River Kennet and some mature gravel pits are all in close proximity. Three further parts of southern England remain as strongholds for Variable Damselfly but again there have been more losses than gains in these areas. In Kent it is found mainly in the marshes and levels in the north-east of the county. In Sussex it can again be found on lowland levels such as Amberley Wildbrooks, the Adur Valley and Pevensey Levels. The species becomes rarer further to the west and there are only three recent locations for the species in Hampshire. These are Sowley Pond in the New Forest, the Moors River north of Bournemouth and a single record in 2005 from the Woolmer Forest. In Dorset,

Llyn Garreg Wen, south-west of Porthmadog, Caernarvonshire, is a well-vegetated lake and one of very few sites for Variable Damselfly and Hairy Dragonfly in the region. *Allan Brandon*

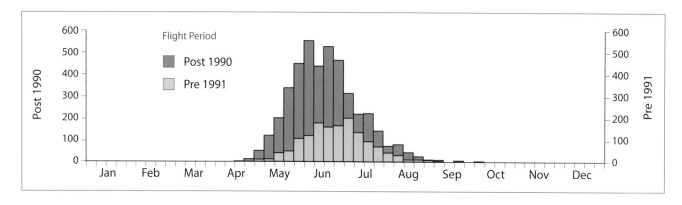

close to the coast. The rich fens of Anglesey are a particular stronghold, while further south in Wales occupied sites include a large shallow lake of natural origin, a complex of shallow pools in an upland bog at about 300m elevation and a meandering and oxbow-rich section of river with surrounding swamp.

In the northern half of England the species appears to be most abundant on larger, deep-water pits, often of glacial or man-made origin. In Cheshire and Shropshire this includes natural meres and artificial marl pits and, in south-east Yorkshire, long-abandoned clay extraction pits. In eastern England many populations are found in gravel pits which have been colonised from nearby fen populations. The common factor linking these sites is again extensive emergent vegetation, frequently giving a fen-like character to the locations.

In central, southern and eastern England, the main habitats include ditches and dykes within grazing marshes or fen. The ditches and dykes are usually slow-flowing, although slower bays and backwaters with luxuriant marginal vegetation can also be occupied on faster-flowing watercourses.

## Conservation status and threats

Variable Damselfly has declined in Britain and is listed as Near Threatened in the Odonata Red Data List but it is Least Concern on the Irish Red List, reflecting its more general abundance there. The greatest threat to this species is the decline in water quality through enrichment, which is linked to agricultural intensification. Pollution from point sources, such as rural houses, can also be a significant driver of enrichment as the catchments of many sites are small. In southern England, many populations are restricted by management of ditch systems that removes aquatic vegetation. In the Somerset Levels, for example, the best sites persist in more remote areas where agricultural influences are limited by poor access.

Summerhill Lough, Cos. Fermanagh and Monaghan. A marl lake with fen and swamp. *Brian Nelson*

## National trends

Variable Damselfly has shown a significant loss of sites throughout much of its English and Welsh range, although this has been balanced by gains in some areas as the species has colonised artificial sites. In southern central England, many former sites would appear to have been lost. The last records from Warwickshire date from the 1930s and the species has similarly disappeared from north Oxfordshire in more recent times. Further south, in the Cothill Fen and Parsonage Moor area on the borders with Berkshire, the species persisted for many years in reasonable numbers. However, there have been no recent records from the site and it is feared lost. Populations with high numbers exist at many sites in Ireland and there is no evidence of any significant reduction in numbers or range there. The situation in Scotland also appears to be relatively stable. Evidence indicates the species requires good water quality and suffers with increase in eutrophication, which is a continuing threat to many populations. Natural succession, especially at artificial wetlands, also causes loss of breeding sites.

However, the species appears to be relatively mobile and there have been significant gains across much of its range since the year 2000. It appears that the species has colonised new sites as they became suitable and a good example of this is the colonisation of Little Paxton Gravel Pits in the Great Ouse Valley in Cambridgeshire.

# Dainty Damselfly
## *Coenagrion scitulum*

### Dainty Bluet

Dainty Damselfly is similar in both appearance and many aspects of its biology to other blue damselflies although, like Southern Damselfly, it is a relatively warmth-loving species. The abdomen of the male is characterised by a 'stalked wine glass' shape on segment 2 and by segment 6 being completely black. Females typically show much more blue on the abdomen than other similar species. It recolonised Britain after an absence of over 50 years and has a one year life cycle, overwintering in the egg stage.

Dainty Damselfly, male.
*Steve Jones*

## Distribution

Dainty Damselfly has a principally Mediterranean distribution, occurring in parts of North Africa, southern and central Europe and east to Turkey, Armenia and Iran. Whilst the species is rather local in some parts of its range, southern European populations are widespread, especially in the west. In northern Europe, there are isolated historic records from sites as far north as northern Germany, some of which refer to now extinct breeding populations. In addition to these old records, the species has been expanding its core range northwards in recent decades, probably in response to climate change. Following a long absence, the species was recorded again from Belgium in 1998 and numerous colonies are now established. In 2003, the first record came for The Netherlands, where a small population now exists. There have been recent records from many southern and western parts of Germany. In Jersey, the species reappeared after a fifty year absence in 2009, when two small colonies were discovered in the south of the island.

In Britain, Dainty Damselfly was first noted in 1946 near Benfleet, Essex, where subsequently a strong colony was discovered at a pond just a few miles away. The species bred successfully in the area scitulum until 1952. The great coastal floods that affected much of the coastline of south-east England in early 1953 exterminated the population and as a result the species was declared extinct in Britain.

A small scale reintroduction, using 160 larvae and four adults from France, was attempted at Hadleigh Country Park on 1 June 1995. One male was later observed flying at the site on 22 July the same year. In 1996 further monitoring revealed two pairs at a neighbouring pond and oviposition took place. In 1997 only one, or possibly two, individual males were seen. Despite further searches in the area over that and subsequent years, no further individuals were located.

During fieldwork for this atlas, Dainty Damselfly was re-discovered on the Isle of Sheppey, Kent, on 21 June 2010 (Brook & Brook, 2011). Although close to the former Essex sites, it seems unlikely that this population is a relict from when those sites were active. The discovery, at the time, of four exuviae in addition to flying adults indicates that colonisation of Kent must have taken place some time prior to 2010. By 2012, the species had been recorded from three hectads on the Isle of Sheppey and the adjacent mainland.

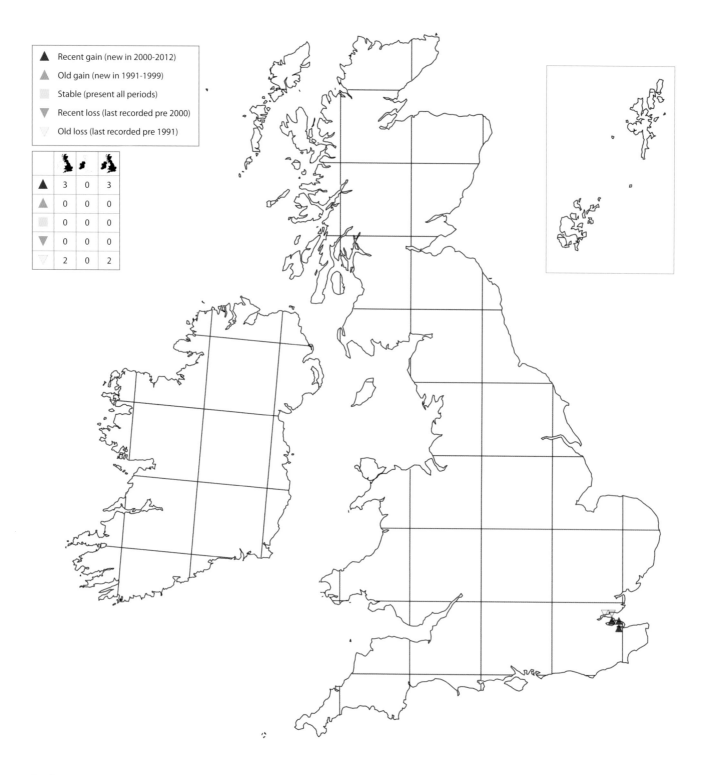

| | UK outline | | |
|---|---|---|---|
| ▲ | 3 | 0 | 3 |
| ▲ | 0 | 0 | 0 |
| ▦ | 0 | 0 | 0 |
| ▼ | 0 | 0 | 0 |
| ▽ | 2 | 0 | 2 |

Legend:
- ▲ Recent gain (new in 2000-2012)
- ▲ Old gain (new in 1991-1999)
- ▦ Stable (present all periods)
- ▼ Recent loss (last recorded pre 2000)
- ▽ Old loss (last recorded pre 1991)

## Habitat

Dainty Damselfly is a warmth-loving species and, over most of its range, it favours sunny, still or slow-flowing waters, typically with rich aquatic vegetation, frequently dominated by water-milfoil or hornwort species. Oviposition takes place into this surface vegetation. Many shallow ponds, ditches and dykes provide a suitable habitat for the species and, in Continental Europe, some recently abandoned gravel pits have also been noted to hold Dainty Damselfly.

In Britain, two of the three main sites for the species are brackish drainage dykes in treeless, coastal grazing marsh.

The dominant submerged water plant here, forming a mat at the water surface, is Spiked Water-milfoil, into which the damselflies oviposit. The margin of these dykes is densely vegetated with Sea Club-rush. One dyke is steep-sided, the other not so. By contrast, the third site is a large pond set in grassland with a few trees nearby. Here the submerged water plants are Canadian Waterweed and Rigid Hornwort, currently covering only a very small area of the pond. In 2012, the largest part of the pond appeared to be devoid of water plants, having been cleared of almost all vegetation since the site was first identified in 2010. The margin is sparsely vegetated with Sea Club-rush, Lesser Bulrush and Common Spike-rush.

Site for Dainty Damselfly on the Isle of Sheppey, Kent. *Gill Brook*

clearance of ponds and dykes, is a potential threat. The original 2010, and best known, site also faces a number of more immediate issues. The high number of visitors to the site has caused discernible trampling of the surrounding vegetation, the effect of which is unclear. The site also holds a significant population of Marsh Frogs, predation by which presents a potential threat.

The Isle of Sheppey and North Kent Marshes contain much apparently suitable habitat for Dainty Damselfly, which may allow it to spread out from its present sites and so buffer itself against any adverse pressures or changes. Most pertinent amongst these is the threat of saline intrusion into coastal wetlands, either insidiously through leaky drainage valves or by an extreme flooding event, such as the one in 1953 that exterminated the Essex population.

## Conservation Status and Threats

Previously categorised as Regionally Extinct, Dainty Damselfly reappeared in Britain too late for its status to be reappraised for the Red List for Britain. It is categorised as Least Concern in the European and Mediterranean Basin Red Lists but rated as Near Threatened in North Africa.

Since it is established in a small area of Kent at present, the new British population must be considered as potentially vulnerable, especially as precise population trends are still unclear. Habitat degradation, including inappropriate

## National trends

Dainty Damselfly was previously recorded from Britain during a short period in the mid-20th century, coincident with a period when annual mean temperatures were frequently above the long-term average. As well as the English records described above, there were also sightings in the Channel Islands, specifically from Jersey in 1940-41 and from Guernsey in 1956. However, all these sightings came to an end and the species was then absent for many

Dainty Damselfly ovipositing in tandem, Kent. *Gill Brook*

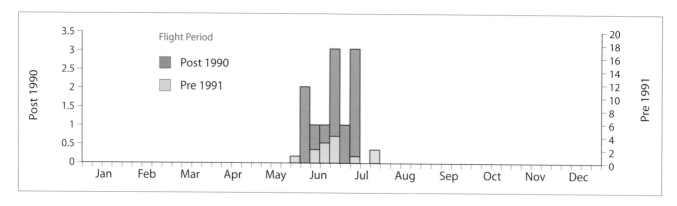

years. As mean annual temperatures began to rise again, the last 15 years of the century saw a significant increase in sightings on the near Continent (Vanderhaeghe, 1999). This trend has continued into the present century and culminated in a return of the species to Jersey in 2009 and to England sometime around 2010. In both areas, established breeding populations are now present, though it is perhaps still too early to judge how they will fare in the longer term. In 2012, approximately 12 individuals were noted at the 'pond' site in North Kent, while poor weather interfered with surveys of the other areas. At one previously occupied site, none was found during 2012-13; however, a new site, close to previous ones, was discovered in 2013.

As yet, no new colonies beyond the ones on the Isle of Sheppey/North Kent Marshes have been discovered in England, but this may perhaps simply reflect a lack of systematic searching. The species is similar to other blue damselflies and could easily be overlooked. Given increasing population trends on the near Continent and the likelihood of continued climate change, it seems highly probable that more colonies will become established.

Private pond, Kent, where Dainty Damselfly has been recorded ovipositing. *Gill Brook*

# Common Blue Damselfly
## *Enallagma cyathigerum*

Common Blue Damselfly is one of several small blue damselflies that can easily be confused. Males can be distinguished by a characteristic black 'lollipop' marking on the top of segment 2 of the abdomen. On the thorax, both sexes have broad, pale antehumeral stripes and lack one of the two short black lateral stripes which are typical of *Coenagrion* damselflies. Females may be green, brown or blue, with 'rocket-shaped' black markings on the abdomen. Emergence can occur in such high numbers that exuviae accumulate one on top of another.

Common Blue Damselfly, male. *Anthony Taylor*

## Distribution

Common Blue Damselfly is a very widespread Palaearctic species, occurring from the Mediterranean to north of the Arctic Circle and eastwards to the Pacific coast of Asia. Until recently it was also thought to occur in North America but genetic studies have shown it to be a separate species, *E. annexum*. Common Blue Damselfly is widespread throughout Britain and Ireland, reaching the Hebrides, Orkney and Shetland Islands. Infilling of records within this range has resulted from the creation of new ponds, lakes and flooded mineral workings.

Broom gravel pits, Bedfordshire, supports a very large population of Common Blue Damselfly with males swarming over the water's surface. *Steve Cham*

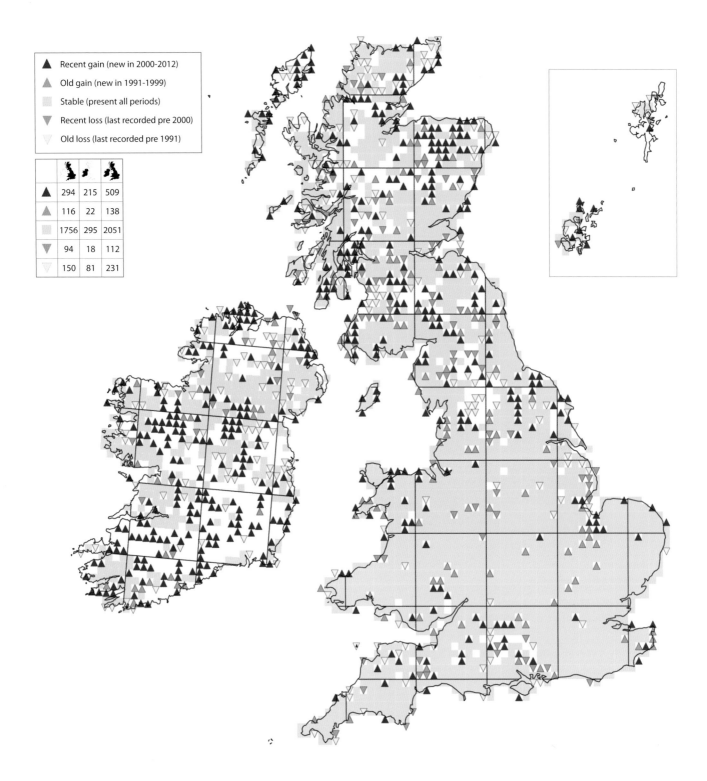

| | 🇬🇧 | ∫ | 🇬🇧 |
|---|---|---|---|
| ▲ | 294 | 215 | 509 |
| ▲ | 116 | 22 | 138 |
| ■ | 1756 | 295 | 2051 |
| ▼ | 94 | 18 | 112 |
| ▽ | 150 | 81 | 231 |

## Habitat

Common Blue Damselfly breeds in a wide range of running and still water habitats. It frequents slow-flowing rivers, canals and large drains and can be especially abundant at lakes, reservoirs, flooded mineral workings and large ponds. It tolerates a wide range of conditions, from acidic to alkaline and from oligotrophic to eutrophic, but is most abundant at neutral-alkaline eutrophic waters typical of lowland areas. It characteristically favours open water habitat more than other blue damselflies and males are commonly seen flying close to the surface well out over the waterbody. The species is generally absent from small ponds and narrow ditches and other watercourses. It occurs at higher altitude in Britain and Ireland than other blue damselflies, occurring, for example, in Ireland at many lakes over 200m above sea level.

This ubiquitous species is highly dispersive, with frequent records away from water or in totally unsuitable breeding habitat. It readily colonises new waterbodies, often before aquatic plants or fish have established. Where large populations of this species are present, there is usually an abundance of submerged aquatic vegetation close to the water's surface, which provides egg-laying sites for females.

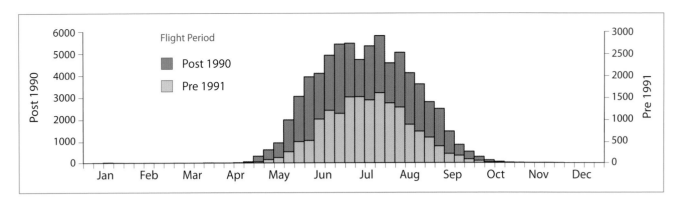

*Above:* Loch Cholla, Colonsay is a deep, peaty, moorland loch with extensive White Water-lily cover. It has a large population of Common Blue Damselfly. *R&B Mearns*

Shore of Lough Mask at Shanvallycahill, Co. Mayo. This habitat of sparse beds of emergent plants in the margins of a large shallow lake is a typical site for Common Blue Damselfly in Ireland. *Brian Nelson*

## Conservation status and threats

It was assessed as Least Concern on both the British and Irish Red Lists. No special conservation or site management measures are required for this abundant species. The species survives very well over long periods in both natural and artificial lakes. The maintenance of open water with some submerged pondweed, supplemented by the continued creation of waterbodies, is all that this species needs. During the later stages of seral succession, when the encroachment of emergent plants reduces the amount of open water, Common Blue Damselflies may disappear altogether from sites.

## National trends

This is the most widespread species in Britain and Ireland. The only information on population change comes from a slight decrease shown by the CEH trends analysis.

Chew Reservoir, Greater Manchester, is a small upland reservoir with Common Blue Damselfly. *Ken Gartside*

# Red-eyed Damselfly

*Erythromma najas*

Large Redeye

Red-eyed Damselfly is a distinctive species, readily identified to genus by the bright red eyes and blue abdominal segments 9 and 10 of the male. Males are conspicuous by their habit of resting on the floating leaves of aquatic plants and mats of algae. The females have reddish-brown eyes and lack the blue tip to the abdomen. Adults appear larger and more robust than most other damselflies. Oviposition takes place in tandem, with both the male and female sometimes submerging completely. The life cycle is two years.

Red-eyed Damselfly, male.
*Steve Cham*

## Distribution

Red-eyed Damselfly is found throughout central Europe from France to Russia and Japan. It is rare in the Mediterranean region yet found around the Baltic as far north as the Arctic Circle. It is absent from Ireland and Scotland.

Berrington Hall pool, Herefordshire. *Will Watson*

Red-eyed Damselfly is widespread across much of southern and eastern Britain south of a line from the Wirral to Flamborough Head. Its range extends to Devon and south Wales as far as Montgomeryshire, where recent range expansion has occurred. Its current distribution fits well with mean July temperatures above 16°C, which suggests that the two year larval development is influenced by temperature.

Red-eyed Damselfly has become increasingly more widespread over the last century. There were few records for this species before 1900, with only scattered colonies from Cheshire to Peterborough and the Home Counties. From 1937 to 1977 an increase in recording resulted in many new records from south-east Yorkshire, the New Forest and especially Surrey and Sussex. By 1990 there had been a great surge of records from an area bounded by Somerset, the Welsh Borders and Cheshire, with a new cluster in Devon. Since then there has been considerable infilling in the core range, yet range expansion westwards and northwards has been slow, with new colonies in Devon, Dorset, south and mid-Wales and south-east Yorkshire.

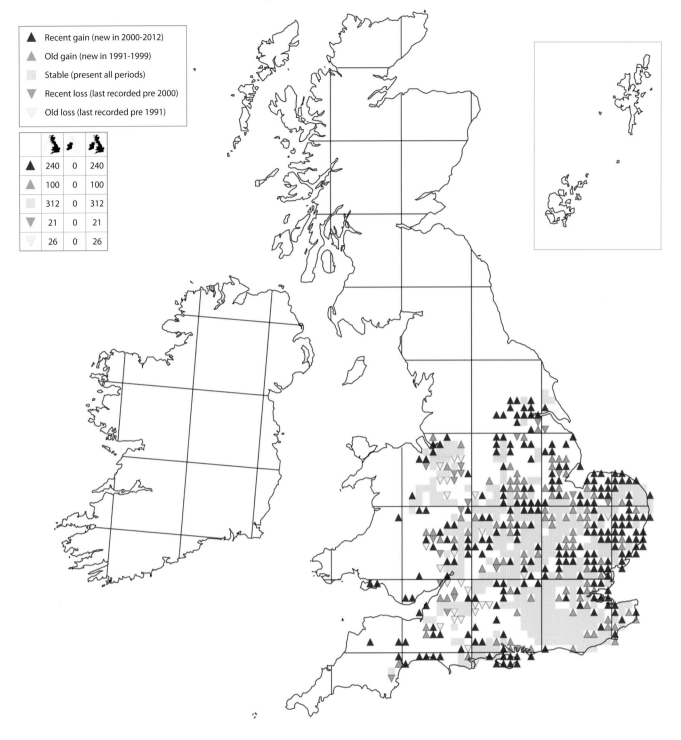

| | | | |
|---|---|---|---|
| ▲ | 240 | 0 | 240 |
| ▲ | 100 | 0 | 100 |
| ▦ | 312 | 0 | 312 |
| ▽ | 21 | 0 | 21 |
| ▽ | 26 | 0 | 26 |

Legend:
- ▲ Recent gain (new in 2000-2012)
- ▲ Old gain (new in 1991-1999)
- ▦ Stable (present all periods)
- ▽ Recent loss (last recorded pre 2000)
- ▽ Old loss (last recorded pre 1991)

## Habitat

Red-eyed Damselfly is typically found at sheltered sites with floating vegetation on eutrophic still waters, slow-flowing rivers or drains and canals. Particularly favoured are plants with spreading flat leaves, such as water-lilies, some pondweeds and Amphibious Bistort. Females oviposit into the submerged stems of these floating aquatic plants. Males can sometimes be found in bankside vegetation when the weather is unsuitable for territorial behaviour over the water but usually they fly into trees for shelter. Emergence takes place both out in the middle of waterbodies on plant parts and other objects protruding above the water, as well as on emergent vegetation at the margins and even on structures like bridges and walls. Any well-vegetated lowland pool in south-east England is likely to have this species wherever floating vegetation is present

## Conservation status and threats

Red-eyed Damselfly is listed as Least Concern in the British Red List. It can be especially abundant at sites with large expanses of floating plants. Overzealous clearance of floating vegetation can therefore be detrimental to the species. For example, a fishing pool near Worcester, where aquatic vegetation was removed to aid fishing, lost this species within a few years. Similarly, at Stover Lake, Devon, the rapid loss of White Water-lily saw adult numbers

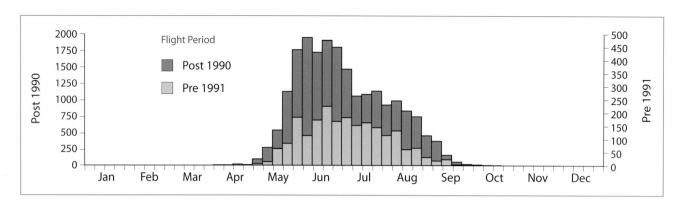

Wrest Park, Silsoe, Bedfordshire, where a series of ornamental lakes and ponds hold a large population. *Steve Cham*

## National trends

The CEH trends analysis (pages 58-63) confirms that there has been a significant increase in this species. It has slowly expanded its range in recent decades. It is on the western edge of its range in Devon, where dispersion along canals and other linear watercourses is likely to have aided expansion. Within two years of its discovery on the Grand Western Canal, Devon in 2004 the species had spread along a nine kilometre stretch. Conversely, a small population first noted in 2005 on water-lilies at Squabmoor Reservoir, Devon, has not spread to Bystock Reservoir, which has a good stand of water-lilies, barely 500m away. This suggests that natural spread between standing waters is limited. Perhaps the incidental translocation of eggs or larvae on plant material, possibly by anglers, is more likely to have spread the species to some areas. These areas include the Bovey Basin, Devon, which was isolated from the nearest known population at the time (in Somerset) by some 85km; the first records from there were in 1978.

drastically reduced within four years and only a small number surviving on a single cultivated water-lily. Control of Fringed Water-lily in Exeter Canal, Devon, where the plant is not indigenous, resulted in a more localised occupancy by Red-eyed Damselfly. These examples emphasise the need for plants with floating leaves, although the species can utilise floating algal mats to some degree.

Hurcott Pool, Kidderminster, Worcestershire, where the lily pads are favoured by Red-eyed Damselfly. *Mike Averill*

# Small Red-eyed Damselfly
## *Erythromma viridulum*

Small Redeye

Small Red-eyed Damselfly males have red eyes and are very similar in appearance to the Red-eyed Damselfly. The female's eyes are brownish. Both sexes have predominantly black upper surfaces and, in males, a blue tip to the abdomen. The sides of the thorax and the base and tip of the abdomen sides are blue in males and initially green in females, developing to blue as they mature. Oviposition is into floating vegetation, usually away from the bank, often in the company of other ovipositing pairs.

Small Red-eyed Damselfly, mating pair. *Steve Cham*

## Distribution

Small Red-eyed Damselfly occurs in a few small areas of the extreme north of Africa, on many of the Mediterranean islands and across most of Europe south of a latitude roughly corresponding to that of the north German coast; it extends as far east as Turkestan. The species used to be rather localised in many north-western parts of Europe but is currently becoming much more common and expanding its range northwards, continuing a trend that began in the

Lower Bruckland Ponds, Devon, provide favoured habitat near the far western edge of its range. *Dave Smallshire*

1980s and accelerated in the early 1990s (Ketelaar, 2002). It reached Denmark in 2001, southern Sweden in 2004, Lithuania in 2007 and Latvia in 2012. In The Netherlands it was very rare until the 1970s but is now common and widespread across the country, where it is regarded as the most expansive species (Dijkstra *et al.*, 2002).

Small Red-eyed Damselfly has now colonised much of south-east England over the last 15 years. It is increasingly more common and widespread south of a line between the River Humber in East Yorkshire, the River Severn Estuary and then Exeter in the southwest (with an outpost in south Wales). It was unknown in Britain before 1999, when it was first discovered in Essex (Dewick & Gerussi, 2000). In 2000, the species was discovered on the Isle of Wight. Genetic studies have subsequently shown that these individuals had a different source to those previously found in Essex (Watts *et al.*, 2010). Within a few years, the species had rapidly colonised many sites within 20km of the south-east coast of England but was also reported as breeding at sites as far inland as Bedfordshire (Cham, 2002). By 2005 it was recorded as far west as Warwickshire (P. Reeve pers. comm.). Colonisation of inland sites continued, with the species rapidly spreading north and west until 2007, when major range expansion appeared to slow down (Parr, 2008). Nevertheless, consolidation of the existing range continues

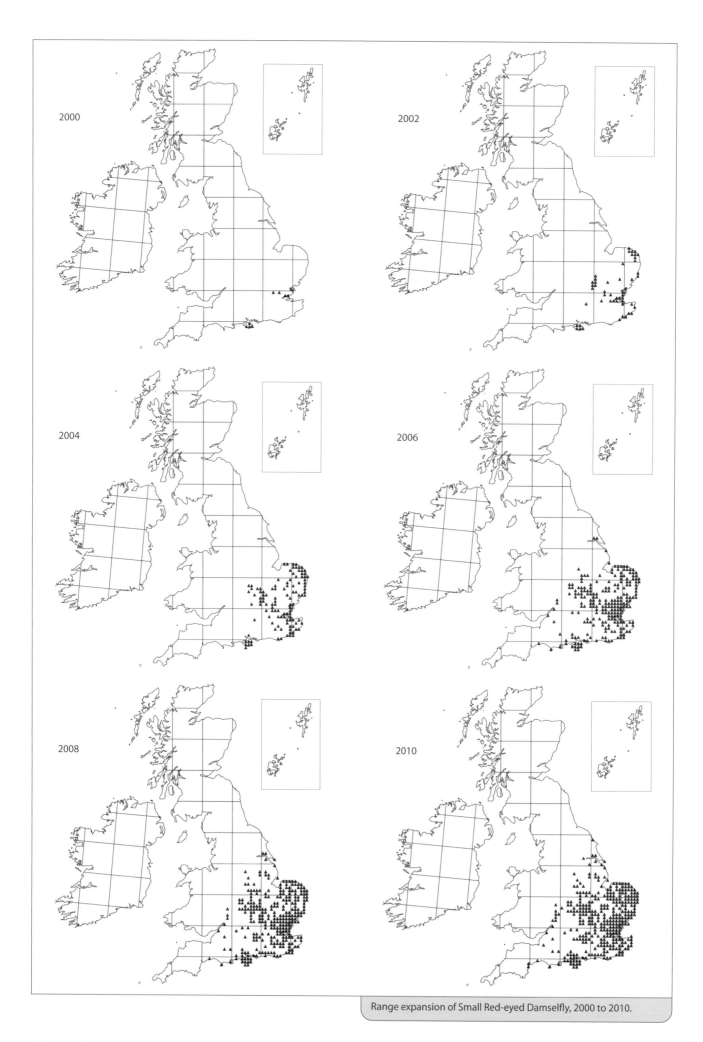

Range expansion of Small Red-eyed Damselfly, 2000 to 2010.

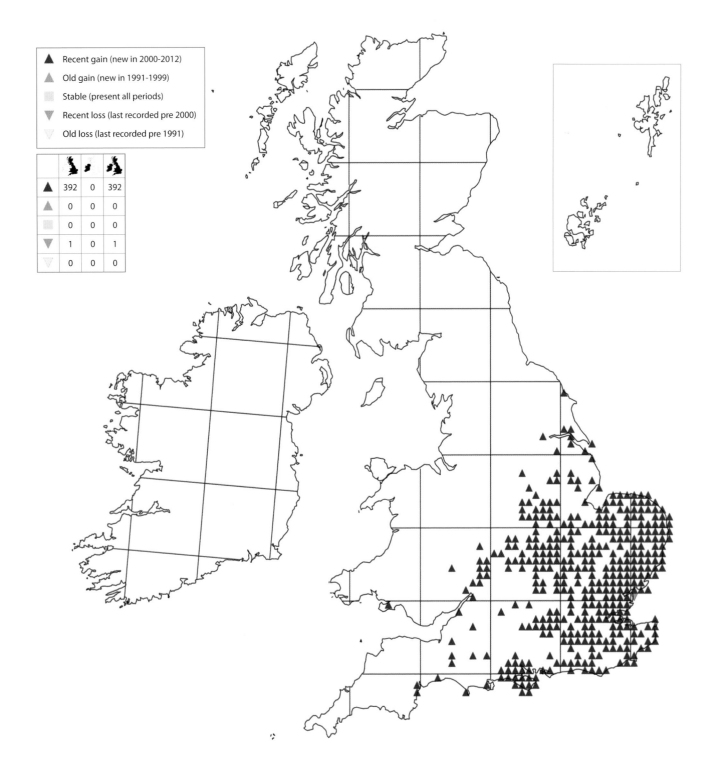

| | ![recent gain] | ![old gain] | ![stable] |
|---|---|---|---|
| ▲ Recent gain (new in 2000–2012) | | | |
| ▲ Old gain (new in 1991–1999) | | | |
| ▦ Stable (present all periods) | | | |
| ▼ Recent loss (last recorded pre 2000) | | | |
| ▽ Old loss (last recorded pre 1991) | | | |

| | | | |
|---|---|---|---|
| ▲ | 392 | 0 | 392 |
| ▲ | 0 | 0 | 0 |
| ▦ | 0 | 0 | 0 |
| ▼ | 1 | 0 | 1 |
| ▽ | 0 | 0 | 0 |

as new breeding colonies become established. Range expansion is thought to have been in response to climate warming and initially it was expanding its British range at roughly 30km per year (Hassell *et al.*, 2014). The first record for Wales was in 2012, when 50+ were found at the Penclacwydd WWT Reserve, Carmarthenshire, during late summer.

## Habitat

Small Red-eyed Damselfly breeds in nutrient-rich lakes and ponds which contain large amounts of submerged plants floating close to the water surface, especially hornwort

(Cham, 2004), floating mats of green algae (Ketelaar, 2002), water-lilies or water-milfoil. In slightly brackish water, floating Fennel Pondweed is sometimes used for perching and oviposition sites (Benton & Dobson, 2007). Open, unshaded sites are favoured and adults will stop flying in overcast conditions when many other dragonfly species are still active. In Europe, it will also breed, although less frequently, on acid moorland pools and running water where aquatic vegetation is abundant (Ketelaar, 2002).

Despite their relatively recent arrival, adult Small Red-eyed Damselflies may be the most abundant damselflies present at sites with optimal conditions. Males readily settle on

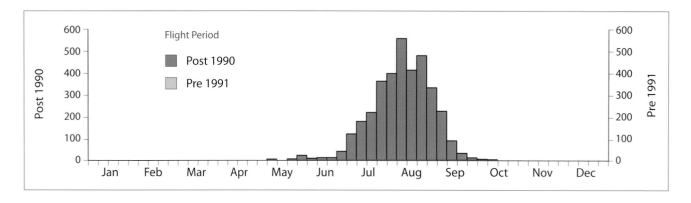

floating plants and are aggressive to both conspecific males and those of other species.

Tandem pairs oviposit, often in groups of hundreds, into large patches of suitable plants close to the water surface. Males remain in tandem with females during oviposition and will pull them clear if menaced by fish or frogs. Larvae live, often at high densities, amongst suspended vegetation, especially hornworts, away from the bankside. Emergence typically occurs on rafts of hornwort and other floating plants, away from the lake margins (Cham, 2004).

## Conservation status and threats

Small Red-eyed Damselfly is currently widespread and expanding its range across Britain. It was not assessed for the British Red List, due to it being a potential vagrant. The species is often abundant at sites and at some it is the most abundant species, therefore not threatened at present. Sites heavily shaded by trees or those that have turbid water that suppresses growth of submerged plants, such as hornworts, are unlikely to support the species. The species is unknown from severely polluted sites.

Flitton Moor pond, Bedfordshire, with large expanses of hornwort that support a large population. *Steve Cham*

## National trends

The rate of spread of Small Red-eyed Damselfly across Britain from south-east England to south Wales has been remarkable. In the early years of colonisation, some particularly favourable sites held very large populations, with 2500 estimated at a site near Lowestoft, Suffolk, in July 2003.

The species continues to be locally abundant and is still increasing its range. The initial colonisation of Britain and rapid range expansion was aided by the species suddenly having access to sites where there was only limited competition from other species.

Populations are now well-established and the indications are that the species is likely to continue to expand its range in Britain, linked with current climate warming trends.

Small Red-eyed Damselflies ovipositing into hornwort at Wrest Park, Bedfordshire. *Steve Cham*

# Blue-tailed Damselfly

## *Ischnura elegans*

Common Bluetail

Blue-tailed Damselfly males have a dark abdomen with a single blue band on abdominal segment 8. Females occur in a number of colour forms with segment 8 either blue or brown. The only species which Blue-tailed Damselfly could easily be confused with is the much rarer Scarce Blue-tailed Damselfly. Copulation is unusually lengthy. The female lays eggs alone into aquatic vegetation and the larvae usually take one year to develop, though at higher latitudes they may take two years.

Blue-tailed Damselfly, female. *Steve Cham*

## Distribution

Globally, this species is common and widespread across Europe and Asia to Japan. In Britain and Ireland, it is a common and widely distributed species but seldom found at moderate to high altitudes, which explains its absence from upland areas. It has possibly increased in upland areas of Scotland up to 450m above sea level. Nelson & Thompson (2004) found it to be the most frequently recorded species in Ireland, being recorded from 72% of hectads, although absent from the uplands, blanket bogs in north Co. Mayo and intensively farmed lowland areas.

## Habitat

Blue-tailed Damselfly can be found in a wide variety of habitat types, including garden ponds, lakes, slow-flowing streams and rivers, canals, ditches and peaty pools. These habitats may have an abundance of submerged, floating and emergent vegetation but the species is often also found in degraded, eutrophic waters with simplified vegetation, including sparse underwater plants.

This species may be found at newly created or restored habitats and is capable of tolerating a degree of pollution and brackish water, where it may be the only species present (Brooks, 2004).

## Conservation status and threats

This species is common, widespread and not considered to be threatened. Therefore it receives no legal protection.

## National trends

This species is common and widespread, though the CEH trends analysis shows a decrease, which some observers have also suggested in recent years.

New Forest roadside pond with a large expanse of New Zealand Pigmyweed that attracts Blue-tailed Damselfly. *Des Sussex*

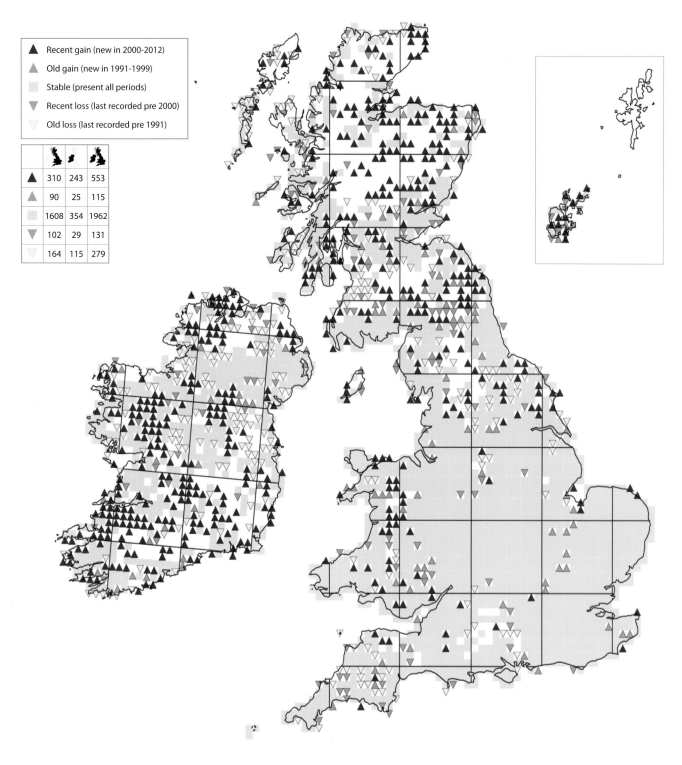

Recent gain (new in 2000-2012)
Old gain (new in 1991-1999)
Stable (present all periods)
Recent loss (last recorded pre 2000)
Old loss (last recorded pre 1991)

| | | | |
|---|---|---|---|
| ▲ | 310 | 243 | 553 |
| ▲ | 90 | 25 | 115 |
| ▦ | 1608 | 354 | 1962 |
| ▽ | 102 | 29 | 131 |
| ▽ | 164 | 115 | 279 |

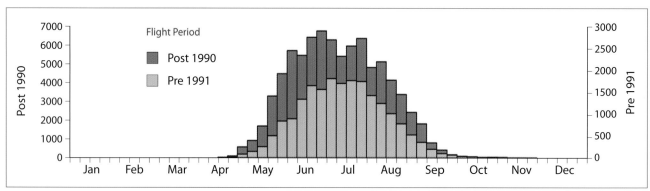

# Scarce Blue-tailed Damselfly

## Ischnura pumilio

Scarce Blue-tailed Damselfly males exhibit the 'blue-tail' typical of *Ischnura* species. Much of the abdomen is black, with segment 9 being blue with two small black marks; a small abutting portion of S8 is also blue. Females develop from a bright orange *aurantiaca* phase to light greenish-brown when mature. Both sexes are smaller than most other damselflies. Females oviposit alone into soft stems growing in very shallow water. Larvae develop in one year, though exceptionally a second generation may emerge in late summer, as happens in southern Europe.

Scarce Blue-tailed Damselfly, *aurantiaca* female. *Steve Cham*

## Distribution

Globally, Scarce Blue-tailed Damselfly is found from the Azores, Madeira and north-west Africa, through Europe and the Middle East across to central Siberia. In Europe, it is widespread in scattered populations, but is most numerous in the south.

The southern and western distribution in Britain and Ireland, which is close to the northern limit of the species' range in Europe, suggests that its distribution may be limited by temperature; the ameliorating effects of the North Atlantic Drift may explain this in part. It is predominantly a Mediterranean species, which has been reported to colonise northwards and eastwards in favourable seasons (Corbet *et al.*, 1960).

In Britain, its range is not unlike that of two other small damselflies, Southern and Small Red, being most numerous between Hampshire and Cornwall. It is also present throughout the southern half of Wales, with a more scattered distribution as far north as Anglesey. In Ireland it is widespread. Significantly, it is the only species of the three smallest damselflies in the British Isles to have reached Ireland, presumably reflecting a successful dispersal strategy. In recent decades, an increasing number of isolated colonies have been discovered east and north

The first ever andromorph female recorded in Britain here seen mating. Forest of Dean, Gloucestershire. *Ingrid Twissell*

of the core range in England and Wales. It is not known whether historical records from areas such as East Anglia refer to migrants or breeders. It is quite probable that many

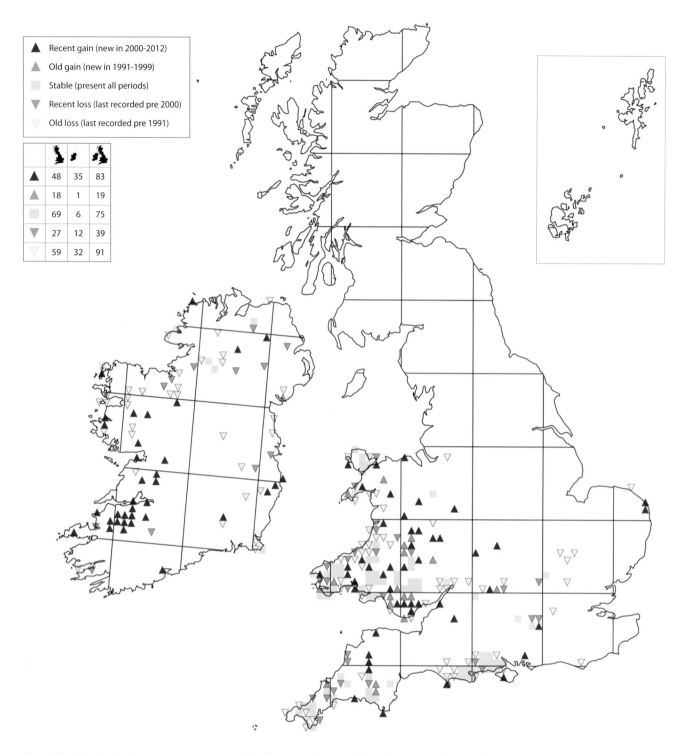

| |  | | |
|---|---|---|---|
| ▲ | 48 | 35 | 83 |
| △ | 18 | 1 | 19 |
| ▦ | 69 | 6 | 75 |
| ▼ | 27 | 12 | 39 |
| ▽ | 59 | 32 | 91 |

Legend:
- ▲ Recent gain (new in 2000-2012)
- △ Old gain (new in 1991-1999)
- ▦ Stable (present all periods)
- ▼ Recent loss (last recorded pre 2000)
- ▽ Old loss (last recorded pre 1991)

short-lived colonies have gone unrecorded, disappearing again as habitat conditions became unsuitable.

Scarce Blue-tailed Damselfly has been well known for many years from the New Forest, Hampshire, with records dating back to 1907. Historical accounts highlight fluctuating populations, which appear to be associated with ditching and timber clearance activities that create shallow water conditions. Recently the species' movement and dispersal has been studied by Allen & Thompson (2009), mainly in the Latchmore Brook area of the Forest. This study showed that populations were more stable where habitat conditions remained suitable, such as seepages utilised by livestock. Other colonies in the Forest are more transient. In north

Hampshire it was known from private land at Eelmoor Marsh, where a strong colony existed between 1999 and 2003; there have been no recent records, though, suggesting that the habitat is no longer suitable. A single recent record from the Isle of Wight may have been a wandering individual from the New Forest, Dorset or possibly the Continent.

In Dorset it has been widespread in the past, with records dating back to the 1940s. At many sites the records have again been sporadic, showing the transient nature of this species. It has been recorded from valley mires for many years, with the creation of quarries, clay and gravel pits, bomb craters and cress beds in the county enabling it to colonise new habitats. Approximately 80% of recent county records come from

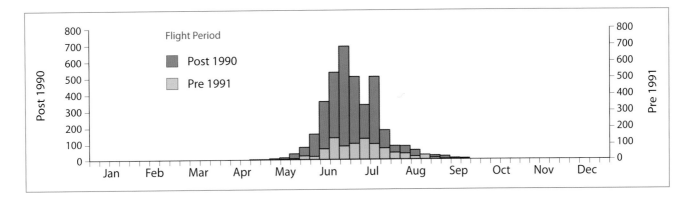

Flight Period
- Post 1990
- Pre 1991

these new sites. It occurs on the army ranges west of Wareham, where its continued presence has been aided by ground disturbance during military manoeuvres.

A similar situation to that in Dorset is found in Cornwall and Devon, where it appears to have spread from natural populations in the valleys of Bodmin Moor and Dartmoor to colonise ponds and streams created or modified as a result of historic tin-mining and more modern china clay extraction. It is now widely recorded from marshy seepages associated with the tin-streaming sites of old mine workings, despite the toxicity at some sites (Jones, 1985). This dramatic increase is reflected in 90% of the Cornish sites being artificial. Elsewhere in Devon it has a chequered history in active and exhausted china clay, ball clay and other quarries, as well as in semi-natural habitat on Dartmoor. The Dartmoor sites comprise flushes, runnels and streams within heathland, especially at 'pinch points' where livestock concentrate to drink or cross.

In South Wales it is most abundant in flushes and seepages arising in the coalfield areas, most likely having colonised from nearby upland sites. In North Wales it occurs at isolated localities, although on the Lleyn Peninsula it is found more widely. The species has a strong population on Anglesey, where it has been regularly recorded for over 30 years. Small, apparently isolated, populations occur in Snowdonia at Cors Bodgynydd, Gwydyr Forest and Lordship Forest, south-

Meeth Clay Pit, Devon, where Scarce Blue-tailed Damselfly Damselfly bred in shallow runnels until extraction ceased and the pit flooded in 2012. *Dave Smallshire*

Salisbury Plain, Wiltshire, where Scarce Blue-tailed Damselfly has recently been discovered breeding in small runnels formed in tank tracks. *Iain Perkins*

west of Bala. In Denbighshire, there was a single sighting in 2009 at Fenn's Moss, while in Brecon it has been known for many years, particularly in the Mynydd Illtyd SSSI. In Cardiganshire it has been recorded from a number of sites, with records dating back to 1899. It is also well recorded in Carmarthenshire, where at some sites it has been recorded almost continuously whereas at others there are gaps in the records. Although this might be explained by irregular recording effort, it is typical of populations that fluctuate as habitat conditions change. In Pembrokeshire, one of the major strongholds for the species in Wales, it is widespread at flushes and shallow ponds, notably at Gors Fawr and in the Mynydd Preseli area. It is well distributed in Glamorgan with regular records dating back to 1905, while in Radnorshire it is widespread at a number of sites where it has persisted for 25 years. There are no recent records from Monmouthshire, where it was recorded in the 1980s, but it is not clear if this is due to loss of breeding sites or a lack of recording effort.

An easterly expansion of its range is almost certainly due to the creation of suitable habitat from quarrying activities, perhaps aided by prevailing westerly airflows to carry dispersing adults. In the Forest of Dean, Gloucestershire, colonies have been recorded at pools, flushes and ditches associated with coal mining activities but these disappeared as the habitat became unsuitable. It was not recorded in the Forest from 2002 until it was rediscovered in 2010 following the clearance of conifer plantations and

Latchmoor flushes, New Forest, Hampshire, holds a large population of Scarce Blue-tailed Damselfly. *Steve Cham*

the creation of new pools. This recent sighting included the first British record of an andromorph blue form female, widely known from continental Europe. This discovery raises the question of whether a recent migration event from the continent had taken place. The sighting of another andromorph female on the east coast of Norfolk in September 2012, together with a typical female near the south Devon coast at Salcombe on 31 August 2012, further suggest immigration. In Gloucestershire and Wiltshire the species has been recorded over a number of years from the Cotswold Water Park in areas of active gravel extraction. Here the habitat conditions change rapidly and the species does not persist for more than a few years at any one site. Numbers have been noted to fluctuate significantly. In Wiltshire, several small colonies were discovered on Salisbury Plain in 2013. Small temporary pools formed in tracks created by military vehicles have created the shallow water conditions favoured by this species.

It was recorded at a quarry north-west of Hereford between 1999 and 2004, perhaps an extension of the Forest of Dean population. In Shropshire, it was recorded breeding at a quarry site east of Ludlow in 2006, 2011 and 2012 with further single sightings elsewhere in the county.

A sand and gravel quarry in Warwickshire, showing Peter and Kay Reeve sampling the shallow water where larvae of Scarce Blue-tailed Damselfly were found. *Steve Cham*

In Berkshire and Oxfordshire it has been recorded at shallow seepage pools in areas of gravel and limestone extraction over a few years while the habitat conditions have been suitable. In Berkshire it has been recorded sporadically in the Aldermaston area, related to gravel extraction where suitable conditions are maintained. After an absence of 14 years it was recorded again in 2011 at Decoy Heath. North of Oxford, it was recorded at Bunkers Hill Quarry, where suitable seepage conditions existed for a short period in the early 1990s, while west of Oxford it was recorded from gravel pits before the habitat became unsuitable. Further east, in Buckinghamshire and Bedfordshire, the species was regularly recorded in the late 1980s at spring-line seepages in chalk quarries but, after persisting for more than a decade, these colonies disappeared as the habitat changed. One of the chalk quarry colonies in Bedfordshire, discovered in 1975, persisted for 30 years before loss of the habitat through succession and lack of management resulted in its demise. The species was discovered in 2002 at an active gravel and sand quarry in Warwickshire, where it persists, yet has subsequently moved around the site as areas have become unsuitable.

## Habitat

Scarce Blue-tailed Damselfly is recorded from a range of semi-natural and artificial habitats across Ireland, Wales and southern England. In England and Wales it often occurs at sites with populations of Southern or Small Red Damselflies. However, wherever Scarce Blue-tailed breeds, the microhabitat is characterised by very shallow water that is maintained during periods of drought and, unlike the other two species, has only sparse aquatic vegetation. The most natural and undisturbed habitat conditions are found in Ireland, where it favours seepages and flushes in heaths, bogs and fens. It also occurs at the naturally-fluctuating shores of large lakes, especially where the shore is sandy. Elsewhere it occurs in mires with shallow flushes and boggy areas with slow-flowing or still water. It prefers small, open and shallow waterbodies and will tolerate a variety of water quality conditions, including both acidic and alkaline. Key habitat conditions are a muddy substrate with sparse vegetation and some open ground and low levels of shade. Such conditions develop in both slow-flowing and still waters, particularly where poaching by livestock or other similar disturbance occurs. Sparse vegetation at tin mining sites may be promoted by residual soil toxicity.

In recent decades it has been reported increasingly from artificial wetlands, such as those created by mineral extraction, as well as new ponds and ditches. These artificial sites have provided opportunities for the colonisation of new areas. Wherever the species occurs, it favours shallow water with slow or no movement, conditions which are often susceptible to drying out. Such shallow waters warm up rapidly during spring and summer, while spring-fed seepages remain ice-free in all but the coldest winters. Similar microhabitat is also found around the shallow margins of streams and ponds kept open by repeated grazing and trampling from livestock. Males can be found perched low down in areas of shallow water with sparse and open vegetation structure.

Ovipositing females are unaccompanied and most often encountered laying eggs into emergent, soft-stemmed, aquatic plants just above the surface in shallow water. Most favoured are soft grasses, rushes and spike-rushes. In very shallow water, females will often lay into a stem right down into the substrate, occasionally partially submerging, which may offer further protection for the eggs. Larvae develop rapidly in the shallow water conditions and are generally found in or on silty, muddy substrates in the early stages of colonisation by plants.

Male Scarce Blue-tailed Damselfly at typical breeding habitat.
*Dave Smallshire*

## Conservation status and threats

At the turn of the 19th century, Scarce Blue-tailed Damselfly was considered to be almost extinct in Britain and Ireland. It currently has widely scattered colonies but is nowhere abundant. The species is classified as Near Threatened in the Red Data list for Britain and Vulnerable in the Irish Red List. Any range expansion over the last decade is largely due to human activities inadvertently creating suitable conditions, while losses have mainly resulted from plant seral succession. Colonies at some new sites are more transient and likely to be associated with early successional stages. Various forms of disturbance which perpetuate bare substrates and openness of vegetation appear to sustain the species at some sites but disturbance and the presence of water need to be maintained if the species is to remain. This species is perhaps the most difficult of all for which to provide sustainable management. Preserving early successional stages is the key to its persistence. Many former sites are in the later stages of succession and have become overgrown. Intensive grazing and poaching by livestock are key factors in suppressing vegetation growth and succession at semi-natural sites, where high numbers of livestock have been encouraged by EU agricultural subsidies in the recent past. Ironically, since the 1990s, agri-environment schemes have led to reduced stocking densities in the uplands, which in combination with other factors has reduced levels of poaching at waterbodies and watercourses.

Depressions which retain water throughout the summer, such as wheel ruts and culverts amongst quarry workings, offer suitable conditions. In the chalk quarries of

Bedfordshire and the clay pit at Smallhanger in Devon, the unofficial activities of four-wheel drive vehicles and motor-bike scrambling have prevented the encroachment of vegetation; the species was lost after their exclusion at the former. Elsewhere in Devon, losses at clay pits have resulted from a cessation of active quarrying and associated pumping (which ensures that pits do not fill with water and that drainage channels continue to flow).

For a species that has such specific microhabitat requirements, which are scarce in Britain and Ireland, the number of dispersing individuals needed to result in new colonies must be considerable. The fact that colonisation of remote sites seems to occur frequently is remarkable. Nevertheless, it should remain a conservation priority to retain existing colonies wherever possible.

The small-scale nature of the habitat conditions are often overlooked during site management work. The species' very presence is indicative of a rare type of habitat. However, the fact that its presence is negatively correlated with high dragonfly diversity could create a conflict of interest when managing sites for other species (e.g. Southern Damselfly) or for maximum diversity. Management needs to be aimed specifically at maintaining early successional stages in shallow water along with open habitat conditions that will favour other specialist species associated with these conditions.

## National trends

The number of sites with the specialised habitat required for this species is restricted and this inevitably limits the availability for new colonisation. The oldest and most sustainable sites are those in semi-natural habitats, typically associated with heathland and moorland. Nevertheless, it is likely that some extensive mining areas may have been occupied for a substantial time, examples including the tin streaming sites of Dartmoor (12th and 13th centuries) and the ball clay workings in the Bovey Basin, Devon (since 1921). A key characteristic of many current breeding sites for this species is their transient nature. Sites can be stable if big enough. There are records spanning 20+ years from sites in Northern Ireland. Such sites are easily gained and lost and populations fluctuate markedly as a result. The CEH trends analysis (pages 58-63) shows a significant decrease.

Given the dispersive nature of this species, some records refer to migrants at potentially suitable sites. At some of these, colonisation has occurred although many are one-off sightings and breeding does not occur.

More than for any other dragonfly species, some breeding sites inevitably will have been missed because of difficulties in gaining access to survey in active quarries. Where, on rare occasions, a recorder has been able to overcome health and safety concerns and gain access permission there is certainly limited evidence that this species breeds within working quarries.

# Large Red Damselfly
## *Pyrrhosoma nymphula*

Large Red Damsel

Large Red Damselfly males have a mainly red abdomen, red eyes and two red antehumeral stripes. Both sexes have black legs that distinguish the species from Small Red Damselfly. Most females are similar to the male but with a rather more robust abdomen and a thin, black dorsal line on all abdominal segments. There are three female colour variants with varying amounts of black on the abdomen. The distinctive larvae normally take two years to develop in Britain.

Large Red Damselfly, female. *Paul Forster*

## Distribution

Large Red Damselfly is widespread throughout much of Europe, extending southwards into northern Greece, south-west Italy and the northern half of Spain and Portugal.

There are also some records from further south in Spain and Portugal as well as in north Morocco. The northern limits are from south-west Norway through southern Sweden to

A well vegetated pond at Duckend NR, Bedfordshire, has a strong population. *Steve Cham*

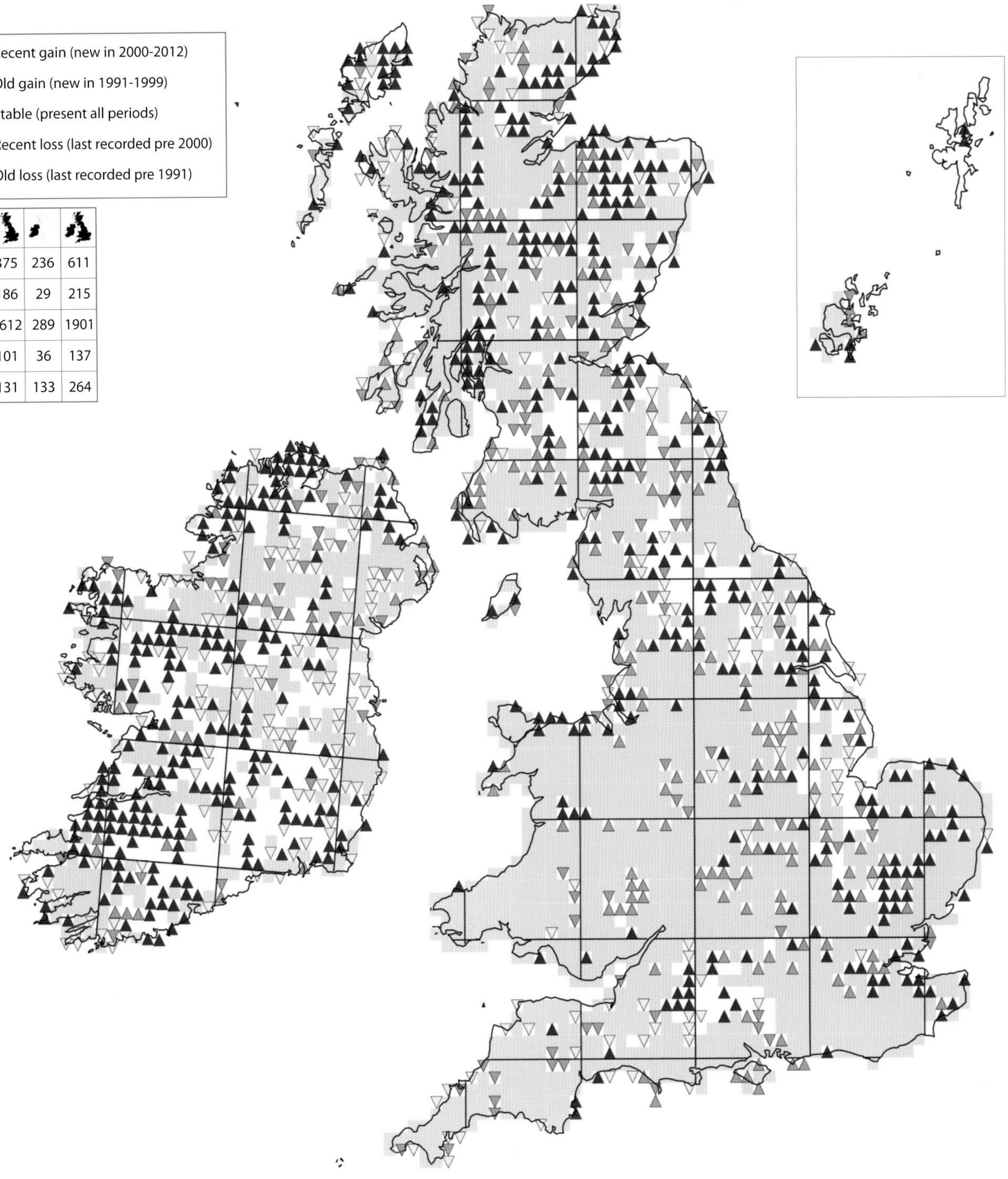
▲ Recent gain (new in 2000-2012)
△ Old gain (new in 1991-1999)
░ Stable (present all periods)
▼ Recent loss (last recorded pre 2000)
▽ Old loss (last recorded pre 1991)

| | | | |
|---|---|---|---|
| ▲ | 375 | 236 | 611 |
| △ | 186 | 29 | 215 |
| ░ | 1612 | 289 | 1901 |
| ▼ | 101 | 36 | 137 |
| ▽ | 131 | 133 | 264 |

Finland and northern Russia. To the east, it extends at least as far as the Ural Mountains but the precise limits are not clear.

In Britain and Ireland, Large Red Damselfly is common and widespread, having been recorded in most counties as well as many offshore islands, including Orkney, the Outer and Inner Hebrides, Isle of Man, the Channel Islands and some of the islands off the west coast of Ireland. It is locally common in parts of eastern England, the Pennines, the English-Scottish border region and eastern Scotland. It is somewhat scarce in counties with extensive chalk geology (e.g. Wiltshire). In Ireland, it is absent from the karst regions of Co. Clare and from areas of intensively farmed land in the south and east. Although not typical of high altitudes in Britain and Ireland, it has been found up to 2000m above sea level in the French Pyrenees (Grand & Boudot, 2006). It is replaced in part of northern Greece, Corfu and southern Albania by Greek Red Damsel (*P. elisabethae*).

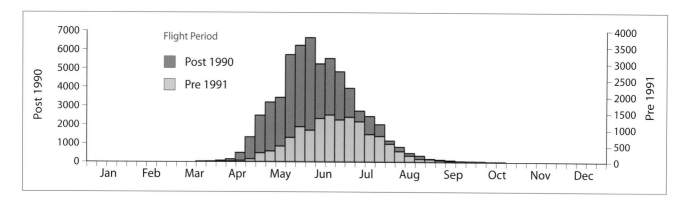

Flight Period

- Post 1990
- Pre 1991

## Habitat

Large Red Damselfly is found in a wide range of still water habitats, including ponds, lakes, canals, ditches, dykes, acid bogs and marshes. It is also found in base-rich waterbodies and can tolerate mild pollution. Like most other species it prefers waterbodies without much overhanging vegetation yet will tolerate some tree cover provided that there is dappled light. In some cases it is the only damselfly present. It has a strong preference for waterbodies that are well-vegetated with floating aquatic plants, particularly Broad-leaved Pondweed.

Lough Alaban, a mesotrophic lake in the west of Co. Fermanagh has a strong population of Large Red Damselfly and Irish Damselfly. *Brian Nelson*

It is also recorded on slow-flowing streams and rivers and in some parts of Britain and Ireland it has been recorded from fast-flowing streams and rivers. The larvae require cover and tend to live near the bottom amongst weeds or debris.

## Conservation status and threats

It is listed as Least Concern in the Red Lists for Britain and Ireland. There are no immediate threats to Large Red Damselfly other than local issues affecting waterbodies. It appears to be a versatile species in that it can occupy a wide range of habitats and in general is locally common rather than abundant.

## National trends

The range of Large Red Damselfly remains fairly stable, although the CEH trends analysis (pages 58-63) shows a slight decrease. Changes since 1990 are generally infilling of records, possibly as a result of increased recording intensity.

Large Red Damselflies mating. *Jonathan Farooqi*

# Southern Migrant Hawker

*Aeshna affinis*

Blue-eyed Hawker

Southern Migrant Hawker is a medium-sized dragonfly similar in appearance to the Migrant Hawker, but with a brighter yellow thorax (due to having the sides plain yellow, often with a blue/greenish tinge, rather than dark with two yellow stripes) and bright blue eyes in males. Females are brown and yellow, but andromorph females have also been found. It is a recent colonist to Britain.

Southern Migrant Hawker, male. *John Curd*

## Distribution

Southern Migrant Hawker has a primarily southern distribution extending across Europe to Mongolia. Up to the end of the 1980s it was recorded only locally in the northern part of central Europe; however, in the mid-1990s sightings significantly increased and the species became abundant in many areas. The species was formerly a very rare vagrant to Britain but now appears to be in the process of colonising. It was first recorded in 1952 with further records in 2006. The first significant influx was in 2010 when males and females were observed predominantly in Essex and Kent on the coastal marshes of the Thames Estuary. An established breeding colony at Hadleigh Country Park on the Thames Estuary in Essex was confirmed in 2011, with adults emerging during 9-14 June that year. This was the first breeding record of Southern Migrant Hawker in Britain. Further colonies are present at Wat Tyler Country Park in Essex and at Cliffe in Kent.

## Habitat

Southern Migrant Hawker specialises in transitional habitats and particularly marshes and low-lying shallow waterbodies that tend to dry out in late summer. It is often associated with emerald damselflies (*Lestes*) and darter

Pond at Hadleigh Country Park, Essex, where Southern Migrant Hawker has been seen patrolling. *Andy McGeeney*

dragonflies (*Sympetrum*), which similarly specialise in these habitats. The larval life stage of Southern Migrant Hawker is poorly known; some authors consider it to be two to three years, including a period of winter diapause, whereas others consider the species to have a one-year life cycle with larvae developing in early spring and emerging as adults in mid summer. Where it does occur in continental Europe it is often seen in very large numbers, with many hundreds present in feeding swarms at dusk. In southern Spain, males have been observed holding territories over

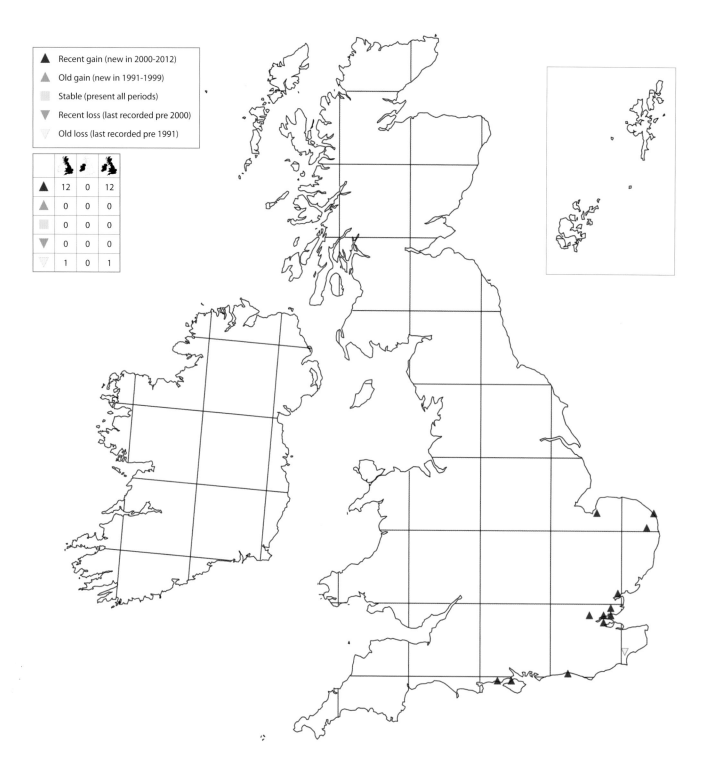

| |  | | |
|---|---|---|---|
| ▲ | 12 | 0 | 12 |
| ▲ | 0 | 0 | 0 |
| ▦ | 0 | 0 | 0 |
| ▼ | 0 | 0 | 0 |
| ▽ | 1 | 0 | 1 |

**Legend:**
▲ Recent gain (new in 2000-2012)
▲ Old gain (new in 1991-1999)
▦ Stable (present all periods)
▼ Recent loss (last recorded pre 2000)
▽ Old loss (last recorded pre 1991)

dry depressions in marshy habitats. When a female is caught, mating takes place on a nearby bush and, after a short period of copulation (a few minutes), the pair remain in tandem (the only European *Aeshna* species to do so), ovipositing in what appears to be quite unsuitable dry habitat. This behaviour was observed at Hadleigh Park in Essex in July/August 2010, the dry oviposition site being fully flooded by February 2011.

## Conservation status and threats

Transitional lowland wetlands are amongst the most threatened of all European habitats. Organisms that specialise in such areas rely upon them drying out in late summer in order to reduce populations of predators such as fish. Unfortunately, such areas are often where water extraction for human purposes takes place, reducing levels at those times of year when Southern Migrant Hawkers are developing. Coastal areas such as the Thames Estuary, where water conditions are brackish, do not have such water extraction problems but continued human activity

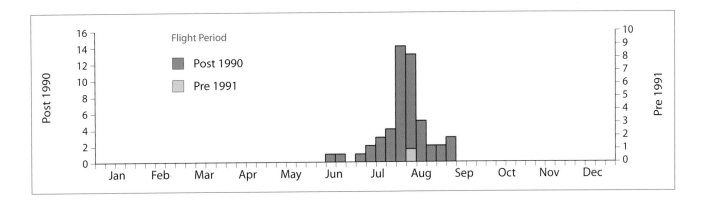

Dyke at Hadleigh Country Park, Essex, where Southern Migrant Hawker has been confirmed breeding. *Steve Cham*

in the form of commercial development remains a constant threat. Flooding of such coastal sites by seawater during extreme surge tides may also be an issue.

## National trends

Southern Migrant Hawker is now established as a resident in The Netherlands and immigration into England in 2010 indicated the early stages of the colonisation process in Britain. It therefore seems only a matter of time before this species will become established with stable breeding populations in Britain.

Southern Migrant Hawker, male. *Ted Benton*

# Azure Hawker

*Aeshna caerulea*

Azure Hawker is a medium-sized hawker. Mature males can be strikingly blue, lacking the yellow abdominal spots of most other blue hawkers. Females have various colour forms: the more frequent brown form has pale yellow abdominal spots whilst the blue form resembles typical males. Body colour can be regulated according to weather conditions, becoming dull in cool/cloudy conditions. They bask frequently, on sunlit boulders, tree trunks and *Racomitrium* moss hummocks, sometimes two or more in close proximity. Larval development probably extends over three years in Scottish populations.

Azure Hawker, female.
*R&B Mearns*

## Distribution

Azure Hawker has a boreal Palaearctic distribution. In Europe it occurs mainly north of latitude 55°. It is recorded above the Arctic Circle and is one of the few species numerous in Eurasia's polar regions. Found throughout Scandinavia (except Denmark) and Estonia, its range extends through Russia to Asia. Isolated post-glacial, relict populations are also present in mountainous areas in Scotland, France, Switzerland, northern Italy, southern Germany, Hungary and Latvia.

Bog pools at Bridge of Grudie, Highland, where Azure Hawker and Northern Emerald breed. *Tony Mundell*

In Britain, the species has only been recorded from montane areas of Scotland. It is absent from Ireland. It was first recorded in 1844 when a specimen was taken 'in the north of Scotland' by a Mr Wilson and given to the noted odonatologist Baron de Sélys-Longchamps (Corbet *et al.*, 1960). Further confirmation came when Robert McLachlan caught two males and a female in 1865 on the south side of Loch Rannoch (Lucas, 1900). Referring to Loch Rannoch and Breadalbane, Lucas stated that the species was 'probably present in the intervening country between these two districts'. Longfield (1949) further affirmed that it was 'entirely confined to Scotland and rare even there, although in good years it is sometimes fairly plentiful in its few known localities'; she mentioned Sutherland, Inverness, Argyll, Perth and Ross as counties in which it had been found. It was discovered in south-west Scotland in 1949 (Ratcliffe, 1949), a location over 150 kilometres from the next nearest known site in Perthshire.

The first evidence of breeding in Scotland was gained in 1952 when larvae were found in numbers at a site in Perthshire (Fraser, 1953). In 1985, a freshly emerged female, found with its exuvia beside a large bog pool near Loch Maree, Wester Ross, was apparently the first observed instance of emergence in Britain (Gabb, 1985). In south-west Scotland, records of adults and larvae increased from 1986 onwards as a result of increased recorder effort (Clarke *et al.*, 1990).

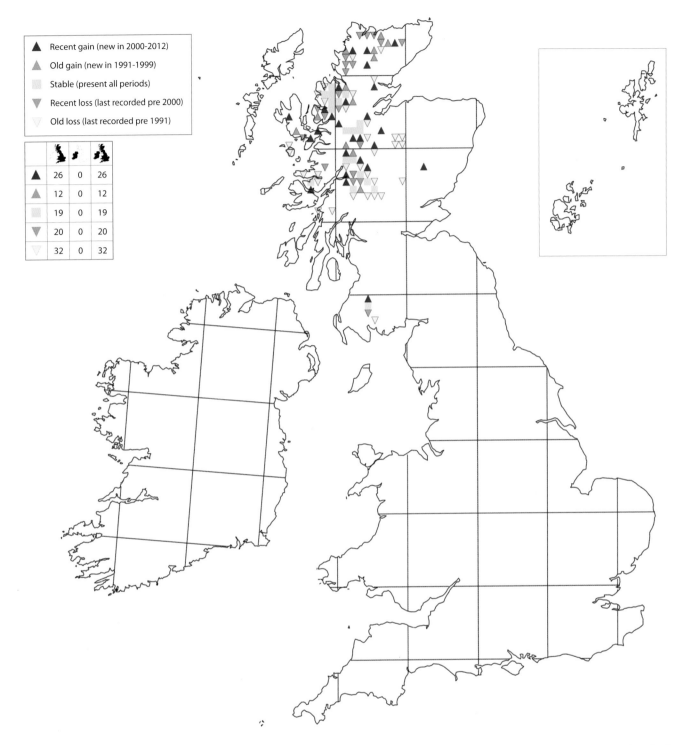

| | ![black triangle] | ![grey triangle] | ![combined] |
|---|---|---|---|
| ▲ Recent gain (new in 2000-2012) | 26 | 0 | 26 |
| ▲ Old gain (new in 1991-1999) | 12 | 0 | 12 |
| ▪ Stable (present all periods) | 19 | 0 | 19 |
| ▼ Recent loss (last recorded pre 2000) | 20 | 0 | 20 |
| ▽ Old loss (last recorded pre 1991) | 32 | 0 | 32 |

Betty and Bob Smith and co-workers collected significant records and gained valuable phenological data from the Loch Maree area, extending the species' known range, notably in the Flow Country of Caithness and Sutherland.

More recently, Azure Hawker has been found at a number of new upland sites in remote areas during surveys for wind farm applications (P. Cosgrove, pers. comm.). Until this time, most of the best-known sites were in more accessible areas that were not necessarily the most productive for the species. Historical records from less accessible areas in the eastern Highlands still need re-surveying, whilst records from central Scotland are considered to be erroneous. The best known and most reliable sites to see the species remain around Loch Maree in Wester Ross.

The species has proved increasingly elusive and hard to find at the most southerly confirmed breeding location in Galloway, although it was seen there in 2010. The felling of modern forests adjacent to known breeding areas may have resulted in changes of adult behaviour.

## Habitat

Azure Hawker breeds in bog pools of varying sizes, with the best sites having a combination of open water with abundant *Sphagnum cuspidatum* bog-moss and thick soupy detritus at the bottom (Clarke, 1994; Smith *et al.*, 2000). The largest populations are found in areas of blanket bog, on plateaux and in valley bottoms, which have many

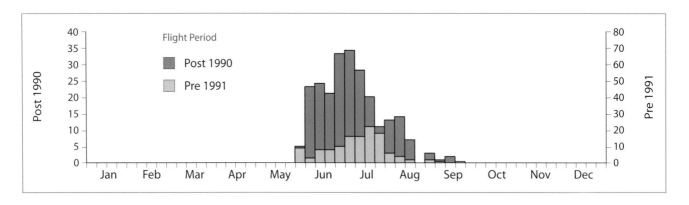

pools scattered over a large area. Sites at the lower altitudes seem to be the most productive, yet they are often in rugged landscapes that are remote, inaccessible and subject to adverse weather conditions. Observations of adults at breeding pools remain relatively few and occur mainly in good weather. This presents challenges for regular recording and limits the opportunities for study into the basic biology of this species. Males seeking females usually move rapidly from pool to pool and may range widely. Females oviposit alone, into bog-moss or soft margins of pools. The paucity of literature and distribution data reflects these difficulties in observing this species.

Larvae of Azure Hawker favour shallow bog pools with 0.15-0.20m depth of water, often very small with a surface area of approximately 1m² (Smith *et al.*, 2000). Pool depths are often hard to assess when bottomed with thick detritus. However, larvae have also been found in much larger pools including many at the Silver Flowe NNR that are ribbon-like, two metres or more across and tens of metres long. Azure Hawker has more specialised requirements than Common Hawker, which has a far wider ecological tolerance, and with which its range completely overlaps. Bogs utilised by Azure Hawkers are rarely found at altitudes above 500m in Scotland, in contrast to Common Hawker. Smith *et al.* (2000) postulate that shallow pools are selected to limit competition with Common Hawker, which prefers deeper pools.

The importance of adjacent woodland as a component of breeding sites in Scotland may have been overstated in previous literature. Sites such as the Silver Flowe had no significant woodland cover until after 1964, yet the species was recorded well before this. The occurrence of the species in the treeless Flow Country further supports this view.

## Conservation status and threats

Azure Hawker is classified as Vulnerable in the Red Data List for Britain. It is restricted to northern Scotland and Galloway and it is possible that it was more frequent in the past. It has suffered in some areas from the increase in conifer planting and associated drainage that this entails. There has been some habitat loss, mainly due to afforestation since the 1940s, but some of the best habitats are too wet to plant. Azure Hawkers were amongst the key invertebrates cited in major studies of the Flow Country when afforestation was a

Azure Hawker breeds in the bog pools under Buachaille Etive Mòr, Glen Etive, Argyll alongside White-faced Darter and Common Hawker. *David Clarke*

major issue (Ratcliffe & Oswald, 1987). Large nature reserves, such as Forsinard, were one of the outcomes to protect this habitat type. Wind farm developments have posed some of the more recent threats, but the risks to dragonflies and their bog pool habitats are taken into account and losses due to these developments will hopefully be minimised.

The drying out of shallower bog pools is an increasing threat, having occurred frequently in spring in the western Highlands since 2000. Higher temperatures, combined with a less equable distribution of rainfall and a more extreme climate, generally pose a threat to this species.

Climate change would seem to pose the greatest threat to this northern species and presage a retreat to higher latitudes and cooler areas. Finding and conserving the areas best buffered against such changes may offer the greatest hopes for its future survival.

## National trends

Azure Hawker has a restricted distribution in Scotland and has been inferred as undergoing a decline. However, progress in revealing its sites and status has been slow, yet steady, in the recording period leading up to this atlas. Increased recording intensity will be required in future years before a true picture can be obtained. Due to the difficulties of recording, the national trend for this species therefore remains unclear.

# Southern Hawker
*Aeshna cyanea*

Blue Hawker

Southern Hawker is a large, colourful dragonfly. Both sexes have characteristic broad, green antehumeral stripes and largely green sides to the thorax. Along the otherwise black abdomen, males have paired, typically apple green, spots that fuse to become complete blue bands on the last two segments, whilst females are brown with bright green markings throughout. Both sexes may have blue abdominal markings. Territorial males sometimes fly quite close to an observer. After laying, eggs remain dormant and hatch the following spring. Larvae typically take two years to develop.

Southern Hawker, male.
*Steve Cham*

Newly emerged Southern Hawker on Water-soldier. *Lorraine Ellison*

## Distribution

Southern Hawker is often common in urban or forested areas in Europe, where it is present from southern Scandinavia and Finland to Italy and Iberia, although more sparse around the Mediterranean. This occupied band extends eastwards into Asia Minor and to the Urals.

In Britain, the species is widespread in England and Wales, albeit more thinly distributed in the north and uplands. There is also a zone of absence or scarcity in the open chalk downland of Dorset, Wiltshire and Hampshire, where its preferred shady ponds are relatively scarce. In Scotland, it occurs principally in the relatively mild mid-west and in the north-east around the Moray Firth, with scattered records along the south-east coast and in the south-west. The scarcity in southern Scotland contrasts surprisingly with the relative abundance of occupied hectads further north.

Southern Hawker is a vagrant to Ireland, the only known record being that of a female found dead in Cork City in October 1988, coincident with a fall of Saharan dust (Nelson *et al.*, 2011). It has also been recorded from a single hectad on the Isle of Man.

## Habitat

Southern Hawker commonly breeds in shallow, often shaded, waterbodies in wooded areas, such as woodland ponds, lakes and canals, where the margins are well-vegetated. It is often found in urban areas, such as ponds in parks, schools and gardens, and is often one of the first species to colonise such sites. The attraction to gardens may be due to their resemblance to woodland glades.

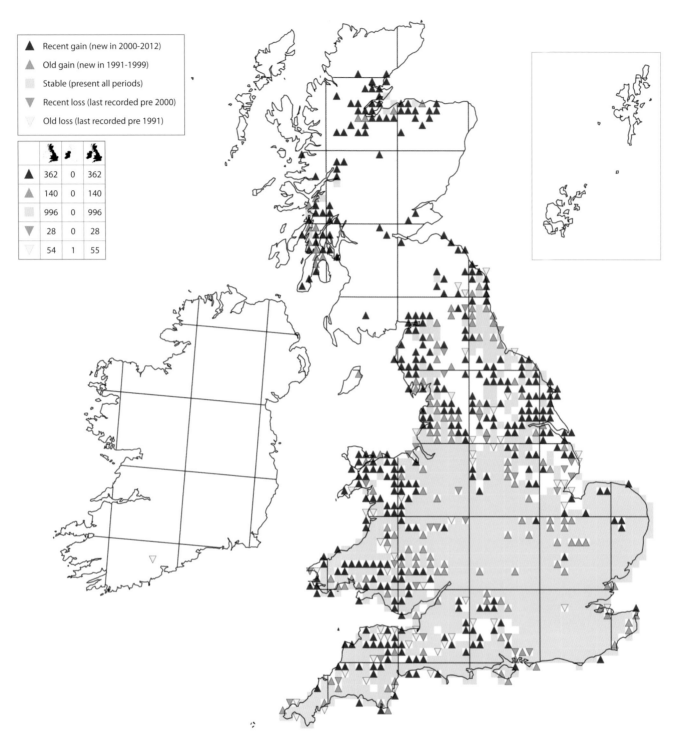

Legend:
- ▲ Recent gain (new in 2000-2012)
- ▲ Old gain (new in 1991-1999)
- ▨ Stable (present all periods)
- ▼ Recent loss (last recorded pre 2000)
- ▽ Old loss (last recorded pre 1991)

Shaded ponds are not often favoured by many other species of dragonfly, so larvae of Southern Hawker can exist at high densities. Adults hunt well away from water and may be found flying back and forth (hawking) along hedgerows, in woodland rides or in urban gardens, often late into the evening. Males will aggressively guard a suitable breeding site for short periods, small ponds being sufficient for only a solitary individual.

Oviposition sites are often mossy logs or stumps close to the margin of the water (Cham, 2004). Soft stems of emergent plants growing at the water's edge are also used. The eggs are laid into soft vegetation, moss or soft wood. Egg-laying females are attracted to solid objects and have

been recorded attempting to lay into camera bags and even human legs and shoes.

In Scotland, larvae have been discovered in splash zone pools, close to the high tidal limit, but which had some freshwater incursion. Such sites included tiny pools on small streams or pools with some seepage, often with little vegetation; the larvae were found under flat rocks. Females have been seen egg-laying into crumbling rocks, the soil between paving slabs, sandy banks and floating woody debris. Many of the recent Scottish records have come from garden or school ponds. Emergence here is later than in England, from late June to August (Batty, 2012).

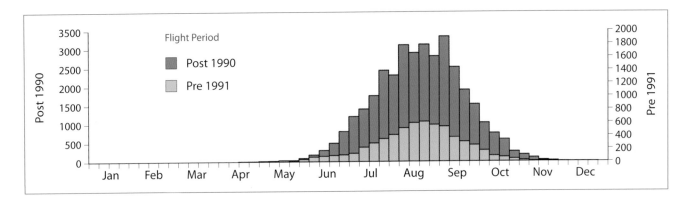

Female Southern Hawker ovipositing into moss. *Kay Reeve*

## Conservation status and threats

Southern Hawker is categorised as of Least Concern in the British Red List. Generally, the main threats to the species are from pollution, dredging and infilling of ponds. In some parts of Northamptonshire, particularly the Nene Valley, it has declined, possibly due to the loss of pond habitats, either through agricultural intensification or increasingly hot summers (Tyrrell, 2006). In general, the species has benefited from an increasing number of ponds in urban gardens and parks.

In Scotland and northern England, it appears to have thrived in the higher temperatures experienced since the previous atlas, so a reversal of that trend could halt its spread, if not cause local extinctions. There is some overlap in the ranges of Southern and Common Hawkers and, in

Woodland pond, Maulden, Bedfordshire: typical of a pond that attracts Southern Hawker. *Steve Cham*

clashes between the two species, the larger Southern Hawker is dominant (Smith, 2012). Moreover, at sites where long-term recording has taken place, a decline in the numbers of Common Hawker has been noted as Southern Hawker numbers have increased (Halliday, 2012).

Pools just above the tideline at Ellary, Argyll and Bute, where Southern Hawker breeds. *Pat Batty*

## National trends

Since the previous atlas, the range expansion of Southern Hawker in Scotland has been dramatic, although it has also spread and there has been infilling with records in its range in the north of England and Wales, with some consolidation in south-west England. Its spread through Wales has not been hampered by high ground such as the Brecon Beacons, the Cambrian Mountains or Snowdonia. In the north of England it has spread up the east and west coasts.

In Scotland, the spread has been in coastal lowlands, both in Argyll and the Inverness region. In the previous atlas it was recorded only from those coastal areas with a relatively mild climate but, in the 1990s, it gradually spread south along the west coast into Kintyre and around the Moray Firth coast in the east. Since 2000, there has been a rapid increase in records from south Kintyre through Lochaber into the Great Glen, where the eastern population has spread into Glen Affric. North of Inverness, breeding sites have been found as far north as Lairg. There are also recent records from south-east Scotland in Fife and east Perthshire but the increase here has not been as great as further north.

# Brown Hawker
*Aeshna grandis*

Brown Hawker is a large, brown-coloured dragonfly with unmistakable amber-coloured wings. Both sexes have two yellow stripes on the side of the thorax and a series of blue spots at the wing bases. The males have a line of tiny blue spots along the length of the abdomen, whereas females have yellow spots. Females oviposit alone and the eggs remain dormant until hatching the following spring. Depending on latitude, larvae take between two and four years to develop.

Brown Hawker, male. *Steve Cham*

## Distribution

Brown Hawker is found across northern Europe and Asia, ranging from Ireland in the west to Lake Baikal in the east and from the Alps in the south to the Arctic Circle in the north. It is absent from the Mediterranean and Black Sea areas, the Iberian Peninsula and western France. It is widespread and common throughout its range.

In Britain, this species is commonly found in the lowlands of southern, central and eastern England as far north as County Durham and west into Lancashire, north-east Wales and south through the Welsh border counties into Avon, Somerset and Dorset. It is absent as a breeding species from Scotland, south-west Wales, Devon and Cornwall. It is common and widespread in a broad band across much of Ireland. Its absence or scarcity over much of Wales, south-west England and western France remains an enigma.

In northern England it is on the edge of its current range in Northumberland where there have been only isolated, mainly historical, records with little evidence of a breeding

Branas Isaf lake, Llandrillo, Denbighshire: the most westerly confirmed breeding site for Brown Hawker in North Wales. *Allan Brandon*

Female Brown Hawker ovipositing into wood. *Steve Cham*

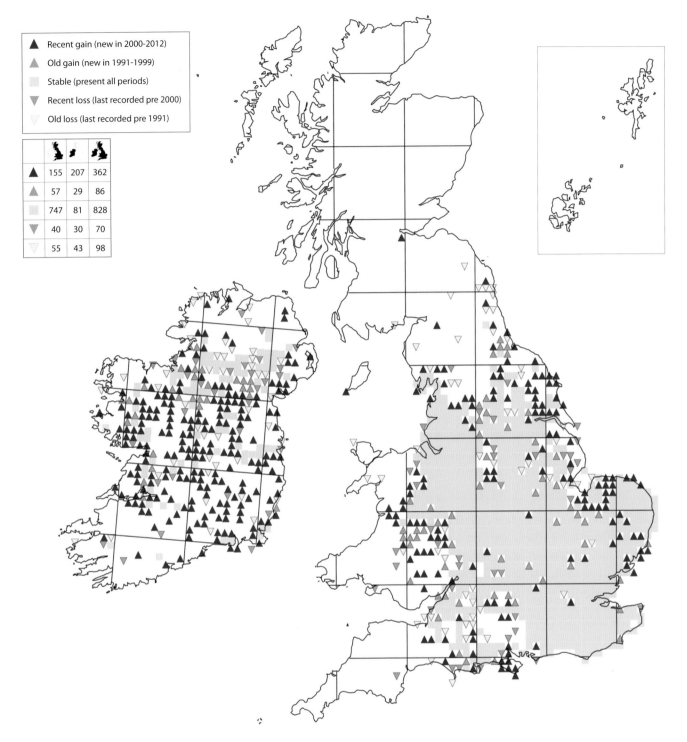

| | | | |
|---|---|---|---|
| ▲ | 155 | 207 | 362 |
| ▲ | 57 | 29 | 86 |
| ▦ | 747 | 81 | 828 |
| ▼ | 40 | 30 | 70 |
| ▽ | 55 | 43 | 98 |

**Legend:**
▲ Recent gain (new in 2000-2012)
▲ Old gain (new in 1991-1999)
▦ Stable (present all periods)
▼ Recent loss (last recorded pre 2000)
▽ Old loss (last recorded pre 1991)

population. The most recent are single records from Morpeth and Alnwick in 2003 and 2004, respectively. In Lincolnshire, it is concentrated to the west of the county with only occasional records in the Lincolnshire Fens. There has been a recent expansion in the region of the River Humber around and to the west of Hull, as well as in North Yorkshire with a concentration of records around the lower reaches of the River Tees. The only recent Scottish record is of a single female ovipositing at Beecraigs Country Park, West Lothian in 2006.

On the west coast of England, Brown Hawker extends to the north of Morecombe Bay with isolated sightings along the southern Cumbrian coast; there is some evidence of a recent northward spread here but to a lesser extent than that shown by other species. There was a single sighting from the Isle of Man in 2003.

Brown Hawker is largely absent from north-west and south-west Wales, where the only recent records were of two singletons in the Colwyn Bay area, and from south-west Wales. However, there is evidence of recent spread westwards from the populations in central-east Wales, around Llandrindod Wells, where it has been present for many years.

In southern England it is common and widespread east of the River Severn, with strong populations in Herefordshire, Worcestershire, Gloucestershire and Shropshire. It is largely

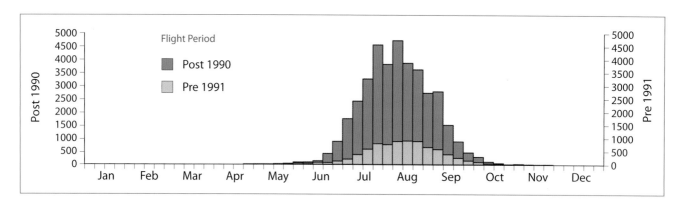

absent from Salisbury Plain but is fairly abundant in surrounding lowland areas in Avon, Somerset, Hampshire and Dorset. Sightings on the Isle of Wight are more likely to refer to migrants than a resident breeding population on the island. To date, the only record west of Dorset and Somerset was a male near Bovey Tracey, south Devon, in August 1999.

Brown Hawker is common and widespread across much of central Ireland and in the lake-rich regions of east Clare, the Corrib-Mask region in Galway and Mayo and counties Sligo, Leitrim, Fermanagh, Cavan and Monaghan. The species is more sparsely distributed in the south-west (Cork and Kerry), the Atlantic fringe of Galway and Mayo, in Meath in the east and across the three northern counties of Donegal, Londonderry and Antrim.

## Habitat

Brown Hawker breeds in slow-flowing rivers, canals, lakes and ponds, provided there is suitable material for the female to oviposit into. The eggs are laid into robust organic material, such as logs or wooden structures that have softened through being in water, or in the roots of submerged trees, larger aquatic plants such as reedmace, Water-plantain and Yellow Iris. It tends to prefer neutral or alkaline habitats. Throughout its range, it tends to be a lowland species and is rarely found breeding above 200m, although dispersing

Felmersham NR, Bedfordshire, is a series of mature gravel pits. Hundreds of Brown Hawker exuviae have been found on the introduced plants of Water-soldier. *Steve Cham*

individuals may be found at higher altitudes. Adults spend time away from water, hunting over meadows and along hedgerows and woodland edges, patrolling a large area with a strong, purposeful flight pattern.

## Conservation status and threats

Brown Hawker is categorised as Least Concern in the British and Irish Red lists as it is widespread and common throughout its range. There are no obvious threats to the species.

## National trends

The CEH trends analysis indicated a decrease in this species, which conflicts with expert opinion. In the previous atlas it was absent from large areas of seemingly suitable habitat and many of these apparent gaps in that range have now been filled. At the edges of all its previously known range, Brown Hawker has shown signs of expansion, especially northwards on the east coast of England. However, the increase in range appears not to be as marked along the west coast. In south-west England the increase in range has been slight, compared to other parts of Britain. A recent record from Scotland, from a lowland area of apparently suitable habitat, is particularly interesting as it might indicate the beginning of range expansion in this area.

Recording during DragonflyIreland produced many new records of the species in central Ireland. The species may well have increased and spread but it is difficult to distinguish any range change from the increased recording intensity.

Brown Hawker emerging. *Lorraine Ellison*

# Common Hawker
## *Aeshna juncea*

Moorland Hawker

Common Hawker is a large dragonfly with a blue-spotted abdomen in males and usually yellow- or green-spotted abdomen in females. Females with male colouration are fairly frequent. Although less obvious in flight, the golden yellow colour of the leading edge wing vein (costa) in both sexes at maturity distinguishes it from similar species. Larval development normally takes two to three years in Britain and Ireland.

Common Hawker, male. *John Curd*

Female Common Hawker ovipositing. *Ian Brodie*

## Distribution

Common Hawker is widely-distributed in northern Europe and ranges up to and beyond the Arctic Circle. Its more southerly European strongholds are in uplands, including the Alps, the mountains of central France and the Pyrenees. Outposts in Portugal and the mountains of Bulgaria are the southern limits. It is one of the few British and Irish dragonflies to have a circumpolar (Holarctic) distribution.

Common Hawker is common and widespread in Ireland. It occurs from sea level to over 500m and is especially numerous in the blanket bogs and heaths in the western half of the island. It is more restricted in the intensively managed lowlands of the south and east due to lack of habitat, although populations can be found in the Wicklow Mountains and less extensive upland areas of Cork and Waterford as well as the coastal wetlands of Co. Wexford.

In Britain, it is widely distributed and usually the commonest hawker, except in agricultural lowlands, north and west of a line between the mouths of the River Tees in the north-west of England and the River Exe in the south-west. In Lancashire, the species breeds only in acidic waters, whether related to upland blanket bog or lowland raised bog. In much of lowland Britain, the Common Hawker is rare or absent,

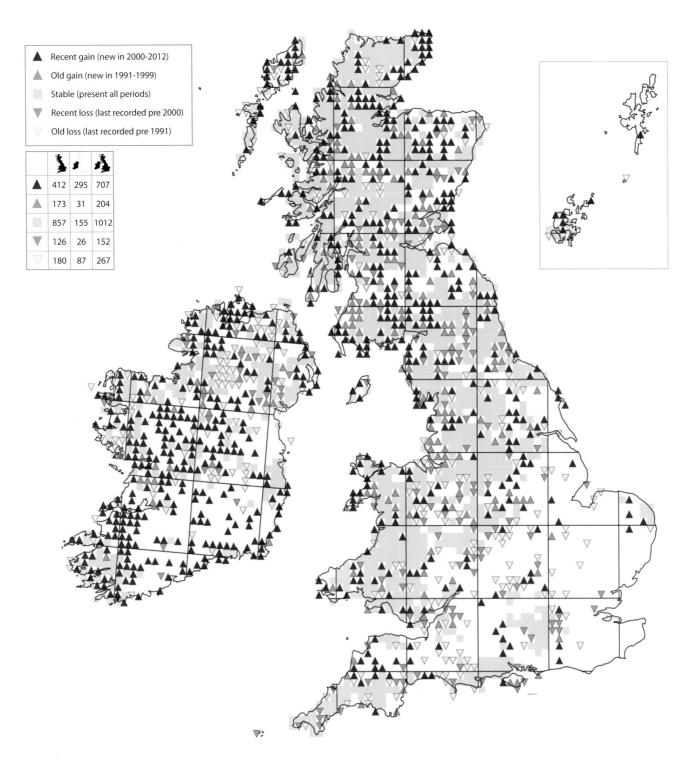

| | | | |
|---|---|---|---|
| ▲ | 412 | 295 | 707 |
| ▲ | 173 | 31 | 204 |
| ▨ | 857 | 155 | 1012 |
| ▼ | 126 | 26 | 152 |
| ▽ | 180 | 87 | 267 |

**Legend:**

▲ Recent gain (new in 2000-2012)

▲ Old gain (new in 1991-1999)

▨ Stable (present all periods)

▼ Recent loss (last recorded pre 2000)

▽ Old loss (last recorded pre 1991)

except in a few remaining areas of bog or heathland with acid mires. Most notably the latter include the Humberhead Moors (Thorne, Crowle, Goole and Hatfield), the New Forest and the Surrey/Berkshire heaths. The species also occurs in a few heathland, grazing marsh and coastal sites in East Anglia. The vernacular name is particularly misleading and in some areas has given rise to erroneous records from inexperienced recorders. It is also thought that some historical records for this species, particularly from eastern England, may have been misidentified, at a time when Migrant Hawker was becoming more common and widespread.

In Scotland, it is widespread and often abundant but it can be rare in farmed lowlands and urban areas,

especially south of the Highlands. It survives in the windswept and exposed environments of the Western Isles and Orkney and is doubtless under-recorded in the more remote hills and islands. The first record for Shetland was a female found dead on 15 September 2009.

## Habitat

In Britain, Common Hawker is most abundant in pools in blanket bogs and acid upland tarns. In Ireland, it is essentially a species of small waterbodies, occasionally in small lakes as well as dune slacks and fen pools where there is a lack of competition.

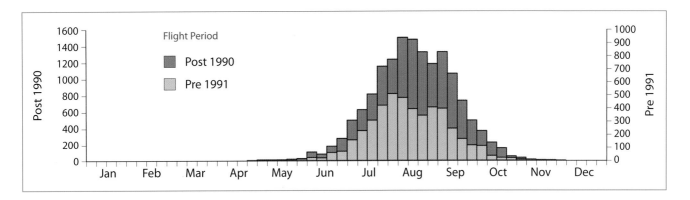

In Scotland, larvae have been found regularly in peaty pools at altitudes of up to 600m or more in all the mountain areas and, exceptionally, at some 1100m on Ben Cruachan, Argyll. This may demonstrate its ability to survive in extreme conditions, although successful emergence in these areas is still to be proven. It will also breed in the slow-moving waters of boggy runnels and streams where there are sections of deeper, quiet, water. Females oviposit alone, sometimes quite late in the day, laying eggs into marginal vegetation, frequently submerging most of the abdomen to do so. Wandering females will also oviposit opportunistically in richer sites, such as park lakes and garden ponds – their larvae competing in the latter especially with Southern Hawkers where both species occur. Less usual breeding sites also include freshwater pools in coastal dunes and dykes within grazing marshes (e.g. in Norfolk). Adults are strong fliers and range widely. They may be encountered feeding, especially in woodlands, at considerable distances from breeding sites.

## Conservation status and threats

Common Hawker is categorised as Least Concern in the British and Irish Red Lists. It is threatened only locally, primarily from habitat destruction, including commercial afforestation of blanket bogs, peat extraction, and urban and industrial encroachment into key habitats such as heathland areas. Such pressures continue and have resulted in the loss of the species from many parts of southern and eastern England especially. Large scale afforestation of upland areas from the mid 20th century onwards has changed the face of many moors and bogs and must have caused some reduction of the breeding habitat. Peat extraction in Ireland will have had major effects, though largely undocumented. No particular measures are needed other than protection of habitats, especially in areas where these have become restricted.

Arenig Fawr pools, Snowdonia, Merionethshire: an area of acidic peaty bog pools occupied by Common Hawker. *Allan Brandon*

Upland pools at Cairnsmore of Fleet, Dumfries & Galloway, occupied by Common Hawker. *R&B Mearns*

## National trends

The CEH trends analysis shows a significant decline in Common Hawker. Whether the current northwards advance of other large hawkers, namely Southern Hawker and Emperor Dragonfly, together with that of the slightly smaller Migrant Hawker, pose a natural competitive threat in sub-optimal habitats remains to be seen.

In Britain and Ireland the species shows no obvious tendency to population movements, either locally or more widely. However, occasional wanderers can occur almost anywhere. Climate change might be expected to have an effect and may be the root cause of unexplained declines at some southern sites.

Over the past twenty years at lowland heathland sites in south-east Berkshire, Hampshire and Surrey the trends have been complex. During the final decade of the 20th century there was a marked increase in the number of records of flying adults and evidence of breeding in this area. However, during the first decade of the new millennium, numbers have steadily declined, despite the continued availability of suitable breeding habitat (J. Ward-Smith, pers. comm.).

Bog pools, Wildmoor, Berkshire. Common Hawker still breeds here but numbers appear to have been declining in recent years. *Des Sussex*

# Migrant Hawker
*Aeshna mixta*

Migrant Hawker is a relatively small hawker. Adult males have a brown thorax with much reduced antehumeral stripes. The dark brown abdomen has paired spots of yellow and cyan. Females are predominantly brown with paired, yellow abdominal markings. Both sexes have a narrow yellow triangle marking on abdominal segment 2. Females oviposit into vegetation, including dead material, sometimes in the drawdown zone away from the water's edge. Eggs overwinter in plant material and hatch the following spring. Larvae develop rapidly and adults emerge within a few weeks.

Migrant Hawker, male. *Steve Cham*

## Distribution

Migrant Hawker is widespread across mainland Europe, where its range extends from northern Africa to southern Scandinavia. It is absent from alpine regions, possibly because the colder temperatures are not conducive to larval development.

In Britain it previously had a predominantly southern and eastern distribution, becoming less abundant across the north Midlands and into Wales and south-west England, where records tend to be predominantly in the south of Devon and Cornwall. However, there has been an increasing number of recent records with confirmed breeding across Wales in Anglesey, Brecknockshire, Caernarvonshire, Carmarthenshire, Glamorgan, Montgomeryshire, Pembrokeshire and Radnorshire. In northern England there have been similar recent increases and it has spread northwards through Durham and Northumberland.

Migrant Hawker was first recorded in Scotland in 2003 from Dumfries & Galloway. It has also been recorded from Ayrshire and regularly from Berwickshire since 2006. Oviposition was recorded on one occasion only. The northern limit of its range is likely to be limited by colder water temperatures that inhibit larval development.

In Ireland, the species was first recorded at Tacumshin Lough, Co. Wexford, during 1997 and it has spread considerably since then. Early records were concentrated along the southern and south-eastern coastal areas but are now spreading inland. It has been recorded in the Co. Clare/Co. Limerick region since 2007 (Nelson, 2011). The species is currently continuing to spread northwards and it has been seen regularly in Co. Down in Northern Ireland since 2006.

## Habitat

Migrant Hawker breeds at a wide range of habitats, from small ponds through to large gravel pits to slow-flowing rivers and canals. Breeding sites have extensive riparian vegetation into which the female lays her eggs along the margins of the water.

The species is able to tolerate brackish waters in coastal regions (Dijkstra, 2006). It was previously thought to avoid acidic heathland pools yet recent records suggest that this is not the case and its presence may be to the detriment of Common Hawker at sites in Berkshire and Hampshire (M. Turton pers. comm., S. Cham pers. comm.).

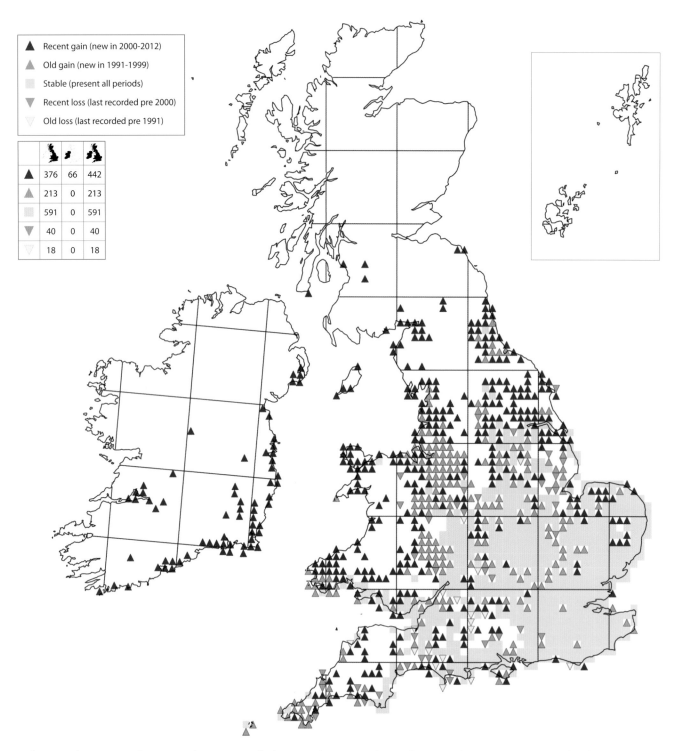

| | | | |
|---|---|---|---|
| ▲ Recent gain (new in 2000-2012) | 376 | 66 | 442 |
| ▲ Old gain (new in 1991-1999) | 213 | 0 | 213 |
| ▥ Stable (present all periods) | 591 | 0 | 591 |
| ▼ Recent loss (last recorded pre 2000) | 40 | 0 | 40 |
| ▽ Old loss (last recorded pre 1991) | 18 | 0 | 18 |

It frequently occurs in large numbers, particularly towards the end of August and early September, when swarms of adults can be found feeding in woodland rides, clearings and over reedbeds, often some distance from the breeding site. Swarms of feeding adults have often been recorded at the emergence of winged ants.

## Conservation status and threats

Migrant Hawker is categorised as Least Concern in the British and Irish Red Lists. The wide habitat preferences of this species and high numbers emerging from many sites mean that it is under no particular threat. The species can occur in large numbers in warm autumns.

Any loss of waterside vegetation may hinder breeding, although the species will oviposit into bare mud and logs, allowing it to colonise many different types of habitat. The rapid larval development is temperature-dependent and it is this factor that is likely to limit expansion in Britain and Ireland.

## National trends

This species gets its vernacular name from its appearance as a migrant species to Britain in the 20th century. Prior to this it was known as the Scarce Hawker, reflecting its rarity at the time. Its increasing abundance resulted in the change of vernacular name, although it soon became established

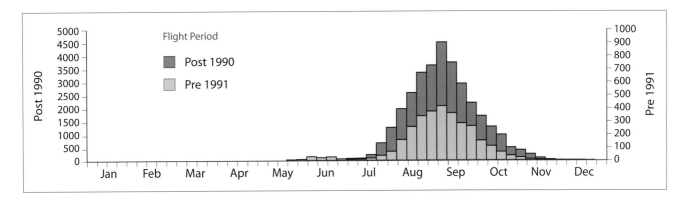

as a breeding species. It is now common and widespread in England, and has also spread into Wales, Ireland and to some extent into Scotland. This range expansion is likely to continue as a result of climate change, especially increasing temperatures in northern regions. Breeding populations are still thought to be augmented by migrants from continental Europe. The CEH trends analysis confirms a significant increase in the species.

There has been significant northwards movement into north-east Yorkshire, and the colonies in Durham and Northumberland that existed pre-2000 show signs of a continued northwards and westwards expansion. It has recently colonised Cumbria and has moved into Dumfriesshire, southern Scotland. Breeding populations are still thought to be augmented by migrants from continental Europe. There are scattered records elsewhere in Scotland but no evidence yet of confirmed breeding colonies.

Female Migrant Hawker ovipositing above the water level. *Brian Smith*

Hundred Acre Piece, Hampshire, has high numbers of Migrant Hawker in late summer. *Steve Cham*

# Norfolk Hawker
## *Anaciaeshna isoceles*

### Green-eyed Hawker

Norfolk Hawker is a large, gingery-brown dragonfly with conspicuous green eyes. It has largely clear wings, two yellow stripes on each side of the thorax and a yellow triangle on segment 2 of the abdomen. Females lay their eggs alone, favouring the leaves and flower stalks of Water-soldier, although other plants are sometimes used. Eggs hatch after 3-5 weeks and larvae normally develop over two years.

Norfolk Hawker, male.
*Steve Cham*

## Distribution

Globally, Norfolk Hawker is widely distributed in lowland areas of central, southern and eastern Europe. It is more restricted in western Europe, including Britain, Spain, Portugal and parts of France. It is absent from Scandinavia, with the exception of Gotland and parts of Denmark.

Within Britain it has always been a scarce and local species of fens and marshes in East Anglia, although it is abundant in some areas. The core range, from which there have been regular records for at least the last ten to twenty years, is an area of 18 hectads in eastern Norfolk and north-east Suffolk. There is some evidence of recent spread from this stronghold, although records well away from the core range are mainly attributable to wandering migrants.

The species currently occupies five river valleys in East Norfolk, with the largest populations in the Broads and in the marshes that border the lower reaches of the River Waveney downstream of Bungay. Areas within the other river valleys currently supporting populations are: River Ant, including marshes adjacent to Alderfen, Barton and Sutton Broads; River Bure, including Woodbastwick, Ranworth and Upton Marshes; River Thurne, including Horsey Mere, Hickling and Martham Broads; Trinity

Female Norfolk Hawker ovipositing into bur-reed in a ditch at Geldeston, Suffolk. *Steve Cham*

Broads and surrounding marshes; Halvergate and Acle (Damgate) marshes; River Yare, including Wheatfen and Strumpshaw Fen.

In 2013, the first records for West Norfolk were received with two individuals seen together at Thompson Water in

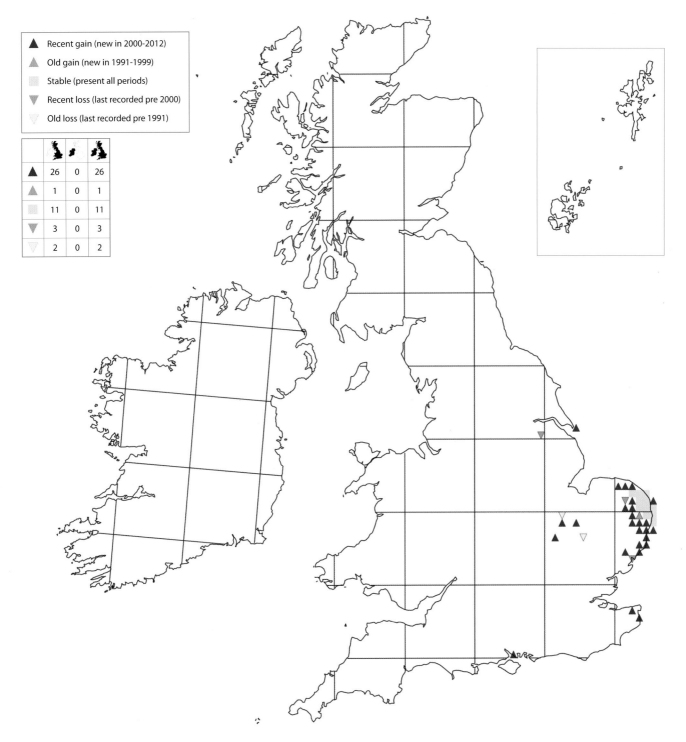

| | 🗺 | ▫ | 🗺 |
|---|---|---|---|
| ▲ | 26 | 0 | 26 |
| ▲ | 1 | 0 | 1 |
| ▦ | 11 | 0 | 11 |
| ▼ | 3 | 0 | 3 |
| ▽ | 2 | 0 | 2 |

July. This followed earlier sightings at Lenwade and Hevingham Great Wood to the north-west of Norwich, sites which are well away from the species' core range. There has been some recent spread to the west of Norwich, which is probably a consequence of habitat improvement between Thorpe Marshes and Cringleford. This has boosted local populations and the species is now moving upstream along the River Yare. There is also some evidence of spread upstream along other rivers, for example the River Waveney on the Norfolk/Suffolk border.

In north Norfolk, Holt Lowes has two casual records of a female Norfolk Hawker dating back to 2001. Both records would appear to refer to the same female that was seen

ovipositing on one occasion. There have been no further records from Holt Lowes but another individual was seen at a private site in the same hectad (TG03) in 2007. In east Norfolk there are several coastal records from Winterton Dunes, spanning a number of years, and one from Trimingham, close to the coast, in 2003. It is reasonable to suggest that continental migrants explain these observations, as well as some of the recent records from Suffolk.

In Suffolk, Norfolk Hawker has occupied marshes adjacent to the River Waveney for many years. There are substantial colonies south of Geldeston Lock and at both Castle and Carlton Marshes. There is also a population at Minsmere

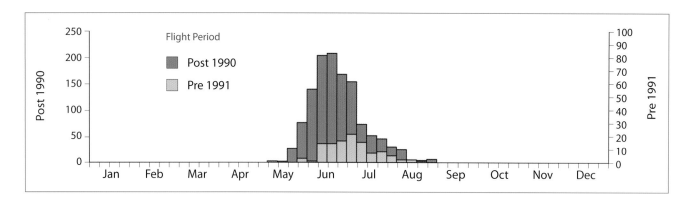

and the Sizewell Belts that has spread south over recent decades, almost to the border with Essex. The increased number of records in Suffolk reflects real range expansion, as well as better recording in recent years.

The coastal records from Landguard Bird Observatory, Suffolk, in 1991; Spurn Bird Observatory, Yorkshire, in 2003; and Titchfield Haven NNR, Hampshire, in 2007, would suggest migrants of continental origin. This could also explain the source of recent sightings in Kent from 2011 onwards. Single individuals were initially reported at Stodmarsh NNR and at Worth near Sandwich Bay, with another at nearby Chislet in 2012. By 2013, several individuals were present at Westbere Lakes, part of the Stodmarsh NNR, indicating that a small colony may be present. A pair was seen mating during July and oviposition

was also observed in two ditches. A 1997 record from Messingham Sand Quarry, north Lincolnshire, is less than 50km from the east coast, so probably represents a further continental migrant.

Historically, the species was also found in the Cambridgeshire fens but was lost from here in 1893. One was then seen at the Ouse Washes in 2002 and another at Woodwalton Fen in 2009. In 2011 a single male was observed flying over Hayling Lake at Paxton Pits Nature Reserve in Cambridgeshire (TL16, formerly in Huntingdonshire). A single female was observed at the neighbouring Rudd Lake the following year. In 2013 a single, immature female was seen at Potton Wood in Bedfordshire on 3 June. This prompted fresh searches at Paxton Pits where at least 30 exuviae were found in an extensive area of Water-soldier on Hayling Lake, thus providing evidence of breeding at this site.

Castle Marshes, Suffolk, support a large population of Norfolk Hawker in the ditches that have Water-soldier. *Steve Cham*

## Habitat

Norfolk Hawker typically breeds in ditches within fens and grazing marshes, occasionally utilising small ponds. The species requires unpolluted water with a rich aquatic flora and is intolerant of brackish conditions. The recent breeding colony at Paxton Pits occupies a mature gravel pit where a dense expanse of Water-soldier represents the main breeding area. Maturing adults have been observed feeding in nearby meadows.

Paxton Pits, Cambridgeshire, where a recently-discovered population of Norfolk Hawker breeds in the large expanse of Water-soldier. *Steve Cham*

Ludham Marshes, Norfolk, is a typical grazing marsh site for Norfolk Hawker. *Pam Taylor*

In England, but not on the continent, the species is particularly associated with an aquatic flora that often includes abundant Water-soldier. This plant indicates good water quality and, although submerged in winter, provides a large surface area of leaf material throughout the year. The importance of Water-soldier to breeding success is not clearly understood and may be purely coincidental. A recent study (Pickwell, 2011) concluded that other aquatic plant communities are also closely associated with the presence of Norfolk Hawker. These are often characterised by Broad-leaved Pondweed, Water-violet, water-milfoil and Frogbit. In all cases, these plant communities represent an abundant and diverse climax flora which often supports a good range of other rare invertebrates.

## Conservation status and threats

The localised distribution of the species makes it vulnerable to extinction and it is protected under Schedule 5 of the Wildlife and Countryside Act 1981 (as amended). It is also listed in section 41 of the Natural Environment and Rural Communities Act 2006 and is ranked as Endangered in the British Red List. Norfolk Hawker was listed as a UK BAP Priority Species in 2007. It is classified as Least Concern in the European and Mediterranean Red Lists but Vulnerable in the North African Red List (Garcia, 2010).

There are likely to be serious implications for the conservation of this species as a result of rising sea level in south-east England. Without improved coastal protection and inland defences, the predicted sea level rise is liable to inundate parts of the Norfolk Broads and coastal marshes with saline water. Such conditions will kill not only Norfolk Hawker larvae but also the aquatic flora and fauna on which they depend. The recent discovery of a breeding population well inland in Cambridgeshire, therefore brings hope of a more secure future for the species in Britain.

During the last century, substantial areas of grazing marsh were lost through conversion to arable land. This significantly reduced the amount of suitable breeding habitat for Norfolk Hawker. The species is thought to have declined during the third quarter of the last century as a consequence of both intensified farming and the eutrophication of aquatic habitats. More recent improvements in sewage treatment and water quality, together with the reversion of arable land to grazing marsh under agri-environment schemes, have served to halt and reverse the previous decline. However, unsympathetic management or neglect of these ditch systems can still impact on Norfolk Hawker. Modern dredging of dykes with machinery not only increases suspended sediment but removes dragonfly larvae and plant material. Pumped drainage systems can also cause fluctuations in water levels; disrupting the micro-habitat conditions that would otherwise be suitable for the species.

## National trends

Since 1990 there have been significant range expansions, as evidenced by the spread southwards in Suffolk and both northwards and westwards in Norfolk. These expansions in range have not happened evenly, with spread along the Rivers Ant and Yare apparently preceding that in other areas. The spread inland and the discovery of a breeding population in Cambridgeshire represents a significant milestone for this species and may offer hope that further range expansion will occur.

# Vagrant Emperor

*Anax ephippiger*

Vagrant Emperor is a medium to large dragonfly. Males have a bright blue 'saddle' near the base of the abdomen, which is less conspicuous or absent in females. Both sexes resemble the equivalent sex of the Lesser Emperor, though in the Vagrant Emperor the eyes are brown and the overall appearance of the body is more sandy than the dark olive-brown typical of the Lesser Emperor. The species has a rapid life cycle, so that early season immigrants have the potential to produce a locally-bred autumn generation, though this has not as yet been observed in Britain and Ireland.

Vagrant Emperor, male.
*R&B Mearns*

## Distribution

Vagrant Emperor is primarily Afro-tropical in distribution and a common dragonfly of Africa, the Middle East, south-west Asia and the Indian subcontinent, with breeding on the European shores of the Mediterranean now also fairly regular. The species has a semi-nomadic lifestyle, the long-lived adults normally following the rains within the inter-tropical convergence zone. This zone around the equator is where the north-east and south-east trade winds meet (though its exact position varies with regional geography and with the season). Given appropriate local wind conditions, wandering migrants may, however, move some considerable distance outside the normal range and reach southern Europe on a regular basis and northern Europe more sporadically. Vagrant Emperor has even been recorded in such unlikely places as Iceland (Olafsson, 1977), the Faroe Islands (Jensen & Nielsen, 2012) and the Caribbean (Meurgey, 2006).

British and Irish records have a bias towards the southern and south-western coastal regions but are very widespread, as would be expected from such a powerful migrant. There is even a record from as far north as Fetlar in Shetland, made during 1970. Some older sightings are close to major ports (e.g. a record from Dublin in 1913) which may

conceivably indicate that some ship-assisted arrivals take place in addition to genuine immigration. It does, however, seem equally plausible that such records result from brightly-lit areas, such as ports, being attractive to incoming night migrants. Vagrant Emperors have indeed been caught on several occasions in moth-traps in Britain and Ireland (e.g. Portland Bill, Dorset, in 1983, Crows-an-Wra, Cornwall in 2011 and Kilpatrick Dunes, Co. Wexford, in 2011; also records from Ireland in 2013, discussed below).

## Habitat

Vagrant Emperor typically breeds in very shallow, often temporary, pools and lakes that usually have high water temperatures, only limited vegetation and no fish or other higher predators. The larvae are able to withstand a considerable degree of salinity. Within Britain, oviposition has only ever been observed at two localities, both within the last few years. At a pool on the North Predannack Downs, Cornwall, egg-laying was noted in both spring and autumn 2011 (Parr, 2011) and oviposition was also noted at Bovey Heathfield, Devon, during autumn 2013. There is no evidence that the Cornish breeding attempt was successful though, as immatures are highly dispersive, it is conceivable

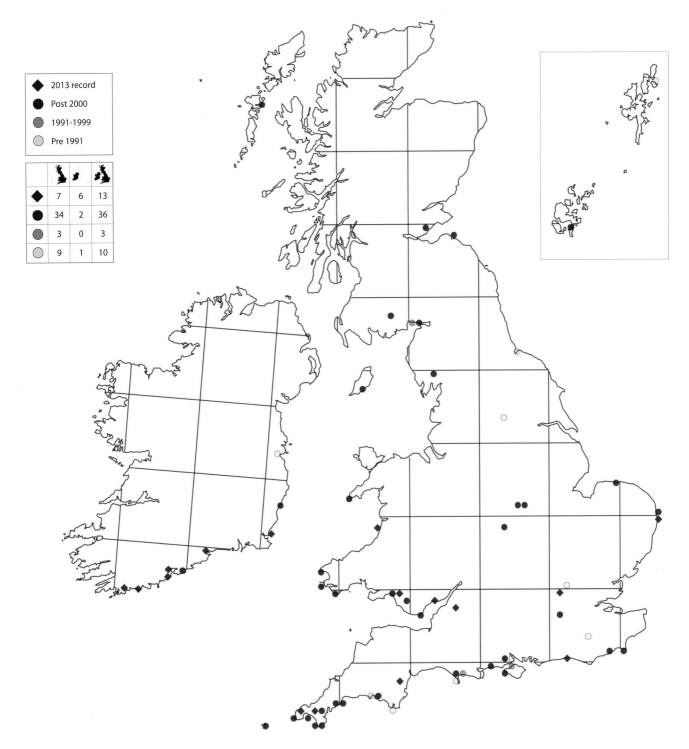

| | 🔷 | 🔷 | 🔷 |
|---|---|---|---|
| ◆ | 7 | 6 | 13 |
| ● | 34 | 2 | 36 |
| ⬤ | 3 | 0 | 3 |
| ⬤ | 9 | 1 | 10 |

◆ 2013 record
● Post 2000
⬤ 1991-1999
⬤ Pre 1991

that if only very small numbers of progeny were produced these could have been overlooked. The species is known to be able to reproduce successfully in central Europe (Vonwil & Wildermuth, 1990).

During migration, individuals may be encountered almost anywhere, though the species tends to avoid woodlands. As with most migrant species, coastal localities are favoured, though this is by no means always the case.

## Conservation status and threats

Vagrant Emperor was not assessed in the most recent Red Lists for Britain and Ireland, by virtue of it occurring only as

a vagrant. Given the species' migratory nature and Afro-tropical or Mediterranean origins, this seems unlikely to change in the near future. There are thus no relevant conservation issues at present.

## National trends

In Britain, the first record of Vagrant Emperor relates to a specimen from Devonport, Devon, in February 1903. Following the first Irish record in 1913 and the second British record in October 1968, the species then started to be seen more regularly and, during the period 1983–1998, it occurred almost annually. Although typically only isolated individuals were involved, during the first three months of

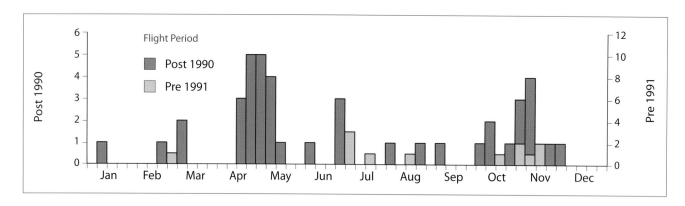

Female Vagrant Emperor ovipositing at Bovey Heathfield, Devon, on 26 October 2013. *Pauline Smale*

1998 some 20 unidentified dragonflies were seen in southern England, many (if not all) of which were likely to have been Vagrant Emperors (Parr, 1998). After 1998, the species returned to being an infrequent migrant for several years. A record in late 2010 was then to be followed by a dramatic surge of sightings during 2011, with several waves of arrivals being noted in both spring and autumn. In all, up to 35 confirmed individuals and many more possibles were reported from Britain and Ireland during this period (Parr, 2011). No further arrivals were noted during 2012, but autumn 2013 then saw another major influx. Although there were many records from England and Wales, the influx was particularly noticeable on the south coast of Ireland. Starting on 24 September, one was caught in west Cork by a cat. Three were then caught in two moth traps the following night at two different Co. Cork localities. In October, single adults were seen at two Cork sites and two, possibly three, at a site in Co. Wexford. One was also seen in Co. Waterford on 12 November. Although no evidence of breeding behaviour was reported, a total of nine sightings is unprecedented for Ireland.

Observations seem to suggest that the frequency of arrivals of Vagrant Emperor to Britain and Ireland is increasing. Given the considerable growth of interest in dragonflies over recent decades, it is possible that some of this apparent increase is simply a reflection of the improved observer coverage that now takes place. However, whereas most historic sightings refer to isolated individuals, the occurrence of several major influxes in recent years may indicate that a genuine increase is taking place, as has also been suspected in some other European countries. The first record of the species from The Netherlands was, for instance, as recently as 1995 (Dijkstra *et al.*, 1995), though there have been several further sightings since then.

Within these overall trends there are signs of periodicity, phases of relative abundance being followed by phases of scarcity. This may be linked to fluctuating patterns of rainfall in areas such as the Sahel and Guinea zones of Africa (Dumont & Desmet, 1990), from where many of our immigrants may ultimately be derived. The species is often reported during periods of winds from northwest Africa or during falls of Saharan dust.

# Emperor Dragonfly

*Anax imperator*

Blue Emperor

Emperor Dragonfly is a large and robust dragonfly. Males have a sky-blue abdomen with a black mid-dorsal line, and an apple-green thorax. In females, the mid-dorsal line is broader than on males and the abdomen is dull green. Adults have a synchronised emergence, typically in early June. Females oviposit unaccompanied into various submerged and floating plants. Larvae usually take two years to complete development but in exceptional circumstances, with abundant food supply, can take one year.

Emperor Dragonfly, male.
*Anthony Taylor*

## Distribution

Emperor Dragonfly is widely distributed from western Europe to central Asia and India. The species also occurs throughout the Middle East, North Africa and tropical Africa. It is widespread throughout the whole of central Europe and the Mediterranean region. In recent decades it has expanded its range northwards into southern Sweden, Latvia and Estonia. In the Atlantic, Emperor Dragonfly can be found on the Azores, Canary Islands, Cape Verde and Madeira, and in the western Indian Ocean it occurs on Madagascar and the Mascarenes.

At the time of the previous atlas, Emperor Dragonfly was largely confined to the low-lying areas of southern England and southern Wales, where it was widespread and not uncommon. Since then it has shown a marked expansion to the west and north into North Wales, north-east England and central Scotland. It is still remains unrecorded from some upland areas of Dartmoor and Exmoor, and the chalk downland areas of Hampshire and Wiltshire. From 2000 onwards it has colonised Ireland, appearing in Co. Wexford in the south-east around 2000 and then showing a rapid spread west and north. It also appeared in Northern Ireland in 2010 and on the Isle of Man in 2011. This dramatic expansion in the Emperor Dragonfly's distribution may be a result of climate change, especially steadily increasing temperatures, allowing the species to colonise and breed in areas where it has not been able to before.

In Scotland it has been recorded regularly from sites in the Borders and Dumfries & Galloway since 2003, with oviposition observed since 2004. In 2006, during a period of good weather, individuals were sighted further north in Scotland but have not been seen at these sites again. Numbers have been reduced since the hard winter of 2010.

Levett & Walls (2011) found that one of the Emperor Dragonflies that they had fitted with a radio transmitter in Dorset travelled a distance of over 5km in 10 days. More extensive radio-tracking of the similar (but migratory) species Green Darner, *Anax junius*, in the United States, showed it capable of travelling over 100km in one day (Wikelski *et al.*, 2006).

## Habitat

Emperor Dragonfly typically breeds in waterbodies that have rich marginal vegetation and a thick growth of aquatic plants, especially pondweeds, with areas of open water.

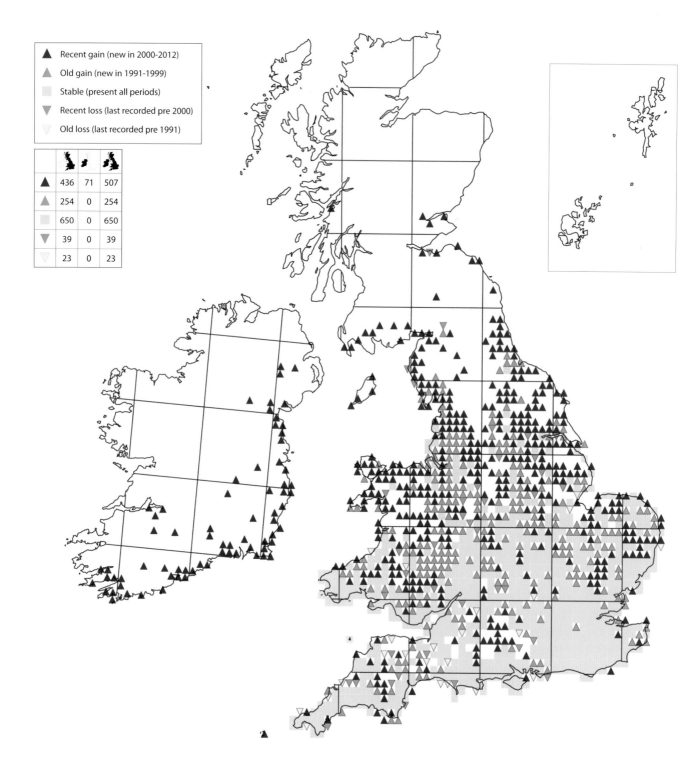

| | ![book map icon] | ![small icon] | ![combined icon] |
|---|---|---|---|
| ▲ Recent gain (new in 2000-2012) | 436 | 71 | 507 |
| ▲ Old gain (new in 1991-1999) | 254 | 0 | 254 |
| ▢ Stable (present all periods) | 650 | 0 | 650 |
| ▼ Recent loss (last recorded pre 2000) | 39 | 0 | 39 |
| ▽ Old loss (last recorded pre 1991) | 23 | 0 | 23 |

Breeding habitats include a wide range of ponds (including large garden ponds), lakes, flooded sand, gravel and clay pits, pools in peat workings, dykes, large ditches, canals and slow-flowing rivers. The species is also tolerant of brackish water and can be found breeding in marshy pools on coastal sand dunes (Mendel, 1992; Randolph, 1992; Smallshire & Swash, 2014).

It readily breeds in newly excavated sites that have little or no marginal vegetation. In such situations the species can be abundant.

## Conservation status and threats

Emperor Dragonfly is listed as Least Concern in the Red Lists for Britain and Ireland. Adult males are highly territorial and will defend a waterbody by regular patrol flights. This behaviour limits the number of adult males seen at a site. However, in favourable habitat, high numbers can emerge before quickly dispersing. Emperor Dragonfly does not appear to be threatened in Britain and Ireland.

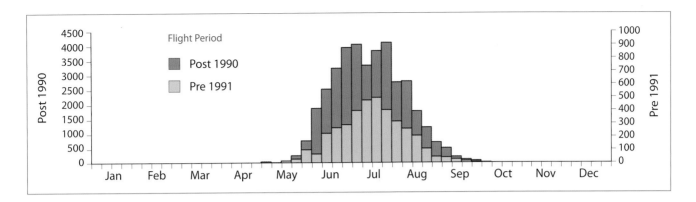

National trends

At the present time, Emperor Dragonfly appears to be widespread throughout its range, with a continuing expansion to the west and north. The CEH trends analysis (pages 58-63) shows a significant increase in this species.

Although it has dramatically increased its distribution in Britain and Ireland since the 1970s and 1980s, many records on the edge of its expanding range have been of single individuals and it has taken many more years before the species has become well-established. Smith (2010) stated that the Emperor Dragonfly was recorded for the first time in 1976 on the Sefton coast in North Merseyside but that the species did not become well-established there until the mid-1990s.

Female Emperor Dragonfly ovipositing. *Adrian Riley*

A series of ornamental lakes at Wrest Park, Bedfordshire: breeding sites for Emperor Dragonfly. *Steve Cham*

# Green Darner
*Anax junius*

## Common Green Darner

Green Darner is a North American dragonfly that closely resembles Emperor Dragonfly in appearance and many aspects of biology. Both sexes have brownish eyes and a 'bull's-eye' mark on the 'forehead', while males lack a central black line on the centre of S2 of the abdomen. The species has a pronounced migratory tendency: many individuals move northward in spring and the progeny of these spring migrants then return south in autumn. Migrants can be blown off course by prolonged periods of strong winds.

Green Darner. *Dave Smallshire*

## Distribution

Green Darner is found from Canada and Alaska (though essentially only as a vagrant at the higher latitudes) southwards through all of the USA to Mexico and as far south as Honduras and Costa Rica. It is also recorded from Bermuda, many islands in the Caribbean, and on Hawaii. Over large parts of its core range it apparently occurs both as a migrant form with a short (a few months) generation time and as a resident form with a longer (one year) generation time. However, the precise balance between these two 'sub-populations' is not well-known and the two forms may not be entirely independent. Similarly, while dragonflies reaching high latitudes early in the season are obviously migrants, just how far south returning migrants may routinely reach in autumn is unknown.

In Europe, it was recorded as a vagrant in Cornwall and the Isles of Scilly during autumn 1998 (Pellow, 1999; Corbet, 2000), when individuals were noted in south-west England following storms associated with the aftermath of Hurricane Earl. Up to eight individuals, including both males and females, were reported between 9 September to 1 October. A male recorded from the Loire Atlantique region of France on 14 September 2003 (Meurgey, 2004) is the only other confirmed record for elsewhere in Europe.

## Habitat

In North America Green Darner typically frequents ponds, lakes and slow-flowing streams, particularly those with plentiful emergent vegetation. On migration it can occur in a wider range of habitats both close to, and away from water. Sightings in south-west England during autumn 1998 were all from coastal or near-coastal localities, as is commonly observed with migrants, and generally involved individuals away from fresh water. Dragonflies were seen either on active migration near the coast, or hunting over open spaces and along sheltered hedges, as in the case of a male at Penlee Point, Cornwall, which remained in the area for some nine days.

## Conservation status and threats

Green Darner was not assessed in the most recent Odonata Red Data List for Britain. The species is a very common dragonfly in North America, but is likely to only occur as an extreme rarity in Europe and there are thus no relevant conservation issues.

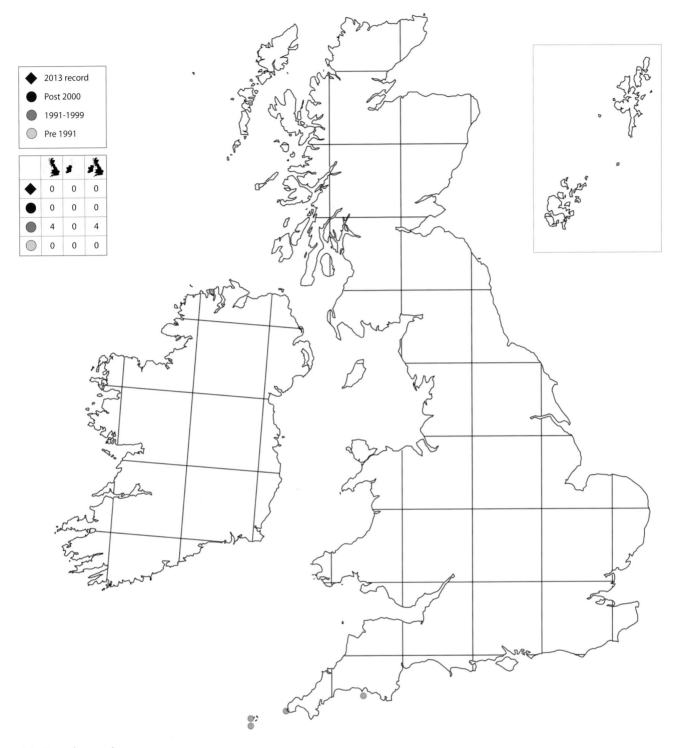

| | 🗺️ | ، | 🗺️ |
|---|---|---|---|
| ◆ | 0 | 0 | 0 |
| ● | 0 | 0 | 0 |
| ⬤ | 4 | 0 | 4 |
| ◯ | 0 | 0 | 0 |

Legend:
- ◆ 2013 record
- ● Post 2000
- ⬤ 1991-1999
- ◯ Pre 1991

## National trends

All the sightings from Britain, plus the one from France, are of recent origin and occurred at a time of exceptional weather. Further vagrants may well appear in future, given the species' abundance and migratory tendency in North America and the forecast for changes in the intensity, timing or path of Atlantic storms.

# Lesser Emperor
## *Anax parthenope*

Lesser Emperor is smaller than the Emperor Dragonfly, with an overall darker appearance. Adult males have a conspicuous blue band (saddle) around the first two abdominal segments. The females are duller than the males and can be distinguished from Emperor Dragonfly females by the brown, rather than green thorax. Vagrant Emperors are also similar but smaller and much paler than the Lesser Emperor, being almost yellow-brown overall. Unlike Emperor Dragonfly, this species oviposits in tandem.

Lesser Emperor, male. *John Curd*

## Distribution

Lesser Emperor is a widespread species of the lower latitudes of Eurasia and the northern part of Africa, described by Askew (1988) as 'local in central Europe and rare in the north... vagrant to Holland... and northern Germany'. However, following a northward spread, which began about 1980 presumably in response to global climate change, it has undergone a dramatic range expansion and is now widespread over much of France and Germany. The first Belgian records for 100 years came in 1983 (Goffart, 1984) and a record in The Netherlands in 1997 was the first definite sighting there since 1938 (Goudsmits, 1997). Sightings of Lesser Emperors have been regular in both those countries since the mid to late 1990s (Dijkstra, 2006).

In Britain, there has been a fairly steady increase in sightings since the first British record in Gloucestershire on June 13 1996 (Phillips, 1997). Likewise, in Ireland, the species' status has clearly changed since the first record in 2000 (Nelson *et al.*, 2001). Although individuals have been recorded near southern coasts, as might be expected for a species arriving from mainland Europe, there has been a surprisingly good spread of records as far north as northern England and even Orkney, Scotland.

## Habitat

This is a generalist species, found in lowland neutral waterbodies including lakes, large ponds, slower-flowing rivers and canals.

Tandem pair of Lesser Emperor egg laying. This behaviour differentiates this species from Emperor Dragonfly where the female egg lays on her own. *Dominique Mouchené*

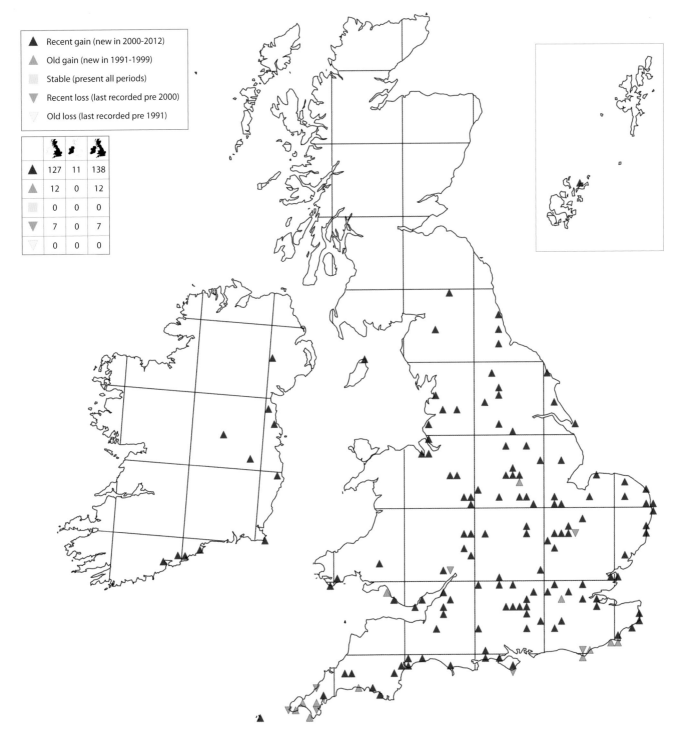

| | ![](dark triangle) | | |
|---|---|---|---|
| ▲ | 127 | 11 | 138 |
| △ | 12 | 0 | 12 |
| ▦ | 0 | 0 | 0 |
| ▼ | 7 | 0 | 7 |
| ▽ | 0 | 0 | 0 |

**Legend:**
- ▲ Recent gain (new in 2000-2012)
- △ Old gain (new in 1991-1999)
- ▦ Stable (present all periods)
- ▼ Recent loss (last recorded pre 2000)
- ▽ Old loss (last recorded pre 1991)

## Conservation status and threats

Lesser Emperor was not evaluated for the British or Irish Red lists. As a generalist species which does not have very specific habitat requirements, it is vulnerable only to the overall, global pressures affecting all dragonflies: wetland loss, drought, pollution and, on a local scale, the stocking of waterbodies with bottom-feeding fish such as carp.

## National trends

Following the first British record in Gloucestershire in 1996 and the first Irish record in 2000, sightings from both islands have become increasingly frequent and widespread. In 2000, there was a record from Orkney, the only Scottish record so far. Breeding was first proved in August 1999 when exuviae were found in Cornwall (Jones, 2000). Oviposition was seen in 2000 in Co. Durham, in 2003 in Co. Waterford (Smiddy, 2004) and in 2005 in North Yorkshire and Devon. By that year, sightings had become sufficiently regular and widespread in Britain for it to be removed from the list of species which is assessed by the national Odonata Rarities Committee (ORC). This was fortuitous as, in the following year, 2006, there was a large influx which also saw several Irish sightings. In 2006 and 2007 there were reports of oviposition from a further nine English counties.

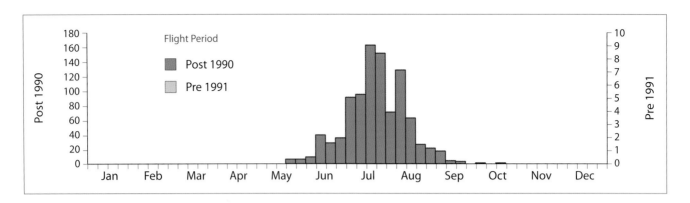

Over the last few years, the numbers of sightings per year in Britain and Ireland have been lower than the 2006/2007 peak, though they remain above pre-2003 levels. This reduction may at least partly be due to records no longer being assessed by the ORC but arrivals in the British Isles have been rather erratic and are clearly dependent on weather conditions on the Continent. In common with many other migrant insects, they are more likely to arrive in association with warm air masses from southern Europe (Parr *et al.*, 2004) and records tend to peak in mid-summer. At present the status of the species in Britain and Ireland is best described as an annual immigrant. Breeding is irregular, although it is quite likely that some breeding attempts have been overlooked. However, given the observed trends, permanent colonisation seems highly likely in the near future. Indeed, the species has been recorded from Dungeness in Kent on an annual basis for well over a decade, though many records here likely still refer to migrants.

The shallow pools of the Lizard, Cornwall attract Lesser Emperor on a regular basis. *Steve Cham*

# Hairy Dragonfly
## *Brachytron pratense*

## Hairy Hawker

Hairy Dragonfly is a small hawker with a noticeably downy thorax. Males have paired blue spots down the abdomen and two prominent green stripes on each side of the thorax; females have paired yellow spots on the abdomen, which is also hairy. This is one of the first species to emerge, often starting in April. Oviposition is typically into the floating stems of decaying emergent plants. Eggs hatch after 3-4 weeks and the larval stage usually lasts two years.

Hairy Dragonfly, male.
*Steve Cham*

## Distribution

The species is found throughout western and central Europe east to the Urals. To the north it occurs in southern Scandinavia but in southern Europe it has a disjunct distribution. There are very few records from the Iberian Peninsula.

Hairy Dragonfly ovipositing at Upton Fen, Norfolk. *Adrian Riley*

In Britain, this was a rare insect until recently but it has now expanded its range significantly. Its distribution in 1983 was centred on the south coast, especially in Sussex and Kent, with other concentrations in the Somerset Levels, south Wales and Anglesey; there were scattered records in East Anglia and elsewhere. At the time of the previous atlas it had a consolidated distribution resulting from expansion outwards from the earlier locations. Additional records confirmed its widespread occurrence across central Ireland.

The current distribution of Hairy Dragonfly is extensive in Ireland, having been recorded in every vice-county except Mid-Cork and also on at least three smaller islands: Gorumna (Co. Galway), Rathlin (Co. Antrim) and Great Saltee (Co. Wexford). It is more localised in Britain, where it has an essentially south-eastern distribution, with outposts in coastal areas elsewhere, perhaps related to the influence of the Gulf Stream. In England the species is found predominantly in the east and south-east, with other concentrations along the south coast (Sussex, Hampshire, Dorset and south Devon), Merseyside and around the Bristol Channel. The main Welsh strongholds are in south Wales, including Pembrokeshire, around Cardigan Bay and Anglesey. It was first found in Scotland near Oban in 1984 (Smith & Smith, 1984), then further south in Dumfries in 1987 and in Knapdale in 1989 (Batty, 1998). It has a westerly distribution

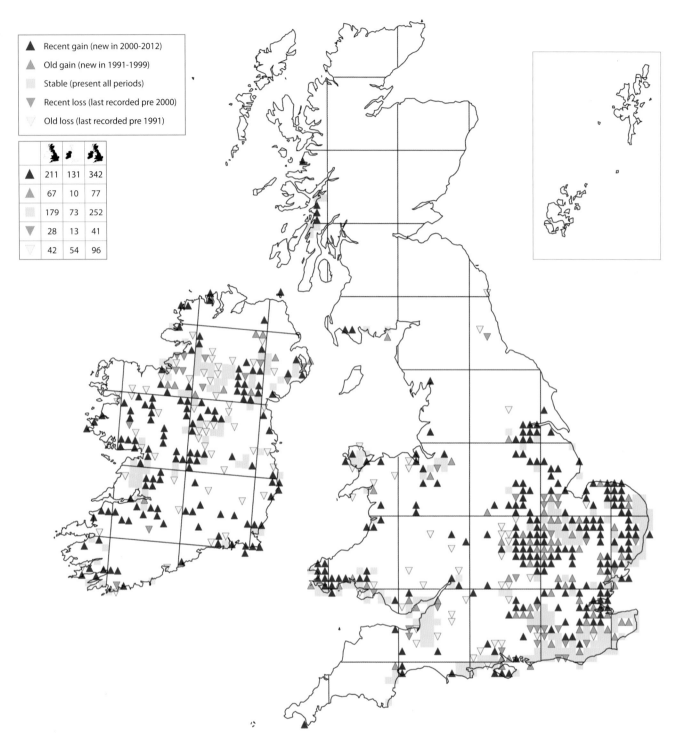

| | | | |
|---|---|---|---|
| ▲ | 211 | 131 | 342 |
| ▲ | 67 | 10 | 77 |
| ▢ | 179 | 73 | 252 |
| ▼ | 28 | 13 | 41 |
| ▽ | 42 | 54 | 96 |

**Legend**

▲ Recent gain (new in 2000-2012)
△ Old gain (new in 1991-1999)
▢ Stable (present all periods)
▼ Recent loss (last recorded pre 2000)
▽ Old loss (last recorded pre 1991)

in Scotland and has increased its known range since the previous atlas. Although this is mainly due to increased recording, it has spread to new sites. Recent reports further north, near Arisaig and on Islay, need further investigation.

## Habitat

Hairy Dragonfly is found where there is a rich, structured habitat, characterised by unpolluted, still or slow-flowing water with open and well-spaced emergent vegetation. Patrolling territorial males typically fly low, in and out of areas of emergent plants looking for ovipositing females. Emergent and bankside vegetation are also important for larvae and emerging adults and also provide shelter for mating adults. Individual adults are often seen feeding in woodland or hedgerows some distance from the breeding site. Although sites are often backed by a shelter belt of trees, scrub or taller vegetation, important grazing marsh sites are characterised by open landscapes with a few trees for shelter. Many sites are linear, such as drainage ditches, canals and slow-flowing rivers, but mature gravel pits and lakes are also used. In Ireland, lakes are the main habitat used.

The presence of floating plant material is important for the species but most of its occupied sites have more than 50% open water. A wide variety of plants is associated with typical habitat, including Common Reed, Reed Sweet-grass, reedmace, bur-reeds, sedges, rushes, Common Club-rush,

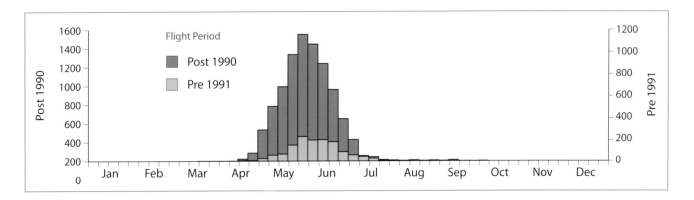

hornworts, water-milfoils, Water-plantain and Water-soldier, with Great Fen-sedge and Greater Tussock-sedge in Scotland. It is usually the richness of aquatic vegetation, rather than individual species, that appears to be important, as this is indicative of good water quality.

Oviposition and the larval stages are dependent on dead and decaying plant material, both floating and submerged. The larvae are typically found clinging to fragments of floating, decaying plant material. Water chemistry at sites is neutral to slightly alkaline, with slightly acid waters only used occasionally, at least in the Midlands (Perrin, 1999).

## Conservation Status and threats

Hairy Dragonfly receives no special protection, being categorised as Least Concern in the British and Irish Red Lists. The gradual expansion since the 1970s may be due to a succession of warm summers and mild winters, as a result of general climate change. However, the maturation of waterbodies, such as gravel pits excavated during the 1960s, has provided new sites for colonisation. In the East Midlands, such habitats have been occupied once emergent vegetation has become established. Some of these sites have become nature reserves and hence receive sympathetic management of the waterbody and vegetation structure.

*Above:* Hairy Dragonfly, just emerged in an area of dense emergent plants. *Steve Cham*

*Below:* Carrick Ponds, Dumfries & Galloway. *R&B Mearns*

Flooded limestone quarry, Stockton, Warwickshire: one of the best sites for Hairy Dragonfly in the area. *Kay Reeve*

In Norfolk, grazing marshes and ditches adjacent to river systems in the Broads provide ideal habitat if they are not over-grazed. Many Hairy Dragonfly sites here are in protected landscapes. Post-war agricultural practices have threatened many coastal grazing marshes important for this species, with conversion to arable and more intensive grassland management and drainage. However, management under agri-environment schemes brought a return to lower stocking densities and the protection of grassland landscapes in areas such as the Somerset Levels and Sussex. These have been to the benefit of Hairy Dragonfly (Tyrrell, 2011).

It is important that breeding sites for Hairy Dragonfly are not subject to excessive vegetation clearance or frequent dredging, since this will affect larval and adult survival. Maintenance of surrounding tall vegetation or trees and scrub, as windbreaks and shelter, is also important.

## National trends

In recent years, populations of Hairy Dragonfly in Britain have expanded away from their former, mainly coastal locations. The CEH trends analysis (pages 58-63) shows a significant increase in this species. Many new inland sites have been colonised, as these have matured and become suitable habitats. The appearance of gravel pits that have been colonised by tall fringing emergent plants has considerably aided this range expansion. The species is currently expanding its range in the Midlands, occupying new sites each year. In Berkshire, the widespread sites occupied since its arrival in the county in 2009 had not changed significantly in character in the years prior to the species arrival, indicating genuine range expansion rather than the exploitation of newly-suitable habitat.

In Scotland, it has increased its known westerly range, mainly due to increased recording, but the species has also spread into new sites. Recent reports further north of these areas need further investigation. Similarly, in Ireland a trend is hard to determine as many of the apparent gains shown on the map are due to increased recording intensity.

Lough Doo, Killarney National Park, Co. Kerry: a mesotrophic lake with open reed swamp, typical lake habitat for Hairy Dragonfly in Ireland. *Brian Nelson*

# Common Clubtail
## *Gomphus vulgatissimus*

Common Clubtail is a medium-sized dragonfly with black and yellow or green markings and with the eyes set apart. It is the only representative of the Gomphidae in Britain and Ireland. Males show a pronounced, characteristic clubbed tip to the abdomen. Following an early synchronised emergence, it disperses and is rarely seen returning to the riverside and therefore easily overlooked.

Common Clubtail, male. *Adrian Riley*

## Distribution

Common Clubtail is widely distributed in Europe from France through the northern Mediterranean to the Urals and as far north as southern Sweden and Finland, where it breeds widely in slow-flowing stretches of rivers, although it can be found at lakes, reservoirs and gravel pits.

In Britain, the main strongholds of the species are within the Severn and Thames catchments, with smaller outliers on the Arun in south-east England and the Dee, Teifi, Twyi and Wye in Wales and the Welsh Borders.

Previously regarded as under-recorded, it underwent an expansion in range over a period from 1978 to 1990. New records came from the upper reaches of the Thames, on the Rivers Kennet, Pang, Loddon and Blackwater. By 1990 it was widespread on the Teme and Avon (major tributaries of the Severn) and new locations had been found on the Teifi (Cardigan) and the Dyfrdwy (the Dee in Wales). It had also spread along the Twyi and along the Arun to the Rother. Despite these range expansions up to 1990, there had also been losses: in East Sussex on the Cuckmere River and from the Moors River in Dorset.

During 1991-1999, there were more new hectad records along the Thames and notably up the River Avon into Warwickshire for the first time. Other new sites included the mid-reaches of the Wye and the addition of more Dee records, which consolidated the position of the latter as a

River Thames, Goring, Oxfordshire: one of the most popular sites to watch emerging Common Clubtail. *Adrian Riley*

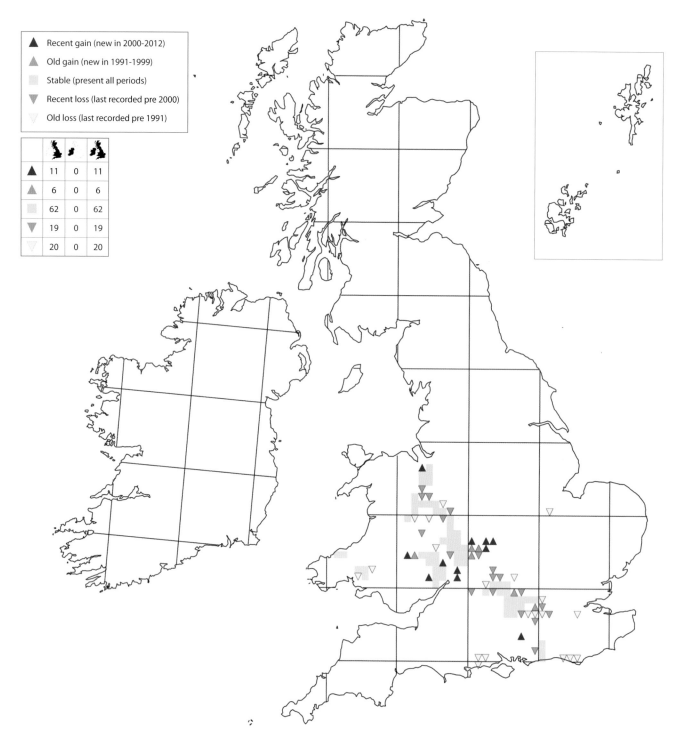

## Habitat

breeding river. However, this period also saw the loss of the last New Forest site at Oberwater (Goodyear, 1994). From 2000, there were records from a further seven new hectads, mainly on the Warwickshire Avon. In 2011 there were further new locations on the Rivers Loddon and Kennet near Reading.

This species' elusive nature makes it difficult to be sure when new locations have been colonised. The discoveries along the River Dee, Twyi and Warwickshire Avon since the 1970s strongly suggest that the range expansion has been real rather than simply a result of increased recording intensity.

In Britain, Common Clubtail breeds almost exclusively in rivers, though there is at least one instance of breeding in standing water. This species inhabits the lower reaches of larger southern rivers where there is accretion of silt for the larvae to burrow into. Although inhabiting large rivers with potentially high flows, the larvae avoid the high velocity areas. The front legs and bulbous antennae are respectively ideally suited to burrowing and detecting prey items in the silt layer (Müller, 1995). The front legs are proportionally longer than the hind legs in comparison with other families.

River Severn, Stourport, Worcestershire, where Common Clubtail occurs with White-legged Damselfly. *Mike Averill*

Rivers need to be of a high water quality and, providing there is no accidental pollution, boats pose no real problem other than the bankside wash they produce, which may reduce emergence success rate. The lowest reaches of rivers tend to be avoided, probably due to raised salinity levels in the tidal regions. A long-running survey on the Severn (Averill, 1989) has shown a wide range of emergence supports, ranging from flat to vertical rocks and from nettles to bur-reed.

Pairing occurs around trees in orchards, woods and hedgerows and females return alone to lay eggs. The presence of these wooded areas, both near the river and further away, is an important factor in the species' locality selection process (Kemp, 1983; Moore, 1991).

Breeding in standing water has only been proven once in Britain, at a pool situated above the River Severn floodplain at Worcester. The exuvia was coated in red sandy silt: very different from the fine grey silt normally coating exuviae from rivers.

River Dee above Farndon Bridge, Clwyd/Cheshire: the only North Wales river holding populations of both Common Clubtail and White-legged Damselfly. *Allan Brandon*

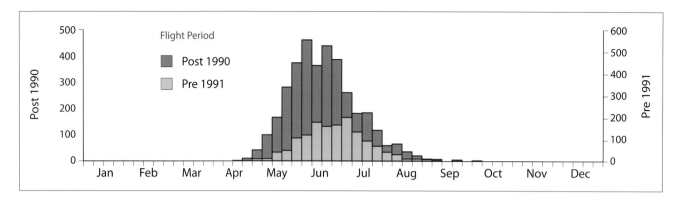

## Conservation status and threats

Common Clubtail is categorised as Near Threatened in the British Red List. Local species action plans have been prepared for the species and its habitat, notably in the stronghold counties of Worcestershire, Shropshire and Cheshire. Conservation plans for this species should consider breeding sites as well as nearby areas of woodland and tall herbs, where feeding and pairing usually take place. Due to the difficulties in finding adults, the important reaches of a river are best determined by larval or exuvia surveys; the latter are also recommended for monitoring site changes over time. The synchronised emergence of this species makes it vulnerable to badly-timed river management practices. Therefore, local BAPs have encouraged careful work on river banks during May and June. Living for up to three years in the silt will make larvae vulnerable to dredging activity.

The synchronised emergence of this species makes it vulnerable to weather abnormalities, boat wash and predation by birds such as wagtails and corvids (Goodyear, 1994). Unseasonal river floods can interrupt or delay emergence, due to changes in the flow rate, water level or temperature of the water.

Rivers are vulnerable to pollution events, where a single incident can exterminate invertebrates for a considerable distance downstream. The lower stretches of rivers typically occupied by Common Clubtail generally coincide with higher human population densities. This increases the risk of pollution events, especially those from an industrial source, be they accidental or deliberate. However, river water quality has improved generally and may have been partly responsible for the recent range expansion in Common Clubtail.

## National trends

Whilst restricted to a small number of river systems in southern Britain, Common Clubtail populations have remained fairly stable since the previous atlas. Adults wander up to 10km from breeding sites, where they are infrequently encountered, so the best measure of abundance comes from larval or exhaustive exuvia counts. A long-term emergence survey on the River Severn near Bewdley, Worcestershire, found annual fluctuations of between 60 and 500 exuviae per 100 metres in favourable reaches. Higher totals in the 1990s were followed by a decline between 2001 and 2007, followed by increases up to 2011.

The difficulties in observing adults at breeding sites has presented a major challenge for survey work. Despite this, new sites have been recorded along tributaries of the major rivers that have large populations and this offers some hope that the species is spreading, albeit slowly.

Common Clubtail emerging on the brickwork at Goring viaduct, Oxfordshire. The wash from frequent boat traffic can pose a threat to larvae emerging low down. *Steve Cham*

# Golden-ringed Dragonfly
## *Cordulegaster boltonii*

## Common Goldenring

Golden-ringed Dragonfly is large and mainly black, with bold yellow bands across the abdominal segments and on the thorax. The eyes are bright green and meet at a single point on the top of the head. Females have a distinctive lance-like ovipositor, projecting beyond the tip of the abdomen, which they 'stab' into shallow water in streams and flushes, laying eggs into the bottom substrate. Depending on latitude, larvae can take between two and five years to develop.

Golden-ringed Dragonfly, male. *Ian McColl*

Golden-ringed Dragonfly, female. *R&B Mearns*

## Distribution

Golden-ringed Dragonfly is the most widely distributed *Cordulegaster* species in Europe. Its range extends from north-west Africa and central Italy to the Arctic Circle, though it may be extinct in Norway. It is more sparsely distributed in north-east Europe, perhaps extending as far east as the Urals.

In Britain it has a marked western and northern distribution, being widespread in Devon and Cornwall and in the hills and mountains of Scotland, northern England and Wales. It is often the only large dragonfly present along upland streams, though it is also common and widespread at streams flowing through lowland heathland and woodland in southern England. It occurs on Anglesey and the larger Scottish islands, with outposts in Orkney and the Outer Hebrides.

There are no records for the Isle of Man and it was unrecorded in Ireland until two females were found in Co. Kilkenny in 2005 and another female in Co. Waterford in 2008 (Nelson, 2011).

## Habitat

The distribution of Golden-ringed Dragonfly seems to be limited by a lack of suitable habitat. Streams and smaller, fast-flowing rivers are the favoured habitat. Occasionally, it is found breeding in runnels and seepages in heathland and moorland. Larvae have also been recorded from drainage ditches. Whilst often quoted to be restricted to streams with acidic water, it has been recorded from calcareous chalk streams in the Test and Itchen Valleys, Hampshire. Territorial males repeatedly patrol stretches of running water, flying close to the surface and frequently

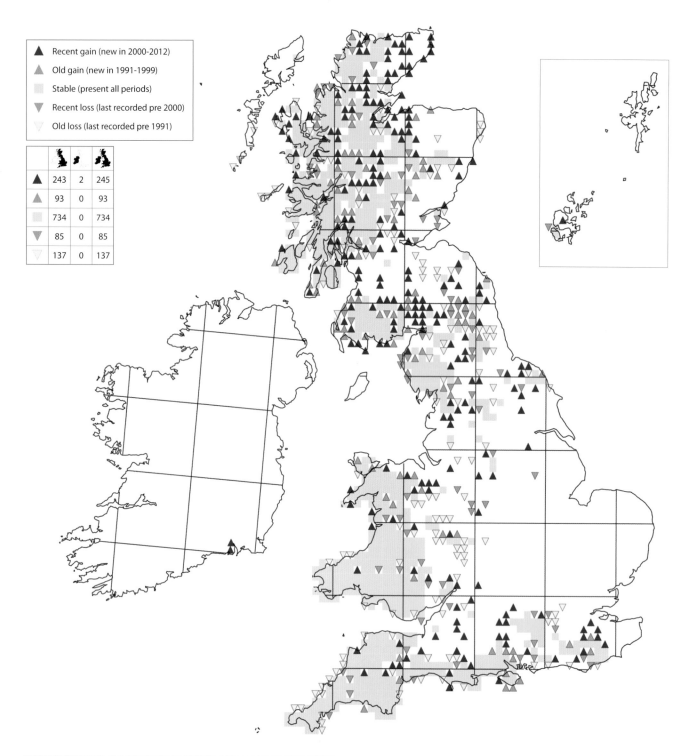

Legend:
▲ Recent gain (new in 2000-2012)
▲ Old gain (new in 1991-1999)
▪ Stable (present all periods)
▼ Recent loss (last recorded pre 2000)
▽ Old loss (last recorded pre 1991)

Female Golden-ringed Dragonfly ovipositing by stabbing the eggs into the substrate. *Adrian Riley*

perching on vegetation close to the water's edge. Territories may be along woodland streams in deep shade, although sunlit areas are generally favoured, especially for perching.

Adults are often encountered away from water, in heathland and along tracks in woodland, scrub and Bracken. In such places adults typically allow a close approach when eating prey, which frequently includes hoverflies, wasps and bees, and can be heard crunching through the chitin of the exoskeleton. Larvae are 'sit and wait' predators, living partially buried in the surface layer of silt and fine debris of the stream bed. The availability of prey items in the various habitats, presumably limited by temperature, may explain the variations in the time larvae take to mature.

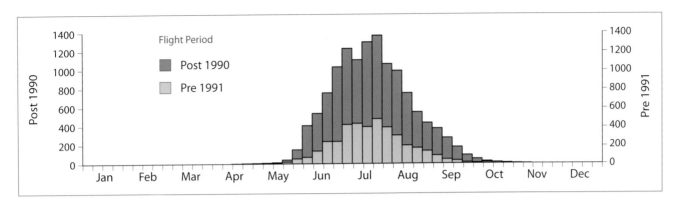

Knoits of Linkins, Dumfries & Galloway, is a deep, still, peaty ditch where Golden-ringed Dragonfly larvae have been found.
*R&B Mearns*

## Conservation status and threats

Golden-ringed Dragonfly is categorised as Least Concern in the British Red List.

Although potentially vulnerable to point-source pollution events, such as leakage from silage stores or slurry tanks, the species does not appear to have suffered in the long term from such events. Another potential threat to this species comes from activities that result in a reduction in water flow, such as through excessive extraction or during drought conditions. Conversely, the management of water flow that encourages riffles and faster-flowing water can benefit this species. This has been demonstrated to good effect in the New Forest, Hampshire, where original meanders have been re-instated following canalisation of some of the streams.

## National trends

The map shows some subtle changes in its distribution in Britain since the previous atlas. Some recent records have filled gaps in the existing range but there are also indications of minor range expansion in southern and northern England. Conversely, there have been apparent losses in the English Midlands and in the uplands on either

Warren Heath, Hampshire: many Golden-ringed Dragonfly larvae have been found along the stream connecting the three reservoirs.
*Steve Cham*

side of the English/Scottish border. There has been high recording intensity in the Midlands and so at least some of this range contraction could be real. However, some apparent losses from the Outer Hebrides, Tiree and Coll could be due to inadequate recording intensity.

It was unaccountably absent from Ireland until recently, although there is much suitable habitat similar to that found in western Britain. Despite records of three females, there have been no further suggestions that a breeding population exists.

# Orange-spotted Emerald
## *Oxygastra curtisii*

Orange-spotted Emerald is a small emerald dragonfly similar in size to other emeralds. In flight it is of a much more dainty appearance. The principal distinguishing feature is the yellow spotting which runs the full length of the dorsal surface of the abdomen and from which the vernacular name is derived. The spots are rather variable and usually appear more prominently on females. There is a prominent pale crest on segment 10 of the male's abdomen. The larval life cycle is two or three years, with emergence taking place in dense vegetation, on branches and on tree trunks.

Orange-spotted Emerald, male. *Damian Pinguey*

## Distribution

Orange-spotted Emerald is the only species in the genus *Oxygastra*, and is endemic to the western Palaearctic. It was first described from English specimens and was considered for a while to be endemic to England. It has not been seen at any of its former localities for many years and is considered Regionally Extinct. The species is locally common in Iberia and France south of latitude 48° north, beyond which it becomes increasingly local. In northern France it almost reaches the English Channel at the Cherbourg Peninsula and there are a few colonies in Belgium. In 2006, Orange-spotted Emerald was rediscovered in Germany and has been the subject of intensive studies there. It becomes increasingly rare further east and there are just a few colonies in Switzerland and Italy. Emergence is between mid-June and mid-July in northern Europe but earlier in southern Spain.

The former British distribution of Orange-spotted Emerald was remarkable. The Moors River in Dorset, in particular a stretch no more than 8km long to the north of Hurn, was the only known breeding site from its discovery in 1820 until its last sighting on 19 July 1963. Other records came from Pokesdown to the south, where specimens were taken in four years between 1878 and 1905. This site is some 3km

Orange spotted emerald, female. *Damien Pinguey*

west of the River Stour and far from the nearest breeding habitat. The Moors River is a tributary of the Stour, from where there were isolated records during the 19th century. Fraser (1940) also stated that '…it was present in fair numbers over boggy pools bordering the Avon River'. The Avon is very close to the Stour and both rivers reach the sea at Christchurch Harbour. Unfortunately, there has never been any confirmation of Fraser's sighting, although there was an unconfirmed sight record from Avon Common in the early 1990s. The only other confirmed record of this

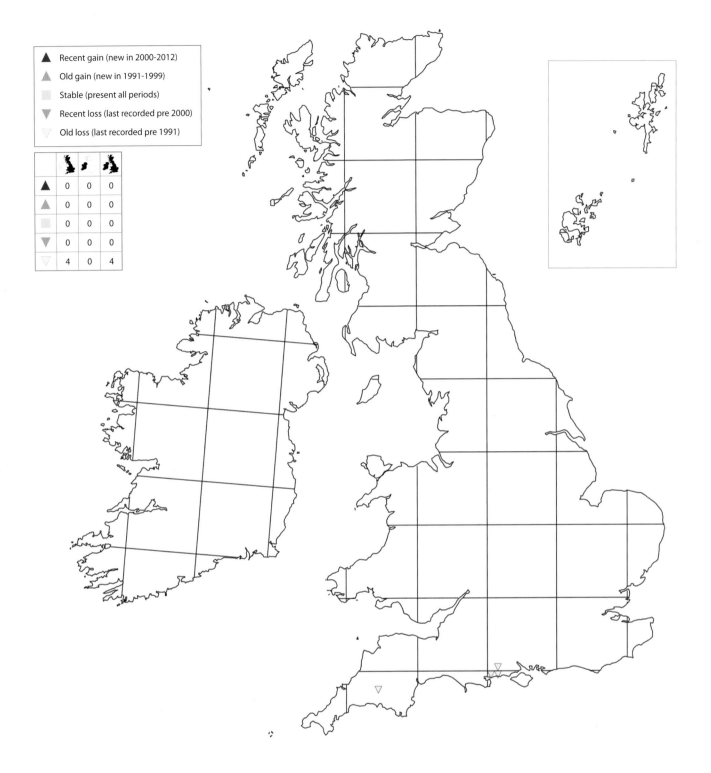

| |  |  |  |
|---|---|---|---|
| ▲ | 0 | 0 | 0 |
| △ | 0 | 0 | 0 |
| ▦ | 0 | 0 | 0 |
| ▼ | 0 | 0 | 0 |
| ▽ | 4 | 0 | 4 |

Legend:
- ▲ Recent gain (new in 2000-2012)
- △ Old gain (new in 1991-1999)
- ▦ Stable (present all periods)
- ▼ Recent loss (last recorded pre 2000)
- ▽ Old loss (last recorded pre 1991)

species came in July 1946, when two males and a female were collected next to the River Tamar north of Gunnislake, Devon; despite searches, no further records have come from this area, which still has suitably calm, tree-lined stretches of river. An 1834 record from the unlikely location of Braunton Burrows, north Devon, has never been authenticated (Fraser, 1940).

## Habitat

Orange-spotted Emerald is essentially a riparian species, favouring small- to medium-sized rivers and streams with tree-lined, deep, slow-flowing stretches. It occasionally breeds in lakes and in Italy it appears to favour such habitat. In northern Europe, larvae are found in tree roots, mainly of Alders. However, in southern Spain, larvae live in leaf litter and detritus that accumulates in deep stretches. Adults usually fly close to the breeding habitat but can occasionally be found feeding over adjacent pasture and open woods. Males hold territory along banks, often flying in and out of shady stretches looking for females; their flight is very rapid and they are often hard to spot. Mating is usually carried out high in the trees and the females return to the water only briefly to oviposit, which they do in shady parts by dipping their abdomens amongst submerged branches or vegetation for only a few seconds.

## Conservation and threats

Orange-spotted Emerald is categorised as Regionally Extinct in the British Red List and Near Threatened (but with a stable population trend) in the European Red List. It is also listed in Annexes II and IV of the EU Habitats Directive.

A specimen taken at Hurn in 1963 proved to be the last record of the species in England, ending a presumed 140-year-plus residence at the Moors River. It had been considered that the principal reason for the demise was that the Palmersford sewage works on the Moors River was enlarged in 1963, leading to reduced water quality and the extinction of the insect. It seems unlikely that this slight degradation would have had any long-term effect on invertebrate populations and more likely that habitat deterioration was responsible for the demise. The river would have had occasional trees, making it suitable for Orange-spotted Emerald. During the 20th century, massive housing development took place, engulfing virtually all of the heathland to the south. Hurn Airport claimed the heath to the west and extensive commercial softwood forestry to the east left a neglected river abandoned between two commercial interests. Tree growth, notably of Sycamore, now shades the majority of the river, transforming it into a woodland brook with most of its interesting dragonfly habitat degraded by neglect. Norman Moore visited the area in the late 1950s and stated then how the area of the river available for Orange-spotted Emerald territories was much reduced. Add to this the fact that the 1962-63 winter provided one of the longest periods of cold weather for 30 years and it is not hard to see how this essentially southern species finally disappeared.

## National trends

Despite increased recording intensity, no proved sightings have been made of Orange-spotted Emerald in Britain since it was last recorded in 1963. In continental Europe, there are a number of established sites in northern France and Belgium and its recent rediscovery in Germany gives some optimism for the re-establishment of this insect in England. Indeed, there were long periods in the past when this species was considered absent before being rediscovered. Lowland rivers are notoriously difficult to survey due to problems of access; furthermore, Orange-spotted Emerald can be hard to find, even in areas where it is common. It is therefore still possible that it could be present in England. There are many small rivers in Devon, Dorset and Somerset which appear to be potentially suitable for this species.

River Tamar above Gunnislake, Cornwall/Devon, provides potentially suitable habitat for Orange-spotted Emerald close to where the species was collected in 1946. *Dave Smallshire*

# Downy Emerald
## *Cordulia aenea*

Downy Emerald is a medium-sized dragonfly with a downy thorax and a metallic emerald-green body with coppery-brown sheen. Mature adults have bright green eyes. Males have a slightly club-tailed abdomen, which in flight is held slightly higher than the thorax. Males patrol the edges of waterbodies with a characteristic rapid flight, interspersed with periods of hovering, especially at small inlets in marginal vegetation. The eggs are laid exophytically and hatch within a few weeks, with larvae normally developing over two to three years.

Downy Emerald, male.
*Steve Cham*

## Distribution

Downy Emerald is widespread throughout much of northern Europe, extending eastwards through Siberia to Japan. In southern Europe, the species is restricted to mountainous areas; it is absent from northern Scandinavia, Iberia and most of the Mediterranean, where its most southerly outposts are in Italy and Greece.

In Britain and Ireland it shows a relict distribution, with highly localised populations in western Ireland, Scotland, Wales and western England and a core range in central-southern and south-east England. A key feature of this distribution is the relative stability of populations at sites where it has been known for many years, including some quite isolated from the main range. In many areas there appear to be populations based on a main or long-established breeding site, with other smaller colonies close by. In most occupied areas there has been relatively little expansion outside the immediate area surrounding the known sites.

In southern England, it remains locally common at pools on wooded heaths and old mineral workings, with the main concentration spreading from Dorset through Hampshire, Berkshire, Surrey and Sussex to Kent. The range extends northwards into south Buckinghamshire, with a strong and long-established population centred on Burnham Beeches and Black Park Lake, from where it has spread to a number of surrounding sites over the last decade. Prior to 2000 in Berkshire, the species was centred around the heathland areas in the south-east and south of the county. Since then it has been recorded at a number of worked-out gravel pits across the centre of the county. The apparent delay in colonisation may be related to the state of maturity of these sites as well as increased recorder effort since 2005. In south Essex it has been long established in Epping Forest, centred on Wake Valley Pond, spreading to most of the woodland ponds throughout the forest, where the species is now regularly recorded.

Away from this core range, populations are more scattered. In Devon, a small isolated population exists around the Bovey Basin, Newton Abbot, where most of the sites are old, flooded claypits, and at two sites in the East Devon Pebblebed Heaths. The only new Bovey Basin site known to have been colonised in the last 25 years is less than 100m from an occupied pond. In north Somerset, it has persisted for many years at Waldgrave Pool, Priddy Mineries. It has colonised the Isle of Wight in the last decade, probably from well-established sites in the New Forest and south Hampshire.

In Gloucestershire, a strong population has persisted at the woodland ponds throughout Forest of Dean and at

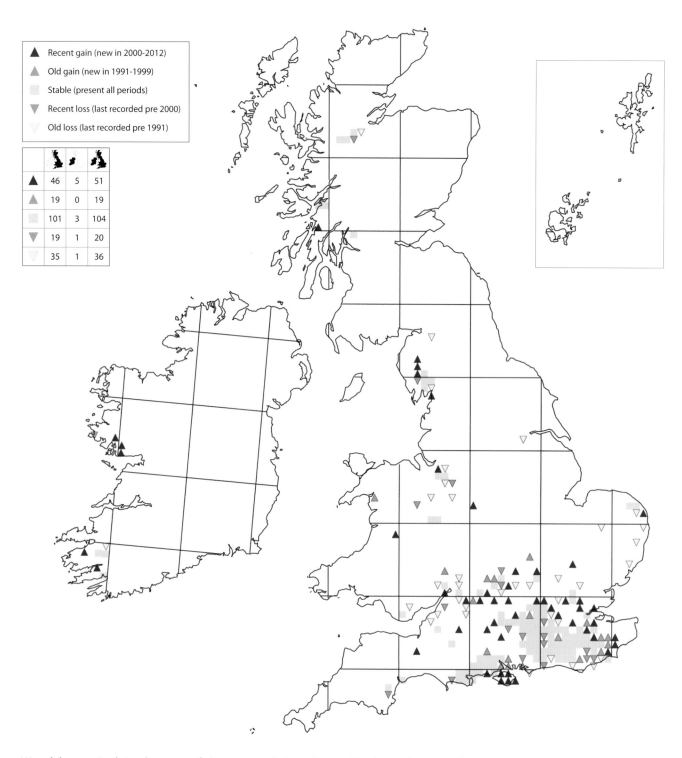

Woodchester Park in the east of the county. It has also spread eastwards into the Cotswold Water Park, where gravel extraction has created sites that have matured with tree-lined margins. In Herefordshire, a single woodland pool site was discovered in 1995, possibly a northern expansion from the Forest of Dean. In Shropshire, it is recorded from several pools south-east of Shrewsbury and, in Cheshire, it has been recorded from several pools in the Delamere Forest area. A single isolated record from Chartley Moss NNR, Staffordshire, in 2000 remains an enigma, being some 40km from the nearest known site.

Since 2000, it has been recorded at a number of new sites in Oxfordshire north of a large population at the lakes in Wychwood Forest, where it has been known for many years. It has now been recorded since the mid-1990s at lakes on large country estates where it may have been undetected due to limited access in former times. More recently it has been discovered at Radley Pits, in an area used for dumping ash from Didcot Power Station. Two of the pools are currently managed as a wetland reserve and, as they have matured and become more wooded, the site has been colonised by Downy Emerald.

In East Anglia a number of sites have been lost over the last 100 years. The somewhat isolated population at the private Captain's Pond in Norfolk has been known for many years. More recently it has been recorded from other woodland

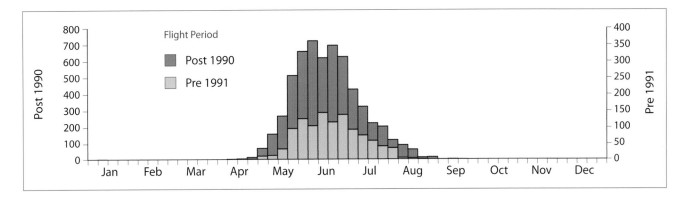

pools nearby, as well as showing initial signs of expanding further afield into the Norfolk Broads area.

A new site at a private, well-wooded, former fishing pit has recently been discovered south of Cambridge, in a county which otherwise lacks suitable habitat for the species. This site is over 70km from the nearest known sites in Essex and Northamptonshire.

A significant population was discovered in 2006 on Ministry of Defence land at Yardley Chase, Northamptonshire, at a series of pools in ancient woodland surrounding ammunition dumps. The sighting of a single individual in 1995 suggests that this population had gone unnoticed for a number of years. Maintenance work by the Forestry Commission to clear scrub and make the ponds more accessible in the years preceding 2006 may have facilitated its discovery here. Individuals, possibly wanderers from this population, have been recorded in the surrounding area and may be the source of a single small colony near Stowe in north Buckinghamshire.

In Bedfordshire there is a strong population, first recorded in 2006, centred on a series of tree-lined pools formed by quarrying Greensand near Leighton Buzzard. These lie on the edge of an extensive area of ancient woodland, from where there was a single record in 1951.

In south Wales, it occurs at Hensol Forest, Glamorgan, where a small isolated population has persisted for over 30 years. In north Wales, a similarly isolated small population was discovered more recently on the edge of Snowdonia National Park at Llyn Tecwyn Isaf. In 2012, a new breeding site was discovered at Llyn Ebyr in Montgomeryshire.

Downy Emerald is recorded from a number of tarns in the Lake District, Cumbria and shows signs of colonising new sites. In Scotland, it occurs with the other two emerald dragonflies, yet remains less widespread, being restricted to three areas. It has persisted for many years at Dubh Lochan, Loch Lomond, from where the first Scottish record came in 1946. Near the west coast, it occurs east of Oban at the Black Lochs, while in the Highlands it has been recorded for many years at a number of lochans in the Glen Affric area, where it is found alongside both Brilliant and Northern Emeralds.

In Ireland it has been known for many years in the south-west at Killarney National Park, Co. Kerry, Glengarriff, Co. Cork, where it was first recorded in 1978, and Glen Inchiquin, south Co. Kerry, where it has been seen regularly since its discovery in 2007. Further north along the west coast, breeding has been confirmed at a small number of lakes in open, treeless blanket bog in the Connemara area of Co. Galway. These follow an isolated sighting there in 1992, suggesting that the species had gone undetected rather than colonising recently.

Captain's Pond, Norfolk, a private site, has one of the most isolated populations of Downy Emerald in England. *Adrian Riley*

## Habitat

In northern Europe, Downy Emerald occurs mainly in oligotrophic to mesotrophic lakes but this has not been studied extensively throughout its British range. Larvae are found in a substrate of coarse, slowly-decomposing plant material, such as leaf litter, and require relatively stable habitat conditions for their development.

In England and Wales, the species is particularly associated with woodland pools, especially where there is extensive deciduous woodland. It is also found at lakes lined with mature trees in historic country estates, as well as at pools and lakes created after mineral extraction. There are some records from canals and slow-flowing rivers, although breeding in the latter remains uncertain. Successful breeding has been recorded at a garden pond adjacent to extensive woodland in the Meon Valley, south Hampshire,

Yardley Chase, Northamptonshire, where a large Downy Emerald population breeds in a number of pools created to protect ammunition dumps. *Mark Tyrrell*

most likely an extension of the strong population in the Botley Wood and Swanwick nature reserve area.

In Scotland, it occurs in sheltered, well-vegetated lochs in a strong association with Caledonian pine forest. At pools in exposed blanket bog in Connemara, Co. Galway, Ireland, larvae have been found in dense layers of decaying Purple Moorgrass leaf litter, while adults use nearby coniferous woodland.

Adults of both sexes are often seen feeding along woodland rides linked to, yet some distance from, the breeding pools. Woodland or tree corridors that link suitable sites have allowed some colonisation to happen. Roosting and mating typically occur out of sight in the tree canopy. Tree density around the water is sometimes quite low but deciduous woodland is often close by. Dappled shade is provided by bankside trees or large stands of fringing emergent vegetation around the margins. The broken nature of a shoreline due to the stands of emergent vegetation, bushes or fishing points can allow quite large numbers of males to hold territory.

In Scotland, Yellow Water-lily, Common Reed, Water Horsetail and the mosses *Fontinalis antipyretica* and *Sphagnum subsecundum* have been noted as common plant species at oviposition sites. In Devon and Surrey, oviposition has been noted into open water under the overhanging branches of willows.

Larval development takes two or three years and bankside plants such as rushes and sedges are used for emergence, with trees sometimes being used. The maiden flight typically takes tenerals into the tree canopy; they mature away from water, feeding and resting in woodland rides and glades.

## Conservation Status and Threats

Downy Emerald is listed as Endangered in the Irish Red List and Least Concern in the British Red list. Although many isolated populations have persisted for a long time, they are at risk should they suffer events that disturb the habitat.

Historical records show some losses from pools and country estate lakes, especially in East Anglia, following significant management work. This has resulted in the loss of the species with no hope of recolonisation from nearby sites. The apparently poor dispersal ability of this species means that the conservation of extant sites is very important.

Where suitable adult and larval conditions occur, the species has persisted for many years with little site management work needed. Over-zealous clearance work, particularly removal of bottom material, is a potential threat to this species. Thinning of trees around breeding pools appears to have no detrimental effect to well-established populations. Eutrophication and disturbance through the activities of Canada Geese and other waterfowl, especially where fed by the public, pose a threat at some sites. At more mesotrophic sites, bottom-feeding by stocked coarse fish results in considerable disturbance of the favoured larval habitat.

## National trends

The CEH trends analysis (pages 58-63) shows a significant increase in this species. Downy Emerald has a relatively low dispersal rate and colonisation of new sites has been mainly in areas close to existing populations. It has shown some signs of northerly spread into the Home Counties of England where pools occur in close proximity to woodland. Concentrations of potentially suitable flooded mineral workings appear to facilitate spread within an area, as the aquatic and intervening habitats mature. Conversely, large expanses of agricultural land with a lack of woodland corridors between woodland pools limits dispersal and range expansion.

In Scotland, the populations are stable with no sign of expansion into new areas. The Irish population is at least stable. New populations have been discovered but it is not possible to determine whether these were previously overlooked or indicative of spread. As with other dragonfly species, it is not impossible that Downy Emerald may have been spread to new sites unintentionally in water from fisheries during fish translocations.

Llyn Tecwyn Isaf, Gwynedd, is the only known site for Downy Emerald in North Wales. *Allan Brandon*

# Northern Emerald
## *Somatochlora arctica*

Northern Emerald is a medium-sized, dark metallic green dragonfly with shining green eyes in mature adults. It closely resembles the Brilliant Emerald but is darker, appearing almost black. The male's abdomen is pinched at the waist and appears swollen towards the tip, ending with calliper-shaped appendages. The face has two yellow spots, one close to each eye, which are not connected by a bar. The female's vulvar scale is comparatively short and lies parallel to the abdomen and not projecting outwards at right angles as in the Brilliant Emerald. The very distinctive hairy larva takes at least two years to develop.

Northern Emerald, male.
*Adrian Riley*

## Distribution

Northern Emerald is found across northern Europe and Asia from Britain and Ireland, through Scandinavia to Siberia and Japan. It has a very localised distribution in western Europe, where it is found in mountainous regions including the Ardennes in Belgium, the Massif Central in France, the Alps and the Pyrenees. It is also found in lowland habitat from The Netherlands and northern Germany to the Baltic states.

Recently emerged Northern Emerald. Near Loch Maree, Ross and Cromarty. *Peter Vandome*

In Ireland, it is found only in Co. Kerry and Co. Cork in the south-west and in Britain it has a scattered distribution in north and west Scotland. The reasons for this disjunct distribution are not known but it could either be a relict one from the early postglacial or the result of separate post-glacial colonisation events.

It was first recorded in Scotland from the Blackwood of Rannoch in 1844 and in Ireland at Killarney in 1849; it is still present at both localities. In Ireland the distribution is limited to Killarney National Park and three areas in particular: the south side of the Upper Lake at Cahernabane, the Galway's River valley above Derrycunnihy and at Glena and Dinish on the western side of Muckross Lake. There has been a single record in 2011 from Garinish Island, Glengarriff, Co. Cork, but where it originated is unknown as suitable habitat is not considered present on the island.

In Scotland, it has been recorded from Caithness to Argyll with outlying sites in the north-west at Loch Merkland in Sutherland and Flanders Moss in Stirlingshire, the most south-easterly site. Its strongholds are in the pine woods of Abernethy, Uath Lochs, Glen Affric, the Loch Maree area, Ardnamurchan and near Loch Arkaig. There has been a single record of an adult on the Island of Muck.

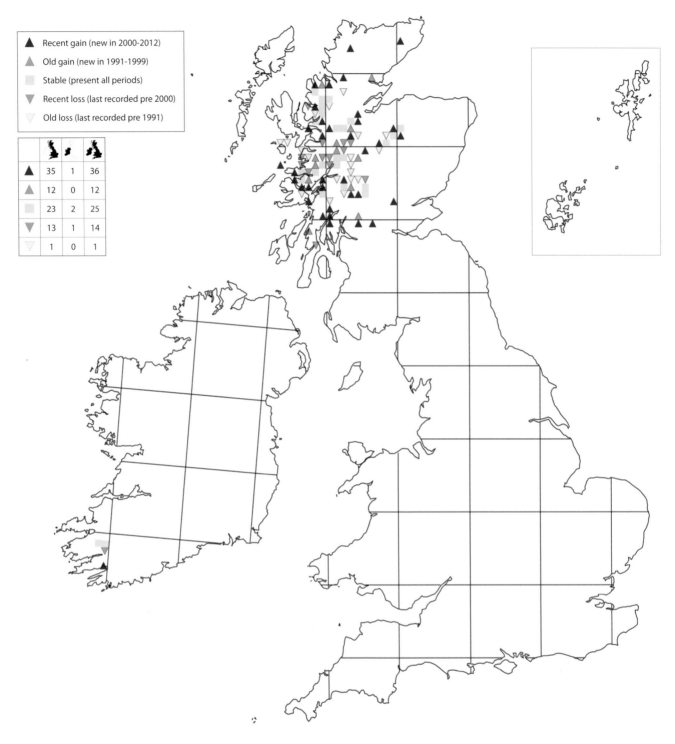

## Habitat

Northern Emerald is a species of peat bogs and runnels. Breeding sites have been found from just above sea level in Argyll to 350m. Irish sites are at low altitude between 20 and 50m above sea level. An unusually high breeding site was recorded in 1989 at 510m above sea level on Meall nan Samhna, West Perthshire, but it has not been seen there subsequently. In Ireland and Scotland, the typical breeding habitat includes bog pools, runnels, seepages and ditches in areas of wet heath, bog or moorland, usually with some water flow. Bog-mosses are present, often forming dense mats, together with emergents such as cotton-grasses and small sedges. Sites typically are small and often with no apparent open water. It occupies acidic to neutral waters (Corbet, 1999). In Ireland, reeds and Bog Myrtle can also be present. Breeding sites are sometimes close to small lakes, such as at Lochan Dubh near Cannich, the Coire Loch in Glen Affric and the lakes in Killarney National Park. However, this is coincidental as Northern Emerald, unlike the other emerald dragonfly species, is not usually found over open water. It was long considered to have an association with boggy clearings in native Scottish pinewoods but it can also be found in birch, willow and oak woodlands. Sites have also been found in boggy clearings in forestry plantations at Callop Wood near Glenfinnan and in Glen Garry. Although adults often hunt in woodland clearings and can be found in the canopy, breeding pools

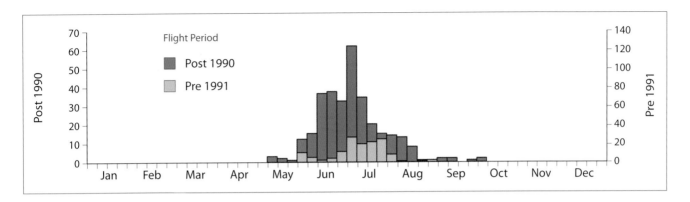

Flight Period
■ Post 1990
□ Pre 1991

Bridge of Grudie, Highland: a noted site for visitors to find Northern Emerald. *Adrian Riley*

can be a considerable distance from the nearest woodland as at Rannoch Moor where the pools are on open moorland.

The larvae live among detritus, beneath floating bog-mosses, in water up to 15cm deep, yet can also be found in very shallow water above the bog-mosses. In larger pools, larvae are usually found in shallower areas with the greatest cover of bog-mosses. Exuviae and emerging adults have been found at sites with no visible water. In times of drought, the larvae retreat deep into bog-mosses and they have been found surviving some 30cm below the surface. Population density appears to be low, with few larvae found in a single bog pool. Both larvae and adults can be elusive and many hours of searching can be spent finding a single larva or exuvia. The largest number of exuviae ever found at a site is 20, in a large area of bog-moss mire, covering approximately 300m by 300m, in Ardnamurchan, Highland, with six people searching for over an hour.

## Conservation status and threats

Northern Emerald is classified as Near Threatened on the British Red List and Endangered on the Irish List. The assessment in Ireland was based on the small number of sites and localised distribution. However, there is no evidence that the species has changed in abundance since

it was discovered in the 19th century, as it still occurs in the original locality which is now within a National Park. In Scotland, there have been significant changes in upland habitats since the mid-20th century, with an expansion of forestry and changes in grazing patterns. Some historical sites from the early 1900s are now covered with extensive forestry plantations. For example, suitable breeding habitat was found to be absent during resurveys at sites such as Tulloch and Glen Spean in the Great Glen area of the Scottish Highlands. Continuing afforestation and drainage of sites are the main threats to the species. Small bog pools and runnels with little water, often scattered in remote upland areas or woodlands, are difficult to locate and protect. With the Scottish Government's current forestry strategy to offset climate change, the pressure for planting areas will continue and sites for this species could be lost. Conversely, the expansion of conifers into formerly open areas could provide some shelter and feeding areas for adults, provided sufficient wetland habitat remains.

Other threats include the cessation of grazing and fencing for conservation management in native woodlands. This can lead to extensive growth of Purple Moor-grass and loose growth of bog-mosses, making sites less favourable. Ideally, sites should remain open to grazing, as at Doire Darach in Glen Orchy.

Dry weather in spring can lead to boggy areas becoming dry, which may affect larval development. The populations in Ireland and south-west Scotland are likely to be under the most threat from climate change.

Bog pool, Rannoch Moor, Highland. *Pat Batty*

## National trends

In Scotland, the known range of the species has expanded both to the north and the south. It is now known from nearly double the number of hectads recorded before 1990. The recent discoveries of breeding sites in Sutherland in 2011 and in Caithness in 2012 could lead to further Scottish records, as both areas have large areas of potential habitat. In southern Scotland most sites only have occasional sightings. The Irish distribution has been essentially stable, although the recent and unexplained record from Co. Cork hints at a broader distribution than currently known.

This improved situation has come about as a result of increased knowledge of the habitat requirements, allowing for better-targeted recording effort, especially for larvae and exuviae, the recording of which is less weather dependent. However, there are still many areas to be investigated, including historic locations, so it is likely that the number of known sites will continue to increase. Populations are small, well-scattered and often in isolated areas of peat bog. Only a small number of known sites produce records on a regular basis, reflecting the accessibility and popularity of sites for recorders. The viability of many colonies still remains unknown, as some sites need to be visited for several years in succession before breeding can be confirmed.

*Above:* Gallavally, Killarney National Park, Co. Kerry: wet heath and bog habitat for Northern Emerald. *Brian Nelson*

*Below:* Cahernabane, Killarney National Park, Co. Kerry: a flat area of wet heath and bog with shallow runnels and habitat for Northern Emerald. *Brian Nelson*

# Brilliant Emerald
## *Somatochlora metallica*

Brilliant Emerald is the brightest coloured of the three extant emerald dragonflies in Britain and Ireland. The adults are often seen at the same sites as Downy Emerald. Whilst the pattern of yellow markings on the 'face' is diagnostic, the bright emerald green metallic colours of the thorax and abdomen are the most eye-catching and distinctive. The larval life is a minimum of two years, probably longer in colder waters.

Brilliant Emerald, male.
*Steve Cham*

## Distribution

Brilliant Emerald is found across Europe from the Pyrenees, northern Italy and Bulgaria in the south to Lapland in the north. It occurs sparsely in the south of this range, mainly at high altitude, and is common in Alpine lakes. Brilliant Emerald has never been seen in Ireland, in contrast to two other emerald dragonfly species. In Britain it is found in two quite distinct and separate populations: in western Scotland and south-east England. These are thought to represent relict populations from two separate colonisations, the first possibly dating from the early post glacial period.

In 1908, the first English record came from Crowborough Warren, Sussex. The population in south-east England is now known to be more extensive than that in Scotland, though the full extent of its distribution in England is far from clear because it is such a difficult insect to observe. The strongholds of its population are concentrated in Berkshire, Surrey and Sussex, although it also occurs in north-east Hampshire at Warren Heath. There are no recent English records north of the Thames and any western extension of its range is probably restricted by the chalk of the Hampshire and Berkshire downs, which provide few habitat opportunities.

In Scotland, it occurs in three main areas (Mill, 2012). It was first discovered in Scotland in the Strathglass region, Inverness-shire in 1869 and still occurs there, at 15 lochan sites in the native pinewoods at Glen Affric, Glen Strathfarra and Cannich. Also in Inverness-shire it is found at 14 sites in the Loch Bran complex east of Loch Ness. The third well separated population is present in the hill lochs on either side of Loch Awe, Argyll (Batty 2013), where it has shown expansion in range in recent years.

## Habitat

In England, Brilliant Emerald is mostly associated with wooded ponds and lakes, yet other habitats are also used. It has been regularly recorded along tree-lined sections of linear waterways, such as the Basingstoke Canal and Wey Navigation in Surrey and the Rivers Arun and Ouse in West and East Sussex, respectively, although exuviae have never been found in either of these rivers and the exact breeding sites are still to be discovered. Scottish populations are associated with lochs adjacent to native pine forests, although the species is also found in sheltered hill lochans some distance from the nearest woodland. Scottish sites are between 150 and 400m, although there are records of a mating pair at 600m on Ben Donachan, Argyll.

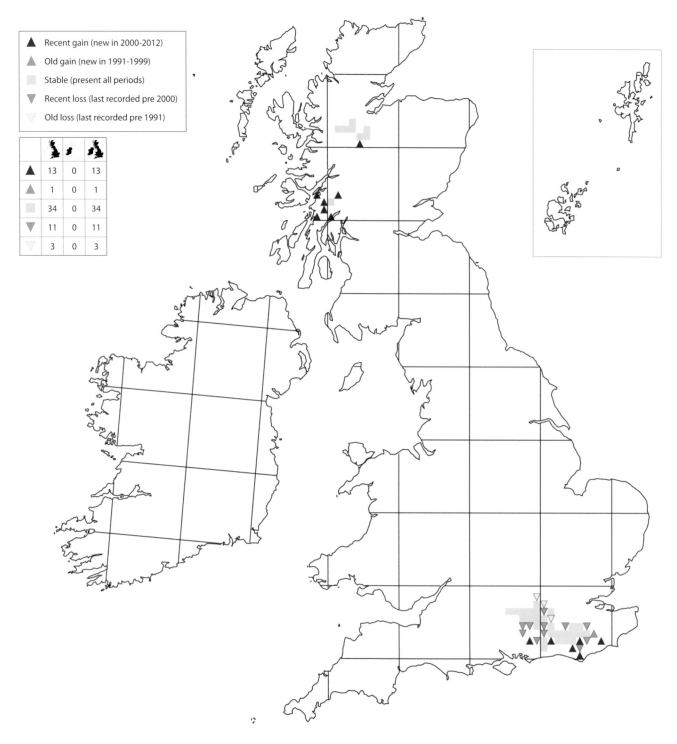

| | {width=20} | , | {width=20} |
|---|---|---|---|
| ▲ | 13 | 0 | 13 |
| ▲ | 1 | 0 | 1 |
| ▦ | 34 | 0 | 34 |
| ▼ | 11 | 0 | 11 |
| ▽ | 3 | 0 | 3 |

▲ Recent gain (new in 2000-2012)

▲ Old gain (new in 1991-1999)

▦ Stable (present all periods)

▼ Recent loss (last recorded pre 2000)

▽ Old loss (last recorded pre 1991)

Black Pond, Esher Common, Surrey: a typical English location for Brilliant Emerald. *Steve Cham*

One requirement for breeding habitat is the presence of shaded areas of calm water with muddy or, preferably, mossy edges where the females oviposit. Shade appears to be important for the development of larvae, which can be found at the edge of water under overhanging banks, in detritus or, occasionally, under stones; such microhabitats provide cryptic hiding places for larval development. In captivity, larvae have not been seen to feed in the open. Scottish sites have either large overhanging, heather-covered peat banks up to a metre or more in height, or extensive floating bog-moss lawns. Breeding sites here are often well-aerated, open lochs with some water movement and larvae can be near the points of inflow or outflow. Some lochans have a stony substrate.

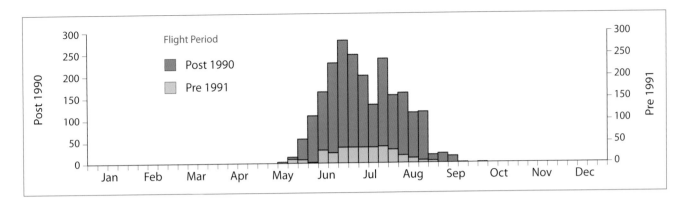

## Conservation status and threats

Brilliant Emerald is listed as Vulnerable in the British Red List in view of the paucity of breeding sites. It has a very restricted distribution in both England and Scotland. It is threatened by any operation that might damage the edge of the breeding habitat or bring changes in water chemistry. In Ashdown Forest, East Sussex, the clearance of some trees from the edges of lakes has led to a reduction in the numbers of territories for breeding males, which favour shady areas in their search for females. The Forestry Commission Scotland manages some sites where forest edge and rides provide sheltered feeding areas.

## National trends

Brilliant Emerald is an elusive dragonfly and most records are of males, with copulation and oviposition rarely observed. Nevertheless, sites are still being discovered. Its status in southern England is considered stable, while in Scotland its known range has expanded in recent years, particularly in the Loch Awe area, Argyll. Additional survey work is required to revisit sites recorded during 1980-90, to determine whether the species is still present. Its elusive nature makes study difficult and further insights into its movement between sites and its breeding behaviour are needed.

*Above:* Coire Loch, Glen Affric, Highland: a typical Scottish location for Brilliant Emerald. *Tony Mundell*

*Below :* Loch Bran, Highland. *Tony Mundell*

# Scarlet Darter
## *Crocothemis erythraea*

### Broad Scarlet

Scarlet Darter is a medium-sized and relatively broad-bodied dragonfly. Mature males are almost entirely bright red, whilst immature males and females are yellow-olive with a distinctive pale stripe on the thorax between the wings. Confusion is possible with the Red-veined Darter, especially the males, but that species lacks the broad abdomen. The Oriental Scarlet *C. servilia* is also very similar but this species has yet to be reported outdoors in Britain and Ireland.

Scarlet Darter, male. *John Curd*

## Distribution

Scarlet Darter has an extensive world range, being found throughout most of Africa, southern, western and central Europe, the Middle East and western Asia as far east as northern India. It also occurs in the Canary Islands and Seychelles, indicative of a high dispersive potential. It is generally common over most of its range.

In western and central Europe, the Scarlet Darter has spread north over the last two to three decades, probably as a consequence of climate change. It is now well established as a breeding species in The Netherlands and Germany, where it had previously been rarely reported (Ott, 2010b). As part of this expansion, the species has now also reached Britain, having been recorded as far north as Cumbria. It has never been reported from Ireland.

The Scarlet Darter is a mobile species that was first noted in Britain during 1995, since when there have been six confirmed records. Arrivals to Britain can potentially occur over quite a long season as the species has two generations in a year in southern Europe. At more northerly breeding sites only a single generation occurs each year.

## Habitat

The Scarlet Darter mostly frequents open still-water habitats, particularly where these are relatively shallow and eutrophic; brackish waters can also be tolerated. In northern Europe, the species is most associated with sites having a warm local microclimate: typically sheltered, shallow, clear waters with good aquatic vegetation. Partially-flooded sand and gravel-pits are thus attractive to the species, as can be stagnant drainage ditches and similar waterbodies. Individuals on active migration may turn up in a wider range of habitats.

## Conservation Status and Threats

Scarlet Darter was not assessed in the most recent Odonata Red Data List for Britain, by virtue of it having occurred only as a vagrant. However, future colonisation of Britain and Ireland seems a possibility, given the strong positive trends being shown in the western European populations. The species has broad habitat requirements, which may assist any ultimate colonisation.

Scarlet Darter, female. *Damian Pinquey*

## National trends

The Scarlet Darter was unknown from Britain prior to 1995, though it had been reported from Jersey in the Channel Islands in the 1940s (Le Quesne, 1946). During early August of the long hot summer of 1995, a male was discovered on the Lizard, Cornwall (Jones, 1996a). In the following years, further solitary migrants were then noted on the Isle of Wight in 1997, in Cornwall during 1998, in Devon and the Isle of Wight during 2000 and in Hampshire during 2002. The most recent record was of a nearly mature male in Cumbria in 2004, since when there have been no further confirmed sightings, though there have been occasional reports of 'possible/probable' individuals. Given the continuing spread of the species on the Continent and its almost annual occurrence on the Channel Islands since 2004, the recent lull in confirmed British and Irish records is unexpected. It is conceivable that the increasing abundance of Red-veined Darter, to which the Scarlet Darter is superficially similar, may have led to the species being overlooked. Whatever the explanation, it seems likely that further confirmed records will be forthcoming in the future.

Scarlet Darter, immature male. *Damian Pinquey*

# White-faced Darter
## *Leucorrhinia dubia*

## Small Whiteface

White-faced Darter is a small, dark dragonfly with red abdominal markings on the male and yellow on the female and immature male. Mature individuals of both sexes have a pure white 'face'. The dark wing-bases, especially of the hind wings, separate it from similar-sized species. Females usually oviposit alone, into tiny patches of free water in between patches of floating bog-moss in acidic pools of at least 30cm depth. The larvae live amongst loose floating bog-moss and their usual greenish colour makes them well-camouflaged. Larval development is believed normally to be two years, although there are rare instances of a one year life cycle.

White-faced Darter, male.
*John Curd*

## Distribution

White-faced Darter occurs widely across much of the northern Palaearctic, ranging from latitude 50 to north of the Arctic Circle. In the south of its range it occurs only at higher altitudes, for example, in the Vosges Mountains of France and the Alps on the French/Italian border. It has limited occurrence in the Pyrenees, which are its southern limit in Europe.

Bridge of Orchy, Argyll and Bute. *Pat Batty*

The mapped distribution in Britain is highly disjunct from southern England to north-west Scotland. The main centres of distribution are in the northern half of Scotland. The species is unknown from southern Scotland, despite the presence of apparently suitable habitats, and has never been recorded from Ireland.

In Scotland, White-faced Darter occurs in at least 27 scattered hectads, from near Bridge of Orchy, Argyll and Bute, northwards to Wester Ross, with an outlying population in Deeside in the east. Its strongholds are in the Loch Maree/ Torridon area of Wester Ross, Glen Affric and Glen Strathfarrar, Abernethy and Monadh Mor north of Inverness. Apart from these, it is known from scattered sites. New colonies have been discovered since 2005 in boggy clearings of forestry plantations at Callop Wood near Glenfinnan, Glen Garry near Loch Ness and Strathpeffer and Balmacara near Loch Carron.

In England and Wales, the species was found at the time of the previous atlas in three separate areas: the Surrey heaths, the north-west Midlands and Cumbria. However, there are now only three strong populations south of Scotland. These are at Fenn's, Whixall and Bettisfield Mosses NNR (Shropshire/Denbighshire), Chartley Moss NNR (Staffordshire) and Scaleby Moss (Cumbria). Population

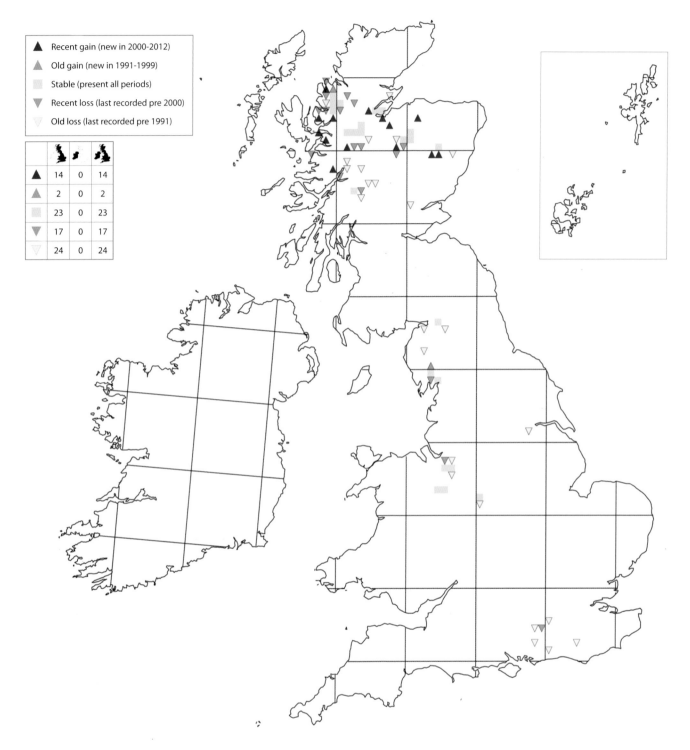

studies at the last two sites, by Beynon (1995, 1977a & b, 1998, 2001) and Clarke (2008 & in prep.), respectively, have shown numbers to fluctuate quite considerably. Both Chartley and Scaleby Mosses have yielded emergence numbers in the low thousands in recent years. Conversely, a minor site on Claife Heights, above Windermere in Cumbria, yields single-figure numbers, although this extensive complex of tarns and mires has long held the species and may yet hold other, undiscovered, pockets of breeding.

White-faced Darter usually shows no tendency to long-distance dispersal. An apparent exception to this, cited by Longfield (1947), refers to numbers coming in from the sea at Scarborough in 1900; occurrences on the Suffolk coast in 1992 and 2001 may have had similar origins. However, in all these instances, it is by no means clear that the dragonflies in question were White-faced Darter, rather than a similar species such as Ruby White-faced Darter *L. rubicunda* or Large White-faced Darter *L. pectoralis*, records of which were confirmed from Suffolk in 2012. Dispersals of various *Leucorrhinia* species in Europe are not unknown: some anomalous or poorly documented British records will always remain problematic in the absence of voucher specimens. Given the diligence of Victorian entomologists, it might be suspected that the lateness of the discovery of some English colonies suggests that they are recent colonisations (e.g. Chartley Moss and Thursley Common

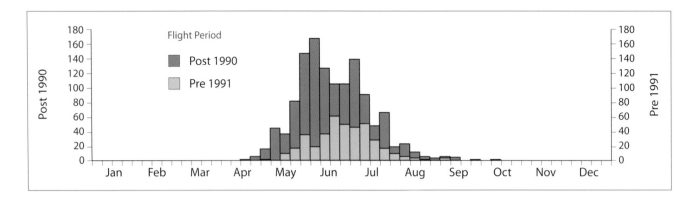

around 1933 and Scaleby Moss in 1946). However, the species was known (and collected) from some sites in northern England before 1850.

## Habitat

Sites for White-faced Darter in Britain commonly have peat substrates and are acidic in nature. The availability of relatively deep water and floating bog-moss that does not fully occlude the water surface seem to be the common components of good breeding sites. Acidity sufficient to prevent fish presence (as predators) has been shown (e.g. by Henrikson, 1988) to be a key factor. More mesotrophic waters are sometimes used in parts of its European range if fish are absent.

The classic habitat of this species, as most often found in Scotland, is a pool complex in a mire associated with open ancient pine/birch woodland. Single isolated pools can be utilised, and may sometimes be quite distant from woodland. This habitat is imitated to varying degrees by flooded peat cuttings in degraded lowland raised mires, such as the 'Mosses' of north-west England, and by other forms of lowland peatlands, such as *schwingmoor*. Recent man-made waterbodies within the general habitat type can be very successfully colonised, provided the bog-moss *Sphagnum cuspidatum* develops, for example, in ditches created as part of management operations of peatland restoration projects and pools created for forestry purposes. Productive pools can be quite small: for example man-made pools around 7m x 5m (and up to 2m deep) can yield several hundred emergents. The species' evident ability to navigate back to emergence pools (Sternberg, 1990) must be an important aspect of its biology.

## Conservation status and threats

White-faced Darter is a Nationally Scarce species and was assessed as Endangered on the British Red List, due to its declining and severely fragmented populations.

The main threat to this species in Scotland continues to be the drainage of peatland areas for commercial forestry, agriculture and development. Isolated bog pools could easily be overlooked and some large relatively inaccessible

areas – as in much of the Scottish Highlands – have still not been adequately surveyed.

Subtle changes in marginal vegetation and bog-moss in pools, as well as water chemistry (pH and solutes), should be looked for at key sites as part of any ongoing management or monitoring. Natural seral succession is a particular threat, especially to smaller sites. These can often be maintained only by active intervention to re-open pools overgrown with bog-moss or to dig additional ones. Tree growth – especially of pine and birch – on otherwise good sites can rapidly convert them to woodland, again requiring positive long-term management to counter this.

To mitigate the processes of decline, White-faced Darter has been the subject of a Local Biodiversity Action Plan in Cumbria since 2001. One of the aims is to re-introduce it to Foulshaw Moss, now a Cumbria Wildlife Trust reserve. A project proposal was prepared in 2008, based on IUCN Guidelines on re-introductions, using Scaleby Moss as the donor population. A major justification for the project was concern over unmanaged vegetation succession in the longer term at the donor site. The project is a partnership between BDS and Cumbria Wildlife Trust, in consultation with Natural England. The methodology is based solely on translocations of larvae and eggs, which commenced in 2010 and, at the time of writing, is showing positive indications. A key resulting task is the monitoring of

Whixall Moss, Shropshire, part of a National Nature Reserve where White-faced Darter and other species have benefited greatly from sympathetic management after peat extraction. *John Curd*

Chartley Moss, Staffordshire, supports a large, isolated population of White-faced Darter. *Steve Cham*

numbers emerging at both sites, mainly through counting exuviae. This has given extensive opportunities for volunteer involvement. Other similar translocations have been proposed elsewhere in England and in 2013 a project began in Delamere Forest, Cheshire.

## National trends

White-faced Darter is a boreal species and one that is most likely retreating due to climate change as well as some habitat loss. The CEH trends analysis (pages 58-63) shows a significant decline. It is probably limited by the availability of suitable sites with the favoured structure of bog-moss. In Scotland, the number of occupied hectads has remained fairly constant since the previous atlas despite increased recorder effort. A current re-introduction project in Cumbria shows promise and, if successful, could be of future conservation importance.

An accelerating rate of loss has been seen in all three occupied areas in England since 1950. The causes of these losses vary. In Cheshire, most of the basin mires were drained for plantation forestry which, on clearance, led to scrub encroachment and over-shading. At the last remaining site, Gull Pool, unexplained increases in water levels led to a rise in pH and a decline of bog-moss and there have been no records from there since 2003. At Thursley Common, Surrey, moderate numbers were present in the 1970s and 1980s but extinction occurred in the late 1990s. The final decline seems to have been precipitated by

a reduction and loss of bog-moss in the breeding pool. Several sites have been lost in Cumbria, four during the mid 20th century. Occlusion of small pools by bog-moss and large scale coniferisation are amongst the causes; a Borrowdale record (Pinniger, 1937) hints at an unrecorded site, long lost through drainage. The species was also lost from the oldest known site, Thorne Moors, South Yorkshire, well before 1950 – probably through peat extraction.

Several short-lived sites have been noted in England. For example, a colony was found at Wisley Common, Surrey, some 25km from the Thursley site, and persisted from about 1955 to 1975. It disappeared after a hot summer dried out the pool. In Cheshire, there are records from three, non-Delamere Forest, sites for single years prior to 1960. A minor population in Cumbria existed at a small tarn near Skelwith Bridge from about 1997-2008. This was a rather atypical site within relatively dense, mixed birch woodland but had bog-moss bordering one side of the pool. Although 80 exuviae were found in 2000, numbers declined steeply thereafter. The site is at least 5km from any known colony and is unlikely to have been long-overlooked. The causes of its decline are not understood. It is most likely that such suboptimal sites began as 'satellites' from established populations and that this is a normal pattern.

# Large White-faced Darter
## *Leucorrhinia pectoralis*     Yellow Spotted Whiteface

Large White-faced Darter is similar to White-faced Darter, but is slightly bulkier and, in males, the coloured spot nearest the tip of the abdomen typically remains yellow even in mature individuals. In females the yellow abdominal spots are more pronounced and larger than in White-faced Darter. The species has been noted as an extremely rare vagrant to the east coast of England, most recently in 2012. Records are apparently associated with irregular migratory movements taking place on the Continent.

Large White-faced Darter, male. *Clive Ireland*

## Distribution

The range of Large White-faced Darter covers the region from Western Siberia to Central Europe, reaching as far west as The Netherlands and parts of France, though these more western populations are often smaller and more scattered than those further east. It has a somewhat more southerly distribution than other European *Leucorrhinia* species, occurring in Scandinavia only in the southern parts, and having isolated populations as far south as the Balkans.

In Britain it has been recorded as a rare vagrant to the east coast. During June 1859 an individual was collected at an unknown locality 'near Sheerness, Kent'; and is believed by some to have been on a boat in the Thames Estuary (Lucas, 1900). More recently two individual males were discovered on the Suffolk coast during early summer 2012: at Landguard on 27 May and at Dockwra's Dyke, Dunwich Heath, over 16-19 June. These sightings were apparently associated with a large movement of the species on the near Continent at this time (Parr, 2013).

## Habitat

Large White-faced Darter typically frequents less acidic and more nutrient-rich habitats than White-faced Darter. It favours clear waters with floating plants and well-developed marginal vegetation, and can thus be found in well-vegetated forest lakes, marshes and fens in addition to peatlands. Migrating individuals may appear in a greater range of habitats.

In Britain, the site at Dunwich Heath where the species was noted in June 2012 comprised a coastal dyke flowing slowly towards the sea, with plenty of reeds and rushes on the edges and large floating mats of Marsh St. John's-wort (Beaumont & Beaumont, 2012).

## Conservation status and threats

The species was not assessed for the most recent Red List for Britain. In Europe, it is considered a threatened and declining species in many areas, being listed on Annexes II and IV of the EU Habitats Directive, although in recent years there have been signs of some localised recovery.

◆ 2013 record
● Post 2000
● 1991-1999
○ Pre 1991

| | | | |
|---|---|---|---|
| ◆ | 0 | 0 | 0 |
| ● Post 2000 | 2 | 0 | 2 |
| ● 1991-1999 | 0 | 0 | 0 |
| ○ Pre 1991 | 0 | 0 | 0 |

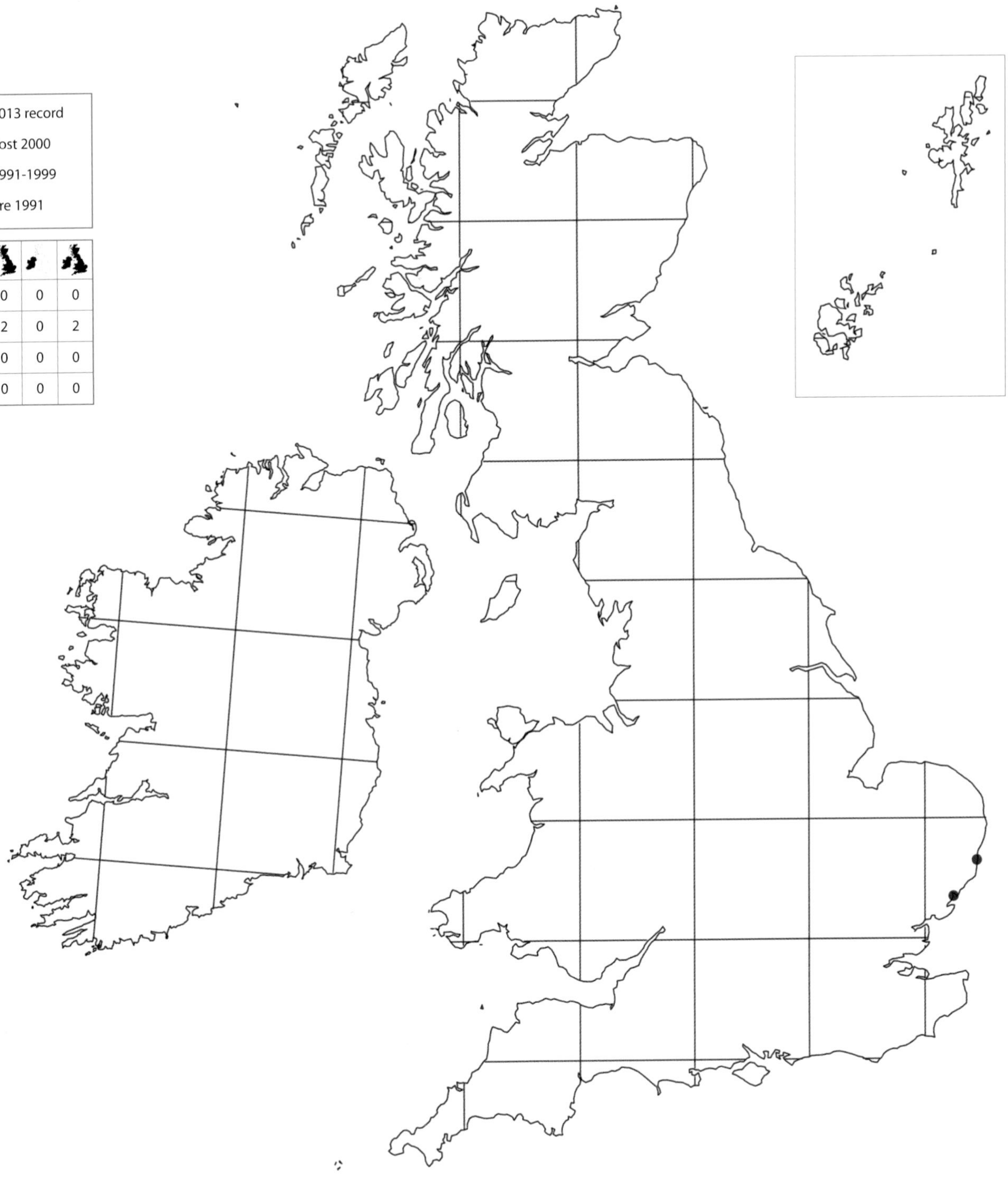

## National trends

Prior to 2012, the only record in Britain relates to an individual in 1859. The discovery of two separate males during 2012 is thus of some interest, though cannot presently be said to indicate any change in status. Populations in The Netherlands have increased in recent years (Parr, 2013), so further occurrences in the UK may occur. There is a suggestion that, unlike other *Leucorrhinia* species, Large White-faced Darter may benefit from climatic warming (Jaeschke *et al.*, 2013).

On the Continent, the migration event that brought individuals to Suffolk in 2012 is known to have also involved smaller numbers of other *Leucorrhinia* species, most notably Ruby White-faced Darter *L. rubicunda*. The future occurrence of additional species of white-faced darters in Britain is thus possible.

# Broad-bodied Chaser
## Libellula depressa

Broad-bodied Chaser is a distinctive dragonfly with a wide, somewhat flattened, abdomen, which in the male develops a blue pruinescence. Females and tenerals are ochre and yellow, females darkening with age and sometimes also developing blue pruinescence. The thorax is brown with broad, cream-coloured antehumeral stripes. The wings have dark, triangular patches at the base. Eggs are laid onto the surface of the water whilst in flight and larvae take one, or more usually, two years to develop.

Broad-bodied Chaser, male.
*Steve Cham*

## Distribution

Broad-bodied Chaser is a common insect across most of Europe, as far north as southern Sweden and southern Finland, and its range extends eastwards into the Middle East and Central Asia.

In Britain, Broad-bodied Chaser is common in southern and central England and Wales. It becomes less common further north, with its main range extending in the west to Cumbria and in the east to Northumberland. It is absent from the uplands of Snowdonia and the Pennines. There have been a number of recent records from southern Scotland. Given the dispersive nature of this species and its recent spread northwards in Britain, it is surprisingly absent from Ireland, although there is an old record from Co. Waterford in 1834.

Female Broad-bodied Chaser ovipositing in a shallow pond. *Steve Cham*

Its range expanded northwards and reached Cheshire in the late 1970s. At the time of the previous atlas it was found mainly to the south of a line between the Mersey and the Wash. By the mid-1990s the first records came from South Yorkshire (east of Sheffield), where the species became established in the years after 2000. Through west Lancashire, a similar spread was observed, with a record from Heysham in 1994, followed by further sightings across to Lancaster from 2005. There were records from several sites in south

Cumbria from 2002, while north Cumbria saw records from 2003. In north-east England, much of lowland Yorkshire was colonised by 2006, with Scarborough being reached in 2009. The spread continued northwards through Durham and Northumberland. The first Scottish record came from Edinburgh in 2003. Oviposition was seen in Dumfries & Galloway in 2006, since when there have been scattered records from the Scottish Borders, Berwickshire, Dumfries & Galloway and Ayrshire.

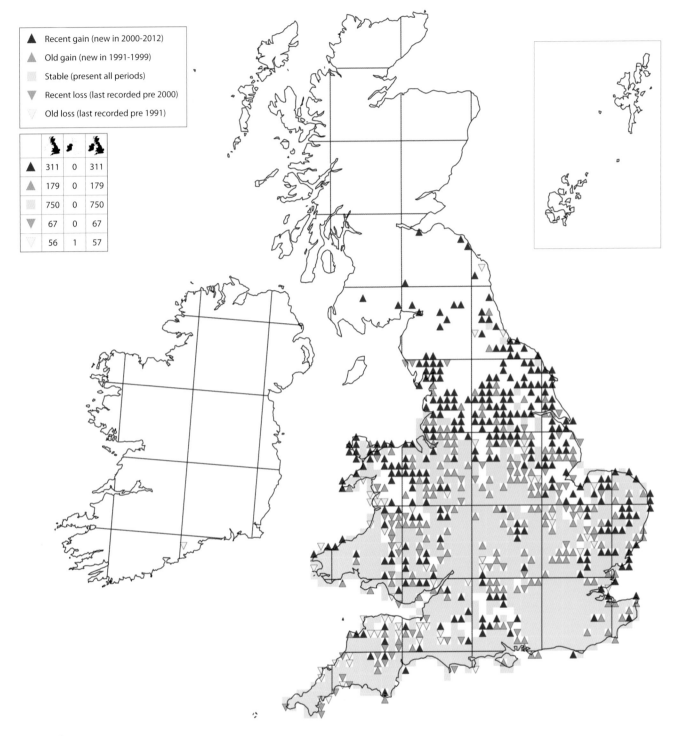

| | ![](recent gain) | | |
|---|---|---|---|
| ▲ | 311 | 0 | 311 |
| ▲ | 179 | 0 | 179 |
| ▦ | 750 | 0 | 750 |
| ▼ | 67 | 0 | 67 |
| ▽ | 56 | 1 | 57 |

Legend:
- ▲ Recent gain (new in 2000-2012)
- ▲ Old gain (new in 1991-1999)
- ▦ Stable (present all periods)
- ▼ Recent loss (last recorded pre 2000)
- ▽ Old loss (last recorded pre 1991)

## Habitat

Broad-bodied Chaser breeds mainly in ponds and lakes with areas of bare margin and clear shallow water, below which the larvae can burrow into mud. The species is often an early coloniser of new ponds and breeding is regularly noted in new garden ponds. It often breeds successfully for a few years at such ponds but then disappears as the waterbody matures and more aquatic vegetation develops. In well-established ponds, lakes and some slow-flowing watercourses, it persists where the margins are trampled by livestock or kept open by some other means. It breeds readily at peaty pools in bogs and is especially common and widespread at such heathland sites in the New Forest,

Berkshire and Surrey. It can be found at elevations up to 300m, suggesting that the freezing of its favoured shallow waters may be a limiting factor in both its altitudinal range and the extent to which it can survive in the north of Britain.

Small ponds usually support only one territorial male at any one time, due to their intensely aggressive behaviour. Larger shallow waters may hold two or more, with regular violent clashes and chases occurring. The males prefer tall perches providing a clear view over the pond, from which to watch for females or other males. The females and immatures are often found well away from water, frequently establishing feeding territories in hedgerows, rides and glades, often well inside woodland. This wandering behaviour is typical of a pioneer species.

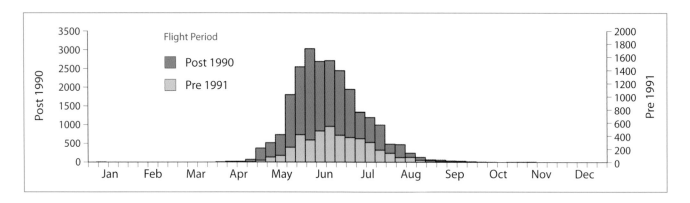

## Conservation status and threats

Although absent from Ireland and restricted to southern areas of Scotland, Broad-bodied Chaser is widespread in most of England and Wales outside the uplands. However, it is more thinly spread in Lincolnshire, West Norfolk, Salisbury Plain and the Berkshire Downs, which is presumably due to a lack of suitable habitat. It was assessed as Least Concern on the British Red List.

*Above:* Twin Bridges Pond, New Forest, Hampshire, is a shallow pond, poached by livestock and supporting good numbers of Broad-bodied Chaser. *Steve Cham*

*Below:* Shallow pond favoured by Broad-bodied Chaser on the edge of a landfill site at Brogborough, Bedfordshire. *Steve Cham*

There have been some apparent losses since the previous atlas from hectads in Cambridgeshire, south Somerset, north Devon and east Cornwall but elsewhere this species appears to be under no specific threat. In the past, it may have suffered as a result of a substantial reduction in the number of farm ponds, although the creation of many new ponds and flooded mineral workings must have counteracted this in some areas. In the New Forest the species remains common and widespread as a result of livestock poaching the margins of the abundant shallow heathland pools.

## National trends

Like other species formerly restricted to southern Britain, the range of Broad-bodied Chaser has expanded significantly at its northern edge since the previous atlas. The CEH trends analysis (pages 58-63) shows a slight increase in this species. Populations seem to be stable in areas where the species is well-established, despite local changes in status as its preferred wetland habitats mature and become less suitable and new ones are created. Much of the recent infilling of records and expansion in range is due to the wanderings of single individuals. Some apparent losses from hectads in East Anglia, south-west England and west Wales may be due to reduced recording intensity.

# Scarce Chaser

*Libellula fulva*

Blue Chaser

Scarce Chaser is a medium-sized dragonfly. Immature males and females have a bright ochre thorax and abdomen, the latter with central, black, bell-shaped markings. Adult males develop blue-grey eyes, a blue pruinescence over the abdomen and a black thorax. Females become dull-brown with age. Both sexes have small dark, triangular patches in the wing-bases and often show dark wing tips, particularly in females. The species typically has a two-year life cycle.

Scarce Chaser, mating pair. *Mark Tyrrell*

## Distribution

Scarce Chaser occurs from southern France, Sardinia, Sicily and Greece northwards to southern Norway and Finland, and eastwards into Asia. It has a scattered distribution in Iberia.

In Britain, it is found only in England, where it has a scattered, yet highly localised distribution south of a line from the Norfolk Broads to the West Midlands. Although the species is absent from Ireland, there is an old record from Co. Kerry in 1849, which is assumed to have been a vagrant.

In the previous atlas, Scarce Chaser was restricted to six discrete areas: i) the Rivers Yare and Waveney in Norfolk and Suffolk; ii) Bristol Avon in Wiltshire and Somerset; iii) Hampshire Avon, Frome and Stour in Dorset and Hampshire; iv) Arun in Sussex; v) Great Ouse in Cambridgeshire and Huntingdonshire; and vi) North Stream and associated ditches near Sandwich, Kent. However, since then there has been a significant spread within and beyond all these areas, together with colonisation of new areas, most notably in the south-west Midlands, Somerset and Devon. While some of this apparent spread can be attributed to increased recording intensity, the species has undoubtedly prospered greatly in the last two decades.

In Northamptonshire, it first appeared on the River Nene in 2005 and has since spread along some 50km from Stanwick Lakes, Higham Ferrers to Ferry Meadows Country Park, Peterborough. It has moved up the River Great Ouse from the strong populations in Cambridgeshire on the Ouse Washes and around Huntingdon into Bedfordshire, appearing upstream of Bedford by 2010. In 2011 there was an isolated record of an immature adult on the River Lea south of Luton, Bedfordshire. New colonies have been found on the Great and Little Ouse in west Norfolk, where some, but not all, of the apparent spread is attributable to

A main drain at Exminster Marshes, Devon, colonised by Scarce Chaser in 2007. *Dave Smallshire*

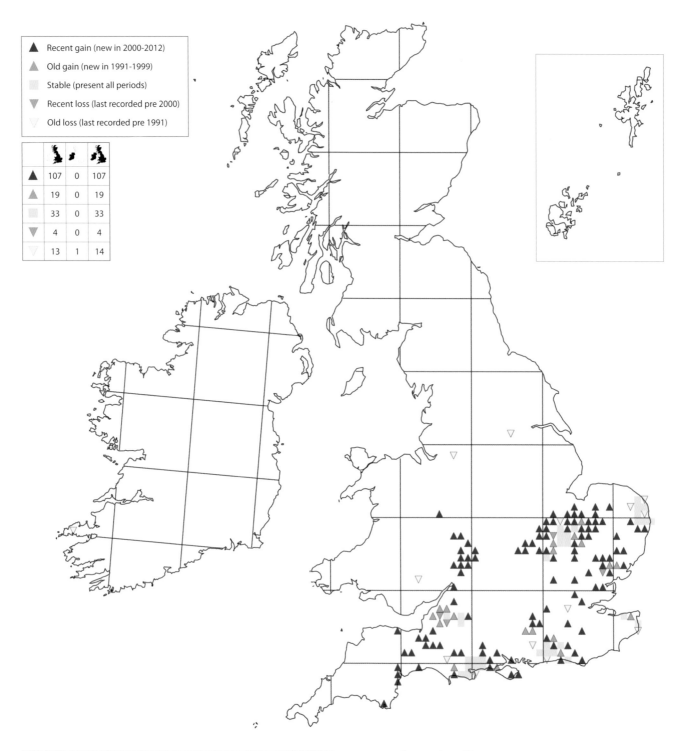

| | ![](black up triangle) | ![](grey up triangle) | ![](up triangle outline) |
|---|---|---|---|
| ▲ Recent gain (new in 2000-2012) | | | |
| ▲ Old gain (new in 1991-1999) | | | |
| ▢ Stable (present all periods) | | | |
| ▼ Recent loss (last recorded pre 2000) | | | |
| ▽ Old loss (last recorded pre 1991) | | | |

| | | | |
|---|---|---|---|
| ▲ | 107 | 0 | 107 |
| ▲ | 19 | 0 | 19 |
| ▢ | 33 | 0 | 33 |
| ▼ | 4 | 0 | 4 |
| ▽ | 13 | 1 | 14 |

River Stour at Bures forms the border between Essex and Suffolk and holds a large population of Scarce Chaser. *Steve Cham*

increased recorder effort. In 1997, it was discovered on the River Stour, Suffolk, from where it has since spread up the Rivers Brett and Gipping and into Essex along the Blackwater navigation and Rivers Chelmer and Colne.

The populations in West Sussex have now expanded into East Sussex, where it was first reported in 2004, and are now firmly established along the Rivers Ouse and Cuckmere. Dorset populations have expanded along the River Stour. In Hampshire, it has been recorded breeding at Blashford Lakes, a series of flooded gravel pits, along the lower reaches of the River Test near Southampton and the River Wey between Bentley and Farnham.

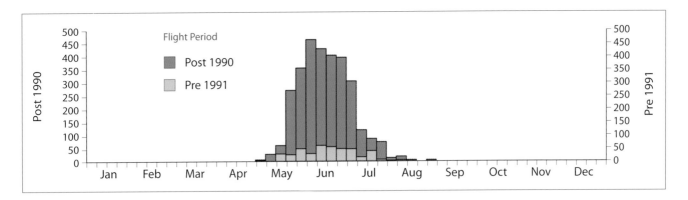

In the south-west, Scarce Chaser has spread southwards from the River Avon into North Somerset since the 1990s. The species was first recorded in 2008 from the Somerset Levels, where it is now present in drains along the Parrett, Tone and Isle. Following its discovery in 2003, there was a considerable expansion in east Devon. It has spread along much of the length of the Grand Western Canal between Tiverton and the Somerset border, with further colonies in the Axe Valley and the lower Exe marshes. Isolated records have also come recently from Dunster on the north coast of Somerset and Kingsbridge in south Devon, with the first record for Cornwall made during 2013 at Marazion Marsh. One of the most dramatic expansions in range has been in the lower Avon Valley in Gloucestershire and especially Worcestershire since 2004, and in Warwickshire since 2010.

## Habitat

The species breeds mainly in mature river systems in flat lowland areas. Slow-flowing, base-rich or neutral rivers are preferred, though nearby gravel pits, ponds, drains and canals are often colonised. Breeding sites are characterised by lush emergent bankside vegetation and adjacent rough meadows or scrub. Emergent plants include Common Club-rush, Reed Sweet-grass, Branched Bur-reed and reedmace (Winsland *et al.*, 1996). The larvae inhabit mud and silt around the base of this emergent vegetation, close to the bank.

In a short term study in Dorset, direct comparisons were made between The Moors River and the Leaden Stour, a system of adjacent associated water meadows, irrigation dykes and ditches. Larvae had a preference for areas where the flow was lower, the pH higher and the temperature was higher all year round, so thus preferred the smaller, quieter

River Avon, Hilperton, Wiltshire, where the range of Scarce Chaser has expanded since 2000. *Steve Cham*

Scarce Chaser, recently emerged adult, one of the first confirmed breeding records for Devon. *David Smallshire*

streams and stretches of slack water (Goodyear, 1995). Habitat preferences appear to be similar in other parts of the country, such as the River Nene, a eutrophic, slow-flowing river in Northamptonshire. Here, Scarce Chasers are found in the highest numbers in sections immediately before a lock, where the flow is slowed and sediment accumulates. Similarly, weirs on stretches of the Worcestershire Avon reduce the flow upstream resulting in slow-flowing water and lush emergent vegetation.

## Conservation status and threats

Scarce Chaser is categorised as Near Threatened in the British Red List, having previously being listed as Vulnerable (Shirt, 1987). The principal threat to the species is extensive clearance of vegetation and mud from watercourses. Over-abstraction of water can result in low flows, de-oxygenation and higher concentration of pollutants, especially during periods of drought. Other threats include excessive shading by trees, as both territorial males and ovipositing females need sunlit bankside areas and open water (Winsland, 1996). The excessive clearance of bankside vegetation and the use of herbicide can degrade habitat for adults. Scarce Chaser seems to be tolerant of mild agricultural run-off and is more tolerant of eutrophication than other riverine species (Winsland *et al.*, 1996). It is hoped that future river management will improve the habitat for this and other dragonfly species by creating slack water and allowing natural meanders.

Scarce Chaser, maturing male. *David Sadler*

## National trends

The range of Scarce Chaser has expanded significantly since the previous atlas, the number of occupied hectads increasing almost fourfold. In the CEH trends analysis (pages 58-63), this species shows the greatest increase, after Small Red-eyed Damselfly. Not only have all the historic occupied areas expanded but significant new areas have been colonised some tens of kilometres from the nearest known sites. This may be a result of one or more factors, including climate change, improvements in water quality and more sympathetic river management. The species has also benefited from the creation and maturing of gravel pits and other suitable standing waters. Further range expansion seems likely.

# Four-spotted Chaser
## *Libellula quadrimaculata*

Four-spotted Chaser is a medium-sized dragonfly, largely brown in both sexes. The abdomen is black at its posterior end, with narrow yellow markings along the sides. Each wing has a dark mark at the node (hence the vernacular name) and there is a black patch at the base of the hind wings. The form praenubila, with enlarged dark wing markings stemming from the node and pterostigma, is found in some populations. The thorax is covered in dense pale hairs. Larvae take two years to develop.

Four-spotted Chaser, male.
*Neil Malton*

## Distribution

The range of Four-spotted Chaser extends across Europe, Asia and North America. It occurs widely in Europe, although it is scarce around the Mediterranean and absent from the mountains and north of Scandinavia. The species' range extends eastwards to China, the Korean Peninsula and the Japanese archipelago.

It is widespread and locally common throughout much of Britain and Ireland. However, it is far from omnipresent and is unaccountably absent or scarce in some regions. It is sparsely distributed in the Pennines, the chalk downlands of Berkshire, Hampshire and Wiltshire, in a band across eastern Wales and in parts of south-west and north-east England. The species is also absent from large areas of northern England, as well as southern and eastern Scotland. There are large areas of southern and eastern Ireland and the upland areas of the Sperrins and Antrim Plateau in Northern Ireland with few occupied hectads. It is present on most of the Inner Hebrides but only occurs locally on the Isle of Man, the Outer Hebrides and Orkney; there are recent records from Shetland.

## Habitat

Four-spotted Chaser breeds in a wide variety of neutral or acidic still-water habitats. The species can be locally very abundant in acidic boggy habitats in western Scotland, Wales, Ireland and England. In Ireland it can occur on base-rich sites, although the preference is still for acidic sites. Water quality may be more important than its acidity. It breeds in boggy pools in lowland heathland, moorland,

The bog pools at Thursley Common, Surrey, support large numbers of Four-spotted Chaser. *Steve Cham*

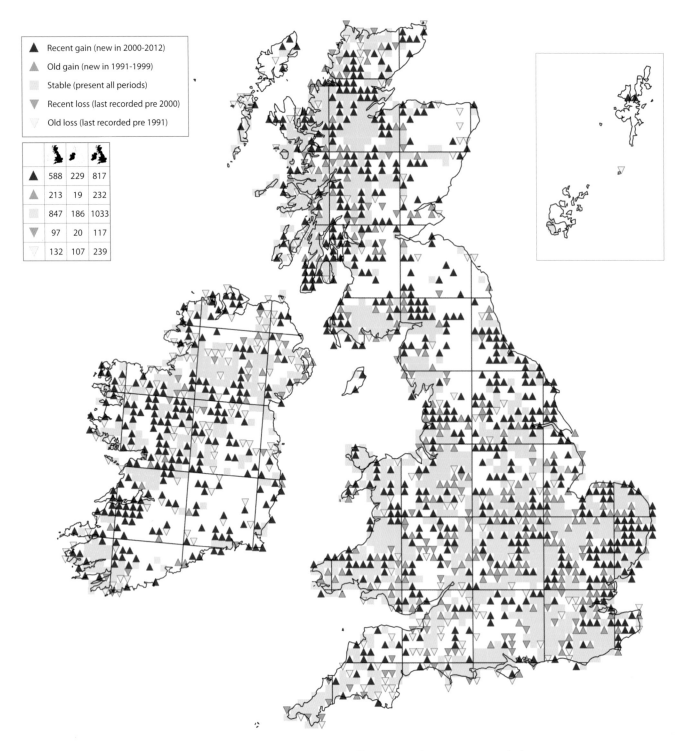

| |  |  |  |
|---|---|---|---|
| ▲ | 588 | 229 | 817 |
| ▲ | 213 | 19 | 232 |
| ▨ | 847 | 186 | 1033 |
| ▼ | 97 | 20 | 117 |
| ▽ | 132 | 107 | 239 |

- ▲ Recent gain (new in 2000-2012)
- ▲ Old gain (new in 1991-1999)
- ▨ Stable (present all periods)
- ▼ Recent loss (last recorded pre 2000)
- ▽ Old loss (last recorded pre 1991)

fens and in the open glades of forestry plantations. It is equally at home in the shallow margins of larger waterbodies such as lakes, reservoirs and flooded sand, gravel and clay pits. Occasionally it breeds in slow-flowing rivers, streams and canals and in the brackish water of coastal dykes in grazing marsh.

Typically, any area of open, standing water with clumps of rushes or tall marginal plants such as reeds provides habitat for the Four-spotted Chaser. Males perch conspicuously on emergent stems or other marginal vegetation, from which they make frequent sorties to feed, fend-off competing males or grab passing females in order to mate.

## Conservation status and threats

Four-spotted Chaser is categorised as Least Concern in the British and Irish Red Lists. At the present time it is widespread and common throughout most of its range. Like many of the generalist dragonflies, Four-spotted Chaser does not appear to be threatened in Britain and Ireland, although populations can be wiped out locally by the destruction of their favoured habitat. Such destruction includes the draining of ponds, and the excessive removal of aquatic and marginal vegetation. Other threats include desiccation during repeated droughts, particularly in the lowlands of eastern England, and the drainage of boggy areas for peat extraction and forestry planting.

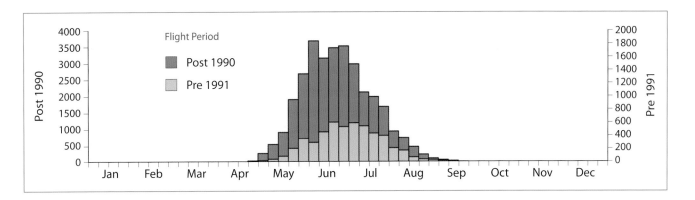

## National trends

The CEH trends analysis (pages 58-63) shows a significant increase. There has also been a substantial net increase in the number of hectads in which Four-spotted Chaser has been recorded since the previous atlas. This is evident in all parts of Britain and Ireland. However, the extent to which this is due to increased recording intensity rather than expansion within its range is difficult to quantify. It is complicated by the largely unknown extent of migration events from continental Europe. Such events have long been reported in the literature, including thousands of Four-spotted Chasers passing Dover, Kent, flying into a north-east wind on 6-7 June 1889 and 'vast numbers' arriving at Margate on 10 June 1900 (Brook & Brook, 2001). However, in more recent times the scale of such migration seems to have diminished, though a significant event, including many individuals, was reported in 1963 (Burton, 1996). Occasional migrants along the coast are still noted. For example, small numbers were seen at Landguard,

Suffolk, coincident with the occurrence of Britain's second-ever Large White-faced Darter in late May 2012.

There are also many reports of extensive migration of Four-spotted Chasers elsewhere in Eurasia, which occur every 10 years or so. These are often preceded by several years of conditions favourable for larval development, during which there are huge population increases. These conditions are then followed by a relatively long period of unfavourable weather conditions which results in a highly synchronized mass emergence of adults. Some of these migration events contain huge numbers of Four-spotted Chasers. One example, reported by Haritonov & Popova (2011), occurred on the steppes of northern Kazakhstan in July 1981 and contained an estimated 100 million dragonflies. Other, even more astounding, events have contained even greater numbers of Four-spotted Chasers (and other dragonfly species to a lesser extent), including an estimated 2400 million individual dragonflies in Germany on 19 May 1862.

White Loch, Annabaglish, Dumfries & Galloway. *R&B Mearns*

# Black-tailed Skimmer
## *Orthetrum cancellatum*

Black-tailed Skimmer is a medium-sized dragonfly, the males of which fly low and fast over open, still waterbodies, often perching on bare ground. Both the immature male and female are yellow and have two black lines running down the length of the abdomen. As the male matures the underlying pattern on the abdomen is covered by a blue pruinescence and it develops a black tip. Females oviposit whilst in flight by dipping the end of their abdomen into the water whilst the male guards her. The larvae take two years to develop.

Black-tailed Skimmer, male. *Mark Tyrrell*

## Distribution

Black-tailed Skimmer occurs across Europe and northern Asia to Kashmir and Mongolia. It is a southern species in Europe and absent from much of Scandinavia.

In Britain, it is relatively common and widespread over much of the southern and eastern counties. There has been a northward expansion in England since the previous atlas, most likely as a result of climate change. It was recorded from Scotland alongside Red-veined Darter in 2006 in Berwickshire and has reached as far north as Fife. It was found again in Berwickshire in 2010.

Given its British distribution, the main distribution in Ireland is surprisingly in the west and centred on the base-rich lakes on limestone. It is present at many of the small lakes on the eastern edge of the Burren and in the Corrib/Mask/Carra lake complex in Counties Galway and Mayo. It is found at scattered sites across the midlands of Ireland and at sites on the east coast from Louth to Cork. The species is largely absent from the south-west and much of the north where limestone is absent but there is some evidence of very recent spread into these areas. It has been known from one site in Co. Donegal for over 30 years but no other permanent sites have been found in that county.

It has recently been seen in Kerry after many years with no records and since 2012 it has been recorded for the first time in three counties in Northern Ireland: Armagh, Antrim and Fermanagh. However, it is not known if any of these are established populations.

White Sands, Lough Graney, Co. Clare. Sandy shore and shallow lake edge; the natural lake habitat of Black-tailed Skimmer in western Ireland. *Brian Nelson*

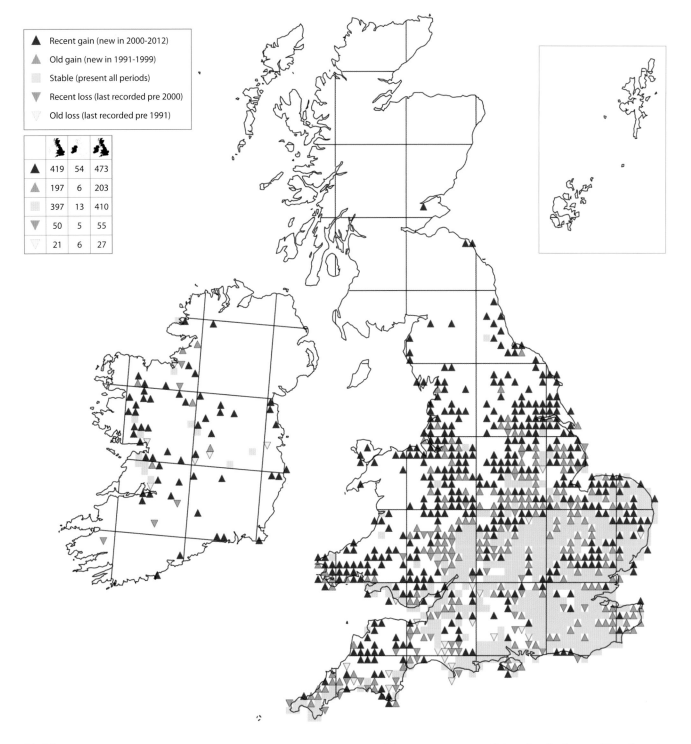

## Habitat

In England and Wales, the Black-tailed Skimmer breeds in a wide range of ponds, lakes, canals, large drains and slow-flowing rivers with areas of bare or exposed ground. It is an early coloniser of pools with bare margins formed as a result of mineral extraction, yet occurs frequently at some well-established heathland pools. In Ireland, the main Black-tailed Skimmer population is associated with the marl lakes (shallow base-rich lowland lakes on limestone that also have bare rocky shores) in the west and midlands. The bare limestone shores and pale marl substrate found on the edges of lakes provide the adults with basking sites. As the water recedes in summer, the shallows created provide

suitable warm water conditions for the larvae. Elsewhere in Ireland it is found at natural ponds in sand dunes, coastal lagoons and extraction pits.

The males are territorial, acquiring and then holding a bankside length of up to 50m. Males settle frequently on bare surfaces close to the water. Females spend a considerable amount of time away from waterbodies feeding along hedgerows and open fields before returning to the waterbody to mate. The female oviposits over water guarded by the male. Larvae live in the shallow edges of waterbodies among the substrate and debris around marginal vegetation, often becoming encrusted with silt and mud, and can travel some distance from the waterbody before emerging.

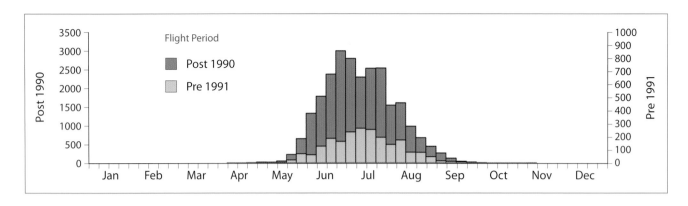

Post 1990

Flight Period

Post 1990

Pre 1991

Pre 1991

Jan  Feb  Mar  Apr  May  Jun  Jul  Aug  Sep  Oct  Nov  Dec

## Conservation status and threats

Black-tailed Skimmer is common and widespread in both Britain and Ireland and is not threatened and thus receives no legal protection. It is classified as Least Concern in the European Red List and in the Red Lists for Britain and Ireland.

It is often an early colonist, favouring open pools in early successional stages, with extensive areas of bare ground. It has benefited particularly from mineral extraction activities. Loss of such bare ground is typical of natural succession. Hence, the management of a waterbody for this species should aim to keep at least some margins clear of vegetation.

## National trends

The CEH trends analysis (pages 58-63) shows a significant increase in Black-tailed Skimmer. This species appears to be expanding its range both northwards and westwards within Britain, possibly as a result of increasing average summer temperatures. Expansion has occurred across south Wales and from the English Midlands north-west into north Wales and and Lancashire and to the north-east into Yorkshire and Durham. In Ireland, the species has expanded its range away from the well-established western range and it has appeared at sites along the east coast from Louth to Wexford since 2004. It is possible that the east coast populations could have been derived from arrivals from Britain, but eastward expansion within Ireland is equally as likely. It has also shown an increase in the north, with first appearances in Co. Armagh in 2012 and both Fermanagh and Antrim in 2013. In the south-west it may also be increasing as it was found for the first time in north Kerry in 2013.

Areas of bare mud around the heathland pools at Thursley Common NNR, Surrey, provide basking sites for Black-tailed Skimmer in an otherwise unsuitable habitat for the species. *Steve Cham*

# Keeled Skimmer
## *Orthetrum coerulescens*

Keeled Skimmers are relatively small dragonflies. Immature adults of both sexes are yellow and superficially resemble darters (*Sympetrum* spp.) Orange pterostigmata and paired whitish lines on top of the thorax distinguish them. Mature males have a predominately pale blue abdomen as a covering of pruinescence develops. They lack the dark tip to the abdomen shown by male Black-tailed Skimmers. Females darken to become brown as they mature.

Keeled Skimmer, male.
*John Curd*

## Distribution

Keeled Skimmer is found from North Africa, across Europe from Iberia and France eastwards as far as western Russia and northern India. In Britain, it is mainly restricted to the heaths of lowland southern England, the lower moorlands of the south-west peninsula, through Wales and Cumbria to scattered sites in western Scotland. The highest densities often occur in extensive areas of lowland heath, such as the New Forest, Hampshire. There are also a few isolated but long-established sites in eastern England, including the North Yorkshire Moors, though it was formerly more widespread here and some sites have been lost to land drainage (Moore, 1986). In Scotland, it was first recorded in 1908 from Methven Moss, the only site in the east, which has since been drained. It has a western distribution from the Loch Maree area in Wester Ross south to Dumfries & Galloway. In Ireland, it is common in the south-west and west and in the Wicklow mountains in the east but is more local elsewhere.

This species has long been recognised as a wanderer; in 1949 the unexpected appearance of a male by a stream in north Somerset was 65km from the nearest known breeding site at the time (Moore, 1980). Phillips (2003) detailed sporadic occurrences in west Gloucestershire,

Bog pools in the New Forest, Hampshire: typical lowland heath habitat for Keeled Skimmer in England. *Des Sussex*

similarly distant from known strongholds, and the current distribution shows a scattering of sightings across the English Midlands. In Britain, most records of Keeled Skimmer near the coast seem to relate to local breeders in coastal heathland. There are a very few records right on the coast, suggestive of immigration, but by and large most unexpected sightings appear to be inland, which probably implies a local origin (A. Parr, pers. comm.). Such dispersal could result in the colonisation of new areas, provided suitable habitat exists.

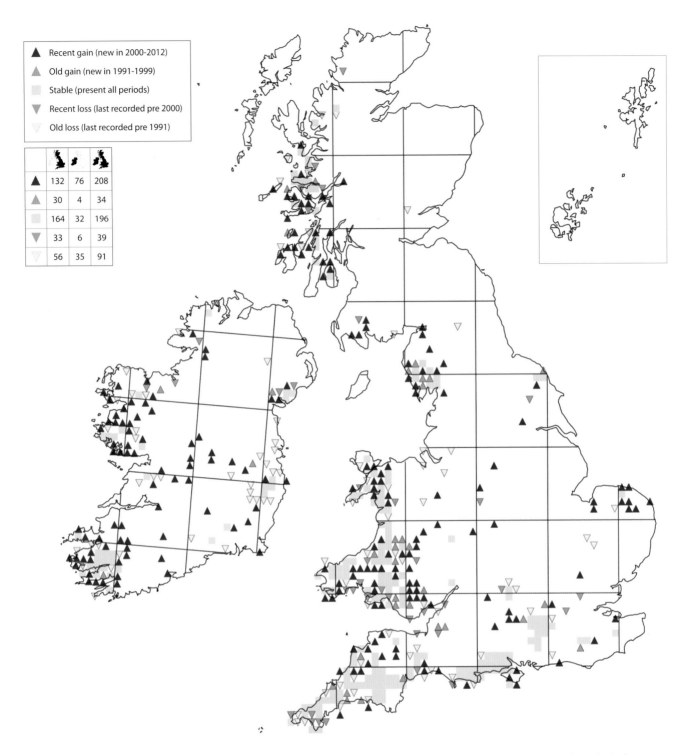

| |  | | |
|---|---|---|---|
| ▲ | 132 | 76 | 208 |
| ▲ | 30 | 4 | 34 |
| ▣ | 164 | 32 | 196 |
| ▼ | 33 | 6 | 39 |
| ▽ | 56 | 35 | 91 |

Legend:
- ▲ Recent gain (new in 2000-2012)
- ▲ Old gain (new in 1991-1999)
- ▣ Stable (present all periods)
- ▼ Recent loss (last recorded pre 2000)
- ▽ Old loss (last recorded pre 1991)

## Habitat

The strongest populations of Keeled Skimmer are found in lowland heathland mires and associated springs, flushes, runnels, streams and small pools where bog-mosses and associated plants such as Bog Pondweed, Bog Asphodel, Marsh St John's-wort and Common Cotton-grass are found. The species also breeds in shallow streams flowing through valley mires in the New Forest. In continental Europe, it can be found in a wide range of habitats including lowland rivers and streams, often in habitats where they are not found in Britain and Ireland.

Areas with large, viable populations of Keeled Skimmers have a plentiful supply of wet, boggy areas interspersed with drier habitat. Given that such often-shallow areas are prone to drying out, large expanses of suitable habitat are ideally required to support viable populations.

Keeled Skimmer also breeds in calcareous fens at some sites, such as Cothill in Oxfordshire. In Ireland, the largest populations are at low levels on south-facing slopes and the overall distribution in Britain and Ireland appears to be the result of oceanic influence on temperature and rainfall.

In Devon, the species currently breeds at altitudes of up to 400m on Dartmoor, being absent from blanket bogs at a

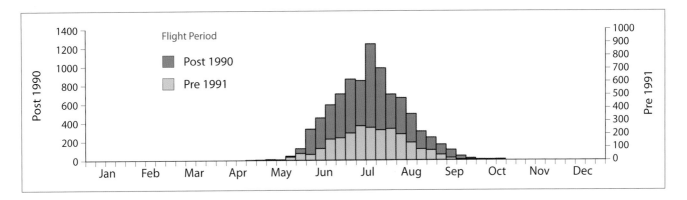

**Flight Period**

- Post 1990
- Pre 1991

higher altitude. This suggests that temperature limits the species' distribution both here and presumably in other upland or northern locations. It is likely that warmer temperatures associated with recent climate change have allowed the species to breed at higher altitudes. Adults typically rest on low vegetation, such as heather and gorse, near the breeding site. The larvae live among detritus or in muddy silt and take two years to develop.

## Conservation Status

Keeled Skimmer is categorised as Least Concern in the Red Lists for Britain and Ireland. It is a locally common dragonfly and its survival is not under immediate threat. The species may be assumed to have been formerly much commoner and more widespread in England when the area of wet lowland heathland was greater. There have been huge losses of heathland in the past to afforestation, development, mineral extraction and agricultural improvement. Natural succession of vegetation from wet heath to scrub may also render the habitat unsuitable. Most populations in eastern England are only able to survive because the habitats are actively managed (Moore, 1986, Merritt *et al.*, 1996).

Many remaining heaths in Britain have legally protected status (SSSIs and often SAC/SPA Natura 2000 sites). Most of these are managed for conservation by non-governmental organisations such as the RSPB and Wildlife Trusts. However, even when heathland is intact and well-managed, the shallow-water larval habitats are vulnerable to drying out during the periods of drought that are a recent feature of climate change (although wetter winters and summer flooding may help to counteract this). The fact that larvae usually take two years to develop exacerbates this problem: two drought-free years in succession are required for successful breeding.

Craigeach Moor, Dumfries & Galloway. *R&B Mearns*

Boggy runnels at Warren Heath, Hampshire. *Ken Crick*

Wet flush at Clee Hill, Worcestershire. *Mike Averill*

## National trends

Compared with the previous atlas, there appears to have been some range expansion, although some of these changes may be as a result of increased recording intensity. There has been an increase in records in the southern half of Wales, with indications of an eastward spread. In England, following habitat restoration work at Holt Lowes, Norfolk, a population increase was recorded. Subsequently, the species has spread to new sites and there is now a well-established colony at Buxton Heath, with regular records of low numbers

from some additional, outlying sites. In Scotland, it has increased its range, doubling the number of hectads since the previous atlas, particularly in Argyll, the islands, Ardnamurchan and in Dumfries & Galloway. This is partly due to increased recording but there is also a real spread into new areas. In eastern Scotland, it has been lost from its sole former site near Perth. In Ireland, given the improved levels of coverage compared with the previous atlas, there has probably been little overall change in distribution.

# Black Darter
## *Sympetrum danae*

Black Darter is a small, dark dragonfly. Mature males are largely black, with yellow markings on the abdomen and stripes on the sides of the thorax. Females and immatures are mostly yellow, with a prominent black triangle on the top of the thorax. The eggs are laid in late summer but hatching is delayed until the following spring. The larvae complete development within two months.

Black Darter, male. *John Curd*

## Distribution

Black Darter is common and widespread throughout most of northern and eastern Europe, although is mainly absent north of the Arctic Circle and in southern Europe. It has a patchy distribution in France, where it is largely restricted to the north-west or mountainous regions. The range extends eastwards through northern Russia, Japan and across North America to Newfoundland.

This is a widespread species of the west and north of both Britain and Ireland, including the Isle of Man, Outer Hebrides and Orkney, although it has never been found in Shetland. It is less frequent in south-east Ireland and south-east Britain, where suitable habitat is largely absent. It occurs widely in peatlands in the north and west but in southern England is largely restricted to mires and boggy ponds in lowland heathland in areas such as Berkshire, Surrey, North Hampshire, the New Forest and Dorset. In Norfolk it breeds in the west of the county at Dersingham Bog, an area of acid valley mire and heathland, and in similar habitat at Grimston Warren and Roydon Common. There are also a number of scattered records elsewhere, although its distribution, especially in the lowlands, is confused by records of wandering individuals that turn up tens of kilometres from the nearest known breeding sites.

Indeed, small numbers of presumed immigrants from continental Europe have been recorded periodically, in association with other darter species, and these explain many of the records on the coast of south-east England especially.

## Habitat

Black Darter is largely confined to upland and lowland bogs and heaths where acidic surface water is retained to allow bog-moss growth and peat formation. Such habitats include raised bogs and blanket, valley and basin mires. Breeding occurs in acidic, nutrient-poor bog pools and the fringes of small lakes with abundant bog-mosses and emergent sedges and rushes. The species does not tolerate poor water quality or shade. Cut-over peat workings, such as at Whixall Moss, Shropshire, Thorne & Hatfield Moors, South Yorkshire, and many across Ireland, can host large breeding populations. Some old flooded clay pits and tin workings on Dartmoor, Devon, and Bodmin Moor, Cornwall, also support large numbers. In all such cases, the abundant growth of bog-mosses is supported by high rainfall or springs. Although it breeds in the lowland heath mires of Purbeck, Dorset, and the New Forest, Hampshire, similar habitat in the East Devon Pebblebed Heaths does not support a breeding population.

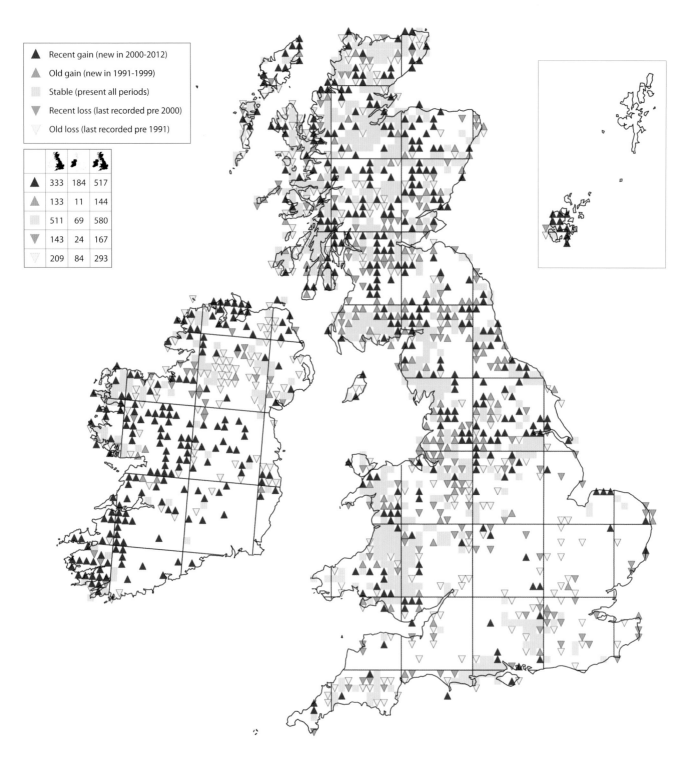

| | ![](black up triangle) | | |
|---|---|---|---|
| ▲ | Recent gain (new in 2000-2012) | | |
| ▲ | Old gain (new in 1991-1999) | | |
| ▦ | Stable (present all periods) | | |
| ▼ | Recent loss (last recorded pre 2000) | | |
| ▽ | Old loss (last recorded pre 1991) | | |

| | 🇬🇧 | , | 🇬🇧 |
|---|---|---|---|
| ▲ | 333 | 184 | 517 |
| ▲ | 133 | 11 | 144 |
| ▦ | 511 | 69 | 580 |
| ▼ | 143 | 24 | 167 |
| ▽ | 209 | 84 | 293 |

An upland pool on the Long Mynd, Shropshire: typical habitat for Black Darter. *Sue McLamb*

The black colouration of the male has a thermoregulatory function, allowing the species to occupy relatively cool upland and high latitude sites. Adults are often encountered basking on rocks and bare ground, where they absorb reflected heat, or on tall vegetation, where they can receive direct radiation from the sun. Wanderers away from breeding sites are often encountered in unsuitable breeding habitat (Smith, 1998).

Oviposition is usually over submerged bog-mosses and other moss species, although occasionally may be over floating plant debris, mud or open water. Shaded areas with overhanging trees are avoided and south-facing sites are preferred late in the season, although north-facing sites are more attractive early in the season when temperatures are higher.

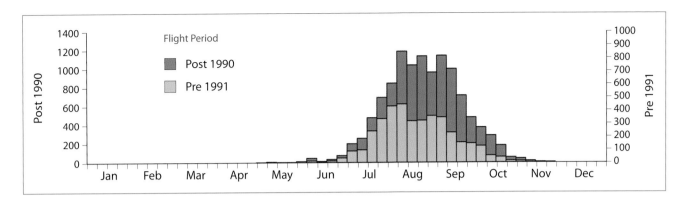

Flight Period

■ Post 1990

□ Pre 1991

Bog-moss surrounding a pool at Warren Heath, Hampshire, attracts large numbers of Black Darter. *Steve Cham*

## Conservation status and threats

Black Darter is categorised as Least Concern in the British and Irish Red Lists, being widespread and abundant at suitable sites throughout western and northern Britain and Ireland and in the heathlands of southern England. Suitable habitats are widespread and the species would appear to be secure.

However, whilst its distribution would appear to be stable, its habitats have undoubtedly been subject to significant threats, including peat extraction, drainage, afforestation, urban development and agricultural intensification. Erosion of blanket bogs as a result of overgrazing has affected the quality of some sites but the effects on this species are unknown. On the other hand, the early indication from restoration trials is that Black Darter has benefited from improvements in habitat quality. Conversely, at some sites in south-east England, for example Epping Forest and heathland in Hertfordshire, the species has been lost through encroachment of scrub and woodland following natural succession resulting from changes in land management; this has resulted in shading and the drying out of breeding sites (Brooks, 1989; S. J. Brooks, pers. obs.). An even more insidious threat is that posed by climate change, through changes in the pattern and amount of rainfall, the essential component of active bogs.

## National trends

The CEH trends analysis (pages 58-63) indicates a significant decline in Black Darter. However, there has been an increase in the number of occupied hectads since the previous atlas, but with no clear evidence that the species has increased its range significantly; this is considered to largely reflect greater recorder effort, especially in Scotland and Ireland. It is possible, however, that the apparent increase in upland districts of England and Wales, which were relatively well recorded prior to 2000, reflects a real change in distribution. The previous atlas recorded a marked range contraction in central and southern England (Moore, 1986) as a result of agricultural intensification, afforestation, drainage and urban expansion onto heathland. These losses may have continued but the picture is confused by the occasional records of wandering individuals. There will have undoubtedly been significant losses of sites in Ireland prior to 2000 due to large-scale peat extraction.

Llyn Tyn-y-mynydd, Cors Bodgynydd SSSI, Gwydyr Forest, Gwynedd: a shallow, peaty, heathland bog lake surrounded by birch scrub mire and partly by conifers. Strong populations of Black Darter are present, together with Keeled Skimmer and an isolated population of Scarce Blue-tailed Damselfly, one of only two colonies known in Snowdonia. *Allan Brandon*

# Yellow-winged Darter
## Sympetrum flaveolum

Yellow-winged Darter is a small darter dragonfly with both sexes having extensive yellow at the wing bases, more so than any other British and Irish darter. The abdomen is orange-red in mature males and yellow in immatures and females. The species is an erratic late-summer migrant to Britain and Ireland, sometimes appearing in high numbers then absent for several years. The life cycle is typically one year, overwintering as an egg. Larval development is rapid, with adults emerging in June and July.

Yellow-winged Darter, male.
*Dave Smallshire*

## Distribution

Yellow-winged Darter is found over much of Eurasia, largely confined to upland areas in the far south; its range extends east through Turkey, Western Siberia, Kazakhstan, Mongolia, China and as far as Korea and Japan. It is generally widespread and common in Siberia and in eastern and central Europe but is more patchily distributed near to its western and southern limits. Here, the species' status and distribution may fluctuate with time as a result of large-scale immigrations. These can establish strong local populations, which then gradually diminish, only for further influxes to re-establish the species.

In Britain and Ireland, Yellow-winged Darter is an irregular migrant. There have been widespread sightings in England and scattered records from Wales but few from Scotland (in 1862, 1945 and 1997) and Ireland (in 1995). The distribution map is heavily dominated by sightings during the significant influx of 1995. Many of the larger immigrations seem to be associated with periods of easterly winds and, correspondingly, there is often an easterly bias to the distribution of records during such influxes. Whilst many immigrants rest soon after reaching land, they clearly continue to move quite considerable distances inland.

Successful breeding has long been suspected at a few localities in England (e.g. Alderfen Broad, Norfolk) following larger invasions in the past (Parr, 1996). Confirmation of breeding was obtained when a single emergent and associated exuvia was recorded at Chartley Moss NNR, Staffordshire, on 22 July 1996 (Beynon, 1998). Proven or likely breeding following the 1995 influx was subsequently also detected at several other sites in England, particularly in East Anglia and the Midlands, as well as in Dyfed, south Wales (Parr, 1997). Such breeding colonies, both historic and modern, have turned out to be highly transient, generally surviving only two or three years at most.

## Habitat

In western Europe, Yellow-winged Darter typically breeds in sunny, shallow, still-water sites that often dry out in high summer. Sites with extensive vegetation, tall grasses, rushes and sedges are particularly favoured. More open waters are also frequented where the edges are very gently sloping, thus allowing large seasonal fluctuations in the waterline. Typical breeding habitat includes fens, swampy hollows, seasonally-flooded meadows, quiet silted-up backwaters of rivers and also old pingo depressions such as those found in the Norfolk Brecklands. The site at Chartley Moss comprised a depression in the peat raft that contained a shallow pool

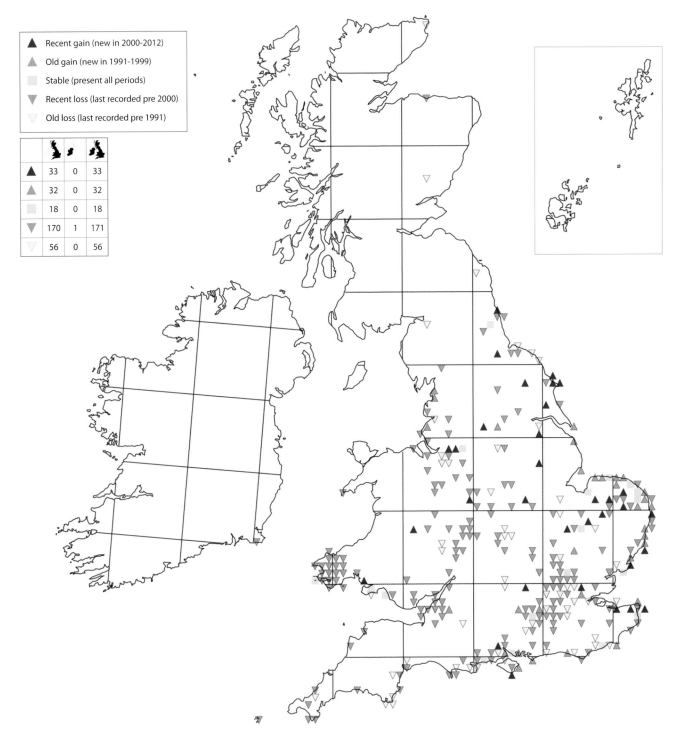

**Legend:**

▲ Recent gain (new in 2000-2012)
△ Old gain (new in 1991-1999)
▦ Stable (present all periods)
▽ Recent loss (last recorded pre 2000)
▽ Old loss (last recorded pre 1991)

| | | | |
|---|---|---|---|
| ▲ | 33 | 0 | 33 |
| △ | 32 | 0 | 32 |
| ▦ | 18 | 0 | 18 |
| ▽ | 170 | 1 | 171 |
| ▽ | 56 | 0 | 56 |

(about 6m wide) of open water surrounded by extensive semi-submerged bog-mosses, containing a dense growth of Cottongrass and Oval Sedge (Beynon, 1998). In parts of its range where it is abundant, a somewhat broader variety of waterbodies may also be frequented. Females typically lay their eggs above the waterline, ovipositing into damp mud. It is possible that eggs laid in sites that do not flood sufficiently over the winter may, perhaps, remain dormant until a later year (Parr, 1998).

Migrants to Britain and Ireland have been seen at typical breeding habitat but may also occur in a variety of surroundings well away from water, some of which broadly resemble breeding habitat (e.g. rank grassy meadows)

whilst others are more diverse. During the large-scale invasion of 1995, some of the highest concentrations of Yellow-winged Darters were noted at Great Yarmouth Cemetery, Norfolk, and on the shingle expanses of Dungeness, Kent (Silsby & Ward-Smith, 1997). These coastal sites apparently represented landing sites for newly-arrived migrants, which later dispersed further.

## Conservation status and threats

Yellow-winged Darter is listed as being of Least Concern in the recent Red Data List for Britain. Given the erratic and transitory nature of British breeding colonies, there are presently no relevant conservation issues.

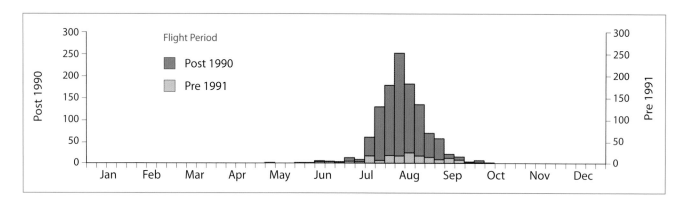

## National trends

Yellow-winged Darter has long been recognised as an erratic, though occasionally numerous, migrant. Particularly favourable immigration years include 1871, 1898, 1926, several years during the 1940s (most notably 1945 & 1947), 1953, 1955 and, more recently, 1995 and 2006 (Parr, 1996; 2007). It is difficult to compare the scale of the different invasions due to a significant increase in recorder effort in more recent years. However, the 1995 influx was particularly dramatic, with well over a thousand individuals being reported (Silsby & Ward-Smith, 1997). Outside these influx years, just the occasional Yellow-winged Darter is seen annually and the species may also go unrecorded for several years in a row.

Yellow-winged Darter immature female. *Dave Smallshire*

Over the last century, there has been no clear change in the frequency of arrivals of Yellow-winged Darter, although there are disproportionately few records from the 1960s-1980s. The pattern differs significantly from other migrant species, such as Red-veined Darter and Lesser Emperor, where immigration has become increasingly more common in Britain and Ireland over recent years. These differences in behaviour most likely result, in part, from the different geographical origins of the various migrants. Red-veined Darter and Lesser Emperor are of essentially southern origin and, in recent years, have been notably affected by climate change, whilst Yellow-winged Darter is of a more easterly origin and hence is not affected in the same way.

Large-scale immigration and future changes in climate may enable longer-lived colonies to develop and allow it to become more permanently established. However, no dramatic change in status is anticipated in the short term. Although productivity at British breeding sites currently appears to be low, colony instability is noted in many marginal parts of the Yellow-winged Darter's range. It could thus reflect an inherent aspect of the species' biology, that it is highly dispersive/migratory in tendency.

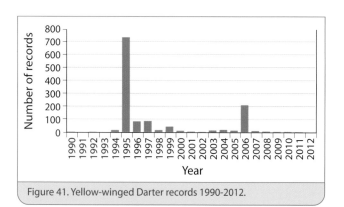

Figure 41. Yellow-winged Darter records 1990-2012.

# Red-veined Darter

## *Sympetrum fonscolombii*

Red-veined Darter can be distinguished from other red darters by the pale pterostigmata, strongly outlined in black, and the eyes with the lower portion tinged blue. The species is a frequent immigrant to Britain and southern Ireland, with breeding recorded in most years. Fully self-sustaining colonies do not typically result, yet a few longer-lived colonies may occasionally become established. An extended bi-modal flight period results from the species' ability to produce two generations in some years.

Red-veined Darter, male.
*John Curd*

## Distribution

Red-veined Darter has an extensive world range, having been recorded from much of Africa, the Azores, Madeira, the Canary Islands, Europe (north to Scandinavia) and parts of southwest and central Asia, including the Indian subcontinent. In Europe it has expanded its range to the north with Denmark's first record in 2003, followed by Latvia in 2010 and Finland in 2011. Around the Mediterranean, it is a characteristic and very common breeding species, while in northern Europe it occurs principally as a migrant. Following large immigrations, breeding attempts may take place, even at quite high latitudes.

In Britain and Ireland, Red-veined Darter was for a long while an uncommon and erratic visitor, primarily to the southern counties of England, but occasionally appearing in greater numbers and extent. Examples include records from as far north as the Firth of Forth, Scotland, during 1911 and records from Co. Cavan, Ireland, in the 1940s. During the mid 1980s the species started to appear more regularly in south-west England and, by the 1990s, this trend had became more pronounced, with records more widespread. Immigrations are now frequent, coming roughly every other year. In 2006, almost a thousand individuals were

noted from Britain and Ireland, with records coming from as far north as Berwickshire in Scotland and as far west as Co. Cork in Ireland.

Recent British and Irish sightings still show a bias towards the south coasts, as might be expected for a migrant of southerly origin. Records are, however, widespread and at least three migration events have reached Scotland in recent years – with individuals noted as far north as Berwickshire during 2006 and East Lothian during 2009 and 2012. Irish records date from 1998 and have become regular in recent years. Some influxes have a strong south-westerly element, with Cornwall being one of the counties where the species is now expected; such a distribution is perhaps indicative of these migrants having an origin in Iberia and/or north-west Africa. Some influxes, by contrast, have a more easterly element, with records from, for example, East Anglia and East Yorkshire. Although a high proportion of the British records are coastal, overall there is a wide scatter of sightings, with inland records becoming increasingly common.

## Habitat

As a strong migrant, Red-veined Darter can potentially turn up almost anywhere, including open ground well away from water. Its most favoured habitat, and the one used for

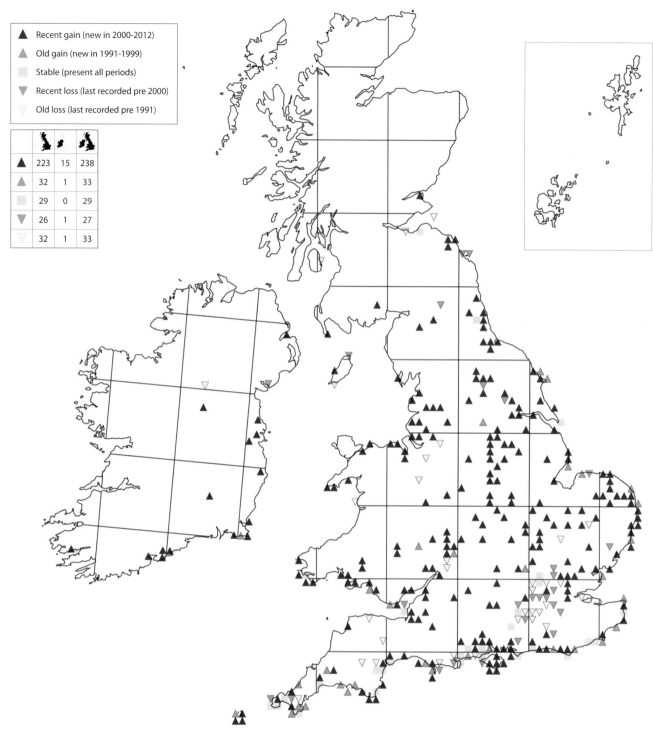

| |  |  |  |
|---|---|---|---|
| ▲ | 223 | 15 | 238 |
| ▲ | 32 | 1 | 33 |
| ■ | 29 | 0 | 29 |
| ▼ | 26 | 1 | 27 |
| ▽ | 32 | 1 | 33 |

Legend:
- ▲ Recent gain (new in 2000-2012)
- ▲ Old gain (new in 1991-1999)
- ■ Stable (present all periods)
- ▼ Recent loss (last recorded pre 2000)
- ▽ Old loss (last recorded pre 1991)

breeding, is exposed sunny, shallow, standing waters with sparse emergent and marginal vegetation. In Britain and Ireland, such habitat is often ecologically recent, and includes balancing ponds, flooded areas in quarries/gravel pits and scrapes on nature reserves that have typically been excavated for wading birds. Other favoured habitat includes coastal lagoons, dune slacks, reservoirs, pools and lakes, while the shallow wetlands of the Cornish moors and downs seem to be particularly attractive to this species. All these habitats warm up quickly in the spring and summer, which obviously is attractive to a species whose strongholds are in hotter climes, and this early warming also allows any eggs and larvae to develop rapidly and emerge in the same year.

In particularly favourable habitat, with good food supplies, breeding Red-veined Darter can produce extremely large numbers of progeny. In 1998, Pellow (1999) reported some 2,000 individuals emerging from the recently created Bake Farm Fishing Lakes in east Cornwall during late summer and autumn, following oviposition earlier in the season. However, more recent occurrences of breeding at this site have not proved as productive, perhaps due to successional changes and fish. A peak daily count of over 200 tenerals and immatures was also noted near Severn Beach in Gloucestershire during late summer 2012. More usually, the numbers of progeny are much lower, in particular at sites where spring emergences are involved. At high latitudes and/or during times of limited food

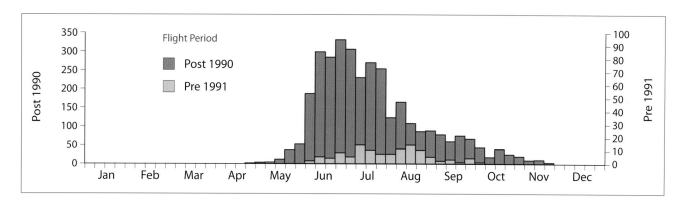

supply development is longer and the larvae may overwinter. However, cold winter conditions tend to result in high larval mortality.

## Conservation status and threats

During spring migration events to Britain, Red-veined Darter will breed on a regular basis. In southern England, progeny will frequently emerge the same autumn, from August onwards, continuing into November if conditions remain favourable. Emergences in the following spring, after a full one year developmental period, are also observed. Partitioning between the two strategies is presumably influenced by factors such as oviposition date, summer weather and larval food supply. Further north in England, a one year life cycle and spring emergences are more typical, though during the very hot summer of 2006

rapid development leading to a second generation within the year was recorded as far north as Brockholes Wetland, Lancashire, and Filey Dams, North Yorkshire.

Breeding attempts have the potential to generate self-sustaining local populations, but the situation is complex. As a strong migrant, the biology of Red-veined Darter may be geared towards producing transient colonies by simply exploiting suitable habitat for as long as it is cost-effective, then moving on. Most, perhaps all, autumn emergers seem to permanently disperse away from their natal site and thus do not contribute to colony sustainability. It is thought that individuals may migrate south but this remains unproven in Europe, although there is evidence that it occurs in Asia (Borisov, 2009). Individuals emerging in spring apparently show greater site fidelity and, in recent years, a few long-lived colonies have been reported from localities where slow development and spring emergence occurred. Notable amongst these are sites at Spurn Point in East

Windmill Farm, The Lizard, Cornwall, where Red-veined Darter breeds in most years. *Steve Cham*

Greenham Common, Berkshire, where the shallow pools have attracted Red-veined Darter to breed and complete a generation.
*Steve Cham*

Yorkshire, where the species was reported annually from 1996 to 2007 (though some records may well refer to fresh immigrants), and at Middleton Nature Reserve, Heysham, Lancashire, where the species was reported annually from 2000 to 2009. However, these sites do not appear to be completely stable. This might reflect their low productivity compared with sites where larval development is fast and autumn emergences are seen. With ongoing climate change, breeding sites may therefore come to show increased stability in the future. However, successional changes and/or changes in hydrology might also be involved in colony stability and therefore future trends may not be so readily predictable.

Despite the still somewhat uncertain status of local breeding, the species is rated as of Least Concern in the current Odonata Red Data List for Britain, by virtue of the continued high levels of immigration, which will serve to renew or replenish any British populations. Red-veined Darter was not assessed in Ireland's most recent Red List.

## National trends

Red-veined Darter was for a long time seemingly only an erratic visitor to Britain and Ireland. In the mid 1980s, the species started to appear more regularly, particularly in south-west England. There was a significant invasion in 1996 that was detected in many other areas of northern Europe, and major arrivals have since been noted in 1998, 2000, 2002, 2006, 2007, 2009, 2011 and 2012, sometimes with more than one immigration event per year. Even in intervening 'quiet' years there are normally several sightings. Local breeding is also now seen on a regular basis, with

many springtime immigrations resulting in the production of a second generation later in the season. In the past, records of successful breeding were considerably more erratic and typically referred to situations where slower larval development (a one-year life cycle) had taken place.

Whilst increased recording intensity might explain some of the increased abundance, this cannot be the full explanation. The immigration events are too dramatic and are not reflected in the fortunes of migrant species of different geographical origin, such as the Yellow-winged Darter. Rather, changes seem to be part of a wider phenomenon, where many species that have their main centre of distribution in southern Europe are becoming increasingly common in Britain and Ireland and other areas of north-west Europe. This is thought to be one of the consequences of ongoing climate change. Increasingly, it is likely that, during larger migration events, any suitable habitat in England or Wales now has the potential to attract the species.

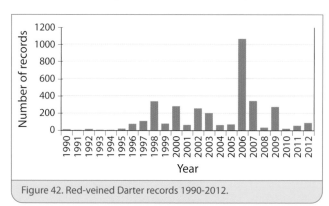

Figure 42. Red-veined Darter records 1990-2012.

# Ruddy Darter
## *Sympetrum sanguineum*

Ruddy Darter is a small dragonfly, superficially resembling the more abundant Common Darter and the Red-veined Darter. It is distinguishable from these species by its all-black legs and, in adult males, a deep, blood-red colouration to the body (hence the Latin *sanguineum*). The abdomen in males is clubbed and this can help separate immature males from females and also from other darter species. Oviposition occurs in late summer with eggs hatching the following spring. The larvae develop rapidly and adults emerge from late June the same year.

Ruddy Darter, male.
*Anthony Taylor*

## Distribution

Ruddy Darter is a widespread species, ranging from North Africa to southern Scandinavia. It is absent from the area of the Alps north of Italy and the Mediterranean Islands. To the east, its range extends to east Siberia.

In Britain, it has a distinctly southern and eastern distribution, extending from south-east England to Dorset, Somerset, the Welsh Borders, the north-west Midlands and the east Midlands. There has been considerable recent range expansion in lowland northern England, where it occurs in Durham, Northumberland and Cumbria. Populations decrease further north and south-west and it is absent from much of Wales, with the exception of mainly coastal regions in the south. It is largely absent as a breeding species in Devon and Cornwall, where presumed migrants appear regularly. The only records from Scotland are from near Reston, Berwickshire, in September 2003. The northern limits of its range are likely to be limited by water temperatures that inhibit larval development.

In Ireland, the species is widespread across the central plain in a broad band from Lough Neagh in the north-east to the Shannon estuary in the south-west. It is also found in the coastal counties from Dublin to Cork. It is absent from large parts of the north, west and south-west and all upland areas.

Although their European ranges are very different, the distributions of Ruddy Darter and the Brown Hawker in Britain and Ireland are remarkably similar. Both species are absent or scarce in Scotland, much of Wales and the far south-west of England but are widespread across lowland England and Ireland. The reasons for this are unclear but are perhaps related to a combination of low winter temperature in the north and high rainfall in the west.

Dune pool, Birkdale, Lancashire. *Phil Smith*

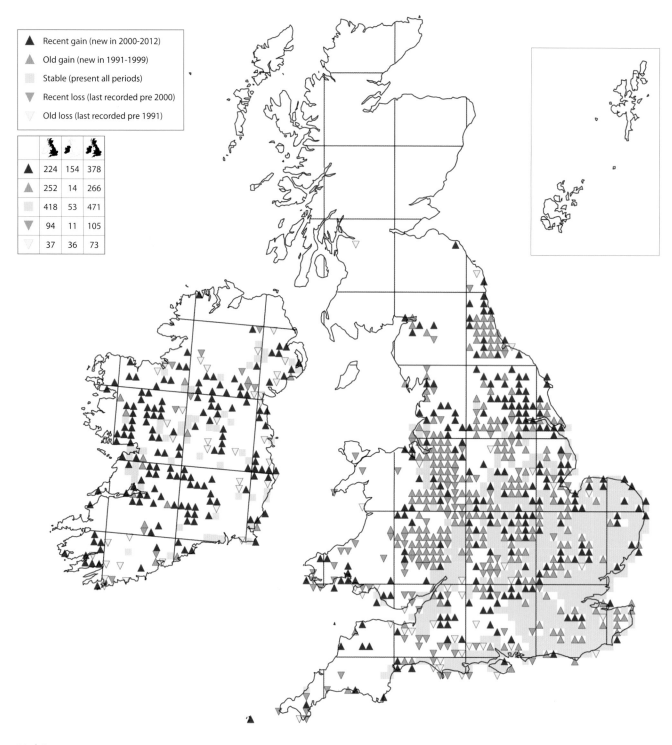

## Habitat

Ruddy Darter favours small, shallow and densely-vegetated ponds, more so than the Common Darter. Narrow ditches and canals with dense emergent plants are also used. Breeding sites are generally those in the late stages of seral succession. It avoids newer gravel pits, but older pits with dense vegetation are colonised. In Ireland, it is associated with temporary ponds of many types, including turloughs and those on lowland fens. Many of these are grazed but, as long as this is not severe, the species can persist. Open conditions are perhaps more important in Ireland to compensate for the cooler climate than in much of Britain. It generally avoids acidic and running waters, although it

may breed in slow-flowing sections of rivers where there is dense vegetation (Cham, 2004; Tyrrell et al., 2006).

Breeding sites generally have water that is shallow and warm enough to allow rapid larval development, with margins or a draw-down zone that comprises dense vegetation and muddy or mossy ground. Oviposition normally occurs in tandem, with the eggs deposited onto muddy or apparently dry margins within the vegetation, often some distance above the waterline.

The life cycle, with rapid larval development in spring, early summer emergence and over-wintering eggs, is particularly well-adapted to sites that dry out in late summer and are

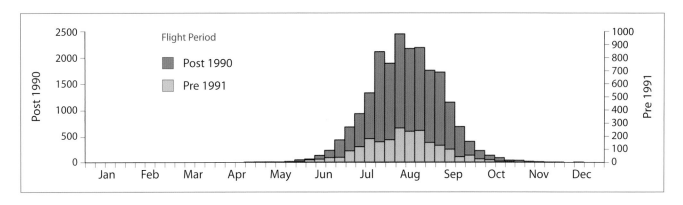

subsequently replenished by groundwater or winter rainfall. Such conditions, in the absence of grazing, often promote dense stands of emergent vegetation and the resulting seral succession will see the disappearance of most other species and, ultimately, this one. The temporary nature of many breeding sites also prevents the persistence of larval predators such as fish. There is often an association between breeding sites for Ruddy Darter and those of the Emerald and Scarce Emerald Damselflies, which have a similar development pattern. More often than not, in England and Ireland, where one of these damselflies is present the Ruddy Darter will also be found.

## Conservation status and threats

Ruddy Darter is categorised as Least Concern in the British and Irish Red Lists.

Some sites for this species have been lost to scrub encroachment and others during pond restoration projects and ditching operations. Whilst the loss of ponds remains a localised threat, the increasing number of ponds and ditches in a late stage of seral succession may have

facilitated range expansion and the species is now more common and widespread than in former decades.

## National trends

The CEH trends analysis (pages 58-63) shows a slight increase in the distribution of Ruddy Darter. Since 2000, it has expanded its range northwards in England, notably in Yorkshire and Northumberland. The outpost populations in Durham may soon join up with the Yorkshire colonies to the south. However, it has failed to colonise much of Wales and in south-west England it remains uncommon. Many recent new records within its more traditional range may be as much to do with increased recorder effort as actual distribution changes.

Higher summer and winter temperatures, together with resultant lower water levels and desiccation of ponds, may explain the expansion northwards. In contrast, wetter conditions in the west and south-west may limit habitat suitability and explain its continued scarcity there.

Thompson Common, Norfolk. The dense emergent vegetation of this area of pingos is attractive to Ruddy Darter, as well as both Emerald and Scarce Emerald Damselflies. *Steve Cham*

# Common Darter
*Sympetrum striolatum*

The Common Darter is a medium-sized perching dragonfly. The abdomen is orange-red in mature males and yellowish in females and in immature adults of both sexes. The wings lack extensive yellow markings and the dark brown, almost black, legs are finely marked with a yellow stripe. Females oviposit in flight, directly into water, either in tandem or alone, usually over aquatic plants just below the surface. Eggs hatch after 10-15 days and adults emerge early in the summer of the following year.

Common Darter, male. *Anthony Taylor*

## Distribution

The Common Darter is common and widespread throughout most of Europe, although it is absent from much of Scandinavia, except southern Sweden and coastal districts of southern Norway. The range extends south to the Mediterranean and parts of North Africa and extends eastwards across Asia to Japan.

Almornes Point, Dumfries & Galloway. *R&B Mearns*

The species is common throughout most of England, Wales and Ireland. In Scotland, it is most likely to be found in coastal and lowland regions, especially in the west, where the winters are milder. It avoids upland regions in northern Britain, as shown by the large gaps in its distribution in the Pennines and the Southern Uplands and Highlands of Scotland. However, its absence is not apparent in upland areas in southern England, Wales or Ireland, suggesting that only higher elevations at higher latitudes are avoided. As with the distributions of many other dragonflies, there are gaps coinciding with the chalk downland of Hampshire and Wiltshire that presumably reflect a scarcity of surface waterbodies. Populations are supplemented by immigrants from continental Europe in most years and occasionally mass migrations occur.

Populations of Common Darter in north-west Scotland and western Ireland tend to have more extensively black legs and markings, particularly on the side of the thorax and underside of the abdomen. Similarly, dark-marked populations of Common Darter are also present along the southern coast of Norway. This led some authors to consider these dark populations to be a distinct species, the Highland Darter *Sympetrum nigrescens*, which seemed to be further characterised by differences in the male genitalia (Lucas, 1912; Gardner, 1955). However, studies of

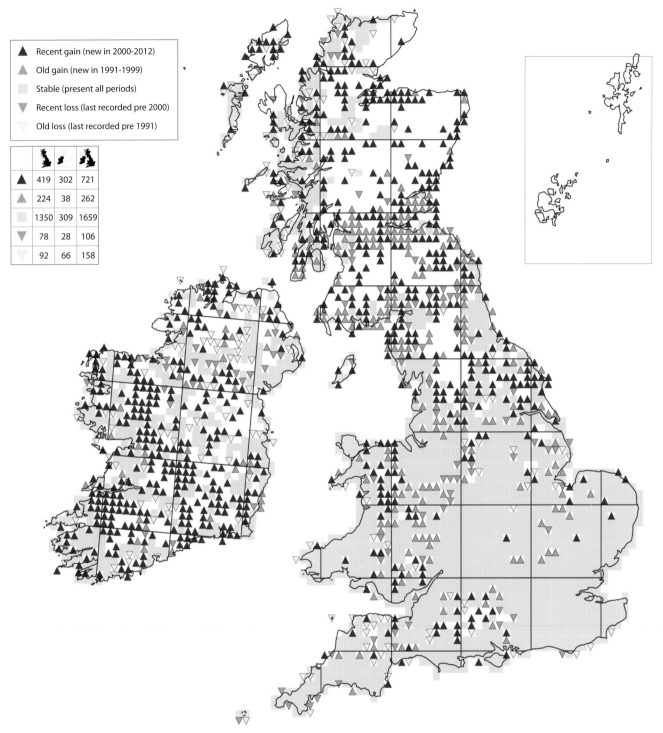

| | 🇬🇧 | 🇮🇪 | 🇬🇧🇮🇪 |
|---|---|---|---|
| ▲ Recent gain (new in 2000-2012) | 419 | 302 | 721 |
| ▲ Old gain (new in 1991-1999) | 224 | 38 | 262 |
| ▪ Stable (present all periods) | 1350 | 309 | 1659 |
| ▼ Recent loss (last recorded pre 2000) | 78 | 28 | 106 |
| ▽ Old loss (last recorded pre 1991) | 92 | 66 | 158 |

British and Irish specimens by Merritt & Vick (1983) suggested that these morphological characters were variable and not reliable in distinguishing the two taxa. This conclusion was confirmed by genetic studies of Common Darters from continental Europe, Ireland (Pilgrim & Von Dohlen, 2007) and Britain (Parkes *et al.*, 2009). The British DNA work showed that, while populations of Common Darter on the north-western Scottish islands do show some genetic differentiation from mainland populations, dark-marked populations on the Scottish mainland show mixed genetic affinities between island populations and those further south. For these reasons the Highland Darter is no longer considered to be a valid species or subspecies but is considered to be a melanic

form of the Common Darter. The dark markings provide an adaptation for living in cold climates, by increasing the efficiency of absorbing radiated heat while the adult is perching on the ground.

As with the previous atlas, all records submitted as Highland Darter are included in the map for Common Darter.

## Habitat

The Common Darter breeds in a wide range of standing or slow-flowing wetland habitats, including ponds, lakes, ditches, canals, large rivers and even bog pools, streams

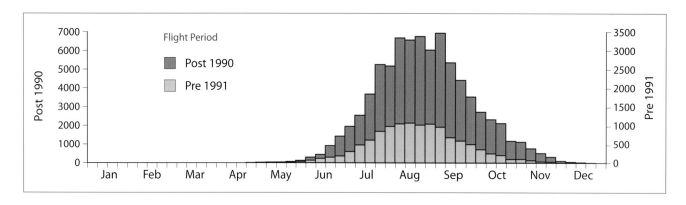

and brackish water. The species will not tolerate poor water quality or shaded sites. It will breed in small pools with extensive mats of filamentous algae and in ponds in early successional stages but breeding sites usually have substantial growth of submerged aquatic vegetation, which is the favoured haunt of larvae. It can be seen ovipositing in rainwater puddles and tidal rock pools but breeding success in such pools is likely to be low or, in the case of the latter, zero. The species can be a rapid coloniser of new habitats and is sometimes the first species seen at new garden ponds.

Tall grasses, Bracken, trees and bushes, which are used by the adults for roosting and foraging, are usually in close proximity but not over-shading the habitat. Adults are often encountered far from breeding sites, in a wide range of wet and dry locations.

## Conservation status and threats

Common Darter is common and widespread in Britain and Ireland and under no serious threat. It is categorised as Least Concern in both Red Lists. Locally, the species may be lost from breeding sites that become seriously polluted or over-shaded by trees.

## National trends

Common Darter has always been common in England and Wales except in mountainous areas. However, since the previous atlas its known range has expanded into the uplands of Wales, the Pennines and Scotland, while in Ireland there has been infilling in what was already an extensive range. The range expansion in upland areas, though the CEH trends analysis suggests a slight decrease in the distribution, is consistent with a response to climate change, especially to milder winter temperatures. At present it is unclear what proportion of the individuals spreading into the eastern Scottish Highlands are of the melanic form, which might be expected to retreat further north and west as the climate continues to warm.

Many populations of Common Darter, like other widespread species in Britain and Ireland, were probably lost from the wider countryside during the 1950s-1970s, due to land drainage and the infilling of ponds, although this is largely undocumented. Conversely, the recent creation of many new suitable wetlands must have benefited this common, generalist species.

Shallow pools covered in filamentous green algae attract many ovipositing pairs of Common Darter. *Steve Cham*

# Vagrant Darter
## *Sympetrum vulgatum*

### Moustached Darter

Vagrant Darter is a small-medium sized dragonfly, the mature male having a brown thorax and bright red, slightly clubbed abdomen, while females and immatures are typically yellow/brown. Some mature females may also develop a red colouration. The head has a short, dark, moustacial stripe running down the outside of the eyes. The prominent vulvar scale of the female is diagnostic. Although fairly common on the near Continent, it is only a rare and sporadic vagrant to Britain and Ireland. The life cycle is one year, overwintering in the egg stage.

Vagrant Darter, female.
*Dave Smallshire*

## Distribution

Vagrant Darter is a common and widespread species in northern and eastern parts of Europe. It occurs throughout much of mid-latitude Europe, ranging east across northern Asia as far as China and Japan. The principal European, nominate, subspecies occurs from southern Scandinavia south to southern France, northern Italy and (as small isolated populations) the Balkans. A pale subspecies – *ibericum* – exists in northern Spain.

Despite its wide distribution in Europe, the species occurs in Britain only as a rare vagrant (hence the common name). It has never been reported from Ireland. There have been about 25 confirmed records, although some other, less-well documented, reports exist. Sightings are largely restricted to the south and east of England, south of a line from Devon to Yorkshire. An apparent concentration of (mostly old) records north of London probably reflects observer coverage effects, though being close to the near Continent, and with the Thames Estuary and outer approaches perhaps exerting a funnelling effect on immigrants, it is conceivable that more dragonflies than average do genuinely reach this area.

## Habitat

Vagrant Darter occurs at many types of standing and slow-flowing waters; it is said to prefer more richly vegetated sites than those preferred by Common Darter (Dijkstra & Lewington, 2006).

## Conservation status and threats

The Vagrant Darter was not assessed in the most recent Odonata Red Data List for Great Britain, by virtue of it having occurred only as a vagrant. This situation seems unlikely to change in the near future and there are thus no relevant conservation issues.

## National trends

Vagrant Darter has long been an erratic visitor to Britain in very small numbers. The first record goes back to the early 19th century, with others then following at irregular intervals. The period around the turn of the 19th/20th century produced several reports and, in more recent times, the great Yellow-winged Darter immigration year of 1995 (Parr, 1996) brought a wave of sightings. Small numbers of individuals were noted at several of the coastal sites where major concentrations of Yellow-winged Darter gathered

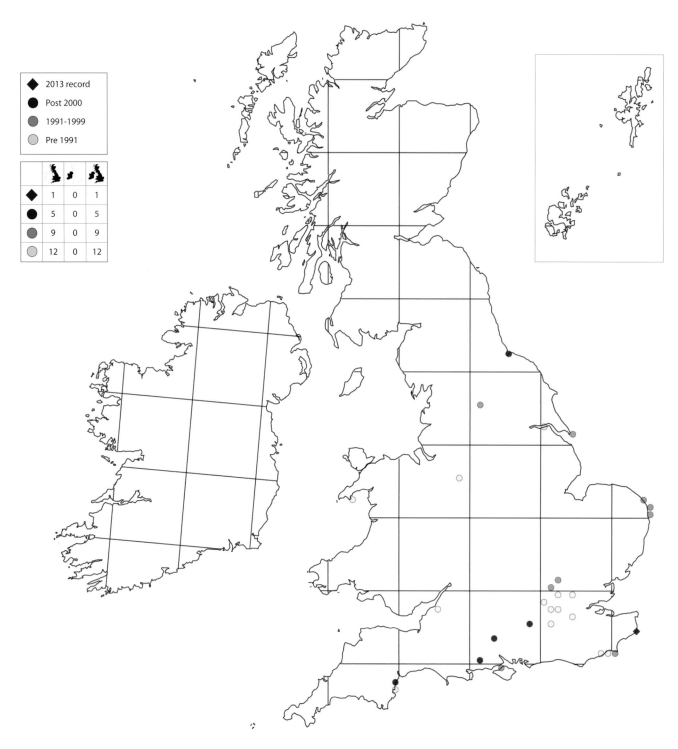

| | 🔶 | ⬤ | 🔶⬤ |
|---|---|---|---|
| 🔶 | 1 | 0 | 1 |
| ⬤ | 5 | 0 | 5 |
| ⬤ | 9 | 0 | 9 |
| ⬤ | 12 | 0 | 12 |

**Legend:**
- 🔶 2013 record
- ⬤ Post 2000
- ⬤ 1991-1999
- ⬤ Pre 1991

(e.g. Yarmouth Cemetery in Norfolk and Dungeness in Kent) and there were reports of singletons inland in Hertfordshire. Occasional observations have continued since then, with the most recent confirmed sightings being a female noted at Dawlish Warren, Devon in September 2007 and a male attracted to a moth-trap at Kingsdown, Kent in September 2013.

Despite it being a common dragonfly on the near Continent, Vagrant Darter is clearly not a particularly frequent visitor to our shores, though due to its close similarity to Common Darter it is possible that some individuals have been overlooked. Given the erratic nature of sightings over a long time period, it seems highly likely

that records of Vagrant Darter in Britain and Ireland will remain sporadic. However, there are some signs of a recent strengthening of the populations in areas such as Norway (Kjærstad *et al.*, 2010) and, to a lesser extent, in Belgium (De Knijf *et al.*, 2003) and The Netherlands (Termaat *et al.*, 2010), which may result in a small increase in the frequency of arrivals to Britain in the future.

# Other species

In addition to the species discussed in the main section of this atlas, there are several that have only reached our shores on a few occasions. Whilst these species do not warrant their own section, they may point the way to future additions to the British and Irish fauna and are worthy of mention here. There have been records of Winter Damselfly and Banded Darter that have occurred since the previous atlas. Records for Yellow-legged Clubtail and Wandering Glider are more historical, although the latter by its dispersive nature could reappear at any time. Other species have fallen just short of our mainland shores or have reached here through anthropogenic means.

## Winter Damselfly
*Sympecma fusca*
Common Winter Damsel

Winter Damselfly, female; this individual was found inside a house in Tonna, Neath Port Talbot, south Wales. *Stephen Coker / Mike Powell*

A female Winter Damselfly was found attempting to overwinter inside a house in Tonna, near Neath, south Wales, during December 2008 (Parr, 2009b). This represents the only British mainland record, although the species has been recorded from the Channel Islands on a few occasions (Long & Long, 2000). The unexpected locality raises the possibility that this individual represents an accidental introduction rather than true migrant. However, there were no obvious ways in which the damselfly could have been accidentally brought into the house in question.

Winter Damselfly is found in a few parts of coastal North Africa as well as on the Mediterranean Islands and throughout much of southern and central Europe north to

The Netherlands and the south coast of Sweden; its range extends east as far as Kyrgyzstan and Tajikistan in central Asia. In more north-eastern parts of Europe and much of Asia the species is replaced by the closely similar Siberian Winter Damselfly *Sympecma paedisca*.

## Yellow-legged Clubtail
*Stylurus flavipes*
River Clubtail

A male of this species was captured near Hastings, East Sussex, on 5 August 1818 (Lucas, 1900). There have been no subsequent records.

## Southern Skimmer
*Orthetrum brunneum*

Southern Skimmer has not yet been recorded from mainland Britain, although one was found on Guernsey in the Channel Islands in July 2001 (Long, 2002). As with the Southern Darter, this primarily southern European species is currently extending its range northwards and the first mainland British record could well be forthcoming in the near future.

## Blue Dasher
*Pachydiplax longipennis*

A female of this common North American species was found dying on the Sedco 706 oil rig in the North Sea off the Shetland Isles in early September 1999 (Parr, 2000). The origin of this individual remains unclear, though it may perhaps have been a genuine transatlantic vagrant. It did not however reach British soil.

## Wandering Glider
*Pantala flavescens*

Wandering Glider is the world's most widely distributed dragonfly, having been noted on all continents except Antarctica. Some populations may undertake truly remarkable migrations, for example between northern India and East Africa (Hobson *et al.*, 2012). Although common whilst breeding or on active migration in parts of North America and in tropical Africa and Asia, it is very scarce in Europe. In Britain, Wandering Glider has been positively recorded on only three occasions – at Horning, Norfolk, in 1823, at Bolton, Lancashire, in 1951 and in Kent in 1989. The Lancashire record refers to an individual known to have been accidentally introduced along with a ship-borne consignment of bananas (Ford, 1954), while the Kent record was from near a major trans-European transport depot and might similarly have resulted from an accidental introduction. The origin of the Norfolk individual remains unclear but could well involve genuine vagrancy. In addition to these confirmed sightings, a dragonfly showing many of the characteristics of Wandering Glider was observed at Brea, Cornwall, on 15 October 1995 (Jones, 1996b). This observation coincided with a major influx of the North American Monarch butterfly (Nelson, 1996). This sighting might easily refer to a true immigrant individual from the USA but remains unconfirmed.

# Southern Darter
## *Sympetrum meridionale*

Southern Darter was treated as a rare vagrant to Britain by a number of earlier authors, but records are based on specimens with very vague data or specimens that have subsequently been found to be misidentified. The species is thus presently not on the official British List, although it was recorded with certainty from Jersey in the Channel Islands during August 1948 (Moore, 1949). Southern Darter is one of a number of species with strongholds in southern Europe whose ranges are known to have been expanding northwards in recent decades, most likely as a result of climate change. It is now seen almost annually on the near Continent and an uncontroversial British record may soon be forthcoming. Given various identification issues, especially for those unfamiliar with the species, Southern Darter may have already occurred in Britain but have gone unnoticed.

Southern Darter, male. *John Curd*

Banded Darter, male. *Dave Smallshire*

# Banded Darter
## *Sympetrum pedemontanum*

Banded Darter is recorded across eastern France and a few small areas of Spain, extending eastwards across much of the mid-latitude Palaearctic zone as far as Japan. In Europe it has been recorded as far north as northern Germany and the Baltic States and as far south as northern Italy, with isolated populations in the Balkans. There has been a significant westward expansion of the species in northern Europe over the last 50 years, with a spread through much of northern Germany into The Netherlands (Wasscher, 1994). In Britain, a single male was seen and photographed on the south side of the Brecon Beacons (at ca. 400m above sea level) near Tredegar, Gwent, in mid August 1995. This was during a period of very significant dragonfly immigration, involving particularly Yellow-winged Darter. The 1995 record and the sighting of a 'possible' in Norfolk during late July 2003 (Parr, 2004), both fit with a westward spread of the species seen in northern Europe in recent years. Continuing range expansion may result in an increase in records over the short to medium term.

# Exotics

It has been known for some time that dragonflies from exotic parts of the world can be accidentally introduced into Europe as eggs or larvae associated with aquarium plants imported by the garden centre or pet trades (e.g. Brooks, 1988; Valtonen, 1985) (Table 9). The expansion of such businesses in recent years has now greatly increased the opportunity for exotic dragonflies, and other taxa, to be imported into Britain. Such imports represent a potential bio-security risk. There are currently several reports of either larvae or adult dragonflies each year (with an even greater number probably going unreported). Typically, most imported aquarium plants are from Singapore, with other south-east Asian countries such as Indonesia, Malaysia and Thailand also featuring prominently; a few shipments come from areas such as Morocco, Israel, Guinea or Madagascar (Parr, 2010). Most exotic dragonflies are thus likely to be of south-east Asian origin and two Asian species in particular seem to be quite frequently introduced – these being Oriental Scarlet *Crocothemis servilia* and Marsh Bluetail *Ischnura senegalensis*. However, nearly 40 exotic species have so far been recorded from Europe and, with numbers continuing to increase, the potential issues become significant!

Usually exotic dragonflies are found indoors and their association with water-plants or fish-tanks helps to highlight their non-British origin. On at least one occasion, however, an exotic damselfly has been found in the wild, when a Marsh Bluetail was found at a garden pond in Kent during late summer 2010 (Parr, 2010). Observers thus need to be aware of exotics when encountering unfamiliar species.

Table 9. Exotic dragonflies recorded in Britain as a result of accidental introductions.

| | |
|---|---|
| Variable Dancer | *Argia fumipennis* |
| Painted Waxtail | *Ceriagrion cerinorubellum* |
| Orange Bluet | *Enallagma signatum* |
| Fragile Forktail | *Ischnura posita* |
| Marsh Bluetail | *Ischnura senegalensis* |
| Green Emperor | *Anax gibbosulus* |
| Lesser Green Emperor | *Anax guttatus* |
| Oriental Scarlet | *Crocothemis servilia* |
| Eastern Pondhawk | *Erythemis simplicicollis* |
| Slender Skimmer | *Orthetrum sabina* |
| Spine-legged Redbolt | *Rhodothemis rufa* |
| Ocean Glider | *Tramea transmarina euryale* |
| (a species of Basker) | *Urothemis bisignata* |

# Appendices

Surrey and Hampshire borders group on a recording field trip to Woolmer Pond Hampshire. Viewed from a dragonfly larva's perspective. *Steve Cham*

# A1 Glossary

## Odonatological terms

**Abdomen** – Posterior section of the body containing ten segments.

**Anal appendages** – The claspers at the tip of the male abdomen used to grasp the female during copulation.

**Andromorph** – Female showing colours of a typical mature male of the same species.

**Anisoptera** – Suborder that comprises the true dragonflies.

**Antehumeral stripes** – The pale stripes, usually a single pair, on the top of the **thorax** of some species.

**Bivoltine** – Completing two generations per year.

**Coenagrionid** – Any member of the group of 'pond damselflies', that includes Large Red Damselfly, the blue damselflies such as Common Blue and Azure Damselfly, and the red-eyed and blue-tailed damselflies.

**Costa** – Vein along the leading edge of the wing.

**Diapause** – State of suspended development that occurs in the eggs or larvae of some species in response to environmental conditions.

**Emergence** – The point in time when a larva leaves the water, sheds its skin / exoskeleton and becomes an adult dragonfly.

**Endophytic** – Refers to eggs laid within organic material.

**Exophytic** – Refers to eggs laid outside of any organic structure.

**Exuvia** (plural: **exuviae**) – The shed larval skin / exoskeleton left after successful emergence. The finding of this proves successful breeding.

**False pterostigma** – The white wing-spot crossed by wing veins that mimics a **pterostigma** in the wing of a female demoiselle.

**Frons** – The upper part of the front of the head, usually more prominent in dragonflies than damselflies.

**Inferior anal appendages** – The lower pair of **anal appendages**.

**Lestid** – Any member of the group of closely-related damselflies comprising the emerald damselflies and the winter damselflies.

**Metapopulation** – A series of spatially separated populations that interact. Emigrants from one population may colonise gaps left where others have declined and thus the metapopulation can have greater stability than any sub-population alone.

**Nodus** or **node** – The kink or notch approximately midway along the leading edge of the wing.

**Odonata** – Insect order comprising both the damselflies and true dragonflies.

**Oviposition, ovipositing** – Egg laying behaviour.

**Ovipositor** – Female apparatus used to lay (oviposit) eggs. A functional cutting ovipositor is used to lay eggs into plant material or other organic matter and is typical of damselflies and hawker dragonflies. Other British species lack a cutting ovipositor and have modified plates that enable them to lay eggs freely into water or directly into substrate. See also **Vulvar scale**.

**Pruinescence** – A waxy bloom that develops to give some species a blue or greyish appearance as they mature.

**Pterostigma** (plural: **Pterostigmata**) – The dark or coloured, often thickened, cell towards the tip of the leading edge of the wing.

**Semivoltine** – Completing a generation in two years.

**Superior anal appendages** – Upper pair of **anal appendages**.

**Teneral** – A newly emerged adult dragonfly that still has a soft cuticle and lacks the full adult colouration.

**Thorax** – Middle section of the body, bearing the wings and legs.

**Voltinism** – Refers to the duration of the larval stage (see **bivoltine** and **semivoltine**).

**Vulvar scale** – The sometimes prominent flap below segment eight in female dragonflies (not damselflies) that lay their eggs freely onto water surfaces.

**Zygoptera** – Suborder that comprises all damselflies.

## Other terms

**Acidic** – Having a pH of less than 7; very acidic waters may have a pH as low as 3.5.

**Alkaline** – Having a pH of more than 7.

**Basin mire** – A fen that has developed in a waterlogged basin; very little open water.

**Balancing pond** – An impoundment to take excess run-off during storm events.

**Blanket bog** – Area of rain-fed moorland with an accumulation of deep peat, dominated by bog-mosses and heathers.

**Borrow pit** – Flooded, usually coastal, excavation that provides material for flood bank, often brackish.

**Brackish** – Slightly salty water often associated with river estuaries and salt-tolerant vegetation (e.g. Sea Club-rush).

**Circum-neutral** – Having a pH of around 7.

**Dune slack** – Depression between sand dunes that can contain brackish/freshwater ponds, sometimes seasonal.

**Dystrophic** – Brownish acidic waters with a high concentration of humic matter and few plants or fish; e.g. bog pool.

**Eutrophic** – Rich in mineral and organic nutrients, encouraging the abundant growth of plants, especially algae, and with low dissolved oxygen content.

**Fen** – Area of wet peat fed by ground water; may be dominated by tall vegetation (e.g. Great Fen-sedge, Black Bog-rush).

**Hectare (ha)** – Area equal to 10,000m$^2$, equivalent to an area of e.g. 100m x 100m.

**Hydroseral succession** – The natural transition of wetland habitat from open water to dry land.

**Hypertrophic** – waterbodies excessively enriched with nutrients; typically cloudy, subject to algal blooms and with very low levels of dissolved oxygen.

**Karst(ic)** – Geological topography on dissolved bedrock, often limestone and typically devoid of surface water.

**Lake (lough or loch)** – Standing water greater than 2ha in extent.

**Lochan** – Scottish name for an inland standing water that is smaller than a loch (q.v.); synonymous with **pond**.

**Lowland heath(land)** – Area dominated by dwarf shrubs (e.g. heathers, gorse), on **acidic** soil and typically below 300m altitude.

**Lowland raised bog** – Dome-shaped wet peatland, typically below 300m altitude. See **Raised bog**.

**Marl** – The pale insoluble mineral deposit found in high pH lakes. Marl lakes are characterised by their high pH, low nutrient status and aquatic vegetation dominated by stoneworts.

**Marsh** – Permanently wet area, not peaty, with grass-like vegetation growing to less than 2m above water level by late summer.

**Mesotrophic** – Clear water with beds of submerged aquatic plants and medium nutrient levels.

**Mineral working** – Active or abandoned sand, gravel or clay pit.

**Mixed woodland** – Woodland containing a minimum of 10% of both broad-leaved and coniferous trees.

**Neutral** – Having a pH of 7.

**Oligotrophic** – Water lacking in plant nutrients and organic matter, with few floating or submerged plants and a high concentration of dissolved oxygen.

**Oxbow lake** – Cut-off river meander, sometimes seasonally wet.

**Peat working** – Area where peat layer has been removed, often flooded; may be **acidic** or **alkaline**.

**Pingo** – Water-filled depressions in parts of Britain and Ireland characterised by often circular shape and raised edges. Some at least are believed to be formed from the melting of subsurface ice at the end of the last Ice Age.

**Pond** – Standing water less than 2ha in extent.

**Poor fen** – Peatland fed by **acidic** groundwater.

**Raised bog** – Acidic, rain-fed dome of peat (decaying bog-moss); may be upland (typically over 300m altitude) or lowland.

**Reservoir** – Impoundment for drinking water, canal feed or irrigation.

**Rich fen** – Peatland fed by **alkaline** groundwater.

**River** – Flowing water greater than 3m wide.

**Runnel** – A small, flowing stream, less than 30cm wide, often associated with springs, flushes and seepages in heathland.

**Saline lagoon** – Area of salt water, may be hypersaline (hence unsuitable for Odonata), with salt-tolerant vegetation.

**Sedimentation pond** – Impoundment used to trap sediment (e.g. clay particles).

**Stream** – Flowing water, 30cm to 3m wide.

**Swamp** – Wet area normally covered by water, with grass-like vegetation (e.g. Common Reed), that may be dominant to the exclusion of other species, growing to more than 1.5m above water level by late summer. [The term is used differently in North America, here referring to forested wetlands.]

**Temporary/seasonal** – Waters that dry up most years.

**Turloughs** – Temporary ponds found in limestone areas of western Ireland. Most are water-filled in winter and dry in summer but they may fill after heavy rain.

**Upland heath** – Moorland dominated by dwarf shrubs (e.g. heathers), typically above 300m altitude (although similar conditions nearer sea level in Scotland).

**Upland raised bog** – Dome-shaped wet peatland, typically above 300m altitude. See **Raised bog**.

**Valley mire (or bog)** – Acidic mire formed in a badly-drained valley.

# A2 Dragonfly and damselfly names

Linnaeus in his original classification and scientific naming system used just two generic names – *Libellula* and *Agrion* – for what are known in Britain and Ireland as dragonflies and damselflies, respectively. The derivation of *Libellula* is uncertain but it apparently originates from a 1554 book entitled *Libri de piscibus marinis* (Corbet 1999): a damselfly larva was illustrated and given the name *Libella fluviatilis*, as its body shape resembled the Hammerhead Shark *Libella marina* that also figured in the book; *Libella* is thought be a diminutive of *Libra* meaning a balance or level. Both *Libellule*, the French word, and *Libellen*, the word in German for the true dragonflies, is derived from the original Linnean usage. The original meaning of *Agrion* in Latin is "of the fields" and is apt for damselflies, which can be found in large numbers in fields at times.

The name dragonfly has been in use for nearly 500 years (Longfield, 1937) and no doubt was coined to describe the large, fast and brightly-coloured insects that caught people's eye. Dragonfly was initially used by authors to describe all Odonata but, in 1853, Selys split the Order into Anisoptera and Zygoptera (Corbet and Brooks, 2008). However, the adoption of the word dragonfly in Britain and Ireland causes confusion, as it applies to both the whole Order Odonata (meaning toothed) and the Anisoptera (meaning unequal wings). Damselfly, originating from the French word *demoiselle*, meaning young or unmarried lady, dates from Selys' split of the Odonata.

The use of common names for dragonflies in Britain was started by Cynthia Longfield in 1937. She coined common names for her Wayside and Wildlife book using a combination of English and scientific names – e.g. Blue Aeshna (Azure Hawker). She wanted to make these insects as accessible as possible and the same justification for using vernacular names still holds today. Before Longfield's names there were local generic names for dragonflies such as "horse-stingers" and "devil's darning needles" (Lucas, 1900). Vernacular names in Britain and Ireland were updated in Hammond (1977) and a further update was issued by the BDS in 1991. These BDS accepted names were further clarified by Mill *et al.* (2004). The names are somewhat prosaic, as they aim to describe the insect's behaviour (e.g. hawker, darter), colouration (e.g. emerald, blue) or pattern (e.g. blue-tailed). The use of descriptors and terms such as 'Common', 'Scarce' or 'Southern' however have occasionally led to problems. For example, the name Common Hawker has given rise to casual observers assuming that frequently-seen large hawker dragonflies must be this species. This has resulted in misidentification and may account for erroneous records in the past away from known areas of distribution.

The names in the Celtic languages of Welsh, Irish (*Gaeilge*) and Scottish Gaelic (*Gaidhlig* pronounced gah-lic) are direct translations of either the English or scientific names and are fairly recent, although there are much older names for dragonflies generically in all these languages. Nelson and Thompson (2004) proposed a mixture of standard BDS common names and approved North American-style names for Irish species but these have not gained wide acceptance. This broadening of style has since continued in Dijkstra and Lewington (2006). The demand for standardisation of English names for continental European species has been driven by both odonatological tourism and the production of identification guides covering several countries. However, at a continental scale this has led to similarities and differences in nomenclature that cause confusion. Nevertheless, provided that the unique scientific names are provided against the relevant vernacular names for all species, confusion can be avoided. It was decided to use current BDS vernacular names throughout this publication, with scientific and current European vernacular names given with the main species texts. A summary of Celtic language and other names is given in Tables 10 and 11.

Table 10. Summary of current damselfly names.

| English name | Irish name | European | Scientific name |
|---|---|---|---|
| **Damselflies** | | | **Zygoptera** |
| **Emerald Damselflies** | **Spreadwings** | **Spreadwings** | **Lestidae** |
| Willow Emerald Damselfly | | Western Willow Spreadwing | *Chalcolestes viridis* |
| Southern Emerald Damselfly | | Migrant Spreadwing | *Lestes barbarus* |
| Scarce Emerald Damselfly | Turlough Spreadwing | Robust Spreadwing | *Lestes dryas* |
| Emerald Damselfly | Common Spreadwing | Common Spreadwing | *Lestes sponsa* |
| Winter Damselfly | | Common Winter Damsel | *Sympecma fusca* |
| **Demoiselles** | **Jewelwings** | **Demoiselles** | **Calopterygidae** |
| Banded Demoiselle | Banded Jewelwing | Banded Demoiselle | *Calopteryx splendens* |
| Beautiful Demoiselle | Beautiful Jewelwing | Beautiful Demoiselle | *Calopteryx virgo* |
| **White-legged Damselflies** | | **Featherlegs** | **Platycnemididae** |
| White-legged Damselfly | | Blue Featherleg | *Platycnemis pennipes* |
| **Coenagrionid Damselflies** | | | **Coenagrionidae** |
| Small Red Damselfly | Small Redtail | Small Red Damsel | *Ceriagrion tenellum* |
| Norfolk Damselfly | | Dark Bluet | *Coenagrion armatum* |
| Northern Damselfly | | Spearhead Bluet | *Coenagrion hastulatum* |
| Irish Damselfly | Irish Bluet | Crescent Bluet | *Coenagrion lunulatum* |
| Southern Damselfly | | Mercury Bluet | *Coenagrion mercuriale* |
| Azure Damselfly | Azure Bluet | Azure Bluet | *Coenagrion puella* |
| Variable Damselfly | Variable Bluet | Variable Bluet | *Coenagrion pulchellum* |
| Dainty Damselfly | | Dainty Bluet | *Coenagrion scitulum* |
| Common Blue Damselfly | Common Bluet | Common Bluet | *Enallagma cyathigerum* |
| Red-eyed Damselfly | Large Redeye | Large Redeye | *Erythromma najas* |
| Small Red-eyed Damselfly | | Small Redeye | *Erythromma viridulum* |
| Blue-tailed Damselfly | Common Bluetip | Common Bluetail | *Ischnura elegans* |
| Scarce Blue-tailed Damselfly | Small Bluetip | Small Bluetail | *Ischnura pumilio* |
| Large Red Damselfly | Spring Redtail | Large Red Damsel | *Pyrrhosoma nymphula* |

Table 11. Summary of current dragonfly names.

| English name | Irish name | European | Scientific name |
|---|---|---|---|
| **Dragonflies** | | | **Anisoptera** |
| **Hawkers** | | | **Aeshnidae** |
| Southern Migrant Hawker | | Blue-eyed Hawker | *Aeshna affinis* |
| Azure Hawker | | Azure Hawker | *Aeshna caerulea* |
| Southern Hawker | Southern Hawker | Blue Hawker | *Aeshna cyanea* |

The Welsh names were taken from the book 'Cyfres Enwau Creaduriaid a Phlanhigion: 3 – Gwyfynod, Glöynnod Byw A Gweision Neidr' edited by Duncan Brown, Twm Elias, Bruce Griffiths, Huw John Huws and Dafydd Lewis ISBN number 978-1-84527-259-3.

| Scottish Gaelic | Irish | Welsh | Authority |
|---|---|---|---|
| **Cuileagan Cruinneig** | | **Mursennod** | |
| | | **Teulu'r Mursennod** | |
| | | | (Vander Linden, 1825) |
| | | | (Fabricius, 1798) |
| | Spré-eiteach Turlaigh | | Kirby, 1890 |
| Cruinneag Uaine | Spré-eiteach Coiteann | mursen werdd | (Hansemann, 1823) |
| | | mursen y gaeaf | (Vander Linden, 1820) |
| | | **Teulu'r Morwynion** | |
| Òigheag Ghleansach | Brídeog Bhandach | morwyn wych | (Harris, 1782) |
| Òigheag Bhrèagha | Brídeog | morwyn dywyll | (Linnaeus, 1758) |
| | | **Teulu'r Mursennod Bach Coeswen** | |
| | | mursen goeswen | (Pallas, 1771) |
| | | **Teulu'r Mursennod Coch A Glas-Ddu** | |
| | Earr-rua an Beag | mursen lygatgoch fach | (de Villers, 1789) |
| | | | (Charpentier, 1840) |
| Cruinneag a' Chinn a Tuath | | | (Charpentier, 1825) |
| | Goirmín Corránach | | (Charpentier, 1840) |
| | | mursen las Penfro | (Charpentier, 1840) |
| Cruinneag Liath | Goirmín Spéiriúil | mursen las asur | (Linnaeus, 1758) |
| Cruinneag Chaochlaideach | Goirmín Luaineach | mursen las amrywiol | (Vander Linden, 1825) |
| | | | (Rambur, 1842) |
| Cruinneag Chumanta | Goirmín Droimriabhach | mursen las gyffredin | (Charpentier, 1840) |
| | Deargshúileach Mór | mursen lygatgoch fawr | (Hansemann, 1823) |
| | | mursen lygatgoch fach | Charpentier, 1840 |
| Cruinneag Ghrinn | Rinnghorm Coiteann | mursen dinlas gyffredin | (Vander Linden, 1820) |
| | Rinnghorm Beag | mursen dinlas fach | (Charpentier, 1825) |
| Cruinneag Dhearg | Earr-rua an Earraigh | mursen fawr goch | (Sulzer, 1776) |

| Scottish Gaelic | Irish | Welsh | Authority |
|---|---|---|---|
| **Tarbh Nathrach** | | **Gweision Neidr** | |
| | | **Teulu'r Gweision Neidr** | |
| | | | Vander Linden, 1820 |
| Tarbh Nathrach Liath | | | (Ström, 1783) |
| Tarbh Nathrach a' Chinn a Deas | Seabhcaí an Phortaigh | gwas neidr y de | (Müller, 1764) |

Table 11. Continued.

| | | | |
|---|---|---|---|
| Brown Hawker | Amber-winged Hawker | Brown Hawker | *Aeshna grandis* |
| Common Hawker | Moorland Hawker | Moorland Hawker | *Aeshna juncea* |
| Migrant Hawker | Autumn Hawker | Migrant Hawker | *Aeshna mixta* |
| Norfolk Hawker | | Green-eyed Hawker | *Anaciaeschna isoceles* |
| Vagrant Emperor | Vagrant Emperor | Vagrant Emperor | *Anax ephippiger* |
| Emperor Dragonfly | Blue Emperor | Blue Emperor | *Anax imperator* |
| Green Darner | | Common Green Darner | *Anax junius* |
| Lesser Emperor | Yellow-ringed Emperor | Lesser Emperor | *Anax parthenope* |
| Hairy Dragonfly | Spring Hawker | Hairy Hawker | *Brachytron pratense* |
| **Clubtails** | | | **Gomphidae** |
| Common Clubtail | | Common Clubtail | *Gomphus vulgatissimus* |
| Yellow-legged Clubtail | | River Clubtail | *Stylurus flavipes* |
| **Golden-ringed Dragonflies** | | **Goldenrings** | **Cordulegastridae** |
| Golden-ringed Dragonfly | Golden-ringed Spiketail | Common Goldenring | *Cordulegaster boltonii* |
| **Emerald Dragonflies** | | | **Corduliidae** |
| Orange-spotted Emerald | | Orange-spotted Emerald | *Oxygastra curtisii* |
| Downy Emerald | Downy Emerald | Downy Emerald | *Cordulia aenea* |
| Northern Emerald | Moorland Emerald | Northern Emerald | *Somatochlora arctica* |
| Brilliant Emerald | | Brilliant Emerald | *Somatochlora metallica* |
| **Chasers, Skimmers, Darters** | | | **Libellulidae** |
| Scarlet Darter | | Broad Scarlet | *Crocothemis erythraea* |
| White-faced Darter | | Small Whiteface | *Leucorrhinia dubia* |
| Large White-faced Darter | | Yellow-spotted Whiteface | *Leucorrhinia pectoralis* |
| Broad-bodied Chaser | Broad-bodied Chaser | Broad-bodied Chaser | *Libellula depressa* |
| Scarce Chaser | Scarce Chaser | Blue Chaser | *Libellula fulva* |
| Four-spotted Chaser | Four-spotted Chaser | Four-spotted Chaser | *Libellula quadrimaculata* |
| Black-tailed Skimmer | Black-tailed Skimmer | Black-tailed Skimmer | *Orthetrum cancellatum* |
| Keeled Skimmer | Heathland Skimmer | Keeled Skimmer | *Orthetrum coerulescens* |
| Wandering Glider | | Wandering Glider | *Pantala flavescens* |
| Black Darter | Black Darter | Black Darter | *Sympetrum danae* |
| Yellow-winged Darter | Yellow-winged Darter | Yellow-winged Darter | *Sympetrum flaveolum* |
| Red-veined Darter | Red-veined Darter | Red-veined Darter | *Sympetrum fonscolombii* |
| Banded Darter | | Banded Darter | *Sympetrum pedemontanum* |
| Ruddy Darter | Ruddy Darter | Ruddy Darter | *Sympetrum sanguineum* |
| Common/ Highland Darter | Common Darter | Common/ Highland Darter | *Sympetrum striolatum* |
| Vagrant Darter | | Moustached Darter | *Sympetrum vulgatum* |

| | | | |
|---|---|---|---|
| Tarbh Nathrach Ruadh | Seabhcaí Ómrach | gwas neidr brown | (Linnaeus, 1758) |
| Tarbh Nathrach nan Cuilcean | Seabhcaí an Deiscirt | gwas neidr glas | (Linnaeus, 1758) |
| Tarbh Nathrach Ballach | Seabhcaí an Fhómhair | gwas neidr mudol | Latreille, 1805 |
| | | | (Müller, 1767) |
| Tarbh Nathrach Dìollaideach | Impire Fánach | gwas neidr crwydrol | (Burmeister, 1839) |
| Tarbh Nathrach Ìmpireil | Impire Gorm | ymerawdwr | Leach, 1815 |
| | | | (Drury, 1773) |
| | Impire Buífháinneach | | (Selys, 1839) |
| Tarbh Nathrach Gaoisideach | Seabhcaí an Earraigh | gwas neidr blewog | (Müller, 1764) |
| | | **Teulu'r Gweision Neidr Tindrwm** | |
| | Lorgearrach na hAbhann | gwas neidr tindrwm | (Linnaeus, 1758) |
| | | | (Charpentier, 1825) |
| | | **Uwch-Deulu'r Gweision Neidr Torchog** | |
| Tarbh Nathrach Òrfhàinneach | Snáthaid Mhór Órfháinneach | gwas neidr eurdorchog | (Donovan, 1807) |
| | | **Teulu'r Gweision Gwyrdd** | |
| | | | (Dale, 1834) |
| Smàrag Umha-dhathte | Smaragaid Umha-dhaite | gwas gwyrdd blewog | (Linnaeus, 1758) |
| Smàrag na Mòintich | Smaragaid an Mhóintigh | | (Zetterstedt, 1840) |
| Smàrag Ghleansach | | | (Vander Linden, 1825) |
| | | **Teulu'r Picellwyr** | |
| | | | (Brullé, 1832) |
| Gathair Bàn-aghaidheach | | picellwyr wynebwyn | (Vander Linden, 1825) |
| | | | (Charpentier, 1825) |
| Ruagaire Leathann | Ruagaire Leathan | picellwyr praff | Linnaeus, 1758 |
| | Ruagaire Tearc | | Müller, 1764 |
| Ruagaire Ceithir-bhallach | Ruagaire Ceathairbhallach | picellwyr pedwar nod | Linnaeus, 1758 |
| | Scimire Earrdhubh | picellwyr tinddu | (Linnaeus, 1758) |
| Uachdarair Dìreach | Scimire na Stuthlán | picellwyr cribog | (Fabricius, 1798) |
| | | | (Fabricius, 1798) |
| Gathair Dubh | Sciobaire Dubh | gwäell ddu | (Sulzer, 1776) |
| Gathair Buidhe-sgiathach | Sciobaire Buí-eiteach | gwäell asgell aur | (Linnaeus, 1758) |
| Gathair Dearg-fhèitheach | Sciobaire Deargfhéitheach | gwäell wythïen goch | (Selys, 1840) |
| | | | (Müller, 1766) |
| Gathair Dearg | | gwäell rudd | (Müller, 1764) |
| Gathair Cumanta | Sciobaire Coiteann | gwäell gyffredin | (Charpentier, 1840) |
| | | gwäell grwydrol | (Linnaeus, 1758) |

# A3 Scientific names of plants and other animals

Plant names follow Stace (2010).

| | |
|---|---|
| Alder | *Alnus glutinosa* |
| Amphibious Bistort | *Persicaria amphibia* |
| Arrowhead | *Sagittaria sagittifolia* |
| Ash | *Fraxinus excelsior* |
| Birches | *Betula* species |
| Bladderworts | *Utricularia* species |
| Bogbean | *Menyanthes trifoliata* |
| Bog-mosses | *Sphagnum* species |
| Bog-myrtle | *Myrica gale* |
| Bog Pondweed | *Potomogeton polygonifolius* |
| Bracken | *Pteridium aquilinum* |
| Branched Bur-reed | *Sparganium erectum* |
| Broad-leaved Pondweed | *Potamogeton natans* |
| Bulrush | *Typha latifolia* |
| Bulrushes | *Typha* species |
| Bur-reeds | *Sparganium* species |
| Canada Goose | *Branta canadensis* |
| Canadian Waterweed | *Elodea canadensis* |
| Carp | Cyprinidae |
| Common Carp | *Cyprinus carpio* |
| Common Club-rush | *Schoenoplectus lacustris* |
| Common Cottongrass | *Eriophorum angustifolium* |
| Common Reed | *Phragmites australis* |
| Common Sedge | *Carex nigra* |
| Common Spike-rush | *Eleocharis palustris* |
| Common Water-starwort | *Callitriche stagnalis* |
| Cottongrasses | *Eriophorum* species |
| Duckweeds | *Lemna* and *Spirodela* species |
| Elder | *Sambucus nigra* |
| Fairy Shrimp | *Chirocephalus diaphanus* |
| Fennel Pondweed | *Potamogeton pectinatus* |
| Floating Pennywort | *Hydrocotyle ranunculoides* |
| Fool's-water-cress | *Apium nodiflorum* |
| Frogbit | *Hydrocharis morsus-ranae* |
| Gorse | *Ulex europaeus* |
| Gorse species | *Ulex* species |
| Great Fen-sedge | *Cladium mariscus* |
| Greater Bladderwort | *Utricularia vulgaris* |

| | |
|---|---|
| Greater Tussock-sedge | *Carex paniculata* |
| Heathers | *Calluna vulgaris*, *Erica* species |
| Hawthorn | *Crataegus monogyna* |
| Hobby | *Falco subbuteo* |
| Hornworts | *Ceratophyllum* species |
| Hoverflies | Syrphidae |
| Jointed Rush | *Juncus articulatus* |
| Lesser Bladderwort | *Utricularia minor* |
| Lesser Bulrush | *Typha angustifolia* |
| Marsh St. John's-wort | *Hypericum elodes* |
| Marsh Frog | *Pelophylax ridibundus* |
| New Zealand Pigmyweed | *Crassula helmsii* |
| Oval Sedge | *Carex ovalis* |
| Parrot's-feather | *Myriophyllum aquaticum* |
| Pondweeds | *Potamogeton* species |
| Purple Moor-grass | *Molinia caerulea* |
| Rainbow Trout | *Oncorhynchus mykiss* |
| Rannoch-rush | *Scheuchzeria palustris* |
| Reed Canary-grass | *Phalaris arundinacea* |
| Reed Sweet-grass | *Glyceria maxima* |
| Rigid Hornwort | *Ceratophyllum demersum* |
| River Water-crowfoot | *Ranunculus fluitans* |
| Rushes | *Juncus* species |
| Sea Club-rush | *Bolboschoenus maritimus* |
| Sedges | *Carex* species |
| Spiked Water-milfoil | *Myriophyllum spicatum* |
| Stoneworts | Charophyta |
| Stream Water-crowfoot | *Ranunculus penicillatus* |
| Sycamore | *Acer pseudoplatanus* |
| Unbranched Bur-reed | *Sparganium emersum* |
| Water-cress | *Rorippa nasturtium-aquaticum* |
| Water-crowfoots | *Ranunculus* species |
| Water-lilies | Nymphaeaceae and *Nymphoides peltata* |
| Water-milfoils | *Myriophyllum* species |
| Water-plantain | *Alisma plantago-aquatica* |
| Water-soldier | *Stratiotes aloides* |
| Water-starworts | *Callitriche* species |
| Water-violet | *Hottonia palustris* |
| Water Fern | *Azolla filiculoides* |
| Water Horsetail | *Equisetum fluviatile* |
| Waterweeds | *Elodea* species |
| White Water-lily | *Nymphaea alba* |
| Willows | *Salix* species |
| Yellow Iris | *Iris pseudacorus* |
| Yellow Water-lily | *Nuphar lutea* |

# A4 Vice-counties

A 'Watsonian' vice-county is a geographical division of Britain used for the purposes of biological recording. Its fixed boundary provides a stable basis for recording by defining units of a roughly equal area. Defined by Watson (1852), they originally covered Great Britain, its offshore islands and the Isle of Man. The larger counties such as Yorkshire and Lincolnshire were subdivided to create recording units of roughly similar size. Especially in Wales, the vice-county names were taken from historic county names. In 1901, Praeger introduced a similar system for Ireland, with vice-county numbers prefixed with the letter H.

Unlike administrative county boundaries, vice-counties remain unchanged, despite frequent local government reorganisations, allowing historical and modern data to be accurately compared. Although Ordnance Survey (OS) grid-based reporting has grown in popularity, vice-counties remain a standard in many biological recording schemes in Britain, allowing data collected over long periods of time to be compared easily (Vincent, 1990).

Table 12. Vice-counties of England and Wales.

| | | | | | |
|---|---|---|---|---|---|
| 1 | West Cornwall (with Scilly) | 25 | East Suffolk | 49 | Caernarvonshire |
| 2 | East Cornwall | 26 | West Suffolk | 50 | Denbighshire |
| 3 | South Devon | 27 | East Norfolk | 51 | Flintshire |
| 4 | North Devon | 28 | West Norfolk | 52 | Anglesey |
| 5 | South Somerset | 29 | Cambridgeshire | 53 | South Lincolnshire |
| 6 | North Somerset | 30 | Bedfordshire | 54 | North Lincolnshire |
| 7 | North Wiltshire | 31 | Huntingdonshire | 55 | Leicestershire (with Rutland) |
| 8 | South Wiltshire | 32 | Northamptonshire | 56 | Nottinghamshire |
| 9 | Dorset | 33 | East Gloucestershire | 57 | Derbyshire |
| 10 | Isle of Wight | 34 | West Gloucestershire | 58 | Cheshire |
| 11 | South Hampshire | 35 | Monmouthshire | 59 | South Lancashire |
| 12 | North Hampshire | 36 | Herefordshire | 60 | West Lancashire |
| 13 | West Sussex | 37 | Worcestershire | 61 | South-east Yorkshire |
| 14 | East Sussex | 38 | Warwickshire | 62 | North-east Yorkshire |
| 15 | East Kent | 39 | Staffordshire | 63 | South-west Yorkshire |
| 16 | West Kent | 40 | Shropshire (Salop) | 64 | Mid-west Yorkshire |
| 17 | Surrey | 41 | Glamorgan | 65 | North-west Yorkshire |
| 18 | South Essex | 42 | Breconshire | 66 | Durham |
| 19 | North Essex | 43 | Radnorshire | 67 | South Northumberland |
| 20 | Hertfordshire | 44 | Carmarthenshire | 68 | North Northumberland (Cheviot) |
| 21 | Middlesex | 45 | Pembrokeshire | 69 | Westmorland with North Lancashire |
| 22 | Berkshire | 46 | Cardiganshire | | |
| 23 | Oxfordshire | 47 | Montgomeryshire | 70 | Cumberland |
| 24 | Buckinghamshire | 48 | Merionethshire | 71 | Isle of Man |

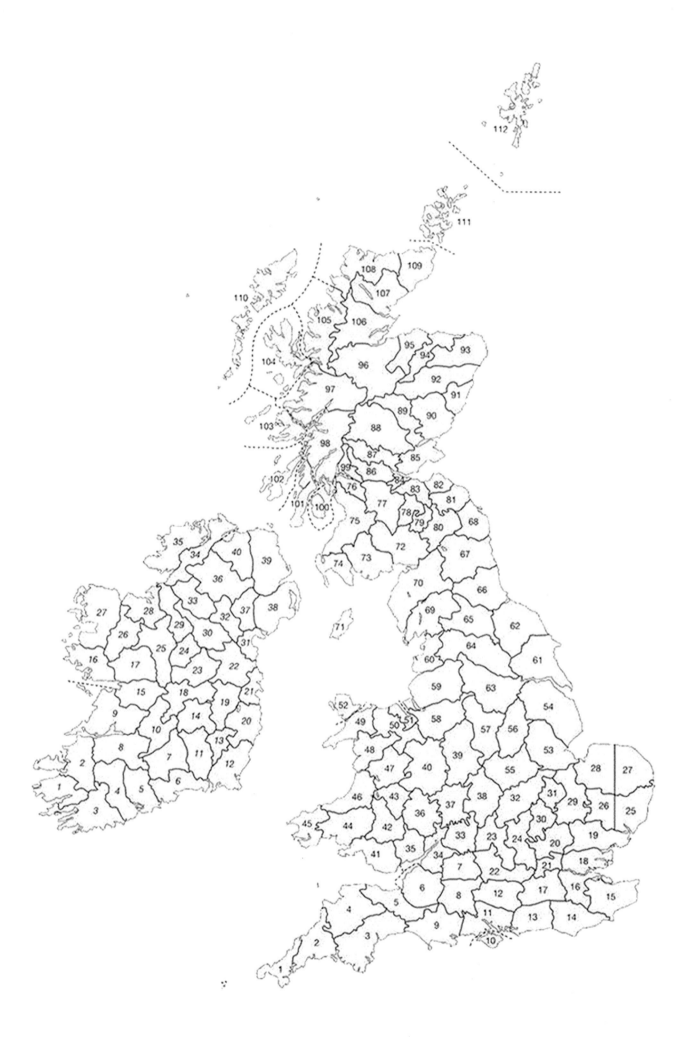

**Table 13. Vice-counties of Scotland.**

| | | | | | |
|---|---|---|---|---|---|
| 72 | Dumfriesshire | 86 | Stirlingshire | 100 | Clyde Isles |
| 73 | Kirkcudbrightshire | 87 | West Perthshire (with Clackmannan) | | |
| 74 | Wigtownshire | 88 | Mid Perthshire | 101 | Kintyre |
| 75 | Ayrshire | 89 | East Perthshire | 102 | South Ebudes |
| 76 | Renfrewshire | 90 | Angus (Forfar) | 103 | Mid Ebudes |
| 77 | Lanarkshire | 91 | Kincardineshire | 104 | North Ebudes |
| 78 | Peeblesshire | 92 | South Aberdeenshire | 105 | West Ross |
| 79 | Selkirkshire | 93 | North Aberdeenshire | 106 | East Ross |
| 80 | Roxburghshire | 94 | Banffshire | 107 | East Sutherland |
| 81 | Berwickshire | 95 | Moray (Elgin) | 108 | West Sutherland |
| 82 | East Lothian (Haddington) | 96 | East Inverness-shire (with Nairn) | 109 | Caithness |
| 83 | Midlothian (Edinburgh) | 97 | West Inverness-shire | 110 | Outer Hebrides |
| 84 | West Lothian (Linlithgow) | 98 | Argyll Main | 111 | Orkney Islands |
| 85 | Fifeshire (with Kinross) | 99 | Dunbartonshire | 112 | Shetland Islands (Zetland) |

**Table 14. Vice-counties of Ireland.**

| | | | | | |
|---|---|---|---|---|---|
| H1 | South Kerry | H15 | South-east Galway | H28 | Sligo |
| H2 | North Kerry | H16 | West Galway | H29 | Leitrim |
| H3 | West Cork | H17 | North-east Galway | H30 | Cavan |
| H4 | Mid Cork | H18 | Offaly | H31 | Louth |
| H5 | East Cork | H19 | Kildare | H32 | Monaghan |
| H6 | Waterford | H20 | Wicklow | H33 | Fermanagh |
| H7 | South Tipperary | H21 | Dublin | H34 | East Donegal |
| H8 | Limerick | H22 | Meath | H35 | West Donegal |
| H9 | Clare | H23 | Westmeath | H36 | Tyrone |
| H10 | North Tipperary | H24 | Longford | H37 | Armagh |
| H11 | Kilkenny | H25 | Roscommon | H38 | Down |
| H12 | Wexford | H26 | East Mayo | H39 | Antrim |
| H13 | Carlow | H27 | West Mayo | H40 | Londonderry |
| H14 | Laois | | | | |

# A5
# Acknowledgement of individual recorders

Aaron, D.; Abah, N.; Abbas, N.; Abbiss, J.; Abbot, A.; Abbott, A.; Abbott, A.M.; Abbott, C.; Abbott, K.; Abbott, R.; Abbott, S.; Abbs, A.; Abbs, M.; Abdulla, M.; Abel, J.; Abel, K.; Abel, M.; Abel, R.; Abraham, F.; Abrehart, T.; Acheson, V.; Ackers, D.; Ackers, G.; Adair, F.; Adair, S.; Adam, B.; Adam, H.; Adam, R.; Adamcik, T.; Adams, A.J.; Adams, B.; Adams, C.; Adams, C.P.; Adams, D.; Adams, E.; Adams, J.; Adams, J.H.; Adams, K.; Adams, M.; Adams, N.; Adams, P.; Adams, P.A.; Adams, S.; Adams, T.H.L.; Adams, W.; Adamson, J.; Addington, R.; Addlesee, H.; Adelson, D.; Adey, J.P.; Adkin, N.R.; Adkin, T.; Adler, M.; Admiraal, P.; Adrain, L.; Agar, N.; Agate, J.; Agg, R.; Agnew, A.; Agnew,A.D.G.; Ahearne, T.; Aide, K.; Aiken, J.; Ainscough, M.; Aitchison, I.; Aitken, A.; Aitken, A.O.; Aitken, I.; Aitken, J.; Aitken, N.; Aitken, S.; Ajax-Lewis, N.; Akers, J.; Akers, N.; Akers, P.; Akers, P.G.; Albani, R.; Albertini, M.V.; Albone, J.; Alder, D.; Alder, G.; Alder, J.; Alder, R.; Alderson, E.M.; Aldis, J.; Aldren, T.; Aldridge, C.; Aldridge, H.; Aldridge, J.;Aldridge, M.; Alexander, B.; Alexander, H.G.; Alexander, J.; Alexander, K.; Alexander, K.N.A.; Alexander, S.; Aley, J.; Alfert, T.; Alford, J.; Alker, P.; Allan, B.; Allan, C.; Allan, D.; Allan, S.; Allen, B.; Allen, B.M.; Allen, C.; Allen, C.A.; Allen, D.; Allen, G.W; Allen, J.E.R.; Allen, K.; Allen, L.; Allen, M.D.B.; Allen, P.; Allen, P.M.; Allen, R.;Allen-Williams, L.; Allenby, A.; Allenby, K.; Allenby, K.G.; Allenby, T.; Allison, G.; Allison, L.; Allison, M.; Allnut, A.C.; Allport, A.; Allsopp, I.; Allum, A.; Almond, J.; Almond, P.; Alred, D.; Alston, A.H.G.; Alyson, A.L.; Ames, W.J.C.; Amor, R.; Amphlett, A.; Amphlett, J.; Amsden, A.; Amsden, A.F.; Anderson, A.; Anderson, B.; Anderson, D.;Anderson, E.; Anderson, G.; Anderson, J.; Anderson, J.D.; Anderson, K.; Anderson, N.; Anderson, P.; Anderson, R.; Anderson, Y.; Anderton, J.; Andress, R.; Andrew, G.; Andrew, H.; Andrew, L.; Andrew, R.; Andrew, S.J.; Andrews, C.; Andrews, D.; Andrews, E.; Andrews, E.W.; Andrews, I.; Andrews, J.; Andrews, M.H.; Andrews, P.; Andrews, R.;Andrews, S.; Andrews, S.J.; Angell, B.; Angle, C.; Annett, H.E.; Anning, D.; Anning, P.; Ansley, J.; Anthony, S.; Antram, C.B.; Antrobus, P.; Apedaile, R.; Appleby, A.; Appleby, T.; Applegate, L.; Appleton, D.; Appleton, G.; Appleton, T.; Appleyard, P.; Aquilina, R.; Archdale, M.; Archer, A.; Archer, E.; Archer, J.; Archer, M.; Archer-Lock, A.; Ardron,P.A.; Arkel, J.; Arkle, J.; Armitage, J.S.; Armitage, P.; Armitt, M.L.; Armour-Chelu, B.; Armour-Chelu, N.H.; Armsby, A.; Armstrong, I.; Arnell, A.; Arnold, F.N.; Arnold, G.A.; Arnold, H.; Arnold, H.R.; Arnold, L.; Arnold, M.A.; Arnold, N.; Arnold, V.; Arnott, J.G.L.; Arthurton, W.; Arundale, J.; Arundale, R.; Ashbee, J.; Ashby, B.; Ashby, C.B.; Ashby,E.B.; Ashdown, W.J.; Ashford, P.; Ashford, S.; Ashley, K.; Ashton, D.; Ashton, L.; Ashton, P.; Ashwell, A.; Ashwell, D.A.; Ashworth, A.; Ashworth, D.; Ashworth, M.; Ashworth, R.; Ashworth, S.; Askem, T.; Askew, D.; Askew, G.; Askew, M.; Askew, R.R.; Aslett, J.; Aspin, W.; Aspin, W.C.; Astbury, A.; Astle, H.; Aston, A.E.C.; Aston, W.H.;Aston-Kilgallon, J.; Atherton, P.; Atkin, C.; Atkin, G.; Atkin, I.; Atkin, J.; Atkin, K.; Atkins, G.; Atkins, J.; Atkins, N.; Atkins, R.; Atkins, V.; Atkinson, A.; Atkinson, D.; Atkinson, J.; Atkinson, J.E.; Atkinson, L.J.; Atkinson, M.; Atkinson, R.; Atlee, H.G.; Attenborrow, R.; Attew, M.; Attia, J.; Attlee, A.; Attlee, H.G.; Attridge, W.; Attside, D.; Atty, D.;Aubrey, P.; Aubrook, E.W.; Auburn, C.; Audcent, H.; Aughney, T.; Aukland, T.; Auld, C.; Aungier, F.; Ausden, M.; Austin, M.; Austin, T.; Averill, M. T.; Averis, A.B.G.; Avery, G.; Avery, L.; Avery, S.; Ayling, K.; Ayres, J.; Ayres, M.; Ayres, M.L.; Ayres, S.E.; Babbs, S.; Bacciu, N.G.; Bacon, J.; Bacon, L.; Badenoch, C.; Badley, J.; Badman, G.; Badmin, J.S.;Baggeley, W.; Baggott, C.; Bagley, D.; Baguley, R.; Bagworth, T.; Bailey, B.; Bailey, D.; Bailey, E.B.; Bailey, G.S.; Bailey, J.; Bailey, M.; Bailey, M.P.; Bailey, S.; Baillie, R.; Baily, P.; Baily, W.E.; Bain, B.; Bain, G.; Bain, R.; Bainbridge, A.; Bainbridge, C.; Bainbridge, I.; Bainbridge, J.; Bainbridge, P.;

Baines, C.; Bainger, C.; Baird, D.; Bairner, S.;Baker, A.; Baker, B.; Baker, B.R.; Baker, C.; Baker, E.; Baker, F.E.S.; Baker, H.; Baker, J.; Baker, M.R.; Baker, N.; Baker, P.; Baker, R.; Baker, R.E.; Baker, T.; Baker, W.B.; Baker-Schommer, M.; Bakere, A.; Bakewell, D.N.; Balchin, C.S.; Balcikanis, G.; Balcombe, J.; Bald, A.; Baldock, C.; Baldock, D.; Baldock, N.M.; Baldock, S.; Baldwin, D.;Baldwin, S.I.; Balfour-Browne, F.; Balkow, K.; Ball, A.; Ball, D.; Ball, G.; Ball, H.N.; Ball, I.; Ball, J.; Ball, M.; Ball, M.E.; Ball, S.G.; Ball, T.; Ballantyne, G.H.; Ballantyne, J.; Balling, C.; Ballinger, B.R.; Ballinger, C.B.; Balmer, K.; Balmont, W.; Bamber, R.; Bamberger, M.; Bamfield, J.; Bamford, R.; Bance, P.C.; Band, C.; Banham, K.; Banks, B.; Banks, C.; Banks, K.; Banks, R.; Banks, S.; Banks, T.; Banks, Z.; Bannister, P.A.; Bannon, J.; Banthorpe, A.; Banthorpe, M.; Banwell, A.; Baptie, M.; Barber, D.; Barber, E.; Barber, G.; Barber, P.; Barber, R.; Barber, S.; Barber, T.; Barbour, D.; Barclay, F.; Barclay, M.; Barclay, R.J.; Bardell-Hedley, P.; Bardwell, L.; Bardwell, M.; Barefoot, J.;Barham, K.; Barker, A.M.; Barker, D.; Barker, G.; Barker, J.; Barker, K.; Barker, L.; Barker, M.; Barker, M.V.; Barker, P.; Barker, S.; Barlow, N.; Barlow, S.; Barlow, T.; Barnacal, B.; Barnard, C.C.; Barnard, D.; Barnard, I.; Barnes, C.; Barnes, D.; Barnes, E.; Barnes, H.; Barnes, J.; Barnes, K.; Barnes, L.E.; Barnes, N.S.; Barnes, R.A.; Barnes, S.;Barnett, D.; Barnett, L.K.; Barnett, R.J.; Barnham, M.; Barnham, V.; Barr, I.; Barratt, A.; Barratt, J.; Barrett, C.G.; Barrett, G.C.; Barrett, J.; Barron, C.; Barron, R.; Barthorpe, I.; Bartle-Rors, H.; Bartlett, I.; Bartlett, P.; Barton, A.; Barton, C.; Barton, J.; Barton, T.; Barton, V.; Barton-Allan, L.; Barwick, M.; Bashford, A.P.; Bashford, R.; Bashforth,S.; Bassett, R.; Batchelor, A.; Batchelor, D.; Batchelor, G.; Bateman, J.; Bater, J.; Bates, A.; Bates, B.L.; Bates, J.K.; Bates, J.W.; Bates, M.; Bates, P.; Bates, R.; Bates, S.; Bates, T.; Bateson, C.; Bateson, G.; Bateson, J.; Bath, W.H.; Bathe, E.C.; Batram, A.; Batt, C.M.; Batt, E.; Batt, S.; Battell, M.; Battell, R.; Batten, N.; Battle, F.; Battle, T.;Batty, A.; Batty, D.; Batty, H.; Batty, L.; Batty, P.; Baum, J.; Baverstock, D.; Baxby, K.; Baxter, E.V.; Baxter, L.; Baxter, P.; Baxter, R.; Bayley, J.A.; Bayley, S.; Baylis, S.; Bayly, N.; Bayne, D.M.; Baynes, E.S.A.; Baynham, D.; Bayton, E.; Beach, T.; Beains, I.; Beal, J.; Beal, R.; Beal, S.; Beale, C.; Beale, J.; Beales, A.; Beaman, G.; Beamsley, N.; Bean, N.; Beard, C.; Beard, M.; Beattie, A.; Beattie, D.; Beattie, J.; Beatty, I.; Beaufoy, S.; Beaumont, A.; Beaumont, E.; Beaumont, J.L.; Beaumont, R.; Beaumont, S.; Beaver, R.A.; Beavis, C.; Beavis, I.C.; Bebbington, J.; Becket, P.A.; Beckett, A.; Beckett, K.; Beckett, P.; Beckett, P.A.; Beckitt, W.; Bedford, K.; Bedford, P.; Bedwell, R.; Beer, T.; Beere, W.; Beesley, C.; Beeson, D.; Beetham, M.; Beevers, D.; Beevers, M.; Beilby, T.; Beirne, B.P.; Belden, P.A.; Bell, A.P.; Bell, C.; Bell, D.; Bell, E.; Bell, H.; Bell, J.; Bell, M.; Bell, M.V.; Bell, N.; Bell, P.; Bell, S.; Bell, S.L.; Bell, T.; Bell-Marley, H.W.; Bellamy, A.J.; Bellamy, B.; Bellamy, G.; Bellamy, L.; Bellamy, M.; Bellingham, M.; Bellis, S.; Belringer,R.M.; Belsey, J.; Belsham, T.; Belton, P.A.; Benatt, B.; Benbow, E.; Benda, J.; Benderskum, C.V.; Bendorf, F.H.; Benford, I.; Benham, D.; Benham, P.; Benjamin, J.; Bennett, A.; Bennett, B.; Bennett, D.; Bennett, G.; Bennett, J.; Bennett, J.P.; Bennett, M.; Bennett, P.; Bennett, R.; Bennett, T.; Bennett-Lloyd, P.T.; Bennion, P.; Benoy, F.; Bensley,V.; Benson, P.; Benson, T.; Benstead Barnes, P.; Benstead, M.; Benstead, P.J.; Bentley, A.; Bentley, C.; Bentley, D.; Bentley, D.P.; Bentley, G.; Bentley, N.; Bentley-Fox, H.; Benton, T.; Beolens, A.; Berrow, S.; Berry, C.; Berry, G.; Berry, I.; Berry, K.M.; Berry, M.; Berry, R.; Berry, W.; Bertenshaw, S.; Bertrand, C.; Berwick, H.; Berwick, M.; Best,C.; Best, J.; Best, M.; Beswick, N.; Betton, E.; Betts, C.; Betts, C.R.; Betts, M.; Beuk, P.; Bevan, D.; Bevan, J.; Bevan, J.R.; Bevan, M.J.; Beverage, D.B.; Beveridge, D.; Beveridge, J.; Bevis, A.; Bew, E.; Beynon,P.R.; Beynon, T. G.; Bhatia, Z.; Bhatti, N.; Bibby, M.; Bicker, A.; Bicker, N.; Bickford, P.; Biddle, L.; Biddle, R.; Bielinski, A.; Bigglestone, S.;Biggs, D.T.; Biggs, J.; Biggs, L.S.; Bigmore, L.W.; Bignal, A.; Bignell, G.C.; Bilcock, D.; Billimore, J.; Billings, M.; Billington, R.; Biltcliffe, C.; Biltcliffe, M.; Bilton, D.; Bilton, D.T.; Binden, C.; Binding, A.; Binding, A.E.; Bindley, K.; Bindon, C.; Bindon, L.; Binge, J.C.; Bingham, D.; Bingham, J.; Bingham, M.; Bingle, A.; Binnion, M.; Binns, A.; Bins, L.;Biott, E.; Birch, C.; Birch, H.; Birch, J.; Birch, S.; Birchall, J.; Birchall, J.E.; Birchall, M.J.; Bircher, R.; Bird, F.; Bird, G.M.; Bird, H.; Bird, J.; Bird, J.N.; Bird, M.; Bird, P.; Bird, P.F.; Bird, T.J.; Birkenshaw, V.; Birmingham, F.; Birtwistle, S.; Bishop, B.; Bishop, E.B.; Bishop, G.; Bishop, P.; Bishop, R.; Bishop, W.; Bison, I.; Bissitt, A.; Black, J.; Black, J.M.;Black, R.; Blackburn, D.; Blackburn, J.; Blackburn, M.; Blackburn, T.; Blackett, D.; Blackledge, A.; Blackledge, D.; Blackman, A.W.; Blackman, P.; Blackman, R.A.A.; Blackstock, T.H.; Blackwell, B.; Blackwell, S.; Blackwood, G.G.; Blackwood, J.J.; Blacow, L.; Bladen, C.; Blades, D.; Blades, L.; Bladon, C.; Bladon, C.M.; Blagden, I.; Blagojevic, M.;Blain, B.; Blain, S.; Blair, A.; Blair, C.G.;

Blair, J.; Blair, K.G.; Blair, P.; Blake, B.; Blake, C.; Blake, J.; Blake, N.; Blake, R.; Blakeborough, B.; Blakeley, D.S.; Blakey, L.; Blamire, S.; Blanco, C.; Bland, B.; Bland, K.; Bland, V.A.; Blane, J.; Blaney, A.; Blanning, P.E.; Blaskett, S.; Blatchley, F.; Blatchley, I.; Blathwayt, L.; Bleay, R.; Blencowe, M.; Blenkarn, S.A.; Blenkarn, S.E.; Blewitt, J.; Blick, M.; Blincow, J.; Blindell, R.; Blindley, K.; Blinkarn, S.A.; Block, S.; Blomley, P.; Blood, E.J.; Bloom, A.; Bloomfield, E.N.; Bloomfield, M.; Bloomfield, P.J.; Bloomfield, S.; Bloss, M.; Bloxham, M.G.; Bluett, A.; Blundell, L.; Blunden, A.; Blunden, T.; Blunt, A.G.; Blunt, G.; Blyth, C.; Blythe, M.E.;Boardman, P.; Boardman, S.; Boardman, T.; Boath, D.; Boath, G.; Boath, J.; Bocock, K.; Bodkin, B.; Bodnar, S.; Boemke, C.; Bolam, G.; Bolas, M.; Bolt, D.C.; Bolt, I.; Bolton, A.E.; Bolton, D.E.; Bolton, J.; Bolton, M.; Bolton, R.; Bolton, S.; Bombus, P.; Bonar, S.; Bond, G.; Bond, I.; Bond, K.; Bone, R.; Bonham, E.; Bonham, P.F.; Boniface, D.;Bonniwell, M.; Boon, C.; Boonstra, H.; Boosey, E.F.; Boote, A.; Boote, M.D.; Booth, A.; Booth, C.; Booth, D.; Booth, F.; Booth, J.; Booth, R.; Booth, S.; Booth, V.; Booty, C.; Booty, D.; Boreham, G.; Boreham, R.I.; Borissow, N.; Boroff, A.; Borradaile, L.; Borrows, A.; Bosanquet, D.S.; Bosanquet, S.D.S.; Bossom, P.; Bostock, E.D.; Bostock, N.; Boston, I.; Boston, P.; Boston, R.N.; Boswell, H.; Botham, S.P.; Bottomer, C.; Bottomer, S.; Bottrell, C.; Bottrell, H.; Boudreau, K.; Boulton, D.; Boulton, L.; Bourke, A.; Bournat, M.; Bovey, S.; Bowcott, J.; Bowden, C.; Bowden, M.; Bowditch, N.; Bowdrey, J.P.; Bowell, W.; Bowen, H.; Bowen, H.J.; Bowen, H.J.M.; Bowen, I.; Bowen-Jones, E.;Bowers, D.J.; Bowers, J.; Bowes, C.; Bowes, G.; Bowey, K.; Bowhill, J.W.; Bowler, J.; Bowlers, P.; Bowley, A.L.; Bowley, J.; Bowley, J.J.; Bowley, R.; Bowley, S.; Bowman, J.; Bowman, N.; Bowman, T.; Bowness, A.; Bowring, D.; Bows, D.; Bowtell, G.; Bowyer, P.; Box, J.; Box, V.; Boxall, P.G.; Boya, J.M.; Boyce, D.; Boyce, D.A.; Boyce, D.C.; Boyd,A.; Boyd, B.; Boyd, C.; Boyd, C.R.H.; Boyd, D.A.; Boyd, G.; Boyd, I.; Boyd, J.; Boyd, J.M.; Boyd, T.; Boyd, T.D.; Boyd, W.C.; Boydell, R.; Boyer, J.A.J.; Boyes, S.; Boyle, A.; Boyle, D.; Boyle, M.K.; Boyle, O.; Boyne, R.; Bracher, W.; Bracken, C.W.; Brackenridge, W.R.; Bradbeer, D.; Bradbeer, J.; Bradbrooke, C.; Bradbury, C.; Bradbury, D.; Braddock,A.; Brade-Birks, S.G.; Bradford, A.; Bradford, R.; Bradley, D.; Bradley, G.D.; Bradley, J.D.; Bradley, M.; Bradley, M.J.H.; Bradley, P.G.; Bradley, R.C.; Bradley, S.; Bradley, V.; Bradshaw, B.; Bradshaw, H.; Bradshaw, R.; Bradshaw, R.L.; Brady, R.; Brain, T.; Braithwaite, M.E.; Brakes, S.J.; Brame, W.; Bramhall, A.T.; Bramhall, R.A.; Bramich, M.;Brandes, S.; Brandon, A.; Brandon, G.; Branney, T.M.E.; Branscombe, J.; Bransden, A.; Branson, A.; Branson, C.; Branston, M.; Brant, C.; Branwhite, R.; Brash, P.R.; Brassley, P.; Bratt, R.; Bratten, J.; Bratton, J.H.; Braven, J.; Bray, E.; Bray, H.; Bray, R.; Bray, R.P.; Brayshaw, S.; Brazier, M.; Brazil, A.R.; Breaks, M.; Breakwell, K.; Breakwell, T.;Breasley, S.J.; Breed, J.; Breeds, J.M.; Breen, D.; Breen, K.; Breeze, S.; Bremner, D.; Brenchley, A.; Brennan, S.; Brereton, T.; Bretherton, M.; Breton, A.; Brett, A.; Brett, E.; Brett, E.C.; Brett, K.; Brett, R.; Brewer, E.G.; Brewster, C.; Brewster, D.; Brewster, M. A.; Brewster, P.; Brian, A.D.; Brian, M.C.; Brice, D.; Bridge, D.; Brierley, B.; Brierley, S.B.; Brierley, S.J.; Briers, R.A.; Brigden, B.; Briggs, C.A.; Briggs, H.M.; Briggs, J.D.; Briggs, R.; Briggs, R.S.; Bright, C.; Brimble, I.; Brimson, C.; Brind, R.; Brindle, A.; Brindle, J.H.; Brinkhurst, R.O.; Brinklow, R.K.; Brinn, D.; Bristow, P.; Bristow, R.; Britnell, A.J.N.; Brittain, J.E.; Britten, E.B.; Britten, H.; Britton, C.; Britton, D.; Britton, R.; Broad, E.; Broad, E.J.; Broad, G.; Brock, P.; Brockhurst, D.; Brocklebank, A.; Brocklebank, H.; Brocklesby, J.S.; Brodie, E.S.; Brodie, I.; Brogan, G.; Bromley, D.; Bromwich, D.; Brook, B.; Brook, G.; Brook, J.F.; Brook, M.; Brook, S.; Brook-Child, K.; Brooke, I.; Brooke, R.; Brooke, S.; Brooker, C.; Brooking, G.; Brooks, B.; Brooks, J.; Brooks, J.E.; Brooks, L.; Brooks, N.; Brooks, P.; Brooks, S.J.; Broome, A.; Broome, T.; Broomfield, M.; Brophy, J.; Brotheridge, D.; Brothers, P.; Brothwell, J.; Broughton, G.; Broughton, M.; Broughton, N.; Brown, A.; Brown, A.F.; Brown, A.J.; Brown, C.; Brown, C.R.; Brown, D.; Brown, E.; Brown, E.S.; Brown, G.; Brown, H.H.; Brown, J.; Brown, J.M.; Brown, L.; Brown, M.; Brown, M.L.; Brown, N.; Brown, P.; Brown, P.G.; Brown, P.J.; Brown, P.W.; Brown, R.; Brown, R.C.; Brown, S.; Brown, S.D.; Brown, T.; Brown, V.; Brown, W.; Brown, Z.; Browne, G.; Browne, L.; Browne, S.; Brownett, A.; Browning, P.; Brownlie, J.; Brownlow, A.; Bruce, C.; Bruce, G.; Bruce, J.; Bruce, P.; Bruce, T.K.; Bruce-Jones, P.; Bruemmer, C.;Bruen, N.; Bruin, D.; Brummage, M.; Brummitt, J.M.; Brunstrom, S.; Brunt, N.; Brunt, R.; Bryan, S.; Bryant, P.; Bryce, M.; Brydson, J.; Bryers, R.; Bryson, G.; Bryson, J.G.; Buchanan White, F.W.; Buchanan, J.; Buck, D.; Buck, F.D.; Bucke, C.; Buckell, L.; Buckham, A.; Buckingham, D.W.; Buckingham, S.; Buckland, L.; Buckland, M.; Buckle, P.J.;Buckle, S.; Buckley, J.; Buckley, Karen L.; Bucknall, A.; Buckstone, A.A.;

Buckthorpe, S.; Budd, A.; Budd, P.; Budd, R.; Budd, S.; Budden, M.; Budworth, D.; Budworth, R.; Buffery, B.; Bugden, C.; Bugge, S.; Bulger, N.; Bull, A.; Bull, A.L.; Bull, K.; Bull, W.P.; Bullard, P.; Bullen, B.; Bullen, S.; Bullen, T.; Bullivant, N.; Bullock, E.F.; Bullock, I.D.;Bullock, J.; Bullock, R.; Bullock, R.J.; Bullock, R.W.; Bulloughs, B.; Bunce, M.A.; Bunce, W.M.; Bundy, A.; Bundy, G.; Bungard, S.; Bunn, D.S.; Bunyan, J.; Burch, S.F.; Burchell, S.; Burdock, A.; Burfield, P.; Burfiend, S.; Burfitt, A.; Burford, P.; Burge, F.; Burges, D.J.; Burgess, J.; Burgess, M.; Burgess, P.; Burgess, R.; Burke, B.; Burkill, H.J.; Burkmar,R.; Burleigh, M.; Burlison, J.; Burn, A.; Burn, A.J.; Burn, A.M.; Burn, D.; Burn, D.S.; Burn, R.; Burnet, S.; Burnett, B.; Burnett, C.; Burnett, S.; Burnham, F.; Burnham, P.M.; Burns, A.; Burns, B.; Burns, K.; Burns, P.; Burns, R.B.; Burns, W.; Burnside, M.; Burr, M.; Burrell, H.; Burrell, J.; Burroughs, D.; Burrows, H.L.; Burrows, P.; Burrows, P.C.;Burrows, I.; Burst, D.; Burston, M.; Burt, D.; Burt, R.; Burt, S.; Burton, A.C.; Burton, C.; Burton, G.; Burton, J.A.; Burton, J.F.; Burton, P.; Burton, P.J.; Burton, S.; Burtt, E.; Bury, C.; Bury, S.; Bushby, M.B.; Bushell, C.; Busuttil, S.; Butchart, A.; Butcher, A.A.; Butcher, J.; Butcher, P.; Butcher, R.; Butler, A.; Butler, A.J.L.; Butler, C.G.; Butler, D.;Butler, E.; Butler, E.A.; Butler, I.; Butler, K.; Butler, M.; Butler, S.; Butler, S.G.; Butt, C.; Buttens, T.; Butter, T.; Butterfield, A.; Butterfield, D.; Butterfield, I.; Butterfield, W.R.; Butterill, G.; Butters, C.; Butters, T.; Butterworth, K.; Button, M.; Button, N.; Buxton, R.; Bybee, A.K.; Byrne, J.; Bywater, J.; Caban, M.; Caban, S.; Cadbury, J.; Cade, M.; Cadman, P.; Cahill, B.; Cahill, J.J.; Cahill, M.; Caiden, M.; Caim, B.D.; Caldicott, T.; Caldock, K.; Caldwell, H.L.; Caldwell, J.; Cale, S.R.; Calender, K.; Callaghan, D.C.; Callaghan, N.; Callaghan, S.; Callan, I.; Callan, I.W.; Callaway, T.; Callf, R.; Callion, J.; Calow, G.; Calvert, R.; Camara, P.; Cameron, E.; Cameron, I.; Cammack, P.; Campbell Smith, J.; Campbell, A.; Campbell, C.; Campbell, E.W.G.; Campbell, G.; Campbell, I.; Campbell, J.; Campbell, J.K.; Campbell, J.M.; Campbell, K.; Campbell, L.; Campbell, M.; Campbell, O.; Campbell, S.; Campbell-Ricketts, H.; Campion, F.W.; Campion, H.; Candlish, P.A.; Cane-Honeysett, N.; Cann, D.; Cannings, F.R.; Cannings, P.; Cannon, C.; Cant, C.; Capewell, J.; Capey, S.; Caplin, M.; Capp, S.; Capper, P.; Capstick, J.; Carder, D.; Cardew, J.W.; Cardy, G.; Cardy, I.; Careon, T.; Carey, J.; Carlaw, M.; Carle, I.; Carley, M.; Carlisle, A.; Carlton, P.; Carlyle, M.; Carman, B.M.; Carman, L.; Carmen, L.; Carney , J.; Caroen, T.; Carpenter, C.; Carpenter, G.H.; Carpenter, P.; Carpenter, R.; Carr, D.; Carr, F.M.B.; Carr, M.; Carr, P.; Carr, R.; Carraro, D.; Carrick, T.; Carrier, P.; Carrigan, C.; Carrington, D.; Carrington, D.G.; Carrington, G.; Carrington, L.I.; Carroll, F.; Carroll, N.; Carroll, S.; Carruthers, D.; Carruthers, S.; Carsewell, I.; Carson, F.; Carson, L.; Carson, M.; Carson, S.; Carstairs, D.N.; Carswell, I.; Carter, A.; Carter, A.E.J.;Carter, C.; Carter, H.; Carter, H.H.; Carter, I.; Carter, J.; Carter, J.W.; Carter, L.; Carter, M.; Carter, N.; Carter, P.; Carter, R.; Carter, S.; Carter, W.; Carthy, B.; Cartwright, B.; Cartwright, L.; Cartwright, M.; Cartwright, R.A.; Cartwright, S.; Cartwright, T.; Carty, P.; Carvell, K.; Carver, R.; Case, P.; Casebourne, W.C.; Casement, P.; Casemore,M.; Casey, A.; Casey, D.; Cash, T.; Casselden, P.; Cassidy, P.; Castell, R.; Castle, D.; Castle, P.; Catchpole, M.; Catley, G.; Catley, G.P.; Catt, M.; Cattanach, F.; Catterwell, M.; Cattliff, E.; Cawley, P.J.; Cawston, J.M.; Cawthorne, D.; Cawthorne, P.; Cawthray, S.; Cebo, J.J.; Cervante, A.; Chadd, P.T.; Chadd, R.; Chadwick, N.; Chalkey, A.;Chalkley, A.; Challis, J.; Chalmel, R.; Cham, S.A.; Chamberlain, A.; Chambers, A.; Chambers, C.; Chambers, D.; Chambers, G.; Chambers, N.; Chambers, P.; Chambers, V.H.; Champion, G.; Champion, G.C.; Champion, M.; Champion, R.; Chandler, D.; Chandler, L.; Chandler, M.; Chandler, P.; Chandler, R.; Chanin, P.; Chantler, P.; Chapman,A.; Chapman, B.; Chapman, B.L.; Chapman, D.; Chapman, E.; Chapman, E.A.; Chapman, F.I.; Chapman, J.; Chapman, M.; Chapman, M.E.; Chapman, P.; Chapman, R.; Chapman, R.A.; Chapman, T.; Chappell, E.G.; Chappell, P.; Charbonnier, H.J.; Chard, A.; Charles, P.J.; Charlesworth, R.; Charlton, P.; Charlton, T.; Charlton-Jones, H.;Charter, E.; Charter, L.; Charters, K.; Chater, A.O.; Chatfield, M.; Chave, J.E.; Checkley, G.; Cheeseborough, I.P.; Cheeseman, L.; Chelmick, D.G.; Chenery, J.M.; Chesham, M.; Cheshier, A.; Cheshire, F.; Cheshire, S.; Chester, J.; Chester, Y.; Chesterton, D.; Chetwynd, H.; Chetwynd, M.; Cheverton, J.M.; Cheyne, D.; Cheyne, E.; Chick, A.;Chiddick, S.; Childs, J.; Childs, P.; Childs, R.; Chilton, I.; Chinery, M.; Chinnery, A.G.; Chittenden, H.; Chitty, L.D.; Chiverton, F.; Chiverton, G.; Chorley, M.; Chown, D.; Chris, E.; Christain, T.; Christer, G.; Christian, G.; Christie, C.; Christie, C.A.J.; Christie, D.; Christie, E.R.; Christie, I.; Christie, L.; Christie, P.; Christlieb, J.; Christmas, M.; Christmas, S.; Church, A.R.; Churchill, C.; Churchill, R.; Churchill, Y.; Churchill, Y.M.; Chuter, I.; Cisman, G.; Ciudiskis,

J.; Clabon, T.; Clapshoe, B.; Clare, P.; Clare, T.; Clark, B.D.; Clark, E.C.; Clark, J.; Clark, L.; Clark, M.J.; Clark, N.; Clark, P.; Clark, S.; Clarke, A.; Clarke, C.; Clarke, D.; Clarke, D.J.; Clarke, E.; Clarke, G.; Clarke, G.E.; Clarke, I.; Clarke, J.; Clarke, K.; Clarke, L.; Clarke, M.; Clarke, P.; Clarke, S.; Clarke, T.; Clarkson Webb, P.; Clarkson, J.; Clarkson, M.; Clarkson, P.; Clarkson, R.; Clarkson-Webb, C.M.; Clarkson-Webb, P.; ClarksonWebb, O.P.; Classey, E.W.; Classey, L.; Claxton, P.; Clay, B.; Claybrough, M.; Clayden, D.; Clayden, D.G.; Clayden, G.; Claydon, D.G.;Claydon, J.; Clayfield, P.; Clayson, S.; Clayson, T.; Clayton, A.; Clayton, G.; Clayton, J.; Clayton, N.; Clayton, P.; Clayworth, K.; Clearing, F.; Cleaver, B.; Clee, A.F.A.; Clegg, H.; Clegg, P. L.; Clegg, R.; Clegg, S.; Cleland, A.; Cleland, G.; Cleland, G.G.; Clemence, J.; Clement, A.; Clements, D.; Clements, D.K.; Clements, H.A.B.; Clements, K.; Clementson, M.; Clemons, L.; Clerici, S.; Clews, B.; Clifford, J.; Clifford, T.; Clift, W.J.; Clifton, J.; Clifton, S.; Clinch, W.; Clinging, R.; Clist, M.J.; Clive, J.R.; Clive, R.; Close, S.; Clotworthy, C.; Clough, J.; Cloyne, J.; Clucas, M.; Clunas, A.; Clutten, B.; Clutterbuck, L.; Coan, H.; Coan, R.; Coates, A.; Coates, D.; Coates, G.N.L.; Coates, K.; Coates, S.; Coats, H.E.; Coatsworth, A.; Cobb, F.; Cobb, P.; Cochrane, K.; Cochrane, M.; Cochrane, S.; Cockbain, C.; Cockbain, R.; Cockburn, A.; Cockburn, C.; Cocker, S.; Cockerill, D.; Cockill, G.; Cocks, W.P.; Cocksedge, B.; Cocoran, S.; Codd, G.M.; Coetzee, E.F.C.; Coghlan, P.; Cohen, K.; Cohme, N.; Coker, A.; Coker, J.W.; Coker, S.J.; Colbert, P.; Colcombe, K.; Coldicott, D.; Coldwell, J.D.; Cole, A.; Cole, A.T.; Cole, C.; Cole, C.B.; Cole, F.; Cole, J.; Cole, M.; Cole, S.; Colegate, V.M.; Coleman, D.; Coleman, L.; Coleman, M.; Coleman, R.; Coleman, S.; Colenutt, S.R.; Coles, H.E.; Coles, R.; Colgate, S.; Collar, Jill E.; Colles, C.; Colley, L.T.; Colley, R.; Collier, I.; Collier, J.; Collier, N.; Collier, R.V.; Collier, T.; Collin, C.J.; Collin, K.; Collin, P.; Collin, R.; Colling, S.J.; Collingwood, N.; Collins, A.; Collins, A.S.; Collins, B.; Collins, C.B.; Collins, G.; Collins, G.A.; Collins, J.; Collins, J.B.; Collins, K.; Collins, L.; Collins, M.; Collins, P.; Collins, R.; Collins, S.; Collinson, M.; Collinson, M.P.; Colman, P.; Colman, S.; Colmer, A.; Colston, A.; Colthrup, C.W.; Colthurst, W.B.; Colvill, D.; Colville, B.; Comerford, P.; Comont, J.; Comont, R.; Condry, W.M.; Coney, D.; Coney, S.; Congreve, A.; Connah, A.; Connelly, M.; Connold, E.; Connolly, K.; Connor, K.; Conroy, J.; Conway, A.J.; Conway, D.; Conway, T.; Coode, E.J.; Cook, A.R.; Cook, B.; Cook, C.; Cook, D.; Cook, D.L.; Cook, H.; Cook, I.; Cook, J.; Cook, K.; Cook, M.H.; Cook, N.; Cook, P.; Cook, R.; Cook, T.; Cooke, M.; Cooke, N.; Coombey, N.; Coombs, F.J.; Cooper, B.; Cooper, D.; Cooper, D.R.; Cooper, E.; Cooper, J.; Cooper, J.D.; Cooper, M.; Cooper, N.; Cooper, R.; Cooper, S.; Cooper, T.; Coote, I.; Cooter, J.; Copeland, A.; Copland, A.; Copley, B.; Copley, V.; Coppock, C.; Coppock, J.; Coppox, C.; Copsey-Adams, J.; Copson, P.J.; Corbet, G.; Corbet, I.; Corbet, N.; Corbet, P.S.; Corbet, S.A.; Corbett, H.H.; Corbett, I.; Corbett, K.; Corbett, P.; Corbett, P.S.; Corbett, S.; Corbin, I.; Corcoran, S.; Cordero, R.P.; Corke, D.; Corke, J.; Corkerton, L.; Corkhill, P.; Corlett, T.; Corley, F.V.; Corley, M.F.V.; Corley, P.; Cormacan, W.; Cormack, D.; Cormack, R.; Cormie, V.; Corner, R.; Cornhill, R.; Cornish, S.; Cornwell, A.; Corran, B.; Corry, J.; Corsie, C.; Corson, P.; Cory, M.; Cory, R.; Cosgrove, P.; Cosnette, B.; Cotgrove, I.; Cottier, P.; Cottis, R.; Cottle, N.W.; Cotton, A.; Cotton, D.C.F.; Cotton, E.; Cotton, M.; Couch, S.C.; Coulcher, C.P.J.; Coulson, D.; Coulson, L.; Coulson-Phillips, A.; Coult, T.; Coulter, J.; Coultherd, P.; Coupar, A.; Coupe, C.; Court, A.; Court, I.; Court, T.; Courtman, J.; Cousins, M.; Coutin, I.; Coventry, H.; Coventry, L.; Covey, S.; Covey, S.J.; Cowan, A.J.; Cowan, C.F.; Cowan, M.; Coward, B.; Coward, T.A.; Cowdy, S.; Cowe, I.; Cowen, R.; Cowie, J.; Cowie, R.; Cowie, S.; Cowin, W.S.; Cowley, B.; Cowley, E.V.; Cowley, J.; Cowlin, J.A.; Cowlishaw, E.; Cowser, R.; Cox, A.; Cox, A.L.; Cox, B.; Cox, H.; Cox, J.; Cox, J.H.; Cox, J.R.; Cox, L.; Cox, M.; Cox, P.; Cox, R.; Cox, R.S.; Cox, S.; Cox, W.E.; Cozens, N.; Cracknell, J.; Cragg, G.; Cragg, J.; Craig, G.; Craig, S.; Craine, E.; Cramb, M.; Cramb, P.; Cramp, J.; Crampton, S.; Crane, M.; Cranefield, P.; Cranfield, J.; Cranney, J.; Cranston, P.; Crassweller, K.; Craven, A.; Crawford, G.; Crawford, J.; Crawford, M.; Crawshaw, J.; Crawshaw, R.; Craythorne, M.; Craze, A.; Creechan, P.; Creed, P.; Crehan, J.; Creighton, M.G.; Cremin, A.; Cremin, R.; Cremona, J.; Cresswell, J.; Crewe, B.; Crewe, J.; Crewe, M.; Cribbin, S.; Crichton, M.I.; Crichton, P.; Crichton, R.; Crick, K.; Cripps, B.; Cripps, N.; Cripps, R.; Critchley, A.; Critchley, M.; Crocker, D.; Crofton, R.; Crofts, D.A.; Croker, J.; Cromie, J.; Crompton, D.W.T.; Crompton, J.; Crook, B.; Crook, J.; Crook, R.; Cropper, R.S.; Crosby, J.; Crosby, P.; Crosby, T.S.; Crosher, J.; Cross, E.J.; Cross, I.C.; Cross, J.; Cross, K.; Cross, S.; Crossley, C.; Crossley, J.; Crossley, R.; Crossman, N.J.; Croton, N.; Crouch, J.; Crouch, S.; Croucher, D.; Crow, P.N.; Crowder, A.; Crowe, F.; Crowle, A.; Crowley, B.; Crowley, M.; Crown, T.; Crowther, N.;

Crowther, P.; Croxton, B.; Crozier, J.; Cruickshanks, K.; Cruikshanks, A.; Crushell, P.; Crutchley, B.; Cu, D.; Cuffe, T.; Cullen, D.; Cullen, J.; Cullen, J.M.; Cullen, M.; Cullens, H.; Culley, S.; Cullinan, P.; Cullum, J.; Culshaw, J.; Cumming, J.; Cundale, J.G.; Cundall, A.; Cunliffe, C.; Cunliffe, J.; Cunningham, J.; Cunnington, A.; Cupit, B.; Curd, C.; Curd, J.; Curnyn, J.; Curran, A.; Curran, E.; Currie, L.; Currie, M.; Currie, N.; Curry, H.; Curson, J.; Curson, L.; Curson, S.; Curtin, M.; Curtis, B.; Curtis, G.; Curtis, I.; Curtis, J.; Curtis, R.; Curzo, J.; Cutt, P.; Cutting, K.; Cutting, L.; Cutts, A.; Cwynarski, M.; D'Alessandro, R.; D'Ayala, R.; D'Oyly, M.J.; D'Oyly, M.; Daborn, R.; Dacheux, S.; Dadds, N.; Daeid, M.; Dafydd, R.; Daguet, C.; Dahl, D.; Dalby, G.; Dale, A.; Dale, C.W.; Dale, J.; Dale, J.C.; Dale, K.; Dale, L.; Dale, M.; Dale, S.; Dale, T.; Dale, W.S.; Dalgleish, P.; Dalglish, A.A.; Dallimore, T.; Dallman, A.A.; Dalton, H.L.; Dalton, R.A.; Daly, R.; Dalziel, D.; Damant, C.; Dana, D.; Danby, J.; Dandy, R.; Daniels, E.T.; Daniels, J.; Daniels, J.L.; Daniels, R.; Daniels, T.; Dannreuther, T.; Dano, L.; Danson, R.E.; Dapling, J.; Darby, E.J.; Darch, P.; Darlaston, M.; Darley, P.L.; Darlington, S.; Darwin, J.; Darwin, K.; Daubney, P.; Daunt, R.; Dave, G.; Davenport, I.; Davey, P.R.; Davey, S.; Davey, S.R.; David, C.; David, I.; David, M.; Davidson, B.; Davidson, I.; Davidson, J.; Davidson, J.R.; Davidson, K.; Davidson, M.; Davidson, N.; Davidson, N.J.; Davidson, P.; Davidson, R.; Davidson, S.C.; Davidson, T.; Davidson, W.F.; Davie, J.; Davies, A.; Davies, C.; Davies, D.; Davies, D.A.L.; Davies, E.P.; Davies, G.; Davies, G.A.N.; Davies, H.; Davies, J.; Davies, J.C.; Davies, L.; Davies, M.; Davies, N.; Davies, P.; Davies, R.; Davies, R.W.; Davies, S.; Davies, T.; Davies, T.A.W.; Davies, W.; Davis, A.; Davis, A.R.; Davis, B.; Davis, D.; Davis, G.; Davis, G.A.N.; Davis, J.; Davis, K.; Davis, K.N.; Davis, L.; Davis, M.; Davis, M.J.; Davis, N.; Davis, O.; Davis, P.; Davis, P.E.; Davis, P.S.; Davis, R.W.; Davis, S.; Davis, T.; Davis, T.A.W.; Davis, W.G.; Davison, G.; Davison, J.; Davison, M.; Davison, P.; Davison, T.; Davy-Dean, J.; Dawes, A.; Dawes, A.P.; Daws, J.; Daws, Jon T.; Daws, R.; Dawson, B.; Dawson, C.; Dawson, D.; Dawson, D.G.; Dawson, I.; Dawson, I.K.; Dawson, J.; Dawson, J.A.; Dawson, J.E.; Dawson, N.; Dawson, R.; Dawson, S.; Day, C.; Day, C.D.; Day, D.; Day, F.H.; Day, G.V.; Day, H.; Day, John J.; Day, K.R.; Day, P.; Day, R.; Day, S.; Dayes, G.; Dayton, N.; Dazley, R.; De Lemos, M.; Deacon, J.; Dean, A.R.; Dean, C.; Dean, M.; Dean, P.; Deans, M.; Dear, L.; Deavin, B.; Defoe, N.; Deighton, A.; Deisler, I.; Delaney, E.; Delaney, H.; Delhanty, J.E.; Dell, C.; Dell, D.H.; Dell, J.; Dellow, J.; Delve, L.; Demidecki, M.; Dempsey, J.; Dempsey, M.; Dempster, J.P.; Dempster, P.; Denard, A.; Denham, B.; Denman, D.; Denning, P.; Dennis, E.; Dennis, G.; Dennis, G.C.; Dennis, M.; Dennis, M.C.; Dennis, R.; Dennison, J.; Dennison, M.; Dennison, R.W.; Denny, K.; Denny, S.; Densley, M.; Densley, R.; Dent, G.E.; Dent, G.R.J.; Dent, J.; Dent, K.; Dent, N.; Denton, J.; Denton, J.S.; Denton, M.L.; Denwood, S.; Denyer, J.; Derby, E.J.; Derbyshire, B.; Derbyshire, P.; Derri, C.; Derrick, L.; Derrick, P.; Dettmar, S.; Deuchar, G.L.; Devery, F.; Devlin, J.; Devonald, S.; Devos, D.; Dewhurst, C.; Dewick, S.; Dewsbury, D.; Dey, D.; Diamond, N.; Diaper, L.; Dicerbo, E.; Dick, D.; Dickens, A .; Dickerson, A.; Dickinson, B.; Dickinson, J.; Dicks, D.E.J.; Dickson, A.; Dickson, B.R.; Dickson, N.; Dickson, P.; Diebel, A.; Dieck, C.; Dietz, N.; Digby, J.; Diggin, J.; Dillon, D.; Dimery, M.; Dimmock, D.P.; Dingle, T.J.; Dinning, J.; Dinsdale, H.; Dinsdale, P.; Disney, S.; Distant, W.L.; Diver, C.; Dixon, A.; Dixon, D.; Dixon, G.; Dixon, H.; Dixon, J.; Dixon, T.; Doan, C.; Doan, R.; Dobbins, G.; Dobbs, A.; Dobbs, G.; Dobbs, R.; Doble, G.; Dobson, C.; Dobson, J.; Dobson, R.M.; Dobson, T.; Dockery, T.; Docketty, C.A.; Dodd, E.; Dodd, I.; Dodd, K.; Dodd, M.; Dodds, G.; Dodds, M.; Dodds, R.M.; Dodgson, A.; Dodgson, J.; Doe, J.; Doherty, J.; Dohrn, M.M.; Doidge, H.; Dolbear, K.; Dolton, M.; Dolton, P.; Donaghy, A.; Donald, F.; Donald, H.; Donald, M.; Donald, P.; Donaldson, R.; Donato, B.; Doncaster, R.; Donelly, A.; Donisthorpe, H.St.J.; Donnelly, A.; Donnelly, T.; Donnison, A.; Donnison, E.; Donnithore, H.S.J.K.; Donnithorne, N.J.; Donovan, J.W.; Donovan, P.; Doody, A.; Doogue, D.; Doran, E.P.; Doran, R.; Doricott, L.; Dorken, D.; Dorney, P.; Dorrell, R.; Dorren, D.; Doubleday, H.; Dougall, T.; Doughty, P.; Dougill, S.; Douglas, A.; Douglas, B.; Douglas, C.; Douglas, I.; Douglas, J.; Douglas, M.; Douglas, R.; Douglas, T.; Doulas, I.; Doust, T.; Dove, I.; Dove, N.R.; Dove, S.; Dove, T.; Doveston, M.; Dovy, C.; Dowding, L.; Dowie, M.; Dowling, D.N.; Dowling, N.; Down, P.; Downer, V.J.; Downer, W.; Downes, J.A.; Downey, M.; Downhill, M.; Downie, A.; Downie, I.; Downing, C.; Downing, D.; Downton, L.; Dowse, D.; Dowse, P.; Doyle, D.; Doyle, J.; Doyle, P.; Doyle, S.; Drage, J.; Drake, C.M.; Drake, M.; Drakeford, T.; Draper, A.; Draper, B.; Draper, F.; Draper, L.; Dray, M.; Drayton, B.; Dresh, C.; Drew, B.; Drew, D.; Drew, R.; Drewery, C.; Drewett, D.; Drewett, H.; Drinan, T.; Drinkall,

N.; Driscoll, J.; Driscoll, R.J.; Driver, A.J.; Driver, C.; Drury, J.; Drury, W.D.; Dryburgh, P.; Dryden, R.; Drysdale, A.; Du Feu, G.R.; Dublon, M.; Duckels, A.S.; Ducker, S.; Ducket, D.; Duckhouse, B.; Duckworth, K.; Duckworth, T.; Duddington, J.; Dudley, C.; Dudley, S.; Dufek, K.; Dufeu, C.; Duffell, M.; Duffie, J.; Duffield, M.; Duffield, S.E.; Duffy, H.; Duffy, M.; Duffy, P.; Duggan, A.; Duggan, R.; Duigan, C.; Duke, S.; Dumbleton, B.; Dummer, G.W.A.; Dunbar, J.; Dunbavin, J.; Duncan, A.B.; Duncan, D.W.; Duncan, M.; Duncan, P.; Duncan, W.; Dunk, P.; Dunkley, J.; Dunkling, G.; Dunlop, G.A.; Dunlop, S.; Dunmore, G.; Dunn, B.; Dunn, D.; Dunn, G.; Dunn, I.; Dunn, J.; Dunn, P.; Dunn, R.; Dunn, R.H.; Dunn, T.C.; Dunnells, D.; Dunning, C.; Dunning, S.; Dunstan, S.; Dunsterville, C.; Dunston, A.; Dunton, C.; Dupe, K.; Durie, T.; Durkin, J.; Durnan, J.; Durnell, P.; Durnford, J.; Durose, K.; Durrant, K.C.; Dutson, G.M.; Dutt, P.; Dutton, A.; Dwyer, A.; Dwyer, C.; Dwyer, P.; Dye, J.; Dyer, B.; Dyer, C.; Dyer, J.; Dyke, R.; Dykes, B.; Dyne, G.; Dyson, B.; Dyson, C.; Dyson, W.; Eades, D.; Eades, R.; Eady, P.; Eagles, R.; Eakin, M.; Eales, H.T.; Eales, T.; Early, J.P.; Earnshaw, B.; Earnshaw, K.; Earp, K.; East, A.; East, J.; Easterbrook, J.; Eastmead, J.; Easton, A.; Easton, J.; Easton, M.; Eastwood, D.; Eastwood, J.; Eastwood, R.; Eastwood, V.; Eatogh, C.; Eaton, D.; Eaton, J.C.; Eaton, M.; Eaves, S.; Ebbs, L.; Eccles, M.; Eccles, M.A.; Eccles, P.; Eccles, P.R.; Eccles, P.T.; Eccleston, M.; Eckley, J.; Eckstein, M.; Eddleston, R.; Eddy, L.; Edelsten, H.M.; Edelston, J.; Eden, R.; Eden, S.; Edey, C.; Edgar, A.; Edgar, B.; Edgar, P.; Edge, J.; Edgeller, M.; Edgington, J.; Edgington, M.J.; Edin, P.; Edison, C.; Edmonds, M.R.; Edmonds, S.; Edmonds-Brown, V.; Edmunds, M.; Edmunds, R.; Edmunds, S.; Edwards, A.; Edwards, B.; Edwards, C.; Edwards, C.J.; Edwards, D.; Edwards, D.A.; Edwards, G.; Edwards, J.; Edwards, J.S.; Edwards, K.; Edwards, M.; Edwards, P.; Edwards, R.; Edwards, S.; Edwards, T.; Eele, P.; Egan, E.; Egan, M.; Egerton, P.; Eggeling, J.; Egglestone, S.; Eke, B.; Ekins, G.; Elcoate, C.; Eldred, L.; Eldridge, P.; Element, D.; Elford, P.; Elias, D.O.; Elias, T.; Elkins, N.; Ellam, C.; Ellams, Z.; Elliot, B.; Elliot, D.; Elliot, M.; Elliot, R.; Elliot, S.; Elliott, A.; Elliott, D.; Elliott, G.A.; Elliott, M.; Ellis, A.E.; Ellis, B.; Ellis, D.; Ellis, D.E.; Ellis, E.; Ellis, E.A.; Ellis, G.; Ellis, H.A.; Ellis, John R.; Ellis, M.; Ellis, P.; Ellis, P.M.; Ellis, R.; Ellis, R.J.; Ellis, S.; Ellis, T.; Ellis, V.; Ellis, W.H.; Ellison, A.; Ellison, G.; Ellison, I.; Ellison, J.; Ellison, L.; Ellison, M.; Ellison, N.F.; Ellison, R.; Elmes, J.; Elphick, D.; Elphick, I.; Elphick, V.; Elsby, K.; Else, J.; Elsey, N.; Elson, S.; Elston, R.; Elton, D.; Elton, G.; Elvidge, N.; Ely, W.A.; Emary, C.; Emary, L.; Embling, B.; Emerson, J.; Emery, D.; Emmett, E.E.; Emms, C.; Enfield, M.; English, G.; English, J.; English, P.; Enlander, I.; Ennis, J.; Enright, M.; Entwisle, M.; Entwistle, P.F.; Entwistle, S.; Erridge, P.; Escriva, A.; Esland, I.; Evans, A.E.; Evans, C.E.; Evans, D.; Evans, D.R.; Evans, E.; Evans, F.; Evans, G.; Evans, G.A.; Evans, I.E.; Evans, I.M.; Evans, J.; Evans, K.; Evans, L.; Evans, M.; Evans, P.; Evans, P.A.; Evans, R.; Evans, S.; Evans, S.B.; Evans, T.; Evans, W.; Evans, W.E.; Evans, W.F.; Eve, H.C.; Eveleigh, T.; Evelyn, M.; Evendon, R.J.; Everett, C.; Everingham, F.; Everitt, J.; Eversham, B.C.; Evison, R.; Ewing, A.; Excell, A.; Exley, J.; Exley, R.; Extence, C.; Eyden, P.; Eyles, T.; Eyre, E.; Eyre, M.D.; Eyre, S.; Eyres, R.; Facey, R.; Fahy, K.; Fair, J.; Fair, S.; Fairbairn, A.; Fairbanks, L.; Fairbrother, V.; Fairchild, D.; Fairclough, K. D. B.; Fairfield, T.; Fairhead, D.; Fairhead, R.; Fairhead, S.; Fairhurst, D.; Fairless, T.W.; Fairlie , F.; Fairness, B.; Fairney, N.P.; Fairweather, D.G.; Fairweather, E.; Fairweather, L.; Faith, C.; Falconer, M.; Falconer, S.; Fale, A.; Falk, S.; Fanning, M.; Fanshawe, M.; Faris, R.C.; Farish, S.; Farley, A.; Farley, E.; Farmer, C.; Farmer, G.; Farmer, I.; Farnaby, J.; Farnworth, D.R.; Farrar, D.A.; Farrell, B.; Farrell, G.; Farrell, L.; Farrell, S.; Farren, J.; Farrow, E.; Farrow, F.J.L.; Farrow, M.; Farrow, N.; Faulkner, A.; Faulkner, C.; Faulkner, J.S.; Fawcett, D.; Fawcett, K.; Fawkes, W.L.; Fay, R.; Feast, D.; Featherstone, B.; Featherstone, G.; Fee, G.; Fee, S.; Fehrsen, J.; Fellman, D.; Fellows, G.; Fellows, R.; Fells, A.; Felstead, G.; Feltham, A.; Feltham, M.; Felton, C.; Felton, R.; Fenby, H.; Fenlon, D.; Fenn, G.; Fennell, T.A.; Fenner, A.; Fentiman, C.; Fenton, A.; Fenton, C.; Fenton, J.; Fenton, R.; Fenton, U.; Ferguson, A.; Ferguson, A.S.; Ferguson, D.; Ferguson, D.M.; Ferguson, H.; Ferguson, J.; Ferguson, L.; Ferguson, M.; Ferguson, N.; Fergusson, D.; Fernee, P.; Fernell, G.; Ferris, K.; Ferry, C.; Fett, A.; Fewster, G.; Ffeil, P.; Ficklin, A.; Fiddler, W.; Fieger, D.; Field, J.; Fieldhouse, D.S.; Fielding, J.; Figgis, O.; Figures, J.; Filby, R.A.; Finch, A.; Finch, G.; Finch, J.; Finch, J.H.; Finch, K.; Finch, M.; Finch, P.; Fincher, F.; Fincher, T.; Findlay, M.; Findley, M.; Finka, L.; Finnemore, M.; Finnemore, T.; Finnen, T.; Finney, E.; Fish, D.; Fisher, A.; Fisher, B.; Fisher, D.; Fisher, D.J.; Fisher, E.M.; Fisher, I.; Fisher, J.; Fisher, M.; Fisher, S.; Fishlock, R.; Fishwick, S.; Fitch, E.A.; Fitchett, A.; Fitchett, G.J.; Fitchett, P.; Fitter, R.S.R.; Fitton, R.; FitzGerald, C.; Fitzgerald, E.; Fitzpatrick,

M.; Fiwek-Smith, C.H.; Flackett, P.; Flanagan, M.; Flannagan, A.; Fleischer, S.; Fleming, J.; Fleming, J.M.; Fleming, M.; Fleming, V.; Fleming-Williams, L.; Flemming, M.; Flenley, D.; Fletcher, D.; Fletcher, G.; Fletcher, J.E.; Fletcher, M.; Fletcher, N.; Fletcher, P.; Fleur, J.; Flinders, I.; Flint, H.E.; Flint, J.; Flint, J.B.; Flint, J.D.; Flint, J.H.; Flint, R.; Flory, J.E.; Flower, L.; Flower, P.; Flowerday, P.; Flowers, M.; Flumm, D.S.; Flynn, C.; Flynn, E.; Flynn, J.; Foale, G.; Fogarty, J.; Foggo, N.; Foley, M.; Follett, P.C.; Follett, S.A.; Fonseca, E.A.; Foot, C.; Foot, E.; Foot, J.B.; Foott, K.G.; Foran, J.; Forbes, B.; Forbes, M.; Forbes, R.S.; Forbes, W.; Forbes-Dale, L.; Ford, B.; Ford, G.; Ford, H.; Ford, J.; Ford, J.B.; Ford, L.H.; Ford, M.; Ford, R.; Ford, R.L.E.; Ford, S.; Ford, W.K.; Fordham, W.J.; Foreman, J.; Forgham, D.B.; Forgham, J.; Formstone, B.; Formstone, J.B.; Formstone, P.; Forrest, B.; Forrest, I.; Forrest, P.; Forrest, P.J.; Forrest, R.; Forrester, M.; Forsdick, P.; Forshaw, D.; Forster, A.P.; Forster, D.; Forster, G.; Forster, J.; Forster, M.; Forster, P.; Forster, P.W.; Forster-Brown, C.; Forsyth, J.; Fortescue, K.; Fortey, J.; Forward, T.; Foss, P.; Foster, A.; Foster, A.P.; Foster, D.; Foster, G.N.; Foster, J.; Foster, J.A.; Foster, K.; Foster, M.; Foster, R.; Foster, S.; Foster-John, P.; Foulds, A.; Fountain, B.; Fowbert, J.; Fowler, A.; Fowler, D.; Fowler, K.; Fowler, N.; Fowler, S.V.; Fowles, A.P.; Fowles, I.F.; Fowles, M.; Fowling, R.; Fox, A.D.; Fox, D.; Fox, I.; Fox, K.; Fox, M.; Fox, R.; Fox, T.; Foxwell, D.J.; Foy, D.; Foyle, E.; Frame, D.; Frame, J.H.; Frampton, K.; Francis, A.; Francis, C.; Francis, I.; Francis, I.S.; Francis, J.; Francis, P.M.A.; Francis, T.; Frank, S.; Frankish, A.; Franklin, B.; Franklin, E.; Franklin, N.; Franks, S.; Frankum, M.; Frankum, N.; Fraser, A.; Fraser, D.; Fraser, E.; Fraser, F.C.; Fraser, J.; Fraser, N.; Fraser, P.; Fraser, P.A.; Fraser, T.J.; Fray, A.E.; Fray, M.; Fray, R.; Fray, R.P.; Free, S.; Freedman, W.; Freeland, M.; Freeman, G.; Freeman, K.; Freeman, M.; Freeman, P.; Freeman, R.; Freeman, T.; Freer, O.; Fremlin, H.S.; French, C.; French, G.; French, J.; French, N.; French, P.; French, S.; Friday, D.; Friday, D.N.; Friday, L.E.; Friday, R.D.; Friend, K.; Friese, J.; Friswell, N.; Frith, M.; Frost, A.R.; Frost, B.; Frost, J.; Frost, M.; Frost, R.; Frost, R.A.; Frost, T.; Froude, C.; Fry, J.; Fry, R.; Fry, R.M.; Fryatt, T.; Fryer, S.; Fuller, D.; Fuller, J.; Fuller, K.; Fuller, P.; Fullforth, V.; Fulton, A.; Fulton, J.; Funnell, D.; Funnell, M.; Furber, S.; Furries, C.; Furse, A.; Furse, J.; Furse, W.J.; Futter, K.; Futter, S.; Gabb, B.; Gabb, P.R.; Gabb, R.; Gabriel, M.; Gaddum, J.H.; Gadenne, N.; Gadogan, H.; Gaffney, J.E.; Gage, B.; Gahan, P.; Gainey, P.; Gale, B.; Gale, N.; Gale, S.; Gallagher, H.; Gallagher, K.; Gallia, E.; Galliford, A.; Gallimore, C.H.; Galliott, M.; Gallon, R.; Galt, K.; Galton, N.; Galtry, K.; Galtry, M.; Gamage, G.; Gamble, G.; Gamble, I.B.; Gamble, J.S.; Gamble, P.H.; Gamble, S.; Gambles, R.M.; Gammage, P.; Gander, L.; Gane, C.W.V.; Gane, D.; Gant, S.; Garbett, A.; Garbett, P.; Garbutt, D.; Garcia, S.; Gardener, F.; Gardener, P.; Gardener, S.; Gardiner, A.; Gardiner, B.O.C.; Gardiner, J.; Gardiner, R.; Gardner, A.; Gardner, A.E.; Gardner, E.; Gardner, M.; Gardner, P.; Gardner, Z.; Garland, K.; Garland, S.P.; Garland, U.; Garner, D.; Garner, G.; Garner, J.; Garner, P.; Garner, R.; Garner, S.; Garner, S.M.; Garnett, P.; Garnett, S.; Garrad, L.S.; Garrard, B.; Garrart, T.; Garratt, G.; Garrett, B.; Garrett, C.; Garrett, S.; Garrett, T.; Garrod, R.; Garry, G.; Garside, A.; Garston, E.; Garvey, L.; Gascoyne, S.; Gaskill, S.; Gasson, M.; Gateley, P.; Gates, C.; Gatis, J.; Gatland, A.; Gauld, S.; Gaunt, R.; Gaunt, R.G.; Gavaghan, J.; Gavan, M.; Gawler, W.; Gawne, W.; Gay, J.; Gay, P.; Gaylor, P.; Geddes, C.; Geddes, R.; Gee, J.H.R.; Geen, V.; Geeson, J.; Geiger, G.V.; Geiger, J.A.; Gemmell, L.; Gemmell, R.; Gendall, E.; Gent, C.J.; Gent, D.R.; Gent, G.; Gent, J.; Gentil, E.; Gentlemen, A.; George, A.M.; George, C.; George, D.; George, J.; George, W.; Gerrard, B.; Gerrard, T.; Gerry, A.; Ghosh, S.; Ghullam, M.; Gibb, K.; Gibbard, C.; Gibbins, C.; Gibbon, D.; Gibbons, C.; Gibbons, H.; Gibbons, N.; Gibbons, R.; Gibbs, D.; Gibbs, D.J.; Gibbs, G.; Gibbs, J.; Gibbs, K.; Gibbs, R.; Gibney, B.; Gibson, C.; Gibson, I.; Gibson, J.; Gibson, N.; Gibson, O.; Gibson, T.; Gibson-Hill, J.; Gibson-Poole, T.E.; Giddings, P.; Gifford, J.; Gilbert, D.; Gilbert, O.L.; Gilbert, R.; Gilbert, T.; Gilbertson, P.; Gilbertson, W.; Giles, G.; Giles, G.B.; Giles, P.P.; Giles, S.; Gilhespy, R.J.; Gilhooley, M.; Gilkes, W.; Gill, A.; Gill, D.; Gill, E.; Gill, J.; Gillam, B.; Gillam, K.; Gillam, M.; Gillatt, W.; Gilles, W.S.; Gillespie, E.; Gillespie, J.A.; Gillham, A.; Gillham, C.; Gillham, M.J.; Gillibrand, R.; Gilligan, A.; Gilligan, N.; Gilliland, J.; Gilmore, D.R.W.; Gilmour, E.F.; Gilroy, E.; Gingell, A.; Gingell, J.; Ginn, N.; Gittens, A.; Gittens, K.; Gittens, T.; Gittings, T.; Gittins, C.; Given, Q.; Gladwin, T.W.; Glass, D.; Glass, R.; Glass, S.; Glaves, D.; Glazebrook, J.; Glazzard, L.; Gleaves, D.; Gledhill, T.; Glen, G.; Glen, S.W.; Glencross, A.; Glendinning, G.; Glenister, P.; Glenny, M.; Glenville, E.; Gliddon, D.; Gloaguen, A.; Glover, J.; Goatman, N.; Gobbett, R.; Goddard, C.; Goddard, D.; Goddard, D.G.; Goddard, J.H.; Goddard, N.; Goddard, P.; Goddard, S.R.; Godfrey, A.; Godfrey, D.; Godfrey, H.; Godfrey, M.F.; Godfrey,

R.D.; Godfrey, S.; Godsmark, H.; Goff, M.; Goff, R.W.; Golaswezski, S.R.; Golden, K.; Goldie, M.; Goldsmith, D.; Goldsmith, J.G.; Gollan, D.; Gomersall, C.H.; Gomes, B.; Gomes, R.; Gompertz, D.; Gondriss, P.; Gonter, M.; Gooch, S.M.; Good, J.A.; Goodall, A.; Goodall, A.L.; Goodall, M.; Goodall, R.N.; Goodfellow, T.; Goodhind, T.S.; Goodley, J.; Goodlife, T.; Goodliffe, R.; Goodman, R.; Goodrich, K.; Goodwin, D.; Goodyear, C.; Goodyear, K.G.; Goodyear, L.; Goom, N.; Gooseman, M.P.; Gordon Smith, P.; Gordon, G.W.; Gordon, I.; Gordon, L.; Gordon, M.; Gordon, P.; Gordon, P.E.; Gordon, P.R.; Goriup, P.; Gorley, M.; Gorman, C.; Gorman, M.; Gorman, S.; Gorton, E.; Gorton, S.; Gosling, J.; Goss, H.; Gossling, T.; Gostick, L.; Gotham, P.; Gough, A.; Gough, B.; Gough, M.; Gould, D.; Gould, F.; Gould, M.; Gould, R.W.; Gould, S.; Goulding, M.; Goulson, D.; Gourlay, D.; Gowenlock, J.; Gowlett, G.; Gowlett, K.; Goy, J.T.; Goy, R.; Grace, A.; Gradwell, A.; Gradwell, A.W.; Gradwell, G.; Gradwell, W.; Graham, A.; Graham, A.N.; Graham, A.W.; Graham, D.; Graham, E.; Graham, E.A.; Graham, J.; Graham, M.; Graham, R.; Graham, S.; Graham, T.; Grainge, C.; Grainger, P.; Grant, D.; Grant, D.R.; Grant, D.W.; Grant, G.C.; Grant, M.; Grant, S.; Grant, T.; Grantham, V.; Graves, P.P.; Graves, T.; Gravett, P.; Gray, A.; Gray, B.; Gray, D.; Gray, D.E.; Gray, H.; Gray, I.; Gray, J.; Gray, J.R.A.; Gray, K.; Gray, M.; Gray, T.; Gray, W.; Grayson, A.; Grayson, F.; Grayson, F.W.; Grearson, J.; Greaves, G.; Greaves, R.; Green, A.; Green, B.; Green, C.; Green, D.; Green, E.; Green, G.; Green, G.H.; Green, G.P.; Green, H.; Green, I.; Green, J.; Green, J.A.; Green, K.; Green, K.J.; Green, L.; Green, M.; Green, N.; Green, P.; Green, R.; Green, S.V.; Green, T.E.; Green, V.A.; Greenacre, B.H.; Greenall, P.; Greenaway, F.; Greenaway, P.; Greenaway, T.; Greenfield, S.; Greenhalf, P.; Greenhill, J.S.; Greenhough, M.L.; Greenland, M.; Greenough, D.; Greenway, C.; Greenway, D.; Greenwood, A.; Greenwood, E.R.; Greenwood, I.; Greenwood, J.; Greenwood, J.J.; Greenwood, P.; Greer, T.; Greeves, L.; Gregory, B.; Gregory, H.; Gregory, J.; Gregory, L.; Gregory, N.; Gregory, S.J.; Gregson, C.; Grenfell, E.; Grennard, P.; Gretton, A.; Greves, D.; Grewcock, D.T.; Grey, B.; Grey, M.; Grey, P.; Gridley, P.; Grieco, G.; Grier, I.; Grierson, R.; Griffin, B.; Griffin, C.; Griffin, L.; Griffin, M.; Griffin, P.; Griffin, S.; Griffin, T.; Griffith, D.; Griffith, F.; Griffith, I.; Griffith, O.; Griffiths, A.; Griffiths, B.; Griffiths, C.; Griffiths, D.; Griffiths, E.; Griffiths, G.; Griffiths, H.; Griffiths, J.; Griffiths, K.; Griffiths, L.; Griffiths, M.; Griffiths, P.; Griffiths, R.; Griffiths, S.; Griffiths, T.; Griffiths, W.; Griggs, P.; Grigson, P.; Griith, C.; Grimes, J.; Grimes, M.; Grimsey, A.; Grimshaw, P.H.; Grimstead, C.; Grindley, C.; Grindley, G.; Grinstead, K.; Grint, J.S.; Griss, D.; Griss, D.I.; Griss, I.D.; Grist, M.; Gristwood, S.; Gritton, R.; Groom, J.; Groom, S.; Groome, G.; Gross, C.; Grove, B.; Grove, S.; Grove, S.J.; Grover, J.; Grover, S.; Groves, A.; Groves, B.; Groves, N.; Groves, R.; Grummitt, G.; Grundy, L.; Gubert, L.; Gudge, A.; Gudge, J.; Guest, J.; Guest, J.P.; Guilford, A.; Guilfoyle, A.; Guilloson, T.; Gumieniak, A.; Gunn, A.; Gunn, D.; Gunn, E.; Gunn, I.; Gunn, M.; Gunn, P.; Gunning, K.; Gurney, D.; Gurney, M.; Gush, G.H.; Guthrie, G.; Guthrie, N.; Gutteridge, P.; Guy, P.; Guy, S.; Guy, S.M.; Gwyn, M.; Gwynn, B.; Gwynn, V.; Gyseman, S.; Hackett, S.; Hackman, J.; Hackney, P.; Hadfield, P.; Hadley, A.; Hadley, L.; Hadley, M.; Hadman, R.; Hadwin, I.; Haes, C.; Haes, E.C.M.; Hageman, G.; Haggar, J.; Haggart, C.; Haggerty, M.; Hague, J.; Haigh, D.; Haigh, R.; Haigh, T.; Haines, D.; Haines, F.H.; Halbert, J.N.; Halcrow, V.; Hale, A.; Hale, A.D.; Hale, I.K.M.; Hale, J.W.; Hale, R.; Hales, M.; Hall, A.; Hall, B.; Hall, C.; Hall, C.G.; Hall, C.R.; Hall, G.; Hall, J.; Hall, K.; Hall, L.; Hall, L.E.; Hall, M.; Hall, M.C.; Hall, N.; Hall, P.; Hall, R.; Hall, R.A.; Hall, S.; Hall, S.B.; Hallet, K.; Hallet, M.; Hallett, C.; Hallett, D.; Hallett, H.M.; Halliday, John B.; Halliday, M.G.; Halliday, P.; Halls, H.; Halls, J.; Halls, J.M.; Halls, M.; Hallsworth, J.; Hallwood, J.; Halpin, J.;Halsall, K.; Halstead, A.J.; Halstead, F.; Halton, S.; Hamalainen, M.; Hamblett, R.; Hambley, J.; Hamblyn, A.; Hamer, G.; Hamill, R.J.H.; Hamilton Meikle, J.; Hamilton, A.; Hamilton, C.; Hamilton, J.; Hamlet, T.; Hamlin, I.; Hamling, L.; Hamm, A.H.; Hammersley, D.; Hammersley, D.P.; Hammond, B.; Hammond, C.O.; Hammond, E.C.; Hammond, H.E.; Hammond, M.; Hammond, M.R.; Hammond, R.; Hammonds, S.; Hampshire, R.; Hamshere, J.; Hamson, R.; Hamzij, M.; Hancock, A.P.; Hancock, B.; Hancock, C.; Hancock, E.F.; Hancock, E.G.; Hancock, L.; Hancock, P.G.; Hancock, S.; Hancock, T.; Hancocks, P.; Hancox, J.; Hancox, P.D.; Hand, H.; Hand, N.; Handford, W.; Handley, C.; Hando, N.; Hands, D.; Hands, T.; Handyside, S.; Hanford, D.M.; Hanlon, D.; Hannah, J.; Hannington, C.; Hanson, T.; Harbid, R.E.; Harbird, R.; Harbird, R.E.; Harcombe, D.J.; Hardcastle, E.; Hardcastle, R.; Harding, B.; Harding, J.; Harding, P.T.; Harding, R.; Harding-Morris, J.; Hardinge, W.; Hards, M.; Hardwick, M.; Hardwick, W.; Hardy, B.; Hardy, C.; Hardy, D.; Hardy, G.; Hardy,

I.; Hardy, J.; Hardy, P.; Hardy, S.; Hare, R.; Hargrave, A.; Hargrave, B.; Hargreave, K.; Hargreaves, B.; Hargreaves, D.; Hargreaves, D.P.; Hargreaves, I.; Hargreaves, R.; Harkes, J.; Harkett, D.; Harle, B.; Harley, R.; Harlington, J.; Harman, T.; Harmer, A.; Harmer, C.; Harmer, J.; Harmer, K.; Harmer, P.A.; Harmer, R.; Harmes, P.; Harold, J.; Harper, J.; Harper, K.G.; Harper, M.W.; Harpley, D.; Harrap, S.; Harries, D.; Harries, H.; Harrington, E.; Harrington, P.; Harrington, R.; Harris, A.; Harris, B.; Harris, C.; Harris, D.; Harris, E.M.D.; Harris, G.; Harris, I.; Harris, J.; Harris, J.E.; Harris, J.I.; Harris, L.; Harris, M.; Harris, P.; Harris, R.; Harris, S.; Harris, U.; Harrison, A.; Harrison, C.; Harrison, G.; Harrison, J.; Harrison, J.P.; Harrison, J.W.H.; Harrison, M.; Harrison, P.; Harrison, R.; Harrison, V.; Harrison-Watts, G.J.; Harriss, P.; Harrold, J.P.; Harrold, R.; Harron, J.; Harrop, A.; Hart, I.B.; Hart, P.R.; Hart, R.; Hart, W.; Harte, E.; Hartley, A.; Hartley, B.C.; Hartley, J.C.; Hartley, T.; Hartwright, J.; Harvard, R.; Harvey, I.; Harvey, I.F.; Harvey, J.; Harvey, M.C.; Harvey, P.; Harvey, P.V.; Harvey, R.; Harvey, R.H.M.; Harvey, S.; Harwood, B.; Harwood, J.; Harwood, N.W.; Harwood, P.; Harwood, W.H.; Haskell, P.; Haskins, L.; Hassall, C.; Hassell, P.; Hastings, D.; Hastings, D.C.; Hastings, J.; Hastings, R.B.; Hatch, C.; Hatch, K.; Hatcliffe, R.; Hathaway, C.; Hathway, R.; Hatsell, C.; Hatton, D.; Hatton, L.; Hatton, W.; Havers, J.R.; Havers, L.; Hawczak, A.; Hawell, J.; Hawes, C.; Hawgood, G.; Hawke, C.J.; Hawker, D.; Hawker, D.M.; Hawkes, B.; Hawkes, R.; Hawkins, A.; Hawkins, C.; Hawkins, I.; Hawkins, J.; Hawkins, K.M.; Hawkins, M.; Hawkins, R.D.; Hawkswell, A.; Hawksworth, A.; Hawley, J.; Hawley, R.; Hawthorn, D.; Hay, R.; Hay, S.; Haycock, A.; Haycock, R.J.; Haycox, S.L.; Haydock, K.; Hayes, C.; Hayes, C.T.; Hayes, H.; Hayes, N.A.; Hayes, R.; Hayhow, S.; Hayhow, S.J.; Hayhurst, S.; Haylers, J.; Hayman, P.V.; Haynes, A.; Haynes, J.; Haynes, P.G.; Haynes, W.J.; Haysom, S.P.; Hayter, S.; Hayter, T.; Hayward, H.H.S.; Hayward, I.; Haywood, D.; Haywood, P.; Hazel, J.; Hazelhurst, G.; Hazell, M.; Hazelwood, A.; Hazelwood, P.; Hazlehurst, G.; Head, M.; Heading, J.; Headley, A.D.; Healey, A.; Healey, B.; Healey, D.; Healey, M.J.; Heap, J.R.; Heard, J.; Heardman, C.; Hearle, A.; Hearle, S.; Hearn, J.; Hearton, J.; Heath, A.; Heath, D.; Heath, J.; Heath, K.; Heath, M.; Heath, P.; Heath, P.J.; Heath, R.; Heathcote, P.; Heather, B.; Heaton, A.; Heaven, K.; Heaver, D.J.; Hediger, E.J.; Hedley, B.; Heery, S.; Hefferan, S.; Heighway, P.; Heijboer, I.; Helison, H.E.; Hellier, K.; Helps, J.; Hemington, G.; Hemingway, D.G.; Hemingway, M.; Hemming, R.; Hemmings, T.; Hemsley, J.H.; Henden,A.; Henderson, A.; Henderson, F.; Henderson, G.; Henderson, L.; Henderson, M.; Henderson, R.; Henderson, T.W.; Hendrie, S.; Hendry, C.H.; Henrickson, L.; Henry, C.; Henry, M.; Henry, N.; Henry, R.; Henson, H.E.; Henson, N.; Henton, A.; Henty, C.J.; Hepinstall, D.; Hepper, D.; Herbert, C.; Herbert, I.; Herbert, J.; Herbert, R.; Herd, D.; Herlihy, D.J.; Heron, K.; Herring, C.M.; Herring, D.H.; Herring, H.; Herring, J.; Herring, J.L.; Herrington, J.; Hersey-Green, G.; Hesketh, I.; Hesketh, R.; Heslop-Harrison, G.; Heslop-Harrison, J.; Heslop-Mullens, M.; Heward, D.; Hewer, T.F.; Hewetson, A.; Hewitson, D.; Hewitt, D.; Hewitt, D.J.; Hewitt, J.; Hewitt, P.M.; Hewitt, R.; Hewitt, S.; Hewitt, S.M.; Hewlett, J.; Hewson, F.; Hewson, R.; Hextell, T.; Hey, A.; Hey, W.C.; Heyes, V.; Heywood, P.; Hiatt, S.; Hibbard, M.; Hibberd, G.; Hickerton, J.; Hickin, N.E.; Hickling, M.; Hickman, A.E.D.; Hickman, B.; Hicks, B.; Hicks, J.; Hicks, L.; Hickson, D.; Hickson, R.G.; Hider, M.; Higgins, B.; Higgins, D.; Higgins, J.; Higgins, M.; Higgins, N.; Higgins, R.C.; Higginson, I.; Higginson, J.; Higginson-Tranter, D.; Higgott, J.; Higgott, J.B.; Higgs, A.B.; Higgs, C.; Higgs, F.; Higgs, G.; Higham, C.; Higham, D.; Highest, J.; Highfield, C.; Hignett, J.; Hignett, S.; Higson, C.; Hiley, A.; Hiley, P.; Hill, A.; Hill, A.A.; Hill, A.G.; Hill, C.; Hill, D.; Hill, G.; Hill, H.; Hill, I.; Hill, J.E.; Hill, L.A.; Hill, P.; Hill, P.J.; Hill, P.M.; Hill, P.P.; Hill, P.S.; Hill, R.N.; Hill, T.; Hillcox, P.; Hillier, H.; Hillier, M.; Hills, S.G.; Hillyer, P.; Hilton, D.; Hilyer, C.; Hince, T.; Hinchcliffe, G.; Hinchcliffe, K.; Hinchcliffe, P.; Hinchcliffe, Z.; Hinchon, G.; Hincks, W.D.; Hind, H.; Hind, M.; Hind, N.; Hind, S.; Hind, S.H.; Hindhaugh, R.; Hindle, D.; Hindle, J.; Hine, A.; Hinks, J.; Hinks, P.; Hintermann, U.; Hinton, J.; Hintze, W.; Hipkin, C.; Hipkin, H.; Hipkin, M.; Hipkin, P.; Hipperson, D.; Hirani, K.; Hirst, W.R.; Hirsthouse, D.; Hitchcock, G.; Hitchcock, G.R.; Hitchcock, J.; Hitckcock, G.; Hnatiuk, M.; Hoare, D.; Hoare, J.; Hobart, D.; Hobart, J.; Hobbs, A.; Hobbs, J.G.; Hobbs, R.; Hobbs, T.; Hobson, D.; Hobson, D.G.; Hobson, G.; Hobson, M.; Hockin, R.; Hocking, B.; Hocking, G.B.; Hodge, P.; Hodge, P.J.; Hodge, T.; Hodge, V.; Hodgers, D.; Hodges, G.; Hodges, J.E.; Hodges, L.; Hodges, M.; Hodges, M.G.; Hodges, P.; Hodges, R.; Hodges, S.; Hodgetts, N.G.; Hodgkins, J.; Hodgkins, J.L.; Hodgkinson, M.; Hodgkinson, R.F.; Hodgson, C.; Hodgson, I.; Hodgson, J.B.; Hodgson, K.; Hodgson, R.; Hodgson, S.B.; Hodkinson, B.; Hodkinson, G.; Hodson, A.;

Hodson, J.; Hoekstra, P.; Hoff, K.; Hogan, D.; Hogan, M.; Hogarth, B.; Hogarth, L.; Hogg, A.; Hogg, J.; Hogg, M.; Hogg, S.; Hoines, P.H.; Holcombe, A.; Holcombe, B.; Hold, A.; Hold, A.I.; Holden, C.R.; Holden, P.; Holden, R.; Holder, A.; Holder, J.; Holding, D.; Holding, M.; Holdsworth, J.; Holdsworth, S.; Hole, J.; Holehouse, M.; Holford, N.; Holland, B.; Holland, J.; Holland, M.; Holland, P.H.; Holland, R.; Holland, S.; Holland, S.C.; Holland, W.; Holliday, J.; Holliday, P.; Holliday, P.H.; Holliday, S.; Holliday, T.; Holling, M.; Hollingdale, J.; Hollingworth, B.; Hollingworth, L.; Holloway, A.; Holloway, D.; Holloway, L.; Holloway, M.; Holloway, R.; Hollowday, E.D.; Hollows, R.; Holman, D.; Holme, R.; Holmes, A.; Holmes, B.; Holmes, E.; Holmes, J.; Holmes, J.D.; Holmes, J.S.; Holmes, J.W.D.; Holmes, L.; Holmes, M.; Holmes, P.; Holmes, P.R.; Holmes, S.; Holmes-Smith, N.; Holt, D.; Holt, M.; Holt, P.; Holt, S.; Holtby, A.; Holtby, K.; Holterman, S.; Holton, N.; Holyfield, S.; Holzer, T.J.; Hom, G.; Homan, R.; Homes, A.; Honeywell, W.; Hook, B.; Hooker, T.; Hooper, A.; Hooson, J.; Hooton, A.; Hooton, G.P.; Hope Jones, P.; Hope, C.; Hope, H.B.; Hope, J.; Hope, P.; Hopewell, A.; Hopewell, B.; Hopgood, D.; Hopkin, S.; Hopkins, D.; Hopkins, G.; Hopkins, G.W.; Hopkins, P.; Hopton, M.; Hopwood, G.; Horan, A.; Horder, A.; Horder, H.; Horlock, M.; Horlor, M.; Hornby, D.; Hornby, M.; Hornby, P.; Hornby, R.J.; Horne, C.; Horne, F.; Horne, J.; Horne, J.M.; Horne, R.W.; Horne, S.; Horner, D.; Horsburgh, L.; Horsefield, A.; Horsefield, D.; Horsfall, A.; Horsnail, P.; Horton, C.; Horton, D.; Horton, G.A.N.; Horton, K.; Horton, P.J.; Hosking, C.F.; Houghton, A.; Houghton, J.; Houghton, J.T.; Houghton, P.; Houghton, S.; House, A.; House, S.; Housman, T.; How, J.; Howard, G.; Howard, L.; Howard, P.; Howard, R.; Howard, S.; Howarth, S.; Howdon, D.; Howe, C.; Howe, E.A.; Howe, J.; Howe, L.; Howe, M.A.; Howe, S.; Howe, S.R.; Howear, P.; Howell, A.C.; Howell, J.; Howells, G.; Howells, L.T.; Howes, C.; Howes, C.A.; Howes, M.; Howes, P.; Howie, A.; Howland, M.; Howlett, D.; Howorth, R.; Hows, M.; Howsham, T.; Howson, J.; Hoyos, E.; Hubball, T.; Hubbard, A.; Hubbard, A.C.; Hubbard, R.; Hubble, D.; Hubbold, A.; Hubbold, S.M.; Huckbody, A.; Hudson, C.; Hudson, J.; Hudson, L.; Hudson, M.; Hudson, N.; Hudson, P.; Hughes, A.; Hughes, C.; Hughes, D.; Hughes, E.; Hughes, H.; Hughes, H.J.; Hughes, H.V.; Hughes, J.; Hughes, J.D.; Hughes, M.; Hughes, M.R.; Hughes, N.; Hughes, P.; Hughes, R.; Hughes, R.A.D.; Hughes, S.; Hughes, T.; Hugheston-Roberts, S.; Hugo, P.; Hulbert, D.; Hull, C.; Hull, E.; Hull, J.E.; Hull, S.; Hulme, D.C.; Hulme, G.; Hulme, I.; Hulme, N.; Hulme, S.; Hulse, H.; Hulson, J.; Hume, J.; Humphrey, C.; Humphrey, J.; Humphreys, B.; Humphreys, J.; Humphreys, L.; Humphreys, M.; Humpidge, R.; Hunley, M.P.; Hunnisett, J.; Hunt, A.; Hunt, D.; Hunt, G.; Hunt, J.; Hunt, J.P.; Hunt, M.; Hunt, M.S.; Hunt, N.; Hunt, N.V.; Hunt, S.; Hunter, A.; Hunter, B.; Hunter, E.; Hunter, G.; Hunter, I.; Hunter, J.; Hunter, K.; Hunter, M.; Hunter, N.; Hunter, S.; Hurford, C.; Hurley, J.; Hurst, A.; Hurst, D.; Hurst, J.; Hursthouse, D.; Hurt, P.; Husk, B.; Huskisson, R.; Hussey, H.; Huston, K.; Hutcheson, M.; Hutchings, A.; Hutchings, A.R.; Hutchinson, G.; Hutchinson, L.; Hutson, T.; Hutt, D.; Hutton, D.; Hutton, J.; Hutton, M.; Huxley, C.; Huxley, L.; Hyde, D.H.; Hyde, G.E.; Hyde, R.; Hyman, P.; Hymer, D.; Hynd, M.; Hynd, W.R.B.; Hynes, C.; Hynes, H.B.N.; Hyre, H.; Hyre, N.J.; Hyslop, A.I'Anson, P.; Iden, M.; Idle, A.; Ikin, H.; Iles, C.; Iles, D.; Iles, I.; Iles, J.; Iles, M.; Iles, S.; Iley, P.; Iliff, D.; Iliff, J.; Iliffe, J.; Iliffe, M.; Iliffe, R.; Ilott, T.; Imlach, J.; Imms, A.D.; Imms, A.W.; Inchliffe, S.; Ing, J.; Ingall, F.; Ingall, R.; Inglis, M.; Ingram, B.; Ingram, L.; Innes, M.; Inns, B.; Inskip, C.; Inskip, M.; Inskip, M.J.; Inskipp, T.; Install, C.; Ireland, C.; Ireland, D.; Ireland, D.T.; Ireland, L.; Ireland, M.; Ireland, P.; Irons, S.; Irven, D.; Irvine, A.; Irvine, C.; Irvine, N.; Irvine, R.; Irving, B.; Irving, D.; Irving, M.; Irving, P.; Irving, R.; Irving, S.; Irwin, A.G.; Ismay, J.W.; Ives, L.; Ives, R.; Ives, R.A.; Iveson, D.; Ivin, C.; Izzard, M.J.; Jack, G.; Jack, S.; Jackson, A.; Jackson, A.C.; Jackson, B.; Jackson, B.E.; Jackson, D.; Jackson, D.L.; Jackson, E.; Jackson, E.E.; Jackson, G.; Jackson, I.; Jackson, J.; Jackson, L.; Jackson, M.; Jackson, N.; Jackson, P.; Jackson, P.K.; Jackson, R.; Jackson, S.; Jackson, W.; Jacob, A.F.; Jacobs, A.; Jacobs, A.F.; Jacobs, C.; Jacobson, J.; Jacques, T.; Jaeger, M.; Jagger, D.; Jakeways, D.; Jakeways, R.; Jakubowski, S.; James, B.; James, C.; James, D.; James, F.; James, G.; James, H.; James, J.; James, K.; James, M.; James, P.; James, R.; James, T.; James, Z.; Jamieson, A.; Janes, R.; Janman, C.; Jannink, M.; Japheth, P.; Jaquin, P.; Jardine, D.C.; Jarman, N.; Jarman, R.; Jarman, R.B.; Jarvis, G.; Jarvis, L.; Jarvis, M.F.; Jarvis, N.; Jayne, A.; Jebbet, D.E.; Jeeves, B.V.; Jefferies, C.; Jefferies, D.; Jefferies, T.; Jeffers, A.; Jeffers, C.; Jeffers, D.; Jeffery, N.; Jeffes, M.; Jeffrey, A.; Jeffrey, C.; Jeffrey, P.; Jeffries, H.; Jeffries, M.; Jeffs, John F.; Jellet, S.; Jenkins, B.; Jenkins, D.K.; Jenkins, H.; Jenkins, J.; Jenkins, J.R.W.; Jenkins, R.; Jenkins, R.A.; Jenkins, S.; Jenks, P.; Jenner, G.; Jenner, H.E.;

Jennings, A.; Jennings, A.D.; Jennings, D.A.; Jennings, M.; Jennings, M.A.; Jennings, P.; Jennings, R.; Jennings, S.; Jennings, T.J.J.; Jennison, P.; Jenny, O.; Jenson, B.; Jenyns, L.; Jepson-Brown, C.; Jermyn, D.; Jermyn, T.; Jessop, L.; Jewell, D.; Jewsbury, L.; Jiggins, S.; Jinman, P.; Joaquin, A.; Jobe, J.B.; Jode, C.; Jode, D.; Jodicke, D.; John, A.D.; John, S.; Johnson, A.; Johnson, A.A.; Johnson, A.C.; Johnson, B.; Johnson, C.; Johnson, D.; Johnson, G.; Johnson, G.C.; Johnson, H.; Johnson, I.; Johnson, J.; Johnson, K.; Johnson, L.; Johnson, M.; Johnson, O.; Johnson, P.; Johnson, R.; Johnson, S.; Johnson, T.; Johnson, V.S.; Johnson, W.F.; Johnston, A.J.; Johnston, H.; Johnston, I.; Johnstone, I.; Johnstone, P.; Jollands, A.W.; Jones, A.; Jones, A.O.; Jones, B.; Jones, B.J.H.; Jones, C.; Jones, C.D.; Jones, C.E.; Jones, C.M.; Jones, C.R.; Jones, D.; Jones, D.G.; Jones, D.H.; Jones, E.; Jones, E.A.; Jones, F.; Jones, G.; Jones, G.H.; Jones, H.; Jones, H.P.; Jones, I.; Jones, J.; Jones, J.H.N.; Jones, J.L.; Jones, J.R.E.; Jones, K.; Jones, M.; Jones, M.R.; Jones, N.; Jones, N.W.; Jones, O.P.; Jones, P.; Jones, P.E.; Jones, P.S.; Jones, R.; Jones, R.A.; Jones, R.E.; Jones, R.H.; Jones, R.J.; Jones, S.; Jones, S.P.; Jones, T.; Jones, V.; Jones, W.; Jones, W.D.; Jones, W.R.; Jordan, H.; Jordan, J.; Jordan, T.; Jourdain, F.C.R.; Jowett, C.; Joy, J.; Judd, E.; Judd, K.; Judd, S.; Judge, S.; Jukes, C.; Julian, S.; Julier, R.; Juniper, B.E.; Jupp, C.; Justamond, M.; Justin, S.H.F.W.; K, J.B.; Kane, L.; Karran, A.; Kate, L.; Kavaliunas, V.; Kay, B.; Kay, D.; Kay, F.; Kay, I.; Kay, Q.O.N.; Kaye, Y.; Keane, R.; Kearns, N.; Keating, A.; Keats, M.; Keay, A.; Keedle, R.; Keeler, P.; Keeley, N.; Keeling, Y.; Keen, A.; Keen, B.; Keen, D.; Keen, L.; Keen, W.; Keenan, S.; Keeping, T.; Kefford, R.W.K.; Keighley, J.; Keighley, M.; Keightley, S.; Keiro, H.; Kelcey, J.G.; Kelham, A.; Kelly, A.; Kelly, C.; Kelly, F.; Kelly, H.M.; Kelly, M.; Kelly, P.; Kelly, R.; Kelly, T.; Kelsall, J.; Kelsey, M.; Kelsh, R.N.; Kemm, H.; Kemp, B.; Kemp, C.; Kemp, H.; Kemp, J.; Kemp, M.; Kemp, R.G.; Kemp, R.J.; Kemp, S.W.; Kemp, T.; Kemp-Gee, J.; Kempster, C.; Kendall, H.; Kendall, N.; Kendall, P.; Kendall, T.; Kennedy, A.; Kennedy, C.; Kennedy, D.; Kennedy, D.L.; Kennedy, K.; Kennedy, R.; Kennedy, S.; Kennedy, V.; Kennerley, J.; Kennerley, P.; Kennison, G.; Kennison, W.; Kenny, G.; Kenny, I.; Kent, D.; Keogh, G.; Keogh, J.; Keogh, N.; Keogh, T.; Kerby, M.; Kernohan, A.; Kernohan, J.; Kerr, J.; Kerr, P.; Kerry, J.C.; Kerry, L.; Kerry, S.; Kersey, R.; Kershaw, L.; Kervegant, D.; Kesby, J.; Keston, A.; Kett, S.M.; Kettell, M.; Kettle, A.; Kettle, R.; Kettle, R.H.; Keverne, J.L.; Key, H.A.S.; Key, R.S.; Keylock, J.G.; Keymer, I.F.; Keys, J.H.; Khan, R.J.; Kiauta, B.; Kilbey, D.; Kilgallen, L.; Killeby, M.; Killick, D.; Killick, J.; Killington, F.J.; Killips, N.; Kilner, M.; Kilroy, J.; Kilshaw, S.; Kimmins, D.E.; Kimpton, A.; Kincaid, M.; Kinder, M.; King, A.; King, D.; King, G.J.; King, J.J.F.X.; King, M.; King, N.; King, N.H.; King, P.; King, R.; King, S.S.; Kingham, D.; Kingham, D.I.; Kingham, D.L.; Kingscott, K.; Kingston, C.; Kinnear, P.; Kinnear, S.; Kinnings, E.; Kinsella, P.; Kinsey, M.; Kirby, B.; Kirby, C.; Kirby, F.; Kirby, M.; Kirby, M.A.; Kirby, P.; Kirby, P.K.; Kirk, J.; Kirk, K.; Kirk, P.; Kirk, S.; Kirk-Bell, S.; Kirkland, P.; Kirkwood, D.S.; Kitchen, C.; Kitchen, M.; Kitchener, P.; Kitcher, C.; Kitching, D.; Kitching, S.; Kitching, T.; Kite, D.; Kite, P.; Kittle, T.; Klymko, M.; Knaggs, A.; Knaggs, D.; Knapp, A.; Knapp, S.; Kneeshaw, J.; Knief, A.; Knight, A.; Knight, C.; Knight, D.; Knight, G.; Knight, J.; Knight, L.; Knight, M.; Knight, P.; Knight, R.; Knight, R.C.; Knight, S.; Knight, Terry D.; Knight, V.; Knights, K.; Knights, R.; Knill-Jones, J.W.; Knill-Jones, R.; Knill-Jones, S.; Knill-Jones, S.A.; Knipe, P.G.; Knisely-Marpole, R.; Knobbs, L.; Knott, H.; Knott, P.; Knott, R.A.; Knowler, J.; Knowler, John T.; Knowles, B.; Knowles, E.; Knox, A.G.; Kohli, M.; Kolodziejek, K.; Koops, J.; Kramer, J.; Krischkiw, P.; Kruszewska, I.; Kruys, I.P.; Kulzer, S.; Kumari, S.; Kwolek, A.; Kydd, B.; Kydd, D.W.; Kyle, D.; Kyme, B.; Labbett, R.; Labram, G.; Lack, J.; Laidlaw, W.B.; Laidler, W.R.; Laing, A.I.; Laing, C.; Laing, S.; Lainson, S.; Lakin, I.; Lally, T.; Lamacraft, D.; Lamb, A.R.; Lamb, J.; Lamb, R.; Lambert, D.; Lambert, I.; Lambert, L.; Lambert, N.; Lambert, R.; Lambert, S.J.J.; Lambeth, C.; Lambrick, C.; Lambrick, C.R.; Laming, H.; Lampard, D.J.; Lampert, N.; Lancaster, P.; Land, D.; Land, H.; Landais, J.; Lane, A.; Lane, A.S.; Lane, C.; Lane, C.J.; Lane, D.; Lane, J.; Lane, R.J.; Lane, S.; Lane, S.A.; Lane, T.; Laney, B.; Laney, T.J.; Lang, I.; Lang, W.D.; Langdon, R.; Langford, J.; Langford, R.; Langham, C.; Langhelt, L.; Langhorne, J.; Langman, M.; Langois, D.; Langton, J.; Langton, P.; Lankester, S.; Lansbury, I.; Lansdell, E.; Lansdown, M.; Lansdown, R.; Lansdown, R.V.; Lansdowne, S.; Lappin, P.; Larcombe, P.; Large, P.; Larkin, P.; Larner, P.; Larsen, H.; Larter, M.; Larter, M.J.; Lashley, B.; Last, W.G.; Latham, C.; Latham, H.A.; Latham, M.; Latham, P.; Latimer, B.; Latty, B.; Lauder, A.; Lauderdale, J.; Laugher, R.C.; Laurie, G.; Laverick, J.; Laverick, M.; Lavers, N.; Lavery, J.; Law, A.; Law, C.; Law, D.; Law, J.; Law, Y.; Lawley, M.; Lawman, J.; Lawrence, A.; Lawrence, B.; Lawrence, M.C.; Lawrence, R.; Lawrence, T.; Lawrie, C.; Lawrie, I.; Lawrie, J.; Lawrie, L.;

Lawrie, T.; Laws, T.; Lawson, A.; Lawson, M.; Lawton, A.; Lawton, H.; Lawton, J.H.; Laycock, H.; Lazenby, A.S.; Le Gros, A.; Le Masurier, P.C.; LeCorre, I.; LeQuesne, W.J.; Lea, E.; Lea, K.; Lea, R.; Lea, V.; Leach, E.; Leach, H.; Leach, S.J.; Leach, T.; Leach, W.E.; Leadbetter, D.; Leadbetter, M.; Leader, C.F.; Leadley, J.; Leadsom, S.; Leaf, A.; Leamy, J.; Leaper, G.; Lear, N.; Leatham, B.; Leather, N.; Leaver, S.; Leavett, R.; Leavett, R.L.; Lecomber, E.W.; Ledbury, R.; Lee, A.; Lee, D.; Lee, E.; Lee, F.; Lee, I.; Lee, J.; Lee, M.; Lee, P.; Lee, R.; Lee, T.; Leece, J.; Leece, J.M.; Leech, D.; Leel, G.; Leeming, D.; Leeming, D.J.; Leeming, N.M.; Lees, A.; Lees, A.J.; Lees, B.; Lees, J.; Leftwich, A.; Legg, A.W.; Legg, K.; Legg, M.; Leggat, K.; Legge, C.; Leicester, P.; Leicester, R.; Leigh, A.; Leighton, C.; Leighton, D.; Leitch, A.J.; Lelliott, T.; Lemmon, R.; Lemmon, T.; Lemoine, F.; Lemon, S.; Lemon, T.; Lenham, S.; Lenton, E.; Leonard, E.; Lerpiniere, J.; Lerwill, K.; Leslie, J.F.; Leslie, M.; Lester, D.; Leszczynski, E.; Letsche, R.; Leven, M.; Levene, J.; Levett, S.; Levis, J.; Levy, B.G.; Levy, C.; Levy, D.; Levy, E.T.; Levy, T.; Lewington, I.; Lewington, R.; Lewis, B.; Lewis, C.; Lewis, D.; Lewis, D.A.; Lewis, D.C.; Lewis, G.; Lewis, G.E.; Lewis, J.; Lewis, M.; Lewis, M.A.; Lewis, M.J.; Lewis, N.; Lewis, P.; Lewis, R.; Lewis, S.; Lewis, W.J.; Leyshon, O.J.; Liddell, E.; Liddell, G.P.; Liddell, P.; Liddell, T.; Lidford, R.; Lidstone-Scott, R.; Liford, G.; Liford, R.; Liford, R.G.; Lightfoot, G.; Lightfoot, K.E.; Lightfoot, R.; Lightley, G.; Liley, M.; Lilley, G.; Limb, K.; Limb, P.; Limb, P.A.; Limbrey, S.; Linch, J.R.; Linden, K.; Lindley, C.; Lindsay, M.; Linehan, M.; Linfield, R.; Ling, S.; Linnett, P.; Linney, F.; Lintin Smith, J.; Linton, I.; List, G.P.; Lister, J.; Lister, J.A.; Lister, K.; Lister, P.; Lister, S.M.; Lister, T.; Liston, A.; Litherland, A.; Litjens, M.; Little, B.; Little, C.; Little, D.; Little, R.; Little, S.P.; Little, W.; Littlewood, N.; Littlewood, S.D.; Lively, M.; Livingstone, A.; Livingstone, D.; Lloyd Thomas, D.; Lloyd, B.; Lloyd, D.; Lloyd, D.F.; Lloyd, H.; Lloyd, S.; Lloyd-Evans, L.; Lloyd-Morgan, G.; Lloyd-Rogers, C.; Lloyd-Williams, J.; Lloyds, J.; Loan, A.; Loates, H.; Lock, L.; Lock, M.A.; Lock, N.; Lockhart, S.; Lockton, A.; Lockton, A.G.; Lockton, A.J.; Lockwood, B.; Lockwood, R.G.; Loder, J.; Lofthouse, T.A.; Logan, N.; Logan, P.; Lomass, I.; Long, A.G.; Long, D.; Longe, D.; Longfield, C.; Longfield, C.E.; Longman, L.; Lonsdale, I.; Lonsdale, L.; Lonsdale, S.; Loose, S.; Looser, A.; Lopato, R.; Lorand, S.; Lorber, P.; Lord, D.J.; Lord, J.; Lord, P.M.; Lothian, D.; Lott, D.A.; Louch, C.S.; Lovatt, J.; Love, L.; Love, M.; Lovegrove, K.; Lovell, S.; Loven, N.; Lovering, I.; Low, M.; Lowe, A.; Lowe, B.; Lowe, C.; Lowe, G.; Lowe, N.; Lowe, P.A.; Lowen, J.; Lowenstein, T.; Lowlings, P.; Lowmass, C.D.; Loxton, R.G.; Lucas, A.; Lucas, B.; Lucas, C.; Lucas, J.; Lucas, M.J.; Lucas, S.; Lucas, W.J.; Lucey, J.; Luck, B.; Luck, H.; Luck, J.; Luckhurst, F.; Lucking, R.; Lucy, E.; Ludlow, H.; Ludwig, D.; Lugg, K.; Lumb, D.; Lumm, D.S.F.; Lundy, V.; Lunn, C.; Lunn, J.; Lupton, P.; Lush, M.; Lusted, C.; Lutley, W.; Lycett, I.; Lyden, J.; Lynas, P.; Lynch, A.; Lynch, C.; Lynch, D.; Lynch, J.; Lynch, S.; Lynes, M.; Lynham, T.; Lynn, C.; Lyon, R.; Lyons, C.; Lyons, G.; Lyons, J.; Lysaght, L.S.; Lyszkowski, R.M.; Lythall, C.; M, M.; MaClean, G.A.; Maas, D.; MacAdam, C.; MacAlpine-Leny, I.; MacDonald, A.; MacDonald, L.; MacDonald, M.; MacDonald, M.A.; MacFarlane Smith, D.; MacGowan, I.; MacGregor, R.; MacIntyre, A.; MacIntyre, N.; MacIver, M.R.; MacKay, A.; MacKay, J.; MacKenzie Dodds, R.; MacKenzie, J.; MacLaughlin, S.; MacLean, C.; MacLean, G.; MacLennan, A.; MacLeod, C.; MacLeod, I.; MacMaster, A.; MacNaughton, F.; MacNeill, N.; MacPherson, F.; MacRae, F.; MacRitchie, B.; MacRitchie, D.; MacVicar, S.M.; Macan, T.T.; Macdonald, B.; Macdonald, R.; Macefield, M.; Macho, I.; Mackay, A.J.; Mackenzie, E.; Mackenzie, N.; Mackenzie, S.; Mackenzie-Dodds, R.; Mackey, B.; Mackie, J.; Mackie, S.; Mackindlay, V.; Mackinlay, L.; Mackinnon, M.; Macklin, R.; Macklin, R.N.; Mackonochie, A.G.; Mackrill, E.; Mackrill, M.; Mackworth-Praed, C.; Maclaurin, A.M.; Maclennan, D.; Macleod, B.; Macrory, M.; Madden, J.; Maddison, P.; Maddock, J.; Maddox, M.; Madge, G.; Madge, S.C.; Madgett, P.; Madin, D.; Magee, G.; Magee, J.; Mager, R.; Maggs, H.; Magnay, A.; Maguire, T.; Mahon, A.; Mahoney, G.; Mahoney, R.; Mahony, R.H.; Mahood, A.; Maiboroda, O.; Maiden, J.; Maidment, C.; Maidstone, R.; Mail, D.; Main, J.; Main, N.; Mainland, D.; Mainstone, C.P.; Mainwaring, D.; Mair, P.; Maisey, A.C.; Maitland, F.; Maitland, G.; Maitland, P.S.; Makeham, A.; Makepeace, S.; Maker, P.; Malard, F.; Malcolm, A.; Malecki, M.; Males, P.; Malet, J.; Mallam, N.J.; Mallet, J.; Malley, A.; Mallinson, L.; Malpass, A.; Malton, N.; Mann, A.J.; Mann, D.J.; Mann, E.M.; Mann, P.; Mann, R.; Mann, R.B.; Mann, S.; Manners, J.; Manning, L.; Manning, R.; Manns, L.; Mansell, A.; Mansfield, D.; Manson, J.; Manson, P.; Manson, S.; Mansson, M.; Manthorpe, J.; Mapplebeck, P.; Marchais, G.; Marchant, J.H.; Marchant, P.; Mardle, D.V.; Marginson, M.; Margot, M.; Marjoram, K.; Marking, J.; Marks, M.; Marks, O.; Markwell, H.;

Marland, A.; Marler, A.; Marmont, A.M.; Marnell, F.; Marole, M.V.; Marquand, E.D.; Marrable, C.; Marren, P.R.; Marriott, D.; Marriott, R.W.; Marrs, B.; Marrs, S.; Marsden, G.; Marsdon, S.; Marsey, C.; Marsh, A.; Marsh, E.; Marsh, L.; Marsh, M.; Marsh, M.C.; Marsh, P.; Marsh, P.J.; Marshall, A.; Marshall, D.; Marshall, H.; Marshall, J.; Marshall, K.; Marshall, L.; Marshall, M.; Marshall, P.; Marshall, R.; Marshall, T.; Marshall, T.F.; Marshall, V.; Marsham, M.; Marston, A.; Marston, K.; Martin, A.; Martin, B.; Martin, C.; Martin, D.; Martin, G.; Martin, H.J.; Martin, J.; Martin, J.C.; Martin, J.P.; Martin, K.; Martin, L.J.; Martin, M.; Martin, N.; Martin, N.A.; Martin, P.; Martin, R.; Martin, S.; Martin, S.A.; Martin, S.J.; Martin, T.; Martin, T.G.; Martineau, A.H.; Masefield, W.; Mash, K.; Masheder, R.; Maskell, J.; Maskell, S.; Maskew, R.; Maskrey, J.; Maslen, R.; Mason, C.; Mason, C.F.; Mason, D.; Mason, J.; Mason, J.L.; Mason, J.M.; Mason, N.; Mason, P.; Mason, R.; Massee, A.M.; Massey, K.; Massey, M.; Massey, P.; Massie, S.; Massini, P.; Masson, J.; Masters, P.; Maston, D.; Matcham, C.; Matcham, H.; Mather, J.R.; Mathers, B.; Mathers, M.; Mathers, P.; Matheson, E.; Mathew, N.; Mathews, B.; Mathews, V.; Mathias, J.; Mathias, J.H.; Matlock, B.; Matson, D.; Matthew, N.R.; Matthews, B.; Matthews, D.; Matthews, J.; Matthews, L.; Matthews, M.; Matthews, M.G.; Matthews, N.; Matthews, R.; Matthews, S.; Mattingley, W.; Matusavage, A.; Maude, D.; Maughan, C.; Maughan, E.; Maughan, M.; Maurice, K.; Mawby, F.J.; Mawby, S.; Mawdsley, T.H.; Mawhinney, K.; Mawkin, S.; Mawson, H.A.P.; Mawson, M.; Maxey, D.; Maxfield, B.; Maxwell, A.; Maxwell, J.; Maxwell, K.; Maxwell, S.; May, D.; May, G.E.; May, M.; May, R.F.; May, T.; Maycock, R.; Mayer, D.; Mayes, C.; Mayes, T.; Mayhead, J.; Mayhew, P.J.; Mayo, M.C.A.; McAdam, G.; McAllister, D.; McAlone, D.; McAvoy, C.; McAvoy, S.; McBain, A.; McBeath, R.; McBurney, L.; McCabe, E.; McCabe, K.; McCabe, L.; McCallum, J.; McCann, D.; McCann, E.; McCann, J.; McCarrick, D.; McCarrick, M.; McCarron, L.; McCarthy, R.; McCarthy, W.N.; McCarty, C.; McCarty, H.; McCleary, J.; McCleary, J.A.J.; McClellan, R.D.; McClure, C.; McColl, A.; McColl, G.; McColl, I.; McComb, A.; McConnell, A.; McConville, A.; McConville, D.; McConway, J.; McCormack, L.K.; McCormack, S.; McCormick, D.; McCormick, P.; McCraw, D.A.; McCreaddie, G.; McCutcheon, D.E.; McDevitt, A.; McDonald, A.; McDonald, G.; McDonald, I.; McDonald, J.; McDonald, S.; McDonnell, I.; McDougall, R.; McDowall, A.; McElheron, A.; McElwaine, G.; McEwan, C.; McEwan, D.; McEwen, E.; McEwen, K.; McFarlan, C.; McFarland, V.M.; McFarlane, A.; McFaul, L.; McFerran, A.; McFerran, D.; McFerran, K.; McGann, M.; McGee, A.; McGee, K.; McGeehan, G.; McGeeney, A.; McGibbon, R.; McGill, M.; McGillivray, J.; McGinn, A.; McGinty, M.; McGovern, A.; McGrath, D.; McGreal, E.; McGregor, C.; McGregor, J.M.; McGregor, T.M.; McGuire, R.; McGurn, P.; McHaffie, P.; McHale, R.; McHugh, E.; McHugh, G.; McHugh, M.; McHugh, P.; McIntosh, J.; McIntosh, L.; McIntosh, L.K.; McIntyre, C.; McKay, C.; McKay, D.; McKean, H.; McKee, N.D.; McKellar, J.; McKelvery, S.A.; McKelvey, S.A.; McKenzie, D.; McKenzie, S.; McKeown, R.; McKerchar, H.; McKillop, R.; McKimm, J.; McKinlay, E.; McKircher, H.B.; McLachlan, R.; McLaggan, A.H.; McLamb, S.; McLaren, J.; McLaughlin, R.; McLean, C.; McLean, I.F.G.; McLeary, J.; McLellan, A.; McLellan, E.; McLellan, J.; McLellan, K.; McLeod, C.E.; McLeod, C.R.; McLoughlin, M.; McLoughlin, V.; McLure, J.; McMahon, N.; McManus, S.; McMillan, J.; McMillan, N.F.; McMullen, M.; McMullin, A.S.; McNair, V.J.; McNamee, M.; McNaughton, G.; McNaughton, J.; McNeill, D.; McNeill, I.; McNeill, S.; McNicholas, D.; McNiven, D.; McOnie, R.J.; McOustra, A.; McQueen, D.; McRae, S.; McSherry, B.; McVeigh, A.; McWilliam, S.; Mckelvey, J.; Mckie, M.; Mclaren, N.; Mead, D.; Meadows, A.; Meakin, T.; Meakins, M.; Mearns, B.; Mearns, J.; Mearns, R.; Measday, A.V.; Measures, D.; Meddins, C.; Medley, R.; Medlock, J.; Mee, J.; Meehan, T.; Meek, E.; Meek, W.; Meers, P.; Megson, G.; Meharg, M.; Meiklejohn, J.; Meiners, P.; Meinhardt, K.; Melhuish, C.; Mella, P.; Melling, T.; Mellings, J.; Mellish, C.; Mellon, C.; Mellor, D.G.; Mellor, M.J.; Mellor, S.D.; Mellows, B.; Mellstrom, L.; Melrose, W.; Melvill, J.C.; Melville, S.; Memory, M.; Mendel, H.; Mendum, T.; Menendez, C.T.; Menichino, N.; Mercer, A.; Mercer, J.; Meredith, G.; Meredith, G.H.; Meredith, J.; Meredith, P.; Merrett, C.M.; Merrett, P.; Merrick, L.; Merrifield, K.; Merrifield, R.K.; Merrill, I.; Merritt, A.; Merritt, R.; Merritt, W.; Merritts, B.; Merry, D.G.; Messa, S.; Messenger, J.; Messinger, A.; Metcalf, F.; Metcalfe, J.W.W.; Methven, D.; Michael, P.; Michaelis, H.N.; Michell, P.; Michelmore, A.P.G.; Michie, B.; Micklewright, S.; Middle, C.; Middleton, A.; Middleton, B.; Middleton, H.; Middleton, J.; Middleton, K.; Middleton, M.; Middleton, R.; Mielcarek, R.; Mighell, J.; Milbank, S.; Milbourne, N.; Milburn, K.; Miles, E.; Miles, J.; Miles, P.M.; Mileto, R.; Milford, P.; Milford, P.J.; Mill, P.J.;

Millard, J.; Millard, T.; Millbank, L.; Miller, A.; Miller, B.; Miller, C.; Miller, D.; Miller, J.; Miller, J.E.; Miller, K.; Miller, K.W.; Miller, Keith F.; Miller, N.; Miller, P.; Miller, P.L.; Miller, R.; Miller, S.; Miller, Y.; Millet, M.; Milligan, Z.; Millington, C.; Millington, S.; Mills, A.; Mills, C.; Mills, D.; Mills, J.; Mills, R.H.; Mills, S.; Milne, B.S.; Milne, E.; Milne, S.; Milne-Redhead, E.; Milner, G.; Milnes, D.; Milnes, J.N.; Milton, F.; Milton, J.; Minchin, M.F.; Minett, C.; Mingin, A.; Mingin, P.; Minihane, J.; Minshall, J.; Minshull, B.; Misselbrook, I.; Mist, B.; Mitchel, D.; Mitchell, B.; Mitchell, B.R.; Mitchell, D.; Mitchell, E.; Mitchell, G.; Mitchell, J.; Mitchell, M.; Mitchell, N.; Mitchell, O.; Mitchell, P.; Mitchell, P.J.; Mitchell, R.; Mitchell, S.; Mitchell, S.H.; Mobarak, J.; Mocroft, S.; Moffat, C.B.; Moffatt, A.T.; Moffatt, B.; Moffatt, F.X.; Moffet, A.; Moir, M.; Mole, S.; Moles, S.; Molly, M.; Moloney, K.; Molyneaux, T.; Molyneux, J.; Monaghan, D.; Monaghan, V.J.; Monckton, S.; Money, J.; Money, S.; Monk, D.; Monk-Terry, M.; Monteith, G.; Montford, A.R.; Moodie, T.; Moody, J.; Moon, A.V.; Moon, H.P.; Moon, J.; Moon, P.; Moon, S.; Moon, S.J.; Moonesay, J.; Mooney, K.; Moorcroft, J.; Moore, B.P.; Moore, C.; Moore, D.; Moore, F.; Moore, H.; Moore, I.; Moore, J.J.; Moore, K.; Moore, K.F.; Moore, L.; Moore, M.; Moore, N.; Moore, N.W.; Moore, P.; Moore, R.; Moore, T.; Moores, C.; Moorhouse, C.; Moorhouse, J.; Moralee, A.K.; Moralee, S.; Moran, S.A.; Moreton, B.D.; Moreton, S.; Morgan, A.; Morgan, D.; Morgan, E.; Morgan, G.; Morgan, H.; Morgan, I.; Morgan, I.K.; Morgan, J.; Morgan, J.E.; Morgan, K.; Morgan, L.; Morgan, M.; Morgan, M.J.; Morgan, N.; Morgan, P.; Morgan, S.A.C.; Morgan, Y.; Moriarity, C.; Morison, D.; Morland, K.; Morley, C.; Morley, D.; Morley, M.; Morris, A.; Morris, C.; Morris, G.J.; Morris, J.; Morris, K.; Morris, L.; Morris, M.; Morris, N.; Morris, P.; Morris, R.; Morris, R.K.M.; Morris, W.; Morrisey, D.; Morrisey, R.; Morrison, A.; Morrison, C.; Morrison, D.; Morrison, J.; Morrison, K.; Morrison, M.; Morrison, P.; Morrison, R.; Morrow, C.; Morss, J.R.; Mortimer, A.; Mortimer, C.; Mortimer, D.; Mortimer, E.; Mortimer, G.; Mortimer, N.; Mortimer, R.; Mortin, J.; Morton, A.J.; Morton, C.; Morton, J.A.; Morton, K.J.; Morton, K.V.F.; Morton, M.; Morton, R.; Morton, W.; Moscrop, C.; Moseley, C.; Moseley, K.; Moseley, K.A.; Mosely, M.E.; Mosley, S.L.; Moss, A.; Moss, N.; Motley, G.S.; Mott, N.; Mott, S.; Mottershead, J.; Mottishaw, J.; Mouland, D.; Mould, A.; Mould, J.; Moulton, C.; Mounsey, J.; Mountain, P.; Mousley, J.; Moverley, T.; Mowat, M.; Mower, D.M.; Mowle, S.; Moxom, D.; Moxon, L.; Moyle, E.K.; Moyse, R.; Muckle, A.; Mudd, R.; Muddeman, J.L.; Muddiman, N.; Mugeridge, R.E.R.; Mugridge, P.; Muir, C.; Muldal, A.; Mulholland, M.; Mulholland, N.; Mulholland, R.; Mulkeen, C.; Mullarney, K.; Mullen, B.; Mullen, E.; Mullen, P.; Muller, A.; Muller, N.; Mullins, B.; Mumford-Smith, J.; Munday, S.; Mundell, A.R.; Mundy, A.V.; Mundy, R.; Murdoch, A.; Murdoch, D.; Murdoch, D.A.; Murdoch, P.; Murgatroyd, S.; Murphy, A.; Murphy, B.; Murphy, C.; Murphy, D.; Murphy, J.; Murphy, J.E.; Murphy, K.; Murphy, M.; Murphy, M.D.; Murphy, P.; Murphy, R.P.; Murphy, S.; Murray, A.M.; Murray, D.E.; Murray, J.; Murray, P.; Murray, R.; Murray, S.; Murray, S.D.C.; Murray, T.; Muscat, D.; Muschamp, J.H.; Muschamp, P.A.H.; Muscott, J.; Muscrop, C.; Muscrop, S.; Museum, L.; Musgrove, A.; Music, J.; Musley, M.P.; Mutch, M.; Muynck, A.; Mycock, R.J.; Myers, A.; Myerscough, M.; Myhill, C.; Nadin, J.; Nagle, T.; Nall, V.; Nash, C.; Nash, M.; Nash, R.; Nash, S.; Nathan, L.; Nattress, B.; Nau, B.S.; Naumanen, S.; Naylor, G.; Naylor, K.; Naylor, M.J.; Naylor, P.; Neal, E.G.; Neal, K.; Neal, R.; Neale, W.; Neate, T.; Neath, B.; Neath, J.; Needham, R.; Needham, T.; Neill, W.; Nelson, A.K.; Nelson, B.; Nelson, C.; Nelson, D.; Nelson, J.; Nelson, J.M.; Nelson, M.; Nelson, P.; Nelson, R.J.; Nelson, S.; Nelson, T.; Nelson, W.; Nelson, W.N.A.; Nesbitt, L.; Nesbitt, M.; Neuburger, T.; Neuman, C.; Nevett, W.; Neville, A.C.; Neville, D.; Neville, R.; New, S.; Newbold, C.; Newbould, J.; Newcombe, J.; Newlands, A.; Newman, A.; Newman, D.; Newman, E.; Newman, G.; Newman, L.; Newman, P.; Newsom Davis, D.E.; Newsome, M.; Newsone, M.; Newstead, S.; Newton, A.; Newton, A.H.; Newton, D.; Newton, G.E.; Newton, J.; Newton, R.J.; Newton, S.; Newton, T.; Neyland, P.; Nichol, C.; Nichol, R.; Nicholls, C.; Nicholls, D.; Nicholls, S.P.; Nicholson, A.; Nicholson, B.; Nicholson, D.; Nicholson, G.; Nicholson, J.; Nicholson, J.B.; Nicholson, N.W.; Nicholson, P.A.; Nicholson, R.; Nicholson, R.A.; Nicholson, S.; Nicol, P.; Nicol, V.M.; Nicole, C.S.; Nicolet, P.; Nielsen, M.; Nightingale, B.; Nightingale, S.; Nisbet, C.; Nisbet, G.; Nisbet, R.G.; Niven, E.; Nixon, A.; Nixon, D.; Nixon, V.; Noad, J.; Noakes, M.; Noar, L.; Nobbs, D.; Nobes, G.; Noble, C.; Noble, D.; Noble, K.; Noel, F.B.; Nolan, M.; Nolan, P.; Noonan, G.C.; Norgate, D.; Norgate, F.; Norledge, J.; Norman, A.; Norman, C.G.; Norman, D.; Norman, G.; Norman, M.J.; Norman, P.; Norman, S.; Norman, T.; Norris, A.; Norris, A.Y.; Norris, D.; Norris, P.; Norris, S.; Norriss, C.; Norriss, T.J.; Nortcott, P.; North, A.; North, A.J.; North, B.; North, M.; North, S.; Northridge, H.J.; Northridge, R.H.; Norton, F.; Norton, J.; Norton, J.A.; Norton, K.; Norwood, P.; Nottage, L.; Nottage, R.; Nottage, R.J.; Nottage, R.L.; Notton, D.G.; Nouvet, S.; Nowers, M.; Noyes, S.; Nugent, E.W.T.; Nundy, J.; Nunn, A.; Nunn, J.D.; Nuttall, D.; Nuttall, S.; Nutton, G.O'Brien, D.; O'Brien, J.; O'Brien, K.; O'Carroll, A.; O'Connell, C.; O'Connor, B.; O'Connor, J.P.; O'Connor, M.A.; O'Connor, T.; O'Donnell, M.; O'Donoghue, P.; O'Donovan, J.E.; O'Farrell, A.F.; O'Flanagan, C.; O'Hara, K.; O'Hare, F.; O'Hehir, S.; O'Keefe, K.; O'Keeffe, C.; O'Kell, M.; O'Leary, P.; O'Mahony, R.; O'Meara, M.; O'Meara, V.; O'Neil, M.A.; O'Neill, B.; O'Neill, J.; O'Neill, M.A.; O'Reilly, P.; O'Riley, J.; O'Riley, P.; O'Rourke, F.J.; O'Sullivan, D.J.; O'Sullivan, J.; O'Sullivan, M.; O'Sullivan, O.; O'Toole, C.; O'Toole, P.; O`Brien, J.; O`Dell, M.; O`Hagan, J.; O`Hara, R.S.; O`Neil, M.A.; O`Neill, M.; O`Toole, C.; Oakenfull, P.; Oakes, L.; Oakley, E.H.N.; Oakley-Martin, D.; Oates, J.; Oates, M.; Oates, P.; Ockenden, J.; Odell, D.; Odin, N.; Offer, D.; Ogilvie, M.; Ogilvie, W.A.; Ogilvy, S.; Okill, J.D.; Okines, D.; Oldfield, P.; Oldroyd, P.; Oleksy, B.; Olin, M.; Oliver, C.; Oliver, D.; Oliver, G.; Oliver, J.; Oliver, L.; Oliver, S.; Oliver, T.; Ollington, T.; Olliver, T.; Olozulu, M.; Olson, P.J.; Omand, D.; Onions, T.; Onslow, N.; Orange, A.; Orchard, A.; Orchard, N.; Orman, V.; Ormand, E.; Orme, B.; Ormerod, J.; Ormond, E.; Orpe, K.J.; Orr, E.; Orton, R.; Orton, T.; Osbaldeston, E.; Osborn, P.; Osborne, J.; Osborne, P.; Osbourne, R.; Osbourne, R.D.; Osley, N.J.; Osman, J.; Ostler, J.; Oswick, D.; Otsu, M.; Otter, J.; Ottley, A.; Ottley, T.; Outen, A.R.; Outram, T.; Overton, C.; Overton, S.; Owen, C.; Owen, C.M.; Owen, D.; Owen, D.M.; Owen, J.; Owen, J.A.; Owen, J.H.; Owen, R.; Owen, R.A.; Owsianka, B.; Oxborrow, B.; Oxenham, J.; Oxenham, J.V.; Pacey, N.; Packer, J.; Packer, L.; Packham, J.; Page, A.E.; Page, C.; Page, J.; Page, M.; Page, P.; Page, S.; Paget, C.J.; Pain, D.; Pain, J.; Paine, B.; Painter, D.; Pait, H.; Palfrey, M.J.; Palin, S.; Palmer, C.; Palmer, D.; Palmer, D.C.; Palmer, E.; Palmer, G.; Palmer, I.; Palmer, L.; Palmer, L.E.; Palmer, L.G.; Palmer, M.; Palmer, M.A.; Palmer, Q.; Palmer, R.; Palmer, S.; Palmer, T.; Palmer, T.W.; Pandolfi, F.; Pankhurst, L.; Pankhurst, R.; Pankhurst, T.; Panter, A.; Panter, G.; Paradine, I.; Pardy, V.; Parfitt, A.; Parfitt, M.; Parfitt, S.; Parker, A.; Parker, A.J.; Parker, A.P.; Parker, B.; Parker, B.N.; Parker, D.; Parker, D.M.; Parker, J.; Parker, J.E.; Parker, J.I.; Parker, M.; Parker, P.; Parker, R.; Parker, T.N.; Parkes, K.; Parkhurst, J.; Parkin, G.; Parkin, J.; Parkinson, A.; Parkinson, D.W.; Parkinson, H.D.A.; Parkinson, L.; Parks, R.; Parmenter, D.; Parmenter, J.; Parmenter, L.; Parmenter, T.; Parnwell, S.; Parr, A.J.; Parr, M.J.; Parr, T.; Parrack, J.D.; Parrott, A.L.; Parry, C.; Parry, D.; Parry, G.; Parry, J.; Parry, P.; Parslow, J.; Parslow, M.; Parslow, R.; Parsons, A.J.; Parsons, D.; Parsons, E.; Parsons, K.; Parsons, L.; Parsons, M.; Parsons, P.; Parsons, R.M.; Parsons, T.; Parsons, V.; Partington, I.; Partridge, J.; Partridge, N.; Partridge, R.; Partridge, V.; Passant, M.; Passey, L.; Paston, S.; Pate, D.; Patel, N.; Paternoster, J.; Paterson, C.; Paterson, D.; Paterson, G.; Paterson, H.; Patient, R.; Patmore, J.; Patmore, S.; Paton, G.; Paton, L.; Paton, V.S.; Patrick, D.; Patrick, E.; Patrick, E.W.; Patterson, D.; Pattinson, R.; Pattison, P.; Patton, L.; Patton, P.; Patton, S.; Paul, C.; Paul, H.; Paul, J.; Paul, L.; Paul, M.; Paul, M.F.; Paull, D.; Pavett, J.; Pavett, P.M.; Pawlett, D.; Pawley, E.; Pawley, S.; Paxman, H.; Pay, A.; Paye, M.; Payne, A.; Payne, D.; Payne, E.M.; Payne, J.; Payne, K.; Payne, R.G.; Payne, R.M.; Payne, T.; Paynter, A.; Paynter, D.; Paynter, R.; Peacey, A.W.; Peachey, C.; Peacock, H.; Peacock, L.; Peacock, M.; Pearce, C.E.; Pearce, K.; Pearce, L.; Pearce, R.; Pearce, S.; Pearman, D.; Pearsall, E.; Pearson, D.; Pearson, F.E.; Pearson, J.; Pearson, M.; Pearson, P.; Pedley, E.; Pedley, I.; Pedlow, A.; Pedlow, J.; Peeling, J.; Peers, M.; Peers, M.F.; Pelc, E.; Pelham-Clinton, E.C.; Pell, D.; Pell, E.; Pell, J.; Pelling, M.; Pellow, K.; Pelten, S.P.J.; Penberthy, D.; Pender, J.; Pender, S.; Pendlebury, R.E.; Pendleton, L.; Pendleton, S.; Pendleton, T.; Penfold, F.; Penfold, N.; Penford, N.; Penhallurick, R.; Penketh, P.W.; Penn, A.; Penn, S.; Penn, V.; Penn-Smith, E.M.; Pennell, J.; Pennell, M.; Pennells, C.; Penney, D.; Penney, H.; Pennie, I.D.; Pennington, D.H.; Pennington, H.D.; Pennington, J.; Pennington, M.; Pennington, M.G.; Pennington, R.; Penrice, W.; Penson, R.; Penson, R. J.; Penson, R.J.; Penton, D.; Pepin, C.E.; Peplow, G.H.; Peppe, W.; Pepper, R.; Pepper, S.; Peppiatt, C.; Percir, J.P.; Percy, J.; Peregrine, P.; Perkins, B.; Perkins, D.; Perkins, J.F.; Perkins, M.D.; Perkins, N.; Perkins, R.; Perkins, R.C.L.; Perrens, C.J.; Perril, D.; Perrin, V.; Perrior, L.; Perris, M.; Perry, A.D.; Perry, A.R.; Perry, D.; Perry, E.; Perry, I.; Perry, J.; Perry, R.; Perry, S.; Pescott, O.; Peterken, A.; Peterkin, M.; Peterkin, T.; Peterman, T.; Peters, A.; Peters, J.; Petley-Jones, R.A.; Petrie, A.B.; Petrie-Hays, N.; Petter, D.; Pettet, B.; Pettitt, M.; Phalasuk, N.; Phelps, S.; Philip, B.; Philip, E.; Philips, E.; Philips, J.; Philips, M.; Phillip, L.; Phillips, A.; Phillips, B.; Phillips, D.A.; Phillips, E.; Phillips, J.; Phillips, J.F.; Phillips, L.; Phillips, M.; Phillips, N.; Phillips, N.J.;

Phillips, P.; Phillips, S.; Phillips, V.; Phillips, V.E.; Philp, B.; Philp, E.G.; Philp, G.; Philp, P.; Philp, T.; Philpott, A.; Philpott, A.I.; Philpott, A.J.; Philpott, C.A.; Phipps, E.; Piatkiewicz, C.; Pickard, B.C.; Pickard, M.; Pickavance, J.R.; Picken, C.; Pickerell, G.; Pickering, F.; Pickering, S.; Pickess, B.; Pickess, B.P.; Pickett, R.; Pickin, A.; Pickles, M.E.; Pickup, A.R.; Pickup, J.; Pickupp, D.; Pickwell, A.; Picozzi, N.; Picton, B.E.; Pidgeon, R.N.; Pierce, G.; Pierce, L.; Pierce, L.C.; Piercey, J.; Piercey, M.; Piercy, D.; Piercy, V.; Piggot, A.; Pike, N.; Pilcher, R.; Pile, J.; Pile, S.; Pilkington, G.; Pilkington, R.; Pilling, L.; Pilsworth, M.; Pimble, A.; Pinchen, B.J.; Pinder, L.C.V.; Pinder, S.; Pinguey, D.; Pinguey, D.K.; Pinhorn, N.; Pinkney, J.; Pinniger, E.B.; Piotrowski, A.; Piotrowski, M.; Piotrowski, S.H.; Pipe, R.; Piper, M.; Pirie, M.; Pisolkar, E.; Pitcher, D.; Pitt, A.; Pitt, F.; Pitt, J.; Pitt, M.; Pitt, R.; Pittkin, D.M.; Pittman, S.; Pitts, J.; Pitts, N.; Pitty, J.; Place, D.; Place, S.; Plank, G.; Plankton, D.; Plant, C.; Plant, C.W.; Plant, S.; Plant, T.; Platt, D.; Platt, G.; Platts, R.; Pleasance, J.; Pleass, N.; Plowden, T.; Pluck, A.; Plumb, A.; Plummer, D.; Plummer, S.; Plumridge, K.; Plumtree, J.S.; Podmore, A.; Pointer, R.; Poland, J.; Polden, A.; Polglase, A.; Polglase, T.; Polkey, A.; Pollard, B.; Pollard, D.; Polley, V.; Pollinger, B.; Pollinger, B.R.; Pollinger, G.; Pollitt, M.; Pollock, G.; Pomeroy, S.; Pont, A.C.; Pontin, A.J.; Pontin, J.; Pool, P.; Poole, A.; Poole, B.; Poole, G.; Poole, J.; Poole, S.; Pooley, M.; Pope, B.; Pope, T.; Popely, L.; Popely, P.; Porritt, G.T.; Porter, B.; Porter, D.; Porter, I.; Porter, J.; Porter, K.; Porter, M.; Porter, M.A.; Porter, P.; Porter, R.; Pothecary, F.; Potter, A.S.; Potter, B.; Potter, G.; Potter, J.; Potter, R.; Potts, J.; Potts, M.; Potts, P.; Potts, V.; Poulter, B.; Poulter, D.; Poulter, R.; Poulton, E.B.; Powell, C.; Powell, D.; Powell, J.; Powell, M.; Powell, R.; Powell, S.; Powell, W.; Power, A.; Power, B.; Power, J.; Powne, J.; Powrie, C.; Powrie, K.; Poyser, S.; Praeger, R.; Prasad, A.; Prater, B.; Pratley, P.; Pratt, A.; Pratt, C.; Pratt, E.A.; Pratt, I.; Pratt, M.; Pratt, M.M.; Precey, P.; Preddy, S.; Preece, M.; Prendergast, A.; Prendergast, E.D.V.; Prendergast, H.D.V.; Prendergast, N.H.D.; Prentice, S.; Prescott, G.; Prescott, M.; Prescott, T.; Prest, D.; Prest, J.; Prestidge, P.; Preston, A.; Preston, C.; Preston, D.; Preston, M.; Preston, R.; Preston-Mafham, K.G.; Prestwood, W.V.; Price, A.; Price, B.; Price, D.; Price, J.; Price, L.A.; Price, M.; Price, N.; Price, P.; Price, R.; Price, S.O.V.; Price, T.; Price, T.R.S.; Price-Thomas, B.; Pridmore, T.; Priestley, M.; Priestley, S.; Prime, D.; Prince, P.; Pringle, N.; Pringle, W.; Print-Lyons, L.; Prior, G.; Pritchard, A.; Pritchard, I.; Pritchard, M.; Pritchard, R.; Pritchard, T.; Pritty, D.G.; Pritty, K.; Probin, B.; Procter, I.; Procter, R.; Proctor, B.; Proctor, C.; Proctor, D.; Proctor, D.A.; Proctor, H.; Proctor, I.; Proctor, J.; Proctor, K.; Proger, J.L.; Prosser, M.V.; Prosser, S.; Proud, A.; Prouse, S.; Prowse, A.; Prowse, S.; Pryce, D.; Pryce, K.; Pryce, K.A.; Pryce, L.; Pryce, R.D.; Pryce-Jones, N.; Prys-Jones, O.; Pugh, D.; Pugh, J.; Pugh, M.; Pugh-Clarke, D.; Pulford, E.; Pullan, D.; Pullar, P.; Pullen, G.; Pumfrett, C.; Pummell, B.; Pummell, B.D.; Pummell, D.; Pumphrey, K.; Purcell, A.; Purchas, W.H.; Purchase, M.; Pursall, J.; Purse, B.; Pursglove, C.J.; Purves, D.N.; Purves, J.; Purves, J.S.; Purveur, R.; Purvis, C.; Putnam, C.D.; Puttock, A.; Pye, D.; Pye, E.; Pyefinch, B.; Pyle, D.; Pyman, G.; Quainton, J.; Qualtrough, A.; Quelch, I.; Quigley, R.L.; Quin, P.C.; Quinn, P.; Quirk, J.; Quirke, M.; Rabbitts, B.; Raby, C.; Rackham, J.; Radcliffe, S.; Radford, A.P.; Radford, D.; Radford, D.J.; Radford, G.; Radford, P.; Radley, D.; Radley, K.; Rae, A.; Rae, C.; Rae, J.; Rae, R.; Rae, S.; Raebel, E.; Rafferty, M.; Rafferty, T.; Raftery, N.; Raftery, V.; Rainbow, B.; Raine, J.P.; Raine, P.; Rainey, J.; Rains, M.M.; Ralph, J.; Ralph, J.D.; Ralphs, I.; Ramage, M.; Rampton, A.; Rance, J.; Randall, H.; Randall, J.; Randall-Jackson, A.; Randolph, S.; Rands, D.G.; Rands, E.B.; Ranger Service, G.; Rangers, S.; Rankin, D.; Rankin, W.T.C.; Ransom, B.; Ransom, T.; Ransome, K.; Ransome, P.; Raper, C.M.; Raper, M.; Rapley, J.; Ratcliffe, D.; Ratcliffe, D.A.; Ratter, M.; Rau, J.; Raven, C.; Raven, P.J.; Raven, S.; Ravensdale, M.; Rawcliffe, C.P.; Rawcliffe, P.; Rawes, K.; Rawes, M.; Rawling, E.; Ray, R.; Raybould, B.; Rayburn, S.; Rayner, B.; Rayner, F.; Rayner, J.; Rayner, J.M.; Rayner, J.W.; Rayner, P.; Rayner, T.; Raynor, R.; Rayward, J.; Rea, B.; Rea, D.; Rea, V.; Read, D.; Read, J.; Read, M.; Read, R.W.J.; Read, S.; Read, T.; Read, V.; Reading, C.; Reading, S.; Rear, D.; Reavey, J.; Reavey, S.; Rebane, M.; Rebecca, G.W.; Redford, G.; Redford, J.; Redford, M.; Redgate, N.D.; Redley, A.; Redman, B.; Redshaw, E.J.; Redshaw, J.; Reece, J.; Reed, A.; Reed, B.; Reed, C.; Reed, D.; Reed, D.K.; Reed, J.; Reed, M.D.; Reed, N.; Reed, P.; Reed, S.; Reed, T.; Rees, D.; Rees, G.; Rees, I.; Rees, J.; Rees, M.; Reeve, B.; Reeve, C.; Reeve, D.; Reeve, K.; Reeve, M.; Reeve, M.S.W.; Reeve, P.; Reeves, K.; Reeves, P.; Reeves, R.; Regan, E.; Reganult, M.; Reid, A.; Reid, B.; Reid, C.; Reid, C.A.M.; Reid, D.A.; Reid, J.; Reid, L.; Reid, M.; Reid, S.; Reid, T.; Reinecke, J.; Reinecke, L.; Renals, T.J.; Renshaw, J.; Renwick, A.; Renwick, N.; Restall, D.; Reuss, N.B.; Revels, R.; Reynolds, A.; Reynolds, F.L.; Reynolds, J.; Reynolds, J.D.; Reynolds, J.R.; Reynolds, S.; Reynoldson, T.B.; Rheinholdt, A.; Rhodes, A.; Rhodes, A.S.; Rhodes, M.; Rhodes, P.; Rhodes, P.J.; Rhodes, R.; Rhone, E.; Rhys-Williams, N.; Ribbands, B.; Ribbon, G.; Ribeaux, N.; Rice, D.J.; Rice, E.; Rice, T.; Rich, H.; Richards, A.; Richards, A.J.; Richards, A.P.; Richards, A.W.; Richards, G.; Richards, J.; Richards, J.P.; Richards, K.; Richards, L.; Richards, M.; Richards, N.; Richards, O.W.; Richardson, A.T.; Richardson, C.; Richardson, D.M.; Richardson, J.; Richardson, K.; Richardson, L.; Richardson, M.; Richardson, M.J.; Richardson, N.; Richardson, N.W.; Richardson, P.; Richardson, P.W.; Richardson, S.; Richardson, T.; Riches, A.; Richmond, D.; Richmond, D.I.; Rickerby, L.; Riddy, M.; Riden, T.; Rideout, K.; Ridgard, M.; Ridge, M.; Ridge, S.; Ridgen, S.; Ridgeway, A.; Ridgill, S.C.; Ridgway, B.; Riding, F.J.; Riding, I.; Ridout, P.; Rieser, C.; Rig, L.; Rigby, D.; Rigby, D.J.; Rigby, J.; Rigby, R.; Rigden, S.; Rigden, S.P.; Rigdon, R.J.; Rigg, S.; Riley, A.; Riley, J.; Riley, M.; Riley, P.; Riley, T.; Rimington, W.; Rimmer, J.; Riordan, E.; Rippey, I.; Ris, F.; Rissbrook, M.; Ritchie, A.B.; Ritchie, P.; Ritchie, R.J.; Ritson, C.; Ritson, K.; Rivett, A.; Rix, S.; Rixson, D.; Roach, S.; Robbin, M.T.; Robbins, J.; Robbins, L.; Robbins, M.; Robbins, S.; Roberts, A.; Roberts, B.; Roberts, B.P.; Roberts, D.; Roberts, E.; Roberts, F.J.; Roberts, G.; Roberts, G.C.M.; Roberts, G.M.C.; Roberts, I.; Roberts, J.; Roberts, J. C.; Roberts, J.E.H.; Roberts, J.L.; Roberts, K.; Roberts, M.; Roberts, N.; Roberts, N.P.; Roberts, P.; Roberts, R.; Roberts, R.H.; Roberts, S.; Roberts, W.W.; Robertson, A.; Robertson, B.; Robertson, D.; Robertson, D.A.; Robertson, G.; Robertson, J.; Robertson, K.; Robertson, K.D.; Robertson, L.; Robertson, L.R.; Robertson, M.; Robertson, P.; Robertson, T.S.; Robeson, K.; Robilliard, T.; Robins, M.; Robinson, A.; Robinson, C.; Robinson, C.A.; Robinson, E.; Robinson, G.; Robinson, H.P.K.; Robinson, I.; Robinson, J.; Robinson, J.P.; Robinson, K.; Robinson, L.; Robinson, M.; Robinson, M.C.; Robinson, N.; Robinson, P.; Robinson, R.; Robinson, S.; Robinson, T.; Robinson, W.K.; Robinson, W.R.; Robson, A.; Robson, B.; Robson, C.; Robson, G.; Robson, J.J.; Roche, N.; Rock, S.; Roden, C.; Roderick, E.; Roderick, H.; Roderick, T.; Rodger, A.M.; Rodgers, D.; Rodgers, R.; Rodway, D.A.; Roe, C.; Roe, K.; Roe, S.; Roebuck, S.; Roex, J.; Rogers, A.; Rogers, C.; Rogers, J.; Rogers, M.; Rogers, P.; Rogers, R.; Rogers, S.; Rolleston, B.; Rolleston, D.B.; Rollinson, L.; Rolls, S.; Rolston, E.; Ronayne, C.; Roocroft, A.; Rooke, R.; Rooke, S.; Roome, B.; Rooney, J.; Rooney, M.; Root, C.; Root, S.; Root, S.M.; Rooum, D.; Roper, C.; Roper, I.M.; Roper, P.; Roper, P.P.; Roper, T.; Rosario-Rabadan, d.; Rose, A.; Rose, B.; Rose, C.; Rose, E.; Rose, F.; Rose, G.; Rose, I.; Rose, J.; Rose, K.; Rosenthal, A.; Rosney, A.S.; Ross, A.; Ross, A.J.; Ross, C.; Ross, D.; Ross, J.; Rossell, T.; Rosser, P.; Rostron, G.; Roth, S.; Rothero, G.; Rotheroe, G.; Rothney, E.; Roughton, J.; Roukin, W.; Roulston, R.H.F.; Roulston, S.; Rouncefield, M.; Rouse, B.; Rouse, H.; Rousseau, J.; Rousseau, R.; Routledge, G.; Routledge, S.; Rowan, S.; Rowden, A.O.; Rowe, B.L.; Rowe, H.; Rowe, J.; Rowe, P.; Rowett, A.; Rowland, A.; Rowland, G.; Rowland, K.; Rowland, K.M.; Rowland, M.B.; Rowland, S.; Rowlands, A.; Rowledge, S.; Rowling, G.; Roworth, P.; Roy, D.; Roy, J.; Royal, M.; Royle, A.; Royle, P.; Royle, R.; Royles, K.; Royles, K.P.; Royston, A.; Rozier, R.; Rubin, M.; Ruddick, H.; Ruddick, T.H.; Rudge, D.; Rudge, W.; Rudkin, P.; Rule, M.; Rumsey, S.; Rundle, C.; Rusbridge, M.; Rush, S.; Russel, R.J.; Russell, C.; Russell, F.; Russell, G.; Russell, H.M.; Russell, J.; Russell, L.; Russell, M.; Russell, P.; Russell, R.; Russell, S.M.; Russell, T.; Russell, V.; Rutherford, C.; Rutherford, C.I.; Rutherford, I.; Rutherford, J.; Rutherford, M.; Rutherford, R.; Rutherford, S.T.; Rutherford, W.; Ryalls, N.; Ryan, B.; Ryan, E.P.; Ryan, F.; Ryan, P.; Ryan, S.; Rycroft, G.; Ryder, S.; Ryder, T.; Ryding, I.; Ryland, K.; Rylands, K.; Rymer, A.; Ryrie, J.L.; Saag, M.; Sadler, D.; Sage, B.L.; Sage, John A.; Sage, M.; Salisbury, G.; Salmon, J.; Salmon, M.A.; Salmon, P.; Salter, B.; Salter, J.H.; Salter, M.; Salway, A.; Sampford, N.; Sampson, C.; Sampson, D.; Samuel, J.E.; Samuel, J.R.; Samuel, M.A.; Samuel, R.L.; Samways, M.J.; Samworth, M.; Sandam, R.; Sanders, D.; Sanders, J.D.; Sanders, T.; Sanderson, D.; Sanderson, J.; Sanderson, M.; Sanderson, M.R.; Sanderson, N.; Sanderson, R.; Sanderson, R.F.; Sandham, R.; Sanford, M.; Sangster, A.; Sankey, J.H.P.; Sankey, S.; Sansbury, B.; Sargeant, A.F.; Sargeant, C.; Saul, K.G.; Saunders, A.; Saunders, A.E.; Saunders, B.; Saunders, D.R.; Saunders, G.; Saunders, J.; Saunders, J.W.; Saunders, L.; Saunders, P.; Saunders, S.; Saunt, G.W.; Sauze, H.A.; Savage, A.; Savage, A.A.; Savan, B.; Savidge, J.P.; Saville, B.; Savory, J.; Sawford, B.; Sawyer, N.L.; Saxton, S.; Sayer, C.J.W.; Sazer, D.; Scally, R.; Scampion, B.R.; Scantleburu, C.; Scarborough, H.; Schmaljohann, H.; Schofield, A.; Schofield, V.; Scholes, T.; Scholey, G.; Schuchard, C.; Scofield, P.; Scott, A.; Scott, A.G.; Scott, C.; Scott, D.; Scott, D.W.; Scott, H.; Scott, I.; Scott, J.; Scott, J.H.; Scott, M.; Scott, P.; Scott, R.; Scott,

T.; Scott, W.; Scott, W.J.; Scott-Bolton, J.; Scott-Langley, D.; Scrimgeour, C.M.; Scroggs, R.; Scroggs, R.W.; Scroggs, R.W.H.; Scruby, M.; Scruton, D.; Scudder, G.G.E.; Scully, F.; Scurr, C.A.; Seabrook, E.A.; Seaby, D.A.; Seaby, W.A.; Seager, E.; Seagon, T.; Seagrave, C.; Seal, P.; Seal, S.; Searle, A.G.; Searle, J.; Searle, J.B.; Searle, S.; Seaton, K.; Seaton, S.; Seaward, D.; Seawright, D.; Secrett, D.; Seddon, E.A.; Seddon, J.; Sedgley, D.; Seilly, D.; Selby, V.; Self, A.; Self, B.; Seligman, P.M.; Sell, M.; Sellers, R.M.; Sellors, G.; Selly, P.; Selman, R.; Selway, E.; Semmens, P.; Semper, A.; Semple, J.W.D.; Senior, J.; Senior, P.; Sennitt, J.; Sennitt, M.; Senter, H.; Sergeant, C.R.; Servante, A.; Service, M.W.; Sevior, A.; Sewell, D.; Sewry, A.; Sexton, S.; Sexton, T.; Seymour, D.; Shackleton, D.; Shackleton, J.; Shacklock, H.; Shadbolt, M.; Shadforth, E.; Shaft, M.; Shakeshaft, P.; Shale, I.; Shallo, E.; Shanahan, M.J.; Shanks, S.; Shannon, G.; Shardlow, M.; Sharkey, G.; Sharp, D.; Sharp, M.; Sharp, P.; Sharp, S.; Sharpe, A.; Sharpe, C.; Sharpe, D.; Sharpe, J.; Sharpe, K.; Sharpe, N.; Sharpe, P.; Sharpes, L.; Sharples, R.; Sharratt, C.; Sharrock, H.; Sharrock, N.; Sharrock, T.; Shattock, M.; Shaughnessy, J.P.; Shaw, A.; Shaw, B.; Shaw, C.; Shaw, C.E.; Shaw, D.; Shaw, E.; Shaw, G.; Shaw, I.; Shaw, K.; Shaw, M.; Shaw, P.; Shaw, P.R.; Shaw, R.; Shaw, S.; Sheahan, M.; Shearing, C.; Shearring, A.; Sheasby, J.; Sheasby, P.; Sheasby, P.G.; Sheehan, P.; Sheikh, R.; Sheldon, D.; Sheldon, S.; Sheldrake, C.W.; Sheldrake, P.; Sheldrake, V.; Shellard, K.; Shellswell, C.; Shelton, B.; Shelton, H.M.A.; Shelton, N.; Shennan, N.M.; Shenston, V.; Shenton, D.; Shenton, D.C.; Shenton, F.W.; Shenton, R.; Shephard, A.; Shephard, R.; Shepherd, A.; Sheppard, C.; Sheppard, D.A.; Sheppard, F.V.S.; Sheppard, J.; Sheppard, L.; Sheppard, R.; Sheppard, S.; Shepperd, J.; Shepperson, C.; Shepperson, D.; Shepperson, J.; Sheridan, M.; Sheriden, M.; Sherman, N.; Sherringham, C.; Sherwin, B.; Sherwin, G.; Shevlin, T.; Shields, L.; Shields, T.; Shiels, S.; Shillaker, R.; Shilland, E.; Shimmings, P.; Shimmings, P.J.; Ship, R.; Shipley, D.; Shires, S.; Shirt, D.B.; Shore, F.; Shorrock, B.; Short, D.; Shorten, M.; Shorter, J.; Shortland, G.; Shortland, J.; Showers, J.; Showler, A.; Showler, D.A.; Shreeves, G.; Shreeves, W.G.; Side, K.; Sides, T.; Sidle, N.; Sidwell, M.; Siewruk, J.; Silcock, L.; Silcocks, A.; Silcocks, T.; Silcox, A.; Silk, H.; Silk, M.; Sillett, A.; Sills, N.; Sills, S.; Silsby, J.D.; Silsby, R.; Silverwood, B.; Silvey, J.; Simmons, H.; Simmons, M.; Simmons, P.; Simms, E.; Simons, R.; Simper, I.; Simpkin, A.; Simpson, A.; Simpson, A.N.B.; Simpson, B.; Simpson, F.; Simpson, G.; Simpson, I.; Simpson, J.; Simpson, P.; Simpson, P.J.; Simpson, R.A.; Simpson, T.; Simpson, V.R.; Sims, A.; Sims, B.; Sims, C.; Sims, I.; Sims, R.; Simson, R.A.; Sinclair, M.; Singleton, R.; Sinnadurai, P.; Sinnott, A.; Sinnott, D.; Sinnott, L.; Skeen, R.Q.; Skelcher, G.; Skelton, J.L.; Skelton, K.; Skelton, M.; Skelton, M.J.L.; Skerritt, J.E.; Sketch, P.; Skevington, M.; Skidmore, P.; Skingsley, D.; Skinner, J.; Skipp, L.; Skirrow, M.; Slack, C.; Slack, F.; Slack, T.; Sladdin, S.; Slade, A.; Slade, B.; Slade, B.E.; Slade, D.; Slade, D.J.; Slade, K.; Slade, L.; Slade, S.; Slaney, C.; Slater, F.; Slater, H.; Slater, I.; Slater, J.; Slater, N.; Slater, P.; Slator, C.; Slattery, M.; Slattery, T.; Slawson, C.; Slaymaker, M.; Slee, R.; Sleeman, D.P.; Sleep, T.; Sley, M.; Sluman, N.; Smale, C.; Smale, J.; Small, C.; Small, D.; Small, H.; Small, J.; Small, M.A.; Small, R.; Small, T.; Smallshire, D.; Smallshire, P.; Smallshire, S.; Smart, B.; Smart, E.; Smart, G.; Smart, M.; Smart, P.E.; Smart, S.; Smellie, W.J.; Smethurst, C.; Smethurst, M.; Smiddy, P.; Smillie, D.; Smith, A.; Smith, A.E.; Smith, B.; Smith, C.; Smith, C.A.; Smith, C.J.; Smith, D.; Smith, D.A.; Smith, D.H.; Smith, D.J.; Smith, E.; Smith, E.J.; Smith, E.M.; Smith, F.; Smith, F.T.; Smith, G.; Smith, H.; Smith, H.A.; Smith, H.R.; Smith, I.; Smith, I.D.; Smith, I.F.; Smith, J.; Smith, J.E.; Smith, J.L.; Smith, J.U.; Smith, K.G.V.; Smith, L.; Smith, L.N.S.; Smith, L.R.; Smith, Les J.; Smith, M.; Smith, M.N.; Smith, N.; Smith, N.D.; Smith, N.W.; Smith, P.; Smith, P.A.; Smith, P.G.; Smith, P.H.; Smith, P.R.; Smith, R.; Smith, R.A.H.; Smith, R.E.A.; Smith, R.E.N.; Smith, R.G.; Smith, R.W.; Smith, R.W.J.; Smith, S.; Smith, S.D.; Smith, S.G.; Smith, S.J.; Smith, T.; Smith, W.E.; Smith, Z.; Smithers, K.; Smithson, T.; Smithurst, D.; Smout, A.; Smout, C.; Smout, M.; Smout, R.; Smout, R.H.; Smyth, F.; Smyth, M.J.; Smyth, W.; Snape, P.; Snell, L.; Snook, D.; Snook, M.; Snow, M.; Snowden, R.; Soames, P.; Soane, I.D.; Sokoloff, P.; Solley, F.; Sollis, D.; Solly, F.; Solman, D.; Somerville, A.; Sommerville, A.; Songhurst, S.; Soons, D.; Soper, P.; Sorensen, J.; Sotherby, R.M.; Soutar, B.; Souter, L.; Souter, M.; South, R.; South, S.; Southall, R.; Southgate, D.; Southgate, F.; Southwood, R.; Southworth, N.; Sowden, S.; Spalding, A.; Spalding, R.; Spalding, S.; Spalding, S.C.; Spano, R.; Spanton, R.; Sparshall, J.; Spavin, S.; Speak, P.; Spear, S.; Speck, M.; Speight, M.C.D.; Speirs, R.A.; Spellacy, N.; Spellman, A.; Spence, B.; Spence, F.; Spence, M.; Spencer, A.G.; Spencer, B.; Spencer, G.; Spencer, J.W.; Spencer, K.; Spencer, R.; Spencer, S.; Spencer, T.; Spencer-Vellacott, P.; Sperring, C.; Speyer, E.I.R.; Spilling, C.; Spinks, P.; Spirit, A.; Spirit, M.G.; Spittal, R.J.; Spong, P.F.; Spooner, B.; Spooner, J.; Spooner, S.; Spottiswood, A.; Spowage, R. M.; Spragge, F.; Spratt, D.A.; Spray, C.; Spriggs, A.I.; Spring, D.; Spring, N.; Springate, S.; Spry, S.; Spyvee, R.; Squires, B.; Squires, B.R.; Squires, F.; Squires, J.; Squires, K.I.; Squires, R.; Squirrell, J.; Squirrell, N.; St Pierre, P.; St Pierre, S.; Stables, H.; Stace, H.E.; Stace, R.; Stacey, A.; Stafford, E.; Stagg, J.; Stainwright, L.; Stallwood, B.R.; Stammers, B.; Stammers, M.; Stamp, C.; Stanbridge, R.; Standbridge, K.; Standbridge, S.; Standen, I.; Standivan, I.; Stanfield, K.; Stanier, H.; Stanley, B.; Stanley, J.M.; Stanley, L.; Stannard, K.; Stannard, P.; Stanners, M.; Stanney, J.D.; Stansfeld, M.A.; Stansfield, R.; Stansfield, S.; Stapleton, A.; Stares, S.; Stark, L.; Starling, L.; Starmore, A.; Stebbings, P.; Steeden, D.; Steedman, J.; Steedman, S.; Steel, C.; Steel, D.; Steel, E.J.; Steele, C.; Steele, E.J.; Steele, G.; Steele, J.; Steele, K.; Steer, J.B.; Steer, N.; Stelfox, A.W.; Stenning, G.; Stenning, J.; Stenning, M.; Stenson, C.; Stenson, L.; Stephen, G.; Stephen, M.; Stephens, D.; Stephens, J.F.; Stephens, M.; Stephens, S.; Stephenson, E.; Stephenson, G.; Sterling, P.; Stern, R.; Steve, R.; Stevens, A.; Stevens, D.; Stevens, D.P.; Stevens, E.; Stevens, J.; Stevens, P.; Stevens, R.; Stevens, S.; Stevens, W.; Stevenson, C.R.; Stevenson, I.; Stevenson, J.; Stevenson, N.; Stevenson, P.; Stevenson, R.; Stevenson, T.; Stevenson, W.J.; Steward, L.; Stewart, A.; Stewart, A.M.; Stewart, B.; Stewart, C.; Stewart, G.; Stewart, I.K.M.; Stewart, J.; Stewart, J.W.; Stewart, K.; Stewart, N.; Stewart, P.; Stewart, R.; Stewart, R.G.; Stewart, S.; Stewart, S.J.; Stewart, W.J.; Stiles, B.; Stiles, K.; Still, E.; Still, E.C.; Still, E.L.; Stillman, R.; Stilwell, R.; Stinger, R.; Stirling, A.; Stirling, A.M.; Stirling, J.; Stirrup, S.; Stobart, J.; Stobbs, A.; Stockton, C.; Stokes, H.G.; Stokes, J.; Stokes, R.M.; Stokoe, R.; Stolworthy, M.R.; Ston, A.J.J.; Stone, B.; Stone, C.; Stone, G.P.; Stone, K.; Stone, N.; Stone, S.; Stone, W.; Stonell, B.; Stones, S.; Stoneybridge, S.; Stonor, C.R.; Storer, B.; Storer, L.A.; Storey, C.; Storey, G.; Storey, M.W.; Storie, N.; Stork, J.; Storrie, N.; Stott, B.; Stott, M.; Stoyle, M.; Stracchan, R.; Strachan, I.M.; Strachan, J.; Strachan, P.; Strachan, R.; Strachen, R.; Strahan, M.; Strange, A.; Stratford, A.; Straw, N.; Street, L.; Street, M.; Streeter, D.; Stretch, B.; Stretton, D.; Stretton, J.; Stretton, T.; Strickland, J.; Strickland, M.; Strickland, P.; Stride, J.; Stride, L.; Stringer, B.; Stringer, R.N.; Stronach, P.; Strother, G.; Stroud, D.A.; Stroud, J.; Stroud, S.; Strudwick, F.; Strudwick, T.; Strugnel, G.; Strutt, A.; Strutt, J.; Strutton, A.; Strutton, M.; Stuart, C.; Stuart, J.; Stuart, R.T.; Stuart, S.; Stubbs, A.; Stubbs, A.E.; Stubbs, M.; Stuckey, P.; Sturdy, P.; Sturgess, P.; Styles, A.; Stythe, R.; Suddaby, D.; Suffern, C.; Sullivan, C.; Sullivan, M.; Sullivan, P.; Summers, P.; Summersby, L.; Summersgill, A.; Summerson, F.C.; Sumner, B.; Sumner, D.; Sumner, D.P.; Sumner, E.D.; Sumner, J.; Sumner, K.; Sumner, T.; Sunter, R.; Surry, R.; Surtees, A.; Sussex, D.J.; Sutcliffe, D.; Sutcliffe, D.W.; Sutcliffe, M.; Sutcliffe, M.J.; Sutcliffe, M.M.; Sutcliffe, R.; Sutherland, E.; Sutton King, P.; Sutton, D.; Sutton, F.; Sutton, G.P.; Sutton, M.; Sutton, M.D.; Sutton, P.; Sutton, R.D.; Sutton, S.; Swabey, D.; Swaffield, K.; Swaine, C.M.; Swainston, A.; Swale, J.; Swales, J.D.; Swales, S.; Swan, D.; Swan, J.; Swan, K.; Swanborough, L.; Swann, B.; Swann, J.; Swanson, S.; Swash, A.; Sweet, N.R.; Sweetman, J.; Swegsda, F.; Swinburne, K.; Swindells, C.; Swindells, R.J.; Swindlehurst, R.; Swinnerton, B.F.A.; Swire, P.; Swire, P.J.; Swire, P.W.; Sykes, M.; Sykes, M.H.; Sykes, N.; Sykes, T.; Sylvester, Y.; Symes, K.L.; Symons, B.; Symons, N.; Syms, J.; Synott, K.; Szczur, J.; Tabiner, H.; Tack, C.; Tagg, D.; Tailby, T.W.; Tait, H.; Tait, N.; Tait, T.N.; Talbot, N.; Talbott, N.; Tallach, N.; Tallack, R.; Tamon, I.; Tams, T.; Tandy, N.; Tankard, R.; Tanner, F.; Tanner, I.; Tanner, R.; Tanner, S.; Tannett, P.G.; Tansey, P.; Tantram, R.; Taplin, J.; Tapping, R.; Tarbat, J.E.; Tardivel, J.; Tardivel, R.; Tarpey, T.; Tarr, S.; Tasker, M.; Tate, M.; Tate, R.; Tatman, S.; Tatner, P.; Tattersall, W.; Tattersley, A.; Taverner, J.; Tayler, P.; Taylor, A.; Taylor, B.; Taylor, B.J.; Taylor, C.; Taylor, D.; Taylor, G.; Taylor, G.A.; Taylor, H.; Taylor, J.; Taylor, J.C.; Taylor, J.E.; Taylor, J.P.; Taylor, J.R.; Taylor, K.; Taylor, L.; Taylor, M.; Taylor, N.; Taylor, N.W.; Taylor, P.; Taylor, R.; Taylor, R.H.A.; Taylor, S.; Taylor, T.; Taylor, T.B.; Taylor, W.T.; Teagle, B.; Teagle, H.; Teagle, J.; Teagle, W.G.; Teague, D.; Teale, S.; Tearle, E.; Teasdale, C.; Tedstone, T.; Teesdale, I.; Teisar, E.; Telfer, D.; Telfer, M.G.; Temple, A.; Temple, K.; Temple, P.; Templeton, L.; Teneva, M.; Tero, C.; Terry, J.; Terry, P.; Terry, S.; Terryle, M.; Tetlow, M.; Tew, I.; Tew, I.F.; Thacker, M.; Thain, C.; Thannett, P.G.; Tharme, A.; Theaker, J.; Theil, A.; Theobald, T.; Thewlis, R.M.; Thicket, L.A.; Thickett, A.J.; Thickett, L.; Thickett, L.A.; Third, A.; Thistlethwaite, C.; Thomas, A.; Thomas, B.; Thomas, C.; Thomas, C.D.; Thomas, D.; Thomas, D.I.; Thomas, D.L.; Thomas, G.; Thomas, G.H.; Thomas, I.; Thomas, J.; Thomas, J.A.; Thomas, K.I.; Thomas, M.; Thomas, M.P.; Thomas, P.; Thomas, P.A.;

Thomas, R.; Thomas, R.M.; Thomas, R.W.; Thomas, S.; Thomas, T.; Thomas, W.; Thomlinson, P.; Thompson, A.; Thompson, B.; Thompson, C.; Thompson, D.; Thompson, G.; Thompson, I.; Thompson, I.S.; Thompson, J.; Thompson, J.A.; Thompson, J.B.; Thompson, J.M.; Thompson, L.; Thompson, M.; Thompson, M.S.; Thompson, P.; Thompson, R.; Thompson, S.; Thompson, T.; Thomson, B.R.; Thomson, E.; Thomson, I.; Thomson, K.; Thomson, R.; Thomson, W.; Thorlby, Tony K.; Thorn, B.; Thorne, A.K.; Thorne, G.; Thorne, K.; Thorne, R.; Thorneycroft, D.; Thornhill, S.; Thornley, A.; Thornton, M.; Thornycroft, N.; Thorpe, D.; Thorpe, J.; Thorpe, R.; Thouless, H.J.; Throup, D.; Thurgate, H.C.; Thurgood, S.; Thurlow, D.; Thurlow, G.; Thurner, M.; Thwaites, W.; Tibbetts, J.; Tickner, M.; Tierney, J.; Tierney, P.; Tilbury, R.; Tilbury, S.; Tillin, N.; Tilling, M.; Tilling, M.R.; Tillley, J.; Tillotson, I.J.L.; Tilmouth, A.; Tilt, J.; Timberlake, C.; Timberlake, K.; Timms, J.; Timms, S.; Tinning, J.; Tinning, P.C.; Tipping, P.; Tipple, D.; Tisdale, M.; Titchmarsh, N.; Titcombe, C.; Tite, R.; Tittensor, A.; Tittensor, R.; Tizzard, P.; Todd, G.; Todd, J.; Todd, J.W.; Tofield, S.; Toft, H.; Tolhurst, D.J.; Tolhurst, K.; Toller, J.; Tomalin, C.; Tomalin, G.; Tomalin, P.; Tomcyzynsky, A.; Tomkinson, P.; Tomlin, E.; Tomlin, J.; Tomlinson, C.; Tomlinson, J.; Tomlinson, S.; Tompkinson, M.; Toms, M.; Tonks, P.; Tookey, T.; Tooley, J.; Toop, C.; Tordoff, G.; Torino, J.; Torney, J.; Tottman, D.; Toulson, N.; Tovey, K.; Towe, C.; Towner, M.; Towns, M.; Townsend, E.; Townsend, M.; Townsend, P.; Toynton, P.; Traer, S.; Trafford, J.; Trail, J.W.H.; Trainer, D.; Trant, C.J.; Trayner, M.; Treacher, P.; Treadwell, P.; Trebble, N.; Tregale, J.; Trelford, A.; Treloar, P.; Treloar, P.T.; Trembath, E.M.; Tremethick, A.; Tremewan, W.G.; Tresize, K.; Trett, M.W.; Trevis, B.; Trevis, G.; Trevor, P.; Trew, C.; Treweke, C.; Tribe, N.; Triggs, N.; Triggs, P.; Trim, D.; Trim, H.; Trinder, G.; Troake, P.; Trodd, P.; Tromans, E.P.; Trotman, K.; Trotman, N.; Troup, R.D.R.; Trubridge, M.; Trueman, I.C.; Trump, R.D.; Truscott, L.A.C.; Trusler, D.; Tubb, J.; Tubb, K.; Tubbs, A.; Tubbs, C.J.; Tucker, D.; Tucker, D.C.; Tucker, J.; Tucker, M.; Tucker, V.; Tudor, L.; Tufts, I.P.; Tulloch, R.; Tulloh, B.; Tully, H.; Tunmore, M.; Tunnah, E.; Tunnard, J.; Tunnicliff, B.; Turkington, C.; Turnbull, I.; Turnbull, N.; Turner, A.; Turner, A.H.; Turner, B.; Turner, D.; Turner, G.; Turner, H.J.; Turner, J.; Turner, J.H.; Turner, John R.G.; Turner, M.; Turner, P.C.; Turner, R.; Turner, S.; Turrell, D.; Turrell, R.E.; Turtle, S.; Turton, M.; Tustin, J.; Tutt, A.; Tutt, D.; Tutt, Z.; Tweddle, S.; Tweedie, W.; Tweedy, L.; Twigg, H.M.; Twinn, H.; Twinn, M.; Twissell, C.; Twissell, I.; Twist, C.; Twyford, A.; Tyler, J.; Tyler, M.; Tyler, M.W.; Tynan, T.; Tynen, M.; Tyner, A.; Tyrer, A.; Tyrie, C.R.; Tyrrell, M.; Tzeschlock, G.Uff, C.; Ullyett, J.; Underwood, A.; Underwood, D.; Underwood, J.; Underwood, M.; Underwood, R.; Unwin, W.C.; Upton, A.; Urbanksi, E.; Urquhart, D.; Urquhart, S.; Urwin, B.; Urwin, W.; Usher, A.; Usher, M.B.; Utting, T.; Valentin, N.; Valgonio, M.; Vallance, D.; Vallance, M.; Vallins, F.T.; Van Der Klei, J.; Vandome, D.; Vandome, P.; Vanstone, I.; Vanstone, M.; Vanstone, R.; Varkala, P.; Varley, J.; Varley, M.; Varney, H.; Varney, P.; Vaughan Jones, A.; Vaughan, A.; Vaughan, H.; Vaughan, I.M.; Vaughan, J.; Vaughan, O.; Vaycey, J.; Veale, W.H.; Veatch, L.; Velasco, M.; Veldman, J.; Venables, A.V.; Venables, H.; Venables, R.; Venus, D.; Verdcourt, B.; Verling, M.; Vernon, D.; Vials, T.; Vicary, G.; Vick, G.; Vick, G.S.; Vickers, B.; Vickers, J.; Vickers, T.; Vigay, J.; Vincent, D.F.; Vincent, E.; Vincent, F.; Vincent, J.; Vincent, M.; Vincent, P.J.; Vincett, J.; Viney, M.; Voaden, J.; Voysey, P.; Vrieling, A.; Vukomanovic, I.; Wackett, C.; Waddell, J.; Wade, P.M.; Wade, V.; Wadge, B.; Wagland, M.; Wagstaffe, R.; Wain, B.; Wain, C.; Wain, C.B.; Wain, D.; Wain, M.; Wain, S.; Wain, W.H.; Wainright, D.; Wainwright, C.W.; Wainwright, D.; Wainwright, R.; Waite, A.; Waite, S.; Wake, A.; Wake, A.J.; Wakefield, H.R.; Wakeley, R.; Wakelin, D.; Wakelin, P.; Wakeling, M.; Wakely, S.; Walden, R.; Waldie, G.; Waldron, J.; Waldron, M.; Wales, M.; Walford, N.; Walker, A.; Walker, B.; Walker, B.D.; Walker, B.J.; Walker, C.; Walker, D.; Walker, D.S.; Walker, E.; Walker, F.A.; Walker, G.; Walker, I.; Walker, J.; Walker, J.J.; Walker, M.; Walker, M.C.; Walker, R.; Walker, S.; Walker, W.; Walkling, K.; Wall, T.; Wallace Pugh, C.H.; Wallace, A.; Wallace, B.; Wallace, D.; Wallace, I.; Wallace, I.D.; Wallace, J.; Wallace, T.J.; Waller, A.; Waller, C.S.; Waller, G.; Waller, I.; Waller, I.J.; Waller, J.I.; Walls, J.; Walls, R.; Walls, R.C.; Walmsley, A.; Walpole, M.; Walsh, A.M.; Walsh, D.; Walsh, D.F.; Walsh, E.; Walsh, F.; Walsh, G.B.; Walsh, J.; Walsh, J.F.; Walsh, P.; Walsh, S.; Walshaw, A.; Walshaw, M.; Walshaw, S.; Walshe, A.; Walter, M.; Walter, M.F.; Walter, T.; Walters, A.; Walters, D.; Walters, J.; Walters, J.M.; Walters, S.; Walther, L.; Walton, A.; Walton, D.; Walton, G.A.; Walton, J.; Walton, K.; Walton, P.; Walton, S.; Wann, J.; Warbrook, J.P.; Warburton, A.; Warburton, B.; Warburton, M.; Warburton, R.; Ward, A.; Ward, B.; Ward, D.; Ward, H.G.; Ward, J.; Ward, K.; Ward, L.; Ward, M.; Ward, N.; Ward, P.; Ward, P.A.; Ward, P.H.;

Ward, R.; Ward, S.; Ward, S.D.; Ward-Smith, A.J.; Ward-Smith, J.; Wardell, B.; Wardell, L.; Warden, D.; Warden, K.J.; Warden, P.; Wardens, C.; Wardens, J.; Wardle, P.; Wardrope, D.; Wardrope, G.; Wardrope, J.; Waring, P.; Waring, T.; Warman, E.; Warman, S.; Warman, S.R.; Warmingham, S.C.; Warmington, K.; Warne, A.C.; Warner, D.; Warner, R.; Warnes, J.; Warnes, M.; Warnock, D.; Warnock, J.P.; Warnock, J.S.; Warren, A.; Warren, D.; Warren, E.; Warren, L.; Warren, M.S.; Warren, R.G.; Warren-Davies, T.; Warrener, S.; Warrillow, S.; Warrington, B.; Warrington, P.; Warrington, S.; Warry, S.R.; Warwick, C.; Warwick, J.; Warwick, S.; Warwick, T.; Wase, F.; Wash, J.; Wash, R.J.; Washington, C.; Washington, D.; Washington, L.; Wasse, J.; Watchman, A.; Watchman, J.; Waterhouse, E.A.; Waterhouse, M.; Waterman, A.; Waters, E.G.R.; Waters, K.; Waters, M.; Waters, R.; Waters, S.; Waterston, A.R.; Waterton, P.; Wathall, G.; Watkins, C.; Watkins, D.; Watkins, E.P.; Watkins, L.; Watkins, M.; Watkins, M.S.; Watkins, O.G.; Watkins, P.; Watkins, R.; Watkins, S.; Watling, M.; Watmore, J.; Watola, G.; Watson Featherstone, A.; Watson, A.; Watson, A.J.; Watson, B.; Watson, D.; Watson, G.; Watson, I.; Watson, J.; Watson, K.; Watson, L.; Watson, M.; Watson, P.; Watson, R.; Watson, R.A.; Watson, W.; Watson, W.R.; Watt, D.; Watt, J.; Watt, K.; Watt, K.R.; Watt, R.; Watt, T.; Wattison, J.T.; Watts, B.; Watts, C.; Watts, C.E.D.; Watts, D.; Watts, F.; Watts, H.J.; Watts, P.; Watts, S.; Watts, T.; Waymont, S.; Weake, M.; Weal, R.D.; Wearing, M.F.; Wearne, G.; Weatherhead, R.; Weaver, A.; Weaver, D.J.; Weaver, G.; Weaver, K.N.; Weaver, R.; Webb, B.; Webb, C.; Webb, D.; Webb, D.F.; Webb, J.; Webb, K.; Webb, N.; Webb, O.P.C.; Webb, P.; Webb, P.C.; Webb, R.; Webber, B.; Webber, G.L.; Webber, J.; Webber, M.; Webber, S.; Webley, J.; Webster, B.D.; Webster, C.; Webster, D.; Webster, E.G.; Webster, H.; Webster, L.; Webster, P.; Webster, R.; Webster, S.; Webster, V.; Wedd, D.; Weddle, R.B.; Weedon, K.; Weeks, A.; Weeks, S.; Weir, A.; Weir, A.J.; Weir, D.G.; Weir, J.; Weir, R.; Weir, S.; Welbourn, B.; Welch, A.; Welch, H.; Welch, M.; Welch, S.; Weldon, J.; Weldrick, J.; Weldrick, Julian C.; Wellenkamp, L.; Wells, C.; Wells, C.E.; Wells, D.; Wells, J.; Wells, L.; Wells, M.; Wells, P.; Wells, R.; Wells, R.P.; Wells, T.; Welsh, J.; Welstead, A.; Welstead, N.I.; Welton, P.; Wendzonka, J.; Wenham, S.; Werndly, M.; Wesley, R.; West, A.; West, B.B.; West, G.; West, J.; West, M.; West, N.; West, P.; West, R.; West, S.; Westdean, G.; Westerberg, S.; Westley, P.; Westmoreland, J.; Westmoreland, L.; Weston, B.J.P.; Weston, J.; Weston, T.; Weston, T.J.; Weston, V.; Westwood, B.; Westwood, D.; Westwood, J.; Westwood, S.; Westwood, W.D.; Wetton, B.; Wetton, P.; Weyl, R.S.; Whale, L.; Whaley, F.W.; Whaley, G.; Whalley, A.; Wharin, C.; Whatmough, J.; Wheeldon, R.; Wheeler, D.; Wheeler, H.; Whelehan, J.; Whellan, J.A.; Whild, S.; Whild, S.J.; Whillock, N.; Whitaker, D.; Whitaker, E.; Whitaker, T.; Whitaker, T.M.; Whitaker, W.; Whitaker, W.J.; Whitburn, M.; Whitby, M.; Whitchurch, T.; Whitcomb, A.D.; Whitcomb, I.; White, A.; White, D.; White, D.J.; White, F.B.; White, G.; White, G.J.; White, G.T.; White, H.; White, H.V.; White, I.; White, J.; White, K.; White, M.; White, M.J.; White, P.; White, R.; White, R.L.P.; White, S.J.; White, T.; Whiteaway, K.; Whitecross, R.; Whitefield, D.; Whitehall, B.; Whitehall, I.; Whitehead, J.; Whitehead, P.; Whitehead, P.F.; Whitehead, R.; Whitehead, R.W.; Whitehead, S.; Whitehead, T.; Whitehorne, D.G.; Whitehouse, A.; Whitehouse, F.I.; Whitehouse, S.; Whitelaw, A.; Whitelegg, J.; Whiteley, D.; Whiteman, C.A.; Whiteside, L.; Whiteside, M.; Whitfield, F.; Whitfield, L.; Whitfield, M.; Whiting, C.; Whitley, P.N.; Whitney, A.; Whittaker, O.; Whittington, A.; Whittle, C.; Whittle, L.; Whittle, M.; Whittles, C.A.; Whitton, D.; Whitworth, S.; Whyle, B.; Whyte, M.; Whyte, P.; Wicken, J.; Wickens, D.; Wickham, J.; Wickham, M.; Wickings, D.; Wicklings, D.; Wicks, D.; Widden, B.J.; Widgery, J.; Wiffen, T.; Wigens, P.; Wiggers, R.; Wigginton, M.; Wigglesworth, B.; Wiggton, M.; Wighton, R.; Wigzell, F.; Wilby, G.; Wilby, J.; Wilby, R.; Wilcox, J.; Wilcox, M.; Wilcox, V.; Wild, A.; Wild, E.H.; Wild, J.; Wild, L.; Wild, O.H.; Wilde, D.; Wilde, I.; Wilde, P.; Wilding, D.; Wildridge, G.F.; Wiley, M.; Wiley, O.; Wilke, D.; Wilkes, K.; Wilkes, N.; Wilkin, V.; Wilkins, J.; Wilkins, P.; Wilkins, R.; Wilkins, T.; Wilkins, V.; Wilkinson, A.; Wilkinson, B.; Wilkinson, C.; Wilkinson, G.; Wilkinson, J.; Wilkinson, K.; Wilkinson, L.; Wilkinson, M.; Wilkinson, P.; Wilkinson, R.; Wilks, J.; Willams, J.; Willams, T.; Willamson, G.R.; Willcocks, P.; Willcox, J.M.; Willet, J.; Willets, K.; Williams Vaughan, J.; Williams, A.; Williams, B.; Williams, C.; Williams, D.; Williams, D.G.; Williams, D.W.; Williams, E.; Williams, E.F.; Williams, G.; Williams, G.A.; Williams, G.E.; Williams, H.; Williams, I.; Williams, J.; Williams, J.H.G.; Williams, J.W.; Williams, K.; Williams, L.; Williams, L.R.; Williams, M.; Williams, M.J.; Williams, N.; Williams, P.; Williams, R.; Williams, R.J.; Williams, S.; Williams, S.G.; Williams, T.; Williams, W.; Williams-Davies, L.; Williamson, B.; Williamson, D.; Williamson, J.;

Williamson, J.R.; Williamson, K.; Williamson, P.; Williamson, R.; Willis, A.; Willis, E.; Willis, J.; Willis, M.; Willis, N.; Willis, T.; Willison, R.; Willits, N.; Willmott, J.W.; Wills, E.; Willsher, J.; Willson, K.; Wilmer, T.; Wilmore, A.; Wilson, A.; Wilson, C.; Wilson, C. J.; Wilson, E.; Wilson, G.; Wilson, H.; Wilson, I.; Wilson, I.B.; Wilson, J.; Wilson, J.D.; Wilson, K.; Wilson, K.D.; Wilson, K.M.; Wilson, L.; Wilson, M.; Wilson, M.C.; Wilson, O.; Wilson, O.S.; Wilson, P.; Wilson, P.H.G.; Wilson, P.J.; Wilson, R.; Wilson, R.J.M.; Wilson, R.M.; Wilson, S.; Wilson, T.; Wilson, T.J.; Wilson, W.; Wilson-Parr, R.; Wilton, D.; Wilton, L.; Wilton-Jones, G.; Wiltshire, J.T.; Winchester, A.; Winder, F.G.A.; Winder, J.; Winder, J.M.; Winder, K.; Winder, M.; Windsor, C.; Wingrove, B.J.; Wingrove, D.; Winnall, N.; Winnall, R.; Winnard, D.; Winnington, A.; Winsch, M.; Winskill, R.; Winsland, D.C.; Wint, J.; Winter, P.; Wise, E.; Wise, N.A.J.; Wise, R.; Wise, T.; Wisniewski, P.; Wistow, R.; Wistow, R.J.; Wiswell, H.; Withers, D.; Withycombe, C.L.; Wittaker, P.; Witter, P.N.; Witts, A.; Wohlgemuth, J.; Woiwood, I.; Wolfendon, I.; Wolffe, A.; Wolstenholme, R.S.; Wolton, R.J.; Wolwood, I.; Womersley, H.; Wood, A.; Wood, B.; Wood, D.; Wood, J.; Wood, N.; Wood, P.; Wood, R.; Wood, S.; Wood, T.; Wood, T.C.; Wood-Homer, H.; Woodbridge, J.; Woodcock, B.; Woodcock, C.; Woodfield, D.; Woodger, J.; Woodhead, D.; Woodhead, F.; Woodhead, J.; Woodhouse, A.; Woodhouse, P.; Woodland, J.; Woodman, G.; Woodman, H.; Woodman, J.; Woodman, S.; Woodmansey, D.; Woodrow, W.; Woodruff, P.; Woods, A.; Woods, J.; Woods, M.; Woods, N.; Woods, P.; Woods, R.; Woods, R.G.; Woods, S.; Woodward, A.; Woodward, D.; Woodward, D.J.; Woodward, F.; Woodward, F.R.; Woodward, G.; Woodward, N.; Woodward, R.; Woodward, R.G.; Woodward, S.; Woodward, S.F.; Wooffe, R.W.; Wookey, G.; Woolcott, J.; Wooldbridge, D.B.; Wooley, V.; Woolfe, J.J.; Woolley, D.; Woolley, E.; Woolley, K.; Woolley, S.; Woolner, M.; Woolnough, M.; Woolnough, P.; Worfolk, T.; Workman, L.; Wormell, P.; Wormwell, C.; Wormwell, K.; Worrall, G.R.; Worrall, L.; Worrall, P.; Worroll, J.; Worsley, B.; Worsley, J.; Worswick, G.; Wortham, P.; Worthington, L.; Worton, L.; Worwood, S.; Woulahan, G.; Wozencroft, J.; Wragg, A.; Wragg, J.; Wragg, M.; Wragg, P.; Wraithmell, A.; Wrench, D.; Wright, A.; Wright, B.; Wright, C.; Wright, D.; Wright, D.E.; Wright, E.; Wright, F.; Wright, G.; Wright, H.; Wright, I.; Wright, J.; Wright, K.; Wright, L.; Wright, M.; Wright, M.T.; Wright, N.; Wright, P.; Wright, R.; Wright, R.N.; Wright, S A.; Wright, S.; Wright, S.A.; Wright, T.; Wright, W.; Wright, W.S.; Wrightson, T.; Wyatt, G.; Wyatt, R.; Wykes, N.; Wyldes, A.; Wylie, W.; Wyllie, J.; Wynde, R.M.; Wyndham Miller, S.; Wyness, L.; Wynn, N.; Wynne, G.; Wynne, I.; Yarnell, R.; Yates, B.; Yates, P.; Yates, S.; Yates, T.J.; Yearsley, K.; Yeates, C.; Yeates, K.; Yeo, M.; Yeomans, E.; Yerbury, J.W.; York, B.; Yost, L.; Youden, G.H.; Youell, S.; Young, A.; Young, G.; Young, H.; Young, I.; Young, J.; Young, M.; Young, M.G.; Young, M.R.; Young, P.; Young, P.A.; Young, S.; Youngman, R.E.; Yuile, P.; Zagni, P.; Zantboer, J.; Zasada, K.; Zienkiewicz, J.; Zonfrillo, B.

The 2014 DRN recorders meeting was held at Bubbenhall near Coventry. *Steve Cham*

# References

Allen, K.A. & Thompson, D.J. 2009. Movement characteristics of the Scarce Blue-tailed Damselfly, *Ischnura pumilio*. Insect Conservation and Diversity 3: 5-14.

Andres, J. A. & Cordero, A. 1998. Effects of water mites on the damselfly *Ceriagrion tenellum*. Ecological Entomology 23: 103-109.

Askew, R .R. 1988. The dragonflies of Europe. Harley Books, Colchester.

Askew, R .R. 2004. The dragonflies of Europe (revised edition). Harley Books, Colchester.

Averill, M.T. 1989. Emergence attitudes in *Gomphus vulgatissimus* (L). Journal of the British Dragonfly Society 5: 37-39.

Averill, M.T. 1998. Dragonfly Roundup. Worcestershire Record No 5 Nov, pp. 13-14.

Batty, P. 1998. *Brachytron pratense* (Muller) in Mid Argyll. Journal of the British Dragonfly Society. 14: 21-27.

Batty, P.M. 2013. The Brilliant Emerald *Somatochlora metallica* (Vander Linden) in Scotland, with particular reference to the Argyll sites and to larval habitat. Journal of the British Dragonfly Society 29: 55-64.

Belden, P. A., Downer, V. J., Luck, J. C., Prendergast, H. D. V. & Sadler, D. 2004. The Dragonflies of Sussex: A guide to their distribution and conservation. Essedon Press, Forest Row, E. Sussex. 81 pp.

Beaumont, E. & Beaumont, A. 2012. Large White-faced Darter *Leucorrhinia pectoralis* (Charpentier) in Suffolk. Atropos 46: 11-13.

Bennett, S. & Mill, P. J. 1993. Larval development and emergence in *Pyrrhosoma nymphula* (Sulzer) (Zygoptera: Coenagrionidae). Odonatologica 22: 133-145.

Bennett, S. & Mill, P. J. 1995a. Pre- and post-maturation survival in adults of the damselfly *Pyrrhosoma nymphula* (Zygoptera: Coenagrionidae). Journal of Zoology 235: 559-575.

Bennett, S. & Mill, P. J. 1995b. Lifetime egg production and egg mortality in the damselfly *Pyrrhosoma nymphula* (Sulzer) (Zygoptera: Coenagrionidae). Hydrobiologia 310: 71-78.

Benton, E. & Payne, R. G. 1983. On the rediscovery of *Lestes dryas* Kirby in Britain. Journal of the British Dragonfly Society 1: 28-30.

Benton, T. & Dobson, J. 2007. The Dragonflies of Essex. The Nature of Essex Series No. 6. The Essex Field Club in association with Lopinga Books. 228 pp.

Bernard, R. & Samolag, J. 1997. Analysis of the emergence of *Aeshna affinis* in the vicinity of Poznan, western Poland. Opuscula Zoologica Fluminensia 153: 1-12.

Beynon, T. G. 1998. Behaviour of immigrant *Sympetrum flaveolum* (L.) at breeding sites in 1995 and subsequent proof of breeding in 1996. Journal of the British Dragonfly Society 14: 6-11.

Borisov, S. N. 2009. Study of dragonfly (Odonata) migrations in the Western Tien Shan mountains using ornithological traps. Entomological Review 89: 1025-1029.

Boudot, J.-P., Kalkman, V. J., Azpilicueta Amorin, M., Bogdanović, T., Cordero Rivera, A., Degabriele, G., Dommanget, J.-L., Ferreira, S., Garrigós, B., Jović, M., Kotarac, M., Lopau, W., Marinov, M., Mihoković, N., Riservato, E., Samraoui, B. & Schneider, W. 2009. Atlas of the Odonata of the Mediterranean and North Africa. Libellula, Supplement 9, Börnsen, Germany.

Bouwman, J. H, Kalkman, V. J., Abbingh, G., Boer, E. P de, Geraerds, R. P. G., Groenendijk, D., Ketelaar, R., Manger, R., & Termaat, T. 2008. Een actualisatie van de verspreiding van de Nederlandse Libellen. Brachytron 11: 103-198.

Bouwman, J.H. & Ketelaar, R. 2008. New records of *Coenagrion armatum* in Schleswig-Holstein (Odonata: Coenagrionidae). Libellula 27: 185-190.

Boyce, D. 2002. Southern damselfly *Coenagrion mercuriale* GB site assessment project. CCW Contract Science. 537. UK BAP Southern Damselfly Steering Group.

Brinn, D. & Nelson, W. N. A. 1986. An early emergence of Odonata from an artificially warmed water source in south Wales. Journal of the British Dragonfly Society 2: 31-36.

British Dragonfly Society 2012. http://www.british-dragonflies.org.uk/sites/british-dragonflies.org.uk/files/libellula%20fulva.pdf

Brook, J. & Brook, G. 2001. Dragonflies of Kent. Transactions of the Kent Field Club, 16.

Brook, J. & Brook, G. 2011. The Dainty Damselfly *Coenagrion scitulum* in Kent. Atropos 42: 9-12.

Brooks, S. J. 1988. Exotic dragonflies in north London. Journal of the British Dragonfly Society 4: 9-12.

Brooks, S. J. 1989. The dragonflies (Odonata) of London: the current status. The London Naturalist 68: 109-132.

Brooks, S. 1999. Field Guide to the Dragonflies and Damselflies of Great Britain and Ireland. British Wildlife Publishing.

Brooks, S. J. & Lewington, R. 2004. (revised edition) Field guide to the dragonflies and damselflies of Great Britain and Ireland. British Wildlife Publishing, Hook, Hampshire, UK.

Brooks, S., Parr, A. & Mill, P. J. 2007. Dragonflies as climate change indicators. British Wildlife 19: 85-93.

Brownett, A. 2005. A re-examination of the status of the Norfolk Damselfly *Coenagrion armatum* (Charpentier): a species of Odonata now presumed extinct in Britain. Journal of the British Dragonfly Society 21: 21-26.

Burton, J. F. 1996. Movements of the dragonfly *Libellula quadrimaculata* Linnaeus, 1758 in North-west Europe in 1963. Atalanta 27: 175-187.

Butcher, R. W. 1927. A preliminary account of the vegetation of the River Itchen. Journal of Ecology 15: 55-64.

Carey, P. D.; Wallis, S.; Chamberlain, P. M.; Cooper, A.; Emmett, B. A.; Maskell, L. C.; McCann, T.; Murphy, J.; Norton, L. R.; Reynolds, B.; Scott, W. A.; Simpson, I. C.; Smart, S. M.; Ullyett, J. M. 2008. Countryside Survey: UK Results from 2007. NERC/Centre for Ecology & Hydrology, 105pp. (CEH Project Number: C03259).

Cham, S. 2002. The range expansion of Small Red-eyed Damselfly *Erythromma viridulum* (Charp.) in the British Isles. Atropos 15: 3-9.

Cham, S., 2004a. Oviposition behaviour of the two British species of red-eyed damselflies *Erythromma najas* (Hansemann) and *E. viridulum* (Charpentier). Journal of the British Dragonfly Society 20: 37-41.

Cham, S.A. 2004b. Dragonflies of Bedfordshire, Bedfordshire Natural History Society, 2004.

Cham, S. 2006. Development and hatching of eggs of the Common Darter, *Sympetrum striolatum* (Charpentier). Journal of the British Dragonfly Society 22: 36-40.

Cham, S. 2007. Field Guide to the larvae and exuviae of British Dragonflies. Volume 1: Dragonflies (Anisoptera). The British Dragonfly Society. Peterborough. 75 pp.

Cham, S. 2009. Field Guide to the Larvae and Exuviae of British Dragonflies. Volume 2: Damselflies (Zygoptera). The British Dragonfly Society, Peterborough. 75 pp.

Chelmick, D. 2009. Species Review 2: The Orange-spotted Emerald Dragonfly *Oxygastra curtisii* (Dale 1834). Journal of the British Dragonfly Society 25: 76-93.

Chelmick, D. 2011a. An Invasion of the Southern Migrant Hawker in 2010. Atropos 42: 3-8.

Chelmick, D. 2011b. The First Breeding record of Southern Migrant Hawker in the UK. Atropos 44: 20-27.

Clarke, D. 1994. Notes on the larva and generation time of *Aeshna caerulea* (Strom) in Scotland, with particular reference to the south-west. Journal of the British Dragonfly Society 10: 29-36.

Clarke, D. J. 1999. The outpost populations of the Banded Demoiselle *Calopteryx splendens* (Harris) in the Solway Firth area, Cumbria; historical perspective and recent developments. Journal of the British Dragonfly Society 15: 33-38.

Clarke, D. J. 2002. Growth and autumnal decline of feeding in captive-reared first-year larvae of the Azure Hawker *Aeshna caerulea* (Ström). Journal of the British Dragonfly Society 18: 9-12.

Clarke, D. J., Hewitt, S. M., Smith E. M. & Smith, R. W. J. 1990. Observations on the breeding habits and habitat of *Aeshna caerulea* (Ström) in Scotland. Journal of the British Dragonfly Society 6: 24-28.

Clausnitzer, H.-J., Clausnitzer, C. & Hengst, R. 2007. Zur Okologie von *Coenagrion tenellum* im Bereich der nordostlichen Verbreitungsgrenze in Niedersachsen (Odonata: Coenagrionidae). Libellula 26: 19-34.

Coker, S. 2002. A Long-Term Plan for *Coenagrion mercuriale* in North-East Pembrokeshire. Printed and circulated by the author.

Collingwood, N. 1997. The dragonflies of Staffordshire. Staffordshire Biological Recording Scheme, 18.

Cooper, A., McCann, T. & Rogers, D. 2009. Northern Ireland Countryside Survey 2007: Broad Habitat Change 1998-2007. Northern Ireland Environment Agency Research and Development Series No. 09/06.

Conrad, F. K. 2010. Red Damselfly – *Pyrrhosoma nymphula* http://www.brickfieldspark.org/data/damselflyred.htm

Corbet, P. S. 1952. An adult population study of *Pyrrhosoma nymphula* (Sulzer) (Odonata: Coenagrioniidae). Journal of Animal Ecology 21: 206-222.

Corbet, P. S. 1954. Seasonal regulation in British dragonflies. Nature, London 174: 655 [erratum 777].

Corbet, P. S. 1957a. The life-history of the Emperor Dragonfly *Anax imperator* Leach (Odonata: Aeshnidae). Journal of Animal Ecology 26: 1-69.

Corbet, P. S. 1957b. The life-histories of two spring species of dragonfly (Odonata: Zygoptera). Entomologist's Gazette 8: 79-89.

Corbet, P. S. 1999. Dragonflies: Behaviour and Ecology of Odonata. Harley Books, Colchester.

Corbet, P. S. 2000. The first recorded arrival of *Anax junius*, Drury (Anisoptera: Aeshnidae) in Europe: a scientist's perspective. International Journal of Odonatology 3: 153-162.

Corbet, P. S. 2003. A positive correlation between photoperiod and development rate in summer species of Odonata could help to make emergence date appropriate to latitude: a testable hypothesis. Journal of the Entomological Society of British Colombia 100: 3-17.

Corbet, P. S. & Harvey, I. F. 1989. Seasonal regulation in *Pyrrhosoma nymphula* (Sulzer) (Zygoptera: Coenagrionidae). 1. Seasonal development in nature. Odonatologica 18: 133-145.

Corbet, P. S. & Brooks, S. 2008. Dragonflies. Collins New Naturalists. London.

Corbet. P. S., Longfield. C. & Moore. N. W. 1961 (reprinted 1985). Dragonflies. Collins New Naturalist. London.

Corbet, P. S., Suhling, F. & Soendgerath, D. 2006. Voltinism of Odonata: a review. International Journal of Odonatology 9: 1-44.

Cordero, A. 1996. A preliminary checklist of Odonata of Galicia, NW Spain. In: Studies on Iberian Dragonflies. Advances in Odonatology, Supplement 1: 13-25.

Cotton, D. C. F. 1982. *Coenagrion lunulatum* (Charpentier) (Odonata: Coenagrionidae) new to the British Isles. Entomologist's Gazette 33: 213-214.

Daguet, C. A., French, G. C. & Taylor, P. 2008. The Odonata Red Data List for Great Britain. Species Status 11: 1-34. Joint Nature Conservation Committee, Peterborough, UK.

d'Aguilar, J., Dommanget, J.-L. & Préchac, R. 1986. A field guide to the dragonflies of Britain, Europe and North Africa. Collins, London, UK.

De Knijf, G., Anselin, A. & Goffart, P. 2003. Trends in dragonfly occurrence in Belgium (Odonata). In: Reemer, M., van Helsdingen, P.J. & Kleukers, R.M.J.C. (Eds.), Proceedings of the 13th International Colloquium of the European Invertebrate Survey. European Invertebrate Survey, The Netherlands, pp. 33-38.

Dewick, S. & Gerussi, R. 2000. Small Red-eyed Damselfly *Erythromma viridulum* (Charp.) found breeding in Essex. Atropos 9: 3-4.

Dijkstra, K.-D., Dingemanse, N. & Edelaar, P. 1995. Zadellibel *Hemianax ephippiger* te Budel: een nieuwe soort voor Nederland. Libellennieuwsbrief 3: 6-7.

Dijkstra, K.-D., Kalkman, V.J., Ketelaar, R. & Van Der Weide, M.J.T. 2002. Der Nederlandse Libellen (Odonata). Nationaal Natuurhistorisch Museum Naturalis. KNNV Uitgeverij Utrecht.

Dijkstra, K.-D. B. & Lewington, R. 2006. Field Guide to the Dragonflies of Britain and Europe. British Wildlife Publishing, Gillingham, Dorset. 320 pp.

Dijkstra, K.-D. B., Kalkman, V. J., Dow, R. A., Stokvis, F. R. and Van Tol, J. 2013. Redefining the damselfly families: a comprehensive molecular phylogeny of Zygoptera (Odonata). Systematic Entomology (2013), DOI: 10.1111/syen.12035.

Dijkstra, K.-D. B., Bechly, G., Bybee, S. M., Dow, R. A., Dumont, H. J., Fleck, G., Garrison, R. W., Hämäläinen, M., Kalkman, V. J., Karube, H., May, M. L., Orr, A. G., Paulson, D. R., Rehn, A. C., Theischinger, G., Trueman, J. W. H., Van Tol, J., Von Ellenrieder, N., & Ware, J. 2013. The classification and diversity of dragonflies and damselflies (Odonata) Zootaxa 3703: 36-45. In: Zhang, Z.-Q. (Ed.) Animal Biodiversity: An Outline of Higher-level Classification and Survey of Taxonomic Richness (Addenda 2013). Zootaxa 3703: 1-82.

DoE. 1995. Biodiversity: the UK Steering Group Report. HMSO, London.

Doi, H. 2008. Delayed phenological timing of dragonfly emergence in Japan over five decades. Biology Letters 4: 388-391.

Drake, C.M. 1990. Records of larval *Lestes dryas* Kirby in Essex during 1987. Journal of the British Dragonfly Society 6: 34-41.

Drinan, T., Nelson, B., Tickner, M., O'Donnell, G., Harrison, S. & O'Halloran, J. 2011. First discovery of larvae of the Downy Emerald *Cordulia aenea* (L., 1758) (Odonata: Corduliidae) in Ireland and the species' use of lakes in treeless blanket bog in Connemara, Co. Galway. Journal of the British Dragonfly Society 27: 1-12.

Dumont, H. J. 2003. Odonata from the Republic of Mongolia and from the Autonomous Region of Inner Mongolia. International Journal of Odonatology 6: 127-146.

Dumont, H. J. & Desmet, K. 1990. Trans-Sahara and trans-Mediterranean migratory activity of *Hemianax ephippiger* (Burmeister) in 1988 and 1989 (Anisoptera: Aeshnidae). Odonatologica 19: 181-185.

Environment Agency 2012a. Web page: environment-agency.gov.uk/news/142101.aspx

Environment Agency 2012b. Web page: environment-agency.gov.uk/research/planning/34383.aspx

Environment Agency. 2013. Environment Agency Pollution Incidents Report September 2013. http://a0768b4a8a31e106d8b0-50dc802554eb38a24458b98ff72d550b.r19.cf3.rackcdn.com/LIT_8547_b70a6b.pdf

Environment Agency (undated) Freshwater Fisheries and Wildlife Conservation A guide to good practice. Web page: environment-agency.gov.uk/static/documents/Leisure/geho1006blak_ee1.pdf

Environment Agency (undated) Stocking Fish: a guide for fishery owners and managers. Web page: environment-agency.gov.uk/static/documents/Business/stocking__eng_172017.pdf

ERA-Maptec. Undated. CORINE Land Cover – Ireland. Land Cover Update for 2006. Final Report. European Environment Agency.

Evans, F. 1989. A Review of the Management of Lowland Wet Heath in Dyfed, West Wales. CSD Contract No. CSD 50/F2C/415. Nature Conservancy Council, Peterborough.

Ford, W. K. 1954. Lancashire and Cheshire Odonata (some further notes). The North Western Naturalist (new series) 2: 602-603.

Fraser, F. C. 1953. *Aeshna caerulea* (Ström) and *Somatochlora arctica* in Perthshire (Odonata). Entomologists' Monthly Magazine 89: 33-36.

Gabb, R. 1985. *Aeshna caerulea* (Strom) breeding at Beinn Eighe N.N.R.. Journal of the British Dragonfly Society 1: 101-102.

Garcia, N., Cuttelod, A. & Abdul Malak, D. (eds.) 2010. The Status and Distribution of Freshwater Biodiversity in Northern Africa. Gland, Switzerland, Cambridge, UK, and Malaga, Spain: IUCN, 2010. xiii+141pp.

Gardner, A. E. 1955. A study of the genitalia of the two species *Sympetrum nigrescens* Lucas and *S. nigrifemur* (Selys) with notes on their distribution. Entomologist's Gazette 6: 86-108.

Gardner, A. E. & MacNeill, N. 1950. The life history of *Pyrrhosoma nymphula* (Sulzer) (Odonata). Part I Life History (Gardner); Part II Final instar nymph and ecological notes (MacNeill). Entomologist's Gazette 1: 163-182.

Garner, P. 2005. The Dragonflies of Herefordshire. Herefordshire Biological Records Centre.

Göcmen, B. 2009. Nature Photography. *Calopteryx splendens* ssp. *intermedia* (Banded Demoiselle / Bantlı Kizböceği). http://fen.ege.edu.tr/~bgocmen/album/picture.php?/931/category/326

Goffart, P. 1984. Observations de *Crocothemis erythraea* et *Anax parthenope* en Belgique durant l'été 1983. Gomphus 1: 1-3.

Gibbins, C. N. & Moxon, J. B. 1998. *Calopteryx splendens* (Harris) at edge of range sites in North-east England. Journal of the British Dragonfly Society 14: 33-45.

Goodyear, K. G. 1994. *Gomphus vulgatissimus* (L) in Oxfordshire and Hampshire. Journal of the British Dragonfly Society 10: 19-20.

Goodyear, K. G. 1995. Comparison of aquatic larval habitat of *Libellula fulva* Müller. Journal of the British Dragonfly Society 11: 42-45.

Goodyear, K. G. 2000. A comparison of the environmental requirements of larvae of the Banded Demoiselle *Calopteryx splendens* (Harris) and the Beautiful Demoiselle *C. virgo* (L.). Journal of the British Dragonfly Society 16: 33-51.

Goudsmits, K. 1997. Een waarneming van de Zuidelijke keizerslibel (*Anax parthenope*, Sélys) in Nederland. Brachytron 1: 59-60.

Groenendijk, D., Mensing, V. & Plate, C. 2008. Ten years dragonfly monitoring in the Netherlands: results and lessons for the future, from International Symposium Monitoring Dragonflies in Europe, unpublished. [abstracts available at http://www.vlinderstichting.nl/pdf/DS_Abstractbook.pdf]

Grand, D. & Boudot, J.-P. 2006. Les Libellules de France, Belgique et Luxembourg. Collection Parthénope. Biotope, Mèze, France. 480 pp.

Gribbin, S. D. & Thompson, D. J. 1991. Emergence of the damselfly *Pyrrhosoma nymphula* (Sulzer) (Zygoptera: Coenagrionidae) from two adjacent ponds in northern England. Hydrobiologia 209: 123-131.

Gyulavári, H. A., Felföldi, T., Benken, T., Szabó, L.J., Miskolczi, M., Cserháti, C., Horvai, V., Márialigeti, K. & Dévai, G. 2011. Morphometric and molecular studies on the populations of the damselflies *Chalcolestes viridis* and *C. parvidens* (Odonata, Lestidae). International Journal of Odonatology 14: 329-339.

Hammond, C. O. 1977. The dragonflies of Great Britain and Ireland. Curwen Books, London, UK.

Haritonov, A. & Popova, O. 2011. Spatial displacement of Odonata in south-west Siberia. International Journal of Odonatology 14: 1-10.

Hassall, C. & Thompson, D. J. 2009. Variation in wing spot size and asymmetry of the Banded Demoiselle *Calopteryx splendens* (Harris, 1780). Journal of the British Dragonfly Society 25: 7-15.

Hassall, C., Keat, S., Thompson, D. J. & Watts, P.C. 2014. Bergmann's rule is maintained during a rapid range expansion in a damselfly. Global Change Biology 20: 475-482.

Hassall, C., Thompson, D. J., French, G. C. & Harvey, I. F. 2007. Historical changes in the phenology of British Odonata are related to climate. Global Change Biology 13: 933-941.

Heijden, A. E. van der. 2000. Een vondst van een populatie Donkere waterjuffers (*Coenagrion armatum*) in De Weerribben. Brachytron 4: 16-19.

Hill, M. O. 2012. Local frequency as a key to interpreting species occurrence data when recording effort is not known. Methods in Ecology and Evolution 3: 195-205.

Hobson, K. A., Anderson, R. C., Soto, D. X. & Wassenaar, L. I. 2012. Isotopic evidence that dragonflies (*Pantala flavescens*) migrating through the Maldives come from the northern Indian Subcontinent. PLoS ONE 7(12): e52594. doi:10.1371/journal.pone.0052594

Holme, J. D. 1995. Notes on *Libellula fulva* Müller on the River Avon near Bristol. Journal of the British Dragonfly Society 11: 20.

Hope, P. 2009. The Small Red Damselfly *Ceriagrion tenellum* (de Villers) and its close relative the Turkish Red Damselfly *Ceriagrion georgifreyi* (Schmidt). Journal of the British Dragonfly Society 25: 41-56.

Horváth, G., Malik, P., Kriska, G. & Wildermuth, H. 2007. Ecological traps for dragonflies in a cemetery: the attraction of *Sympetrum* species (Odonata: Libellulidae) by horizontally polarizing black gravestones. Freshwater Biology 52: 1700-1709.

Hubble, D. S. & Hurst, D. 2003. Management of small dug ponds for Odonata conservation and colonization in an area of valley mire and wet heathland (Bourne Valley, Dorset). Journal of the British Dragonfly Society 19: 24-34.

IPCC, 2013. Climate Change 2013: The Physical Science Basis. Contribution of Working Group I to the Fifth Assessment Report of the Intergovernmental Panel on Climate Change [Stocker, T.F., D. Qin, G.-K. Plattner, M. Tignor, S. K. Allen, J. Boschung, A. Nauels, Y. Xia, V. Bex & P.M. Midgley (eds.)]. Cambridge University Press.

Isaac, N. J. B. 2012. Extracting trends from biological recording data. In National Biodiversity Network Conference. London. doi:doi:10.6084/m9.figshare.428369

Isaac, N. J. B., van Strien, A. J., August, T. A., de Zeeuw, M. P., & Roy, D. B. 2014. Extracting robust trends in species' distributions from unstructured opportunistic data: a comparison of methods. Methods in Ecology and Evolution, in press.

IUCN 2005. Guidelines for Using the IUCN Red List Categories and Criteria. Prepared by the Standards and Petitions Subcommittee of the IUCN SSC Red List Programme Committee.

IUCN Red List 2010. http://www.iucnredlist.org/apps/redlist/details/165524/9

Ivinskis P. & Rimšaitė J. 2009. Odonata of Purvinas wetland in eastern Lithuania. Acta Biologica Universitatis Daugavpiliensis 9: 39-42.

Jaeschke, A., Bittner, T., Reineking, B. & Beierkuhnlein, C. 2013. Can they keep up with climate change? Integrating specific dispersal abilities of protected Odonata in species distribution modelling. Insect Conservation and Diversity 6: 93-103.

Jeffries, M. 2001. The Northumbrian Frontier of the Banded Demoiselle *Calopteryx splendens* (Harris). Journal of the British Dragonfly Society 17: 55-58.

Jenkins, D. K., Parr, M. J., Moore, N. W., & Silsby, J. 1998. Management guidelines for the southern damselfly. In Species Management in Aquatic Habitats (ed. C.P. Mainstone). Environment Agency, Bristol.

Jensen, J.-K. & Nielsen, O. F. 2012. Brun kejserguldsmed *Anax ephippiger* (Burmeister, 1839) (Aeshnidae, Odonata) fundet på Færøerne i 2011. Entomologiske meddelelser 80: 3-6.

JNCC. 2013. Third Report by the United Kingdom under Article 17 on the implementation of the [Habitats] Directive from January 2007 to December 2012 Conservation status assessment for Southern Damselfly (*Coenagrion mercuriale*). http://jncc.defra.gov.uk/pdf/Article17Consult_20131010/S1044_UK.pdf

Johansson, F. & Brodin, T. 2003. Effects of fish predators and abiotic factors on dragonfly community structure. Journal of Freshwater Ecology 18: 415-23.

Jones, S. P. 1985. A note on the survival of dragonflies in adverse conditions in Cornwall. Journal of the British Dragonfly Society 1: 83-84.

Jones, S. P. 1996a. The first British record of the Scarlet Dragonfly *Crocothemis erythraea* (Brullé). Journal of the British Dragonfly Society 12: 11-12.

Jones, S. P. 1996b. 1995: a year of exotic invaders. Cornwall Dragonfly Group Newsletter 6: 8-10.

Jones, S. P. 2000. First proof of successful breeding by the Lesser Emperor *Anax parthenope* (Sélys) in Britain. Journal of the British Dragonfly Society 16: 20-23.

Kalkman, V. J. & Lopau, W. 2006. Identification of *Pyrrhosoma elizabethae* with notes on its distribution and habitat (Odonata: Coenagrionidae). International Journal of Odonatology 9: 175-184.

Kalkman, V. J., Boudot, J.-P., Bernard, R., Conze, K.-J., De Knijf, G., Dyatlova, E., Ferreira, S., Jović, M., Ott, J., Riservato, E. & Sahlén, G. 2010. European Red List of Dragonflies. Luxembourg: Publications Office of the European Union.

Kemp, R. G. & Vick, G. S. 1983. Notes & observations on *Gomphus vulgatissimus* (Linnaeus) on the River Severn and River Thames. Journal of the British Dragonfly Society 1: 22-25.

Kemp, R. G. 1988. Is *Gomphus vulgatissimus* (L) exclusively a riverine species in the British Isles? Journal of the British Dragonfly Society 4: 8-9.

Ketelaar, R. 2002. The recent expansion of the Small Red-eyed Damselfly *Erythromma viridulum* (Charpentier) in The Netherlands. Journal of the British Dragonfly Society 18: 1-8.

Kjærstad, G., Andersen, T., Olsvik, H. A. & Brittain, J. E. 2010. Døgnfluer, øyenstikkere, steinfluer og vårfluer. In Kålås, J. A., Viken, Å., Henriksen, S. & Skjelseth, S. (Eds.) Norsk rødliste for arter 2010. Artsdatabanken, Trondheim. Pp. 227-234.

Khrokalo, L. & Krylovskaya S. 2008. Distribution and current status of *Coenagrion armatum* (Charpentier, 1840) in Ukraine. IDF-Report 13 (2008): 1-16.

Kosterin, O. 2009. English translation of: E. I. Malikova. 1995. Strekozy (Odonata, Insecta) Dal'nego Vostoka Rossii. International Dragonfly Fund Report 22: 1-22.

Kuussaari, M., Heliölä, J., Pöyry, J., & Saarinen, K. 2007. Contrasting trends of butterfly species preferring semi-natural grasslands, field margins and forest edges in northern Europe. Journal of Insect Conservation 11: 351-366.

Lawton, J. H. 1970. A population study on larvae of the damselfly *Pyrrhosoma nymphula* (Sulzer) (Odonata: Zygoptera). Hydrobiologia 36: 33-52.

Leipelt, K. G., Suhling, F. & Gorb, S. N. 2010. Ontogenetic shifts in functional morphology of dragonfly legs (Odonata: Anisoptera). Zoology 113: 317-325.

Le Quesne, W. J. 1946. The dragonflies of Jersey. Bulletin annuel de la Société Jersiaise 14: 213-216.

Levett, S. & Walls, S. 2011. Tracking the elusive life of the Emperor Dragonfly *Anax imperator* Leach. Journal of the British Dragonfly Society 27: 59-68.

Long, M. & Long, R. 2000. Non-British damselflies in Jersey. Atropos 9: 95-96.

Long, R. 2002. Southern Skimmer *Orthetrum brunneum* (Fonsc.) on Guernsey. Atropos 15: 10.

Longfield, C. 1948. A vast migration of dragonflies into the south coast of Co. Cork. Irish Naturalists' Journal 9: 133-141.

Longfield, C. 1949. (second enlarged edition) The dragonflies of the British Isles. Warne, London, UK.

Lucas, W. J. 1900. British Dragonflies. Upcott Gill, London. 356pp.

Lucas, W. J. 1912. British Odonata in 1911. Entomologist 45: 171-173.

Luck, J. 2011. Sussex Dragonfly Society Newsletter – Spring 2011, online http://webjam-upload.s3.amazonaws.com/sds_newsletter_spring_2010_opt_d6c5c9b1c15c4668ad1755d09c8f244c_4152_.pdf

Mendel, H. 1992. Suffolk dragonflies. Suffolk Naturalists' Society, Ipswich. 159pp.

Macan, T. T. 1964. The Odonata of a moorland fishpond. Internationale Revue der gesamten Hydrobiologie 49: 325-360.

Macan, T. T. 1974. Twenty generations of *Pyrrhosoma nymphula* (Sulzer) and *Enallagma cyathigerum* (Charpentier) (Zygoptera: Coenagrionidae). Odonatologica 3: 107-119.

Macan, T. T. 1975. VIII. Fishponds: Structure of the community in the vegetation of a moorland fishpond. Verhandlungen der Internationale Vereinigung für Theoretische und Angewandte Limnologie 19: 2298-2304.

Marren, P. R. & Merritt, R. 1983. Scarce species status report 2. A review of *Coenagrion hastulatum* (Chartpentier) in Britain. Journal of the British Dragonfly Society 1: 16-19.

Martens, A. 1993. Influence of conspecifics and plant structures on oviposition site selection in *Pyrrhosoma nymphula* (Sulzer) (Zygoptera: Coenagrionidae). Odonatologica 22: 487-494.

Mayo, M. C. A. & Welstead, A. R. 1983. *Coenagrion mercuriale* (Charpentier) on the flood plains of the River Itchen and River Test in Hampshire. Journal of the British Dragonfly Society 1: 20-21.

McGarrigle, M., Lucey, J. & Ó Cinnéide, M. (eds) 2010. Water Quality In Ireland 2007-2009. Environmental Protection Agency, Wexford, Ireland.

McGeeney, A. 1986. A Complete Guide to British Dragonflies. Jonathon Cape, London.

McLachlan, R. 1884. The British Dragon-flies annotated. Entomologists Monthly Magazine 20: 251-256.

Merritt, R., Moore, N. W. & Eversham, B. C. 1996. Atlas of the Dragonflies of Britain and Ireland. HMSO, London. 149pp.

Merritt, R. & Vick, G. S. 1983. Is *Sympetrum nigrescens* a good species? Journal of the British Dragonfly Society 1: 7-8.

Met Office. 2014. Seasonal Central England Temperature, 1659 to 2013. http://www.metoffice.gov.uk/hadobs/hadcet/ssn_HadCET_mean_sort.txt

Meurgey, F. 2004. Première observation d'*Anax junius* (Drury, 1773) en France (Odonata, Anisoptera, Aeshnidae). Martinia 20: 13-15.

Meurgey, F. 2006. *Anax ephippiger* (Burmeister, 1839), a new species for the West Indies. Argia 8: 21-22.

Michiels, N. 1992. Consequences and adaptive significance of variation in copulation duration in the dragonfly *Sympetrum danae*. Behavioral Ecology and Sociobiology 29: 429-433.

Michiels, N. & Dhondt, A. A. 1988. Direct and indirect estimates of sperm precedence and displacement in the dragonfly *Sympetrum danae* (Odonata: Libellulidae). Behavioral Ecology and Sociobiology 23: 257-263.

Michiels, N. & Dhondt, A. A. 1989. Differences in male and female activity patterns in the dragonfly *Sympetrum danae* (Sulzer) and their relation to mate-finding (Anisoptera: Libellulidae). Odonatologica 18: 349-364.

Michiels, N. & Dhondt, A. A. 1991. Sources of variation in male mating success and female oviposition rate in a nonterritorial dragonfly. Behavioral Ecology and Sociobiology 29: 17-25.

Mill, P. J. 2012. The Brilliant Emerald *Somatochlora metallica* (Vander Linden) and its close relative the Balkan Emerald *S. meridionalis* (Nielson). Journal of the British Dragonfly Society 28: 75-91.

Mill, P. J., Taylor, P. & Parr, A. J. 2004. Vernacular names for the dragonflies of north-western Europe. Journal of the British Dragonfly Society 20: 73-76.

Mill, P. J. 2010. Species Review 3: The Large Red Damselfly *Pyrrhosoma nymphula* (Sulzer) with notes on its close relative the Greek Red Damselfly *Pyrrhosoma elisabethae* Schmidt. Journal of the British Dragonfly Society 26: 34-56.

Mill, P. J., Brooks, S. & Parr, A. 2010. Dragonflies (Odonata) in Britain and Ireland. In: Silent Summer: The State of the Wildlife in Britain and Ireland (ed. Maclean, N.). Cambridge University Press, Cambridge. pp. 471-494.

Miller, P. L. 2004. Common Darter *Sympetrum striolatum* (Charpentier), pp. 143-144. In: Brooks, S.J. & Lewington, R. (eds) Field guide to the dragonflies and damselflies of Great Britain and Ireland. British Wildlife Publishing, Hook.

Midttun, B. 1977. Observations of *Somatochlora arctica* in Western Norway. Norwegian Journal of Entomology 24: 117-119.

Moore, B. P. 1949. *Sympetrum meridionale* Sélys (Odon., Libellulidae), new to the Channel Islands. Entomologist's Monthly Magazine 85: 23.

Moore, N. W. 1980. *Lestes dryas* Kirby – a declining species of dragonfly (Odonata) in need of conservation: note on its status and habitat in England and Ireland. Biological Conservation 17: 143-148.

Moore, N. W. 1991. Where do adult *Gomphus vulgatissimus* (L) go during the middle of the day? Journal of the British Dragonfly Society 7: 40-43.

Moore, N. W. 1986. Acid water dragonflies in eastern England – their decline, isolation and conservation. Odonatologica 15: 377-385.

Muller, O. 1995. Ökologische Untersuchungen an Gomphiden (Odonata: Anisoptera) unter besonderer Berücksichtigung ihrer Larvenstadien. Cuvillier, Göttingen.

Nelson, B. 1999. The status and habitat of the Irish damselfly Coenagrion lunulatum (Charpentier) (Odonata) in Northern Ireland. Entomologist's monthly Magazine 135: 59-68.

Nelson, B. 2011. A review of notable records of Irish odonates post DragonflyIreland (2004-2010), including confirmation of the Golden-ringed Dragonfly Cordulegaster boltonii (Donovan) on the Irish list. Journal of the British Dragonfly Society 27: 105-131.

Nelson, B., Ronayne, C. & Thompson, R. 2003. Colonisation and changing status of four Odonata species, Anax imperator, Anax parthenope, Aeshna mixta and Sympetrum fonscolombii, in Ireland 2000-2002. Irish Naturalists' Journal 27: 266-272.

Nelson, B., Ronayne, C. & Thompson, R. 2011. Ireland Red List No. 6: Damselflies & Dragonflies (Odonata). National Parks and Wildlife Service, Department of the Environment, Heritage and Local Government, Dublin, Ireland.

Nelson, B. & Thompson, R. 2004. The Natural History of Ireland's Dragonflies. The National Museums and Galleries of Northern Ireland.

Nelson, B., Thompson, R. & Morrow, C. 2001. Dragonfly Ireland. Internet publication. (Current version http://www.habitas.org.uk.dragonflyireland/)

Nelson, J. 1996. The Monarch Danaus plexippus (L.) influx into Britain and Ireland in October 1995. Atropos 1: 5-10.

Olafsson, E. 1975. Drekaflugan Hemianax ephippiger (Burm.) (Odonata), ovæntur gestur a Islandi. Natturufroedingurinn 45: 209-212.

Ormerod, S. J., Rundle, S. D., Lloyd, E. C., & Douglas, A. A. 1993. The influence of riparian management on the habitat structure and macroinvertebrate communities of upland streams draining plantation forests. Journal of Applied Ecology 30: 13-24.

Ott, J. 2007. The expansion of Crocothemis erythraea (Brullé, 1832) in Germany – an indicator of climatic changes. In: Tyagi, B.K. (Ed.) Odonata: Biology of Dragonflies. Scientific Publishers (India), pp. 201-222.

Ott, J. 2010a. Monitoring Climatic Change with Dragonflies. BioRisk 5. Pensoft Publishers, Sofia.

Ott, J. 2010b. Dragonflies and climatic change – recent trends in Germany and Europe. BioRisk 5: 253-286.

Ott, J., Schorr, M., Trockur, B. & Lingenfelder, U. 2007. Species Protection Programme for the Orange-spotted Emerald (Oxygastra curtisii) in Germany – the example of the River Our population. Pensoft, Sofia.

Ottolenghi, C. 1987. Reproductive behaviour of Sympetrum striolatum (Charp.) at an artificial pond in northern Italy. Odonatologica 16: 297-306.

Parker, D. E., Legg, T. P. & Folland, C. K. 1992. A new daily Central England Temperature Series, 1772-1991. International Journal of Climatology 12: 317-342.

Parkes, K. A., Amos, W., Moore, N. W., Hoffman, J. I. & Moore, J. 2009. Population structure and speciation in the dragonfly Sympetrum striolatum/nigrescens (Odonata: Libellulidae): an analysis using AFLP markers. European Journal of Entomology 106: 1279-184.

Parr, A. J. 1996. Dragonfly movement and migration in Britain and Ireland. Journal of the British Dragonfly Society 12: 33-50.

Parr, A. J. 1997. Migrant and dispersive dragonflies in Britain during 1996. Journal of the British Dragonfly Society 13: 41-48.

Parr, A. J. 1998a. Winter dragonfly sightings in Britain during early 1998. Atropos 5: 13-16.

Parr, A. J. 1998b. Migrant and dispersive dragonflies in Britain during 1997. Journal of the British Dragonfly Society 14: 52-58.

Parr, A. J. 2000. Blue Dasher Pachydiplax longipennis (Burmeister) on an oil rig in the North Sea. Atropos 10: 3-5.

Parr, A. J. 2004. Migrant and dispersive dragonflies in Britain during 2003. Journal of the British Dragonfly Society 20: 42-50.

Parr, A. J. 2007. Migrant and dispersive dragonflies in Britain during 2006. Journal of the British Dragonfly Society 23: 40-51.

Parr, A. J. 2008. Migrant and dispersive dragonflies in Britain during 2007. Journal of the British Dragonfly Society 24: 62-70.

Parr, A. J. 2009a. The Willow Emerald Damselfly Lestes viridis (Vander Linden) in East Anglia. Atropos 38: 6-9.

Parr, A. J. 2009b. Winter Damselfly Sympecma fusca Vander Linden in West Glamorgan. Atropos 37: 28-31.

Parr, A. J. 2010. Records of Exotic Odonata in Britain during 2010. Atropos 41: 39-42.

Parr, A. J. 2011. The year of the Vagrant Emperor Anax ephippiger (Burmeister). Atropos 44: 3-10.

Parr, A. J. 2012. Migrant and dispersive dragonflies in Britain during 2011. Journal of the British Dragonfly Society 28: 56-65.

Parr, A. J. 2013. The Large White-faced Darter Leucorrhinia pectoralis in Britain during 2012. Journal of the British Dragonfly Society 29: 40-45.

Parr, A. J., de Knijf, G. & Wasscher, M. 2004. Recent appearances of the Lesser Emperor Anax parthenope (Sélys) in north-western Europe. Journal of the British Dragonfly Society 20: 5-16.

Parr, M. J. & Parr, M. 1979. Some observations on Ceriagrion tenellum (de Villers) in southern England (Zygoptera: Coenagrionidae). Odonatologica 8: 171-194.

Pellow, K. 1999. An influx of Green Darner Anax junius (Drury) into Cornwall and the Isles of Scilly: the first European records. Atropos 6: 3-7.

Pellow, K. 1999. Some observations of a breeding population of Red-veined Darter Sympetrum fonscolombii (Sélys) in Cornwall during 1998. Journal of the British Dragonfly Society 15: 23-30.

Perrin, V. L. 1999. Observations on the distribution, ecology and behaviour of the Hairy Dragonfly Brachytron pratense (Müller). Journal of the British Dragonfly Society 15: 39-45.

Phillips, J. 1987. Lesser Emperor Dragonfly Anax parthenope (Sélys) in Gloucestershire; the first British record. Journal of the British Dragonfly Society 13: 22-24.

Phillips, J. 2003. Recent records of Orthetrum coerulescens (Fabricius) Keeled Skimmer from the Forest of Dean. Gloucestershire Naturalists' Society Journal 48: 299-302.

Pickwell, A. 2011. The influence of salinity on the distribution and survival of the Norfolk Hawker dragonfly (Aeshna isosceles Müller, 1767) in the Norfolk Broads. Final Report to the Broads Authority, Norfolk.

Pilgrim, E. M. & Von Dohlen, C. D. 2007. Molecular and morphological study of species-level questions within the dragonfly genus Sympetrum (Odonata: Libellulidae). Annals of the Entomological Society of America 100: 688-702.

Pinhey, E. C. G. 1961. A survey of the dragonflies (order Odonata) of eastern Africa. British Museum, London, UK.

Prendergast, N. H. D. 1988. The distribution and abundance of Calopteryx splendens (Harris), C. virgo (L.) and Platycnemis pennipes (Pallas) on the Wey river system (Hampshire & Surrey). Journal of the British Dragonfly Society 4: 37-44.

Preston, C. D. & Croft, J. M. 1997. Aquatic Plants in Britain and Ireland. Harley Books, Colchester.

Prince, P. & Clarke, R. 1993. The Hobby's breeding range in Britain. What factors have allowed it to expand? British Wildlife 4: 341-346.

Proctor, M. 2013. Vegetation of Britain and Ireland. Collins New Naturalists. London.

Purse, B. V. 2001. The ecology and conservation of the southern damselfly (Coenagrion mercuriale). PhD Thesis. University of Liverpool, Liverpool, UK.

Purse, B. 2002. The Ecology and Conservation of the Southern Damselfly (Coenagrion mercuriale Charpentier) in Britain. R&D Technical Report W1-021/TR. Environment Agency, Bristol.

Randolph, S. 1992. Dragonflies of the Bristol Region. City of Bristol Museums and Art Gallery and Avon Regional Environmental Records Centre, Bristol, UK.

Ratcliffe, D. A. 1949. *Aeshna caerulea* in Kircudbrightshire. Scottish Naturalist 61:175.

Ratcliffe, D. A. & Oswald, P. H. (eds). 1987. The Flow Country: the peatlands of Caithness and Sutherland. Peterborough: Nature Conservancy Council.

Richards, M. 1998. Odonata Survey of Part of Abernethy RSPB Reserve. RSPB, unpublished report.

Riservato, E., Boudot, J.-P., Ferreira, S., Jović, M., Kalkman, V. J., Schneider, W., Samraoui, B. & Cuttelod, A. 2009. The status and distribution of dragonflies in the Mediterranean. The IUCN Red List of Threatened Species – Regional Assessment. IUCN, Gland, Switzerland and Malaga, Spain. 33 pp. Also at: http://cmsdata.iucn.org/downloads/mediterranean_dragonflies_en_web.pdf

Robert, P.-A. 1958. Les Libellules (Odonates). Neuchâtel, Delachaux et Niestle.

Rodwell, J. S. (ed) 1991. British Plant Communities. Volume 2: Mires and heaths. Cambridge University Press, Cambridge.

Rouquette, J. R. 2005. Conservation requirements of the Southern Damselfly in chalkstream and fen habitats. Science Report SC000017/SR. Environment Agency, Bristol.

Rouquette, J. R. & Thompson, D. J. 2007. Patterns of movement and dispersal in an endangered damselfly and the consequences for its management. Journal of Applied Ecology 44: 692-701.

Roy, H. E., Adriaens, T., Isaac, N. J. B., Kenis, M., Martin, G. S., Brown, P. M. J., Hautier, L., Poland, R., Roy, D. B., Comont, R., Eschen, R., Frost, R., Zindel, R., Van Vlaenderen, J., Nedved, O., Ravn, H. P., Grégoire, J.-C., de Biseau, J.-C. & Maes, D. 2012. Invasive alien predator causes rapid declines of native European ladybirds. Diversity and Distributions 18: 717-725.

Rüppel, G. 1985. Kinematic and behavioural aspects of flight of the male banded agrion, *Calopteryx (Agrion) splendens* L. In Gewecke, M. & Wendler, G. (eds). Insect Locomotion. Verlag Paul Parey, Berlin, pp.195-204.

Rüppel, G., Hilfert-Rüppel, D., Rehfeldt, G. & Schutte, C. 2005. Die Prachtlibellen Europas. Die Libellen Europas. Vol. 4. Die Neue Brehm – Bücherei: 654. Westarp Wissenschaften, Hohenwarsleben.

Sahlén, G., Bernard, R., Rivera, A.C., Ketelaar, R. & Suhling, F. 2004. Critical species of Odonata in Europe. International Journal of Odonatology 7: 385-398.

Samraoui, B., Bouzid, S., Boulabahl, R. & Corbet, P.S. 1998. Postponed reproductive maturation in upland refuges maintains life-cycle continuity during the hot dry season in Algerian dragonflies. International Journal of Odonatology 1: 119-135.

Schiel, F.-J. 2006. Nachweise einer zweiten Jahresgeneration von *Erythromma najas* (Odonata: Coenagrionidae). Libellula 25: 159-164.

Schloemer, S., Dalbeck, L., & Hamm, A. in press. Diversity of species in Beaverponds: The effect of the Eurasian Beaver *Castor fiber* L. on Dragonflies and Damselflies (Odonata).

Schorr, M., & Paulson, D. 2014. World Odonata List. http://www.pugetsound.edu/academics/academic-resources/slater-museum/biodiversity-resources/dragonflies/world-odonata-list2/ (accessed 11 February 2014).

SEPA. 2009. Scottish Environment Protection Agency: Scotland's Water Environment Review 2000-2006. http://www.sepa.org.uk/science_and_research/data_and_reports/water/water_environment_review_2006.aspx

Shirt, D. B. 1987. British Red Data Books: 2 Insects. Nature Conservancy Council, Peterborough.

Silsby, J. 1993. A review of *Hemianax ephippiger*, the Vagrant Emperor. Journal of the British Dragonfly Society 9: 47-50.

Silsby, J. 1996. 1995: a bumper year for Darter immigrants. Atropos 1: 10-11.

Silsby, J. & Ward-Smith, J. 1997. The influx of *Sympetrum flaveolum* (L.) during the summer of 1995. Journal of the British Dragonfly Society 13: 14-22.

Siva-Jothy, M. 2004. Banded Demoiselle *Calopteryx splendens* (Harris). In Field Guide to the Dragonflies and Damselflies of Great Britain and Ireland. 4th ed. (ed. Brooks, S. & Lewington, R.). British Wildlife Publishing, Hook, Hampshire, pp. 61-62.

Smallshire, D. & Swash, A. 2014 (third revised edition). Britain's Dragonflies. A field guide to the damselflies and dragonflies of Britain and Ireland. WILDGuides Ltd., Old Basing, Hampshire, UK.

Smiddy, P. 2004. Some records of rare Odonata species in east Cork and west Waterford: 2002-2003. Irish Naturalists' Journal 27: 357.

Smith, E. M. & Smith, R. W. J. 1999. The Status of *Coenagrion hastulatum* (Charpentier) in Scotland, with notes on larval sampling. Journal of the British Dragonfly Society 15: 1-9.

Smith, E. M. & Smith, R. W. J. 2001. Review of Sites and preliminary Action Plan for *Coenagrion hastulatum*, Scottish Natural Heritage Commissioned Report No F96AC304.

Smith, E. M. & Smith, R. W. J. 1984. *Brachytron pratense* (Muller) and other Odonata of the Black Lochs, Argyll. Journal of the British Dragonfly Society. 1: 51-54.

Smith, P. H. 1998. Dispersion or migration of *Sympetrum danae* (Sulzer) in South Lancashire. Journal of the British Dragonfly Society 14: 12-14.

Smith, P. H. 2010. Dragonflies and climate change. Coastlines 2010 (1): 17.

Smith, R. W. J., Smith, E. M. & Richards, M. A. 2000. Habitat and development of larvae of the Azure Hawker *Aeshna caerulea* (Ström) in northern Scotland. Journal of the British Dragonfly Society 16: 1-16.

Speyer E. R. 1909. On the occurrence of *Somatochlora metallica* in Sussex. Entomologist's Monthly Magazine 45: 227-233.

Stace, C. 2010 (third edition). New Flora of the British Isles. Cambridge University Press, Cambridge.

Starmore, A. 2008. Submerged oviposition behaviour in the Large Red Damselfly *Pyrrhosoma nymphula* (Sulzer) on the Isle of Lewis. Journal of the British Dragonfly Society 24: 45-50.

Stevens, J. & Thurner, M. 1999. A 1998 survey to further investigate the status and distribution of the Southern Damselfly (*Coenagrion mercuriale*) in Hampshire: Hampshire Biodiversity Partnership.

Stoks, R. & McPeek, M. A. 2003. Predators and life histories shape *Lestes* damselfly assemblages along a freshwater habitat gradient. Ecology 84: 1576-1587.

Stoks, R., McPeek, M. A. and Mitchell, J. L. 2003. Evolution of prey behaviour in response to changes in predation regime: Damselflies in Fish and Dragonfly Lakes. Evolution 57: 574-585.

Strange, A. & Burt, S. 1998. Southern Damselfly *Coenagrion mercuriale* Survey at Itchen Valley Country Park. Unpublished report.

Strange, A. 1999. Distribution of Southern Damselfly on the River Itchen: Ecological Planning and Research for English Nature and Environment Agency.

Sulzer, J. H. 1776. Abgekiirze Geschichte der Insekten nach dem Linneischen System 24.

Sykes, T. 2000. Biodiversity Action Plan for Hampshire: Volume 2. Available from: www.hampshirebiodiversity.org.uk/pdf/PublishedPlans/SouthernDamselflyjjDTP.pdf

Szabo, J. K., Vesk, P. A, Baxter, P. W. J., & Possingham, H. P. 2010. Regional avian species declines estimated from volunteer-collected long-term data using List Length Analysis. Ecological Applications 20: 2157-2169.

Tailly, M. 2002. *Calopteryx splendens erevanense* Akramovski, 1948. http://users.telenet.be/tailly/armenodon/description_erevanense.htm and see also http://users.telenet.be/tailly/armenodon/calop_sple_erevan.htm

Termaat, T., Kalkman, V. J. & Bouwman, J. H. 2010. Changes in the range of dragonflies in the Netherlands and the possible role of temperature change. BioRisk 5: 155-173.

Thompson D. J., Rouquette J. R. & Purse B. V. 2003. Ecology of the Southern Damselfly. Conserving Natura 2000 Rivers Ecology Series No. 8. English Nature, Peterborough.

Thompson, R. & Nelson, B. 2014. Guide to the Dragonflies and Damselflies of Ireland. National Museums Northern Ireland, Cultra.

Tingley, M. W., & Beissinger, S. R. 2009. Detecting range shifts from historical species occurrences: new perspectives on old data. Trends in Ecology & Evolution 24: 625-33.

Tyrrell, M. 2011. Species Review 5: The Hairy Dragonfly *Brachytron pratense* (Müller). Journal of the British Dragonfly Society 27: 13-27.

Tyrrell, M., Emary, C., Brayshaw, S., Sutcliffe, D. & Showers, J. 2006. The Dragonflies of Northamptonshire, Northants Dragonfly Group.

Tyrrell, M., Emary, C., & Piper, M. 2009. The Beautiful Demoiselle *Calopteryx virgo* (Linnaeus) in Northamptonshire: eastwards expansion & habitats. Journal of the British Dragonfly Society 25: 100-106.

Valtonen, P. 1985. Exotic dragonflies imported accidentally with aquarium plants to Finland. Notulae Odonatologicae 2: 87-88.

Vanderhaeghe, F. 1999. Een beknopt overzicht van de huidige verspreiding en status van *Coenagrion scitulum* (Rambur, 1842) in België en Noord-Frankrijk. Gomphus 15: 69-85.

Van Strien, A. J., Termaat, T., Groenendijk, D., Mensing, V., & Kéry, M. 2010. Site-occupancy models may offer new opportunities for dragonfly monitoring based on daily species lists. Basic and Applied Ecology 11: 495-503.

Vincent, P.J. 1990. A Biogeography of the British Isles: an Introduction. Routledge, London. (Recording species distributions, pp. 48-73.)

Vonwil, G. & Wildermuth, H. 1990. Massenentwicklung von *Hemianax ephippiger* (Burmeister, 1839) in der Schweiz (Odonata: Aeshnidae) Opuscula Zoologica Fluminensia 51: 1-11.

Walsh, S. 2012. A summary of climate averages for Ireland 1981-2010. Climatological note No.14. Met Éireann, Dublin.

Ward, L. & Mill, P. J. 2004. Distribution of the Banded Demoiselle *Calopteryx splendens* (Harris) in northern England: an example of range expansion? Journal of the British Dragonfly Society 20: 61-69.

Ward, L. & Mill, P. J. 2005. Habitat factors influencing the presence of adult *Calopteryx splendens* (Odonata: Zygoptera). European Journal of Entomology 102: 47-51.

Ward, L. & Mill, P. J. 2007. Long range movements by individuals as a vehicle for range expansion in *Calopteryx splendens* (Odonata: Zygoptera). European Journal of Entomology 104: 195-198.

Ward, L. & Mill, P. J. 2008. Substrate selection in larval *Calopteryx splendens* (Harris) (Zygoptera: Calopterygidae). Odonatologica 37: 69-77.

Ward-Smith, A. J., Sussex, D. J. & Cham, S. A. 2000. Flight characteristics of the Brilliant Emerald *Somatochlora metallica* (Vander Linden) in south-east England. Journal of the British Dragonfly Society 16: 24-28.

Ward-Smith, J. & Sussex D. 2006. Population expansion of Small Red Damselfly *Ceriagrion tenellum* (Villers) in south-east Berkshire. Journal of the British Dragonfly Society 21: 55-67.

Wasscher, M. T. 1994. Areaaluitbreiding van *Sympetrum pedemontanum* (Allioni) in Noordwest Europa in de periode 1953-1985. Contactblad Nederlandse Libellenonderzoekers 22: 11-15.

Watts, P.C., Keat, S. & Thompson, D.J. 2010. Patterns of spatial genetic structure and diversity at the onset of a rapid range expansion: colonisation of the UK by the small red-eyed damselfly *Erythromma viridulum*. Biological Invasions 12: 3887-3903.

Wikelski, M., Moskowitz, D., Adelman, J. S., Cochran, J., Wilcove, D. S. & May, M. L. 2006. Simple rules guide dragonfly migration. Biology Letters 2: 325-329.

Wildermuth, H. 2008. Die Falkenlibellen Europas. Westarp Wissenschaften 2008.

Winsland, D. 1983. Some observations of *Erythromma najas*. Journal of the British Dragonfly Society 1: 6.

Winsland, D. 1996. Dragonfly Wildlife Report. British Wildlife 7: 184-185.

Winsland, D. C., Moore N. W. & Silsby J. 1996. Management Guidelines: Scarce Chaser – *Libellula fulva* Müller Southern 1764. In the Species and Habitats Handbook, Environment Agency.

Woodrow, W. 2009. Monaghan Irish Damselfly and Water Beetle Survey 2009. Unpublished report to Monaghan County Council and The Heritage Council.

Yu, X. & Bu, W. 2011. Chinese damselflies of the genus *Coenagrion* (Zygoptera: Coenagrionidae) Zootaxa 2808: 31-40.

Zahner, R. 1960. Über die Bindung der mitteleuropäischen Calopteryx-Arten (Odonata, Zygoptera) an den Lebensraum des strömenden Wassers. II. Der Anteil der Imagines an der Biotopbindung. Internmationale Revue der gesamten Hydrobiologie 45: 101-123.

Zoder, S. 2010. *Libellula fulva* Müller, 1764 (Spitzenfleck) am Unteren Inn (Odonata, Anisoptera, Libellulidae). Mitteilungen der zoologischen Gesellschaft Braunau 10: 91-94.

# Index

Index to damselfly and dragonfly species, species accounts are shown in **bold**.

Printed in the UK by
Gomer Press Limited.